THE
MINISTER'S MANUAL

SEVENTY-SEVENTH ANNUAL ISSUE

THE MINISTER'S MANUAL

2002

Edited by

JAMES W. COX

JOSSEY-BASS
A Wiley Company
San Francisco

Editors of THE MINISTER'S MANUAL

G. B. F. Hallock, D.D., 1926–1958
M. K. W. Heicher, Ph.D., 1943–1968
Charles L. Wallis, M.A., M.Div., 1969–1983
James W. Cox, M.Div., Ph.D.

Library of Congress Cataloging Card Number

25-21658
ISSN 0738-5323
ISBN 0-7879-5003-3

FIRST EDITION
HB Printing
10 9 8 7 6 5 4 3 2 1

CONTENTS

PREFACE

The Minister's Manual 2002 presents sermonic contributions from a wide range of preachers, teachers, and writers. They come from many geographical, denominational, and theological backgrounds. I am convinced that although they do not always agree on every issue, they speak responsibly and their thoughts deserve careful consideration. They share our common faith and enrich our personal understanding and devotion. Nevertheless, they speak for themselves, and their views do not necessarily represent, in all cases, those of the publisher, the editor, or the Southern Baptist Theological Seminary.

I am grateful to the seminary, where I have taught since 1959, for providing valuable secretarial assistance in producing the manuscript. I wish to thank especially Linda Durkin and Marianne Bickley for their faithful and efficient assistance. Also, I wish to thank the authors and publishers from whose works I have quoted. It is hoped that the rights and wishes of no one have been overlooked. Again, I am deeply grateful.

James W. Cox
The Southern Baptist Theological Seminary

SECTION I

GENERAL AIDS AND RESOURCES

CIVIL YEAR CALENDARS FOR 2002 AND 2003

2002

January	February	March	April
S M T W T F S	S M T W T F S	S M T W T F S	S M T W T F S
1 2 3 4 5	1 2	1 2	1 2 3 4 5 6
6 7 8 9 10 11 12	3 4 5 6 7 8 9	3 4 5 6 7 8 9	7 8 9 10 11 12 13
13 14 15 16 17 18 19	10 11 12 13 14 15 16	10 11 12 13 14 15 16	14 15 16 17 18 19 20
20 21 22 23 24 25 26	17 18 19 20 21 22 23	17 18 19 20 21 22 23	21 22 23 24 25 26 27
27 28 29 30 31	24 25 26 27 28	24 25 26 27 28 29 30	28 29 30
		31	

May	June	July	August
S M T W T F S	S M T W T F S	S M T W T F S	S M T W T F S
1 2 3 4	1	1 2 3 4 5 6	1 2 3
5 6 7 8 9 10 11	2 3 4 5 6 7 8	7 8 9 10 11 12 13	4 5 6 7 8 9 10
12 13 14 15 16 17 18	9 10 11 12 13 14 15	14 15 16 17 18 19 20	11 12 13 14 15 16 17
19 20 21 22 23 24 25	16 17 18 19 20 21 22	21 22 23 24 25 26 27	18 19 20 21 22 23 24
26 27 28 29 30 31	23 24 25 26 27 28 29	28 29 30 31	25 26 27 28 29 30 31
	30		

September	October	November	December
S M T W T F S	S M T W T F S	S M T W T F S	S M T W T F S
1 2 3 4 5 6 7	1 2 3 4 5	1 2	1 2 3 4 5 6 7
8 9 10 11 12 13 14	6 7 8 9 10 11 12	3 4 5 6 7 8 9	8 9 10 11 12 13 14
15 16 17 18 19 20 21	13 14 15 16 17 18 19	10 11 12 13 14 15 16	15 16 17 18 19 20 21
22 23 24 25 26 27 28	20 21 22 23 24 25 26	17 18 19 20 21 22 23	22 23 24 25 26 27 28
29 30	27 28 29 30 31	24 25 26 27 28 29 30	29 30 31

2003

January	February	March	April
S M T W T F S	S M T W T F S	S M T W T F S	S M T W T F S
1 2 3 4	1	1	1 2 3 4 5
5 6 7 8 9 10 11	2 3 4 5 6 7 8	2 3 4 5 6 7 8	6 7 8 9 10 11 12
12 13 14 15 16 17 18	9 10 11 12 13 14 15	9 10 11 12 13 14 15	13 14 15 16 17 18 19
19 20 21 22 23 24 25	16 17 18 19 20 21 22	16 17 18 19 20 21 22	20 21 22 23 24 25 26
26 27 28 29 30 31	23 24 25 26 27 28	23 24 25 26 27 28 29	27 28 29 30
		30 31	

May	June	July	August
S M T W T F S	S M T W T F S	S M T W T F S	S M T W T F S
1 2 3	1 2 3 4 5 6 7	1 2 3 4 5	1 2
4 5 6 7 8 9 10	8 9 10 11 12 13 14	6 7 8 9 10 11 12	3 4 5 6 7 8 9
11 12 13 14 15 16 17	15 16 17 18 19 20 21	13 14 15 16 17 18 19	10 11 12 13 14 15 16
18 19 20 21 22 23 24	22 23 24 25 26 27 28	20 21 22 23 24 25 26	17 18 19 20 21 22 23
25 26 27 28 29 30 31	29 30	27 28 29 30 31	24 25 26 27 28 29 30
			31

September	October	November	December
S M T W T F S	S M T W T F S	S M T W T F S	S M T W T F S
1 2 3 4 5 6	1 2 3 4	1	1 2 3 4 5 6
7 8 9 10 11 12 13	5 6 7 8 9 10 11	2 3 4 5 6 7 8	7 8 9 10 11 12 13
14 15 16 17 18 19 20	12 13 14 15 16 17 18	9 10 11 12 13 14 15	14 15 16 17 18 19 20
21 22 23 24 25 26 27	19 20 21 22 23 24 25	16 17 18 19 20 21 22	21 22 23 24 25 26 27
28 29 30	26 27 28 29 30 31	23 24 25 26 27 28 29	28 29 30 31
		30	

Church and Civic Calendar for 2002

January

1	New Year's Day
5	Twelfth Night
6	Epiphany
10	League of Nations Anniversary
13	Baptism of the Lord
17	St. Anthony's Day
21	Martin Luther King Jr.'s Birthday, Observed
25	Conversion of St. Paul

February

1	National Freedom Day
2	Presentation of Jesus in the Temple
10	Race Relations Sunday
12	Shrove Tuesday Lincoln's Birthday
13	Ash Wednesday
14	St. Valentine's Day
17	First Sunday in Lent
18	Presidents' Day
22	Washington's Birthday
24	Second Sunday in Lent St. Matthias, Apostle
26	Purim

March

3	Third Sunday in Lent
17	St. Patrick's Day
24–30	Holy Week
24	Palm Sunday
25	The Annunciation
28	Maundy Thursday Passover
29	Good Friday
31	Easter

April

7	Low Sunday
25	St. Mark, Evangelist

May

1	May Day Loyalty Day Law Day
1–5	Cinco de Mayo Celebration St. Philip and St. James, Apostles
5–12	National Family Week
9	Ascension Day
12	Mother's Day
17	First day of Shavuot
19	Pentecost
26	Trinity Sunday
27	Memorial Day

June

2	Corpus Christi
9	Children's Sunday
11	St. Barnabas, Apostle
16	Father's Day
24	The Nativity of St. John the Baptist
29	St. Peter and St. Paul, Apostles

July

1	Canada Day
4	Independence Day
22	St. Mary Magdalene
25	St. James the Elder, Apostle

August

1	Civic Holiday (Canada)
14	Atlantic Charter Day
15	Mary, Mother of Jesus
24	St. Bartholomew, Apostle
26	Women's Equality Day

September

2	Labor Day
7	Rosh Hashanah

16	Yom Kippur	11	Veterans Day
21	St. Matthew, Evangelist and		Armistice Day
	Apostle	17	Bible Sunday
	First day of Sukkoth	28	Thanksgiving Day
29	St. Michael and All Angels	30	St. Andrew, Apostle
			First day of Hanukkah

October

December

6	World Communion Sunday		
14	Columbus Day, Observed	1	First Sunday of Advent
18	St. Luke, Evangelist	8	Second Sunday of Advent
23	St. James, Brother of Jesus	15	Third Sunday of Advent
24	United Nations Day		Bill of Rights Day
27	Reformation Sunday	22	Fourth Sunday of Advent
28	St. Simon and St. Jude,	25	Christmas
	Apostles	26	Boxing Day (Canada)
31	Reformation Day		St. Stephen, Deacon and
	National UNICEF Day		Martyr
		27	St. John, Evangelist and
			Apostle

November

1	All Saints' Day	28	The Holy Innocents, Martyrs
2	All Souls' Day	31	New Year's Eve
10	Stewardship Day		Watch Night

The Revised Common Lectionary for 2002

The following Scripture lessons are commended for use in public worship by various Protestant churches and the Roman Catholic Church and include first, second, and Gospel readings, and Psalms, according to cycle A from January 6 to November 24 and according to cycle B from December 1 to December 29. (Copyright 1992 Consultation on Common Texts)

Epiphany Season

Jan. 6 (Epiphany Sunday): Isa. 60:1–6; Ps. 72:1–7, 10–11; Eph. 3:1–12; Matt. 2:1–12

Jan. 13: Isa. 42:1–9; Ps. 29; Acts 10:34–43; Matt. 3:13–17

Jan. 20: Isa. 49:1–7; Ps. 40:1–11; 1 Cor. 1:1–9; John 1:29–42

Jan. 27: Isa. 9:1–4; Ps. 27:1, 4–9; 1 Cor. 1:10–18; Matt. 4:12–23

Feb. 3: Mic. 6:1–8; Ps. 15; 1 Cor. 1:18–31; Matt. 5:1–12

Feb. 10: Isa. 58:1–9a, 9b–12; Ps. 112:1–9 (10); 1 Cor. 2:1–12, 13–16; Matt. 5:13–20

Lenten Season

Feb. 13 (Ash Wednesday): Joel 1:1–2, 12–17; Ps. 57:1–17; 2 Cor. 5:20b–6:10; Matt. 6:1–6, 16–21

Feb. 17: Deut. 30:15–20; Ps. 119:1–8; 1 Cor. 3:1–4; Matt. 5:21–37

Feb. 24: Lev. 19:1–2, 9–18; Ps. 119:33–40; 1 Cor. 3:10–11, 16–23; Matt. 5:38–48

Mar. 3: Isa. 49:8–16a; Ps. 131; 1 Cor. 4:1–5; Matt. 6:24–34

Mar. 10: Deut. 11:18-21, 26-28; Ps. 31:1-5, 19-24; Rom. 1:16-17; 3:22b-28 (29-31); Matt. 7:21-29

Mar. 17 (Transfiguration Sunday): Exod. 24:12-18; Ps. 2; 2 Pet. 1:16-21; Matt. 17:1-9

Holy Week

Mar. 24 (Palm/Passion Sunday): Liturgy of the Palms—Matt. 21:1-11; Ps. 118:1-2, 19-29. Liturgy of the Passion—Isa. 50:4-9a; Ps. 31:9-16; Phil. 2:5-11; Matt. 26:14-27:66

Mar. 25 (Monday): Isa. 42:1-9; Ps. 36:5-11; Heb. 9:11-15; John 12:1-11

Mar. 26 (Tuesday): Isa. 49:1-7; Ps. 71:1-14; 1 Cor. 1:18-31; John 12:20-36

Mar. 27 (Wednesday): Isa. 50:4-9a; Ps. 70; Heb. 12:1-3; John 13:21-32

Mar. 28 (Holy Thursday): Exod. 12:1-4 (5-10), 11-14; Ps. 116:1-2, 12-19; 1 Cor. 11:23-26; John 13:1-7, 31b-35

Mar. 29 (Good Friday): Isa. 52-53:12; Ps. 22; Heb. 10:15-25; John 18:1-19:42

Mar. 30 (Holy Saturday): Job 14:1-14; Ps. 31:1-4, 15-16; 1 Pet. 4:1-8; Matt. 27:57-66

Mar. 30 (Easter Vigil): Gen. 1:1-2:4a; Ps. 136:1-9, 23-26; Gen. 7:1-5, 11-18; 8:6-18; 9:8-13; Ps. 46; Gen. 22:1-18; Ps. 16; Exod. 14:10-31; 15:20-21; Exod. 15:1b-13, 17-18 (resp.); Isa. 55:1-11; Isa. 12:2-6 (resp.); Bar. 3:9-15, 32; 4:4 (alt.); Prov. 8:1-8, 19-21; 9:4-6 (alt.); Ps. 19; Ezek. 36:24-28; Ps. 42-43; Ezek. 37:1-14; Ps. 143; Zeph. 3:14-20; Ps. 98; Rom. 6:3-11; Ps. 114; Luke 24:1-12

Easter Season

Mar. 31 (Easter): Acts 10:34-43; Ps. 118:1-2, 14-29; Col. 3:1-4; John 20:1-18; Matt. 28:1-10; Isa. 25:6-9; Ps. 114; 1 Cor. 5:6b-8; Luke 24:13-49

Apr. 7: Acts 2:14a, 22-32; Ps. 16; 1 Pet. 1:3-9; John 20:19-31

Apr. 14: Acts 2:14a, 36-41; Ps. 116:1-4, 12-19; 1 Pet. 1:17-23; Luke 24:13-35

Apr. 21: Acts 2:42-47; Ps. 23; 1 Pet. 2:19-25; John 10:1-10

Apr. 28: Acts 7:55-60; Ps. 31:1-5, 15-16; 1 Pet. 2:2-10; John 14:1-14

May 5: Acts 17:22-31; Ps. 66:8-20; 1 Pet. 3:13-22; John 14:15-21

May 12: Acts 1:6-14; Ps. 68:1-10, 32-35; 1 Pet. 4:12-14; 5:6-11; John 17:1-11

May 19 (Pentecost): Num. 11:24-30; Ps. 104:24-34; Acts 2:1-21 or 1 Cor. 12:3b-13; John 20:19-23 or John 7:37-39

May 26 (Trinity Sunday): Gen. 1:1-2:4a; Ps. 8; 2 Cor. 13:11-13; Matt. 28:16-20

June 2: Gen. 6:9-22; 7:24; 8:14-19; Ps. 46; Rom. 1:16-17; 3:22b-28 (29-31); Matt. 7:21-29

June 9: Gen. 12:1-9; Ps. 33:1-12; Rom. 4:13-25; Matt. 9:9-13, 18-26

June 16: Gen. 18:1-15 (21:1-7); Ps. 116:1-2, 12-19; Rom. 5:1-8; Matt. 9:35-10:8

June 23: Gen. 21:8-21; Ps. 86:1-10, 16-17; Rom. 6:1b-11; Matt. 10:24-39

June 30: Gen. 22:1-14; Ps. 13; Rom. 6:12-23; Matt. 10:40-42

July 7: Gen. 24:34-38, 42-49, 58-67; Ps. 45:10-17; Rom. 7:15-25a; Matt. 11:16-19, 25-30

July 14: Gen. 25:19-34; Ps. 119:105-112; Rom. 8:1-11; Matt. 13:1-9, 18-23

July 21: Gen. 28:10-19a; Ps. 139:1-12, 23-24; Rom. 8:12-25; Matt. 13:24-30, 36-43

July 28: Gen. 29:15-28; Ps. 105:1-11, 45b; Rom. 8:26-39; Matt. 13:31-33, 44-52

Aug. 4: Gen. 32:22-31; Ps. 17:1-7, 15; Rom. 9:1-5; Matt. 14:13-21

Aug. 11: Gen. 37:1–14, 12–28; Ps. 105:1–6, 16–22, 45b; Rom. 10:5–15; Matt. 14:22–33

Aug. 18: Gen. 45:1–15; Ps. 133; Rom. 11:1–2a, 29–32; Matt. 15: (10–20) 21–28

Aug. 25: Exod. 1:8–2:10; Ps. 124; Rom. 12:1–8; Matt. 16:13–20

Sept. 1: Exod. 3:1–15; Ps. 105:1–6, 23–26, 45b; Rom. 12:9–21; Matt. 16:21–28

Sept. 8: Exod. 12:1–14; Ps. 149; Rom. 13:8–14; Matt. 18:15–20

Sept. 15: Exod. 14:19–31; Ps. 114; Rom. 14:1–12; Matt. 18:21–35

Sept. 22: Exod. 16:2–15; Ps. 105:1–6, 37–45; Phil. 1:21–30; Matt. 20:1–16

Sept. 29: Exod. 17:1–9; Ps. 78:1–4, 12–16; Phil. 2:1–13; Matt. 21:23–32

Oct. 6: Exod. 20:1–4, 7–9, 12–20; Ps. 19; Phil. 3:4b–14; Matt. 21:33–46

Oct. 13: Exod. 32:1–14; Ps. 106:1–6, 19–23; Phil. 4:1–9; Matt. 22:1–14

Oct. 20: Exod. 33:12–23; Ps. 99; 1 Thess. 1:1–10; Matt. 22:15–22

Oct. 27: Deut. 34:1–12; Ps. 90:1–6, 13–17; 1 Thess. 2:1–8; Matt. 22:34–46

Nov. 3: Josh. 3:7–17; Ps. 107:1–7, 33–37; 1 Thess. 2:9–13; Matt. 23:1–12

Nov. 10: Josh. 24:1–3a, 14–25; Ps. 78:1–7; 1 Thess. 4:13–18; Matt. 25:1–13

Nov. 17: Judg. 4:1–7; Ps. 123; 1 Thess. 5:1–11; Matt. 25:14–30

Nov. 24 (Christ the King): Ezek. 34:11–16, 20–24; Ps. 100; Eph. 1:15–23; Matt. 25:31–46

Advent and Christmas Season

Dec. 1: Isa. 64:1–9; Ps. 80:1–7, 17–19; 1 Cor. 1:3–9; Mark 13:24–37

Dec. 8: Isa. 40:1–11; Ps. 85:1–2, 8–13; 2 Pet. 3:8–15a; Mark 1:1–8

Dec. 15: Isa. 61:1–4, 8–11; Ps. 126; 1 Thess. 5:16–24; John 1:6–8, 19–28

Dec. 22: 2 Sam. 7:1–11, 16; Luke 1:47–55; Rom. 16:25–27; Luke 1:26–38

Dec. 25 (Christmas Day): Isa. 9:2–7; Ps. 96; Titus 2:11–14; Luke 2:1–14 (15–20) or Isa. 62:6–12; Ps. 97; Titus 3:47; Luke 2:(1–7) 8–20 or Isa. 52:7–10; Ps. 98; Heb. 1:1–4 (5–12); John 1:1–14

Dec. 29: Isa. 61:10–62:3; Ps. 148; Gal. 4:4–7; Luke 2:22–40

Four-Year Church Calendar

	2002	2003	2004	2005
Ash Wednesday	February 13	March 5	February 25	February 9
Palm Sunday	March 24	April 13	April 4	March 20
Good Friday	March 29	April 18	April 9	March 25
Easter	March 31	April 20	April 11	March 27
Ascension Day	May 9	May 29	May 20	May 5
Pentecost	May 19	June 8	May 30	May 15
Trinity Sunday	May 26	June 15	June 6	May 22
Thanksgiving	November 28	November 27	November 25	November 24
Advent Sunday	December 1	November 30	November 28	November 27

Forty-Year Easter Calendar

2002 March 31	2012 April 8	2022 April 17	2032 March 28
2003 April 20	2013 March 31	2023 April 9	2033 April 17
2004 April 11	2014 April 20	2024 March 31	2034 April 9
2005 March 27	2015 April 5	2025 April 20	2035 March 25
2006 April 16	2016 March 27	2026 April 5	2036 April 13

2007 April 8	2017 April 16	2027 March 28	2037 April 5
2008 March 23	2018 April 1	2028 April 16	2038 April 25
2009 April 12	2019 April 21	2029 April 1	2039 April 10
2010 April 4	2020 April 12	2030 April 21	2040 April 1
2011 April 24	2021 April 4	2031 April 13	2041 April 2

Traditional Wedding Anniversary Identifications

1 Paper	7 Wool	13 Lace	35 Coral
2 Cotton	8 Bronze	14 Ivory	40 Ruby
3 Leather	9 Pottery	15 Crystal	45 Sapphire
4 Linen	10 Tin	20 China	50 Gold
5 Wood	11 Steel	25 Silver	55 Emerald
6 Iron	12 Silk	30 Pearl	60 Diamond

Colors Appropriate for Days and Seasons

White. Symbolizes purity, perfection, and joy and identifies festivals marking events in the life of Jesus, except Good Friday: Christmas, Epiphany, Easter, Eastertide, Ascension Day; also Trinity Sunday, All Saints' Day, weddings, funerals. Gold may also be used.

Red. Symbolizes the Holy Spirit, martyrdom, and the love of God: Good Friday, Pentecost, and Sundays following.

Violet. Symbolizes penitence: Advent, Lent.

Green. Symbolizes mission to the world, hope, regeneration, nurture, and growth: Epiphany season, Kingdomtide, Rural Life Sunday, Labor Sunday, Thanksgiving Sunday.

Blue. Advent, in some churches.

Flowers in Season Appropriate for Church Use

January: carnation or snowdrop	July: larkspur or water lily
February: violet or primrose	August: gladiolus or poppy
March: jonquil or daffodil	September: aster or morning star
April: lily, sweet pea, or daisy	October: calendula or cosmos
May: lily of the valley or hawthorn	November: chrysanthemum
June: rose or honeysuckle	December: narcissus, holly, or poinsettia

Quotable Quotations

1. Doubt isn't the opposite of faith, it is an element of faith.—Paul Tillich
2. Too humble is half proud.—Hanan J. Ayalti
3. Too many young people are beginning to regard home as a filling station by day and a parking place for the night.—William Joyce
4. Our doubts are traitors, and make us lose the good we oft might win by fearing to attempt.—William Shakespeare
5. The secret of being miserable is to have leisure to bother about whether you are happy or not.—George Bernard Shaw

6. The church is the only society in the world that exists for the benefit of those who are not its members.—William Temple

7. Some, perhaps even most, people spend more time thinking about the right color for the bathroom wall than about the right way to conduct their lives.—Joshua Halberstam

8. Sour godliness is the devil's religion.—John Wesley

9. Worship is transcendent wonder.—Thomas Carlyle

10. Religion is a way of walking, not a way of talking.—Dean Inge

11. Of all the home remedies, a good wife is the best.—Frank McKinney Hubbard

12. We become that we think of ourselves.—Abraham Joshua Heschel

13. Life is what happens to us while we are making other plans.—Thomas la Mance

14. For an idea that does not at first seem insane there is no hope.—Albert Einstein

15. They say hard work never hurt anybody, but I figure why take the chance.—Ronald Reagan

16. Before God can deliver us we must undeceive ourselves.—Augustine of Hippo

17. God may forgive you your sins, but your nervous system won't.—Alfred Korzybski

18. Science without religion is lame; religion without science is blind.—Albert Einstein

19. It is easier to love humanity as a whole than to love one's neighbor.—Eric Hoffer

20. In short, the Man Christ Jesus has the decisive place in Man's ageless relationship with God. He is what God means by "Man." He is what man means by "God."—J. S. Whale

21. Faith is the hand that takes the blessing. But don't look too much at the hand.—Dwight L. Moody

22. A suburban mother's role is to deliver children obstetrically once, and by car forever after.—Peter de Vries

23. Legalism is simply law growing cancerously.—E. G. Selwyn

24. If you must love your neighbor as yourself, it is at least as fair to love yourself as your neighbor.—Nicholas de Chamfort

25. Conscience is the inner voice that warns us somebody may be looking.—H. L. Mencken

26. I firmly believe that the future of civilization is absolutely dependent upon finding some way of resolving international differences without resorting to war.—Dwight D. Eisenhower

27. Optimist: a man who gets treed by a lion but enjoys the scenery.—Walter Winchell

28. The stupid neither forgive nor forget; the naive forgive and forget; the wise forgive but do not forget.—Thomas Szasz

29. Freedom is nothing else but a chance to be better, whereas enslavement is a certainty of the worst.—Albert Camus

30. Love does not consist in gazing at each other, but in looking together in the same direction.—Antoine de Saint-Exupery

31. The person who has a firm trust in the Supreme Being is powerful in his power, wise by his wisdom, happy by his happiness.—Joseph Addison

32. We know accurately only when we know little; with knowledge, doubt enters.—Goethe

33. Winners got scars, too.—Johnny Cash

34. A doctrine of black supremacy is as evil as a doctrine of white supremacy.—Martin Luther King

35. To abandon religion for science is merely to fly from one region of faith to another.—Giles and Melville Harcourt

36. Hope is the poor man's bread.—George Herbert

37. Anxiety is simply part of the condition of being human. If we were not anxious, we would never create anything.—William Barrett

38. He who goes with wolves learns to howl.—Spanish proverb

39. If you criticize a mule, do it to his face.—Herbert V. Prochnow

40. Behold the turtle. He makes progress only when he sticks his neck out.—James Bryant Conant

41. You grow up the day you have your first real laugh at yourself.—Ethel Barrymore

42. No one gossips about other people's secret virtues.—Bertrand Russell

43. Failure is instructive. The person who really thinks learns quite as much from his failures as from his successes.—John Dewey

44. Only one petition in the Lord's Prayer has any condition attached to it: it is the petition for forgiveness.—William Temple

45. A great grief has taught me more than any minister, and when feeling most alone I find refuge in the Almighty Friend.—Louisa May Alcott

46. All happy families resemble one another; every unhappy family is unhappy in its own way.—Leo Tolstoy

47. It is never too late to give up our prejudices.—Henry David Thoreau

48. The so-called new morality is too often the old immorality condoned.—Lord Shawcross

49. As the flower turns to the sun, or the dog to his master, so the soul turns to God.—William Temple

50. Injustice is relatively easy to bear; it is justice that hurts.—H. L. Mencken

51. The chief pang of most trials is not so much the actual suffering itself as our own spirit of resistance to it.—Jean Nicolas Grou

52. Friends provoked become the bitterest of enemies.—Baltasar Gracián

Questions of Life and Religion

1. What forms does idolatry assume today?
2. Is humility an enemy of self-esteem?
3. How does hope differ from wishful thinking?
4. Is it best to be honest with God and with others?
5. In what ways does the Holy Spirit continue the work of Christ?
6. What is heaven like?
7. Are we always guilty when we feel guilty?
8. How does God guide us?
9. How can we help those who grieve?
10. Are grace and good works in conflict?

11. How can we know what God is like?
12. Does one have to *feel* forgiven to *be* forgiven?
13. What are we afraid of?
14. How broad is God's family?
15. When do we have faith?
16. Can evil overthrow faith in a loving God?
17. What is the responsibility of Christians toward people of other religions?
18. Why is the Lord's Supper or Communion also called "the Eucharist"?
19. Why is ethics a necessary element in religious experience?
20. What is eternal life?
21. In what sense are we all equal or unequal?
22. How can we bring envy and jealousy under control?
23. Do we have responsibility for our environment?
24. How does Jesus Christ figure into the final events of human history?
25. What does God intend in the doctrine of election?
26. Is education optional for Christians?
27. How can we deal with our doubts?
28. What is the total biblical teaching on divorce?
29. Is faith a useful factor in the healing process for disease or illness?
30. How is discipline related to the religious life?
31. What do modern-day disciples do as followers of Christ?
32. How can we conquer depression?
33. What are our sources of help in decision making?
34. Are there useful ways for healthy people to think about death?
35. How does the fourth Gospel equate crucifixion and glorification?
36. Is there a necessary conflict between modern science and the biblical account of creation?
37. How are faith and obedience related to God's covenant of grace?
38. Is conversion a once-and-for-all experience?
39. When is conscience a safe guide and when is it not?
40. What are the different meanings of *confession* and why is it useful?
41. Does Christian experience enlarge the experience of community?
42. Is absolute separation of church and state possible or desirable?
43. Can we experience salvation apart from the Church?
44. How can children teach us about God?
45. Is capital punishment unjustly and ineffectively administered?
46. What is the meaning of *blessing*?
47. Why do we baptize?
48. Is anger ever right?
49. What can we say in favor of aging?
50. How are addiction and free will related?
51. When do believers experience "the absence of God"?
52. What can be done to diminish or eliminate abortions?
53. What are the main challenges facing the Church in this new century?

(These questions were suggested by and treated extensively in *Handbook of Themes for Preaching,* edited by James W. Cox, Westminster/John Knox Press, 1991.)

Biblical Benedictions and Blessings

The Lord watch between me and thee when we are absent from one another.—Gen. 31:49

The Lord our God be with us, as he was with our fathers; let him not leave us nor forsake us; that he may incline our hearts unto him, to walk in all his ways and to keep his commandments and his statutes and his judgments, which he commanded our fathers.—1 Kings 8:57–58

Let the words of my mouth and the meditation of my heart be acceptable in thy sight, O Lord, my strength and my redeemer.—Ps. 19:14

Now the God of patience and consolation grant you to be like-minded one toward another according to Christ Jesus; that ye may with one mind and one mouth glorify God, even the Father of our Lord Jesus Christ. Now the God of hope fill you with all joy and peace in believing, that ye may abound in hope, through the power of the Holy Ghost. Now the God of peace be with you.—Rom. 15:5–6, 13, 33

Now to him that is of power to establish you according to my Gospel and the teaching of Jesus Christ, according to the revelation of the mystery, which was kept secret since the world began but now is manifest, and by the Scriptures of the prophets, according to the commandments of the everlasting God, made known to all nations for the glory through Jesus Christ forever.—Rom. 16:25–27

Grace be unto you, and peace, from God our Father, and from the Lord Jesus Christ.—1 Cor. 1:3

The grace of the Lord Jesus Christ and the love of God and the communion of the Holy Ghost be with you all.—2 Cor. 13:14

Peace be to the brethren, and love with faith, from God the Father and the Lord Jesus Christ. Grace be with all them that love our Lord Jesus Christ in sincerity.—Eph. 6:23–24

And the peace of God, which passeth all understanding, shall keep your hearts and minds through Christ Jesus. Finally, brethren, whatsoever things are true, whatsoever things are honest, whatsoever things are just, whatsoever things are pure, whatsoever things are lovely, whatsoever things are of good report; if there be any virtue, and if there be any praise, think on these things. Those things which ye have both learned and received, and heard and seen in me, do; and the God of peace shall be with you.—Phil. 4:7–9

Wherefore also we pray always for you, that our God would count you worthy of this calling and fulfill all the good pleasure of this goodness, and the work of faith with power; that the name of our Lord Jesus Christ may be glorified in you, and ye in him, according to the grace of our God and the Lord Jesus Christ.—2 Thess. 1:11–12

Now the Lord of peace himself give you peace always by all means. The Lord be with you all. The grace of our Lord Jesus Christ be with you all.—2 Thess. 3:16–18

Grace, mercy, and peace, from God our Father and Jesus Christ our Lord.—1 Tim. 1:2

Now the God of peace, that brought again from the dead our Lord Jesus, that great shepherd of the sheep, through the blood of the everlasting covenant, make you perfect in every good work to do his will, working in you that which is well-pleasing in his sight, through Jesus Christ, to whom be glory for ever and ever.—Heb. 13:20–21

The God of all grace, who hath called us unto his eternal glory by Christ Jesus, after that ye have suffered a while, make you perfect, establish, strengthen, settle you. To him be glory and dominion for ever and ever. Greet ye one another with a kiss of charity. Peace be with you all that are in Christ Jesus.—1 Pet. 3:10–14

Grace be with you, mercy, and peace from God the Father, and from the Lord Jesus Christ, the Son of the Father, in truth and love.—2 John 3

Now unto him that is able to keep you from falling, and to present you faultless before the presence of his glory with exceeding joy, to the only wise God our Savior, be glory and majesty, dominion and power, both now and ever.—Jude 24:25

Grace be unto you, and peace, from him which was, and which is to come; and from the seven Spirits which are before his throne; and from Jesus Christ, who is the faithful witness, and the first begotten of the dead, and the prince of the kings of the earth. Unto him that loved us, and washed us from our sins in his own blood, and hath made us kings and priests unto God and his Father, to him be glory and dominion for ever and ever.—Rev. 1:4–6

SERMONS AND HOMILETIC AND WORSHIP AIDS FOR FIFTY-TWO SUNDAYS

SUNDAY, JANUARY 6, 2002
Lectionary Message

Topic: Epiphany—Greater Gifts
Text: Matt. 2:1–12
Other Readings: Isa. 60:1–6; Ps. 72:1–7; Eph. 3:1–12

You see it in every Sunday school Christmas pageant: three kings adorned in Burger King crowns and velour bathrobes. They carry a strange collection of boxes and bottles, intended to represent the gifts the Magi carried on their way to the manger, accompanied by half-remembered verses of "We Three Kings." Tradition even gives the Magi names and mini-biographies: Gaspar, King of Tarsus, brought a small chest filled with frankincense; Melchior, King of Arabia, gave gold to baby Jesus; and Balthasar, King of Ethiopia, came with a flask of myrrh. If, during lesson time, Sunday school teachers say anything further about the three kings, the two points they make most frequently are (1) Jesus is the King of Kings, and that's why other kings honored him; and (2) we give presents to one another at Christmas because we are following the example of the three kings bringing gifts to Jesus.

These sanitized, G-rated renditions of the Christmas story threaten no one's peace of mind—but they are not based on the biblical account of the Magi. Matthew's Gospel calls them wise men, not kings. They were almost certainly astrologers rather than royalty. The Bible mentions three gifts, but not how many givers there were. We do not know their real names, nor where they came from. As for the first of the lessons usually derived from the episode, it should be noted that at least one king—Herod—wanted to kill baby Jesus rather than worship him.

We like this simplistic reading of the story because it makes us feel good. We enjoy getting out the Camcorders and taping the kids as they dress up and entertain the church. We use the story to justify holiday extravagance. Like the rest of our culture, we worship at the altar of consumerism, and like the rest of our culture, we do it without much thought of honoring the infant Messiah. But what if we divested the story of its glue-on beards and foil-wrapped nostalgia? What if we considered the action as it might play out in the contemporary world? The result would be an Epiphany that shows forth not only the Christ who came for Jew and Gentile but also the real cost of honoring the King of Kings.

I. *The wise men gave their time.* One reason the gifts of the magi are celebrated twelve days after Christmas is to remind us that it took *time* for the wise men to see the star and then make their way to Jerusalem and Bethlehem. It took them time to study Old Testament prophecy concerning the Messiah, time to contemplate the significance of this sign in the heavens, time to figure out the best route in crossing the desert. The stable in Bethlehem was not a thirty-minute break in a whirlwind tour of the Holy Land. It wasn't an event sandwiched between soccer practice and an orthodontist's appointment. But time is one of the rarest commodities in our society; we never have enough and are loathe to commit any more of what we do have. Two-career couples speak defensively of spending "quality time" with their children, even though they don't spend "quantity time." Indeed, time is something we *spend.* It is a treasure as surely as gold, frankincense, and myrrh—and Jesus says, "Where your treasure is, there will your heart be also." It was not the price of the gifts that gave the Wise Men a face-to-face encounter with the Son of God; the shepherds, after all, had no costly presents. It was rather the *time* they gave to the endeavor that gave the Magi access to the Savior of the world. As the prophet Jeremiah wrote, "You will seek me and find me when you seek me with all your heart" (Jer. 29:13). How much time are we willing to give in order to encounter the King of Kings?

II. *The wise men gave their security.* Travel was dangerous in the ancient world, and the wilderness was no place for the timid. Scorpions, wild animals, and the possibility of getting lost or dying of thirst posed natural threats to safety. Robbers and slave traders were even worse menaces to one's security. There were no cell phones to summon help. The Wise Men took enormous risks to see the infant Redeemer. Their jeopardy became greater when they sought directions from Herod and then failed to report back to him. Life would have been easier and safer if they had stayed home; they could have studied the Scriptures and the stars and prayed private prayers of thanksgiving that the King of the Jews had been born. But like Paul they were willing to suffer the loss of all things, and count them as refuse, for the surpassing worth of knowing Christ Jesus the Lord (Phil. 3:8). Although it is true that more Christians have been martyred in the last one hundred years than in the previous nineteen hundred years combined, very few of us in North American churches have experienced genuine suffering for our faith. How much would we be willing to risk? Epiphany may be a time to sing the old hymn, "Jesus, I my cross have taken," with its line, "Perish every fond ambition, all I've sought, or hoped, or known; yet how rich is my condition: God and heaven are still my own!"

III. *The Wise Men gave their devotion.* When they reached the stable in Bethlehem, Matthew tells us, they *saw* the child, they *fell down and worshiped* him, they *opened their treasures,* and *they offered him gifts.* Surely this scene is a foretaste of what the writer of Revelation describes: throngs around the throne of God doing the same things as the Magi did—plus singing hymns of praise. In the beginning of Jesus' life, a sample of humanity—Jews and Gentiles, natives and foreigners—were blessed to see the Lord's face and worship him. At the culmination of history, all who have sought the Lord Jesus from every time and place will do the same. The joy of being in Christ's presence will be reward enough.

Gold, frankincense, and myrrh? Perhaps we should say gold, frankincense, and *more,* for that is what the Wise Men offered Jesus. And so should we, confident that in exchange we will receive the best gift of all: our Lord Immanuel.—Carol M. Norén

ILLUSTRATIONS

DEVOTION.   During the war with the Philistines, King David said longingly, "O that someone would give me water to drink from the well of Bethlehem that is by the gate!" (2 Sam. 23:15). It wasn't just physical thirst that David felt; it was also a longing for peace and freedom in his besieged home. Three of his men sneaked behind enemy lines to obtain water from that well and brought it to the king. We can imagine their astonishment when he refused to drink it. Instead, he poured it out as a sacrifice to God, likening it to the blood of the men who risked their lives to get it. The water itself would be priceless to a thirsty man, but David valued even more highly the devotion of those who brought it.—Carol M. Norén

GIFTS.   Giving and receiving gifts reveals something important about the relationship between the giver and recipient. The amount spent (in time or money) is not the telling feature. More revealing is the nature of the gift. Does it show how well the giver knows and understands the receiver? Does it evoke shared memories or anticipate a future between them? The saddest gifts are those that suggest that the two parties don't know each other at all and are unwilling to invest the effort to do so. The gifts of the Wise Men all suggest that the Wise Men knew something about the Messiah from studying Old Testament prophecies, and their presents looked to Jesus' present and future needs.—Carol M. Norén

SERMON SUGGESTIONS

Topic: God's Triumph
Text: Isa. 60:1–6
(1) It comes despite Earth's darkness. (2) It has a growing appeal and attraction. (3) Its purpose finds its ideal and ultimate fulfillment in Jesus Christ.

Topic: God Has a Plan
Text: Eph. 3:1–12
(1) For ages God's plan was shrouded in mystery. (2) This plan was carried out in Jesus Christ. (3) God used the apostle Paul to bring God's plan to fruition for Jew and Gentile alike. (4) God's plan requires us today to respond creatively to the continuing and special needs of our time.

CONGREGATIONAL MUSIC
1. "O Morning Star, How Fair and Bright," Philipp Nicolai (1599)
    WIE SCHOEN LEUCHTET DER MORGENSTERN, Philipp Nicolai (1599)
    This "queen of chorales" relates both to the prophecy of Isaiah and to the account of the star in the East seen by the Magi. It should be sung majestically but joyously. Because of its unusual length, its stanzas could be sung alternately by choir and congregation.
2. "Hail to the Lord's Anointed," James Montgomery (1822)
    WEBB, George J. Webb (1837)
    Montgomery's free paraphrase of Psalm 72 absorbs the psalmist's perceived intent with liberal use of romantic imagery. This hymn would function well at the opening of Epiphany worship.
3. "Make Me a Captive, Lord," George Matheson (1890)
    DIADEMATA, George J. Elvey (1868)
    This noble hymn on the paradoxes of the Christian faith relates particularly to the first verse of the Epistle lesson (Eph. 3:1), in which the apostle uses the imagery of being imprisoned in the Lord's arms. It can be sung in response to the Ephesian reading.
4. "What Star Is This?" Charles Coffin (1737); trans. John Chandler (1837)
    PUER NOBIS NASCITUR, M. Praetorius (1609)
    This Epiphany carol treats the story of the Wise Men and the star in a lighter vein than the first hymn. In the worship of certain churches, this hymn might be more accessible to the singers of the congregation.—Hugh T. McElrath

WORSHIP AIDS

CALL TO WORSHIP.   "O God, May your people worship you as long as the sun shines, as long as the moon gives light, for ages to come" (Ps. 72:5 TEV).

INVOCATION.   We swing wide the gate of the new year, Lord, as, with minds set on the things of God, we enter the challenges set before us. Gather every day of our year unto meaning, so that our moments and hours may be God-honoring, beginning with this first act of corporate worship in the new year. In the ageless name of the Son, we pray.—E. Lee Phillips

OFFERTORY SENTENCE.   "The silver is mine and the gold is mine, saith the Lord of hosts" (Hag. 2:8).

OFFERTORY PRAYER.   Heavenly Father, the gospel teaches that where our treasure is, there our hearts will be also. Help us invest the treasure of our gifts and resources where you would have our hearts reside. We bring these offerings in your service and in Jesus' name.—Kenneth M. Cox

PRAYER.   O God, whoever else you are in the mystery and greatness of your being, you are love. You are the fountain of all love. "We love because you first loved us." To what radical love you keep calling us: to be forgiving to the utmost, to return good for evil, to pray for those who spite us, to persevere through every estrangement, to be available and vulnerable, even to dying on a cross. Who among us is equal to such a challenge? Only in the meaning and experience of your love in Christ crucified can we ever respond to such a high calling.

As we sense your love reaching out to us and to all others, we reach out to one another. We pray for our family and friends with whom we work and play; for those who give leadership to our church in its various ministries; for those who are lonely because they are bereft of loved ones or rejected by others; for those broken with pain and discouraged by illness, and for their family and friends who faithfully keep vigil and pray for their wholeness; for those who are perplexed by difficult decisions; and for those who have the great responsibility of governing others in our nation and in all nations. With them may we hear your call to the righteousness that alone exalts.

In all things draw us to yourself, O God, that our work may be for us not a burden but a delight. Let us not serve in the spirit of bondage as slaves, but in the cheerfulness and gladness of children rejoicing in the doing of your will through the grace of our Lord Jesus Christ.—John Thompson

SERMON

Topic: Can God Work Through You?

TEXT: Num. 11:24–30; Acts 2:1–21

Our text today comes from the book of Numbers. It deals with a large body of material beginning in Numbers 11:1 and extending to 19:22. These are the murmuring stories, the hard, hard times when God's people rose up in anger and complaint and rebellion.

It was not a pretty picture. God led his beloved people out of slavery, across the Red Sea, and into the wilderness. They were on their way to the Promised Land. But a not-so-funny thing happened to them on the way to this new land. Numbers gives us a picture of the dark side of this chosen people. They are pictured as faithless, rebellious, angry—blind to the leadership of God in the wilderness. Alongside this picture is another tradition. God, despite their spitting and clawing and resistance, led them, his reluctant children. And despite their stupidity and childishness and unfaith, he guided them, he sustained them, and he brought his people finally to the new land.

But a great deal of the book of Numbers deals with the murmurings of the people. They began when Israel faced the Red Sea in front of them and Pharaoh's attack in back of them. Moving from Egypt to Sinai, they griped and grumbled every step of the way. "O that we had meat to eat! We remember the fish we ate in Egypt for nothing, the cucumbers, the melons, the leeks, the onions, and the garlic; but now our strength is dried up and there is nothing at all but this manna to look at" (Num. 11:4–6). They complained about the bitter, diseased water. They complained about the sickness they felt in the hot, dry desert. They complained about their enemies, who seemed like giants while they seemed like grasshoppers before them. They hated Moses for getting them into this mess. They despised his assistant, Aaron. And over and over, like a litany, they would say to themselves and to one another, "How in the world did we ever get ourselves into such a mess as this?"

So, by the middle of the eleventh chapter, Moses had had enough. Following the leadership of God, he had struck out on a journey with a ragtag band of ex-slaves without a road map. They had followed a pillar of cloud by day and a pillar of fire by night—not exactly the AAA way. But Moses believed this had been God's doing. Now he had had enough. He was tired—very tired. He kept thinking, "If I hear one more time how great it was back in Egypt, I am just going to turn the reins over to somebody else. If I hear one more time griping, murmuring, crying, and complaining, I will strangle somebody in the name of the Lord."

> Moses heard the people weeping throughout their families, every man at the door of his tent; and the anger of the Lord blazed hotly and Moses was displeased. Moses said to the Lord, "Why has thou dealt ill with thy servant? And why have I not found favor in thy sight, that thou dost lay the burden of all these people upon me? Did I conceive all these people? Did I bring them forth that thou shouldst say to me, 'Carry them in your bosom, as a nurse carries the suckling child, to the land which thou didst swear to give to their fathers?' Where am I to get meat to give to all these people? For they weep before me and say, 'Give us meat, that we may eat.' I am not able to carry all these people alone; the burden is too heavy for me. If thou wilt deal thus with me, kill me at once, if I find favor in thy sight, that I may not see my wretchedness." [Num. 11:10–15]

The strangest thing happened: God heard the frustrations of Moses. He told Moses to call together the seventy elders, the leaders of Israel: "Bring them to the tent of meeting. Have them stand with you, and I will come down and talk with them." And this is significant: "And I will take some of the spirit which is upon you and put it on them, and they shall bear the burden of the people with you, that you may not bear it yourself alone" (Num. 11:17).

So it came to pass that the burden of leadership was dispersed. It rested on Moses and the seventy elders. God "took some of the spirit that was upon him and put it upon the seventy elders; and when the spirit rested upon them, they prophesied" (Num. 11:25).

But it got out of hand. There were two men—Eldad and Medad—not elders, who decided they would share Moses' burden, too. They began to prophesy. The people were furious. They came to Moses saying, "Guess what: Eldad and Medad are prophesying as though they are somebody. Tell them to stop." There was a long pause and Moses said, "Are you jealous for my sake? Would that all the Lord's people were prophets, that the Lord would put his spirit upon them!"

We are living in a time of much murmuring. Our angers are barely beneath the surface. *Road rage* is a current word. We sue one another at the drop of a hat. We set up impossible standards for our leaders—and it doesn't matter who it is. Look at our response to the tragedy at Columbine High School. We blame everybody: the parents, the principal of the school, the school board, video games, strange clothing, body piercing, tattoos, wild music, movies drenched with violence, no prayer in the schools, crummy churches, ineffective pastors, a society with not enough rules, too many guns, too much money, houses too big, working mothers, absentee fathers, lack of values, the morals of the president of the United States. It is an onomatopoetic word: it sounds like the thing it describes. Murmuring, murmuring, murmuring, murmuring.

So God answered Moses and God dealt with the murmuring of his people. His solution? He called seventy elders from the tribes and gave them part of the responsibility that Moses had totally assumed. Eldad and Medad decided they would be part of the answer and no longer a part of the problem. So, on their own they began to prophesy—to help their leaders out.

When the elders and Eldad and Medad began to work, the burden was not too great. The responsibility was shared and the people of Israel moved forward. The murmuring did not stop. It never does. But the people moved forward, because the journey was the people's journey, not Moses' journey.

Do you remember what happened in the early days of the Church? There was murmuring in the Church. Widows were being neglected. Pastors were too busy. There was more work than there were hours in the day. So they began to solve the problem with the election of the first deacons. They elected seven persons of good report—persons of responsibility—to share the load, to make sure that all the people's needs were attended to, to take some of the burden off the back of the pastor, and to assume that part of the health and work of the Church belonged to them.

Baptists in the sixteenth century hammered out a principle that came out of the New Testament (1 Pet. 2:5, 9; Rev. 1:6; 5:10; 20:6). They called the Church the priesthood of all believers. There is no pecking order, they said, in the Kingdom of God. Now we know that this has always been more dream than reality. This is why the well-heeled and the rich and famous are treated one way and everybody else is treated another way (see James 2). The ways of the world do invade the life of the Church everywhere. But the dream says that the ground at the foot of the cross is level, and everybody stands on that same ground.

Through the years we have misunderstood this marvelous doctrine. We have taken it to mean that anybody could march into any meeting anywhere and do anything they pleased. After all, we are all priests. But this is a total misunderstanding. The early Baptists believed that everybody was *responsible* for the growth and movement of the Kingdom of God. If the Church falls down it is everybody's fault. If the Church moves ahead, you are to be part of that movement. God counts on us to make this possible. To assume the mantle of priest is to wear the mantle of responsibility. The deacons in the early Church took on part of the burden of the pastor. They did not add to the burdens of the Church.

Alongside this passage from Numbers, I have read a marvelous passage from Acts 2. It was the great dream. In verse 1, they were all together in one place. In verse 2, a sound came like the rush of a mighty wind and it filled all the house. In verse 3, each one of them felt the tongues of fire resting on them. In verse 4, all were filled with the Holy Spirit. In verse 5, every nation was represented. In verse 6, a multitude came together and they all heard in their own language. In verse 9, we are given a list of the languages and the differences the Spirit spoke to each person, one by one. In verse 12, all were amazed, and in verse 17, those wonderful words of Joel are quoted: that God's Spirit will be poured out on all flesh, that sons and daughters shall prophesy, that young men shall see visions and old men shall dream dreams, and that even maids and janitors will find the Spirit poured out on them. "And whoever it is—whoever it is—that calls on the name of the Lord Jesus will be saved" (Acts 2:1–21).

It was a revolutionary event. Why? Because it began something that is still trying to touch each and every one of us. The Spirit of God does not rest only on the ordained, duly qualified, seminary-trained, well-heeled, and educated—period. No. In Acts 6, seven deacons were chosen to complete the Spirit's work. The Spirit of God is like the wind that touched everything and everybody, and when you are touched, you will get up like Eldad and Medad and make a difference. No more murmuring. No more murmuring. Now you will assume responsibility. You will take your place in that long, long line that makes a difference.

So, at long last we come to the point of this sermon: Can God work in your life? Can the Spirit move in your life? Can you make a difference where you are? Will you be one of the seventy who said we will share the load, we will put our murmuring aside, we will make a difference. Will you be like Eldad and Medad—the unlikely ones—who came forward and said, You can count on me. Will you be one of the servants in Acts 6?—Roger Lovette

SUNDAY, JANUARY 13, 2002
Lectionary Message

Topic: We Too Believe, and So We Speak

TEXT: Acts 10:34–43

Other Readings: Isa. 42:1–9; Acts 10:34–43; Matt. 3:13–17

One popular method of biblical interpretation today is sometimes called "dynamic translation of the text." The action of the text is not only paraphrased in contemporary language but also "recontextualized" in the present world. For example, in a dynamic translation of the story of the Good Samaritan, those who didn't stop to give help might be yuppies and elected officials, and the Samaritan might be a homeless person with AIDS. Although dynamic translation can render a text more vivid and evocative, one of its dangers is that important words can get lost in translation.

This morning's reading, taken from the tenth chapter of Acts, is a passage we often recontextualize—and no wonder, given the interesting characters and exciting action. Our focus might be on the experience Cornelius had, in which an angel told him to seek out Simon Peter (10:1–8), or on Peter's vision of animals clean and unclean (10:9–16). The point often made about these portions is that God may command us to do unexpected things—even things that are contrary to what we were taught growing up—and we must do what God calls us to do. The outpouring of the Holy Spirit onto Gentiles and Jews alike is borrowed to support God's evenhanded dealing with all people. The baptism of Cornelius and his acceptance into the community demonstrate the invisible changes that have already taken place.

This method of Bible study pays more attention to actions than to speech. It is thus regrettable, for it is Peter's *speech* in verses 34–43 that enables us to make sense of the action. Let's take a closer look at what is said.

I. *It is about Jesus Christ.* These nine verses present salvation history in succinct form. Peter's words tell the story of Jesus, beginning with the announcement by John the Baptist and Jesus' baptism. Cornelius learns that Jesus was from Nazareth; that he had a ministry of preaching and healing; that he was crucified, buried, and raised on the third day; that he called followers into ministry; and that he will return as judge of the living and the dead. Peter does not talk about his vision, about how he felt before and during the event, and about how it compared with others' religious experiences. No, it is not Peter's prior experiences that make sense of his encounter with Cornelius, but rather remembering who Jesus Christ is and what Jesus has done. Peter baptized Cornelius because it was consistent with the Risen Lord's command to spread the gospel to all. If we consider how little biographical information we have about Peter, Paul, and the other apostles, it becomes apparent that they consider themselves part of God's story but of no great significance on their own.

II. *It is a confession of faith.* There is a remarkable correlation between this testimony in Acts and the Apostles' Creed. Elsewhere in the New Testament, we discover converts making confessions of faith and the people of God presenting their beliefs in summary form. In Acts 2, Peter presents the gospel in miniature in his Pentecost sermon. The Ethiopian eunuch of Acts 8 heard Philip expound on Isaiah 53:7–8 and responded by confessing, "I believe that Jesus Christ is the Son of God." The hymn of Philippians 2:5–11 recapitulates the story of Jesus in poetic form. During his sermon on Mars Hill (Acts 17:22–33), Paul re-presents the heart of the gospel in terms a non-Jewish audience could understand. In whatever way the truth is worded, the essentials of the Christian faith remain the same: Do we believe in our own small lives and limited experience? No, we believe in the person and work of Jesus Christ. This belief is stated still more tersely in John 3:16 and 2 Corinthians 5:19. Modern affirmations that focus on our feelings and circumstances rather than on Jesus Christ do not have the power of the Word and Spirit to change lives.

III. *It is the basis for how we engage in ministry and the rest of life.* It is the fashion today for companies, colleges, and other institutions to have mission statements. Such statements provide the foundation for action and decision making; they are a "gold standard" by which other propositions are assessed. The New Testament shows that the mission statement of the Church is not based on one disciple's dream, another's vision, or still another's life experience, but rather on who Jesus Christ is and what he has done and will do. Our confession of faith is the lens through which we view the vicissitudes of the world around us and respond to it. As the apostle Paul wrote elsewhere, "We too believe, and so we speak" (2 Cor. 4:13). Unless we are centered on the reality of who Christ is, we as the Church have nothing to say, nothing to do, and no future before us. Thanks be to God for speaking his Incarnate Word, Jesus Christ.—Carol M. Norén

ILLUSTRATIONS

EXPECTATIONS.   A story is told of two primary grade teachers. The first teacher was told that the students in her class were unusually gifted; the second teacher was told that the children in her class were of below-average ability. Both teachers believed the reports given to them, even though both classes were a mix of average, gifted, and below-average students. The teacher who believed that the children were gifted taught with enthusiasm, encouraging the children to live up to their abilities—and they did! The teacher who believed that her students would not amount to much taught them as though they were dull and incapable—and they too met her expectations. In both cases the teachers acted on what they were told; words produced belief and belief led to predictable results.—Carol M. Norén

WHO ELSE IS WRONG?   A few years ago, former televangelist Jim Bakker published his book *I Was Wrong.* The book traces the rise and fall of the PTL ministry and Bakker's marriage to Tammy Faye. He wrote, "As the true impact of Jesus' words regarding money impacted my heart and mind, I became physically nauseated. I was wrong. I was wrong! Wrong in my lifestyle, certainly, but even more fundamentally, wrong in my understanding of the Bible's true message. Not only was I wrong, but I was teaching the opposite of what Jesus had said." Many of Bakker's critics did not read the book but nevertheless claimed it was another scam. In truth, however, Bakker's confession is something like Simon Peter's, because in this passage, Peter too was confessing, "I was wrong." He acknowledged that he had misunderstood God's Word, and he too used his mistake as an opportunity to tell someone what Jesus said and did.—Carol M. Norén

SERMON SUGGESTIONS

Topic: God's Kind of Servant
TEXT: Isa. 42:1–9
(1) Brings forth justice (v. 1). (2) Is sympathetic toward those who struggle (vv. 2–4). (3) Though unlikely and unworthy, is enabled and used by God to achieve God's high purposes (vv. 5–9).

Topic: Why Be Baptized?
TEXT: Matt. 3:13–17
(1) Jesus had a special reason to be baptized (vv. 13–15). (2) Although we share an aspect of Jesus' reason for being, our purpose is special for us (Acts 2:38; Gal. 3:27).

CONGREGATIONAL MUSIC
1. "Give Glory to God, All You Heavenly Creatures," Ps. 29; vers. Calvin Seerveld (1983)
   ARLES, Charles H. Gabriel (c. 1925)
   The militant mood of this simple Gabriel tune reinforces the notion of the earth-shaking power of the voice of God which is set forth as the principal theme of Psalm 29.
2. "God Is Working His Purpose Out," Arthur C. Ainger (1894)
   PURPOSE, Martin F. Shaw (1931)
   As response to the reading of Isaiah's prophecy (42:1–9), this hymn that affirms the certainty of the universal spread of God's glory would be appropriate.
3. "Songs of Thankfulness and Praise," Christopher Wordsworth (1862)
   SALZBURG, Jaakob Hintze (1678)
   This Epiphany hymn refers to all the themes of the season found in Holy Scripture. It is

stanza 2 that relates specifically to the event recorded in the Gospel lesson (Matt. 3:13–17), that is, the baptism of Jesus.

4. "Holy God, We Praise Your Name," vers. *Te Deum*, Ignaz Franz (eighteenth century) GROSSER GOTT, *Katholisches Gesangbuch* (c. 1774)

Suitable for the opening of worship, this free paraphrase of the great Latin paeon of praise, the *Te Deum*, also relates in particular to this day's reading from Acts (10:34–43).—Hugh T. McElrath

WORSHIP AIDS

CALL TO WORSHIP.   "Praise the Lord, you heavenly beings; praise his glory and power. Praise the Lord's glorious name; bow down before the Holy One when he appears" (Ps. 29:1–2 TEV).

INVOCATION.   Just for a while, Lord, let us behold thy glory. Just for a while let us feel the divine presence. Just for a while let us be so quiet that the Spirit of God can move across the depths of our souls and change us from within. Give us in these few minutes what we need until we meet again, and steel us with courage to receive the gift.—E. Lee Phillips

OFFERTORY SENTENCE.   "Whoever shares with others should do it generously" (Rom. 12:8 TEV).

OFFERTORY PRAYER.   Lord, please guide our offering to build God's Kingdom on Earth, that the Holy Spirit might bless giver and recipient and that Jesus Christ might be honored.— E. Lee Phillips

PRAYER.   Lord, make us instruments of your peace. Where there is hatred, let us sow love; where there is injury, pardon; where there is discord, union; where there is doubt, faith; where there is despair, hope; where there is darkness, light; where there is sadness, joy. Grant that we may not so much seek to be consoled as to console; to be understood as to understand; to be loved as to love. For it is in giving that we receive; it is in pardoning that we are pardoned; and it is in dying that we are born to eternal life.—St. Francis of Assisi

SERMON
Topic: The Parts and the Whole
TEXT: Isa. 6:1–8

It is a confession that comes and goes. It is a confession we are made abundantly aware of and then it seems to fade away. We begin to believe it does not describe us. We have corrected the problem. It is no longer applicable, and then it happens again. Yet no matter how many times there is evidence for it, we want to forget it as quickly as possible.

I am talking about Isaiah's confession. He has come to the Temple in the year that King Uzziah died—perhaps as the citizens of Syria recently had done. Isaiah went to the Temple to grieve the death of his King. But in that moment of worship, he had, in our modern language, a religious experience. He saw the Lord sitting on a throne, high and lifted up. He immediately fell down in reverence and awe, and he felt the earth move under his feet. The voice of the Lord spoke. Isaiah trembled and imagined that he was in big trouble. He had gotten in over his head. He was not supposed to be there. He did not deserve to be there. He was unworthy to be there. He was a man of evil and impure thoughts, and he lived in the midst of other people who were unclean. He believed he was going to die. The people were tainted with evil and sin, and Isaiah knew he was a sinful man.

Every Sunday we come in here and confess that we know we are sinful people and that we live in the midst of an unclean and sinful world. Yet every time there is a news report that an airline has intentionally and deliberately refused to make necessary and vital repairs to its airplanes, somebody asks the question, in all sincerity, "How could somebody do that?" As if we really don't believe that evil exists in all of us and is affecting our actions and our thoughts!

My history books told me that there was a time when people began to think that Darwin and Freud were going to make us progress upward and onward to become the brightest and best, that progress was society's most important product, and that with all of the new railroads, the telephone, the planes and cars, the age of perfectibility of humanity was in sight. Churches had crusades to win the world for Christ by the end of the 1920s. But we also had World War I, the depression, and World War II and the Hitler gas chambers. Humanity was getting better and better, so how could these things happen? Woe is me, for I am a man of unclean lips and I dwell in the midst of a people of unclean lips.

The Christian faith calls it the doctrine of original sin, and it is the affirmation that we are all affected by the power of evil, in the same way that we are all affected by the power of the air we breath. We affirm that God made us good, but we also affirm that we did not stay that way and that now all who are part of the human race, all who are human beings, are conflicted. There is a jungle within us. There are powers, forces, urges, and wants within us that are destructive, selfish, mean, and brutish. But these are not the only forces in us. There are noble, kind, generous, and peaceful spirits within us as well. Any business, any group that believes people are basically good and will do the right thing if left to their own choices has simply refused to see the power of evil within us.

On one of his Mars Hill tapes, Ken Myers talks with a religious observer of culture who suggests that one of the great changes that has happened in public education is that education has accepted as true the affirmation that children are basically good. It has accepted the notion that all claims of knowledge are just one's personal opinions and that all moral standards are just local traditions. Every time one person tries to teach another person some absolute, some moral code, some relationship between the parts and the whole, that person is imposing on the other person his or her own prejudices and biases. If parents bring their children to worship, they are imposing on the children their own religious biases. And our culture suggests that children would really be better off if they were allowed to pick their own religious values. In other places and in other ages, it was understood that there were necessary and important boundaries and limits that needed to be taught to children so that the evil within them might be contained. Now children are seen as innocent, good, wonderful creatures who have within them marvelous possibilities and gifts, and we ought not to impose any limitations or restrictions on them because those biases and prejudices might crush or destroy their unique characters. So, every no, every rule, every limitation is now fought as a restriction of somebody's right to be free, is resisted because it may cramp somebody's development. Listen to the debate about a dress code in school. Wearing identical clothing restricts children's right to express their own personalities in school. Any suggestion that what is being limited and restricted is demonic and an expression of evil is ruled out because that judgment is seen as simply bias, prejudice, the expression of an arbitrary, obsolete value system.

So, of course when high school students from a progressive, upper middle class high school go on a shooting spree and kill hordes of other students who have been teasing, bullying, ridiculing, hazing them, all anybody can do is walk around for more than a year asking the question over and over again, "Why did this happen? How did this happen?" The categories and the descriptive models are not available. The culture celebrates the young girl who acknowledged her Christian faith before being shot, but it has a great deal more difficulty using the Christian faith category to explain the evil within the other or the event.

Over and over, we go through the same cycle: culture keeps trying to break down the religious experience into something less mysterious, into something it can understand, manage, and explain. The culture wants to be able to analyze and control the mystery of this encounter with a Holy God. Father, Son, and Holy Ghost—the mystery of the Trinity, the power and love of God. Over and over, even the Church has tried to explain this so that the world could understand it. President Tom Gillespie of Princeton Theological Seminary says that one of the great blessings that will come from the postmodern age is that the Church will suddenly be freed from the self-imposed burden of trying to explain its theology to the world. Now Christian faith can just boldly declare the mystery of the triune nature of God's love as a mystery of the encounter of faith and not worry what the world will say about the logical implications of that three-in-one language. The Church will know that the world has gotten itself into such a mess that nobody's arguments will hold water. Every generalization will be attacked as a grab for power. Every statement of moral conduct will be opposed by others. The work of trying to defend the Christian faith in the public arena will be just as impossible as the work of trying to defend any other worldview or comprehensive system of knowledge. All of them will be lumped together as just somebody's current theory.

The Christian witness in the years to come is going to be seen in terms of the kind of boundaries, limits, and standards we are willing to accept, that make us look funny in the eyes of the world around us. The power of our witness to Jesus Christ just evaporates when we, too, try to diminish or ignore the power of evil.

One woman took her spiritual journey very seriously. She was a member of a new church in a dynamic community—a university community of the brightest and best people, high-tech, creative. They were into small-group ministry. All members were assigned to prayer circles and Bible study groups. Into the church came an older man who had been active in ministry in another denomination. He volunteered to lead a prayer circle. He began to make comments and suggestions that the woman did not think were appropriate. She told the minister and staff. They told her they were supposed to be pastors to all the people in the church, so they took a kind of nonjudgmental stance. Finally, the woman took her charges to the next level, where she asked for action. Action is now being suggested.

Where was the recognition that we are sinful people living in the midst of unclean people? Jesus suggests that when evil appears his disciples need to confront that evil and seek to put limits on it. If anyone sins against you, confront them. If they will not repent, take elders with you and confront them.

If Dr. Gillespie from Princeton is right, we are entering a wonderful time for Christian people. We can teach and preach our description of reality and our understanding of human nature and know that we will not be supported by the schools, by the politicians, by the government, by the intellectual community. We will be one more group competing with every other group, and our witness and our impact will be through how we live in response to what we say we believe.

Look around. There is no shortage of evidence of evil. We are sinful people, people of unclean lips, and we live in the midst of unclean people. The evil in us has been overcome by the love of God in Jesus Christ, and as we gather in that name and in that power, the Spirit and the grace of God come into us and grant us the power and the vision to begin to be transformed into the image and likeness of Jesus Christ. It is a journey of sanctification. It is a blooming of the new creation, like the coming of a flower. It is a lifetime journey into a new kingdom and a new creation. By the power of the Holy God at work in us, the evil in us is refined, purified, confronted, and consumed, so that we come closer and closer to the intention and purpose for which God created us.

Nobody has yet found a way to explain God-in-three-persons, Blessed Trinity, in a way that is satisfying to the philosophy department of any major university. Nobody has yet, that I know of, found a way to explain how God is sovereign over all, yet we have free will. We have wasted a lot of time over the centuries trying to defend ourselves from the criticisms of society. Now that rational attacks on rationality have gone so far that nothing rational can be explained satisfactorily, we are back where the early Church began—making claims that we believe: that we have been created by a good and loving God, that we are walking contradictions, partly truth and partly fiction. Good and evil afflicts us all. The evil within us and all creation has been met and overcome by the love and mercy of God in Jesus Christ, and as we gather in obedience and faith in Jesus Christ, the Holy Spirit of God, the Spirit who makes us one with Jesus Christ works in us and through us to purge and purify us and make us new creations. We claim it, we don't need to explain it; we need to be prepared to live it.—Rick Brand

SUNDAY, JANUARY 20, 2002
Lectionary Message

Topic: A Star Witness
TEXT: John 1:29–42
Other Readings: Isa. 49:1–7; Ps. 40:1–11; 1 Cor. 1:1–9

A phrase that has come into use within the last ten years or so is "culture wars." It can be used to denote many conflicting claims within contemporary life, but in the Christian Church, it often refers to disputes over worship style and evangelism. There is the assumption that aging World War II vets, Baby Boomers, Gen-Xers, and Millennials have different world views and preferences—and these preferences must be taken into account if we're going to be effective in carrying out the Church's mission. We tinker with new music, alternative days and times for worship services, formal versus informal styles, preaching from the center aisle rather than from the pulpit. We assume that people are shopping around for a church that matches their aesthetic preferences, and perhaps that is true to some extent. In many ways, we let the culture set the agenda for the church while learning to speak the language of the people to whom we are trying to minister.

Could it be our priorities are out of order? In our attempt to "be all things to all people, that [we] might by all means save some" (1 Cor. 9:22), there is always the danger of becoming a market-driven enterprise rather than a gospel-driven enterprise. If we look to the witness of John the Baptist, as recorded in this morning's text, we find he did not wear a garment of camel's hair rather than cotton because the color was more flattering to his skin tones. He was not concerned with making his listeners feel comfortable and welcome so that they'd come back to hear him a second time. By today's standards, John the Baptist was doing things all wrong! And yet, in spite of his rough language and eccentric appearance, John the Baptist was doing exactly what God called him to do. He is a model witness for us as we consider ways to proclaim the Gospel today.

I. *John lived courageously.* John the Baptist ministered in a hostile environment. The Pharisees sent spies to see if they could catch him in error, and the Roman government certainly wasn't cheering about the Messiah of whom John spoke. His listeners didn't enjoy being called "a brood of vipers," and there must have been scoffers among the crowds when he preached and baptized. He appears to have been homeless, scavenging off the land and heedless of his future. Self-preservation was not part of his *modus operandi.* There is nothing in Scripture to suggest John the Baptist was *unkind,* but his bravery in speaking out against deceit and sin cost him his life.

We would do well to ask ourselves how we understand our mission in an indifferent or hostile culture. The courage of John the Baptist should incite us to do whatever God calls us to do without regard for prestige, personal safety, or self-interest.

II. *John spoke the truth about Jesus.* All Israel had been waiting for the promised Messiah. John was appointed to be "the voice of one crying in the wilderness" to prepare the way of the Lord. He proclaimed who Jesus was: the "one who was before me," the Lamb of God who takes away the sin of the world, and the Son of God. His Jewish listeners would have recognized this last as a messianic title, but they would have been startled by the appellation "Lamb of God" with its associations with Passover. The Passover lamb, after all, was sacrificed to remember God's deliverance from the plague of the first-born. In speaking this truth about Jesus, John was announcing that the Christ would not be the political leader hoped for by Israel, but rather the Savior of the world, the one who would deliver them from the penalty of sin.

Do we soft-pedal the truth about Jesus as it has been revealed to us? A minister at one of America's megachurches talks about Christ as healer and leader, but not as Savior and Lord. When another evangelist asked him why he didn't use the latter terms, the minister said people won't accept that they need *saving,* but everyone wants to be *healed*—and the term *Lord* is a turn-off. All our language is imperfect and limited, but like John the Baptist, we should endeavor to proclaim *all* of who Jesus is, and not limit ourselves to the terminology that is fashionable and acceptable in the marketplace.

III. *John embodied humility.* John the Baptist and Jesus were related; their mothers were kinswomen. On the basis of Luke's Gospel, we might almost claim John had known Jesus since before his birth. John the Baptist could have been tempted, therefore, to make much of their connection and bask in the Messiah's reflected glory: behavior akin to that of James and John when they asked Jesus for seats of honor in the Kingdom of God. But John the Baptist embodies humility in his witness. Twice in this passage he acknowledges, "I myself did not know him," meaning, presumably, that he had no previous insight that Jesus was the

Son of God, until the Spirit revealed it to him. Furthermore, John tells the Pharisees that he is not worthy to untie the thong of Jesus' sandal, that Jesus ranks before him, that Jesus baptizes with the Holy Spirit while he, John, only baptizes with water. The Gospel reports that two of John's disciples left John after hearing his witness, and went to follow Jesus. Still later John remarks, "he (Jesus) must increase, but I must decrease."

Do our churches practice the same humility and servant-hood as John the Baptist? Are we honest with each other and the world about our failings, our ignorance, our occasional short-sightedness? Are we as willing to speak of the way Christ has changed our lives as we are the way others ought to let Christ change them? A contemporary bumper sticker echoes the humility of John: "Christians aren't perfect, just forgiven." Courage, honesty, and humility do more to present the grace of Jesus Christ than one style of music as opposed to another. Thank God for witnesses like John the Baptist.—Carol M. Norén

ILLUSTRATIONS

TESTIFYING CONFESSIONALLY.   Several years ago I participated in a short-term mission in the red-light district of Hamburg, Germany. We helped run a coffee-house ministry at the Salvation Army citadel, organized a daycare center for children of prostitutes, and did street evangelism every evening. This last consisted of singing, distributing tracts and invitations to the coffee house in different languages, and giving personal testimonies. Very soon I noticed that people ignored or jeered at speakers who told "triumphant" faith stories. By contrast, when persons testifying spoke confessionally, acknowledging his or her need for Christ and how they perceived God at work in them, passersby drew nearer and wanted to hear them. One might say that people are likely to be resentful of someone who brags of perfect health, but everyone wants to know of a good doctor.—Carol M. Norén

PAUL'S CONFESSION.   The apostle Paul had a sterling pedigree, which is documented in Acts 22:1–3, 25–28 and Philippians 3:4–7. It is curious, then, that Paul "boasts" far more about his error in persecuting Christians prior to his conversion, and repeats the story of God smiting him on the road to Damascus. On the face of it, such stories put the apostle in a very unflattering light. But Paul openly admits his early rejection of the Messiah in order that God's patience and prevenient grace may be cast in sharper relief. Paul acknowledges his ongoing battle with sin (Rom. 7) as a means of sharing the good news that "there is now no condemnation for those who are in Christ Jesus."—Carol M. Norén

SERMON SUGGESTIONS

Topic: Patience and Its Fruits
TEXT: Ps. 40:1–11
(1) Intolerable circumstances (v. 2). (2) Ineffective remedies (v. 6). (3) Inspiring considerations (v. 5). (4) Intentional proclamations (vv. 7–10).

Topic: How Christ Has Blessed Us
TEXT: 1 Cor. 1:1–9
(1) He has brought us God's grace (v. 4). (2) He has enriched us with an experience we can openly share (vv. 5–7). (3) He has enabled us to trust God for a glorious future (vv. 8–9).

CONREGATIONAL MUSIC

1. "O Day of Rest and Gladness," Christopher Wordsworth (1862)

   CRUEGER, W. H. Monk (1868)

   ES FLOG KLEINS WALDVOEGELEIN (seventeenth century); harm. G. R. Woodward (1904)

   This hymn for the opening of morning worship reflects some of the thoughts in the Old Testament lesson (Isa. 49:1–11), especially the idea of reverent adoration of "the Holy One of Israel."

2. "Great Is Thy Faithfulness," Thomas O. Chisholm (1923)

   FAITHFULNESS, William M. Runyan (1923)

   A comforting song extolling the faithfulness of God, it relates to the assertion that God is indeed faithful in both the Epistle reading (1 Cor. 1:1–9) and the Old Testament lesson (Isa. 49:1–7). It could be sung either to introduce or follow either of these readings.

3. "Behold the Lamb," Dottie Rambo (1979)

   BEHOLD THE LAMB, Dottie Rambo (1979)

   Drawing on the passage in today's Epistle reading (John 1:29–42), this contemporary song could be sung immediately following that reading. A quiet singing of the final refrain could be quite worshipful.

4. "I Waited Patiently for God," Ps. 40; vers. Bert Polman (1980)

   MERTHYRTYDFIL, Joseph Parry (1870)

   The first two stanzas of this metrical version of Psalm 40 are based on the first portion of the psalm assigned for this day's worship. It could be sung instead of reading the psalm lesson.—Hugh T. McElrath

WORSHIP AIDS

CALL TO WORSHIP.   "I waited patiently for the Lord; and he inclined unto me, and heard my cry. . . . And he hath put a new song in my mouth, even praise unto our God: many shall see it, and fear, and shall trust in the Lord" (Ps. 40:1, 3).

INVOCATION.   Now O Lord, mercifully deal with us for we are sinners in need of forgiveness and strugglers in need of faith, and our hope is in God who made heaven and earth and loves us beyond telling.—E. Lee Phillips

OFFERTORY SENTENCE.   "Ascribe to the Lord the glory due his name. Bring an offering and come before him: worship the Lord in the splendor of his holiness" (1 Chron. 16:29 NIV).

OFFERTORY PRAYER.   Small beginnings make large differences, Father. Take our meager gifts and our larger offerings and through them do great things for the kingdom of Christ, we pray.—Henry Fields

PRAYER.   Clear our vision this morning, we pray, Lord. We are so blinded by what is visible around us that we fail to see the things of the Spirit that make the large difference in how we live and move and have our being. We need this morning to be able to see beyond the darkness of the material world into that which is luminously spiritual. All about us are barriers that prohibit our view of the wide vistas you desire us to see. Enable us this morning to see beyond the barriers that we may envision what is real and eternal.

Let us see beyond the barrier of the quick satisfaction of hate to the long joy of forgiveness.

Let us see beyond the appetite for more to the pleasure of self-control.

Let us see beyond greed to the luxury of giving.

Let us see beyond blinding pride to the healthiness of humility.

Let us see beyond profit to usefulness.

Let us see past the heat of desire to the light of renunciation.

Let us see past the glaring light of power to the beauty of service.

Let us see past the poisonous growth of selfishness to the wonder and power of selflessness, we pray in Jesus name.—Henry Fields

SERMON

Topic: The Greatest of These

TEXT: 1 Cor. 13

What would Jesus tell the disciples in His last hours with them? What challenge would He leave with them? Jesus said, "By this shall all men know that you are my disciples, if you have love one for another."

"By this" Jesus said, not by your power, not by your wealth, not by your success, not by your attractiveness, not by your impressive statistics, not by your beautiful buildings, but by your love. This is how people will know that you are my followers. For love is the key to the Christian life, the distinguishing mark of discipleship.

But what is love? We use this same word to refer to affection and attraction, to devotion and emotion, to feeling and to fancy. We say we love God and love the Braves and love oysters, using the same word for each. But what does the word really mean? In our text for today which Harnack calls "the greatest, strongest, and deepest thing Paul ever wrote" and which G. Campbell Morgan says is "one of the most remarkable passages that ever came from the pen of man," Paul paints a portrait of real Christian love.

I. *Unequaled in its richness.* First, Paul says that love is unequaled in its richness (vv. 1–3). There were five things which the saints at Corinth considered to be key to life: oratory, prophecy, miracle working, philanthropy and martyrdom. Notice how Paul relates love to these five things. Paul is not comparing love to these five things as if to say that love is better than they are. He is saying that if you have all five of these things, but do not have love, you really have nothing. All other virtues, all other characteristics, all other qualities, all other gifts, all other attainments are nothing without love. Love is absolutely essential.

The church has lost much of its spiritual power. Why? Because while gaining material wealth and social prestige, it has lost its love.

Take away love, and the church is a failure. Take away love, and life is a drag. Take away love, and our eloquent words are meaningless. Take away love, and our earth is a tomb. Take away love and you have nothing. Love is unequaled in its richness.

II. *Unending in its response.* In the first phrase of verse 4, Paul tells us, secondly, that love is unending in its response. The word "patient" means "longsuffering" and it carries with it the idea of persistency. What Paul is saying is that love, real love, is unending in its response.

Notice how Paul illustrates this in verses 5–6. When Paul says that love is not jealous, he means that the achievement of others cannot make love waver. When Paul says that love is not boastful or arrogant or rude, and does not insist on its own way, he means that one's own achievement cannot make love waver. When he says that love is not irritable or resentful, he means that injuries caused by others cannot make it waver. When he says that it does not rejoice in the wrong but rejoices in the right, he means that sin or failure on the part of others cannot make it waver. Nothing can make love waver—not the achievement of others, not one's own achievement, not the injury caused by others, not the failure of others, nothing!

III. *Unequivocal in its reaction.* But then there is a third thing Paul tells us about love—it is unequivocal in its reaction. The second phrase in verse four, which the New American Standard translates "Love is kind," is expressed in another translation like this: "Love looks for a way of being constructive." Love not only passively endures all that life throws at it. Love reacts to life with positive action. In every situation, in every person, love looks for a way to be constructive. It is unequivocal in its reaction.

How often our love simply contemplates and considers instead of acting. One poet describes the pathos of our day when he writes, "I was hungry, and you formed a humanities club and discussed my hunger. Thank you. I was imprisoned, and you crept off quietly to your chapel to pray for my release. I was naked, and in your mind you debated the morality of my appearance. I was sick, and you knelt and thanked God for your health. I was homeless, and you preached to me of the spiritual nature of the shelter of God's love. I was lonely, and you left me alone to pray for me. You seemed so holy, so close to God. But I am still very hungry, and lonely, and cold. . . ."

When in the rush and busyness of life you are willing to stop just for a minute and reach out a hand of compassion to someone in need, that's love. And Jesus said, "By this shall all men know that you are my disciples, if you love one another."—Brian L. Harbour

SUNDAY, JANUARY 27, 2002
Lectionary Message

Topic: Heroes Versus Headship
TEXT: 1 Cor. 1:1–18
Other Readings: Isa. 9:1–4; Ps. 27:1, 4–9; Matt. 4:12–23

> Isn't he beautiful? Beautiful, isn't he?
> Isn't he wonderful? Wonderful isn't he?

The opening lines of a Vineyard song that praises God could easily have been the theme song of the early Christians in the city of Corinth. They would not have sung it to exalt the deity but rather to praise a favored leader of their chosen clique within the church. How easy it is to slip into following one whom God provides as teacher and mentor for us on our faith journey and then to revere him or her as wonderful, even beautiful, instead of the Provider himself. Appreciation and admiration of human leadership can become a subtle but sure distraction from the one who alone is worthy of our praise. Before we know it, we are worshipping the hero instead of the head of the Church. Such was the case in the Corinthian church in A.D. 56.

I. *Setting things straight.* Paul had his work cut out for him. He had to exhort the first-century converts. This passage is one among many in which Paul counsels and instructs the Corinthians on important issues of Christian faith and conduct. Unlike the church in

Philadelphia, the Corinthian church was not known for its brotherly love, and Paul had to appeal to them to resolve their differences, present a united front, and be knit together.

(a) In verse 11 we learn that Chloe's household had brought word to Paul that there was trouble on the homefront. Word got around when there were family problems. Interpreters agree that the word *quarreling* is too weak a translation to describe the divisions of this young church family. The differences were more like *factions* (also used in 11:19) or the word *hairesis,* from which we get heresy, and its root meaning is "choose." Such problems arise when Christians become totally absorbed in one aspect of the truth to the exclusion of the whole truth as it found is in Jesus, thus reaching the danger point. Their selectivity had produced splinter groups, or *schismata,* and open strife.

(b) Three, even four groups had formed and taken on the names of their leaders. "I am of Apollos," "I am of Paul," "I am of Cephas," and "I am of Christ" had become their slogans. F. F. Bruce[1] says that each phrase was used by members as a watchword to identify themselves. Out of a sense of loyalty, they made these claims against one another and lost their focus on Christ, who had come only to be one of them. Their watchwords totally distracted them from the Living Word and diluted the power of the cross (v. 17). A competitive spirit contradicts the message of the cross.

(c) Like the Sons of Zebedee asking to be placed on the right and left of Jesus, we too desire to be in places and with people who are viewed as impressive and important. We flock to our magnificent megachurches and we name-drop in order to be identified with popular Christian leaders. We can easily become wooed by the servant instead of the Word, who became flesh for us. Like James and John in Mark 10:35–41, who pleaded for a more prestigious position, we don't have a clue as to what we are doing when we try to join the ranks of Deity! Like them, we ask with such boldness, as though we could ever handle such a position! We have all we can humanly handle to keep a solid standing on the level ground at the foot of the cross. The job of the churches is to become a united front, not just "those people up front."

II. *The power for living in harmony is found in the cross alone.* To others it is foolishness. To those who are being saved it is the life-giving power to live as the Church and fulfill our purpose, according to verse 18.

(a) Paul Little[2] maintains that one thing is a major difference between Christianity and other religions, namely that Christ offers us his power to live as we should. He gives us forgiveness, cleansing, and his own righteousness, all as a free gift. He reconciles us to God. He does something for us that we cannot do for ourselves. Essentially, every other religious system is a do-it-yourself proposition—like a set of swimming instructions for a drowning person—whereas Christianity is a life preserver. Christ rescues us so that we can pass on the life preserver to another drowning victim.

(b) The lesson is that living as an effective leader requires transparency so that who we are and what we do and say do not block the cross but show the way to the cross. A leader's purpose is not to be served but to serve, in a way that does not draw people to themselves but rather moves people one step closer to Christ as the Way and the Truth and the Life. The apostle Paul said it best: "Less of me and more of Christ."

---

[1]*Paul: Apostle of the Heart Set Free*
[2]*Know What You Believe*

(c) Jesus does not ask us to do the impossible but equips us to become all he designed the Church to be in fulfilling our mission. In the cross we have the power to accomplish that task. Fellowship is a blessing from God, not a building block for popularity. We are to complement each other with our spiritual gifts, build up and edify the body for ministry, and be a unified force as we go out into the world with the good news of salvation for all.—Sally Gill

ILLUSTRATIONS

CHRIST UNITES US.   Corrie ten Boom,[3] survivor of the Holocaust, knew that the hardest task Christians are called to is to love one another and live in unity. As she prepared to go before a group to give witness to the power of the cross in her life, she saw a former Nazi guard in the crowd. She recognized him as one who had tortured her and her sister in a German concentration camp. She felt paralyzed as she realized the impossibility of speaking about God's forgiveness while feeling such strong emotions of hatred for this man. She prayed and stepped forward to speak as God began a heart-changing work within her. He opened the floodgates of his forgiveness and freed her to embrace the former guard as a redeemed brother in Christ. The power of the cross found victory again.

JOINED TO CHRIST.   Arthur John Gossip[4] says that we are "saved not by one cross but by two—Christ's and our own. We must be crucified with Christ, die with him, and rise with him into a new way of life and being." Galatians 2:20 says this is possible because I have a life that Christ now lives in me.

SERMON SUGGESTIONS

Topic: A Song of Light, Joy, and Freedom
TEXT: Isa. 9:1–4; Matt. 4:12–17
(1) The burden of the past: (a) as a people, (b) as an individual. (2) The dawning of hope: (a) through divine providence and intervention, (b) through the divine presence recognized, (c) ultimately, through Jesus the Christ.

Topic: A Plea for Unity
TEXT: 1 Cor. 1:10–18
(1) The problem: idolatrous rivalry. (2) The consequence: hindrance to the gospel. (3) The solution: finding our unity in the undivided Christ.

CONGREGATIONAL MUSIC

1. "In the Cross of Christ I Glory," John Bowring (1825)
   RATHBUN, Ithamar Conkey (1851)
   This hymn could set the tone for a service in which the Epistle reading (1 Cor. 1:10–18) is the basis for the sermon. The apostle Paul's declaration that the cross, though foolishness to those who are dying, is the power of God for salvation, finds an echo in this vibrant hymn.

---

[3]*Tramp for the Lord* (Fort Washington, Pa.: Buckingham Christian Literature Crusade, 1974), pp. 114–116.
[4]Wirt and Beckstrom, *Topical Encyclopedia of Living Quotations* (Minneapolis: Bethany House, 1982), p. 48.

2. "Jesus Calls Us O'er the Tumult," Cecil F. Alexander (1852)
    GALILEE, William H. Jude (1887)
    Here we have a familiar hymn that relates admirably to the calling of the disciples found in the Gospel lesson (Matt. 4:12–23). Singing it quietly following the Gospel reading could be quite effective as an application of the biblical lesson to the experience of the singer.
3. "The People Who in Darkness Walked," Isa. 9:2–3; vers. John Morison (1781)
    LOBT GOTT, IHR CHRISTEN, Nikolaus Hermann (1554)
    The first two stanzas of this metrical setting of the first few verses of Isaiah 9 relate to the portion of the chapter assigned as this day's Old Testament lesson. It could be effectively used as an antiphon, with the first stanza being sung before the reading and the second stanza after the reading.
4. "O Lord, You Are My Light," Ps. 27; vers. *Psalters* (1887, 1912)
    ARTHUR'S SEAT, John Goss (1827)
    This Bible song paraphrases the first six verses of Psalm 27. The singing of its stanzas could be alternated with the reading of the psalm verses selected for this day's lesson.—Hugh T. McElrath

WORSHIP AIDS

CALL TO WORSHIP.   "The Lord is my light and my salvation; whom shall I fear? The Lord is the strength of my life; of whom shall I be afraid?" (Ps. 27:1).

INVOCATION.   Almighty Father, as we gather in this sacred place, we pray that you will open our hearts to the remembrance of past blessings, that we may not forget how you have led us across the years to the present moment. Focus our thoughts this morning on what you are yet doing among us so that we may not lose heart in the daily walks we must take. Point us toward the future, with all its promise and hope, so that we may not lose our sense of destiny as we continue the journey of faith.—Henry Fields

OFFERTORY SENTENCE.   "Lay up for yourselves treasures in heaven, where neither moth nor rust doth corrupt, and where thieves do not break through and steal: for where your treasure is, there will your heart be also" (Matt. 6:20–21).

OFFERTORY PRAYER.   Remind us this morning, Father, that we give in order that lives may be changed, families strengthened, and our world made a better place in which to live. Remind us that our coins and dollars feed the hungry, comfort the lonely, minister to the dying, and give a face to Jesus among the multitudes around the world. Prick us with generosity and inoculate us against selfishness as we give now in the name and for the cause of Jesus.—Henry Fields

PRAYER.   "God so loved the world, that he gave his only begotten Son, that whosoever believeth in him should not perish but have everlatsting life."
    Almighty Love, we thank thee for this song and its story. What a world it is to live in, if the greatest sorrow that we have, the darkest doubt, the most severe affliction, the heaviest burden, may all be brought to Calvary! We may know what pain means, and what the accomplishment of the divine desire shall mean in the glory that is to come. If we are in such a

world, all within the bosom of thine own love, all within the gracious circumference of thine own pity, all within the warmth of thine own eternal springtime and hope, *how shall we live?* What heroisms we may have within us, unborn, shall suddenly spring into life, and what latent manhood and womanhood are there shall breathe forth songs for everybody. Lord, may we live in this atmosphere! Forgive us that we have been in any other atmosphere, "for God so loved the world." There is something more than the troubles we have brought here this morning, something more than the thing that dogs us from place to place and follows us. There is something more than the fact of our personal failure.

O God, thou art and thou hast so loved the world that we accept it all and give up doing alone and working alone and bearing alone, and we accept thine offered partnership in our life, through Jesus Christ. Amen.—Frank W. Gunsaulus

SERMON
Topic: Being Yourself Before God
TEXT: Luke 18:9–14

The point of this story is that the tax collector knew who he was and was honest with himself and honest with God. But the Pharisee, the religious man, was not honest about who he was or what he needed. The man we see in the parable—righteous, smug, respectable—is only a sham; he is not the real man at all.

Now, before any of us get our defenses up, let's all admit that we are part tax collector and part Pharisee—every one of us. There is a part of our lives in which we are honest and open—sometimes brazenly so—and there is a part that even we ourselves do not know, a hidden part, a subconscious part, a part that plays tricks on us so that occasionally we think we need to see a psychiatrist. So, let's all take some comfort in the fact that we are like the tax collector and can sometimes make amazing confession about ourselves, and then let's make this one of those confessions: that there is a darker side of our Dr. Jekyll and Mr. Hyde makeup, one that we cannot seem to help, that is all sham and pretense and not so nice. We are both tax collector and Pharisee. Part of us is open and honest, and part of us is hidden and deceitful.

That's true, isn't it?

What Jesus wants his audience to see—want *us* to see—is the importance of being completely open with God, of coming before the Holy and throwing back the doors of our hearts and saying, "Here, Lord, this is the way I really am." This is what the tax collector did. We don't know what he was like outside the temple. He may have played a good game out there. He may have strutted around like a peacock, with great rubies and diamonds on his fingers from the money he made collaborating with the Romans, acted as if he were the toughest hombre in the world. But in the Temple, when he was alone with his thoughts and God, he put aside all charades and bared his breast in an act of contrition and cried in agony of soul, "Lord, be merciful to me, a sinner." Chalk one up for the tax collector. He got down to the bare essentials with God.

Maybe it's Jesus' way of saying to us, "You haven't really gotten down to brass tacks, you haven't really discovered who you are, until you admit that you are a sinner in the eyes of God."

Are we better than the tax collector? In our eyes, or in Jesus' eyes? The best we do is never good enough. The image of God is completely disfigured in us. But once we have admitted that—once we have beat on our breast and cried, "Lord, be merciful to me, a sinner"—we are able to hear the good news that Christ has died for sinners and that God, for Christ's sake, has forgiven us. That's the joy, and we don't feel it until we have faced the truth about ourselves, until we have "come to ourselves" as the prodigal did and admitted who we are before God.

We don't want to admit it. The "old man," the unborn side of us, keeps throwing up smokescreens about what good people we are and what nice thoughts we have and how good all our intentions are. But that is all part of the evil in the world, part of the web of darkness in which Jesus saw us caught.

You see the problem with being this way, don't you? We hide behind all these bushes in our subconscious and then we don't know who we really are and what would really make us happy. We fool ourselves along with everybody else we are trying to fool. God isn't fooled, but we are. The Pharisee in us prevents us from being completely honest with God, and then we don't feel better from being in Gods' presence, and when we go down to our houses we are not blessed as the tax collector was. Like the Pharisee, we might as well have stayed home; it didn't do him a bit of good to go up to the Temple and practice his deceit with God. We are no more whole than when we came.

How do we get our lives together? We begin the way the tax collector did. We come into the presence of God and stop pretending that we are good. We stop pretending that we are on top of everything. We simply admit, "Lord, I'm a sinner." That's the bottom line. No falsification, no facade, no pretense. And then we wait before God until we know who we really are, until God gives us a feeling for who we are and what our strong suits are. Then we give thanks and make our promises and get up and go away as different persons.

That's important, to go away different. The tax collector did. He came before God, admitted his brokenness, felt the healing presence of holiness and love, and went away blessed.

The choice is ours. We are both the tax collector and the Pharisee. We decide which one we are going to be each time we come into the presence of God. But as Jesus showed us, there isn't much point in bothering if we are only going to play the Pharisee.—John Killinger

SUNDAY, FEBRUARY 3, 2002
Lectionary Message

Topic: The Pursuit of Happiness
TEXT: Matt. 5:1–12
Other Readings: Isa. 58:1–12; Ps. 112:1–10; 1 Cor. 2:1–16

The pursuit of happiness is an obsession for many Americans. We go to great extremes to find the best ways to achieve this elusive dream.

You know the roads, don't you? Some people travel down the way of possessions, believing that accumulating more and more material goods will lead to happiness. Others take the path of popularity, convinced that if they are well-liked, all will be well. A few journey down the road of power, assuming that control over others leads to happiness. And of course there are those who simply try to escape it all because they sense that none of these other roads offers any hope.

Then along comes Jesus with a different way to be happy. He wore no designer robe and drove no custom-made chariot. He was a leader of no army, but he did take his band of followers to the top of a hill and told them how to have happiness. We call these teachings the Beatitudes. Each teaching begins with the word *blessed,* which means "happy." See what Jesus teaches us about the pursuit of happiness.

I. *The world says we will be happy when we are in control; Jesus said we will be happy when we realize that we cannot control.* Many people assume that if they can have their way in life they will be happy. This leads them to try to control their family, job, or church. After all, doesn't it make sense that I will be happy if I can have things my way?

Listen to Jesus. Look at his list of Beatitudes: the happy are the poor in spirit, the mourners, the meek, those who are hungry and thirsty for righteousness, and the persecuted. There is no control there! Instead you see a list of people who realize that they are out of control. This realization frees us to turn over control of our lives to a loving God who wants to save us. The lesson is simple: happiness comes when we turn over the control of our lives to the God who loves us, saves us, and wants what is best for us. As long as we try to pursue and control our happiness, it will not happen. On the other hand, when we give up that control and become poor in spirit, the blessings start to flow.

II. *The world says that happiness comes when we fill up our lives; Jesus said that happiness comes when we empty them.* Filling our lives to the brim seems to be the American way. We fill our homes with possessions, our time with appointments, our minds with information, and our hearts with dreams and goals. We may be full, but are we happy?

The Beatitudes send a different message. Empty your life and you will find happiness. What? That's right: empty your life so there is room for it to be filled with God's love and grace. If life has become too crowded for you because of a constant desire to fill your emptiness, maybe you are not giving God room to live in your heart. Empty it out, clear out a space, become poor in spirit and hungry for righteousness, and see if being filled with God's Spirit will not give greater meaning to your life. This is the road to blessing.

III. *When we stop pursuing, we start receiving.* The pursuit of happiness just leads to more pursuit. Happiness is never a destination to be achieved but a journey to be experienced. When we let go of our insatiable quest for control and when we stop trying to fill our lives to the brim, we make room for God to surprise us. Jesus described these surprises. We receive the kingdom of heaven when we know that we are poor, satisfaction when we admit our hunger, and inheritance of the Earth when we live with a God-controlled meekness.

As long as we are trying to build our own kingdom, we will never experience the kingdom of heaven. It is only when we acknowledge our own poverty that we can find the door to this new kingdom. Once we realize that we are not in control, we can live in the kingdom where God is in control. Only after we have emptied our own lives of all the distractions that clutter our hearts can we be filled with the ways of this new kingdom, which lead to blessing and happiness. The answer, then, is not in the pursuit of happiness, but in seeking first the Kingdom of God (Matt. 6:33). It is in the experience of the Kingdom that we will find our happiness.—David W. Hull

ILLUSTRATIONS

IDENTITY.   When Wendell Wilkie was a young schoolteacher, he once used a creative approach to teach his class about the American way of life. He gave each student three buttons and told them that these buttons represented life, liberty, and the pursuit of happiness. His assignment was for the students to return the next day with a report on the three buttons. The following morning one youth was particularly troubled as he held out two buttons and reported, "Mr. Wilkie, I have life and liberty, but my momma sewed pursuit of happiness onto my brother's britches."—J. Winston Pierce[1]

FULFILLMENT.   A coffee company helped us to think of life as "filled to the brim." Therefore, we might want to consider the concept of emptying and filling in terms of making coffee. You never want to start brewing new coffee with yesterday's remains still in the pot. Empty out the old before putting in the fresh. In the same way, it is only when we acknowledge the emptiness of our poverty, hunger, thirst, and tears that we can be filled with the great gladness of God's grace.—David W. Hull

SERMON SUGGESTIONS

Topic: What God Really Wants from Us
TEXT: Mic. 6:1–8 TEV
(1) God's gracious providence (vv. 4–5). (2) Our inadequate response (vv. 6–7). (3) God's specific requirements (v. 8): (a) to do what is just, (b) to show constant love, (c) to live in humble fellowship with God.

Topic: How God's Wisdom Works
TEXT: 1 Cor. 1:18–31 REB
(1) By using the cross of Christ as the instrument of our salvation. (2) By using people without rank or standing in the world to do his will and work.

CONGREGATIONAL MUSIC

1. "Nature with Open Volume Stands," Isaac Watts (1797)
   GERMANY, William Gardiner's *Sacred Melodies* (1815)
   This hymn, considered by some to be Isaac Watts's greatest, could open worship as well as relate to the Epistle lesson (1 Cor. 1:18–31), in which the apostle extols the power and wisdom of the preaching of the cross (see stanza 3).
2. "Lord, Who May Dwell Within Your House," Ps. 15; vers. Christopher Webber (1986)
   CHESHIRE, Este's *Psalmes* (1592)
   This modern metrical version of Psalm 51 could be "lined out" by a good solo singer acting as precentor. The old psalm tune, CHESHIRE, from one of the earliest English psalters, lends itself to this sort of historic treatment.
·3. "What Does the Lord Require?" Albert F. Bayly (1949)
   SHARPTHORNE, Erik Routley (1968)
   One of the best contemporary hymns to come from the pen of Bayly, a British clergyman, so closely follows the Old Testament lesson (Mic. 6:6–8) that singing it could well take the place of the reading. The first two stanzas, which are in question and answer form, could be sung antiphonally between choir and congregation.

---

[1] *To Brighten Each Day* (Nashville: Broadman Press, 1983), p. 222.

4. "O How Blest Are the Poor in Spirit," Matt. 5:3–12; para. Richard Avery and Donald Marsh
BEATITUDES, Avery and Marsh (1979)
Antiphonal singing of this contemporary Scripture song is naturally suggested by its form
with refrain. The choir or a soloist could sing the Beatitude verses and the congregation could
respond with the refrain.—Hugh T. McElrath

WORSHIP AIDS

CALL TO WORSHIP.   "O Lord, who may abide in your tent? Who may dwell in your holy
hill?" (Ps. 15:1).

INVOCATION.   In the depths of our hearts, O God, we ask these questions, for who is
worthy of worshiping you? By your grace, you open the door for us and invite us inside, so
that we can become what you want us to be and do what you want us to do. So, here we
are. Bless us that we may be blessings.

OFFERTORY SENTENCE.   "You know the generosity of our Lord Jesus Christ: he was rich,
yet for your sake he became poor so that through his poverty you might become rich" (2 Cor.
8:9 REB).

OFFERTORY PRAYER.   Great giving God: as an act of worship we offer to you our
resources—our money, our time, our abilities, and our plans.
God, here are our lives! Accept us as you do our other offerings and use us in the spread-
ing of your Word, the doing of your will, and the coming of your Kingdom.
O God, here are our lives!
We pray in the name of your incomprehensible offering to us, your Son, Jesus Christ.—
C. Welton Gaddy[2]

PRAYER.   In moments of honesty, Father, we look at ourselves and wonder what about
us you could possibly love. We have heard your call to rise up and follow Christ, yet we hear
that call as if it were an echo from afar, not a present call to action. We know that we are sinful and filled with evil struggles, yet we pretend that we are monarchs above all others.
Stained with evil, we consider ourselves robed in purity. Wandering and often lost in the darkness of the world, we set ourselves up as guides for our fellow human beings. O Father, in
our sane moments when we really look inside our souls, we see that we are those who fit
Jesus' description of blind folks leading the blind.
How can we escape your justice? How can we be pleasing to you with all our faults, sins,
and misshapen attitudes? How thankful we are this morning that though you see us as we
are, you still love us and call us on to higher levels of living. Give us the gifts we need to rise
to what you would have us become, that we may be true sons and daughters of our Father
of love and strength.
Make us aware of the mission of your church in this community, Father. Lead us as we

---

[2]*Prayers*

seek to be evangelists of the highest order to those about us. Open our eyes to the many needs that cry out for solution. Inspire us to walk in the ways of Jesus as we move in and out among the people in our area of influence. Show us how to truly build your Church so that it may stand against all forces that would crush it in these days and in the days to come.

Let those among us who suffer illness be aware this morning of the presence of the great physician. Let those who sorrow be met by the Comforter of life. Let those who are lonely experience the presence of life's greatest friend. Let those who are lost hear today the voice of the Good Shepherd calling their name and beckoning them to come home to the Father. Speak through our voices the words of encouragement and hope, so that others might regroup and try again. Work through our hands to alleviate pain and suffering, so that life for some may be made whole again. Move through our prayers, so that even our least prayerful thoughts may be a force to uplift another and give them strength.

Now bless us powerfully as we yield to the presence of your Spirit and worship you.—Henry Fields

SERMON
Topic: The Call to Greater Things
TEXT: John 1:43–51

When Nathanael encountered Jesus, he discovered that Jesus already knew all about him. Jesus knew Nathanael's nature and personality. He referred to Nathanael as "an Israelite in whom there is no deceit" (John 1:47). Here is a man, Jesus said, who has no guile, nothing false in him. Jesus knew Nathanael from a distance, and Nathanael, somewhat startled, asked of Jesus, "Where did you get to know me?" (John 1:48).

I. *In the same way God also knows you and me.* God knows us just as well as—even better than, in fact—Jesus knew Nathanael. He knows our hurts, our pains, our doubts, our struggles, and our questions about life. He knows our fears, our insecurities, our hopes, our dreams, and our aspirations. He knows what is in our hearts, whether it be love or hate, forgiveness or bitterness, purity or deceit, beauty or ugliness.

There is no new teaching. God said of the prophet Jeremiah, "Before I formed you in the womb I knew you" (Jer. 1:5). The word translated *knew* means "to know" in the biblical sense—a profound and intimate knowledge, as a husband and wife know each other. Such is the way of God with us.

Remember that the psalmist said, in the verses we read together earlier, "O Lord, you have searched me and known me . . . and are acquainted with all my ways" (139:1, 3). Yes, God knows every dark corner, and every bright corner, of our lives—those deep recesses of the soul that we will not reveal even to our best friend. The Lord knows you, even if you think you don't know him.

II. *God sees us where we are.* "Where can I go from your Spirit?" the psalmist asked. "Or where can I flee from your presence? If I ascend to heaven, you are there. If I make my bed in Sheol [the world of the dead], you are there. If I take the wings of the morning and settle at the farthest limits of the sea, even there your hand shall lead me, and your right hand shall hold me fast" (Ps. 139:7–10). There is no getting away from God's watchful, searching eyes.

Nathanael asked Jesus, "How do you know me?" Jesus answered, "Before Philip called you, when you were under the fig tree, I saw you." The word translated *saw* in "I saw you" means "to know, to be acquainted with." There is some symbolism at work here. In Jewish thought and literature, to dwell under a fig tree is symbolic of dwelling in peace, security, or safety (Mic. 4:4; Zec. 3:10; 1 Kings 4:25). Just when we think we are sitting under our own little private fig tree, God lets us know that he sees us and is acquainted with all our ways. He comes to us to rouse us from our spiritual slumber and to remind us of our calling.

God sees where we are in our lives, in our spiritual journeys. He knows how we got where we are. He knows the problems, temptations, and difficulties we had to overcome to get to where we are today. But he is also well acquainted with all our capabilities, opportunities, and promise. Jesus knew the promise Nathanael had as a disciple, even though Nathanael did not yet know the one he was destined to follow. The Lord sees you where you are, and he sees where you can be in the future.

III. *Most important, God calls us to greater things.* To become a disciple and follow the Master is to begin an exciting journey. Jesus said to Nathanael, "Because I said to you, 'I saw you under the fig tree,' do you believe? You will see greater things than these." As a sidebar and historical note, Nathanael (also known as Bartholomew) was from the town of Cana. Today a beautiful church (I have a picture of it) called the Church of Nathanael stands in the city of Cana in honor of the disciple. If Nathanael could only have known the great things that were to come after him because he responded to the Master.

You may have thought that there is nothing good left to be or that you have nothing good to offer God in his service. But the Lord sees ahead to where you cannot see. He has a plan. He calls you to greater things. The Lord calls you to life abundant, full of peace and joy and happiness. He calls you to spiritual heights, far above what you can imagine—if you are willing to follow him in faith and find your life in service to him. God calls us out of ourselves, so to speak, to better, greater, more glorious things. He calls us to be the best that we were created to be. He calls us to a grander, more noble purpose in life than we may have ever imagined.

But the abundant life that God offers is contingent upon our faith, testimony, and openness to him. Notice Nathanael's profession of faith in Jesus: "You are the Son of God! You are the King of Israel!" (John 1:49).

Perhaps you have been off somewhere under your own little fig tree, so to speak, not thinking much about your life and spirituality. The good news is that God says to us here today, just as Jesus said to Philip and Nathanael long ago, "Follow me" and "You will see greater things than these."

Won't you hear that call, and won't you, after the example of Philip and Nathanael, decide to follow him too? Today?—Randy Hammer

SUNDAY, FEBRUARY 10, 2002
Lectionary Message

Topic: The Light of the World

TEXT: Isa. 58:1–12

Other Readings: Ps. 112:1–9 (10); 1 Cor. 2:1–12 (13–16); Matt. 5:13–20

"You are the light of the world" (Matt. 5:14). What did Jesus mean when he said these words? I wonder if his followers got it. More important, do we know what it means to "let your light shine" before the world? Jesus often used Isaiah as the text for his preaching. Maybe we can turn to this Old Testament prophet to find the meaning of being the light in our world today.

I. *The darkness of shallow religion* (vs. 1–5). God was upset with the people. Ritual had replaced relationship. Fasting was being done in the name of faith, but the people were just going through the motions of religion. The right motivation was not present. The depth of relationship that God desired with the people was just a shallow pool of ritual. The harmony between men and women that should flow from an experience of the Holy had sunk to a low point. What was the problem? Is this still an issue for us today? See what you think.

(a) *Selfishness had replaced sharing.* "Behold, in the day of your fast you seek your own pleasure" (v. 3). The purpose of fasting is to create a personal situation in which the focus of life is placed on God. But at the very time that they were going through the ritual of fasting before God, the people's focus was on fulfilling their own pleasure. They could not get beyond their desire to please themselves. Of course, that same danger exists in the Church today. Worship is designed to focus our minds and hearts on God, yet how many times do we come wanting our own desires for pleasure to be met? The ministry of the Church is an opportunity to share our gifts with others, but so often we think only about how our own needs are being met.

(b) *Control had replaced compassion.* Selfishness always leads to a desire to control. People who constantly seek their own pleasure will grab for power to ensure that they get their own way. Imagine how the heart of God was grieved when the people oppressed all the workers even during the holy time of fasting (v. 3). Imagine also how a tear comes to the eye of God when church becomes a place of manipulation, power struggles, and control because people desperately want to hold on to their selfish desires.

(c) *Hatred had replaced hospitality.* The indictment of God seemed to get worse. The selfishness of the people had escalated to control and oppression. God rebuked them for their fighting. Imagine the people of God fasting in a spirit of worship and at the same time quarreling, fighting, and hitting with a "wicked fist" (v. 4). Yet we have not learned much in the hundreds of years that have passed since these words were written. Churches are still places where fighting and hatred instead of love are found. God speaks to us the same message that was spoken years ago. This darkness of shallow, empty religion is unacceptable.

II. *The shining light of ministry* (vv. 6–12). As the sun breaks the darkness of night at dawn, so the words of the Lord pierce our shallow religion and call us to a deeper faith. "Then shall your light break forth like the dawn . . ." (v. 8). When is "then"? We back up a few verses to see that God wants us to live in the ways that had been forgotten. We let our lights shine when we are engaged in ministry to others.

(a) *Sharing.* The fasting that God requires is for us to "share [our] bread with the hungry" (v. 7). This ministry of sharing with others begins to move the emphasis away from meeting our own selfish pleasures and allows the light of God to shine through us as we help others. Our world is not impressed by the self-centeredness of the Church. People do respond to the shining light of sacrificial love that is willing to share food with the hungry and life with the dying.

(b) *Compassion.* If an oppressive, controlling, power-hungry religion is a sign of darkness in the world, a community of faith based on compassion is a ray of wonderful light. The ministry call of God is for us to "cover the naked" when we see them (v. 7). Instead of hiding our eyes from the injustice and oppression in the world, we are called to minister with compassion to the needs of others.

(c) *Hospitality.* The darkness of hatred is overcome by the light of hospitality. The depth of this hospitality is seen in the admonition to "bring the homeless poor into your house" (v. 7). The time for quarreling and fighting is over; the time for God's healing hospitality has begun.

III. *Conclusion.* Isaiah helps us understand what Jesus meant by calling us the light of the world. He was calling us to ministry—the same ministry of sharing, compassion, and hospitality that our Lord demonstrated while on the Earth. With this ministry comes a promise for a new dawn: "If you take away from the midst of you the yoke, the pointing of the finger, and the speaking of wickedness, if you pour yourself out for the hungry and satisfy the desire of the afflicted, then shall your light rise in the darkness and your gloom be as the noonday" (vv. 9–10).—David W. Hull

ILLUSTRATIONS

A LIGHT TO GUIDE.   Watching a lamplighter moving along the road on a distant hill, John Ruskin commented, "That is what I mean by being a real Christian: you can trace his course by the lights he leaves burning."

COMMUNITY.   During World War II, five hundred soldiers were attending a performance of *Rigoletto* in an Italian opera house. An air raid caused all of the lights to go out, leaving the room in darkness. A GI took out his flashlight and began to shine it toward the stage. Soon the rest of the soldiers joined him by doing the same thing. The conductor bowed, waved his baton, and continued the performance. Our calling as a church is to be a community of shining lights in the world.—David W. Hull

SERMON SUGGESTIONS

Topic: Equipment for Proclamation

TEXT: 1 Cor. 2:1–12

(1) The preacher's goal—to preach Christ crucified. (2) The preacher's strength—the power of God. (3) The preacher's interpreter—the Holy Spirit.

Topic: How to Mean Something for God

TEXT: Matt. 5:13–20

(1) Be like salt and preserve what is good. (2) Be like light and point the way to God. (3) Be like a true and faithful teacher who teaches by example what pleases God.

CONGREGATIONAL MUSIC

1. "O Day of God, Draw Nigh," Robert B. Y. Scott (1937)

   OLD 134th, *Genevan Psalter* (1551)

   A good contemporary mainline hymn to set the theme of justice and righteousness, "O Day of God, Draw Nigh" is a fitting response to any and all four of this day's Scripture lessons.

2. "Awake, My Soul, and with the Sun," Thomas Ken (1711)

   MORNING HYMN, Francois H. Barthelemon (1785)

   Besides ideally serving as opening praise for morning worship, this venerable hymn relates to the themes of this day's readings: the habits and behaviors of the righteous person.

3. "Sleepers Wake, a Voice Astounds Us," Philipp Nicolai (1599)

   "Awake, Awake, for Night Is Flying"

WACHET AUF, Philipp Nicolai (1599)

Similarly appropriate for the beginning of morning worship, this majestic "King of Chorales" in its third stanza relates to 1 Corinthians 2:16 in the Epistle reading for this day.

4. "How Blest Are Those Who Fear the Lord," Ps. 112; vers. *Psalters* (1887, 1987)

MELCOMBE, Samuel Webbe (1782)

This rather strict paraphrase of Psalm 112 could be alternately sung and read in worship as follows: stanza 1, sung; vv. 3–4, read; stanza 3, sung; vv. 7–8, read; stanza 5, sung; v. 10, read; stanza 6, sung.—Hugh T. McElrath

WORSHIP AIDS

CALL TO WORSHIP.   "Praise the Lord! Happy are those who fear the Lord, who greatly delight in his commandments. . . . They rise in the darkness as a light for the upright; they are gracious, merciful, and righteous" (Ps. 112:1, 4 NRSV).

INVOCATION.   Father, we come into this sanctuary this morning as individual parts of a wonderful congregation. Each of us brings with us some need or joy or disappointment or sadness, an irritating illness, some problem bigger than we can manage by ourselves. We do not ask that our every desire and wish be granted. We do ask that we be given strength and light to manage life so that what we do reflects our faith and glorifies the Lord Jesus.—Henry Fields

OFFERTORY SENTENCE.   "Whatever you are doing, put your whole heart into it, as if you were doing it for the Lord and not for men, knowing that there is a master who will give you an inheritance as a reward for your service. Christ is the master you must serve" (Col. 3:23–24 REB).

OFFERTORY PRAYER.   Thank you, Father, for a giving church. We truly want to give, need to give, and will today give something to help in the ongoing work of Christ among us and around the world. Help us know our true ability and grant us the grace to let this knowledge guide our giving, we pray in Jesus' name.—Henry Fields

PRAYER.   How wonderful it is to come into your presence and find reception, help, hope, and love, Father. Broken and wounded we come. Sad and angry we come. Searching and longing we come. Sinful and lost we come. In these holy moments, abiding for a while in your presence, may we find the entrance to the salvation of our needs.

Our hurts we bring with us—painful, sore, running wounds we cannot heal. Some of them have been inflicted upon us by the brokenness we have experienced in family, in community, and even in faith. No matter what the source of the hurt, we need healing that only you can provide, healing that comes as we learn to forgive what others have done to us. Help us to forgive those who have failed to keep their promises to us, those who have failed to abide by their commitments and thereby have placed a heavy burden on us that we resent.

Forgive us for not always keeping our promises, for committing to situations and failing to abide by the commitments, for promising that we would never do things and then doing them anyway, for denying that we've done things even when the responsibility was completely our own.

Let truth, integrity, and peace rule our hearts and homes, our places of worship and work, and all our relationships. In the name of Jesus, who never taught us anything but the truth and who never made us a promise he could not keep, meet us today, we pray.—Henry Fields

SERMON

Topic: The Love That Keeps Us Going
TEXT: Luke 19:28–48

You wonder how he did it, don't you? Where he found the inner strength to go through with it, knowing what he knew. He could see the writing on the wall. Jerusalem would be the end of the way for him. His blood would stain its paving stones.

Jerusalem, which he loved.

He cried as he looked at the city. Only twice do the Gospels say that Jesus shed tears. Once was at the grave of his friend Lazarus. The other time was here, as he entered the city for the final conflict. A friend of mine experienced a most notable thing on his first trip to the Holy Land. He had gone to Jericho and then had traversed the fifteen miles of crooked, hilly roads to Jerusalem, approaching the city as Jesus did so many years ago. Passing through the little village of Bethany, he made the sharp turn in the road just over the brow of the hill above the Mount of Olives, and there it was, the gleaming Dome of the Rock and the entire city laid out in panorama before him. "For the first time," he said, "I could see why Jesus wept. He could see the whole city spread out before him, like a picture, and it would reject him and he would die for it."

How did he do it? How could he go through with it, knowing he would die?

If we think about it, this is one of the most meaningful aspects of the Incarnation—Jesus' identification with the hard, sheer, unrelenting obduracy of human existence. We can relate to this, can't we? For we have experienced the hardness, the occasional difficulty of just going on.

Life *is* hard. People *do* suffer. Sometimes it is all we can do to put one foot in front of the other and keep on going. And love is the energizer that makes it possible. Love gives us the courage to enter a city where death is waiting, to hold together a life that has gone to pieces, to continue on our journeys despite sickness and despair and desertion. Jesus wept over Jerusalem because he loved it. "O Jerusalem, Jerusalem! If only you could have known what would make you happy!" And the love carried him on, like a river carrying a man to sea.

It is God's love that really keeps us going, even when we don't know it. God's love for the world enabled Jesus to enter Jerusalem and withstand tortures and crucifixion.

God's love is the real goal of everything—being gathered up in the oneness and joy of the eternal.

This is why we are forever searching, struggling, looking, says Carlo Caretto. We are looking for the love of God, which is the fulfillment of all life.

Jesus had found this. He was in touch with it. It is why he was able to enter the doom-laden city. It is why he could go to the cross. He knew the secret of everything!

God is love, not an idol. God is not merely a power or a king. God is love. And life, for all its hardness, is not nearly so hard when we know this.

It is the love that overcomes the world—and the love that keeps us going.—John Killinger

SUNDAY, FEBRUARY 17, 2002
Lectionary Message

Topic: Spiritual Growth

TEXT: 1 Cor. 3:1–9

Spirituality is "in" these days. In the Christian world you can find many books, workbooks, and study guides related to spiritual growth. Small groups all across the country are composed of people who hunger to grow spiritually. Even outside of the church world, our culture has a renewed interest in matters that are spiritual. The abundance of television shows and movies that deal with the supernatural and spiritual world give evidence of a society that is no longer satisfied with the cut and dried logic of science. We hunger for the spiritual dimension of life.

So how do we grow spiritually? The apostle Paul answered that question as he wrote to the church at Corinth. His teaching will help all of us in our spiritual growth.

I. *Jealousy stunts spiritual growth* (vv. 1–4). The words of the apostle were harsh. He admitted that he could not call his listeners spiritual. Instead he referred to them as "babes in Christ." Something had stunted their growth, keeping them in spiritual infancy. The problem was their "jealousy and strife." Let's unpack these words and see why spiritual growth is choked by envy.

(a) *Self-centered.* The symptom was jealousy, the disease was self-centeredness on the part of the Corinthians. Even though they had accepted Christ as their Savior, they had not allowed the Lord to transform their outlook on life. Paul said they were still "of the flesh." This term refers to a self-centered approach to life as opposed to a God-centered or spiritual approach to life. The focus of the Corinthians was still on themselves. They believed in Jesus but they cared mostly about themselves.

We struggle with the same self-centeredness today. Everywhere we turn we are faced with messages that tell us to "look out for number one." Churches are filled with carnal (fleshly) Christians who believe in Jesus but who have not been willing to turn loose a life that is oriented toward the self. People like this may act in a pious way, speak the language of Zion, or lead in the church, but they do not possess real spirituality. A self-centered focus stunts our growth and keeps us spiritual infants.

(b) *Divisive.* This focus on self led to divisions and strife in the Corinthian church. It always does. When we think we are most important, then only our way is right and others must be wrong. Members of the church took sides, claiming allegiance to leaders Paul and Apollos rather than to Christ as Lord.

The tragic history of the Christian church is one of division and splitting. People who work to bring disunity in the church are not spiritual. The work of the Spirit is to unify, not divide. Yet we continue to struggle with this kind of Christian immaturity two thousand years after the Church began. Sometimes the most disruptive people in the church will cloak their actions under the term *spirituality.* Remember what Paul wrote. Jealousy and strife lead to division, and these are characteristics of the flesh, not the Spirit.

II. *Humility accelerates spiritual growth* (vv. 5–9). After beginning with a rebuke for the negative behavior of the Corinthians, Paul lifted up a positive model for us. True spiritual growth happens when we take on an attitude of humility. Our focus is no longer on the self but on others. It makes all the difference in the world.

(a) *Service to others.* Paul moved from the divisive atmosphere that swirled around himself and Apollos and called for the people to take another look at the ministry of these two men. They were servants who gave of themselves so that the Corinthian people might believe in Christ. In this service the two men played different roles. "I planted," said Paul, referring to his ministry of introducing the gospel to the people. "Apollos watered" described the way that Apollos came along later to build on the ministry of Paul. One was not better than the other. Instead, the focus was not on the value of each man but on their common mission in Corinth. They each had different assignments, brought varying gifts to the table, and worked at different times. Servant leadership was the thread that ran through their work.

Real spiritual growth begins to erupt in a church when a servant mentality prevails. Instead of worrying about who gets the credit, a focus on ministry will begin to turn self-centered hearts toward the needs of others. This new approach of humility on the part of the people allows God to work in our midst. We grow beyond baby food when we begin to serve others.

(b) *Reliance on God.* The greatest step in our spiritual growth occurs when we learn the truth of Paul's phrase, "but only God gives the growth." The best gardener can plant the right seed, fertilize the soil, and water the ground, but the gardener can do nothing to actually make a plant grow. Only God can do that.

True spirituality happens with the humility that knows that even our service focused on others is not accomplished with our own strength. As long as we are doing good deeds for others but privately patting ourselves on the back for our wonderful works, we are still self-centered (of the flesh). Spiritual maturity happens when we learn that simple gardening message: only God gives the growth. We are then set free to live in the power of God's Spirit.

III. *Conclusion.* Do you hunger for spiritual growth? Don't try to guard your own desires with a self-centered lifestyle. You will remain a spiritual infant. Instead, become a gardener sowing the seeds of service and ministry to others, and let God cause you to grow.—David W. Hull

ILLUSTRATIONS

DIVISION IN THE CHURCH.   A man was stranded alone on a desert island for many years. When he was finally rescued there were three buildings on the island. "What are these three buildings?" the rescuers asked. "This one is my home," the man replied. "This second one is my church," he offered. "And this third building?" asked the rescuer. "That is the church I used to attend!" Division in the church is a sign of spiritual immaturity.—David W. Hull

THE REAL NEED.   In the days when the Czar ruled over Russia, the leader took a walk in his palace garden. In the far corner of the garden the Czar noticed a soldier standing guard. Confused by the location of this soldier, the Czar asked the man why he was stationed in such a place. The sentry did not know but said that he had been ordered to this post by his commander. The Czar continued to be curious. He asked the commander, who also did not know. After some research the Czar learned the origin of the assignment. Almost one hundred years earlier, when Catherine the Great ruled over Russia, she had planted a rose bush in that very location. To protect her plant she stationed a guard to watch over it. The only problem was that the plant had long since died. What Catherine needed was not a guardian standing tall and strong and offering protection. She needed a gardener bending, stooping, and helping the plant to grow.—David W. Hull

SERMON SUGGESTIONS

Topic: The Choice Is Yours!

TEXT: Deut. 30:15–20

(1) Each of us is born with a variety of instincts, urges, appetites, and desires. (2) When these God-given drives are perverted, unchecked, and undisciplined, they can lead to our ultimate destruction, or at least can rob us of happiness, peace, and success that could have been ours. (3) Our destiny, however, is in our own hands: (a) the way: "choose life" (v. 17); (b) the means: "loving the Lord your God," "obeying him," "holding fast to him" (v. 20).

Topic: The Final Authority

TEXT: Matt. 5:21–37

(1) The importance of the Law (vv. 17–20). (2) The significance of Jesus in the interpretation of the Law: "But I say to you . . ." (vv. 22, 28, 32, 34, 39, 44).

CONGREGATIONAL MUSIC

1. "Word of God, Across the Ages," Ferdinand Q. Blanchard (1952)

   AUSTRIAN HYMN, Joseph Haydn (1797)

   Start today's musical worship with this outstanding contemporary hymn exalting the Word of God—the prevailing theme of the psalter reading.

2. "I Have Decided to Follow Jesus," Garo Christians (c. 1950)

   ASSAM, Indian Folk Song, arr. William J. Reynolds (1959)

   The reading of the challenge to choose between life and death (Deut. 30:15–20) could be answered by the unaccompanied singing of this simple folk song.

3. "Teach Me, O Lord, Your Way of Truth," Ps. 119:33–36; vers. *Psalter* (1912)

   ST. CRISPIN, George J. Elvey (1862)

   This paraphrase of parts of the lengthy Psalm 119 could well be used both on this Sunday and on the one following as an effective introduction to the psalter reading.

4. "What Gift Can I Bring," Jane Marshall (1980)

   ANNIVERSARY SONG, Jane Marshall (1980)

   Relating in spirit both to the Epistle lesson (1 Cor. 3:1–9) by suggesting gratitude for others who have planted and watered, and to the Gospel lesson (Matt. 5:31–37), in which reconciliation with another is prerequisite to offering acceptable gifts to God, this modern hymn could appropriately be sung between the two readings.—Hugh T. McElrath

WORSHIP AIDS

CALL TO WORSHIP.   "Happy are those whose way is blameless, who walk in the law of the Lord. Happy are those who keep his decrees, who seek him with their whole heart" (Ps. 119:1–2 NRSV).

INVOCATION.   Grant to us, O God, the insight to see and believe that your way is always the best way among many possible choices, and give us the grace and courage to follow the way that our hearts tell us is right.

OFFERTORY SENTENCE.   "From everyone to whom much has been given, much will be required; and from the one to whom much has been entrusted, even more will be demanded" (Luke 12:48b NRSV).

OFFERTORY PRAYER.   Help us, gracious Father, to measure our stewardship obligations by the abundance of your love for us, and may we return gifts of love, service, hours, and money for the blessing of others and for your glory.

PRAYER.   Bless us, our Father, in all our work and in all the relations of life. Sanctify the life of the home. May its memories abide with us to strengthen us in the hour of temptation, to comfort us in the hour of sorrow. May children love and honor their parents, and may parents be tender and considerate with their children, knowing how delicate is the soul of the child and how easily harshness casts it down. Pour out a spirit of kindness and goodness in the home so that all its members may be bound each to each in bands of mutual love and service that may not be broken. Bless us in the larger world where we toil and suffer. We thank thee for work and the opportunity to work. Grant that our labor may be congenial to us, that we may do it with ease and a sense of mastery. Let us not be enslaved to our tasks, but may we feel ourselves greater than they and ready for still nobler efforts. Save us from sullen discontent, from fruitless war with the circumstances of our lot. Make our hearts obedient, that by the untoward things of experience we may win a larger and a freer life. Give us the spiritual vision and a desire to pass beyond ourselves, to think of the needs of others, to make the world a little better than we found it. Put within us Christ's yearning for the redemption of the world. Kindle within us his passion for the souls of men. Uphold us with the faith that thou hast called us into fellowship with him, as thy coworkers in the achievement of thy purpose of good. In this faith let us cheer the mourner, raise up the fallen, relieve the needy, forgive the wrongdoer, and praise the lover of simplicity and goodness. While we give to others, give thou to us, that we may grow more and more in the spirit of helpfulness and generosity, both in word and deed, and unto thy name we will ascribe praise and honor and glory, world without end.—Samuel McComb

SERMON
Topic: The Extravagance of God
TEXT: Matt. 10:1–16

At first reading, I don't like this story very much. It feels unfair. It's bad business, poor economic policy.

My sympathy is with the earliest workers hired—the 6:00 A.M. to 6:00 P.M. crowd. They labored all twelve hours in the workday and they got paid the same coin as those who worked only nine hours, six hours, three hours, and, unbelievably, one hour! It seems quite unjust.

But this is not a story about economic theory or business practice. "The Kingdom is like this," says Jesus in verse 1. But it's still strange. I think it was strange to the world in which it was first heard. Matthew alone has the story. The other three Gospel writers didn't know it, forgot it, or chose to ignore it.

Now, the situation itself is not strange. Vineyards needed harvesting in first-century Palestine—especially in the fall. The grapes ripened and then, very quickly, the rains came. If the crop was not gathered promptly, it could be ruined and lost to the rains. It was likely that the landowner in Jesus' story was in a race against time.

How is this story about life in the Kingdom?

It's about the grace of God—what D. S. Cairns once called "the extravagant goodness of

God." On each end of the story, Matthew remembers that Jesus said, "The first will be last and the last will be first." So God's grace means no favored status. Whether we're early or late, first or last, we're all of equal value in the eyes of God.

The Gospel is hope for nobodies and somebodies and anybodies! We are blessed and forgiven, not on the basis of what we deserve or earn but on the basis of the freedom and compassion of God.

When I'm on the receiving end of grace, I'm glad there's no partial or probationary payoff. But with you and others, I'm not so sure. There is in every one of us a twelve-hour worker or an older brother (to remember that other story about the prodigal in Luke 15). They're a lot like these two—and a lot like us.

The older brother could have rejoiced that his younger sibling was lost and is found, was dead and is alive!

But he didn't.

So, who was in the crowd to hear this story? Who were the all-day workers? Who was the older brother?

Maybe the Pharisees and the Scribes, who never got the point that it's a gospel of grace, and they hammered Jesus for hob-nobbing with tax collectors and harlots and other sinners.

Or maybe he told this story for the disciples. They would need it later on, because more and more Gentiles and ex-pagans would start coming into what was a Jewish-Christian church. And there would come a time when older leaders would be replaced by younger ones who would come to the vineyard much later in the day.

I think Jesus told this story for all of us who rejoice in the grace of God for ourselves but who may not be so happy to see others receive it.

So let me leave you with two truths about this extravagance of God. First of all, *grace is God's risk with us.* There are no guarantees about how we're going to turn out. There was no way to know how Simon Peter or James or John or Judas would turn out. But Jesus didn't wait to embrace them, to invite them, to teach them, to partner with them.

So Jesus stayed in hot water with a lot of religious and respectable people. They knew: you can't let a man with a theology of grace run loose. Sooner or later they'd have to rein him in, shut him up, get rid of him.

It's interesting that right after he told this story about the grace of God, Jesus talked about death and resurrection again—for the third time in Matthew's Gospel.

But Jesus bet the whole future of the Kingdom of God on ordinary, sinful people who would believe stories like this one and change their lives. Karl Barth says that too much of our preaching is about an obligation to be met in order to receive a gift. The Word of the New Testament is about a gift that will lead to an obligation!

It's God's risk, but the first word of salvation is *grace!*

A second truth about the extravagance of God is this: grace is God's faithfulness to us—because God is not in debt to any of us. Oh, we may think so. (The rich young ruler who came and went just before Jesus told this story may have gone away sorrowing because he couldn't bargain with God.) But you can't bargain with God. God's grace means you don't have to! God will be faithful to you no matter what!

It is New Testament theology that God's faithfulness to you is not based on your earning or deserving or bargaining but on God's own extravagance! And you can build a lifetime on that! Elton Trueblood has said that the only people who can truly understand the gospel are those who are at least forty years old. That may not be universally true, but it's easy to understand what he meant. By the time you're forty years old, you've lived long enough to fall flat on your face several times. You know how desperately you need the grace of God, and how powerful and plentiful it is!

This little story startled its hearers, and it startles us, too The extravagance of God is strange and wonderful! Frederick Buechner says it well: The grace of God means something like this: Here is your life. You might never have been, but you are because the party wouldn't have been complete without you. Here is the world. Beautiful and terrible things will happen. Don't be afraid. I am with you. Nothing can ever separate us. It's for you I created the universe. I love you.

There's only one catch: like any other gift, the gift of grace can be yours only if you'll reach out and take it.

Maybe being able to reach out and take it is a gift too.—William L. Turner[3]

SUNDAY FEBRUARY 24, 2002
Lectionary Message

Topic: The Right Thing to Do
TEXT: Matt. 5:38–48
Other Readings: Lev. 19:1–2, 9–18; Ps. 119:33–40; 1 Cor. 3:10–11, 16–23

What rights do we have? The laws of our land protect us and give us certain rights in our free society. Many of us are quick to claim these rights as protection against injustice. You have heard it often: "I have my rights!" Jesus put a new twist on understanding our rights in this passage from the Sermon on the Mount. He calls us to move beyond our rights to see the needs of others. This new focus is the very basis of Christian caring.

I. *A focus on my rights* (vv. 38, 43). Jesus reminded the people of their rights. The Law of the Old Testament provided for the rights of the people. Two different quotes helped the people remember the ways of justice in their land.

First, there was the concept of "an eye for an eye and a tooth for a tooth." This law protected the rights of both the victim and the accused. The law meant that a victim did have the right to get even when someone had hurt him. It also meant that the accused person had the right to limited retaliation. For example, if a man killed his neighbor's cow, the victim could not come and kill all of the cattle of his neighbor in retribution. The victim could get even, but could not get ahead in the battle of revenge. This law was most useful in protecting a balance of justice in a time when anarchy could easily have reigned.

Second, Jesus referred to the commandment of old, "You shall love your neighbor and hate your enemy." This law gave people the challenge to love their neighbors, but it also gave them the right, or permission, to hate those who were their enemies. Such a law made it perfectly acceptable for Jews to hate Samaritans, because they could be classified as enemies. You can imagine the shock that rippled through the town when Jesus used the parable of the good Samaritan to answer the question, "Who is my neighbor?" (Luke 10:29–37). The

---

[3]*Wishful Thinking: A Theological ABC* (New York: HarperCollins, 1973), pp. 33–34.

people thought they had a right to hate the Samaritans. Jesus began to redefine the Samaritans as neighbors.

In both of these cases, the Law of the Old Testament helped to establish rights for the people, thus maintaining justice in the land. Although Jesus did not come to abolish these laws, he did challenge the people to have a different focus. Any time we concentrate on our rights, we focus on ourselves. Jesus asks us to look in another direction.

II. *A focus on the needs of others* (vv. 38–48). Do you see the shift in the approach of Jesus? He knows we have rights that are protected by laws. But rather than making these rights the primary emphases of our lives, we are called by our Lord to look beyond our rights to see and meet the needs of others. This is not an easy passage to swallow. However, the way we hear the words of Jesus will make all of the difference in our caring for the world. The word *care* comes from *kara,* which means "to lament, weep, grieve." When we see the needs of others and let these needs bring tears to our eyes, lament to our hearts, and grieving to our minds, then we can get beyond our own rights and get on with the business of caring for others.

(a) *We have a right to retaliation, to get even with those who have hurt us.* Look beyond that right to the need for reconciliation on the part of a brother or sister, and turn the other cheek even if you have the right to strike back (v. 39).

(b) *We have a right to our own possessions.* Certainly we are allowed to protect our own things against other people who might want to take them away. Look beyond your right to protect your possessions and see the needs of others who may have much less than you (v. 40).

(c) *We have a right to our own time.* A Jewish citizen could be forced by a Roman soldier to help carry a load for only one mile. After all, citizens had rights to their own time. Look beyond your own rights to time and see if the extra use of your time will help meet the needs of someone else (v. 41).

(d) *We have a right to our own money.* No one should be able to take it from us. Look beyond your rights to see if you can invest in the lives of others who really need some of the financial resources you could offer (v. 42).

(e) *We have the right to hate our enemies.* Look beyond that right and see the human hurts of those you now despise. Begin to love them, not because you have to but because they need to be loved (v. 44).

III. *Conclusion.* Christian caring is when we move beyond our rights to see and meet the needs of others. Isn't that what Jesus did? He had every right to hate a sinful world and protect his life. Instead he saw our needs and reached out to meet them on the cross. He cared for us and he calls us to care for the world. It is the right thing to do!—David W. Hull

ILLUSTRATIONS

WHAT MADE THE DIFFERENCE.   In the early days of our country, Peter Miller was a Baptist pastor in Pennsylvania. In his community, Michael Wittman was a bitter enemy who did everything he could to destroy the ministry of Miller. After the Revolutionary War, Michael Wittman was sentenced to death. Miller walked seventy miles to see his friend George Washington to plead for the life of Wittman. Washington said, "No, Peter, I cannot grant the life of your friend." Miller replied, "My friend? He is the bitterest enemy I have!" Washington exclaimed, "What! You have walked seventy miles to save the life of an enemy? That puts the matter in a different light. I'll grant your pardon." Peter Miller went home with Wittman, no longer an enemy but a friend.—David W. Hull

LOVE DEFINED.   W. Oscar Thompson Jr. had a very simple definition for love: "Love is meeting needs." To live out this kind of love, we must look beyond our rights to see and meet the needs of others.[4]

SERMON SUGGESTIONS

Topic: Holiness on Two Levels
TEXT: Lev. 19:1–2, 9–18
(1) In the way we worship (vv. 1–4). (2) In the way we treat our neighbor (vv. 9–18).

Topic: God's Building
TEXT: 1 Cor. 3:10–11, 16–23
(1) The foundation, already laid, is Jesus Christ. (2) The building itself has needed the work of apostles and others to continue the unending task of construction. (3) We, as individual believers, God's Temples, will be judged on the quality of the materials we bring to what we build.

CONGREGATIONAL MUSIC

1. "Christ Is Made the Sure Foundation," Latin (seventeenth century); trans. John M. Neale (1851)

UNSER HERRSCHER, Joachim Neander (1680)

WESTMINSTER ABBEY, Henry Purcell (c. 1680)

This ancient hymn is based on the Pauline notion of Christ as the only foundation for our faith, found in the Epistle reading (1 Cor. 3:10–11).
2. "Be Just in Judgment, Fair to All," Lev. 19:15–18; vers. Calvin Seerveld (1985)

TORONTO, Calvin Seerveld (1985)

The various laws laid down in the book of Leviticus come alive in meaning when set to poetry and music, as in this metrical version of Leviticus 19:15–18. The Old Testament reading could stop after verse 17 and the remainder of the lesson could be sung.
3. "Teach Me, O Lord, Your Way of Truth," Ps. 119:33–36; vers. *Psalter* (1912)

ST. CRISPIN, George J. Elvey (1862)

Again, this metrical version of excerpts from Psalm 119 could effectively be sung to either introduce or follow the psalter reading.
4. "We Are Travelers on a Journey," Richard Gillard (1974)

BEACH SPRING, *The Sacred Harp* (1844)

The general sentiment of this contemporary hymn resonates well with the readings from the Sermon on the Mount, this Sunday's Gospel lesson. It would be effective if sung unaccompanied in response to that reading.—Hugh T. McElrath

---

[4]*Concentric Circles of Concern* (Nashville: Broadman Press, 1981), p. 84.

WORSHIP AIDS

CALL TO WORSHIP.   "Teach me, O Lord, the way of your statutes, and I will observe it to the end. Give me understanding, that I may keep your law and observe it with my whole heart" (Ps. 119:33–34 NRSV).

INVOCATION.   Lord, because where two or three are gathered together in your name, you promise to be in the midst of them, we boldly claim your presence in our midst today, to judge, cleanse, and bless, in Jesus' name.—E. Lee Phillips

OFFERTORY SENTENCE.   "Honor the Lord with your substance and with the first fruits of all your produce" (Prov. 3:9 NRSV).

OFFERTORY PRAYER.   Lord, allow this offering to prioritize our beliefs, so that in giving we affirm the highest and holiest, leaving behind the transitory and temporary, as did Jesus, our Savior.—E. Lee Phillips

PRAYER.   O God, by whom the meek are guided in judgment and by whom light rises up in darkness for the godly: Grant us, in all our doubts and uncertainties, the grace to ask what you would have us do, that the Spirit of wisdom may save us from all false choices, that in your light we may see light and on your straight path we may not stumble; through Jesus Christ our Lord.—*The Book of Common Prayer*

SERMON
Topic: The Radiance of Christ
TEXT: Matt. 17:9

Even church members who believe that anything that tells us more about Jesus Christ is supremely important for our life today may find this story puzzling. It doesn't seem to correspond to anything in our own experience, so we are apt to lodge it in the fuzzy department of our faith. Jesus healing a leper, Jesus dying on a cross, even Jesus rising from the dead—all these present a fairly clear picture for our understanding. But transfiguration—what on Earth does that mean? That's exactly where we must begin our search for understanding: on Earth this story *is* almost meaningless, for it is one of those moments in the Bible when heaven breaks through.

Let's admit right away that the word *transfiguration* is intimidating. One might say that it is an obfuscating polysyllable. Yet apparently Matthew, Mark, Luke, and John could find no other word to describe what happened on that mountaintop.

The word occurs nowhere else in the entire Bible. Something happened to Jesus that day, something we need to know about. All these evangelists place the story at an important turning point in Jesus' life—the moment when he turned from the popular campaign in Galilee and deliberately set off for Jerusalem, where he knew he would run headlong into his enemies and be crucified; the moment when his disciples confessed he was the Christ and were horrified by the kind of Christ he was: not a conquering warrior but a suffering servant.

The story is filled with symbolism and imagery, reminding us of the Old Testament pictures of Moses communing with the Lord on Mount Sinai and emerging from a cloud with his face shining; of Elijah being caught up to heaven in a chariot of fire.

If we want to understand Jesus, if we want to know who he was and what he does for us—and that is, I submit, as important for us as knowing who we are or what these forces are that shape our world today—then we must not only listen to his words and ponder what happened to him, but we must also be open to those moments when we receive from him a revelation that I am calling the "radiance of Christ." There are moments when heaven breaks through and Christ is transfigured for us—when, as John put it, "we behold his glory."

For Peter, James, and John (who at this point were not, we must remember, holy men with haloes on their heads and "St." prefixed to their names, but ordinary mortals, like you and me, trying to make out who Jesus was and what he meant), this transfiguration of their Lord was such a moment. They couldn't describe it in the plain prose of a journalist or historian. They had to speak of his face "shining as the sun, and his raiment white as the light." Instead of giving us a theological footnote to the effect that they now realized that Jesus had come to fulfill the revelation of the Law and the prophets, they spoke of seeing Moses and Elijah and conversing with them. Instead of reporting that they now believed Jesus to be greater than the most revered of Old Testament figures, they wrote, "A bright cloud overshadowed them: and behold a voice out of the cloud, which said, 'This is my beloved Son . . . hear ye him." And instead of explaining how they came to believe in the unique authority of Christ, they tell of the cloud covering them for a moment; and then, when they had lifted up their eyes, they saw no man but Jesus alone. You will notice that this radiant Christ is not transporting them in a moment of ecstasy right out of this world. Rather, he brings them down to Earth with a jolt: "Tell the vision to no man, until the Son of Man be risen from the dead." The Jesus of the vision was on his way to Calvary and Easter morning.

When you rise to confess your faith in the words of the Apostles' Creed, I don't believe you are thinking through the precise meaning of every clause, yet you are saying something about Christ, something beyond words that is probably expressed only in the music of a hymn or the silence of Holy Communion. You are responding to what I am calling the "radiance of Christ."

The same thing happens when you listen to a sermon. You may not follow the preacher's arguments, or you may follow perfectly but disagree. He may believe, poor soul, that he is explaining the Gospel reading, but what creates or nourishes belief is something beyond the power of human words. It is the radiance of Christ that comes shining through the arguments, the stories, the illustrations—as was said of John the Baptist: "He was not the light, but was sent to bear witness to the light." When that happens, mere human words are transfigured and we are in the presence of Christ.

Listen to St. Paul speak of our face-to-face encounter with the living Christ: "We all reflect, as in a mirror, the splendor of the Lord; thus we are transfigured into his likeness, from splendor to splendor. Such is the influence of the Lord who is Spirit."

The Christian is not called to stay on the mountaintop. We come down. We emerge from the sanctuary into a world that more and more seems to us lunatic and crying out for help. That's where we have to take the radiance of Christ, as healers, peacemakers, givers, ambassadors of his love. Then indeed it will have been good for us to have been here.—David H. C. Read

SUNDAY, MARCH 3, 2002
Lectionary Message

Topic: Live One Day at a Time

TEXT: Matt. 6:24–34

Other Readings: Isa. 49:8–16; Ps. 131; 1 Cor. 4:1–5

What occupies your time the most? Your thoughts and concerns about what happened yesterday? Are you worried about something today? Maybe you are afraid of what tomorrow might bring. Jesus warned against worrying about what is going to happen tomorrow. Yet for some individuals, yesterday is a real problem.

We must learn to live fully in the present. Yesterday is gone, tomorrow is a hope, and only today can be fully experienced. I believe that many in our society and in our churches are struggling with their present existence. They are calling out for a word they can use to face the challenges of the day. People want to know if there is any purpose to life. Some feel like a peanut in the bleachers at Yankee Stadium after the game is over and the crowd has gone home. We must guide individuals to use the gifts of the power to remember, the ability to anticipate, and the courage to experience the present. Each of these powers has a function in our lives and we must learn how to relate them to each other.

I. *Living in the past.* Jesus warned us about living in the future and I believe this warning applies as well to the past. One is just as bad as the other. The past can leave us stunned and disabled. We can miss the present when we continue to live out past victories. We remind ourselves of the things we have accomplished and do not build on the positive events in our lives. At the same time, we can be disabled and unable to function in the present because of previous defeats and failures. We are afraid of taking another chance in life. Failure has a way of petrifying us.

II. *Living in the future.* We can apply the terms *stunned* and *disabled* to the future. Many are those who have great ambitions and good intentions for tomorrow that never become realities. We can miss out on the things of today as we dwell on the bad things that might happen tomorrow. Some of us are dazed by big plans and dynamic ideas, yet we put little effort into developing a plan of action and making it a reality. Others are paralyzed by tomorrow because they have convinced themselves that something terrible is going to happen. They expect the worst, and when it doesn't happen, they are disappointed. The future should be used to energize us for the present.

III. *Live in the present.* When Jesus mentioned that we should not worry about tomorrow, I do not believe he meant to be unconcerned about today. Those who are seeking to accomplish God's will for their lives today are not obsessed with tomorrow. Those who have their heads in the clouds or have cold feet are not likely to be living fully in the present.

Youth have the tendency to live in the future and older people tend to live in the past. I believe that the challenge for all Christians should be to live today to its fullest, not holding on to the past nor living with a pie-in-the-sky attitude that everything is going to be all right. When we concern ourselves with today's problems and opportunities, we will have peace about what might happen tomorrow.

The present must always be more important to us than the past and the future, not the other way around.

Christ mastered the secret of living fully in the present. The Gospels show that he was oblivious to the past and aware of the future and never lost sight of what was happening around him. It is much easier to talk about a goal than to accomplish it. So many of us are not living in the present.

Where are you living? Where do you spend most of your time? In the past? Memory is a wonderful part of our lives, but it should not become our master. We should learn from the past and not try to live there. The past should shed light on the present, but not control it.

We need to be living in the present. History for an individual is not a cycle, repeating itself. Life passes by us only once, and if we miss it, it is gone forever. We have a hard time remembering the past fully and can only anticipate the future, but we can experience the present and have at least some ability to change it or to change ourselves. I believe that one of the secrets of life is to live in the present.

If we become sensitive to the present, we will have a better understanding of what God is calling us to do.

Tell yourself that you don't have to bear three-days' load today. Pray for strength for today and trust God for tomorrow. There is special strength in saying, "This one thing I do."

We have a rich heritage of doctrines, traditions, and resources in our churches. But the true test is, Is there life in the body? Are we alive and willing to accept the challenges of today?—William P. Cubine

ILLUSTRATIONS

THIS DAY.   The best thing about the future is that it is offered to us one day at a time. A friend of mine, Dr. Boreham of Australia, whom I got to know when I visited that country, told in one of his books of an occasion when he was staying in a home for a few days and noticed that written on one of the windowpanes, as though with a diamond, were these words from one of the Psalms: "This is the day that the Lord hath made. Let us rejoice and be glad in it." When he went down to breakfast he said to his hostess, "I am curious to know why that text is written on my window." She said, "I was going through great trouble and sorrow. When the morning came I wished it were evening and when the evening came I wished it would all end. Then I did a thing that you will laugh at me for doing. I just let the Bible open of itself and the first words that took my eye I received as a message from God. The message that met my eye was this: 'This is the day that the Lord hath made. Let us rejoice and be glad in it.'" I thought to myself, That gives me a clue for my life. I am worrying. I am brooding over the past. I am grumbling about the present. I am terrified of the future. I will just grasp the opportunity of this day and live out this day.—Leslie D. Weatherhead[1]

THE POWER OF "ALMOST."   Always remember . . . that you are a mortal being; that humans have innate limitations; that they never *completely* overcome groundless fears and anxieties; and that life is a ceaseless battle against irrational worries. If you fight this battle intelligently and unremittingly, however, you can *almost* be free from *almost* all your needless concerns. What more can you ask of a good life?—Albert Ellis and Robert A. Harper[2]

---

[1]*Prescription for Anxiety*
[2]*A Guide to Rational Living*

SERMON SUGESTIONS

Topic: God Remembers

TEXT: Isa. 49:8–16a, especially v. 16a

(1) Circumstances that can cause us to feel godforsaken (v. 14). (2) Changing conditions that can create hope (vv. 8–12). (3) Appropriate response to God's providence (v. 13). (4) The explanation of God's action (v. 16a).

Topic: Not Until It's Over!

TEXT: 1 Cor. 4:1–5

(1) God has committed the truth of Christ to us as believers. (2) Inevitably, we as congregations or individuals are wide open to criticism, even condemnation, by rivals, chronically suspicious persons, or perceptive observers. (3) Though we may be able to make a good case for our beliefs and actions, the real truth will come with the coming of the Lord.

CONGREGATIONAL MUSIC

1. "All My Hope Is Firmly Grounded," Joachim Neander (1680); trans. Fred Pratt Green (1886)
   MICHAEL, Herbert Howells (1930, 1977)

   The spirit of the Psalter reading (Ps. 131) and the actual teaching of the Gospel lesson (Matt. 6:24–34) are caught up in this noble new hymn of praise. The original German text of the seventeenth century is given fresh significance by the twentieth-century translation set to a bold but quite singable twentieth-century tune.

2. "Seek Ye First," Karen Lafferty (1972) (setting of Matt. 3:33)
   SEEK YE, Karen Lafferty (1972)

   One of the most appealing contemporary Scripture songs, this minihymn could be used effectively as a response to the reading of the Gospel lesson. Its appeal can be enhanced upon repetition by singing one or both stanzas with the alleluia descant.

3. "In Christ There Is No East or West," Michael A. Perry (1982)
   MCKEE, African American spiritual; adapt. H. T. Burleigh (1939)

   This hymn is different than the one by John Oxenham that starts with the identical first phrase. It relates appropriately to the Old Testament reading (Isa. 49:8–16a), in which the writer forecasts the hopeful return of the children of God from the east, north, and south (region of Aswan). The restoration of Israel can thus be transposed to the New Testament notion of Christ as the source of all unity.

4. "We Are Called to Be God's People," Thomas J. Jackson (1973)
   AUSTRIAN HYMN, Franz Joseph Haydn (1797)

   This hymn is quite relevant to the admonition of the apostle Paul (1 Cor. 4:1–5) to be servants of Christ who are always faithful when entrusted with sacred responsibilities. Each stanza focuses on a different kind of responsibility as (1) God's people, (2) God's servants, and (3) God's prophets.—Hugh T. McElrath

WORSHIP AIDS

CALL TO WORSHIP.   "Let Israel hope in the Lord from henceforth and for ever" (Ps. 131:3).

INVOCATION.   O God, you have promised never to leave or forsake your people. The ways of your providence are full of mystery, we know. But give us the faith to wait patiently and worship with belief as your plans come to fruition.

OFFERTORY SENTENCE.   "Bear ye one another's burdens, and so fulfill the law of Christ" (Gal. 6:2).

OFFERTORY PRAYER.   Today, O Lord, you have given us another opportunity to bring before you a portion of the fruits of our labors, so that your Kingdom may grow as the needs of many at home and abroad are met with compassionate love in many practical ways.

PRAYER.   Clear our vision this morning, we pray, Lord. We are so blinded by what is visible around us that we fail to see the things of the Spirit that make the large differences in how we live and move and have our being. We need this morning to be able to see beyond the darkness of the material world into that which is luminously spiritual. All about us are barriers that prohibit our view of the wide vistas you desire us to see. Enable us this morning to see beyond the barriers so that we may envision what is real and eternal.

Let us see beyond the barrier of the quick satisfaction of hate to the long joy of forgiveness.

Let us see beyond the appetite for more to the pleasure of self-control.

Let us see beyond greed to the luxury of giving.

Let us see beyond blinding pride to the healthiness of humility.

Let us see beyond profit to usefulness.

Let us see past the heat of desire to the light of renunciation.

Let us see past the glaring light of power to the beauty of service.

Let us see past the poisonous growth of selfishness to the wonder and power of selflessness, we pray in Jesus' name.—Henry Fields

SERMON
Topic: With All Your Heart
TEXT: Rom. 10:1–3

George Hunter describes "how the West was lost" in his book on reaching secular people with the gospel. He notes the causes of the decline of church influence in the West, including the rise of science, the cultural-intellectual renaissance, and the age of the Enlightenment. He declares that the age of Enlightenment is over, along with Modernism. We have entered the postmodern age. These days, leaders tend to be qualified by passion and charisma rather than by their cold logic and deep intellect.

I am not so sure that this new age has just arrived. People have always followed passionate leaders. I saw an old film from the 1930s of Adolf Hitler's speeches to the German masses. My German was too rusty to follow the logical rationale of his message, but I certainly could comprehend his passion. This little man who rose from obscurity to threaten all human existence rode on the power of his passion. The poor acoustics of the outdoor speech and the limited quality of the electronics required careful articulation and strong vocal projection, but there was more to his speeches than volume and enunciation. Hitler spoke with passion. Perhaps the best evidence of the total depravity of the man was in the conviction with which he spoke of the superiority of the Arian race and the destiny of the German nation.

When Jesus was asked to identify the first commandment, he cited the *shema,* from Deuteronomy 6:4, which calls for us to love God "with all your heart." *Heart, soul, mind,* and *strength* have distinctive Old Testament meanings, but the intention was to dramatize the dimensions of the whole person. Our devotion to God must be total. No part of you can be reserved as secular. All that you are must be committed in love to the God of our salvation.

I. *We need to get our hearts straight.* In the Bible, the heart is more than an organ of human anatomy. It is the center of the self, the seat of emotion and understanding. The romanticized, sentimental symbol of the heart in love ballads and movies does not fit well into our faith response to God. Our love for God is the highest kind of human commitment. It does not mesh with the cheap emotionalism or the erotic romance of the entertainment media.

Last week I was listening to the local Christian radio station while driving into town. The song was one I remember well from the church music I heard and sang in the 1950s. It was melodic and deeply emotional, like most good music; but something about the song did not fit with the words. Then it struck me: the music was patterned after one of the pieces in *Naughty Marietta,* a musical drama I had sung in on tour with the Baylor Chapel Choir. What bothered me was not the words, the theme, or even the melody. It was the association. The romantic love ballad was unworthy of the kind of love I would offer God.

I have serious reservations about the meaning of love in today's media as a baseline for our human relationships. A part of growing up in marriage was to discover that romance is only a part of a much larger, much more complex relationship. In the real world, love has to deal with all of the human emotions, including anger and frustration. Love involves pain as much as pleasure, self-sacrifice as much as self-fulfillment, and fear along with security. I am not cynical about marriage. In fact, if the love that binds us together in Christian marriage is nothing more than sentimentality and romance, it never measures up to the real world in which we live out our covenant.

II. *Holy love is distinct from romance.* To love God with all of your heart calls for a passionate commitment that goes to the core of your being. When the *shema* calls for us to love God with our whole heart, we need to look higher than the movies and popular music of our time.

Paul was a passionate man. His Epistles reveal more than cold logic. The apostle to the Gentiles spoke about his love for his people, Israel: "I have great sorrow and unceasing anguish in my heart." Again he spoke from the heart: "My heart's desire and prayer to God for them is that they may be saved." His description of the great salvation that came with the person of Christ calls for his reader to confess with the lips and believe with the heart. Finally, he said, "Everyone who calls on the name of the Lord shall be saved." The Law was never intended as an impersonal, cold set of rules imposed on the world by an uncaring God, but limiting the Law to lip service devoid of all human passion was a problem confronted by both Jesus and Paul. What you believe is of critical importance, but how you believe is also critical. A half-hearted, superficial faith is no faith at all.

Like most teens, Jimmy was full of fun and energy, and he was struggling to find himself and what he wanted to do with his life. He was not a bad kid, but periodically he got with the wrong crowd and followed bad examples. I recall several times when we were growing up when Jimmy made a public declaration of his sin and pled for the prayers of the church for his salvation. He was baptized at least three times, but he never seemed to find peace with God. Later in life he had similar difficulties with marriage and vocation. When he died of a cerebral hemorrhage in his forties, I wondered if he had been tormented by a brain disorder all of those years, and I wondered if he had ever found peace with God. No one could ever say that Jimmy was not passionate about religion or that he did not feel strongly about God. The heart is more than emotion. The heart is the core of your being.

The heart is both law and gospel. To love god with all your heart is to commit your whole life to the service of God. It is personal and emotional. We are indeed persons with emotions, but we need to put aside our judgment of one another. God looks on the heart, but most of us have difficulty seeing what is going on in the heart of another person. People who go about in quiet desperation are not necessarily emotional, but we should not judge people who are reserved or quiet as lacking in heart.

The only way you can love God is from the heart, and that is the only way you can understand or serve God. Religion is always more than a name on a card in a file, more than a code for conformed behavior. Christ went to the cross in his passion for people like us. The only way we can be his disciples is to take up the cross in passion to follow him.—Larry Dipboye

SUNDAY, MARCH 10, 2002
Lectionary Message

Topic: Preparing for a Disaster
TEXT: Matt. 7:21–29
Other Readings: Deut. 1:18–21, 26–28; Ps. 31:1–5, 19–24; Rom. 1:16–17; 3:22b–28 (29–31)

Experts in building design have developed new approaches in construction to prevent loss of lives and property when a tornado or hurricane strikes. Proper preparation is a vital part of reducing the high cost of disasters when they occur. Jesus was aware of preparing for the events of life when he told the story about two men who built their houses. The story was meant to illustrate the importance of having built a solid foundation for our lives when the problems of life come upon us.

The movie *Titanic* won most of the year's Oscars for its outstanding production. The largest ocean liner of its day was promoted as unsinkable, but beneath the great ship's trimmings lay a fatal flaw. It was not until eighty years later that scientists understood why the ship sank so quickly. The brittle steel from which the ship was constructed was probably the cause for the disaster. One researcher who made this discovery, Steve Blasco, put it this way, "Shipbuilding technology had outstripped metallurgy technology."[3]

A vital part of any new adventure in science is to have a backup system in the event of an emergency. The *Titanic* was not prepared. There were not enough life jackets or lifeboats, and no emergency drills had taken place on the cruise.

How prepared are you for the disasters that may come in your life? I believe that we must each establish a firm foundation and build on it a reliable structure if we are to survive. For

---

[3]*Reader's Digest,* Aug. 1995, pp. 155–160.

some of us, life may seem routine and uneventful for a long time. For others, every day seems to bring a new test of survival. For all of us, there will come times of loneliness when we are separated from others on whom we have depended for support.

In this parable, Jesus tells about two builders who are constructing houses. They may have been building near a dry streambed that was no threat, until the rains came and the water began to rise. As the waters rushed down from the mountains and into the valley, one of the houses fell. Why? Because one man had not taken time to dig down to the bedrock for his foundation. The house built on the sand could not withstand the force of the water. From the outside, the houses looked the same, but one builder had nothing left when the waters went down. Jesus is saying that life is like a house. We need a good solid foundation to support the rest of our lives.

Jesus said we are to listen to and act on the wisdom he gives if we want to make it through the crises of life that will surely come to each of us. What are some of the important spiritual structure designs we need to develop in our lives to be prepared for such difficult times?

I. *Find the answer to "Who am I?"* Each person has a need to know who they are and where they came from. We cannot live our lives apart from others. To know that we are God's creation is not enough. We need to be reconnected with God through Jesus Christ. God wants to restore us to a right relationship with him and make us joint heirs with Christ. We have been created in his image (Gen. 1:27) and have a special place in this world (Ps. 8:4–8). How much does God love us? So much that he gave his Son to die for us (John 3:16). God wants us to be his representatives here on Earth (2 Cor. 5:20).

II. *Find the answer to "Why Am I Here?"* God has a plan and a purpose for each of us. He will not force his will on us, but the Holy Spirit does move in our lives to reveal what we ought to do. There are other people in this world to whom God would have us relate through ministry. Jesus taught and lived that persons are more important in life than material things. He said, "Whatever you wish that men would do to you, do so to them" (Matt. 7:12). Life takes on a new meaning when we have a purpose for living. Christ wants to give us a challenge that is more than material security and personal pleasure. Some people live for things and others have things to live for. Which of these two walks in life best describes your life?

III. *Find the answer to "Where am I going?"* Jesus says to all of us, "Seek first his Kingdom and his righteousness and all these things shall be added to you" (Matt. 6:33). There are those in the world today who live and will die as Christopher Columbus did: they don't know where they are going or where they are, and when it is all over, they won't know where they have been.

William James once said, "The best use a man can make of his life is to spend it for something that will outlast it." Most of us need to focus our lives if we hope to leave something in this world for others. T. S. Eliot said that listless, aimless, weary people of our age are waiting for a knock at the door. Maybe you are struggling right now for someone to give you a new reason for living. Without a purpose for living, we experience futility and boredom.

Are you preparing for the storms of life that in all probability will hit you? Life will go on no matter how great the crisis. Remember that Christ stilled the storm on the Sea of Galilee, and he will provide the support you need to survive. After all, what we need to survive the storms is the same thing we need each day of our lives.—William P. Cubine

ILLUSTRATIONS

READY AND NOT READY.   The difference between life and death can be seen as we compare the sinking of the *Titanic* and the mishap of *Apollo 13*. The designers of *Apollo 13* were aware of possible failures in their spaceship and provided backup support that avoided disaster. The designers of the *Titanic* lacked full understanding of the nature of the steel used in building their ship, and because of their overconfidence in their work, they failed to provide sufficient lifesaving devices.—William P. Cubine

THE CHOSEN SITE.   The durability of the one house and the collapse of the other are not ascribed to the strength or weakness of the walls, as in the rabbinic parable, or even to the careful laying of a foundation or its lack, as in Luke, but only to the chosen location. Thus everything depends on where a man "settles" and builds his "house," that is, his life. We are reminded of Paul's saying about the one foundation on which alone it is safe to build (1 Cor. 3:11). Unlike Paul, however, Matthew is thinking not of Jesus' death and Resurrection as the seat of all salvation, but of Jesus' *teaching* as presented in the words of the Sermon on the Mount (see the discussion of vv. 28–29). He goes on to state explicitly that the man who has merely heard these words has not built on them, but the man who lives them has. Unlike 1 Corinthians 3:11, Matthew 16:18 refers to Peter as the "rock," precisely because he transmits and interprets Jesus' words authentically to the community. Of course the contrast must not be exaggerated.—Eduard Schweizer[4]

SERMON SUGGESTIONS

Topic: When God Speaks

TEXT: Deut. 11:18–21, 26–28

(1) He demands total and continual attention to his word: (a) by the consent of the heart and (b) by constant reminders. (2) However, the choice and its consequences are up to us.

Topic: Questions About the Gospel

TEXT: Rom. 1:16–17; 3:22b–30

(1) Are we ashamed of the gospel? (2) Can the gospel accomplish a life-changing salvation? (3) What can we do to experience the promised benefits of the gospel?

CONGREGATIONAL MUSIC

1. "Be Strong in the Lord," Linda Lee Johnson (1979)
   STRENGTH, Tom Fettke (1979)
   Voicing the basic idea of the last verse of the psalm for this day, this contemporary hymn would be an effective response to that reading. The choir could sing the stanzas, with the congregation joining in on the exhilarating refrain.
2. "How Firm a Foundation," K in Rippon's *Selection* (1787)
   FOUNDATION, the Sacred Harp (1844)

---

[4]*The Good News According to Matthew*

This strong hymn of faith can be sung in connection with the Gospel reading about the wise and foolish builders. Its reassuring message focuses on the truth that the righteous can depend on God's faithfulness.

3. "My Hope Is Built," Edward Mote (1834)
   SOLID ROCK, William B. Bradbury (1863)

Relating to the principal theme of the Gospel, Epistle, and Psalter lessons, this classic gospel song would be appropriately sung in any part of the worship service. Because it is well-known, a stanza or two could be sung without instrumental accompaniment.

4. "Word of God, Across the Ages," Ferdinand Q. Blanchard (1952)
   AUSTRIAN HYMN, Franz J. Haydn (1797)

The Old Testament reading concentrates on the importance, in commandment and teaching, of the Word of God, which is to be hidden in the heart and passed on from generation to generation. This hymn on God's Word could serve appropriately both for the opening of worship and in connection with the Old Testament lesson.—Hugh T. McElrath

WORSHIP AIDS

CALL TO WORSHIP.   "Be of good courage and he shall strengthen your heart, all ye who hope in the Lord" (Ps. 31:24).

INVOCATION.   Loving God, we often come to you with fears, but you graciously remind us that we can dare to live with courage, for in our times of deepest need you give us strength. So, let this service of worship focus our hearts on you and your faithful promises.

OFFERTORY SENTENCE.   "Live in love as Christ loved you and gave himself up on your behalf, an offering and sacrifice whose fragrance is pleasing to God" (Eph. 5:2 REB).

OFFERTORY PRAYER.   We give, Father, so that others might receive. Sometimes others give that we might receive. Today we do not know how the equation is working. All we know is that we cannot afford *not* to bring tithes and offerings, for they are the means whereby you bring blessings on gift, giver, and receiver. Let this offering today become busy doing your work, we pray in Jesus' name.—Henry Fields

PRAYER.   O God, we remember with sadness our want of faith in thee. What might have been a garden, we have turned into a desert by our sin and willfulness. This beautiful life which thou hast given us, we have wasted in futile worries and vain regrets and empty fears. Instead of opening our eyes to the joy of life, a flower, or the face of an innocent child and rejoicing in it as in a sacrament, we have sunk back into the complainings of our narrow and blind souls. O deliver us from the bondage of unchastened desires and unwholesome thoughts. Help us to conquer hopeless brooding and faithless reflection, and the impatience of irritable weakness. Toward this end, increase our faith, O Lord. Fill us with a more complete trust in thee, and with the desire for a more wholehearted surrender to thy will. Then every sorrow will become a joy. Then shall we say to the mountains that lie heavy on our souls, "Remove and be cast hence," and they shall be removed and nothing shall be impossible to us. Then shall we renew our strength and mount up with wings as eagles; we shall run and not be weary, we shall walk and not be faint. We offer this prayer in the name of Jesus Christ, our Lord.—Samuel McComb

SERMON
Topic: Seeking Divine Guidance
TEXT: Prov. 3:5–6; 1 John 1:5–10

So, how do we get guidance for the future? Why, you know! Many turn to Ouija boards, crystal balls, fortune-tellers, tea leaves, cards, horoscopes, and astrologists. Do we find direction from the stars? Where do we go for guidance in making decisions for life? I wish there were a machine labeled "Divine Guidance." The instructions might read, "Put your question in the slot and out will come the divine answer." But it just isn't that simple, is it?

Nevertheless, the writer of the Book of Proverbs asserts, "Trust in the Lord with all your heart and he will direct your path." An ancient rabbi, Bar Kappara, stated that this text is the "hinge" on which all the essential principles of Judaism rest. Trust in God is the hinge on which most of our life really does depend. This is a text that many of us memorized in childhood. This call to trust is for those who already believe in God. It is addressed not to those outside the faith but to those who are within it.

"Trust in the Lord with all your heart, but lean not on your own understanding." Ah, that's the rub, isn't it? Some of us lean too much on our own understanding. The injunction to trust in the Lord would not be necessary if everyone did. The idolatry of self arises from those who puff themselves up and feel they have enough insights to make all the necessary decisions regarding life without any divine guidance. They feel no sense of dependence on God or others. They feel sufficient in their own abilities.

Go a step further with me into our theme and encounter those who say that the vastness of the universe makes it impossible for us to be known. "How could there be a God who is concerned about us on this tiny speck in the universe?" they ask. Light, traveling at 186,000 miles per second, takes fifty million years to reach our planet from a distant star.

Others throw up a warning flag that points to the accidents, suffering, and pain in the world. To these persons, the enigma of suffering denies the love and providence of God.

Still others declare that even if there is a God, we can't really communicate with him. "Why," they laughingly declare, "we can't even talk to each other. How can we communicate with God?" (Oh, I know there are some people who drive down a street and claim that God finds a parking place for them.)

Well, when we lean on our own understanding, it does seem to make for some tough going, doesn't it? Nevertheless, this ancient writer instructs us, "In all your ways acknowledge him and he will direct your path." The words *acknowledge* and *trust* are derived from a rich Hebrew word whose root meaning is "to see" or "to know." This word involves much more than just physical vision or intellectual knowledge, though that is part of its meaning. This is knowledge in its totality. This knowledge encompasses the heart, will, and mind. It is similar to Jesus' declaration of loving God with all your heart, soul, mind, and strength. When you and I acknowledge God with all our capacity, then his direction will be clear.

If we acknowledge God with all our heart, we will be humble. If we acknowledge God with all our heart, we will also seek to learn to live in harmony with the universe, like the rest of nature does. When we acknowledge God in all our ways, we discover, paradoxically, that in our dependence on God we also receive freedom.

God has created our world with the possibility of accidents, because he has given us freedom. Without freedom we would not be authentically human.

If we acknowledge God with all our hearts, we commit our total self to him.

The Wisdom writer has assured us that if we acknowledge God with all our heart, he will direct or make straight our paths. This is the promise we have from God if we love him with all of our being. This promise assures us of the providence of God. The writer does not tell us how, but his promise of guidance is enough. How do we determine the guidance of God? Let me offer some brief suggestions.

First, we need to follow the light we have within us. This might be called *spiritual intuition*.

Second, we need to use our reasoning powers. I don't know why we think that using our minds is counter to what God wants us to do. Why do we think that God is always going to guide us by imparting something from outside ourselves?

Third, we need to study the Scriptures. Let me quickly send up a warning flag here. Don't use the Scriptures like a Ouija board. The Bible is not some book of magic that we thumb through for quick answers. When you search the Scriptures, you will find the eternal principles and teachings about how God has worked in the lives of other people in the past. Seek to understand how you can relate these principles and teachings to your own life.

Fourth, wait patently for God.

Fifth, draw on the resources of the Church.

Finally, remember how mysteriously and unexpectantly God moves. We never know for certain how God works in people's lives. He works in different ways for different people, because each person is different. The affirmation from the ancient writer of Wisdom is, "Trust in the Lord with all your heart. Acknowledge him in all your ways and he will direct your path."—William Powell Tuck

SUNDAY, MARCH 17, 2002
Lectionary Message

Topic: The Mountains and Valleys of Our Lives

TEXT: Matt: 17:1–9

Other Readings: Exod. 24:12–18; Ps. 2; 2 Peter 1:16–21

It was six days after the confession of Peter (Mark 8:27–30) that Jesus took Peter, James, and John and led them up onto a high mountain, possibly Mount Hermon (Mark 9:2). Here he "was transfigured," his garments had a strange whiteness, and a divine voice was heard by the disciples. Mark 14:4 refers to the time as two days before the Passover.

We all experience spiritual mountaintops and deep valleys in our lives. It is a moving experience to be lifted up into the presence of God, but most of life is lived in the valley of everyday reality. We need both experiences in order to appreciate both the greatness of God and the needs of those around us. It has been said that all sunshine creates a desert.

Our text for today is about individuals who had a personal encounter with Christ and their lives were changed. The history of Christianity is the story of how men and women have experienced radical changes in their lives after a personal experience with Christ. We are so much a part of the world into which we have been born that when we are lifted up into a spiritual encounter with Christ it is not always easy to go back to the daily tasks of life. The world has a way of conditioning us to be like it, and Christ comes to release us from this conformation and to transform us into his agents of reconciliation and love. We are to have, as Paul stated, "that mind which was also in Christ Jesus."

You may ask, how can this take place in our lives, which are so filled with the pressures of our society? To have a mountaintop experience, several things in our lives need to be changed. Only Christ can release us from our sins. This is the beginning of our religious activities and the start of a growth process in our spiritual pilgrimage. This experience gives us the freedom to respond to the will of God, who is in heaven, and to live life here on Earth as God would direct us. This experience with God cleanses us from guilt and rebellion, which frees us to stop thinking about ourselves and to reach out to others who are in the valley with us.

Within this mountaintop experience with God we are freed from the fear of death and to think about the matter of living. This freedom comes through our release from the sins that burden us. We have a message of hope rather than fear to tell the world, but until we have experienced this release, we have a problem convincing others. On the mountaintop with Christ we can come to know that neither life nor death, troubles nor persecution, illness nor loneliness, nor any other creature can separate us from the love of God in Christ Jesus. We need this experience so we can go back to the valley of living in this world.

To experience Christ personally is to be motivated to live in a positive way in order to help others overcome the stranglehold of evil on their lives. Paul reminds us, "Do not let yourselves be overcome by evil, but overcome evil with good" (Rom. 12:21). We cannot rest on our spiritual oars and coast through life thinking only of ourselves. The disciples openly admitted that for them it would be better to stay on the mountain, but Christ led them back down to the valley to minister to the people. He told them to say nothing until after he had been raised from the dead. After the Resurrection, Christ gave them a commission that is the same for us today. He said, "Go, therefore, and make disciples of all nations, baptizing them in the name of the Father and of the Son and of the Holy Spirit, and teaching them to obey everything that I have commanded you. And remember, I am with you always, to the end of the age" (Matt. 28:19–20).

It is great to worship God, but those who have been changed by a worship experience must express love. I believe that one of the weaknesses of modern Christianity is that we go to church and worship, but Monday through Saturday we ignore those around us who we are to love. Christ stated clearly what we need to do in the valley when he told the parable about the last judgment (Matt. 25:34–46). One of the best expressions of our love for God is to feed the sheep as Christ commanded. However, we can sometimes get so caught up in the needs of others that we either forget or get too busy to retreat back to the mountaintop. As Christians we need times of retreat into the presence of God in order to be recharged spiritually and go back into the world of the hurting. It takes a great deal of effort to balance our spiritual lives with God and meeting the needs of others.

We need the wisdom that is the gift of God to help us know what things in this world can be changed and what cannot. Let us recommit our efforts by seeking to change the things that can be changed instead of getting depressed and frustrated by giving our full energy to trying to change the things that cannot be changed.

Individuals can be transformed by Christ even today. The good news is that we can live today with power from God to overcome all that is evil in this world, because we have personally experienced Christ as the Risen Savior. The question that faces us today is, Have we been released from transfixtion so that we are motivated to reach out to others? Are we overcoming evil with good, or letting evil overcome us?

It is time now to start letting God's will become our mandate and direction. When we personally find peace with God, we can then guide others to the one who can change them with a mountaintop spiritual encounter.—William P. Cubine

ILLUSTRATIONS

YEARS IN THE VALLEY.   I remember the first time I "saw" Jesus. She was a delicate black woman with a determined disposition, a member of the housekeeping staff in the hospital where I completed my clinical pastoral education. The first time I saw her—saw him!—she was seated at the bedside of a child, holding her hand, wiping her brow, telling her Bible stories, and singing sweet melodies.

It was her lunch hour. She'd sacrificed it every day so that she might spend time with selected patients. I told my supervisor. He said, "Bernice! She's been doing that for, oh, I'm not sure, some sixteen years, I suppose. Some witness to Christ crucified, don't you think?"—Albert J. D. Walsh

FOR BETTER UNDERSTANDING.   Knowing that they hear the voice of God, the disciples, in intense fear, fall face down on the ground; they dare not see the awful majesty of God. But with the voice the vision has reached its climax and fulfilled its purpose. Jesus comes to the cowering disciples, touches them reassuringly, and tells them to rise and cease to fear; the glorious manifestation of the Father has ended. So they dare to raise their eyes; now they see no signs of the divine majesty or the ancient leaders of Israel. They see Jesus alone in his familiar human form. Now they should understand him better; they have the answer to their deep inward rebellion at the idea of a suffering Christ: the Old Testament supports his teaching; the Father wills the Cross; they should listen to what Jesus says about it.—Floyd V. Filson[5]

SERMON SUGGESTIONS

Topic: The Ideal Ruler
TEXT: Ps. 2
(1) Must point to God as the ultimate ruler (vv. 1–7). (2) Can be seen only and definitively in Jesus the Christ (vv. 8–11). (See Matt. 3:17 and 17:5, and Isa. 42:1.)

Topic: Why We Hope
TEXT: 2 Pet. 1:16–21
(1) Because of prophetic voices. (2) Because of eye witnesses of the majesty of Jesus Christ.

---

[5]*The Gospel According the Matthew*

(3) Because of the trustworthiness of the movement of the Holy Spirit in the hearts and minds of those who have brought the message to us.

CONGREGATIONAL MUSIC

1. "Christ, Whose Glory Fills the Skies," Charles Wesley (1740)

 RATISBON, Freylinghausen's *Gesangbuch* (1740)

 A glorious hymn for the opening of worship, this great Wesleyan paean relates to the majestic glory of God mentioned in the Old Testament reading, the Epistle, and the Gospel lesson. It would be best used with the reading in Exodus (24:12–18).

2. "Christ Upon the Mountain Peak," Brian Wren (1962)

 MOWSLEY, Cyril Taylor (1985)

 SHILLINGFORD, Peter Cutts (1962)

 The Transfiguration of Jesus found in both the Epistle and the Gospel lessons is the theme of this fine contemporary hymn. Sung to either modern tune, it would be effective as a response to either reading.

3. "O Wondrous Type! O Vision Fair," Latin (fifteenth century); trans. John M. Neale (1861)

 WAREHAM, William Knapp (1738)

 Appropriately sung in connection with the Transfiguration of our Lord, this hymn pulls the singer into the company of Peter, James, and John, who worship and adore him.

4. "Wherefore Do the Nations Rage," Ps. 2; vers. *Psalter* (1912)

 MONSEY CHAPEL, Dick Van Halsema (1952)

 Psalm 2 receives a powerful metrical interpretation in this song. The modern tune captures the rough spirit of the words, which could be sung section by section in alternation with the reading of the words, as follows: stanza 1, vv. 1–3; stanza 2, vv. 4–6; stanza 3, vv. 7–9; stanza 4, vv. 10–12.—Hugh T. McElrath

WORSHIP AIDS

CALL TO WORSHIP.   "Create in me a pure heart, O God, and renew a steadfast spirit within me. Do not cast me from your presence or take your Holy Spirit from me. Restore to me the joy of your salvation and grant me a willing spirit, to sustain me" (Ps. 51:10–12 NIV).

INVOCATION.   As we come to you, O God, we confess our deep need. We have experienced so much that can cause us to lose sight of you and your love. So, we pray that you will renew and strengthen our faith and our commitment to your will in all circumstances, as we worship you.

OFFERTORY SENTENCE.   "Every good and perfect gift is from above, coming down from the Father of the heavenly lights, who does not change like shifting shadows" (James 1:17 NIV).

OFFERTORY PRAYER.   Lord of life, add resolve and commitment to our stewardship today, that what we give will match what we do in a harmony of redeeming faith.—E. Lee Phillips

PRAYER.   God, we thank thee for this universe, our great home—for its vastness and its riches, and for the manifoldness of the life that teems upon it and of which we are part. We praise thee for the arching sky and the blessed winds, for the driving clouds and the constellations on high. We praise thee for the salt sea and the running water, for the everlasting hills, for the trees, and for the grass under our feet. We thank thee for our senses, by which we can see the splendor of the morning and hear the jubilant songs of love and smell the breath of the springtime. Grant us, we pray thee, a heart wide open to all this joy and beauty, and save our souls from being so steeped in care or so darkened by passion that we pass heedless and unseeing when even the thornbush by the wayside is aflame with the glory of God.

Enlarge within us the sense of fellowship with all living things, our little brothers, to whom thou hast given this Earth as their home in common with us. We remember with shame that in the past we have exercised the high dominion of man with ruthless cruelty, so that the voice of the Earth, which should have gone up to thee in song, has been a groan of travail. May we realize that all creatures live not for us alone but for themselves and for thee, and that they love the sweetness of life even as we, and serve thee in their place better than we in ours.

When our use of this world is over and we make room for others, may we not leave anything ravished by our greed or spoiled by our ignorance, but may we hand on our common heritage fairer and sweeter through our use of it, undiminished in fertility and joy, so that our bodies may return in peace to the great mother who nourished them, and our spirits may round the circle of a perfect life in thee.—Walter Rauschenbusch

SERMON
Topic: Whenever We Wish to See Jesus
TEXT: John 12:20–23

So one day some Greeks stroll on up to Philip with this request, "Sir, we wish to see Jesus," which is, quite frankly, and at least at face value, a simple enough appeal. And perhaps plain old-fashioned common courtesy would dictate that Philip respond by saying something like, "Well, sure, why not? I'd be glad to introduce you to Jesus!"—which would miss the mark completely. Because you see, for John, that simple plea—"Sir, we wish to see Jesus"—represents far more than the desire to hold a chit-chat with the Christ.

No, John's Gospel is pressing us in another direction altogether. On hearing the request, "Sir, we wish to see Jesus," John teases us into asking some questions, such as, "What exactly does it mean to see Jesus?" or "Where do we see Jesus?"

I wouldn't necessarily expect you to know this but, for some five chapters prior to the account about the Greeks, the recurring issue is what in the world people are to make of Jesus. Everyone, from religious officials to his own followers, expresses serious reservations about who Jesus might possibly be. In fact, at one point they become so frustrated that some of them shout, "How long will you keep us in suspense? If you are the Christ, tell us plainly!"

Anyway, here's the point. People were perplexed whenever they looked at, watched, or listened to Jesus. Few witnessed his life and recognized the Redeemer. Most either walked away scratching their heads or bent down to pick up stones to toss at the presumptuous preacher from Nazareth.

Confusion was the most common reaction to any encounter with this character called

Jesus. In fact, as John recounts the otherwise joyous day of Jesus' entrance into Jerusalem, with the great crowd singing praise to highest heaven, he says that Jesus' "disciples did not understand these things."

Well, that's not quite so. Actually, what John says is that Jesus' disciples did not understand these things *at first*; but when Jesus was glorified, they remembered that these things had been written of him and had been done to him. So, in John's Gospel, the glorification of Jesus is when we can witness the truth of his character as the Christ of God.

In essence, what we are given is a Gospel in which we see people wondering who Jesus might be. Theirs was a world with far too much sickness, far too many conflicts, far too little justice, and far too little comfort. Dread disease, families in crisis, rampant violence, and that old demon death.

So Jesus came on the scene, with a relatively slow start. Throughout his ministry, however, the hearts of those who heard him preach began to pound just a little harder. As they witnessed healing, exorcisms, and miracles, their minds began to swim with dreams of the Messiah. They wondered if maybe, just maybe, Jesus could be that Christ. And then one day, in the tiny village of Bethany, they were left breathless. Gazing with gaping mouths, they watched as Lazarus, who was once dead as a doornail, stepped free from his rocky tomb!

For most people, that's all it took and their minds were made up. They now looked at Jesus and saw the one who could conquer death. And if death was not a deterrent to his power, than surely he could free them from every other form of adversity.

By the time Jesus traveled the stone's throw from Bethany to Jerusalem, the ranks of his followers had swollen considerably. I would imagine that's why John recorded the Pharisees as saying, "You see, you can do nothing. Look, the whole world has gone after him!"

"The hour has come," said Jesus, "for the Son of Man to be glorified. Very truly, I tell you, unless a grain of wheat falls into the Earth and dies, it remains just a single grain, but if it dies, it bears much fruit. . . . And I, when I am lifted up from the Earth, will draw all people to myself." You see, the cross is like a magnet, not because it holds some fascination as a tool of torture, but because of the one who is nailed fast to the wood. To see Christ is to see this cross. Nothing speaks more clearly of Jesus' character as the cross.

"Sir, we wish to see Jesus." Yes, of course. But sometimes the Jesus we see doesn't sit so well with us. Oh, we have no problem with the Good Shepherd Jesus or the miracle-working Jesus or the in-the-garden Jesus or the "What a friend we have in Jesus" Jesus.

But what about the Jesus who speaks of judgment? And what about the Jesus whose hands and feet and side are scarred? Or the Jesus whose brow has been marred by a thorn-plaited, makeshift crown?

Only this crucified Christ can save us from whatever we need most to be saved from. Save us from each other. Save us from ourselves. Save us from death both beyond the grave and before.

"Sir, we wish to see Jesus." Well, there are those occasions when we are actually given a glimpse of this Christ of Calvary: in the life of some saint, in some work being carried out in Christ's name and for Christ's sake and disclosing Christ's real presence and power. These are the memorable moments, frequently unanticipated, that always leave us with the impression that we have looked upon something, someone, sacred.

"Sir, we wish to see Jesus." Well, maybe so. But first we must concede that to see Jesus is to receive him as he has chosen and chooses to disclose himself.

We might hope for a Savior to shelter us from the pains and general anguish of life, but what we're given is a Christ whose body bears the scars of a divinely suffering sympathy.

The character of Christ is defined by Calvary. He said the same, didn't he? "And I, when I am lifted up from the Earth, will draw all people to myself." And because that's true, each and every manifestation of Christ will make its appearance in the long shadow of a cross. In that form, I've seen him, and so have you.—Albert J. D. Walsh

SUNDAY, MARCH 24, 2002
Lectionary Message

Topic: You Must Decide!
TEXT: Matt. 21:1–11; Matt. 26:14–27:66
Other Readings: Ps. 31:9–16; 118:1–2, 19–29; Isa. 50:4–9a; Phil. 2:5–11

Two of the great special seasons in the Christian church year are Advent and Lent. Lent is the penitential season of forty days beginning on Ash Wednesday and ending on the eve of Easter. Today, Palm Sunday, marks the first day of what we call Holy Week and it is my hope that this message will help you, as you look forward to Easter, to experience a fresh blessing because you have put out a special effort for something to transpire between you and Christ on that special day.

The Scriptures for today deal with the change of attitude of the crowd from when it greeted Jesus as he entered Jerusalem on what we now call Palm Sunday to that Friday when they shouted, "Crucify him!"

Why did the attitude of the crowd change so radically? The first day of the week Jesus was greeted with great admiration and praise as he rode unassumingly into the city of Jerusalem on a little colt. It was Passover time and the pilgrims and natives of the city stopped their work and shouted with joy. They cut branches from the trees and waved them in the air. They took off their garments and put them in his pathway. They raised their voices as they shouted, "Praise to the Son of David." Then, only five days later, they cried, "Let him be crucified!"

When I read these words, the question comes to my mind, Why did they change so much? I am aware that a crowd can very easily change its actions, but this was a completely opposite viewpoint. I believe that today we can learn something relevant from this event if we take a closer look. Yes, I believe that this very old story could assist us in making this Easter more meaningful, if we can catch an insight.

The response of the people on that Sunday was the result of Jesus' ministry over a three-year period. He had become a well-known person in Palestine. He had performed all types of miracles. He had spoken and taught with an authority that impressed the people, and they had responded to him. They were looking to him as a person who could free them from the Roman rule. He became their hero and redeemer because of what he had previously done for them.

The religious and political leaders of Jerusalem viewed Jesus in a different way. They monitored him in a much closer manner than the common people who supported him. Jesus was more of a threat to the religious leaders than to the Romans. He was a threat to their power and income because of his criticism of their practices. The religious leaders had controlling power in all the areas of the people's existence. The common people knew that you just did not cross these leaders without paying a price. The crowd on Palm Sunday may have been reacting out of emotion rather than weighing the ultimate cost of standing with Jesus against the religious and political leaders of the day.

We today must face this reality in our modern society. The blessings of God are great when we do not have to pay a price to be accepted by those with power. This is when the water hits the wheel, and we must decide which voices we will follow. Christ offers some wonderful promises for the future, and commits to standing beside us. For many, the here and now is more important than the future. Immediate gratification is the norm and we sometimes are willing to compromise for it.

As a coin has two sides, so does the Christian life. One side is receiving the gift of eternal life and the promise of heaven. The other side is the demands that come with the gift. Often we don't want to acknowledge or commit to these demands. We want things always to be comfortable and pleasant. Jesus promises to comfort us, yet at the same time he calls us to take up the cross and follow him (Matt. 16:24). To follow Christ in everyday life means to give up some things we really enjoy. Christ said that we cannot serve two masters. It a joy and blessing to accept Christ into our lives as Savior, but it is a difficult process to make him Lord of our lives. One of the difficulties of following Christ is that it is voluntary and not a matter of Christ forcing this response on us.

The depth of our love for Christ is directly related to our following him in life. Jesus told the parable of the Last Judgment in Matthew 25:31–46 and emphasized loving others who are not like us. We sometimes have a hard time accepting the fact that God loves those whose theology, race, ethnicity, and social status are different from ours. I am convinced that the secret of accepting others is Christian love. We cannot limit our love only to loving God. This is where Jesus makes a difference. If you practice this approach to life, you may lose more than you will gain here on Earth, but it is the Christian way of life. It is sticking with Jesus every day and not just when it is to our advantage.

We face a decision this morning: Will we follow Christ only when it has some advantage for us or will we follow his example even though it may cost us something? It will not be easy. Jesus didn't have it easy when he was here on Earth. Can you see yourself in the crowd on Palm Sunday? Will you see yourself in the crowd on Good Friday?

We need to decide to accept both the blessings and the demands that Christ confronts us with today. Let Christ change you in this Holy Week, and Easter will have a deeper meaning for you.—William P. Cubine

ILLUSTRATIONS

HIS TRIUMPH.   For one brief hour, his absolute, downright honesty triumphed over all the subterfuge of men, his love for mankind triumphed over their lust for power, and his spirit triumphed over the selfishness of the world. Now, it may have been only a temporary triumph, for it led right into the hands of the enemy; it played their game, it gave them their opportunity, and the triumph ultimately ended in the darkness of Good Friday. But let us not forget today—and this, I think, is the new note in the Palm Sunday story as I would sound it this year—let us not forget that it was indeed triumph when the lover of the world for one moment overcame all the forces and powers of evil and destruction.—Theodore Parker Ferris

FOR US!   All that, from the arrest in the Garden of Gethsemane on—the spitting and ill-treatment of the high council, the crown of thorns, the scourging, the mocking, and finally the tortures of the crucifixion and the abandonment by all, at last by God himself—all that "Christ had to suffer." God wanted it so, God did that, and all the persons suffering on the stage of this story—Judas, Caiaphas, the roaring crowd of people, the soldiers, and Pilate—they are all only instruments in God's hand who do what God wants to have done and what God wants to have done for our sakes. You can understand it only in the moment when you add to everything, "for me." Only then does it cease to be horrible, only then do you notice that you are horrible; but God who does all this is the Love that seeks and saves you.—Emil Brunner[6]

SERMON SUGGESTIONS

Topic: A Festal Theme Forever
TEXT: Ps. 118:10–2, 19–29
(1) God is good. (2) God's love for us has no end.

Topic: Surviving in a Competitive World
TEXT: Phil. 2:5–11
(1) Think like Jesus. (2) Act like Jesus. (3) Win like Jesus.

CONGREGATIONAL MUSIC

1. "Hosanna, Loud Hosanna!" Jeannette Thelfall (1875)
   ELLACOMBE, *Wurttemberger Gesangbuch* (1784)
   One of the hymns most frequently used for Palm Sunday, this venerable song concentrates on the singing of "Hosanna!" at Jesus' triumphal entrance into Jerusalem. In the third stanza, the singing congregation joins the biblical event and identifies with the singing children.
2. "Open Now Thy Gates of Beauty," Benjamin Schmolck (1732); trans. C. Winkworth (1863)
   UNSER HERRSCHER, Joachim Neander (1680)
   Relating especially to the reading in Psalm 118, this grand chorale can appropriately function as a call to worship at the beginning of the service.
3. "I Seek My Refuge in You, Lord," Ps. 31; vers. Marie J. Post (1985)
   COLERAINE, *La Scala Santa* (1681); arr. Erik Routley (1985)
   Verses 4 and 5 of this contemporary metrical paraphrase of Psalm 31 are parallel to the reading (vv. 9–16). If the tune is unfamiliar, the fourth verse could be sung by the choir, followed by verse 5 sung by the congregation and choir.
4. "As He Gathered at His Table," Paul A. Richardson (1986)
   STUTGART, Christian F. Witt (1715)
   STUART, Paul A. Richardson
   As an accompaniment to the Gospel reading on the Lord's Supper, this modern hymn recalls the deeper meanings of the actions and symbols in the Supper's observance. The pre-

---

[6]*I Believe in the Living God*

ferred tune is STUART, composed by the author of the text and intended for unison singing. The seven stanzas could be sung alternately by a soloist (or choir) and the congregation.

5. "All Praise to Christ," E. Bland Tucker (1938)

ENGELBERG, Charles V. Standford (1904)

One of the great hymns to come from the twentieth century, "All Praise to Christ" is based on the Epistle lesson—Phil. 2:5–11—and finds suitable expression in the rousing unison tune, ENGELBERG, also from the early twentieth century.

6. "At the Name of Jesus," Caroline M. Noel (1870)

KING'S WESTON, Ralph Vaughan Williams (1925)

As masterful a setting of Philippians 2:11–12 as the preceding hymn, this hymn is sometimes preferred because of its stately tune by the great British composer Ralph Vaughan Williams.—Hugh T. McElrath

WORSHIP AIDS

CALL TO WORSHIP.   "The stone which the builders rejected has become the cornerstone. This is the Lord's doing; it is wonderful in our eyes" (Ps. 118:22–23 NIV).

INVOCATION.   We wander Lord, but now we return. We forget Lord, but now we remember. We thought we were so powerful, but now we are humbled. See us as we are, Lord, and through this worship hour lift us to where we need to be because we would see Jesus (John 12:21).—E. Lee Phillips

OFFERTORY SENTENCE.   "Remember the words of the Lord Jesus, how he said, 'It is more blessed to give than to receive'" (Acts 20:35).

OFFERTORY PRAYER.   Yes, Lord, we have been blessed in receiving many gracious gifts through your providence. Now bless us again as we open our hearts and our hands to let you give your blessings to others by means of what we do now.

PRAYER.   The morning has broken, Father, and with it we step into the holiest week of the year, walking in the steps of Jesus as his life comes to a climax crowned with redeeming Crucifixion and eternal Resurrection. Father God, who created such a wonderful gift for all mankind, we need some creating work done in us. This morning we ask that you create in us a clean heart and a renewed mind, giving us a fresh spirit and a strong resolve to serve Kingdom causes. As Jesus saw the needy city opening before him on that first Palm Sunday, make us see the needy circles all around us in the world in which we live. Open our eyes to see the fate of the lost, those who live apart from faith in the Lord, and invigorate us to be ambassadors of salvation news as we go out to find them in their darkness and gently lead them to the light of the highway of real life.

Open our eyes to see those who are depressed and disappointed and spiritually at a dangerous low. Lead us to walk beside these strugglers, to gently guide them through their darkness until together we emerge into the light of grace and love and truth.

Open our eyes to the displaced folks of the world—those who have lost home, family, and even identity. Sweep our gaze across the world and enable us to discover how to help both the strangers among us and the strangers in strange lands.

Open our eyes to those of the fellowship who feel left out and lonely and ignored. Give us the ability to open our arms to them, to include them in our structures and thus help them belong among the good things that happen with God's people.

Open our eyes this morning to future possibilities for serving you. Give us a vision that will capture us, motivate us, and inspire us across the years, that we may, in the strength of the Christ of Palm Sunday, ride on to victory, purpose, and triumph. Amen.—Henry Fields

SERMON
Topic: The Strange Power of God
TEXT: 1 Cor. 1:17; Phil. 2:5–8

Weakness is not a quality that any of us admires, not in one another and certainly not in our God. Who seeks to worship at the altar of weakness? The old argument against idolatry seems to have been thrown in the face of Christians in the shadow of the cross. The reason that a piece of wood or stone is an inadequate deity is the same reason that brings uncertainty to bear on the death of the Son of God on Good Friday. The Old Testament vibrates with the glory and power of our God. The Lord answered Job out of a whirlwind. This is the God who "laid the foundation of the Earth." "The heavens are telling the glory of God; and the firmament proclaims his handiwork." "The Earth is the Lord's and the fullness thereof." "God is our refuge and strength." But Christians proclaim that the same God of glory is the Father of Jesus the Christ, who died on the cross. Can you understand the confusion and even the ridicule that emerged from identifying the God of glory with the crucified savior? The folly of the cross was the weakness it implied about God. D. M. Baillie noted, "The Gospels were written at a time when Christians could look back and glory in the Cross as ordained by the purpose of God; but they do not conceal the fact that to Jesus Himself, when He looked forward and saw that it was likely, and even when He embraced it by faith, it appeared as an unspeakable tragedy."

What do you say about the cross? Was the humiliating death of Jesus a great tragedy that Christians managed to theologize into a symbol of hope, or was the cross a positive effect of the power and purpose of God in Christ? The Gospels never picture Jesus as a helpless victim of circumstances. Even on the cross he was more Lord than pawn of history. Yet no figure is more tragic and no person ever appeared to be more defeated than the Crucified One. Where is the power of the cross?

Let me raise another question of relative importance: Where is the power of the rulers and owners of our world? The power of God, which is identified with the humiliation of Christ, is strange indeed, but what kind of power do we seek? Where are the Caesars who ruled the great Roman Empire? Where are the mighty armies of Napoleon? For that matter, where is the financial kingdom of Howard Hughes? No generation has ever enjoyed the technical power we possess, yet we live in captivity to our own power. The gospel is not suggesting nonsense in the world of the cross. If we examine our lives carefully, I suspect that there is less reason and purpose in our concept of power, or even in the goals we set for ourselves, than we can find in the cross. The political real estate of the Earth has shifted from one owner to another through the generations of human history, and no one has been powerful enough to hold it. The maps of Europe, which I studied in elementary geography classes, are no longer valid. Yet God is still Lord of creation.

Perhaps the time has come to recognize the power of God in the cross. "The way of the cross," which we have sung and praised but seldom lived, is a commitment to abandon the world's concept of power in favor of pouring out our lives for our God. The word Paul uses is *rare*. The *kenosis* of God in Christ is the strange power of God. No one admires weakness, but no power can stand before the grace of our God.—Larry Dipboye

SUNDAY, MARCH 31, 2002
Lectionary Message

Topic: What Does It Mean?

TEXT: John 20:1–18

Other Readings: Isa. 25:6–9; Ps. 114; 118:1–2, 14–29; Matt. 28:1–10; Luke 24:13–49; Acts 10:34–43; Col. 3:1–4; 1 Cor. 5:6b–8

Be honest! Would you believe the story of Easter if you had never been exposed to the Christian faith? Probably not! There are many skeptics in our world today who do not believe in the Resurrection of Christ. After all, how many individuals do you know who died and were buried and came back to life?

The story of Easter is not a fable. That Christ overcame the grave is a documented event. With this assurance in mind, let us think about some revealing truths the Resurrection has for us today.

I. *He lived up to his claims* (Matt. 20:19; 27:63; Mark 9:31; Luke 18:33; 24:46; John 14:18–19; 20:9). In the Gospel of John, Jesus claims to be the Resurrection and the Life as he seeks to comfort Martha in her sorrow over the death of Lazarus (John 11:25, 26). This victory over the grave clearly shows that the power of God is greater than all the power of evil in the world. God and Christ truly were the same, as he stated in his ministry. This fulfillment of his promise to us assures us that with God all things are possible here on Earth as well as in heaven. It is hard for us to grasp the love and power of God—that he would come back to those who had rejected him and continue to be patient with us today when we go our own way.

The Resurrection was in keeping with the claims and character of Jesus Christ. If this prediction had not become a reality, all he said and did could be cast aside as lies.

II. *God accepted Jesus' death for our sins* (Isa. 1:18; 53:12; John 3:16; 1 Cor. 15:12–23; 1 Pet. 2:24). God was in Christ reconciling the world to himself. We humans do not have power to bridge the gap between God and ourselves that was created by sin. The sending of Christ as a substitute for our sins was God's last effort to restore a broken relationship. Paul says in Ephesians 1:7 that we have redemption and forgiveness through Jesus' blood, and again, in Ephesians 2:13, he says that we are brought near to God by the blood of Christ.

Reconciliation is needed in each of our lives, and by the Resurrection this is made possible. The Resurrection means that we are cleansed (Heb. 9:4), justified (Rom. 5:90), loosed from our sins (Rev. 1:5), purchased by God (Rev. 5:9), sanctified (Heb. 10:10), at peace with God (Col. 1:20), and redeemed from all iniquity (Titus 2:14).

III. *We become the extension of his love* (Matt. 28:19–20; John 14:12–14; 16:24; 21:15–17; Acts 1:8). Jesus was the incarnation of God. He lived on Earth and revealed to everyone what God was like. When he ascended into heaven he commissioned each of us as his followers to continue his work here on Earth. He promised that with the help of the Holy Spirit we would be able to do the things he did, and greater things because of the power that would be available to us.

Christ offered himself as an example and invites us to follow in his footsteps (1 Pet. 2:21). We are to glory in his cross (Gal. 6:14). We are to preach Christ crucified (1 Cor. 1:23) and to "proclaim the Lord's death till he comes," by observing the Lord's Supper, or Communion (1 Cor. 11:26).

The world is waiting to hear the message of the Resurrection and the grace of God for all people, and we are commissioned to share that message because of the Easter event. The world is looking to us as Christians and wants to see Jesus lived in our lives much more than they want us to tell them about Christ. We must daily seek to reach out to the least of these our brethren (Matt. 25:31–46). Our lives must show love and not judgment if we want them to hear the message of hope we have to share with them about Christ the Resurrected.

Let us celebrate the joy and hope of Easter. "Lift up your heads, O ye gates; and be ye lifted up, ye everlasting doors: and the King of glory shall come in. Who is this King of glory? The Lord strong and mighty, the Lord mighty in battle. Lift up your heads, O ye gates: even lift them up, ye everlasting doors; and the King of glory shall come in" (Ps. 24:7–9).

He promised that he would come back. He accomplished God's plan for our reconciliation. Now let us continue the ministry of reconciliation that has been given to those of us who have accepted so great a salvation.

Go in peace! Go in joy! Go to serve!—William P. Cubine

ILLUSTRATIONS

THE ONE OBJECT. David Brainerd describes, in that wonderful *Journal* of his, the method of his work among the North American Indians: "I never got away from Jesus, and him crucified; and I found that when my people were gripped by this, I had no need to give them instructions about morality. I found that one followed as the sure and inevitable fruit of the other." Yes, indeed; for Jesus, once known and understood and loved, brings with him into a man's life a different atmosphere, in which spontaneously the evil things begin to droop and the fine things burst into bloom. Christ irrelevant? He is as relevant to every one of us, in our deepest and most intimate needs, as the daily bread we have to eat to keep ourselves alive.

Christianity, therefore, is right, absolutely right, when it refuses, in spite of a barrage of criticism, to be deflected from the one object for which it exists, which is *to hold up Jesus*. It must be the most hopeless, sterile, soul-destroying thing imaginable to have only arguments, advice, and moral points of view to offer to the world to help it in its troubles; but to have Christ to offer—a living and accessible and all-sufficing Christ—how different that is, how redemptively effective, how gloriously charged with hope! "I am coming to you with Christ," said Paul.—James S. Stewart

THE SCOPE OF THE GOSPEL. You may be utterly sure that the divine hand, which created you at the first, can recreate you and will recreate you at the last.

This is the measureless, exhilarating scope of the gospel you and I have received from Christ. It embraces not only today and tomorrow and next year and all the "threescore years and ten," but reaches out also into the far vistas of eternity and the glories of the New Jerusalem. Surely, given a faith of such dimensions, we have no right to be dull, conventionalized, lackluster Christians. We ought to be rejoicing and exulting in it—yes, even when the road grows rough beneath our feet and perplexities thicken around our path—triumphing in it as we fare onward on our way, reinforced by its splendor and guided by its marvelous light. And to the God who has created us for this high destiny, to the dear Christ who has called us to be joint heirs with himself, and to the Holy Spirit who kindles immortal longings in our hearts, be praise, thanksgiving, and glory now and for ever.—James S. Stewart[7]

SERMON SUGGESTIONS

Topic: The Good News Inside and Out

TEXT: Acts 10:34–43

(1) God's universal purpose (vv. 34–35). (2) God's particular message (vv. 36–38). (3) God's special witnesses (vv. 39–43).

Topic: Of Yeast and Unleavened Bread

TEXT: 1 Cor. 5:6–8

(1) The expanding power of germinal evil (v. 6). (2) The redemptive power of sincerity and truth (vv. 1–8).

Topic: Everything Is Different

TEXT: Col. 3:1–4

(1) What God has done for us in Christ (v. 1). (2) The new possibilities now open to us (vv. 2–3). (3) Our guarantee for the future (v. 2).

CONGREGATIONAL MUSIC

1. "Alleluia, Alleluia! Give Thanks," Donald Fishel (1971)
   ALLELUIA NO. 1, Donald Fishel (1971)
   This contemporary text proclaims the good news of Easter. Like spirituals and choruses, it contains little progression of thought but sets forth a few truths that are significant. Though the stanzas could be sung in harmony, this song would best be rendered in unison, possibly by a children's choir.

2. "Give Thanks to God for All His Goodness," Ps. 118; vers. Stanely Wiersman (1982)
   GENEVAN 98/118, *Genevan Psalter* (1551); harm. Claude Goudimel (1564)
   This metrical paraphrase stays so close to the content of the original Psalm 188 that it (possibly omitting stanza 2) could well be sung to the steady rhythm of the tune to which the psalm was sung in John Calvin's Geneva, and appropriately substituted for the Psalter reading.

3. "The First Lord's Day," William N. McElrath (1959)
   SPRING BROOK, William N. McElrath (1959)
   Although written with preadolescents in mind, this twentieth-century hymn on the Resurrection, and the joyful response of praise its truth engenders, has become popular among all ages for Easter worship. The following singing of the three stanzas and chorus could be

---

[7]*King Forever*

effective: refrain ("We sing for joy"), stanzas 1 and 2 without refrain, stanza 3 and refrain, refrain repeated.

4. "We Welcome Glad Easter," Anon.
   ST. DENIO, Welsh tune (c. 1839)
   This anonymous hymn, also appropriately sung by young people, captures the glad note of Easter praise, enhanced by the singable Welsh tune, ST. DENIO. It could suitably follow the Gospel lesson as well as the reading from Acts 10.

5. "When Israel Fled from Egypt," Ps. 114; vers. Henrietta T. Harmsel (1985)
   ANDRE, William B. Bradbury (1853)
   The simplicity of this Bradbury tune should make possible a spirited singing of this paraphrase of Psalm 114. It follows the original so faithfully that it could easily replace the Psalter reading.

6. "Christ Is Alive," Brian Wren (1968)
   TRURO, Thomas Williams's *Psalmodia Evangelica* (1789)
   This hymn of realistic contemporaniety examines some of the implications of the Spirit of the living Christ as it touches modern life. It would be quite appropriately sung in connection with the Epistle reading (1 Cor. 5:6–8).

7. "Sound Aloud the Trumpet," Janie Alford (1979)
   MARTHA'S SONG, Hal H. Hopson (1985)
   A unison song of Easter adoration, this hymn encloses two inner stanzas of narrative within its outer stanzas of praise. As such, with its rousing tune composed for the text, it would be suitable as a response to the Old Testament reading in Isaiah.

8. "Jesus Christ Is Risen Today," Latin (fourteenth century) in *Lyra Davidica* (1708)
   LLANFAIR, Robert Williams (1817)
   Often confused with Wesley's "Christ the Lord Is Risen Today," this venerable hymn has a similar form, with interspersed alleluias and a tune suitable for either hymn. An antiphonal performance, with a choir singing the text of each stanza and the congregation responding with the alleluias, would be both appropriate and exciting.

Other well-known Easter hymns used are "Christ the Lord Is Risen Today," by C. Wesley; "Low in the Grave He Lay," by Robert Lowry; "The Day of Resurrection," by John of Damascus; and "The Strife Is O'er," Latin, translated by Francis Pott.—Hugh T. McElrath

WORSHIP AIDS

CALL TO WORSHIP.   "This is the day on which the Lord has acted, a day for us to exult and rejoice" (Ps. 118:24 REB).

INVOCATION.   Lord, fill us with the light of faith, as glowed from the tomb when Christ arose, for the light of his presence vanquishes the darkness of every tomb in which we may find ourselves, and leads to God.—E. Lee Phillips

OFFERTORY SENTENCE.   "He that spared not his own Son, but delivered him up for us all, how shall he not with him also freely give us all things?" (Rom. 8:32).

OFFERTORY PRAYER.   O Lord our God, receive our praises and prayers, and these our offerings which we present before thee, and with them ourselves, our souls and our bodies, a living sacrifice, holy and acceptable to thee; through Jesus Christ our Lord.—*Minister's Worship Manual*

PRAYER.   O thou who art the first and the last, our God and our King, our never-failing comfort and companion, we adore thee today for this Easter light and this Easter warmth and we thank thee that these symbols of the springtime of the soul have come to us again for our blessing, for our inspiration, for our guidance, and above all for the sanctification of our lives. O Lord, we approach thee with great humility, remembering how vast is this theme and how we are permitted with our finite natures to come so close to an infinite reality. The whole universe today seems to resound with a vast "Amen" from heaven when all that our Savior did and all that he spoke is made eternally true by his rising from the dead. Father, in heaven, we pray thee as thou gavest thine only Son and as thou gavest him unto us—so not by our labors and our deserts but by our gifts we are going homeward. We pray to thee that the Resurrection warmth may come over all the coldness and iciness of our lives, melting it; that the Resurrection light may come over all the darkness, driving gloom away. We pray in the name of our Lord and Savior, Jesus Christ. Amen.—Frank W. Gunsaulus

SERMON
Topic: A Word with Which to Wipe Our Eyes
TEXT: Isa. 25:6–9

If you find these words familiar, it could be that you've heard them read at someone's funeral. In that hour, these dramatic words are intended to convey the conviction of hope. Tears and anguish are the things we associate with grief; and here, in this passage, the prophet declares that one day God will dispose of death, wiping tears of sorrow from all faces. It is a word we want and need whenever that dark cloud of bereavement casts a long shadow over our lives.

"It will be said on that day," proclaims God's prophet. The phrase "that day" carries the weight of such great human, heartfelt expectation. And what, I wonder, was the exact nature of the crisis or calamity? What deep and desperate condition caused this prophet and people to strain their eyes, staring into the far horizon of a distant future?

"It will be said on *that day*." On hearing the prophet's words I am once again mindful of those times from my childhood when I looked—even, longed!—for some future day. A day that held so much promise I could sometimes hear the laughter, feel the love, smell the table setting.

A birthday, Thanksgiving, Christmas. The day my best friend, Junior, would come and we would play from dawn to dusk. I recall the excitement of anticipating that first day of summer vacation, with the promise of pond fishing and searching out tunnels throughout Frankie Kasak's hay loft. And I would yearn for "that day."

"It will be said on that day." And while I trust that the prophet knew what he was talking about, I wonder about the word *said*: "It will be *said*." *Said*? Doesn't that seem so, well, flat? That day is nothing normal; there is nothing ordinary about that day. That day is the fulfillment of every human and heartfelt dream of deliverance from destruction, decay, even death. That day brings something so terrifyingly terrific that I can only imagine eyes stunned and wide, tongues momentarily stopped.

Then again, maybe the prophet means something else altogether. It could be that he never intended to convey the image of a very cool, casual, "It will be said." I would think the prophet would have meant something like, "It will be shouted," or even, "It will be sung!"

Sometimes all we can do is sing—when our souls are gifted with a graceful word, a word that somehow wipes tears from our eyes, a word that in some wonderful way restores to our crestfallen hearts a holy hope. At such times, in the presence of a power we can barely comprehend, we can do nothing other than sing: "Christ the Lord is risen today! All creation, join to say: Alleluia!"

Meanwhile, the world continues to produce its own madness. Slaughters at a mosque, furnaces fired up to receive human lives, another child pulls a trigger, and parents try to pick up the pieces of a tragic loss. The horrific and frightening sickness of the world can cause us to question, "Has God been hidden? concealed? withdrawn?" Yet doesn't this passage, this prophetic proclamation, imply that at long last God has come, and will come again onto the scene?

And then there's that other phrase: "We have waited for him . . . the Lord for whom we have waited." Repeated as if to make sure we heard just how deeply this longing has been felt and this looking has gone on. "We have waited . . . we have waited."

Recall those moments of personal desperation and darkness when, from some cavern deep in the solitude of your being, your very soul cried out, "Save me!" I don't know the circumstances. In truth, it doesn't matter much. What matters is that you remember how much pain you genuinely felt, lost in that condition. And did God come calling? And did your heart receive healing? And did you know, once again, that you were being sustained by unseen arms? You would have known salvation had it come—or better, when it came!

But notice here just *who* is the source of this salvation. That's what we must never fail to recall. It is God! God is the only source of salvation. Some other god might bring us material comfort, or ego strength, or personal empowerment. Only God can, has, will bring salvation.

There is a healing that runs so deep, so high, and so wide, only God could be its author and perfecter. Salvation is that salve with which God cures the corruption of the human soul. Salvation is the balm with which God restores our worst brokenness. Salvation is the medicine with which God mends the wounds of human misery.

"This is the *Lord* for whom we have waited." This must be something more than simple parallelism, saying the same thing differently: "This is our God . . . this is the Lord." To sing "This is the Lord" is to personalize the God who has come, and comes, to claim his children.

The *Lord!* Yes, a title, *kyrios.* He who rules over all, in all, for all! But more, much more. A nameless God would be a fraud. This God of salvation has given us his name: Yahweh, or Jesus. The name that is above every name, and yet the name of one who is mindful of your name and my name. "This is the Lord for whom we have waited."

So, "Let us be glad and rejoice in his salvation."

Biblical scholar Walter Bruggemann would remind us that the prophets of Israel were not carping social critics with some program to push. They were, instead, poets. All they had were words.

Even so, inspired by a gracious God, these poetic prophets painted the Lord's promise all over the canvas of human history. To behold that painting is to receive the vision that alone can speak to the sanctuary of every human soul. Isaiah paints that picture, extends that promise, offers that poetic vision to us.

In the proclamation of the gospel, we have received that for which the prophets and their people could only look forward: the message of God's own "D-Day!" And it looks like a carpenter nailed to a cross, a rocky tomb emptied of death, cowering disciples now confidently declaring the presence of the Risen Christ.

And the faith with which we can invest in the future "V-Day" is itself a gift of God. It is God's power planted deep in our souls which can and will sustain us throughout our days of desperation, both personal and global.

Yet in Christ we have received that promise. Then how much hope we must have compared to those who once walked without the benefit of the blessing that is uniquely ours: "Christ in you, the hope of glory!"—Albert J. D. Walsh

SUNDAY, APRIL 7, 2002
Lectionary Message

Topic: Seeing Is Not Believing
TEXT: John 20:19–31
Other Readings: Acts 2:14a, 22–32; Ps. 16; 1 Pet. 1:3–9

An eyewitness account of an accident or other event usually serves as a good measure or foundation for what has or has not occurred. The eyes see, the brain records the image, and the mouth speaks the testimony therein. However, in the New Testament we are in essence told to no longer view life and the world on the basis of what our visual sense places in our way. Our natural eyes are now duplicitous and deceitful. We can no longer trust or count on the two God-given orbs located in our head to provide us with a clear and accurate picture of what is tried and true. Instead, as this passage of John demonstrates, our eyewitness report is truthful and right because of the one who dwells in us.

I. *For those gathered in the locked room, fear was natural.* No longer could they see Christ the Messiah, their protector. He was now dead and so were their hopes. However, when he appeared they believed and rejoiced. Both the negative and positive reactions of the disciples would be no different for any of us. As human beings, we are totally dependent on our five senses to guide us through life. Until we see with the naked eye, our ability to receive something as real or forthright is a virtual impossibility.

The words that Christ spoke to the disciples, as well as his scarred hands and side, gave them the strength and courage to believe that he was indeed the same one who had died a few days earlier. Christ's appearance brought forth the hope that the disciples perceived had died at his Crucifixion.

Jesus' imparting of himself to the disciples by means of the Holy Spirit equipped and empowered them to serve. For humankind, the words of Christ are life. They are the hope by which we are to live. We cannot see Christ with the natural eye. Yet he is alive and active within us, giving us the power to hope, the power to live, and the power to serve. The working of the Holy Spirit within us furnishes us with the capability to see beyond what is in front of us. Our eyes are now the eyes of the Spirit, granting us the privilege to look at the impossible and regard the possible. This new view allows us to believe the unbelievable.

II. *Thomas, who was not present at the first appearance of the Resurrected Christ, refused to consider the report of the others.* Though these men were friends of his, Thomas adamantly declined to accept their eyewitness account. Thomas's disbelief at their statements is much like the way you and I are inclined to respond. At times persons share information with us that we wholeheartedly reject simply because we lack the capability to believe the report to be true. It matters not that the person or persons who are supplying us with the information are honest; we must see this thing for ourselves.

Believing Christ to be all that the Bible says he is requires that we accept the statements that Christ and the Holy Spirit are at work within us as authentic. This is difficult because we are by nature inclined to believe only in that which is tangible. Yet God's desire is that our vision be refocused and transfixed on him, the one whom we cannot see but by faith know to be present.

Christ's second appearance, when Thomas was present, gave the naysayer opportunity to see for himself that what his friends had told him previously was indeed true. In the United States, the state of Missouri takes as its motto, "The Show-Me State." Thomas could have been from Missouri. The assertions of his friends became a reality only when Christ showed Thomas his wounds and invited Thomas to touch his hands and side. It was the visible Christ who caused Thomas to believe that the Savior was risen. Sometimes, like Thomas, we cannot fathom the presence of Christ in our lives until he appears in our view or invades our circumstances. Some of us must see Jesus for ourselves; otherwise, no matter what someone else has to say, we simply cannot and will not believe. But God asks us—implores us, really—to believe without seeing. He asks that we simply believe because he is God. Our blessings come when we neither refute the visibility of God's handiwork in our lives nor demand evidence of God's presence, but rather accept, believe, and receive his presence as a given.

III. *The Gospel writer tells us that he has written these words so that we could believe that Jesus is the Christ, the Son of God, and so that believing we may have life* (v. 31). Life for the follower of Christ rests on and in his or her conviction that the words in the Bible are true. Moreover, we are compelled to live our lives no longer in the flesh but in the spirit, having received the gift of the Holy Spirit. Our natural eyes do deceive us; they do indeed play tricks on us. This is why we are required to lean and rely on the eyes of the Spirit, that we would receive sight and insight into the world around us. Trusting in the flesh and depending on humankind will cause us to lose sight of the one and only wise and true God.

Our faith in God is predicated on our willingness to behold the invisible and envision the visible.

IV. *The famous hymn writer John Newton wrote, "Amazing grace, how sweet the sound that saved a wretch like me; I once was lost, but now am found, was blind, but now I see."* May we see the glorious light from heaven and embrace its power to inform, conform, and transform not only us but the whole world.—Cheryl Greene

SERMON SUGGESTION

Topic: God's Witnesses

TEXT: Acts 2:14a, 22–32, especially v. 32

(1) David, the prophetic witness. (2) The apostles, eye witnesses. (3) Believers today, experiential witnesses.

CONGREGATIONAL MUSIC

1. "O Sons and Daughters, Let Us Sing," Jean Tisserand (fifteenth century); trans. John M. Neale (1851)

O FILII ET FILLAE, trad. French tune (fifteenth century)

This narrative Easter carol with alleluias is particularly appropriate when sung with the Gospel reading about Jesus' encounter with "doubting Thomas." Stanzas 6 to 9 deal specifically with Thomas. They could be sung framed by stanza 1 at the beginning and stanza 5 at the end.

2. "Protect Me, God, I Trust in You," Ps. 16; vers. Michael Saward (1970)

MEPHIBOSHETH, M. Christian T. Strover (1973)

An alternation of reading and singing this modern paraphrase and tune could be singing in alternation with the reading of the psalm, as follows: sing stanza 1, read vv. 3–4; sing stanza 3, read vv. 7–8; sing stanza 4, read vv. 9–10; sing stanza 6.

3. "O Savior, Precious Savior," Frances R. Havergal (1870)

ANGEL'S STORY, Arthur H. Mann (1881)

Based primarily on Jesus' words to Thomas ("Blessed are those who have not seen and yet have believed," John 20:29b), this hymn could appropriately follow the reading of the Gospel lesson. The last half of each stanza is repetitious and refrain-like, so could effectively be sung antiphonally between choir and congregation.

4. "When All Thy Mercies, O My God," Joseph Addison (1712)

WINCHESTER OLD, Este's *The Whole Book of Psalms* (1592)

This grand old hymn of morning praise could follow the Psalter reading in grateful response for the goodness of life bestowed by a loving God.—Hugh T. McElrath

WORSHIP AIDS

CALL TO WORSHIP.   "You show me the path of life. In your presence there is fullness of joy; in your right hand are pleasures forevermore" (Ps. 16:11 NRSV).

INVOCATION.   We confess that we come to worship you as those unworthy of the joy and pleasures that we may experience here today. Yet you forgive us and show us again the bright paths of obedience and service, and you strengthen us for every good work. To that end, renew us for your glory and praise.

OFFERTORY SENTENCE.   "You are so rich in everything—in faith, speech, knowledge, and diligence of every kind, as well as in the love you have for us—that you should surely show yourselves equally lavish in this generous service."

OFFERTORY PRAYER.   Open our eyes again, O God, so that we can clearly see the cost of your love for us. Prepare our hearts to meet the challenge of the needs of those around us as well as those far away from us. Help us to see both the small things and the great things that love can do.

PRAYER.   Our practice of religion too quickly becomes routine, Father. The enthusiasm with which we begin this journey of faith has a way of diminishing as we journey down the road of time. This morning, call us back to the basic concepts that brought us into faith in the first place. Make us willing instruments of your will. In our lives may there be built true channels through which your grace may flow out to the world. Help us to harness our gifts and talents in such a way that they will be instruments used to build your Kingdom among people and not become focused on our selfish desires. Direct our deeds so that they will be counted as building blocks for the city of your truth. Somehow, here this morning, instill in all of us the knowledge that our life counts for something in making this a better world in which to live, work, and worship aright.

So that this may happen, we take this hour to commit our lives to following the higher, better pathways through life; our wills to being more strongly focused on your purposes for us and creation; and our thoughts to concentrating on noble truths by which to live daily. Because we have come before you to worship this morning, we pray that our lives will be better for the living of tomorrow, that our wills will be stronger to do right, and that our spirits will be more open and sharing because we have worshiped together with others.

Grant especially to those who contend with sorrow or distress the blessings and consolation of your presence. Grant us victory in the struggles of life, and may we be more than conquerors through him who loved us and gave himself for us.—Henry Fields

SERMON
Topic: Easter Living
TEXT: Col. 3:5–14

I. *Forgiveness.* The first Easter action word is *forgiveness.* Forgiveness extends and expands Easter. Paul could look back over his own life and see how the forgiveness of ordinary disciples had been used to change his life. Paul, or Saul of Tarsus, as he was first known, had not been an easy man to forgive. He had hated the Christians. As a devout Pharisee, Paul was convinced that Jesus and his followers were enemies of the faith of Israel. He tried, using every way he could think of, to undermine and destroy the Church. Christians were imprisoned. The Church was persecuted. Saul was totally unprepared, however, for the way Stephen, the first Christian martyr, died. Death by stoning was particularly brutal. Each person present stepped forward to hurl a large stone at the person who had been condemned. Saul stood by, consenting to Stephen's death. Those who were doing the stoning placed their outer garments at Saul's feet. While this happened, Stephen looked with love upon his executors and then lifted his face in prayer: "Lord, do not hold this sin against them" (Acts 7:60). Saul couldn't forget that prayer for forgiveness.

He intensified his efforts and carried his persecution to Damascus. On the way, Saul had an experience that changed his life. There was a brilliant, blinding light. Paul fell to the ground and heard a voice say to him, "Saul, Saul, why do you persecute me?" (Acts 9:4). Paul cried out, "Who are you, Lord?" (Acts 9:5). He heard the words of forgiveness and grace, "I am Jesus, whom you are persecuting; but rise and enter the city, and you will be told what you are to do" (Acts 9:5–6). Paul was led, blinded and confused, into the city of Damascus. He was in an upper room along a street called Straight for three days and three nights. He could neither eat nor drink. Then a frightened, timid disciple named Ananias slowly climbed the steps to that upper room and took the persecutor's hands and said to him, "Brother Saul, the Lord Jesus who appeared to you on the road by which you came has sent me that you may regain your sight and be filled with the Holy Spirit" (Acts 9:17). Something like scales fell from Paul's eyes. He rose, took food, and was baptized. That was the beginning of a ministry that would include spreading the Church throughout the Empire and writing a significant portion of the New Testament. Paul's conversion began with the experience of Christ on the road to Damascus, but it was Paul's memory of Stephen and the words of forgiveness and grace of Ananias that helped convince Paul that resurrection and forgiveness were real.

Now Paul was writing from another little room—a Roman prison. He was writing to a small, obscure congregation in Colossae in the Lycus River Valley of modern Turkey. In chapter 3 he talks about resurrection living. He had experienced the reality of forgiveness himself, because he had forgiven those who had betrayed and falsely accused him (which had led to his being in prison instead of out proclaiming the gospel). Paul was writing to the Colossians, a people who had been confused by false teachers and bewildering doctrines. He told them that, as they held to the centrality of Christ and the victory of the Resurrection, they must never forget the releasing power of forgiveness—"forgiving each other; as the Lord has forgiven you, so you must also forgive" (Col. 3:13).

Forgiveness is an Easter action word. It cannot be forced. We are called not to create forgiveness but to be channels; not to block or withhold forgiveness, but to let God's forgiveness flow through us.

II. *Kindness. Kindness* is the second Easter action word. In the third chapter of Colossians, Paul teaches us something really important about Easter. The Resurrection is not just an event in the life of Jesus Christ. It is not just a future experience for Christians. Through faith in Jesus Christ, each of us is given a here-and-now and the possibility of a new creation, a new beginning, in which we put off the old nature and put on a new existence. As authentic Easter people, certain attitudes and actions are no longer appropriate for us.

As Easter people it is no longer appropriate for us to treat other human beings as objects of gratification of physical lust and desire. That is why Paul says in verse 5, "Put to death therefore what is earthly in you: immorality, impurity, passion, evil desire, and covetousness, which is idolatry." It is not that sex is evil—it is not. Genesis, chapter 1, verse 27, says, "male and female he created them." What is wrong is the abuse of sex, sex as a weapon, as a method of dominating or controlling or degrading another human being. What is wrong is regarding sex as a toy to be taken lightly. This is a verse that we need to hear because we are living in a society that is sexually abusing our children like no other society in human history. A little girl growing up today has one chance in four of being raped or sexually abused before she reaches high school. Paul writes, "In these you once walked, when you lived in them. But now put them all away" (Col. 3:7–8).

Easter living means refusing to let our communication be contaminated by old negatives: "anger, wrath, malice, slander, and foul talk." Paul writes, "Do not lie to one another, seeing that you have put off the old nature with its practices and have put on the new nature" (Col. 3:9–10).

III. *Love.* The word *Love*—agape—means unconditional caring and commitment. In the New Testament, agape is used to mean God's love. Paul says, "Above all these, put on love, which binds everything together in harmony" (Col. 3:14).

God's agape, revealed as ultimately victorious and triumphant in the Resurrection of Jesus Christ, is available to us here and now, for Easter living. We are to "put on love." It binds everything together in perfect harmony.—Joe A. Harding

SUNDAY, APRIL 14, 2002

Lectionary Message

Topic: Walking, Talking, and Eating

TEXT: Luke 24:13–35

Other Readings: Acts 2:14a, 36–41; Ps. 116:1–4, 12–19; 1 Pet. 1:17–23; Luke 24:13–35

Bill Gorski of Richmond, Virginia, refers to the shopping mall as the "poor man's spa." Rain or shine, Bill and a group of his friends meet every day except Sunday to walk the mall. Bill and his wife, Eloise, began the practice years ago, upon their doctor's advice. Since his wife's death, Bill has continued the routine, though he remarked, "It isn't the same." On Bill's recent visit to our church for the baptism of a great-grandchild, he shared these thoughts as we sat at a table during the reception. "As beneficial as walking is, I do believe the talking as we walk—especially since Nana's death—is just as beneficial, and perhaps more so." He paused as his eyes filled with tears. When he could speak again, he continued: "I had so hoped she could live longer. There were so many things we had planned to do. I don't think I will ever get past the loss of her." His friends were not present to share his grief, but those of us at the table were, and we cared about his pain. I knew that on Monday he would be back in Richmond with his friends—walking, talking, and eating at McDonald's. I also knew that our Lord is walking with him on the way he is going.

I. *Christ walks with those in sorrow.* A very long time ago, some other hurt and disappointed people were returning home from Jerusalem. Their hearts were heavy and their steps were slow as they went down Jericho Road. Like Bill and his friends, they talked as they walked. They too were saddened by the death of someone dear to them, someone on whom they had placed high hopes and wishes. Their conversation was about what had just happened in their holy city. A tragic and untimely death had robbed them of their friend. As they shared their hurt, a stranger joined them on the journey. "What is this conversation that makes you so sad?" Perhaps their body language gave them away. We can be sure the stranger already knew the answer to the question. Cleopas remarked that the stranger was surely not from Jerusalem if the events of the last three days were unknown to him. He began to tell of Jesus of Nazareth, whom he described as a prophet mighty in deed and word. Cleopas spoke of what Jesus said and did, and had difficulty connecting this with the sad ending of the story: Jesus' cruel, untimely death. Why should it have happened that way? We never know to whom we're talking! It's good that these were kind and favorable words, don't you think? Have you ever asked a question incognito—a very personal question the answer to which would pertain to you? For example, in the days when prejudice against women ministers was respectable in my denomination, I used to risk the question, "What do you think of women in ministry?" The answer was often such that I remained a stranger to the speaker. Other times, I rather enjoyed the response, and especially enjoyed someone trying to frame it diplomatically.

The sadness of these travelers was evident. Jesus was supposed to redeem Israel, but now their hope had vanished. He was dead—and not only dead, but no one could find his body! There was a story floating around that he was alive—a story told by some women about angels they allegedly saw. On their word the men checked it out, but when they left to come home, no one had seen Jesus yet. By now these sad folk had reached the Emmaus exit on the Jericho Road and turned toward home. Their companion was going on down the road, but they said to him, "It's late, and you're tired. Stay with us. You are welcome." They could not find their friend Jesus in Jerusalem, but there was a stranger at hand for whom they could do a kindness. After seven and a half miles, all were tired and hungry. Never mind that the stranger had just called them foolish and slow-hearted, accusing them of not believing in their own prophets. He had literally dumped the whole load on them, beginning with the books of Moses and the prophets, and up to the very present. Perhaps after hearing and saying all this, some nourishment was in order for all three travelers.

II. *Christ breaks bread with the hungry.* I can recall a summer vacation at a cottage on Albermarle Sound when my husband dumped the whole load on two friends and me as we sat at a table. A retired minister, he was recovering from heart surgery and had a need to preach—and preach he did. When he finally stopped, one friend commented, "He's covered from Genesis to Revelation! Is he using us as guinea pigs or something?" Maybe the Emmaus couple had similar thoughts. Nevertheless, after the teaching, a meal was served. Their stomachs were filled, their eyes were opened, and they recognized their guest. They confessed that they had felt something as he preached and opened the Scriptures for them. The Word of God brings light and restores lost hopes and dreams. The bread of life strengthens us for the journey. With swift steps and light hearts, they returned to Jerusalem and found the eleven disciples and others with them. In the opening of Scripture, in the breaking of bread at a table in Emmaus, and in the midst of other followers back in Jerusalem the Risen Christ was present. The Lord of Life was there, and he blessed them and commanded them to tell the story.

III. *Christ calls us to walk and talk and break bread in his name.* We too go up to Jerusalem with high hopes—swift steps taking us to some event with great anticipation. When disappointment and confusion result, if we remember we can certainly identify with the people on the Emmaus Road. "We had hoped this was the one to save Israel," but he could not even save himself. This was a painful disappointment. We can take encouragement from knowing that Jesus is on the road with us. We can take heart in knowing that he can turn our hurts into rejoicing and give us some great news to share with others. We are "Easter People," that is, people of the Resurrection, with whom Jesus is walking and talking. Jesus is the unseen guest at our tables. Let us be thankful that he is not unknown to us but is revealed in countless ways every day. An anonymous poet wrote:

> Dark clouds have silver linings
> And even teardrops glisten;
> And sad songs have sweet melodies
> If we will only listen!
> Raindrops shine like diamonds fair
> Thistles have a lovely flower;
> And hope like a cheery sunbeam
> Springs in the darkest hour.

Let's tell each other and the whole world the story of the Risen Christ, who has promised, "Lo, I am with you always." It's a story people are waiting to hear.—Bess Gibbs Hummings

ILLUSTRATIONS

INTIMACY.   One of the most popular devotional writings in contemporary Western Christianity is "Footprints in the Sand." Christian bookstores sell it emblazoned on refrigerator magnets, potholders, wall plaques, clocks, key rings, and bookmarks—so there's clearly a market for it. I've often asked myself why this simple bit of writing has claimed the appreciation of millions of people. It occurs to me that in our mobile society, where people often do not put down roots in a community, the intimacy of someone always walking by your side (or carrying you) has enormous appeal. The Lord who speaks to the narrator of "Footprints" does not judge or belittle, but corrects and reassures. This is what the Risen Christ did with the people walking on the road to Emmaus. And intimacy with the divine and constant friend may be what evangelism should present today.—Bess Gibbs Hummings

TRANSFORMATION.   In the 1989 edition of the *United Methodist Hymnal*, a hymn by Michael Peterson retells the events of Luke 24:13–35. The first stanza is striking in its originality and insight:

> On the day of resurrection to Emmaus we return;
> While confused, amazed, and frightened, Jesus comes to us, unknown.

That's how many of us feel about Easter, truth be told. Like those disciples, we have heard reports of the Resurrection, but the power of that truth has not transformed our lives. We may still view life from the perspective of Good Friday, without hope. The final stanza depicts the transformation that can take place in believers:

> Opened eyes, renewed convictions, journey back to scenes of pain;
> Telling all that Christ is risen, Jesus is through us made known.

This is good news indeed! Not only is the Risen Christ restored to us, and with him our hopes for tomorrow; but we are also made participants in revealing the good news to others.—Bess Gibbs Hummings

SERMON SUGGESTIONS

Topic: The Promise for All of Us
TEXT: Acts 2:14a, 36–42
(1) An assured affirmation (v. 36). (2) An anguished response (v. 37). (3) A promising alternative (vv. 38–40). (4) An awesome achievement (vv. 41–42).

Topic: God Always the Same
TEXT: 1 Pet. 1:17–23, especially v. 20
(1) Then—"before the foundation of the world." (2) Now—"at the end of the ages." (3) Why—"for your sake."

CONGREGATIONAL MUSIC
1. "Hope of the World," Georgia Harkness (1954)
    O PERFECT LOVE, Joseph Barnby (1889)

This noble prayer hymn can suitably relate to both the Epistle and the Gospel lessons appointed for this day. The third stanza is a prayerful response to the experience of the two disciples on the Emmaus road (Luke 24:13–36). The entire hymn can be a response to the passage in 1 Peter, especially verse 21, which declares that through Christ's saving blood, our hope is in God.

2. "What Shall I Render to My God," Charles Wesley (1780)

   ARMENIA, Sylvanus B. Pond (1841)

   Wesley's paraphrase of Psalm 116:12–18 could appropriately accompany the Psalter reading for this day. The ARMENIA tune, which is in a flowing style, could be sung by a soloist in alternation with the congregation's singing.

3. "The Church's One Foundation," Samuel J. Stone (1860)

   AURELIA, Samuel S. Wesley (1864)

   The singing of this venerable hymn would be effective as either an introduction or a response to the reading in Acts about the birth of the Church and the preaching of Peter.

4. "My Tribute," Andrae Crouch (1971)

   MY TRIBUTE, Andrae Crouch (1971)

   This hymn by a contemporary African American is one of the many that could be used in connection with the question of the psalmist (116:12). Other possibilities are "What Offering Shall We Give," by Isaac Watts (1709) and "What Gift Can We Bring," by Jane Marshall (1982).—Hugh T. McElrath

WORSHIP AIDS

CALL TO WORSHIP.   "I love the Lord, because he hath heard my voice and my supplications. Because he hath inclined his ear unto me, therefore will I call upon him as long as I live" (Ps. 116:1–2).

INVOCATION.   You have bound our hearts and lives to you, O Lord, for you have heard our prayers for forgiveness and for your loving presence in our times of deepest need. We love and worship you because you first loved us, showing us your grace and salvation in Jesus Christ. Now accept, we pray, our gratitude and praise this hour and always.

OFFERTORY SENTENCE.   "And Jesus sat over against the treasury and beheld how the people cast money into the treasury" (Mark 12:41a).

OFFERTORY PRAYER.   How do we measure up, Lord Christ? Your total life was a gift for us. Now, in the spirit of your giving, we can give, and reflect a measure of your love for us.

PRAYER.   Hear our prayer, O God, as we ask you to open the lives of your people so that the power of your Risen Son may have fuller impact on our daily round of common tasks. May this great fact of history become through us a moving certainty, so that all believers may no longer be mere children of Earth but have their citizenship in the unseen. Make the nearness of the living Christ more real so that our coldness may be overtaken by warmth, our stumbling corrected by our being lifted up, and our tears and sorrow wiped away through hope. May we become humble in his presence, and through our surrender to his call may we rise to share in the victory of his will in every decision and crisis of life. Change our lives so that we ourselves may become life changers who bear others' burdens, offer a cup of water to a thirsty one, and nourish always a vision of the larger good. Help us to work, and pray, and serve until we shall all come "in the unity of faith unto the measure of the stature of the fullness of Christ." Lord, we believe; bear with us through our unbelief. O Risen Savior, lead us to believe in you that we may own your life.—Donald Macleod

SERMON
Topic: On the Beach
TEXT: John 21:1–19

The disciples were despondent. The world had collapsed around them. Their Lord had been crucified. I suppose we can assume that by the time this story takes place, at least a week after the Resurrection, the disciples had heard of the Resurrected Christ. We can also assume that some had seen him, if we think of the upper-room story and this one as sequential. But obviously they did not yet know the significance of the Resurrection for their own lives. They were still confused and bewildered. So they did what any intelligent person would do in such circumstances: they went fishing.

But they caught nothing—and they probably were not surprised, considering how things had been going lately. But here comes the first lesson in this amazing, rich story. The disciples, some of them, had been recruited by Jesus to be "fishers of men." You remember, Jesus said, "Follow me, and I will make you fishers of men." In this story, after the Resurrection they were symbolically doing what they were called to do. After the Resurrection, they went fishing. Only they failed. They couldn't do it without Jesus.

So who showed up but Jesus himself. Coming to the shore, the disciples noticed a stranger standing there. He asked, "Catch anything?" which is the question everybody asks a fisherman. The disciples' answer was typical of fishermen. They said, "Not much happening out there." They had caught nothing. They had fished all night and had caught nothing.

The stranger then said, "Cast your net on the right side of the boat." They did it, and caught a whole mess of fish. The disciple named John said to Peter, "It's the Lord! It's gotta be the Lord! There's only one person who can fish like that!"

So, what this story is saying is that without Jesus empowering and guiding us, we, as disciples, are ineffective. We are impotent without Jesus' presence with us. With Jesus present, which is what the Resurrection makes possible, disciples can bring all humankind into the Kingdom. A hundred and fifty-three species equals, allegorically, all the races, all the nations of the world. So with Jesus' empowerment, everyone will be captured by the preaching of the gospel.

That is the way the story opens. It proclaims that Jesus is with us. Jesus is with us to empower us and to guide us in doing what he has called us to do. Without him, we can't do it. That is the first part of the story. You could call it "The Kettle of Fish." The second part of the story could be called "The Charcoal Fire." This is the part of the story that I want us to focus on.

The disciples got off the boat and joined Jesus on the beach. Jesus was standing by a charcoal fire. Now, you are not to miss that detail. This was no ordinary fire; this was a charcoal fire. The last time we read about a charcoal fire in the Gospel of John, it was outside the palace of Caiaphas, the high priest of Jerusalem. The soldiers were standing around a charcoal fire warming themselves. Peter was lurking a little ways off. The soldiers saw Peter standing in the shadows. The light from the fire illumined his face. They thought they recognized him. They asked him, "Aren't you a disciple of Jesus?" Peter said, "No." They asked him three times, beside a charcoal fire, "Are you a disciple of Jesus?" And three times Peter said, "No."

For Peter, the sight of a charcoal fire would have brought back that dreadful memory. Jesus was standing on the shore beside a charcoal fire. Peter, who had impulsively jumped out of the boat when he had seen that it was Jesus and had ran through the shallow water to the shore, must have stopped dead in his tracks when he saw Jesus standing beside a charcoal fire.

Jesus said nothing to Peter. He took the fish and cooked them breakfast. Then he took the bread, broke it, and gave it to them. Now they knew for sure: this was the Lord!

Three times Peter denied Jesus around a charcoal fire, and three times Jesus forgives Peter around a charcoal fire. That's what is happening here. Forgiveness is happening here. "Feed my sheep" means "You've got your old job back. You are restored." Forgiveness means forgetting the past and starting over again.

Then the story ends with a riddle. It is about the only time that Jesus uses a riddle. Jesus says to Peter, When you were young, you girded yourself and walked where you would; but when you are old, you will stretch out your hands and another will gird you and carry you where you do not wish to go.

What does that mean? The author of the Gospel of John puts in his own interpretation. He puts it in parentheses so you will know that this is just his interpretation. He says that it is a prediction of Peter's crucifixion. Peter will die, like Jesus, on a cross in Rome. But Peter will tell the Romans, "I am not worthy to die as my Lord died." John says it is a prophesy, a prediction of the way Peter will die."

When you are old, you will stretch out your hands—as in the Crucifixion.

But there is something else here. Look at the riddle again. When you are young, you are like Peter was. You are confident, brash, and boastful, sure of your powers, sure that you can do anything in this life. Remember that Peter said to Jesus, "I will never leave you. Others will betray you, I am sure, but I will never leave you." And he left him.

There is a time in our lives when we think we can do anything. We believe that usually when we're young. Then sooner or later we fail; we fall on our faces. That is when we learn we cannot do it all.

It was exactly that way with the disciples. Days before the Crucifixion—in fact, days before this scene takes place—the disciples were walking with Jesus toward Jerusalem. Jesus was going to be crucified. And what were the disciples doing? Boasting, bragging, competing with one another as to which one of them is the greatest.

Now look at them. Look at what happened to them just a few days later. Every one of them failed to deliver on their boasting. Every one of them failed. Peter is just the representative disciple. He is the most likable of all the bumblers, but he is still a bumbler, just like us.

I believe that what this means—this fishing and catching nothing and then Jesus showing up to show them how to do it—it means we need grace to do what we are called to do. And at some point in our lives, when we are able to say, "I am a sinner and I cannot do this on my own; come Lord Jesus, help me"—that's when we grow up.—Mark Trotter

SUNDAY, APRIL 21, 2002

Lectionary Message

Topic: Submit Yourself to Victory

TEXT: 1 Pet. 2:19–25

Other Readings: Acts 2:42–47; Ps. 23; John 10:1–10

I. SITUATION: *Believers are instructed to submit to authority.* In this passage, the apostle Peter gives instructions to Jewish Christians who were in a position of servitude to submit to their masters—even in situations where they were treated wrongfully. The passage should be read as not just about historical servants and masters, but also about authority relationships in general. We are all in some respects both in and under authority. For example, we may be employees under the authority of an employer, as well as parents in authority over our children.

Submission to authority figures—even when they are wrong—is a difficult instruction to follow, but it is really our key to operating successfully under authority, both naturally and spiritually. We must focus not on an authority who does wrong as our enemy, but on the spirit behind the wrongdoing (Eph. 6:10–13). We cannot control another person's actions, but as believers in Christ we can take authority over any spirit that is not like God (Luke 10:19). We do this by prayer, living in agreement with God's Word, putting faith in God's Word, and confessing God's Word over our lives and over the situations we face. Our key to victory is to keep our thoughts, words, and actions in line with scriptural instructions (Gal. 5:22–26; Matt. 5:3–7:14; Eph. 4:17–6:9). When we submit ourselves to God during times of personal injustice and resist the urge to retaliate in an ungodly manner, then the Spirit and power of God will be free to operate on our behalf, and the forces of the enemy will have to flee from us (James 4:7). The real issue here is whether or not we trust God to act on our behalf when we obey Scripture. Far too often we end up in defeat because we use ungodly means to defend ourselves during times of injustice, then we pray for God to rescue us. However, we cannot have victory over Satan if we use the devil's means to defend ourselves (Mark 3:23–26).

II. COMPLICATION: *Submission is a* lifestyle *to which God calls us.* Peter teaches that if we suffer because of something we did wrong, we get no special recognition for it. However, if we suffer wrongly and *endure it patiently,* then that is commendable. He asserts that we are *called* to be patient through suffering and to continue doing good when wrong is being done to us. This is part of our job description as Christ's disciples. This is exactly what our Lord Jesus Christ did for us, not only as a vicarious act, but also as an example for us to follow.

Christ submitted to unjust authority without responding negatively because he refused to be distracted from his mission. He knew the authority he had over humankind. He was moved by neither afflictions or discomforts to his own flesh or emotions, nor by the people who were responsible for such affliction. He was willing to take on temporary physical suffering in order to secure eternal life for all those who would trust in him.

This focus on eternal life versus eternal separation from God is the reason death to self is so important (Luke 9:23–25; Gal. 2:20; Col. 3:3). If we seek to save our lives—to satisfy our desires or go to any lengths to preserve our own comfort—we will not be able to last long in true service to the Lord. The cost of serving the Lord is that our flesh will be discomforted. The enemy—our adversary the devil—seeks to use anything he can to distract us from God's purposes. Sadly, he often succeeds at this plot, as we spend our time doing things that appear successful for a short time yet bear little enduring fruit in the lives of other people and have no eternal significance. All Satan has is the temporary: the *now*. He attempts to keep us trapped in focusing on present, fruitless things because if he is successful at this we will not live in the light of eternity and perhaps our own soul and the souls of many whom we are destined to reach with the gospel may be lost.

III. Resolution: *Submission is a position of power and triumph.* Submission to authority is the way to reign in life. In the case of unjust authority, as we endure without sin in our thoughts, words, and actions, we avail ourselves to be instruments of God through which his power can flow to triumph over the works of the enemy. The key is to focus (as Jesus did) on completing God's work, not on defending ourselves. We must remember that if we have committed ourselves to serving the Lord, and if we occupy ourselves with doing that, then when someone treats us wrongfully, they interfere with the purpose of God, hence becoming his enemy. God can remove hindrances that get in the way of his purpose (Acts 12:1–24).

Through his uncompromising willingness to be a sacrifice in life and death for the sins of the world, Jesus is our Savior eternally as well as our Healer at present. The blows that unjustly cut through him released the blood that is the balm that heals for wholeness all who live for and believe in him: "By his stripes you are healed" (Acts 12:24).

The end of verse 23 is worth noting: "He committed himself to him who judges righteously." This is true faith. If we believe that "the eyes of the Lord are in every place keeping watch on the evil and the good" (Prov. 15:3), then we need not be preoccupied with the evil done to us. If we believe that "God always causes us to triumph" (2 Cor. 2:14), then persecution does not shake us, for we know that we will overcome the persecution. If we believe "no weapon formed against us shall prosper" (Isa. 54:17), then we do not fear or fret when the weapon is formed. "All things work together for those who love God, for those who are called according to his purpose" (Rom. 8:28). We can spend all our time loving God, cooperating with his purpose, and resting in faith. Why? Because he will cause even the wrong committed against us to work out for good (see the story of Joseph in Gen. 37:1–46:30).—Audrea Ivy

ILLUSTRATIONS

BURNING COALS.   Paul understood our human nature and mixed motives better than we sometimes realize. At the end of Romans 12, after exhorting his readers to bless those who persecute them, he quotes Proverbs 25:21–22 as a sly motivation for returning good for evil: "By so doing you will heap burning coals upon his head." The thought of making an enemy feel ashamed of his or her abuse of authority is alluring, as is the glow of self-righteousness that would probably follow. The best reason for blessing those who persecute us is our love for the Lord who commands us to do so.—Audrea Ivy

DEALING WITH INJUSTICE AND EVIL.   Our generation is quite resistant to the idea of submitting to an authority that is believed to be unjust and evil. "What about Hitler?" they ask. "What about racist regimes and repressive governments?" Without minimizing the evils these represent, we should remember the temptation to externalize evil and locate it outside ourselves. A more useful and immediate question might be, "What about the ways I abuse my own authority over others?"—Audrea Ivy

SERMON SUGGESTIONS

Topic: Believers—After the Spirit Came!

TEXT: Acts 2:42–47

(1) They worshiped together (v. 42). (2) They were awestruck (v. 43). (3) They were generous in sharing their possessions (vv. 44–45). (4) They made worship a daily experience, both at home and in public gatherings (vv. 46–47a). (5) Consequently, they witnessed daily the turning of many to the Lord in conversion (v. 47b).

Topic: What Makes the Good Shepherd Good

TEXT: John 10:1–10

(1) He is committed to the good of the sheep (v. 7). (2) He gives the sheep security (v. 9a). (3) He gives the sheep productive freedom (vv. 9b, 10a).

CONGREGATIONAL MUSIC

1. "My Shepherd Will Supply My Need," Isaac Watts (1719)

    RESIGNATION, *Beauties of Harmony* (1814)

    Of the many paraphrases of the great Shepherd Psalm, Watts's "My Shepherd Will Supply My Need," set to an old shape-note tune, is one of the most appealing.
2. "Surely Goodness and Mercy," John W. Peterson (1958) and Alfred B. Smith (1958)

    GOODNESS, John W. Peterson (1958) and Alfred B. Smith (1958)

    For a modern version of Psalm 23, use this hymn that could appropriately be sung at the close of worship. The refrain alone could constitute an impressive response to the benediction.
3. "Day by Day," attr. Richard of Chichester (thirteenth century)

    GODSPELL, Stephen Schwartz (1971)

    This contemporary setting of an ancient prayer could be sung in connection with the Epistle lesson, especially 1 Peter 2:11, exhorting us to follow the steps of Jesus, our example. It could be introduced by a soloist (possibly as a response to prayer) and repeated by the congregation.
4. "Savior, Like a Shepherd, Lead Us," *Hymns for the Young* (c. 1830)

    BRADBURY, William B. Bradbury (1859)

    The shepherd motif is found in the Gospel reading (John 10:1–10) as well as in the psalm for the day. To make the message more alive in an all-too-familiar song such as this children's hymn, a phrase-by-phrase antiphonal treatment (choir and congregation) would be effective.—Hugh T. McElrath

WORSHIP AIDS

CALL TO WORSHIP.   "Surely goodness and mercy shall follow me all the days of my life: and I will dwell in the house of the Lord forever" (Ps. 23:6).

INVOCATION.   Grant, O Lord, that we indeed will dwell in your house as long as we live and then dwell in the house not made with hands, eternal in the heavens. In the meantime, and particularly in this service of worship, may we be touched with the reality of your goodness and mercy, so that we may live victoriously in the days to come.

OFFERTORY SENTENCE.   "Then he said to them, 'If any want to become my followers, let them deny themselves and take up their cross daily and follow me'" (Luke 9:23 NRSV).

OFFERTORY PRAYER.   Our offerings seem so small, Lord, considering what Jesus did for us. Teach us, we pray, that the meaning and imitation of his life may become real in what we are and do day by day among those about us. To that same end, show us how what we give can fulfill a vital part of our Christian service.

PRAYER.   The power and richness of rebirth surrounds us in this springtime season, Father. How we need to see the place of beginning again as well as experience its presence in our personal lives. For some, the winds of winter have blown hard across their spirits and left coldness, which needs the thaw of spring. For others, the chill of listlessness has not been chased away by the warm, gentle zephyrs of springtime. For yet others, the bleakness that comes from being lost in this adventure of life—lost without a guide, lost without a savior—makes all seasons harsh and difficult. Let this hour be the beginning of springtime in our souls.

Let this be the time when our hopelessness gives way to hope. It is easy to lose hope when the circumstances of life pound us hard and leave us in vales of sorrow and valleys of loss. In those places, we cannot see the horizon before us, only the moment in which we exist. Let the showers of hope fall fresh on saddened spirits here this morning so that rebirth in hope can steady their lives.

Let this be a time when our failures give way to possibilities. When we fail, we too often stand and stare at the failure until it consumes our thought, saps our energy, and brings meaningful life to a halt. We get locked in the freezer of our failures. Today, give us a vision of what we can accomplish, and remind us that no failure is useless, that it teaches us what will not work, thus opening doors to other possibilities. Give us eyes to see what you would have us attempt to do in your strength. Then the season of failure will be past and the glory of new beginnings will be real.

Let this be a time when our losses are forgotten and life's real treasures are found. Remind us, Father, that what we consider as loss just may not be as important as we have made it. Tied to the things of this world, we feel pain when that which we have gathered unto ourselves is lost to us, be it material wealth, relationships, knowledge, or some other measure of value. This morning, bring us to understand that the eternal values, high moral standards, and noble character fashioned after the ways of Christ are the treasures that cannot be stolen and will not deteriorate. In the light of such truth, new birth will come to our very souls.

Let this be a time when old sins are laid aside in the warmth of truth, through the door of forgiveness, by the wonder of grace. Our sins become our burdens. They stifle the very life out of us and force us to carry the heavy load of guilt far into the night of our sinning. Some more than others need to be made aware this morning that sins are forgiven, burdens are lifted, and blind eyes are made to see when we come into the presence of the Lord in all humility and in confession. Here, on this spring day of new beginnings, let us see the cross, high and lifted up; let us meet the Savior outside the open tomb and walk from this day forward in renewed strength that can come only from following after him.—Henry Fields

SERMON
Topic: Worship in the Sanctuary
TEXT: John 4:24

When Christians assemble for worship, what is going on—or what ought to be going on? Are there some specific meanings that can be identified with this experience?

I. *Awakening.* The first answer that I would give is that worship has to do with *awakening.* Without intending a pun, it really is true that most of us come to church asleep. That is, we are possessed with many capacities that are latent within us and that deserve to be aroused and turned to useful service. A ringing sentence from Paul's Epistle to the Romans could appropriately be inscribed on every order of worship or written across every sanctuary door: "You know what hour it is, how it is full time now for you to wake from sleep." Paul then went on: "For salvation is nearer to us now than when we first believed."

The point is that worship should lead repeatedly to personal awakening. Something within us should stir that has not been activated before. This does not necessarily mean that one's blood will boil because of severe disagreement with the preacher (although that possibility cannot be ignored). It more readily means that an individual should gain fresh insight into how his one (or many) talents can come alive for his own enrichment and the enrichment of the world about him. This might be characterized as a progression from slumber to service. Worship's purpose is to make life vital and vibrant—not to leave it the same as it was before.

Whatever the elements of worship—music, liturgy, art, homily—their primary purpose is evocative. Singly or in combination, they should evoke responses from the participants. (In this connection it is well to note that those who guide worship—preachers, musicians, readers—also should find worship an awakening experience.)

The entire Christian community ought to realize from its worship what has been identified as "a moving of the Holy Spirit." This is to say that there ought to come a sense of alertness and awareness that people are not helpless, after all; their God-given talents can be set free, for their benefit and that of the world. Music, silence, the spoken word all contribute to this end, evoking this understanding.

II. *Making us human.* A second major redefinition of worship lies in a direction being charted today by a number of thoughtful people. Fundamentally, worship is intended to make us human.

What does it mean to be human? Obviously, many answers are appropriate. But for Christians at worship and in daily living, the answer is that being human means having the capacity to love and be loved, having sensitivity to appreciate all of God's people, and having freedom to express deeply held feelings and emotions. God made us this way—as human beings—but both circumstances and self manage to repress and inhibit each person's full humanity. We require a liberation, a release; worship can become that for us.

Without worship, we have few structures to assist us in fulfilling our truest selves. Worship thus aids in the realization of who we are. The deepest gratification a minister ever feels is when someone says, "Today's sermon [or service] spoke right to me." Such testimony signifies that human emotions and attitudes have been allowed to come into their own. The individual knows that he or she has been addressed personally—and such knowledge counts for much in our time.

III. *Pointing.* Worship also points us in the right direction. In and through all else that it accomplishes, worship turn us from our sundry idolatries to the living God. It helps us with our perspective; it gets us on the right track again. We both find and are found by the power who created us and whose we are. In the words of one scholar, we are "eternalized"; our minds are lifted to the "unchanging."

IV. *The mystery and wonder of God.* We need not be ashamed to acknowledge mystery at this point, nor to admit that we stand at the edge of the unknown. "God is spirit, and those who worship him must worship in spirit and truth," states the Gospel of John, and it seems to be an apt summary of things as we find them. This is why attitudes such as reverence and humility traditionally have characterized Christian worship, although latitude must be allowed for diversity in expression of these things. There is nothing automatically irreverent about the sound of trumpets, drums, and cymbals in the sanctuary, even given a jazz beat. The truth is, there are innumerable ways to confront the mystery and wonder of the Living God. Many of these ways should be pressed into service for us, and should be permitted to speak to us.— John H. Townsend

SUNDAY, APRIL 28, 2002
Lectionary Message

Topic: A New People
TEXT: 1 Pet. 2:2–10
Other Readings: Acts 7:55–60; Ps. 31:1–5, 15–16; John 14:1–14

1. *The Christian abroad.* Some of you may have had the experience of participating in worship abroad. This may have involved the fascinating experience of worshipping with another culture in its own manner and using its own language, or it may have meant attending services in an English-language church or chapel. When visiting the latter, one sometimes discovers many fellow Americans, and perhaps a corresponding group of British or Australian members, and feels almost instantly at home. However, because of the near-universality of the English language in the world, churches that use English also attract people from other countries who may feel more comfortable using English than the local tongue for worship and Bible study. This means that these "ex-pat" communities are truly international. While they ostensibly provide a little bit of home for those living abroad, they in fact bring Americans into greater contact with Christians from other cultures, giving them the opportunity not only to learn different ways of seeing the faith (and to discover that what is familiar to us may not be as universal as we would like to believe), but also to discover that being a Christian is something of an ethnic identity itself, whatever one's nation of origin.

2. *"In Christ there is no East or West."* When the First Letter of St. Peter was written, Christianity was already something of a world religion. We of course know the story of Pentecost, in which converts to and students of Judaism had gathered from all over the known world in the Holy City for the Jewish festival and were amazed to hear the newly gifted apostles preaching to them in their native tongues. At that time, *koine* Greek, rather than English, was the vehicle for preaching and even worship in the disparate congregations set up around the Mediterranean rim. St. Paul frequently refers to the way the New Faith had broken down barriers and made one people out of many. His primary example was Jew and Gentile, but his

words have lived on in the encounters of Roman and Barbarian, European and African, American and Asian, and may some day be used when the gospel is shared in outer space!

3. *"God's own people."* Peter goes on to tell us, "You are a chosen race, a royal priesthood, a holy nation, God's own people." He adds, "Once you were not a people, but now you are God's people." His experience seems to have been something like that which I had serving abroad, and which many others may have serving or being part of multiracial and multiethnic faith communities even within the United States. In witness and worship, in service and in the adventure of discipleship, Christians have much in common and forge a bond of love and courage that transcends the apparent boundaries of race and nation. In fact, Christians find that they constitute Paul's idea of a "new race" or nationality. In 2 Corinthians 5:20, he even suggests that "we are ambassadors for Christ, since God is making his appeal through us." This idea that we are representatives of a "foreign government," of a king whose sovereignty is not of this world, can be true wherever a Christian community finds itself—in the heartland of America or on a distant shore.

4. *The marks of our "nationality."* What are the characteristics of this new people we have become? What is the mark of our citizenship? It is first of all that our King lives in us, that we are his servants, but that in a special way we share his kingship. Ours is a Kingdom in which freedom and responsibility are balanced, where love and justice complement each other, and where the apparent contradictions of a cross and victory, a tomb and life, are the source not of confusion but of hope and joy. Our war of independence took place on Calvary and in the empty tomb, in our constitution of Holy Scripture and in the Church's historic creeds, and our Fourth of July is the soon-to-be celebrated festival of Pentecost, when this new nationality was born. And the truly bizarre and wonderful part of this nationality that we are part of is that it has no earthly country to call its homeland, no borders or national sovereignty to claim as its own. It exists wherever two or three of us are gathered with our King—in the midst of us, just as he promised.

5. *A global Church for the global village.* Let us remember that however comfortable or proud we may feel in or about a country, a nationality, a place, or even a congregation, we Christians are essentially a nomadic people, wandering the Earth, challenging its rulers, upsetting its comfortable assumptions, and generally helping the Kingdom of God to break into the world. In Christ we have achieved much more than a global village, with its implications for culture and commerce. We have become a new and alternative identity for the sake of the world: the Church, giving to that world the hope of redemption and resurrection because of and to the glory of our King. We are "dual nationals" as we live on earth: *in* the world but not *of* it, loving it because God has made it, but not destined to be here forever. Our King has something and someplace other prepared for us, and sooner than we think, he will call his faithful ambassadors home.

May Jesus Christ our King bless this strange and wonderful multicolored tribe we have become—his Church, his royal priesthood, his own people.—Tyler A. Strand

ILLUSTRATIONS

THE KINGDOM OF GOD.   Every movement that has broken into history has had a watch-cry. No cause or crusade can succeed without a slogan. Men on Madison Avenue lie awake at night thinking up cliches and catch words. In the American Revolution it was "No taxation without representation!" In the French Revolution it was "Liberty, Equality, and Fraternity!"

In the First World War it was "Make the world safe for democracy!" In the Civil War it was "With liberty and justice for all!" In Christianity it is "The Kingdom of God," the rule of God in the heart of the individual and the reign of God in society.—Joseph R. Sizoo

FAITH.   I am perfectly aware of the danger we see in a man who rashly identifies his will with the will of God. Kipling once said in a rather amusing vein that there was only one thing more terrible in battle than a regiment of desperadoes, and that was a company of Scottish Presbyterians who rise from their knees and go into action convinced that they are about to do the will of God. I hope the Lord will spare us from that.—Theodore Parker Ferris

SERMON SUGGESTIONS

Topic: Like His Master
TEXT: Acts 7:53–60
(1) Stephen spoke the truth of God (Acts 6:8–7:53). (2) Stephen offended those set in opposition to the truth of God (Acts 7:54). (3) Stephen died forgiving his killers (Acts 7:60).

Topic: Getting the Crucial Matters Straight
TEXT: John 14:1–14
(1) Our ultimate destiny. (2) Our exclusive guide. (3) Our ongoing task.

CONGREGATIONAL MUSIC

1. "Come, My Way, My Truth, My Love," George Herbert (1633)
   THE CALL, Ralph Vaughan Williams (1911)
   Relating particularly to John 14:6, this old text to a modern tune could function as a call to worship. Sung first by soloist or choir, the congregation could join in singing the last two stanzas.
2. "You Are the Way," George W. Doane (1824)
   DUNDEE, *The Scottish Psalter* (1615)
   Also based on John 14:6, this entire hymn is beautifully developed as a confession of faith in Jesus: the Way, the Truth, and the Life. Should the tune be unfamiliar, it could be lined out by a precentor in the style in which these psalm tunes were originally sung.
3. "Jesus, Still Lead On," Nicholaus L. von Zinzendorf (1778); trans. Jane Borthwick (1846)
   SEELENBRAUTIGAM, Adam Drese (1698)
   This outstanding German hymn would be effective as a response to the Psalter reading (Ps. 31:1–5) since in a different way it expresses the same truth of dependence on God in a time of stress.
4. "We Are God's People," Bryan Jeffery Leech (1976)
   SYMPHONY, Johannes Brahms (1862); arr. Fred Bock (1976)
   Based on many Scriptures, including the Epistle lesson (1 Pet. 2:2–10), this sturdy hymn could well be used as the opening hymn of worship. The choir might sing a stanza or two of this famous Brahms tune before the congregation is asked to join in.—Hugh T. McElrath

WORSHIP AIDS

CALL TO WORSHIP.   "In thee, O Lord, do I put my trust; let me never be ashamed; deliver me in thy righteousness" (Ps. 31:1).

INVOCATION.   O Lord, let our hearts be open to your truth now, that we may feel and see and know the riches of your Kingdom that reaches beyond our limited love, our myopic vision, and our cherished prejudices, through the Christ for all the world.

OFFERTORY SENTENCE.   "Thanks be to God for his indescribable gift" (2 Cor. 9:15 NIV).

OFFERTORY PRAYER.   No offerings of ours can begin to compare with the gift of your only Son, gracious God. Yet because of this wonderful gift, we now bring ourselves and a portion of our material possessions and tokens of our gratitude and love.

PRAYER.   O Spirit of the living God, you are Savior and friend of all who hear your name. This is our word of greeting as we gather once again to hail and celebrate your wondrous works for the sake of men and women everywhere. We praise you for your sovereign power in the universe you have made, but chiefly we rejoice because you have come close to us in Jesus and formed us into Christian families who take care of the blessings of home in the sure order of our Father's world. We thank you for the story of the Scriptures in which the solitary are set in families and when this fellowship consists of believing souls, the Church and the nation are abundantly enriched and internally strong. We bless you for the design and support of your Kingdom, which comes to those who commit themselves to its duty and service and brings the scattered people of each community into bonds of trust and faith.—Donald Macleod[1]

SERMON
Topic: Hope Against All Hope
TEXT: Ps. 130; John 11:1–45

Can you remember a time when you were really discouraged? A time when all the odds were against you? A time when you felt there was no hope? If so, then you are not alone. If you can recall such a time when there seemed to be no hope, then you can relate to the psalmist who said, "From the depths of my despair I call to you, Lord" (Ps. 130:1 GNB).

If you can recall such a time of hopelessness, then you can understand how Mary and Martha of Bethany felt when their beloved brother Lazarus died.

Had we been there on that hillside on that day long ago, we would have been able to see the hopelessness in the eyes of Mary and Martha when they said to Jesus, "If only you had been here, Lord, our brother would not have died!" (John 11:21). Hope—they needed some hope. But what is this hope that is such a longed-for commodity when the chips are down?

I. *Hope is looking up to the Lord from the deepest depths of despair.* Indeed, if you are as low as you can go, where else is there to look except up to the Lord for help? Like the psalmist, we can call to the Lord to help us. We can wait before the Lord in worship and eager anticipation of his help.

Hope is confidence that there is a divine presence at work in the world that wants only what is best for you. As the prophet Jeremiah said to the Lord, "You are my hope in the day of doom" (Jer. 17:17 NKJV). Hope is looking up to the Lord from the deepest depths of life.

---

[1]*Princeton Pulpit Prayers*

II. *Hope is trusting in the Lord's Word.* "I wait for the Lord," the psalmist said, "and in his word I hope" (Ps. 130:5). Many have been the times when I have been discouraged and when I felt there was no hope for my present situation. But then when I turned to the Scriptures and read of the psalmist who struggled with problems or despair and was victorious, I gained new hope.

When I turned to the Gospels and read the words of Jesus, I found new strength. If we, as Jesus says, believe in the word of the Lord, we too shall "see the glory of God" manifested in our lives. We shall gain new hope.

III. *Hope is remembering that with the Lord there is steadfast love [mercy].* "Hope in the Lord," the psalmist says, "for with the Lord there is mercy" (Ps. 130:7 NKJV). Hope is remembering the loving kindness of God.

As William Shakespeare put it in *The Merchant of Venice,*

> The quality of mercy is not strain'd.
> It droppeth as the gentle rain from heaven

The Old Testament book 1 Chronicles records how, when David one time did something to anger the Lord, the court prophet went to David on the Lord's behalf and offered him three different forms of punishment for his sin: three years of famine, three months of running from the armies of his enemies, or three days of punishment from the Lord himself. David replied, "Let me not fall into human hands. . . . Let me fall into the hand of the Lord, for his mercy is very great" (1 Chron. 21:13).

IV. *Hope par excellence is revealed in Jesus Christ, God's great message of hope to the world.* God can breathe new life into even situations that seem hopeless and dead.

With God there is always hope, even in the face of death. "But even now," Martha said to Jesus standing before the tomb of her brother Lazarus, "even now I know that God will give you whatever you ask of him" (John 11:22). And the story goes that Jesus cried, "Lazarus, come out!" (John 11:43). And the dead man came out. Religious pilgrims are still visiting the tomb of Lazarus two thousand years later.

The Christian message is that anyone who sees and believes in God as revealed in Christ will never be without hope. As Paul so eloquently puts it in Romans, "Neither death, nor life, nor angels, nor rulers, nor things present, nor things to come, nor powers, nor height, nor depth, nor anything else in all creation, will be able to separate us from the love of God in Christ Jesus our Lord" (Rom. 8:38–39). That, my friends, is Christian hope, hope that is possible, even against all evidence of hope.—Randy Hammer

SUNDAY, MAY 5, 2002
Lectionary Message

Topic: What We Want, What We Get

TEXT: John 14:15–21

Other Readings: Acts 17:22–31; Ps. 66:8–20; 1 Pet. 3:13–22

I. *What they want.* To put this reading in some perspective, let's imagine it as a bad news briefing. Picture the company executive telling the managers that their division is being downsized by the head office, or the surgeon telling the family members that the operation didn't go as expected and there are going to be some complications. The people in both rooms are stunned and frightened at first, then they begin to ask questions—What's going to happen? How bad will it be? How long do we have? They want answers, they want clarity, they want reassurance. But so many times they can't have any of those things, because the future simply isn't clear enough.

Our text today comes in the Farewell Discourses, the stretch from John 13:31–17:26 in which Jesus begins talking and, except for a few questions by the disciples, doesn't stop. He starts right off telling them that he is only going to be with them a little longer and that they will look for him but find him no longer. This seems to shock them, and their questions indicate how confused they are: Lord, where are you going, and Why can't I follow you? Lord, we don't know where you're going, so how could we know the way? Lord, if you'll show us the Father, then we'll be satisfied. They want answers, they want comfort, they want their friend and teacher with them.

II. *One command.* What they get, instead, is one command and one promise. These two elements are pretty much all there is to the Farewell Discourses. Like Pachelbel's Canon, these chapters state a simple theme, then restate, then elaborate, then invert, then reprise. "If you love me, keep my commandments." "Those who love me will keep my words." "If you keep my commandments, you will abide in my love, just as I have kept the Father's commandments and abide in his love." OK, then what is the command? "This is my commandment, that you love one another as I have loved you."

Think about the other Gospels for a second. What sorts of ethical instructions does Jesus give? Even in Mark, which contains a lot less of Jesus' teachings than Matthew or Luke, the readers are told to stay away from the love of money, to forgive so that they can be forgiven, to avoid divorce, and to give generously. In John, there is only one commandment: love one another as I have loved you, and it isn't handed down until the night when Jesus tells them he's going away.

But you know, sometimes that's enough. As a novice youth director, I was called to the emergency room to sit with a woman whose husband had come in with a heart attack, and I remember how desperately I wanted to tell her that everything would be all right. It didn't seem enough just to be there then; now I know better. Sometimes it makes all the difference to know that someone loves you, to know that you won't have to stand in those dark places by yourself. That's his command: love one another as he loved you, with all he had, to the point of laying down his life.

III. *What is the promise?* I will not leave you orphaned; I am coming to you. I suppose that what the disciples really wanted to hear in that moment was, "I'm not really leaving," but that wasn't possible. "I'll only be gone a little while" confused them: If you're coming back, how is it that we will see you, but no one else will? He then tells them about the Paraclete.

What they wanted was their teacher with them, telling them what they needed to hear. What they got was another teacher to remind them of all that Jesus taught. What they wanted was the presence of their friend, sharing the good and bad times with them like always. What they got was someone to be inside them and among them always, encouraging them in the good times, stiffening their courage for the bad times. They wanted assurance and clarity about the future. They didn't get that, but they got the presence of the Spirit that would never leave them, so they would never face the future alone.

You can think of this one promise like God's big villa with about a zillion rooms, and all Jesus' friends as invited guests. You can think of it as an ancient grapevine on the side of a hill, with Jesus as the trunk and the believers as the uncountable branches and twigs growing on it. The images in Jesus' message all have the same point: you are in me and I am in you and that will never change, no matter what the future holds.

IV. *What they wanted was for their life to stay the same.* Change makes us all afraid, doesn't it? They didn't want to hear the bad news. What they got was a command to make Jesus' love the standard of conduct between them, and what they got was a promise that through the Spirit, Jesus would always be with them. And that was enough—not just for the twelve, but for all believers from then until now.—Richard Vinson

ILLUSTRATIONS

ANOTHER PARACLETE.   The most important point to note is that this is *another* Paraclete (v. 16), implying that Jesus fulfilled the same role while he was with the disciples. The Holy Spirit, therefore, is the continued divine presence assisting the disciples to perform the mission of Jesus in the world. He will remain with them and within them. He will teach them everything and make them remember all that Jesus has said (see the comment on 2:22). The fourth Gospel itself is thus evidence of the work of the Paraclete in the Johannine church.— George W. MacRae[1]

FREEDOM IN THE SPIRIT.   It is confusing to hear Jesus talking about obeying commandments and being free in the Holy Spirit at the same time. For many people, this is an either/or proposition: Either we are bound by someone else's commandments, or we are free to choose for ourselves. In the Gospel of John we are given a very different picture: Obedience and Christian freedom in the Spirit are intimately related to each other.—Dennis C. Benson[2]

SERMON SUGGESTIONS

Topic: A Sermon for Pagans
TEXT: Acts 17:22–31 NRSV
(1) You are extremely religious. (2) You still have a vacant place in your heart for a god as yet unknown to you. (3) I bring you the message of the Lord of heaven and Earth, who calls you and all people to repent in view of the coming and Resurrection of Jesus Christ.

Topic: Guidelines for Doing Right
TEXT: 1 Pet. 3:13–22 NRSV
(1) Do not be intimidated. (2) Be ready to give an honest account for your faith. (3) Keep your conscience clear.

---

[1]*Invitation to John*
[2]*The Bible Creative*

CONGREGATIONAL MUSIC

1. "Come Down, O Dove Divine," Bianco da Siena (fifteenth century); trans. Richard F. Littledale (1867)

DOWN AMPNEY, Ralph Vaughan Williams (1906)

This rich hymn invoking the Holy Spirit of love and truth naturally relates to the Gospel lesson in John. It is also not unrelated to the apostle Paul's preaching in the Acts passage: "For in him we live and move and have our being" (17:28a).

2. "My Hope Is Built on Nothing Less," Edward Mote (1834)

SOLID ROCK, William B. Bradbury (1863)

The singing of this excellent gospel hymn witnessing to the hope and assurance in the hearts of Christian worshippers could meaningfully follow the Epistle reading in 1 Peter where the apostle is exhorting the persecuted believers to be ready to testify to the hope that is in them. It is sometimes good to sing all the stanzas before finally lifting the stirring refrain as a climactic expression of firm faith in Christ.

3. "Come, All You People, Praise Our God," Ps. 66; vers. *Psalter* (1912)

ADOWA, Charles H. Gabriel (1910)

A free paraphrase of the exact verses of the Psalter lesson (66:8–20), this song could be sung as a call to praise at the beginning of worship. It would also be appropriate as an offertory hymn.

4. "Lead Me, Guide Me," Doris Akers (1953)

LEAD ME, Doris Akers (1953)

This African American gospel hymn could be used in connection with the reading in Acts where the apostle Paul calls for repentance and confession of error on the part of his hearers. A meaningful use of this song would be to have one or more soloists sing the stanzas, with the congregation joining in on the unison refrain.—Hugh T. McElrath

WORSHIP AIDS

CALL TO WORSHIP.   "Bless our God, O peoples; let the sound of his praise be heard" (Ps. 66:8 NRSV).

INVOCATION.   Our hearts reach out to you in praise, O God, for you have richly blessed us. We have understood more and more that even our difficult times, faced with faith in you, enriched our lives. Lord, increase our faith to your glory.

OFFERTORY SENTENCE.   "To the Lord belong the Earth and everything in it, the world and all its inhabitants" (Ps. 24:1 REB).

OFFERTORY PRAYER.   We know, O God, that what we bring as offerings belongs to you already, but as a gesture of our love and a token of your providence in our lives, we bring our money and our very selves and present them to you.

PRAYER.   O God, you have prepared for those who love you such good things as surpass our understanding: Pour into our hearts such love toward you that we, loving you in all things and above all things, may obtain your promises, which exceed all that we can desire; through

Jesus Christ our Lord, who lives and reigns with you and the Holy Spirit, one God, for ever and ever.—*The Book of Common Prayer*

SERMON
Topic: The Search for a New Face
TEXT: 2 Cor. 3:18; 4:6

Few things are as fascinating as a human face. Consider how it focuses the whole person, as if nothing from the neck down really matters. After all, only the face can welcome or reject, smile or scowl, laugh or cry. For all of our "body language," only facial features register such emotions as fear, anger, shame, scorn, and pain. It is here, and only here, that we eat and drink, see and hear, speak and sing, taste and smell, breathe and kiss. No wonder we look into the face as a mirror of the soul and refer to the great issues of life in terms of "saving face" and "losing face," or of "facing up to" our past, present, and future.[3]

In an effort not to fall on our face, we lavish enormous attention on its physical appearance. Hairstyling and cosmetics have become huge industries with devoted patrons. The local press reported recently that in Mountain Brook alone there are twenty-four beauty shops grossing $5.6 million per year for hairdos, manicures, and massages, not counting the purchase of grooming products in department, grocery, and drug stores.[4] Laser technology has been enlisted to zap spider veins, "resurface" wrinkled skin, and remove everything from assorted blemishes to unwanted hair. "Medical spas" specializing in "facial rejuvenations" have sprung up recently, leading to five million cosmetic procedures last year, up more than 800 percent in a decade.[5]

The most intense search for a new face has been stimulated by rapid strides in aesthetic surgery.[6] Begun primarily to meet the needs of men, the specialty concentrated until recently on such practical tasks as rebuilding noses collapsed by syphilis, reconstructing whole sections of the face blown away by modern warfare, and reshaping the noses of Irish, Jewish, and African immigrants to hasten their ethnic assimilation. But in the last fifteen years, the field has shifted from repairing damage to enhancing beauty, with facelifts, cheek implants, eyelid nips, and chin tucks becoming commonplace. Instead of being prompted by a midlife aging crisis, these procedures are now viewed as preventive maintenance that often begins in the teen years and is repeated regularly. It is not surprising that the number of aesthetic surgeries doubled between 1984 and 1999 and has doubled again since then.[7]

We are now on the verge of the made-to-order designer face. The French artist Orlan (b. 1947) has made her face a "compendium of art-historical 'quotations,' incorporating the

---

[3]David F. Ford, "Facing," in *Self and Salvation: Being Transformed* (New York: Cambridge University Press, 1999), pp. 17–29.

[4]Julie Ross Cannon, "Beauty and the Brook," *The Birmingham News*, Jan. 23, 2000, p. 19-A.

[5]Cathy Booth, "Cosmetic Surgery: Light Makes Right," *Time*, Oct. 11, 1999, pp. 67–70.

[6]Sander L. Gilman, *Creating Beauty to Cure the Soul* (Durham, N.C.: Duke University Press, 1998) and *Making the Body Beautiful: A Cultural History of Aesthetic Surgery* (Princeton: Princeton University Press, 1999); Elizabeth Haiken, *Venus Envy: A History of Cosmetic Surgery* (Baltimore: Johns Hopkins University Press, 1997).

[7]Claudia Kalb, "Our Quest to Be Perfect," *Newsweek*, Aug. 9, 1999, pp. 52–59; Stephanie Paulsell, "Fearfully and Wonderfully Made," *Christian Century*, Oct. 13, 1999, pp. 964–967.

chin of Botticelli's Venus, the lips of Moreau's Europa, the eyes of Gérôme's Psyche, the brow of Leonardo's Mona Lisa."[8] No wonder Lucianne Goldberg said of her friend and co-conspirator Linda Tripp's recent makeover, "It looks like she's had a head transplant."[9]

I. *The Futility of a Faceless Existence.* Does all of this attention lavished on outward beauty achieve the desired results? As one who has traveled widely and had extensive contact with almost every world culture, I have not found more beautiful women or more handsome men than in America. While I can gladly celebrate the great strides we have made to maintain an attractive appearance, I fear that there is a deeper beauty that we have neglected in all of this blasting and peeling and cutting on the surface of the skin. We are not given a distinctive face at birth, since all babies look virtually alike; rather, we grow a face over many years until, by the time we are fifty, we have the face we deserve. Finally the face becomes a map of our mysterious depths, an icon of our hidden identity, a sacrament of our true spirit. That is why the Bible uses the face as a synonym for one's very being, so that to send a messenger "before thy face" (Mark 1:2) is to confront the whole person. Like it or not, we carry our life in our face.[10]

Go anywhere that people gather and study their faces. Look at how many are hard, sullen, or sad, or artificially painted to disguise the absence of joy. As the prophet put it, "The look on their faces testifies against them" (Isa. 3:9 NEB). Many a face sags from the load of a bitter legacy, as in Edwin Markham's "The Main with the Hoe" made famous by Millet's painting:

> Bowed by the weight of centuries he leans
> Upon his hoe and gazes on the ground,
> The emptiness of ages in his face,
> And on his back the burden of the world.[11]

Sometimes we become part of the "faceless masses" through no fault of our own, but other times we deliberately "de-face" the image of God by rebelling against the Creator who shaped it deep within the human spirit. In Goethe's *Faust,* the bitter face of Mephistopheles is described with the searing indictment, "It was written on his brow that he had never loved a human soul."[12] The Bible speaks graphically of how we may "turn away our faces" in indifference, as did the Israelites who forsook God's habitation, the Temple (2 Chron. 29:6); or of how we may "hide our faces" in shame (Isa. 53:3), as did Adam and Eve in the Garden of Eden (Gen. 3:8); or how we may "harden our faces" in rebellion, as did those who refused to repent of their injustices and falsehoods (Jer. 5:3).

How often we try to make the face a mask of our true condition. Just as Jezebel painted her face in a vain effort to disguise her wickedness (2 Kings 9:30), we often try to appear beautiful on the outside precisely because life is so ugly deep within; or like the pious contemporaries of Jesus, we go to the opposite extreme and disfigure our faces to look dismal

---

[8]Holly Brubach, "Beauty Under the Knife," *Atlantic Monthly,* Feb. 2000, p. 99.

[9]Cited by Maureen Dowd, "A Fake Somebody," *New York Times,* Jan. 2, 2000, p. 9-WK.

[10]Christopher Nugent, "The Face as Theology," *Theology Today,* Oct. 1984, 4(3).

[11]Stanza 1, cited in John Bartlett, *Familiar Quotations,* 13th ed. (Boston; Little, Brown, 1955), p. 755.

[12]Cited by R. Roy Keaton, "What Does Your Face Reveal?" *The Lion,* Dec. 1957, p. 44.

so that we may win the praise of others for our great sacrifices (Matt. 6:16); or we feign the glamour of celebrities in the hope that we may have our moment in the spotlight. But all of these are disguises that mock reality because the outer that is seen does not reflect the inner that is unseen.

Remember that Satan comes to us not so much as a person but as an impersonator, a mask-wearer, the lord of the false face. The Grim Reaper is pictured as having no face at all because spiritual death is finally faceless, devoid of the life-giving image of God. How many tragic faces are all around us with the mark of Cain upon their brow? (Gen. 4:15). Look in the mirror, my friend, and behold your face. Is it darkened with jealousy, downcast with despair, confused with doubt, snarling with contempt, passive with apathy? Look at your face and ask what it says about your soul!

II. *The light on the Lord's face.*[13] In the Hebrew Scriptures, the highest expression of spirituality was conveyed by the phrase "to seek God's face" (Ps. 27:8), which meant to commune with his very presence. A few individuals were said to have actually seen God's face (Gen. 32:30), although such an intimate encounter was viewed as dangerous (Judg. 13:22–23) or even deadly (Exod. 33:20), much as it was for the subjects of an ancient potentate, who would not dare to look upon his countenance unbidden but would prostrate themselves before his feet with their faces in the dust. To overcome this instinctive fear of majesty, God literally grew a human face in Jesus of Nazareth and allowed ordinary people to gaze on it to their heart's content. It is interesting that we are told nothing in the Gospel story about the physical features of Jesus' face, yet the record is full of references to the many ways in which his face revealed what we need to know about the mind and heart of God.

For one thing, *it was a compassionate face.* We know that it blazed in indignation over the disfiguring blight of disease (Mark 1:41). Yet it was a tender face that conveyed the welcome and forgiveness of God to a fallen woman of the streets (Luke 7:47–50). To the rich young ruler Jesus turned a loving face that nevertheless demanded total renunciation of self for Jesus' sake (Mark 10:21). When Jesus reached Jerusalem for the last time, his face became a tear-stained face as he wept over the unresponsiveness of a city that was squandering its chance for peace and choosing instead the path of self-destruction (Luke 19:41–44). Behold the many ways in which the grace of God was perfectly expressed by that singular face.

Again, we know that for all of its graciousness, *his was also a resolute and determined face.* Luke tells us that when Jesus began the last, fateful journey of his life, "he set his face to go to Jerusalem" (9:51) even though his followers warned him of the folly of such a venture (John 11:7–8, 16). This description is reminiscent of the Servant of the Lord in Isaiah who "hid not his face from shame and spitting" (50:6) but rather "set his face like a flint" because he was confident of God's ultimate vindication (50:7–9). The courage and commitment etched in the firm visage of Jesus never flinched or faltered, even when his face was slapped to coerce a false confession (John 18:22–23), spat on in derision by his tormentors (Mark 14:65; 15:19), or pierced with a crown of thorns in mockery (Matt. 27:29). When finally he "bowed his head" in death, it was not as a defeated victim but as a triumphant conqueror with the cry of victory on his lips, "It is finished!" (John 19:30).

---

[13]This wording was suggested by a sermon by Edgar DeWitt Jones, "The Light on the Lord's Face," in *The Protestant Pulpit,* compiled by Andrew Watterson Blackwood (New York: Abingdon Press, 1947), pp. 211–217.

Supremely, *his was a face radiant with the glory of God.* On the Mount of Transfiguration, "as Jesus was praying, the appearance of his countenance was altered" (Luke 9:29) "and his face shone like the sun" (Matt. 17:2). In this transfiguration, three startled disciples were permitted to "behold his glory, glory as of the only Son from the Father" (John 1:14), a glory that lurked around the edges of his earthly ministry from beginning to end (John 17:4–5). So luminous was God in his life that even during the noonday darkness of Calvary, a Roman centurion could look up into that bloody face and see the Son of God (Mark 15:39).

The apostle Paul captured the whole point of our brief effort at portraiture by suggesting that God's light shines into our hearts when we see "the light of knowledge of the glory of God in the face of Jesus Christ" (2 Cor. 4:6). To put it as concisely as possible, *only by facing Jesus are we faced by God in such a way that we get a new face!*[14] That is why the old gospel song entreats:

> O soul, are you weary and troubled?
> No light in the darkness you see?
> There's light for a look at the Savior,
> And life more abundant and free!
> Turn your eyes upon Jesus,
> Look full in His wonderful face;
> And the things of earth will grow strangely dim,
> In the light of His glory and grace.[15]

III. *Till we have faces.*[16] The only way we may permanently alter our faces is to transform our lives from within by those same qualities of mercifulness, steadfastness, and holiness that transfigured the face of Jesus. To be sure, we can temporarily decorate the face with cosmetics to produce a pleasing effect, but we know that such beauty is only skin deep and will not last even for a day. No matter how many times we peel the skin or pamper the flesh, zap the blotches or carve the profile, we are, as Simone de Beauvoir saw so clearly, fighting a losing battle with the bitch-goddess Vanity. The inner sources of beauty, by contrast, shape our faces slowly over time. It is only long-lived character that gives beauty to the face that never fades.

Surface beauty, as such, is not bad unless it becomes a daily obsession and an end in itself. But is this all we want our faces to display? It was said of the Suffering Servant that "he had no form or comeliness that we should look at him, and no beauty that we should desire him" (Isa. 53:2). Think of those who, like the Servant, have allowed the pathos and tragedy of life to become etched deeply into the furrows of their face. Abraham Lincoln was hardly handsome and Mother Teresa was certainly no beauty, but God's infinite pity and humanity's vast hurt were crowded into every crevice of their countenance, making them strangely beautiful to behold because their faces were full of strength—the strength of a resolute determination to love even the unlovely. We are here on the threshold of a great para-

---

[14]Ford, "Facing," 1999, pp. 24–25.
[15]Helen H. Lemmel, "Turn Your Eyes Upon Jesus," stanza 1 and refrain.
[16]The title of "a myth retold" by C. S. Lewis, *Till We Have Faces* (London: Geoffrey Bles, 1956).

dox, according to which we most truly admire those faces that have been shaped by a lifetime of self-effacement.

In the early days of the New Testament Church we are introduced to Stephen, a man "full of grace and power [who] did great wonders and signs among the people" (Acts 6:8). But because he sought to set Jesus above the customs of his people (6:13–14), he was hauled before the religious authorities to defend himself, resulting in one of the greatest sermons recorded in the New Testament (7:2–53). Acts tells us that, despite the fact that a secret plot had been instigated against him (6:11), that a mob had been stirred up to oppose him (6:12), and that false witnesses had been secured to twist his words (6:13), as he made his defense, "all who sat in the council saw that his face was like the face of an angel" (6:15). Obviously this was a moment when Stephen would have been justified to have a face full of fear, exasperation, resentment, even contempt for his accusers. What was the source of this angelic countenance that he maintained even as his tormentors became enraged, ground their teeth against him, and reached for rocks to end his life? It came from gazing into heaven, where he "saw the glory of God, and Jesus standing at the right hand of God" (7:55).

The apostle Paul, who was present as a persecutor at Stephen's martyrdom (8:1), later developed the fundamental insight that we gain a radiant face by looking on the glorious face of Jesus. First he reminded his readers that when Moses came down from Mount Sinai, he was forced to wear a veil because his face was so aglow from talking with God (Exod. 34:29–35)—a brightness that soon faded because it was based on the limited understanding of an earlier era (2 Cor. 3:7–15). By contrast, when we behold the glory of the Lord through the living Spirit of the Risen Christ, we are gradually "being changed into his likeness from one degree of glory to another" (3:16–18) because God "has shone in our hearts to give the light of the knowledge of the glory of God in the face of Jesus Christ" (4:6).

High above Franconia Notch in the White Mountains of New Hampshire is an outcropping of rock formed during the Ice Age that from a distance precisely resembles the features of a noble human face. Once worshiped by the Indians as a profile of the "Great Spirit," the protuberance has long been known as "The Old Man of the Mountain" or, from the title of a beloved tale by Nathaniel Hawthorne, "The Great Stone Face."[17] The story tells how a lad named Ernest lived out his life in that valley looking for someone to fulfill the ancient prophecy that a great man would arise among them whose countenance would exactly resemble that of the Great Stone Face. The more Ernest gazed at the mountain peak for hours on end, watching its visage change with the shifting light and shadows, the more he longed to meet one whose face would embody its impressive features.

But his hopes were disappointed time and time again. First there was a local nicknamed Gathergold who had gone away to become an exceedingly wealthy merchant and returned to live in an opulent mansion, but his sordid face had the Midas look of "wrinkled shrewdness." Then there was a native son who had become an illustrious military commander with the nickname Old Blood and Thunder but whose face was full of trucelent energy expressive of an iron will rather than the gentle wisdom and tender sympathies that marked the Great Stone Face. Next there was an eminent statesman nicknamed Old Stony Phiz who returned

---

[17]William Clarvat, Roy Harvey Pearce, and Claude M. Simpson (eds.), *The Centennial Edition of the Works of Nathaniel Hawthorne*, Vol. 11 (Columbus: Ohio State University Press, 1974), pp. 26–48.

with "a weary gloom in the deep caverns of his eyes, as of a child that had outgrown its play-things, or a man of mighty faculties and little aims, whose life, with all its high performances, was vague and empty, because no high purpose had endowed it with reality."

As these great pretenders came and went, each failing the test of a noble face, Ernest quietly grew old meditating on the lessons of the Great Stone Face that crowned the brow of the mountain. The wrinkles that now furrowed his brow "were inscriptions that time had graved, and in which he had written legends of wisdom that had been tested by the tenor of a life." When he shared his thoughts with friends and neighbors, "his face would kindle, unawares, and shine upon them, as with a mild evening light." On one such occasion, when he went at sunset to discourse with a gathering of the inhabitants in a sylvan glen, "his words had power, because they accorded with his thoughts, and his thoughts had reality and depth because they harmonized with the life which he had always lived. . . . They were the words of life, because a life of good deeds and holy love was melted into them." As he spoke, "the face of Ernest assumed a grandeur of expression, so inbred with benevolence" that a great poet who had accompanied him, moved "by an irresistible impulse, threw his arms aloft, and shouted—'Behold! Behold! Ernest has himself the likeness of the Great Stone Face!'"

If pondering the noblest features of nature's brow for a lifetime could shape the face of Ernest, how much more can we be transformed by "looking unto Jesus" (Heb. 12:2) until we take on his likeness and others literally see Jesus in us. The self-effacement through which we can find a new face like that of Christ is well expressed by a plaque on the wall of Memorial Church in Harvard Yard which honored the ministry of Andrew Preston Peabody with this inscription:

> His precept was glorified by his example
> while for thirty-three years
> he moved among the teachers and students of Harvard College
> and wist not that his face shone

—William E. Hull

SUNDAY, MAY 12, 2002
Lectionary Message

Topic: Family of Suffering
TEXT: 1 Pet. 4:12–14; 5:6–11
Other Readings: Acts 1:6–14; Ps. 68:1–10, 32–35; John 17:1–11

It feels very strange for a person in my position to pick up a text on suffering and seek to say something meaningful about it. Living in the most affluent nation that has ever existed, taking for granted comforts that as a child I would have never expected to enjoy, what can I say about suffering? And living in an environment that tolerates Christians, how can I relate to this text that speaks about suffering for the sake of Christ?

Surely we have all suffered. Pain, disease, heartache, tragedy, and mental illness fall to us and to our loved ones without regard to when and where we live. But most of us have never been "reviled for the name of Christ," nor suffered physical abuse for the name of Christ, nor undergone great financial hardship for the name of Christ. In what sense can we say that we have shared in Christ's sufferings?

I. *We share in Christ's sufferings when we are partners with those who really are suffering.* We are not persecuted because of our faith, but some people are, and we can help support them. Paul called the Philippians his partners in ministry because they helped him financially again and again. We can send our money to congregations in other places who struggle to stay afloat. We can donate our time and our energies to ministries that will relieve suffering. We can build homes for the homeless and we can lobby against policies that help create homelessness.

II. *We share in Christ's sufferings when we approach suffering as a part of discipleship.* Peter suggests throughout this letter that we should think of unmerited suffering as a way of following in Christ's footsteps. This doesn't make the pain go away, of course, and it can be overdone. Once a wealthy man who was driving me from the airport to my hotel in his Mercedes told me how he had been disenfranchised by those in power because of his commitment to Christ and to truth. But perhaps it helps us a little to think, as we suffer, that Christ did, too, and that our experience gives us something in common with him.

III. *Peter gives us some practical advice about how to get through the tough times.* Don't think it strange that you suffer, he says—but we often do think so. Here's how it goes: How could this happen to us? We're the good guys. Or maybe we aren't; maybe God is angry with us. Or maybe being good doesn't really count for much, if the good guys can suffer this much. You see what I mean? If you start with his advice—don't think it strange that you suffer—you may avoid needless guilt or too much cynicism.

IV. *Don't think you're alone.* Suffering has a way of making a person feel isolated. Pain, grief, anguish—it all tends to make us focus on ourselves, on where it hurts, and in the process we feel more and more alone. Peter says we should remember that there is a family out there suffering along with us. You have brothers and sisters undergoing the same kinds of suffering as you. Pray for them as they pray for you. Take comfort in the solidarity of their commitment to you and to Christ, and give them the same comfort.

V. *Don't think it is eternal.* When we are in pain, every moment lasts a lifetime. When we are lonely, every night stretches out for a year. When our hearts are broken or when we are afraid, we think it will never stop. But it will. We know, though we don't like to think of it, how short are our lives and how quickly our good times and bad will end. Peter reminds us that our suffering is "for a little while," and though it may not feel brief, it is.

VI. *Don't think God doesn't care.* Suffering makes us feel isolated not only from other people, but also from God. Peter knew this and urged his readers, and us, to put all our cares on God. Don't fall prey to the hungry lion who wants to tell us that God has forgotten, that God is far away, that God is unconcerned about us. God is with us. God is part of our family of suffering that stretches all over the world. Remember the parable of the sheep and the goats? Every hungry and thirsty person, every sick and persecuted person, every poor and deprived person bears the face of Christ, because he has decided to identify himself with all who suffer for any cause. God is with us; God is part of our fellowship of suffering.

When you suffer, think of it as an experience that can potentially bring you closer to Christ. Remember that others are sharing your experience, some to a lesser and some to a greater degree, and that God is with you. When you hurt, don't try to go it alone—reach out to God and to your brothers and sisters, and that will help you make it through.—Richard Vinson

ILLUSTRATIONS

PRAYER IS REAL.   What if we are only talking to ourselves when we pray? There are many answers, of which we choose only two. The first, a blurted prayer, "O God, help me!" certainly doesn't "feel" as if we were speaking to our reflection in a mirror. We know full well that we are not God and that there are times when we cannot help ourselves. The threat that provokes the prayer certainly isn't the bubbling up of some internal chemistry. It is *objective* in very fact: our best friend has just betrayed us, or death has just knocked at the door. Then why brand the prayer merely *subjective?* We pray to Someone who is beyond betrayal and death.—George A. Buttrick[18]

ROOTAGE.   You will not get what you want just for the asking. If you do nothing about it, nothing will happen. On the other hand, if you pray about it, you may get it, but you may not. You may get something even greater than what you asked for. You may get what I wish all of us could get, myself included, and that is a deeper rootage in things. One of the reasons that we are so likely to snap in heavy storms, the way trees do, is that our roots don't go deep enough. You may get a deeper rootage, and the deeper your rootage is, the greater your lifting power will be; that is, the deeper you go into the very nature of existence, the more realistic you will be about life and suffering, joy and sorrow, death and defeat; the greater will be the lifting power you will have when the time comes for you to raise some great burden that you would never choose but which has been laid upon you.—Theodore Parker Ferris

SERMON SUGGESTIONS

Topic: Prelude to Pentecost
TEXT: Acts 1:6–14
(1) Political nostalgia (v. 6). (2) The promise of a superior power (v. 8a). (3) The universal challenge (v. 8b). (4) The vital assurance (vv. 9–11). (5) The crucial step (vv. 12–14).

Topic: Jesus' Prayer for Us
TEXT: John 17:1–11
(1) That we may have eternal life (vv. 1–3). (2) That we may know that to know Jesus, the Son, is to know God, the Father (vv. 6–8). (3) That we may be protected by the Father and the Son (v. 11b). (4) That we may live with one another in the unity of love (v. 11c).

CONGREGATIONAL MUSIC

1. "Hail the Day That Sees Him Rise," Charles Wesley (1739) and Thomas Cotterill (1820)
   LLANFAIR, Robert Wilson (1817)
   Generally regarded as the most popular of all Ascension hymns in English-language worship, "Hail the Day" relates, of course, to the reading in Acts and could well open the singing worship for this day. It lends itself naturally to antiphonal treatment.
2. "How Firm a Foundation," Anon. from Rippon's *Selection* (1787)
   FOUNDATION, Funk's *Genuine Church Music* (1832)

---

[18]*The Power of Prayer Today*

This strong hymn of comfort and encouragement can relate to the Epistle lesson, especially 1 Peter 4:13 with its reference to the "fiery ordeals" that will come to test the faithful. Accordingly, special emphasis could be brought to stanza 4 of the hymn—"When through fiery trials"—by having the congregation sing it heartily in unison without instrumental accompaniment.

3. "Let God Arise and by His Might," Psalm 68; vers. *Psalter Hymnal* (1987)

GENEVAN, *Genevan Psalter* (1539)

Here we have the great historical setting of Psalm 68 from the original metrical Psalters. The Psalm 68 tune, known as "the Huguenot Marseillaise," became the battle song of the Calvinist Reformation. An exceedingly long hymn, the three stanzas that parallel today's Psalter lesson would be 1, 2, and 9.

4. "Bind Us Together," Bob Gillman (1974)

BIND US, Bob Gillman (1974)

The use of this contemporary prayer song would be quite appropriate in response to the prayer of Jesus that his followers be one (John 17:1–11).—Hugh T. McElrath

WORSHIP AIDS

CALL TO WORSHIP.   "Sing the praises of God, raise a psalm to his name; extol him who rides on the clouds. The Lord is his name, exult before him" (Ps. 68:4 REB).

INVOCATION.   As we sing the songs of Zion, O God, may we think of the words and let our hearts be lifted up to you and let our melody encourage one another, for your glory.

OFFERTORY SENTENCE.   "And He said to them, 'Take heed what you hear. With the same measure you use, it will be measured to you; and to you who hear, more will be given'" (Mark 4:24 NKJV).

OFFERTORY PRAYER.   Lord of all, let this be the offering that goes from sanctuary to slum, from local church to foreign mission field, from few to many, presenting the love of God for all.—E. Lee Phillips.

PRAYER.   O God, when we move through the valley of suffering, sorrow, and disappointment, help us to be quiet, to trust in the goodness of thy being and love, to wait upon thee, to do nothing quickly or rashly, and then to go forward believing that all things will work together for good to those who love thee and try to do thy will. We ask this in the name of him who, when things did not go well for him, thought about it, asked that the cup might be taken from him, and then said, "Thy will, not mine be done."—Theodore Parker Ferris

SERMON

Topic: Hannah—Dedicating a Child and a Home

TEXT: 1 Sam. 1:19–28

A parent-child dedication service can be a meaningful experience. Only time will tell how meaningful it is. For we all know that words spoken in commitment must be lived out with deeds done. It is easier to say the words than to live them. For our homes to be Christian will take hard and dedicated work.

It is important that we give it, for the home is the greatest theological seminary in the world. Our children will learn more about God from the home and in the home than in any other place. We don't really have to say much to teach children about God. Our attitudes at home, the deeds we do there, and the values we live by there, are all teaching our children how important God is or isn't. What we live for and the way we live defines their understanding of God. It is very important that we commit ourselves to making our homes Christian.

What is involved in that? This question is why I want to talk about Hannah, the mother of Samuel, who came and dedicated her child to God. In doing so, she pointed out three important principles to know as we try to keep our homes Christian.

I. *We must never forget who gives us our children.* Hannah had been the laughingstock of the community for a long time because she wanted to have children but didn't. In those days, childlessness was a bad thing. So Hannah prayed earnestly to God for a child, and Samuel was born. She went to God's house and praised God. She thanked him for his goodness, and in doing that she showed that she remembered where Samuel came from. He was God's precious gift to her. She was thankful for him, and for all the days of her life Hannah would not forget that God gave her the blessing of a child.

We say that's common sense, we know that. Children are the gift of God. By the way, parents are, too. All of us are created in the image of God. That's common sense, but it is worth remembering. It ought to tell us a couple of things.

For one thing, we ought to act like the children of God at home. How is it in our homes? Do we put on a good show at church, but at home is a different matter? Do we as parents, young people, and children strive to act like children of God? Are we kind, patient, and sympathetic? Do we love one another? One of the needs in the home is for us to remember whose we are. We are God's and we need to act like it.

The other application of this lesson is this: We need to *treat* each other as children of God. One of the tragedies of our time is child abuse by parents who beat and neglect their children. We wonder how this could happen. Sometimes we fall into the mistake of believing that children are our possessions. Children are not possessions; they are persons created in the image of God. They are his, and they are to be treated with respect, dignity, and courtesy. Do we try to be sympathetic? Do we try to understand? Do we listen? Do we provide for their needs? Do we try to love them? Do children try to treat parents the same way? To understand them, to be sensitive to their needs? It's a mutual way of living in the home—to try to treat one another with the respect and dignity due a child of God, because that's who everyone is.

II. *We must seek to be good stewards of our children's lives, to train them well.* This is what Hannah did when she came to dedicate Samuel to the Lord. She realized that motherhood was a great privilege, but it was also a tremendous responsibility. It mattered to God what she did with Samuel. It was important for her to train Samuel in such a way that he would know who his God was.

That is an important aspect of parenting. God lends us our children and expects us to be good teachers and trainers of them, to prepare them for that time when he will want them back. It's like putting my money in a bank. I trust that banker to take good care of my money, to be a good steward of it, to use it well. If he loses it, misplaces it, or steals it, then I won't like that; I'll try to have him put in jail. I certainly will take my money out of that bank. In a sense, God gives us children, and he expects us to be a good steward of their lives. He expects us to train them to be his children. Is that what we are doing in our homes?

Do we teach our children to pray? Do we pray with them? Do we read our Bibles with our children and help them to understand it? Do we teach our children to love all people regardless of color of skin or where they were born? Do we teach our children to be kind to one another, to be sensitive to the needs of others? Are we teaching our children that it matters what is right and what is wrong, that to live honestly is the best way to live? Are we teaching our children to support the church by supporting it ourselves?

III. *We need to give our children away to God.* That was what Hannah did. She left Samuel in the care of Eli, because she wanted Samuel to grow up to serve God. How she loved Samuel to do that for him! She wanted Samuel to know God and wanted God to have Samuel, and she gave him away. "As long as he lives," she said, "he is lent to the Lord" (v. 28). Samuel did grow up to be a great prophet and leader of Israel, and I think you can trace it back to these moments when Hannah said to God, "Here is Samuel, he is all yours."

This is what we are here to do as parents. God gives us our children, but only for a while. A day will come when he will ask for them back. Are we preparing them for that moment when God will want them in his service? Are we trying to develop our children to try to follow the will of God or our wills? Are we trying to teach them that joy in life is doing what he wants?—Hugh Litchfield[19]

SUNDAY, MAY 19, 2002
Lectionary Message

Topic: Prophet's Wish
TEXT: Num. 11:24–30
Other Readings: Ps. 104:24–34; Acts 2:1–21 or 1 Cor. 12:3b–13; John 20:19–23 or 7:37–39

It's Pentecost Sunday! In my church, that means bright red felt flames on a white background hanging on the ends of the pews and two huge banners at the front of the church, one a white dove descending on a blue field, the other a brightly colored tree of life. It means red stoles on the choir, red paraments around the platform, and a children's sermon with wind in it somehow. It generally means reading Acts 2 and figuring out how to talk about speaking in tongues to Baptists who don't do it themselves. It doesn't usually mean thinking about Eldad, Medad, and the seventy elders of Israel. We have to get our bearings, I think.

Today we're in the desert with Moses and the Israelites. They had been on the road from Egypt to the Promised Land for two years, and they were not happy campers. In fact, the first part of this chapter says that the whole band was wailing and whining because they had only manna to eat. Every evening when Moses would take a little stroll around the camp, checking things out, all the folks would be sitting out in front of their tents saying "Oh, life was so much better back in Egypt, where we had all the fish and fresh vegetables we could eat." Hey, there is only so much of this a leader can take, and one day Moses just snapped. He asked the Lord, "What did I ever do to deserve this? Am I a criminal and this is my punishment from

---

[19]*Sermons on Those Other Special Days* (Nashville: Broadman Press, 1990), pp. 85–91.

you? I can't bear these people one day longer. If you want to kill me, do it now and quickly, but don't keep torturing me with this bunch."

This was not the first time the Israelites had whined, nor is it the first time Moses had sat down in the road and tried to quit. Brothers and sisters, it is just a fact of life: people will whine and leaders will get burned out. If we'd been Israelites eating manna for two years straight, we'd have whined, too, and if we had been Moses trying to herd these yowling cats through the wilderness for two years straight, we'd have given God our notice and checked out. So what's the remedy: a long vacation? therapy? a transfer to another parish?

What God does is take seventy of the whiners and give them a good dose of the Spirit. Moses rounded them up and had them stand around the tent where the presence of God always appeared. Imagine a prayer meeting where they all complained about the temperature and the menus for church suppers and the lack of spiritual depth in Moses' preaching lately. But then God descended in the cloud that went in front of the people every day and took some of the Spirit—the same Spirit that rested on Moses—and gave it to the seventy. And those whiners got fired up; they started prophesying. We aren't told what their topics were: Did they all preach about the same thing, I wonder? Did each point out the sins of the one on his right? Did they all talk at once? Was anyone edified by hearing seventy sermons in one service? More to the point, what was it like for Moses to know that for once there were more folks than just Moses listening to God's voice and passing it along? Did he think, finally, they know what it felt like? Maybe they could understand now.

Two of the seventy whining cats had escaped the roundup, as cats will do, and had missed the prayer meeting. But their names were on the list, so God dosed them up, too, and they prophesied, and soon there was a complaint about unlicensed preaching going on. "Are you crazy?" said Moses, "I wish all God's people were prophets."

And that's what we came to hear today, brothers and sisters: the wistful voice of a tired man of God, worn out from his years on the road absorbing all the complaints of the faithful, wishing that all of his whining cats could hear God's Spirit and then pass the Word along. Just think of it: a whole community of prophets, all tuned in to God's will, all deeply concerned about the needs of their neighbors, all faithfully passing along the wisdom God gave them. What could we do for each other, if everyone took it as his or her responsibility to know and to speak and to implement the will of God? What could we do for our community if everyone took it as his or her responsibility, like the prophets of old, to preach justice and do justice? What if the Spirit came upon us and left not one person who only passively took, who only soaked up ministry like the Israelites gathered manna—What if the Spirit changed all the whiners into prophets?

"In those days," says the Lord, "I will pour out my Spirit on all flesh, and your sons and your daughters will prophesy." That's Pentecost—that's today. "To each is given the manifestation of the Spirit for the common good." That's Pentecost—that's today. "You are not in the flesh; you are in the Spirit, since the Spirit of God dwells in you." That's Pentecost, today and every Sunday. God's Spirit dwells in each of you, and dwells in all of us together. In the one Spirit we were all baptized into one body, Christ's body, and we all drank deeply of the one Spirit. What Moses wished for should be true with us—all God's people empowered by the Spirit to know and do the will of God. Can we join him in that prayer? I think we're likely to be surprised by God's response.—Richard Vinson

ILLUSTRATIONS

SPIRITUAL GROWTH.   Two things above all hinder our spiritual growth. On the one hand, our fretful concern about the state of our soul's health, and on the other, our self-seeking impulses that, in spite of all our prayer and meditation on God's Word, in spite of all our attempts at self-improvement, ever lurk within us, driving us to take ourselves more seriously than God, to consider our honor as more important than the honor of God, so that our pride refuses to bend beneath the yoke of the humility of Christ. As long as we are thus worldly and self-willed, Christ cannot take form and shape within us. There is no room for him. Our souls are blocked by the pressure of the world and of the self. If we do not begin to make ourselves of no account, then our Christian life will inevitably be impoverished.—Emil Brunner[20]

POWER FROM ON HIGH.   A daughter watched beside her mother's bedside through long weeks of illness, night after night, day in and day out. When it was over she said, "I didn't know it was in me to do all that." Who knows her own limits of strength? When we think we have reached the end of our string and then hold on with prayer, we touch "him who by the power at work within us is able to do far more abundantly than all that we ask or think" (Eph. 3:20 RSV).

It is this power from on high that came on the disciples at Pentecost. It is this power that made John Wesley feel his "heart strangely warmed" at Aldersgate and changed him from a seeking and rather stilted young priest into the formative spiritual force of the eighteenth century. It is this power that is the basic need of the Christian Church in the twenty-first century. As one critic has said, the church has increasingly efficient organization and buildings, but it lacks inspiration. Too many of us are trying to run our churches without the Holy Spirit.—Ralph W. Sockman

SERMON SUGGESTIONS

Topic: What Is Your Special Gift?

TEXT: 1 Cor. 12:3b–13

(1) The source (vv. 4–6). (2) The purpose (v. 7). (3) The variety (vv. 8–11). (4) The unity (vv. 12–13).

Topic: What to Do When You're *Really* Thirsty

TEXT: John 7:37–39

(1) Life's unsatisfied thirsts. (2) The drink that truly satisfies. (3) The living water that overflows.

CONGREGATIONAL MUSIC

1. "O Worship the King," Robert Grant (1833)
     LYONS; attr. Johann M. Haydn (eighteenth century)
     This grand hymn—a free paraphrase of Psalm 104 (which therefore could well replace the

---

[20]*The Great Invitation*

Psalter reading)—makes a wonderful opening for a service of worship. There are many descants and good free accompaniments available for use with the LYONS tune.

2. "Breathe on Me, Breath of God," Edwin Hatch (1878)

TRENTHAM, Robert Jackson (1888)

Based on the experience of the disciples with the Risen Christ, this prayer hymn could be sung as a natural response to the Gospel lesson (John 20:19–23). Congregational singing could be varied by having a soloist sing one or more of the stanzas.

3. "Wind Who Makes All Winds That Blow," Thomas H. Troeger (1983)

ABERYSWYTH, Joseph Parry (1879)

Thomas Troeger, a striking contemporary hymn poet, had the Acts passage (2:1–21) in mind when he wrote this compelling hymn. Singing it to the Parry tune can be a powerful prayer for the Spirit's coming to renew the Church.

4. "Like the Murmur of the Dove's Song," Carl P. Daw Jr. (1982)

BRIDEGROOM, Peter Cutts (1969)

One of the most appealing modern Pentecost hymns is this one by another fine American hymnist, Carl Daw. Its popularity is enhanced by the long expressive lines of the BRIDEGROOM tune. Unison antiphonal singing, phrase by phrase between choir and congregation would be effective, with everyone coming together on the refrain: "Come, Holy Spirit, Come."—Hugh T. McElrath

WORSHIP AIDS

CALL TO WORSHIP.   "I will sing unto the Lord as long as I live: I will sing praise to my God while I have my being" (Ps. 104:33).

INVOCATION.   O God, our Father, make this truly a house of prayer and song today. May we call upon you in the confidence that you hear the desires of our hearts and the words of our lips. Help us to surrender to you our selfishness and greed, so that nothing will hinder our proper worship.

OFFERTORY SENTENCE.   "But you shall receive power when the Holy Spirit has come upon you; and you shall be witnesses to me in Jerusalem, and in all Judea and Samaria, and to the end of the earth" (Acts 1:8 NKJV).

OFFERTORY PRAYER.   Teach us, good Lord, to serve thee as thou deservest: to give and not to count the cost, to fight and not to heed the wounds, to toil and not to seek for rest, to labor and not to ask for any reward, save that of knowing that we do thy will.—St. Ignatius Loyola

PRAYER.   (1) Pray for one another. Ask God to bless the persons next to you and those before and behind you. Ask that they be given strength for their tasks, courage to do what is right, faith to believe in themselves and others, and peace as a presence for their journey.

(2) Pray for the Church universal and this congregation in particular. Ask that you discover your place in the Church, your mission in Christ's name, your calling from God.

(3) Pray for the strugglers in life—those who are deep in sorrow, those who suffer debilitating illnesses, those who are restricted by disease, those whose loneliness seems never to

end, those in the depths of depression and despair. Ask that the comforter of all comforts bless them in their struggles and needs.

(4) Pray for the ones who have discovered the strength of joy. Pray that such good medicine will be shared with those around them, given to drastic situations, found available to everyone as we seek to enter the nearer presence of the Lord.

(5) Pray for the uncommitted among us—those who linger on the outskirts of faith, those who need to make clear-cut decisions about their relationship with the Lord, those who know that the road to really belonging to the Church leads through membership in the congregational family. Pray for those who were once alive to the fellowship of Christ and are now strangers to his presence and joy, that this may be the beginning of a new day in their faith journey. Pray that sacred vows will be made and meaningful dedications and commitments will come to all gathered with us today.

(6) Give praise to Father God for this hour, thank him for his goodness and mercy. Utter thanksgiving for every blessing already received and those yet waiting for us just beyond the moment. Thank him for what he will yet do in our midst as we wait expectantly before him with longing and hope.

Hear our prayers, O Lord, we pray.—Henry Fields

SERMON
Topic: A New Age upon Us
TEXT: Acts 2:1–21

Happy birthday, everyone! A glorious anniversary to you all! Today we celebrate a new beginning in world history. We rejoice in a world no longer ruled by the tyrannies and illusions of the present time, and we now surrender to the blessings of unity and understanding. We celebrate today the founding of a colony of heaven; we announce a beachhead established in our world bearing the force and energy of liberation. Pentecost represents the birthday of the Church, the community of a Messianic age set among the structures and agencies of this old age, reconciling, healing, demonstrating in a broken and divisive world the possibilities of challenging, dynamic, loving community. Happy birthday, new world. Happy birthday, new community.

That great narrative we read a few moments ago describes the power and dynamics of this new world we celebrate. The allusion of Luke, who wrote this narrative, to a reconciled humanity—referring to Parthians and Medes, Arabs and Jews, Greeks and Capadocians—envisions the ends of the Earth and all its national, creedal, racial, geographical, and tribal polarities embraced by the love of Christ and forged by the Spirit into a single, mutually encouraging and focused missionary community. Luke proclaims the universal possibilities of a torn and fragmented world finally healed by outgoing servant love. He knows it will be a gathering we have never experienced before. That is Peter who spoke those stormy and explosive words from the prophet Joel—those images suggesting new beginnings, like blood, fire, smoke, visions—radical discontinuities, the language of the apocalypse. These words illustrate a creation so new, so revolutionary, that it can be described in language no less charged and vivid.

This Pentecostal vision, this birth through the Spirit of the new age, draws us again into the world of the biblical promise. The roots of our identity as Christians, the cornerstone of our existence, rests on our hope. We Christians cherish the living legacy of the Hebrew prophets, for instance, because they envision new futures amid fierce and frequently murderous resistance. Remember the prophet Isaiah? He was a spokesman for the future if ever there was one. He promised a peaceable kingdom where the lion would lie down with the lamb, the infant would play over the viper's nest, where swords would be beaten into ploughshares and spears into pruning hooks, where we would neither learn nor engage in war anymore. Why is hope in such a place so striking? Because Isaiah's promise of peace comes while the evidence screams, "No way!" Isaiah and his people find themselves surrounded by empires, warlords, and tyrants hungering to invade their nation, slaughter the citizenry, and bend them to slavery. In the face of catastrophe, Isaiah sees history turned upside down, a reversal of violence and inhumanity, a peaceable world community through and beyond anticipated defeat and ruin.

Or Joel: the prophet included in our lesson this morning, the source of the vision in that very first Christian sermon, that passionate oration delivered by Peter to counter the bystander's accusation that the Spirit-filled Christian community was drunk and debauched so early in the morning. Joel: for all his wild imagery, what more vivid futuristic panorama could Peter have chosen for a festival of the Holy Spirit? Joel's words come to us from an agricultural land, a farming culture, devastated by drought—crops shrunken and burned as if by fire—but even worse, a land plagued by locusts devouring, mutilating, ravaging everything in their fierce and frenzied invasion. Joel spoke from amid a frightened and ruined people; starvation slinked and terror ruled among them. But Joel spoke for a future against a future mocked. He gathered a starving and desolate community, leaned on his God because finally that was all they had, and they were delivered. Hope against hope. Pentecost, you see, if it does nothing else, forges our vocation as a prophetic community reminding the world of a startling new future in which the dissonance of the human race will become the unity of the human family. That is the promise of Pentecost. That is the mission of God and God's Church.

How, then, do we celebrate this anniversary? How do we, a people born at Pentecost, keep alive to the promptings and power of the Spirit? We do it, I think, by remaining true to our Pentecostal beginnings, by committing ourselves to, working for, and exemplifying among ourselves and to the world's skeptical bystanders a new future for God's world.

And for all the apocalyptic imagery of the New Testament, the language of radical hope, we know that the immediate future is a function of staying power and will be built brick by brick, step by painful step. We know that the future of God in our time will come by perseverance and tenacity.

So, friends, how shall we celebrate Pentecost? How shall we rejoice in the new age forged by the Spirit? Let me offer an old-fashioned exhortation: Do not get discouraged about the possibilities for making a difference in God's world. Heaven knows that we in the churches, in our eagerness for survival, can get as inertia-bound as any human aggregation this side of heaven. But Pentecost reminds us that we are in existence not simply to survive in a risky time, but to stand and speak for a new future in this time. That is who we are: a community of the future—love's future. Pentecost envisions that future in radical terms. God grant, as the prophet Joel promises, that the Spirit may pour out on each of us and on this congregation as a whole, that young and old, male and female, may see visions, dream dreams, and live recreated in God's Spirit-transformed world.—James W. Crawford

SUNDAY, MAY 26, 2002

Lectionary Message

Topic: Blessing by the Trinity

TEXT: 2 Cor. 13:10–13

Other Readings: Gen. 1:1–2:4a; Ps. 8; Matt. 28:16–20

The New Testament never used the word *trinity,* and never raised, much less resolved, all the pertinent questions about how God's multiplicity and unity are connected. The later Church experimented with definitions, tried to wall off blind alleys, and fought over nuances, but the New Testament does none of this. Instead, our Scriptures mostly give us the Trinity in hymns and blessings, and in this case, in a benediction. Paul always ended his letters with a prayer or two, but the Trinitarian form is unusual for him. Is this a meaningless variation, or is he perhaps trying to put more folks on his side: "All the saints greet you, and the Father, Son, and Holy Ghost send their best, too"?

I. If you read the first ten verses of this chapter, you might never guess that Paul would wind up the letter with more than a perfunctory benediction. This chapter has the tone of a showdown; it sounds like something I'd yell at my kids: "All right, this is the last time I'm going to tell you to go to bed; don't make me come up there again." When Paul wrote 2 Corinthians 13:10–13, the believers he wrote to were at odds with him and with each other. They had insulted him, ignored his advice, and questioned his apostolic credentials. 2 Corinthians 13:10–13 was Paul's fiery self-defense, which he winds up with a stern warning. He was going to come back to see them and they were going to get to the bottom of this. If they wanted to back Paul into a corner, by golly, he'd have his miracles ready; if they wanted proof that he had the power of the Spirit, he would show them—but they wouldn't like it. It seems a long way from "Any charge must be sustained" and "I will not be lenient" to "grace, love, and communion be with you all." How does Paul get there?

II. First, he knows that they belong to Christ, even if they don't know that: "Do you not realize that Jesus Christ is in you?" This is grace: the favor of God, the very presence of God, freely offered, loyally maintained by virtue of God's character, and mediated through Jesus. Grace, said Paul, was what held him up through all of the beatings, imprisonments, disasters, and illnesses he had experienced in order to preach the gospel. Grace was what enabled him to live with his "thorn in the flesh" and with the realization that God would not answer his prayer to remove it. Grace is free, but not worthless; grace is ever present, but not insipid. The grace of the Lord Jesus could resurrect these troubled believers, making their chaotic community into an icon of the living Jesus. Paul could offer them "the grace of the Lord Jesus Christ" because he knew that despite their attitudes, grace was transforming them.

III. Paul cared about those folks, even in his anger and hurt. He told them, "Examine yourselves. . . . Test yourselves. . . . I hope you will find out that we have not failed." If they found themselves estranged from God, then Paul's faith was in question. If they were divided, then Paul's heart was torn. This is love: a commitment more than a feeling, a decision to be smack in the life of someone else. Listen to what he says a little earlier in this letter: "Here I am, ready to come to you this third time. . . . I will most gladly spend and be spent for you." Paul's love mirrors God's love here, because he will not abandon them and will not stop trying to do them good.

IV. Love doesn't mean that Paul will be happy with their sorry ways of living; love means he won't quit trying to move them toward God: "Put things in order, listen to my appeal, agree with one another!" Love moves Paul to push them toward communion, toward a common life with a common purpose.

In 2 Corinthians 13:10–13, Paul spends a lot of time explaining himself, and as he draws near the end, he feels a little self-conscious about it: "Have you been thinking all this time that we have been defending ourselves before you?" Well, yes, the reader responds. "Everything we do," says Paul, "is for the sake of building you up." In the end, Paul cares less about what they think of him than about how they fit together as a community: "I fear that there may be quarreling, jealousy, anger, selfishness, slander, gossip, conceit, and disorder. I fear that when I come again, my God may have to humble me before you, and that I may have to mourn over many who have sinned but haven't repented." When Paul prays, "May the communion of the Holy Spirit be with all of you," it is a passionate desire for God to re-create them, to blow away the barriers to unity and shape them into the body of Christ.

Paul knows that the Corinthian believers belong to Christ, and that God's grace through Christ is at work in them. He has committed himself to work for their good, even if it means pouring himself out for them, so he knows that they have seen something of God's love in how he, Paul, has loved them. And he hopes with all his heart that they can set aside the things that divide them from each other and from him and become a whole fellowship, a real communion of God's Spirit, sharing the kiss of greeting without pretense. Isn't that how we know the Trinity in our lives—not as words in a creed but as the goodwill, the sacrificial deeds, and the fervent prayers of other believers?—Richard Vinson

ILLUSTRATIONS

FAITH AND THE TRINITY.   The doctrine of the Trinity, which has had many harsh things said about it in recent years, has to be understood as the Church's attempt to describe in a brief formula how it came to know God and the only way a Christian can rightly know God. He is the God who from the beginning has been calling man into a covenant relation with himself—the only relationship in which life in this world makes sense and has a future. When his call from beyond our world was insufficient, he came to us in a person of our own flesh and blood and in him knocked on the door of our human life. He came in search of us in Jesus Christ, and where men let themselves be found, he took possession of their very selves, filled them with his Spirit, and through them extended his search for man. The Trinity describes God's invasion of our world, and the question for us is how we shall respond to this invader. Faith in him is surrender to his invasion, openness to the life he brings, readiness to let the life that comes to us from him go on through us to others.—James D. Smart[21]

A NEW REVELATION.   Jesus Christ is the one in whom human selfhood fully came to its own and lived its fullest life, as human life ought to be lived, because his human selfhood was wholly yielded to God, so that his whole life was the life of God. That was the one life which was wholly divine and wholly human. He lived his life in such a way that it was the life of God incarnate; but also, since the initiative is always with God, he lived it as he did

---

[21]*The ABC's of Christian Faith*

because it was the life of God incarnate. And thus through him there came to those who knew him a new revelation of God.

But what happened through him did not come to an end when "the days of his flesh" ended, though his disciples thought it would and were appalled at the prospect of his being taken from them. Very soon afterwards they made two great discoveries. They discovered, first, that the divine presence of which they had become aware while their Master was with them in the flesh had come back to them, and was going to continue, in a far deeper and more marvelous way, in a way that was independent of his actual presence in the flesh, though not independent of his having lived on earth in the flesh.—D. M. Baillie[22]

SERMON SUGGESTIONS

Topic: Answers to the Big Question

TEXT: Ps. 8, especially v. 4

(1) God uses the frailest—even infants—to praise him (v. 2). (2) God uses, to his honor and glory, mere mortals as his agents directing the affairs of his creation.

Topic: Some Doubted

TEXT: Matt. 28:16–20

(1) Devotion to Jesus persists despite doubt (vv. 16–17). (2) Jesus still entrusts his imperfect followers with a message for all the world (vv. 18–20). (3) Jesus reassures us of his unfailing presence until the end of the age (v. 20b).

CONGREGATIONAL MUSIC

1. "We Believe in One True God," Tobias Clausnitzer (1668); trans. Catherine Winkworth (1868)
    RATISBON, J. G. Werner's *Choralbuch* (1815)
    This hymn is a metrical version of the Trinitarian articles of the Apostles' Creed. It is therefore appropriate for use on Trinity Sunday in connection with either the Epistle reading or the Gospel lesson, both of which speak of the Triune God—Father, Son, and Holy Spirit.
2. "Maker, in Whom We Live," Charles Wesley (1747)
    DIADEMATA, George T. Elvey (1868)
    This less-known Wesleyan hymn appeared under the title "To the Trinity" in the author's collection of 1747. It is organized symmetrically to exploit the Trinitarian form in its first three stanzas, with a climax in the final stanza addressed to the "Eternal, Triune God." It would serve as a grand opening for worship.
3. "Lord, You Give the Great Commission," Jeffery Rowthorn (1978)
    ABBOTS LEIGH, Cyril V. Taylor (1941)
    No more significant hymn could be found to accompany the Gospel reading (Matt. 28:16–20) than this challenging text set to the majestic tune ABBOTS LEIGH. The hymn is rich in its references to aspects of the Great Commission. In those churches where this long broad melody is unfamiliar, the members of the choir should probably sing the first stanzas before the congregation joins them on the remainder of the hymn.
4. "Lord, Our Lord, Your Glorious Name," *Psalter* (1912)
    CHAUTAUQUA, William F. Sherwin (1877)

---

[22]*God Was in Christ*

This metrical paraphrase of Psalm 8 omits no thought of the original psalm. Therefore, it could be sung in place of the Psalter reading. Sung originally to "Day Is Dying in the West," the familiar hymn tune beautifully and effectively supports the words, which climax with "How great your name!"—Hugh T. McElrath

WORSHIP AIDS

CALL TO WORSHIP.   "O Lord, our Lord, how excellent is thy name in all the Earth! Who has set thy glory above the heavens" (Ps. 8:1).

INVOCATION.   No words of ours, O Lord, can adequately picture you, but you have revealed yourself to us, and we worship you for your great glory and for the love you have given to us in Jesus, in whose name we pray.

OFFERTORY SENTENCE.   "Each of you has been blessed with one of God's many wonderful gifts to be used in the service of others. So use your gift well" (1 Pet. 4:10 CEVJ).

OFFERTORY PRAYER.   You have given to each of us a special gift, O God, that we might bring your blessings to others. Help us to recognize the importance of the gift of giving and the joy of this part of our stewardship.

PRAYER.   Our memories are quickened this morning as we come into this worship setting, Father. Special times such as this Memorial Day send our thoughts into the past to recall the many young men and women who have heeded the call to serve our nation in defense of freedom. While many returned to chosen endeavors, others perished in far-flung fields and on seas of battle. How we wish that the endless rows of white crosses did not dot the cemeteries of the world. How we wish that the hearts of loved ones did not still break when they recall the price that their child, companion, friend, or relative paid that we might enjoy continued freedom. Yet we cannot recall the events of the past in order to change them. All we can do is express the deepest, heartfelt gratitude for what was done for us, and vow before you that we will strive to prevent such devastation from ever occurring again. Give us the courage to stand before evil and defeat it in your strength, we pray. Open our minds and souls to seeking every avenue available to remedy situations in the world short of armed conflict.

May we who have been presently entrusted with freedom's heritage guard our trust well so that future generations will enjoy the enormous benefits that freedom brings. May their memories of us be memories of a noble people who managed our trust well.

Now, as we worship, hear our prayers for the needs of those around us—the sick, the lonely, the sorrowing, the depressed, the struggling, the frightened, the tempted, and the lost. May each person find that your grace is sufficient to meet their needs, and then some.—Henry Fields

SERMON
Topic: A Gift Remembered—A Name Forgotten
TEXT: Matt. 26:6–13 KJV, NASB

Tomorrow is Memorial Day across the vast expanse of this great nation of ours.

The southern states were slow to observe Memorial Day because it was originally declared in 1868 by the Commander in Chief of the Union Army, John A. Logan, "for the purpose of strewing with flowers or decorating the graves of comrades who died in defense of their country during the late rebellion." No matter that subsequently that day has also honored all those who died in later wars. No matter that the blood of our grandfathers, fathers, brothers, husbands, and sons mingled with other American blood in the trenches of France, on the shores of the Pacific, in the snows of South Korea, or in the jungles of Vietnam. We'll never forget those dark hours of shame and disgrace, those hours of defeat and exploitation. But if we spitefully refuse to remember one, we forget all the others.

Remembering and forgetting—ah, how fickle we are. We lock up within the safety deposit boxes of our minds all the unkind words, all the injurious deeds, all the brusque rebuffs of a lifetime, waiting for an occasion to bring them out of hiding and heap them like coals of fire on another's head. And how quickly we forget the kind word, the gentle touch, the soft smile, the sympathizing tear.

It need not be so; and this is part of the good news we call the gospel. It results in gratefulness and commitment. But it does not happen automatically, and that is the reason for focusing on an unnamed woman who appeared in an unusual set of circumstances and did a most remarkable thing. Although her name has been forgotten, her deed, her gift, has been remembered. Just as Jesus predicted, "Wherever this gospel is preached in the whole world, what this woman has done shall also be spoken of in memory of her" (Matt. 26:13 NASB).

I. *A timely gift.* Notice, first of all, the timeliness of the woman's gift. Like our natural remembering and forgetting, we tend to get caught up in the drama of that last week in Jesus' life. We sense the bitterness of his opponents. We gasp at the treachery of Judas Iscariot. We are captured by the sense of intrigue and tragedy that leads Jesus to the cross. All is pointing toward Calvary and, beyond that, to an empty tomb.

Wedged in between the plotting of the leaders and the betrayal of Judas is this striking story: A woman appeared as an uninvited guest and stole the whole show when she broke a vial of costly perfume and anointed the head of Jesus. What presumptuousness! What wastefulness! Yet how timely was her gift!

Here, squeezed between the leaders who were seeking an opportunity to seize Jesus and kill him, and Judas, who was looking for a good opportunity to betray him, is the clue we are seeking. It is found in an unnamed woman who offered to Jesus in the most opportune moment a timely gift. There would be ample opportunities to minister to the needs of the poor; but *now* was the moment for Jesus! Now was the time of decision! This was her one chance, and she seized it, and her gift is remembered.

II. *An appropriate gift.* Next, notice the appropriateness of the woman's gift. To the untrained eye of the observer, what more useless gift could have been given to Jesus? Here is a poor, tired, itinerant preacher who is on his last go-round. What use does he have for expensive perfume?

No wonder his disciples were indignant. "What a waste! What a dreadful loss!" Certainly more useful and practical things could have been done with that gift.

Yet, to the eye that sees not the moment but the panorama of God's purpose, what a good deed the woman has done to Jesus! Or as the Revised Standard Version states, what a "beautiful thing" (v. 10). How good and how fitting under the circumstances.

Could not our discipleship also benefit from such an appropriate responsiveness? How often we give him part of ourselves instead of the whole and discover that *part* is simply not suitable for his purposes.

III. *A precious gift.* Third, let's notice the preciousness of the woman's gift. Although Matthew only told us that the perfume was "very costly" and could have been sold for a "high price," Mark filled in some of the details for us. Mark recorded that the perfume was "pure nard," which might have been sold for "three hundred denarii"; but even these details are lost on us who are unacquainted with Palestinian customs and measurements.

Nard was an expensive imported fragrance produced in India and brought to Palestine by caravans of traveling merchants. A denarius was a day's wages for an ordinary laborer. Thus, three hundred denarii would be approximately a year's wages for the common Palestinian worker.

We must be cautious, however, that we do not miss the point. Preciousness is not measured by some absolute monetary yardstick. A gift valued at $300 is not inherently superior to one valued at $200, or even $1, for that matter, especially as that gift is viewed through the eyes of the Master.

No wonder the story of the unnamed woman has been told again and again. Devotion like that inspires others to give their best and leads the lost to the Savior. Love never calculates. Love never thinks how little it can get by giving. Love's one desire is to give to the uttermost limits, to give the best.

IV. *The anonymous giver.* Why has she remained the nameless woman whose deed will never be forgotten?

Here is the final secret that now stands revealed in the pages of Holy Scripture. Her gift has been remembered and her name has been forgotten because she didn't allow herself to get in the way of her gift. Her gift was important not because of who gave it but because of to whom it was given.

There were others who cast their wealth into the Temple treasury that day as Jesus and his disciples stood by and watched. But it was an unnamed widow who cast in two mites who caught his eye and received his commendation. Others gave out of their surplus, but she gave out of her poverty, putting in all she had to live on. Her gift will be remembered, though her name has been forgotten.

And what of us? Shall we too seize our opportune moment and give our most appropriate and precious gifts to Jesus? Shall we too be remembered because we give to him our best?—Michael Fink

SUNDAY, JUNE 2, 2002
Lectionary Message

Topic: The Judgment Day Surprise!
TEXT: Matt. 7:21–29 NIV
Other Readings: Gen. 6:9–22; 7:24; 8:14–19; Ps. 46; Rom. 1:16–17; 3:22b–28 (29–31)

In life we all face surprises. Sometimes they are good and we enjoy them. Examples of these good surprises are having an unexpected birthday party thrown for you, being given a promotion that was never sought, finding out that your new stock has just skyrocketed in value, or something as simple as running into an old and dear friend and enjoying a pleasant walk down memory lane.

But some surprises are unwanted and unhappy experiences. Such examples are discovering that your company is downsizing and that you are on the list to be laid off, having the doctor tell you that cancer was discovered during your annual physical, or—one of the worst of all surprises—getting a phone call that offers the shocking news of the sudden and tragic death of a beloved child.

In the passage for this week, Matthew 7:21–29, we find Jesus explaining how the final, destiny-determining judgment for all humankind, often referred to by the Old Testament prophets (Isa. 2:11, 17; Joel 2:1; Mal. 3:17; 4:1), will be to many people—even many professing Christians—a huge and disastrous surprise. Many will find out—to their shock and dismay—that they are being excluded from the kingdom of heaven.

I. *The nature of the surprise.* As we open to Matthew 7:21, we find Jesus coming to the end of his Sermon on the Mount and ending with the flourish of a dramatic and surprising announcement: "Not everyone who says to me, 'Lord, Lord,' will enter the kingdom of heaven, but only he who does the will of my Father who is in heaven." In other words, he says—in a passionate warning of love—that those who plan to enter the kingdom must do more than claim his lordship; they must know and do the Father's will. And of course Jesus clearly implies that all he has just shared in the Sermon on the Mount ("these words," v. 24) is the Father's will. Jesus always claimed that he did and said nothing except as directed by the Father (John 8:28).

Then Jesus reinforces these shocking words with a powerful analogy between building a physical structure (a house) and building our lives (our characters). He says, "Therefore everyone who hears these words of mine and puts them into practice is like a wise man who built his house on the rock. The rain came down, the streams rose, and the winds blew and beat against that house; yet it did not fall, because it had its foundation on the rock" (Matt. 7:24–25).

What is surprising about all of this? The surprise is that many who call Jesus Lord will not be saved! To use this word, *Lord,* in this eschatological judgment context ("on that day," v. 22) is to recognize Jesus—at least verbally—as the Messiah. But even more, it is to acknowledge him as the judge who is making the ultimate decision about one's eternal destiny! These people think they are true disciples and claim they are, but they are not. What a devastating surprise to find out on judgment day!

II. *The magnitude of the surprise!* Now, the fact that people—apparently sincere—who call Jesus Lord will not be permitted into the kingdom is a surprise in itself, but the greater surprise is the sheer magnitude of the group's size and the degree of their miscalculation. It's a huge group that thinks they hold a valid ticket to the kingdom—yet they will be caught off guard and turned away. Jesus says: "Many will say to me on that day, 'Lord, Lord. . . .' Then I will tell them plainly, 'I never knew you. Away from me, you evildoers'" (Matt. 21:22–23). A reading of Matthew 25:41 suggests that this sending away involves being thrown into eternal fire and lost forever. What a change in destiny: from being one step away from the kingdom to being thrown into hell!

How can it be? How can so many people be so deceived? But according to Jesus, this will tragically be the case in the judgment! Many will make the claim that Jesus is their Lord, but under careful scrutiny it will be found that they are merely giving lip service.

This warning of Jesus should cause us all to pause and ask about the authenticity of our own claim to the kingdom and the soundness of our own profession of Jesus' lordship!

III. *The apparent injustice of the surprise.* But there appears to be an injustice here! Jesus tells these individuals who call him Lord "evildoers!" But the fact is that those who are rejected *appear* to be doing the good works that Jesus called for. In fact, when rejected, they cry foul in loud protests, claiming that they have indeed done the will of the Father and carried out the counsel of Jesus. They say, "Lord, Lord, did we not prophesy in your name, and in your name drive out demons and perform many miracles?" They sound off as if to say, "Hey, wait a minute Lord! Don't you remember all of the terrific things we did for you?" The force of their question in the Greek implies that they expect a positive answer.

And don't they have a point? What wonderful accomplishments they have apparently achieved—and all in Jesus' name! Haven't they done just what Jesus commanded them to do in the Sermon on the Mount: acts of righteousness and giving to the needy (Matt. 6:1-3)? Haven't they done the kinds of things suggested in the judgment context of Matthew 25:34-46? They seem to qualify fully for the kingdom—yet here is Jesus turning them away (v. 23). Obviously this is not only a surprising turn of events, but a devastating fate for these many people who thought they would receive a rich reward for their efforts. But is it really an injustice?

IV. *The justness of the surprise.* Jesus now explains not only that many who claim rights to the kingdom will be turned away, but *why*. He explains that this is done not on a whim or as an act of spite, but as a righteous act performed by a just judge. Notice his comments: "Then I will tell them plainly, 'I never knew you. Away from me, you evildoers!'"

Notice that he offers two reasons for their rejection. First, they never really "knew" Jesus. Despite the fact that these outcasts called him Lord, which was a claim to intimacy, allegiance, and submission, they really didn't know him in a deep, personal, saving way as Lord and best friend. Their knowledge of him was extremely superficial. That's why Jesus said, "I never knew you. Away from me. . ." (v. 23). The Greek for the verb in the phrase "I never knew you" can mean "I never recognized you" or "I never became acquainted with you." Jesus seems to suggest that while they may have thrown his name around, as though he were their friend, they did not treat his name as a saving, sacred name (see Acts 4:12; John 14:6-7).

The second reason that so many of these false disciples will justly be excluded from the kingdom is that they are evildoers (v. 23), despite their charade as godly disciples. The term *evildoers* (*anomia* in Greek), literally means "lawless ones." In 1 John 3:4, *lawlessness* is a clear definition for "sin." So these folks were full-blown, unrepentant sinners.

Yet, in Jesus' story of the coming judgment day, the rejected individuals apparently did some outwardly good things in his name. They claimed to have done good deeds by his power, that is, in his name (v. 22), but Christ dismissed this claim by sharply denying that these individuals had worked in partnership with him. Why were they and their purported good works evil? Because they were not done as acts of obedience to God's will and they were not done in Christ's power; rather, they were done to earn personal merit and glorify self. We know this because when they were rejected, they immediately recited all of the good things they had done: "Lord, Lord did we not" do this and that for you? Notice also that they did not put forward their faith in Jesus and their reliance on his atoning life, death, and saving grace as the basis for their entitlement to heaven (see Eph. 2:8-9a). In fact, their works were likely done through Satan, who works through sinful human beings to perform "counterfeit" miracles and wonders in order to deceive those who reject God's truth and love (2 Thess. 2:8-11; Rev. 16:13-14).

So, they were indeed justly rejected. But they shouldn't have been surprised by it. Jesus makes the requirements for the kingdom very clear. Remember Jesus' words earlier in this passage: "Not everyone . . . will enter the kingdom of heaven, but only he who does the will of my Father who is in heaven" (v. 21). This is the theme that Jesus drove home again when he shared the closing analogy of the wise and foolish builders (Matt. 7:24–27): "Therefore everyone who hears these words of mine and puts them into practice is like a wise man who built his house on the rock."

How can we avoid the judgment day surprise? By taking Jesus seriously!—Kenneth B. Stout

ILLUSTRATIONS

HEAVEN'S BUILDING CODE.   Today, most communities have building codes that require foundations to be of a certain depth, thickness, and quality. These are to protect people from themselves—that is, from their own carelessness—and from unscrupulous builders who might use inferior products and measurements when building the foundation for their homes. When we built our new home a few years ago, we had to have an authorized building inspector come and check out the concrete foundation that had been laid by our building contractor, to see if it met the code before anything could be constructed on it. We were glad for this code and this inspection process because we learned of a huge, expensive house not far away that looked impregnable but apparently had not been properly built or inspected and, consequently, crumbled after a couple of years of occupancy, causing great destruction. The instructions of Jesus in the Sermon on the Mount are not just suggestions, but vital guidelines—a kind of heavenly building code—for building strong, durable foundations for our lives, foundations that can help us withstand life's storms and take us securely through the judgment and safely into the kingdom!—Kenneth B. Stout

THE IMPORTANCE OF SPECIFIC OBEDIENCE.   Remember that Cain brought a gift of produce to the altar to worship God (an apparently good deed) but was rejected outright because it was not the specific gift (an animal sacrifice representing Christ's death) that God had requested. Cain was considered an evildoer because he ignored God's Word and did his own thing, whereas his brother, Abel, carefully listened to and obeyed God's request. He brought a slain animal for sacrifice—and was accepted as righteous (Gen. 4:3–7). If we respect God's words and carefully obey them through the grace and strength he provides through Christ, we can be certain of his favor and our happiness.—Kenneth B. Stout

SERMON SUGGESTIONS

Topic: Total Security
TEXT: Ps. 46
(1) God is our ultimate security (vv. 1–2). (2) What God permits and does is enough to make many fear and tremble (vv. 8–9). (3) To those in doubt or rebellion, God cries, "Give in; admit that I am God" (v. 10).

Topic: Religion to Be Proud Of
TEXT: Rom. 1:16–17
(1) It is good news of salvation. (2) It is for all. (3) It expresses the righteousness of God and results in righteous living.

CONGREGATIONAL MUSIC

1. "A Mighty Fortress Is Our God," Martin Luther (1529); trans. Frederick Hedge (1852)
   EIN FESTE BURG, Martin Luther (1529); harm. J.S. Bach (c. 1730)

No more thrilling start could be made to a service of worship than the singing of this, the greatest hymn about the greatest man in the greatest period of Church history. It is a free paraphrase of Psalm 46 and thus particularly appropriate.

2. "If You Will Trust in God to Guide You," Georg Neumark (1641); trans. C. Winkworth (1863)
   WER NUR DEN LIEBEN GOTT, Georg Neumark (1657)

This strong hymn with its reference to building on the rock that will not move would be quite suitable as a response to the Gospel reading about the wise man who built his house on a rock.

3. "We Have a Gospel to Proclaim," Edward Burns (1968)
   MENDON, trad. German melody; arr. Samuel Dyer (1824)

In connection with the Epistle lesson in Romans (1:16–17) in which the apostle Paul declared that he was not ashamed of the gospel, this hymn spells out the elements of that gospel. The internal stanzas dealing with the Incarnation, Crucifixion, Resurrection, and Ascension of Jesus could be sung antiphonally by two sections of the congregation, and stanzas 1 and 6 could appropriately be sung by all.

4. "My Hope Is Built," Edward Mote (1834)
   THE SOLID ROCK, William B. Bradbury

This grand gospel hymn that relates both to the Old Testament lesson about Noah and the flood and to the Gospel reading of the parable about the security of building a house on rock can be effective.—Hugh T. McElrath

WORSHIP AIDS

CALL TO WORSHIP.   "God is our refuge and strength, a very present help in trouble" (Ps. 46:1).

INVOCATION.   You have never failed us or forsaken us, O God, though sometimes we thought you had forgotten us. We thank you for coming to our aid in many ways—through a remembered verse of Scripture, the kind words of a friend, or the uplifting words of a hymn or sermon. Because we need you every day in every way, we come to you now and ask that your presence answer the yearnings and cries of our hearts.

OFFERTORY SENTENCE.   "And the king will answer, 'Truly I tell you: anything you did for one of my brothers here, however insignificant, you did for me'" (Matt. 24:40 REB).

OFFERTORY PRAYER.   Grant, we beseech thee, almighty God, that our gifts, being dedicated to thy service, may be used for the good of thy Church and the welfare of thy people; through Jesus Christ our Lord.—*Minister's Worship Manual*

PRAYER.   Here we are, Father, part of the huddled masses yearning for that something more that completes life. In our brokenness we come, having tried in our own strength to make life work our way, only to see it fall apart. In our sorrow we come, having been wounded by the events of life, which tear at our hearts, bringing pain to our days and tears to our nights. In our lostness we come, having chosen pathways of lesser value to follow and missing your highway of life. In our guilt we come, drowning in those emotions and feelings that haunt us with their condemnation because we know our actions, words, and thoughts were evil. In our loneliness we come—lonely many times even when we stand in the midst of people, lonely for that home where things are right and which always seems just out of sight over the horizon. In hope we come, believing that you and you along have the words of life, know the way we should go, care for us with an unending concern, save us to the uttermost, and prepare a place for us where neither moth nor rust can corrupt and where thieves cannot break through and steal. In expectation we come, believing that you will not leave us or forsake us, that you will not leave us comfortless, that you will not forever hide your face from us, that you will love each of us as if there were only one of us to love.

So here we are, Father, each of us here for his or her particular reason. We need to experience in this hour what we cannot find anywhere else except in the presence, power, and worship of you, the God and Father of our Lord Jesus Christ. O God of our fathers, God of all revelation, God of every person's salvation, God of unending grace and love, come to us even now, we pray, as we wait reverently and expectantly together in Jesus' name.—Henry Fields

SERMON

Topic: Discovering Yourself

TEXT: Gen. 37:1–11; Mark 10:17–22

Joseph is our model today for discovering some lessons on knowing where we are. Joseph is no ideal example of a person who had his life all together. He was a flawed hero. The biblical record about Joseph covers chapters 37 through 50 in Genesis. This long epic presents an account of Joseph's struggle to find himself. As a young man, he struggled to know where he was. The negative reaction of his brothers to his dreams about the whole family bowing down to him is not surprising. His superior attitude and favorite-son position did not generate admiration or strengthen family unity. His arrogance and conceit only created hatred and jealousy. He was a pampered young man whose colorful coat with its long sleeves was not suitable for a working man but for the leisure class. The rest of the family was engaged in hard manual labor while Joseph assumed the role of a princely lord who had a favored position with his father. His self-conceited attitude indicates that he was still trying to discover who he was.

Joseph demonstrates that we don't discover where we are simply by knowing some information or facts about ourselves. Joseph already told them too frequently that he was the firstborn and favorite son of his father. He was the son of Rachel and the dreamer of grandiose dreams. But that information was not sufficient to reveal the real Joseph.

If we are going to learn where we are, we need self-control. As Joseph matured through his hard lessons, his behavior indicates that he had inner strength. Joseph was made a slave in Potiphar's house. Under Joseph's management, the household prospered. Potiphar's wife tried to seduce Joseph, but he rejected her temptation and fled out of the house, leaving behind his outer garment. When you consider Joseph's circumstances, it may have been better for him if he had yielded to the sexual advances of Potiphar's wife. "Who does he think he is?" she may have thought. "Slaves don't have rights. They are property." Whatever their masters wanted they were supposed to do. Joseph was a young man who knew the urges of the flesh, but he also had high moral standards. He executed self-control at a difficult moment in his life.

Move further into the story of Joseph and you will find that not only did Joseph demonstrate self-control but he also seemed to have an inner peace and a sense of being in tune with God. Even when he was sold into slavery, put in prison, and seemingly rejected at every turn, he seemed to be at peace with himself and sought to make the best of the situation. The way Joseph advanced in Potiphar's house shows him making the best he could of where he was. The Scriptures say that Potiphar's house was blessed because of Joseph, and he did the best he could, even in prison.

Joseph's inner peace came from an awareness that God was directing his life. Even when his life was difficult, he believed that God was present to sustain him. Later, when Joseph rose to a position of great power in Egypt, he gave God the credit for all that had happened. God was working in his life during the times of affliction as well as in the times of prosperity.

God doesn't remove all problems and difficulties from our lives, but he remains with us in the midst of all of these struggles and gives us his peace. "My peace," Jesus says, "give I unto you."

Joseph also discovered that difficulties and problems are a part of life. Here was a young man who had been the favorite son of his father. He had his every need met. He thought he was the center of the world. His brothers became jealous, plotted at first to kill him, but decided instead to sell him into slavery. Things went from bad to worse, for the household slave was soon cast into prison. His circumstances seemed to have reached bottom. But in the midst of all of the difficulties, he continued to have faith in God. Joseph was certain that God's purpose for his life would triumph.

Joseph learned that in the midst of all of his difficulties and problems—even slavery and imprisonment—God was with him. He was sure that God was in control. He believed in the providence of God. "You meant evil against me," Joseph later said to his brothers, "but God meant it for good, to bring it about that many people should be kept alive, as they are today" (Gen. 50:20). He acknowledged God's presence in the bad as well as the good. God doesn't deliberately send evil, suffering, pain, and failures into our lives. But as Paul reminds us, "God can work in all things to bring about good" (Rom. 8:28).

Joseph, who had experienced so much abuse at the hands of his brothers, developed into a forgiving person. His brothers had plotted to put him to death but decided to sell him as a slave, and he was taken in chains to Egypt. In Egypt he rose to high positions, first in Potiphar's house as a slave and then as Pharaoh's right hand man as the Minister of Agriculture. Later his brothers came down from Canaan during a famine in their country and sought to buy food from him. What did he do? Did he take vengeance on them? No, he discovered through a test, in which he put his silver cup in Benjamin's sack, that Judah and the other brothers had also changed and were willing to remain as slaves rather than see their brother Benjamin enslaved. Joseph revealed who he was to his brothers and forgave them for what they had done twenty years in the past.

When you and I have experienced difficulties, hurts, and abuses from others, one of the great lessons of a mature person is his or her willingness to forgive.

Finally, one of the great truths in the story about Joseph is that God was always going before him. Whether he was a slave or in prison, he trusted God. He didn't spend all of his time looking back to Canaan, where his family was and where everything had been ideal for him. He could have spent all of his time thinking about "how wonderful life was back then." Instead, he focused on where he was now and looked to the reality of God's presence to sustain him. He trusted God to go before him into the future. In quiet trust, he leaned on God for assurance.

Jesus has called us to come follow him into the future. He offers to lead us. When we follow him, we will surely know where we are.—William Powell Tuck

SUNDAY, JUNE 9, 2002
Lectionary Message
Topic: Inclusion for an Age of Exclusion!
Text: Matt. 9:9–13 (See also Mark 2:14–17; Luke 5:27–32 NASB)
Other Readings: Gen. 12:1–9; Ps. 33:1–12; Rom. 4:13–25

This passage is an interesting and inspirational story of Matthew's decisive response to Jesus' invitation to become one of his twelve disciples. It shows Matthew to be a powerful model of immediate and wholehearted commitment. Now, we could focus today on Matthew (also called Levi, Mark 2:14) and his wonderful example and have a great sermon. But this morning I suggest that Matthew's call to discipleship and his response to it have even more value when viewed as a revelation of the new kind of teacher that Jesus was (Matt. 7:28–29; 9:10) and of the exciting good news he was presenting (Matt. 4:16–17).

I believe that a careful examination of the narrative will show that Jesus was using the story of Matthew to unveil the wonderful truth that his message about the kingdom included everyone—even those sinners who were normally excluded! (Matt. 9:12–13). In other words, by the way Jesus treated Matthew in this story, he was communicating the message of an *inclusiveness* almost unheard of in that time. Notice the evidence.

I. *First, the very act of calling Matthew to be a disciple projects inclusiveness.* Matthew was a tax collector living in Capernaum (v. 9). Since he is described as "sitting in the tax collector's booth" (Matt. 9:9), commentators generally conclude that he was probably not a door-to-door agent but more of a customs official. He likely collected revenues or excise taxes from caravans and travelers passing along the main road, which crossed the border between the territories of Herod and Philip Antipas.

Now, tax collectors—including revenue agents—were not looked at with favor by most of the Jewish people. They were usually considered unpatriotic for helping their pagan conquerors collect taxes among their own people. They were also considered to be contaminated by their involvement with Gentiles and secular Jews. But mostly they were hated because they often oppressed and defrauded their own people for selfish financial gain. As a result, they were treated as social and religious outcasts.

What a surprise, then, when Jesus called Matthew—one of these despised tax collectors—to be one of his disciples, and in a very public way. The record says of Jesus, "He saw a man called Matthew, sitting in the tax collector's booth, and he said to him, 'Follow Me!' And he got up and followed him" (Matt. 9:9). It was considered a scandalous act for Jesus to make such a man a part of his inner circle, but Jesus did it intentionally. He did it to show that he was no ordinary teacher and that he would not abide by old taboos.

II. *Second, the act of going to Matthew's home and eating with him projects inclusiveness.*

Matthew was so pleased that Jesus accepted him and invited him to be one of his followers that he sponsored a huge party at his home in honor of Jesus. In the Gospel of Matthew, the details aren't as clear on this point as they are in Mark's and Luke's accounts of the same story (Matt. 9:9–10; Mark 2:14–17; Luke 5:29–30). Luke reports, "And Levi [Matthew] gave a big reception for him [Jesus] in his house; and there was a great crowd of tax collectors and other people who were reclining at the table with them. The Pharisees and their scribes began grumbling at Jesus' disciples, saying, "Why do you eat and drink with the tax collectors?" (vv. 29–30).

Now, it is quite amazing that Jesus actually went to Matthew's home and ate with him. This is groundbreaking stuff! It appears to have been the first time that Jesus so openly manifested the inclusiveness of his ministry. Meanwhile, the Pharisees and other opponents began to attack Jesus. They felt that to associate with such people was to open oneself to contamination and impurity, but to go to their homes and eat with them was even more galling. At this time, and in this culture, going to someone's home and eating with him was seen as a clear sign of intimacy and friendship. So the fact that Jesus ate with Matthew was seen by the Pharisees as gross impropriety and immorality. This is why they grumbled so loudly to Jesus' disciples, "Why is your teacher eating with tax collectors and sinners?" (Matt. 9:11).

Jesus, by his example, unabashedly proclaims that it is fully appropriate to go to the home of a sinner, and he rejects the idea of ranking and categorizing people based on superficial prejudices. Matthew was sincerely seeking a better life and opening up to the Holy Spirit—certainly a valid reason to visit him. Jesus explained his actions to the grumbling Pharisees this way: "It is not those who are healthy who need a physician but those who are sick" (Matt. 9:12).

III. *Third, the act of accepting and dining with Matthew's friends projects inclusiveness.* Jesus not only went home and ate with Matthew, but he freely accepted, dined alongside of, and spent precious time with Matthew's friends. Remember, according to Luke's account of this same story, Matthew threw a big reception for Jesus and invited a great crowd of his friends (Luke 5:29). But this great crowd was made up not primarily of nice, upstanding people, but of tax collectors and sinners (Matt. 9:10). These were the people whom Matthew knew and associated with, so it was only natural for him to invite them. They were his friends and workmates, and he wanted them to meet Jesus—a very different kind of spiritual leader, with whom he had come to feel comfortable. He was confident that his friends would enjoy and appreciate Jesus as much as he did—and apparently they did, and so had a wonderful banquet.

Now, to dine with Matthew—who had agreed to be Jesus' follower—was one thing, but to break bread and spend time with Matthew's many friends was quite another, especially since Matthew's friends were *sinners,* a term meaning "irreligious people" or, as one commentator described them, "notoriously evil people." The term *sinner* in this setting was generally understood to refer to tax collectors, adulterers, robbers, Gentiles, and the like.

But again, Jesus did not shy away from associating with these sinners. His consistent argument was that these were the very people he should be spending time with (Matt. 9:12). He responded to the condemning Pharisees with a known rabbinic phrase: "Go and learn what this means: '*I desire compassion and not sacrifice*'" (Matt. 9:13). This was a partial citation of Hosea 6:6, where Hosea expressed concern about a religion that is all about externals at the expense of mercy. In citing this passage, Jesus was suggesting that the Pharisees were so overly concerned about ceremonial and external purity that they were ignoring the real needs of struggling sinners and were therefore wrongly excluding them from God's mercy and forgiveness. The fact is that many of these so-called sinners were hungering and thirsting for righteousness (as Matthew had been) and consequently were closer to true righteousness than the self-satisfied Pharisees. Once Jesus made clear his attitude toward Matthew, other tax collectors and sinners became a large percentage of his audiences and some of his strongest supporters (Luke 15:1–2).

Notice that Jesus did not fear being "corrupted" by these worldly friends of Matthew, but rather saw this party as an opportunity to affect them with his purity and love, that is, to open a door of dialogue. And no doubt he took advantage of it. Perhaps Jesus was invited to speak and share the good news with them. Surely Matthew wanted to show off Jesus and make clear to his friends why he was giving up tax collecting and making other major changes in his life. The fact is that by rubbing shoulders with these unchurched friends of Matthew, Jesus was again signaling his inclusiveness and his desire to bring all people into the kingdom of heaven.

In the end, then, we learn that Jesus' call to Matthew was a message to all the world, and especially to us—the Church—that discrimination must be replaced by inclusivness if we are to proclaim the gospel after the pattern of our Lord!—Kenneth B. Stout

ILLUSTRATIONS

WHEN EVERYONE IS IMPORTANT.   Every four years when there is an election here in the United States, politicians are eager to reach out to and include as many groups of people as possible—even groups whom they have neglected (and perhaps even disagreed with) during the previous four years. Eager for their vote, these politicians suddenly begin visiting these groups and their communities, speaking to them, making great promises to them, catering to them in every way imaginable—all in order to gain their support and get elected. In our most recent election, in 2000, this was especially evident. Because the election was so very close, politicians of both major parties, at every level, made sure that they were as all-inclusive as possible during their campaigns. They sought out Catholics, Muslims, Jews, African Americans, gun owners, soccer moms, Hollywood stars, sports heroes, single parents, the religious right, and the social left. How sad, that, as a nation, we can have such a vigorous spirit of inclusiveness when it is for selfish and political purposes, yet after elections these same groups—some with serious needs—are often neglected by our political leaders and the country at large. This kind of pseudo-inclusiveness is far different from that which was taught and practiced by Jesus Christ when he was on the Earth. He truly cares about all people and wants to include them in his eternal plans.—Kenneth B. Stout

BEWARE OF THE EVIL OF PREJUDICE.   Many of us will remember the terrible airplane tragedy that occurred off the New York coast several years ago, when a jumbo jet was blown apart by a massive and mysterious midair explosion. Everyone on board was lost. Long before there was any solid evidence of foul play, many Americans—including some crash investigators—began speculating that the explosion may have been caused by a terrorist bombing or nighttime missile attack. Almost immediately, rumors began to circulate that it was likely carried out by someone from the Middle East, perhaps an Arab or Muslim who hated the United States. There was a terrible rush to judgment that concluded that the perpetrator must be someone from that part of the world because, in the minds of many, that is where terrorists come from. And, unfairly, certain people who were associated with the flight and of Middle Eastern origin were targeted as suspects. One man in particular was detained and accused. In the end, however, it was determined that the explosion was not caused by a terrorist attack at all but most likely by a fuel tank explosion caused by an electrical spark given off by faulty wiring. Later it was acknowledged that unwarranted prejudice against people of Middle Eastern origin had driven the rush to judgment and given rise to the false accusations. How careful we must be not to hold prejudices against whole groups of people because of the actions of a few.—Kenneth B. Stout

SERMON SUGGESTIONS

Topic: A Journey by Stages

TEXT: Gen. 12:1–9

(1) God had plans for Abram (v. 1). (2) God made promises to Abram (vv. 2–3). (3) Abram remembered the God who had called him (vv. 7–8).

Topic: How to Win with God

TEXT: Rom. 4:13–25

(1) Like Abraham, hope against hope in God's promise for the significance of your life. (2) Like Abraham, trust in God's grace for your relationship to him, a faith that counts for righteousness.

CONGREGATIONAL MUSIC

1. "I Sing the Mighty Power of God," Issac Watts (1715)

   ELLACOMBE, *Gesangbuch der H.W.K. Hofkapelle* (1784)

   FOREST GREEN, English melody; arr. Ralph Vaughan Williams (1906)

   This great Wattsian hymn breathes the spirit of the Psalter reading (Ps. 33:1–12) and could well serve as a response to it. Alternately, it could be used to inaugurate singing worship, using either of its fine tunes.

2. "Immortal Love, Forever Full," John G. Whittier (1806)

   SERENITY, William V. Wallace (1856)

   The fifth stanza of this poetic hymn (beginning with the words, "The healing of his seamless dress") relates directly to Jesus' healing of the woman with the issue of blood by her touch of his garment. This hymn could thus be effectively used in connection with the Gospel lesson in Matthew 9.

3. "Faith of Our Fathers," Frederick W. Faber (1849)

   ST. CATHERINE, Henri F. Hemy (1864)

   Abraham's faith as recorded both in the Old Testament lesson (Gen. 12:1–9) and in the Epistle (Rom. 4:13–25) can receive an appropriate response in the singing of this hymn that exalts the faith of our fathers.

4. "Make Me a Channel of Blessing," Harper G. Smyth (1903)

   EUCLID, Harper G. Smyth (1903)

   God promised Abraham that he would be blessed in order to be a blessing to countless others (Gen. 12:2). This gospel song could well serve as a response to the Old Testament reading. To avoid repetition that often becomes meaningless, the first three questioning stanzas could be sung before singing the refrain.—Hugh T. McElrath

WORSHIP AIDS

CALL TO WORSHIP.   "The counsel of the Lord stands forever, and the plans of his heart to all generations" (Ps. 33:11 NKJV).

INVOCATION.   Give us today, O Lord, clearer insight into your will for all people of all kinds, and give us a deepening love that will enable them to know your love and plans for them.

OFFERTORY SENTENCE.   "Set your mind on God's Kingdom and his justice before everything else, and all the rest will come to you as well" (Matt. 6:33 REB).

OFFERTORY PRAYER.   God give us the willingness to support those causes that reflect your justice and show the meaning of your Kingdom here on Earth. To that end, bless the offerings we bring today.

PRAYER.   Lord, make us instruments of your peace. Where there is hatred, let us sow love; where there is injury, pardon; where there is discord, union; where there is doubt, faith; where there is despair, hope; where there is darkness, light; where there is sadness, joy. Grant that we may not so much seek to be consoled as to console; to be understood as to understand; to be loved as to love. For it is in giving that we receive, it is in pardoning that we are pardoned, and it is in dying that we are born to eternal life.—Attributed to St. Francis, *The Book of Common Prayer*

SERMON
Topic: Roots and Wings
TEXT: Luke 18:9–17

Today we are observing Children's Sabbath—a day set aside in churches and synagogues across the country to focus on God's call to care for the most vulnerable ones in our midst: our children.

Children's Sabbath celebrates not just teens but all young people, and in fact it's a day not simply for them but for all of us. To embrace and care for our children is to embrace something essential about all our lives.

Do you remember what it's like to be a teenager? It is a time when the world is opening up in countless ways as young people discover their strengths, their talents, and their enthusiasms.

I remember often feeling that I couldn't measure up. Little League was over, so I was no longer spending large stretches of my life in right field. But athletes were increasingly the stars of my little world, and I wasn't one. At some time in my teens I fully discovered the opposite sex, but even by the end of my teens I was still trying to overcome my shyness when I was with those mystical creatures. I eventually did fall in love, and before my teens were over, was dropped by the young woman I was sure was the love of my life.

Of course I experimented with all sorts of things—clothes, behavior, attitudes. No, I didn't inhale. But there were other, fairly minor league ways to get into mischief. And when I did wander from the straight path, I was fortunate enough to have in the adults around me a healthy balance of love and limits, of firm discipline and forgiveness.

I remember plenty of happy times and some disappointments—so much to learn, experience, and explore. Underneath it all, though, I think I most remember being unsure, unsettled, sometimes lonely. "Who am I?" I kept wondering. In this huge, confusing world, where do I fit in?

The children and teens we honor today are themselves launched on the same perilous quest we all share, to discover who they are as children of God, to grapple with the destructiveness and evil that come their way, to face the temptations everywhere to sell themselves short and not believe in who they are.

In fact, by all appearances, we as a society are profoundly ambivalent about our children. On the one hand, we dote on them. We buy them things, lots of things. We cheer them on, urge them to achieve, nudge them constantly into being more mature and goal oriented, driving ourselves to the brink of exhaustion to provide for them.

Our society is drawing nearly every adult out of home and community and into a stressful world of work, and often what is lost is the time love takes, the time for attention.

We are only beginning to measure the impact of such a violent culture on our children. One study by the American Psychological Association finds that the average child watched eight thousand televised murders and one hundred thousand acts of violence before finishing elementary school. And one in six youths between the ages of ten and seventeen has seen or knows someone who has been shot.

So, much of this violence is the consequence of a driven culture and economy that prize success above everything else. We push, we spend, we pack our days ever tighter, and somehow many of us seem to be making it. But what are the consequences for the vulnerable among us, for our children and our teens, for our souls, for the children within us?

We and our children need what we might call a stress-free zone, a zone where the drivenness and anxiety around us are held at bay, where we and our children can simply be with each other.

In our Gospel lesson, Jesus is pushing us to see a truth that seems almost impossible to accept. Look, he says, at these two people who have come into the Temple to pray. There's the Pharisee: a fine, upstanding man who has done everything right—fasting, saying his prayers, paying his tenth to the Temple. He's what we might call the archetype of the traditional Episcopalian—well-educated, honest, responsible, making his full pledge to Trinity Church—and he simply thanks God for making him who he is.

And then there's the tax collector: as sleazy and pushy as they come, always on the make, despised and distrusted by everyone. He's probably just finished squeezing some money out of someone else when he slips into church, and something happens. He starts beating his breast and saying, "God, be merciful to me, a sinner."

And then Jesus throws the curve: It's the tax collector who goes away with God's blessing, not the good, decent Pharisee.

This isn't a parable of who's good and who's bad, but of who's blessed and who isn't. It isn't about a good Pharisee and a bad tax collector, but about a God who loves us with abandon, no matter what. And it seems that the one requisite of being blessed, of receiving God's love, is needing it, and knowing that we need it. That's all the tax collector had going for him.

But then, the very next words in the Gospel after this passage are the story of people bringing their children to Jesus. When the disciples try to push them away Jesus says, "No, don't stop them, for to such as these belongs the Kingdom of God." He goes on to say, "Whoever does not receive the Kingdom of God as a little child will never enter it."

Do you see the connection? The key to discovering what life is about, to receiving God's blessing, is being in a position of neediness, of vulnerability. It's when we can be as open as that tax collector, as needy as a little child, that we can receive the peace and love that God wants to give us.

And it is the mission of the Church to be a place where we and our teens can experience that kind of acceptance.

There is an old saying that what our children need most from us are roots and wings. They need to know who they are, where they belong, who their people are, what their values are, where they will find life's meaning; and they need to be helped to fly, to go with the air that will carry them, to know their strengths and their limits, to have a vision of where they are headed. It is our task as a church to be a place where our children can find both of these things, and both of them—roots and wings—are gifts from the family and the Church.— Samuel T. Lloyd III

SUNDAY, JUNE 16, 2002
Lectionary Message
Topic: Our Readiness for Service—The Real Test

TEXT: Matt. 9:35–38; 10:8 NIV
Other Readings: Gen. 18:1–15 (21:1–7); Ps. 116:1–2, 12–19; Rom. 5:1–8

Over and over again we are reminded in Scripture that we are Christ's ambassadors and witnesses to the world. We are responsible for sharing the gospel where we live and among the people with whom we associate every day (2 Cor. 5:20). But are we doing it—and are we doing it successfully? Do we have the right motivations, attitudes, strategies, and message to evangelize the world around us effectively? In other words, are we truly ready for Christian service?

I suggest that a brief look at Matthew 9 will help us answer these questions, because in this chapter we find what it takes to be ready for this task, especially as we focus on verses 35 to 38. In this passage we are given a captivating look at how Jesus himself presented the gospel to the population centers of his day. It's the record of his own Galilean outreach, just before sending out the twelve apostles.

I. *Jesus' motivation for ministry in Galilee.* It is very clear that Jesus' ministry in Galilee was motivated by a powerful love and desire to seek out people who need help, hope, and deliverance from sin and disease. Notice the record: Jesus went through all the towns and villages, teaching in their synagogues, preaching the good news of the Kingdom and healing every disease and sickness. When he saw the crowds, he had compassion on them, because they were harassed and helpless, like sheep without a shepherd (Matt. 9:35–36 NIV).

Now, this account tells us a lot. The historian Josephus notes, for example, that there were some 204 cities and villages in Galilee alone at that time. Each location was thought to have at least fifteen thousand people; that meant a total population of more than *three million!* But Jesus took the initiative and, driven by selfless love for people, went with vigor and enthusiasm to seek and save the lost (Luke 19:10).

II. *Jesus' attitude toward the people of Galilee.* Remember that as Jesus traveled from place to place he drew enormous crowds. But even more impressive than that fact was the marvelous way he reacted to them. This reaction had nothing to do with celebrating his rapidly growing reputation or showing off his amazing rhetorical skills and miracles; rather, it has to do with his attitude toward the people and his attention to their needs.

According to Matthew, Jesus' attitude and reaction to the people was always the same: "When he saw the crowds, he had compassion for them" (Matt. 9:36). To Jesus, these crowds were more than masses of people; they were individuals with urgent needs and great potential. Jesus saw these individuals as the average person did not: as "harassed and helpless, like sheep without a shepherd" (9:36b). He looked below the surface, beyond the income level, and behind the mask and saw them as they really were: bullied and oppressed.

He saw them as harassed by the Romans, by Jewish traditions, by injustice, by crushing poverty, and by their own piercing guilt. He also saw them as helpless. Their attempts to reform the brutal and dominating systems of society were futile, and personal choices were limited. Finally, Jesus saw them as sheep without a shepherd (9:36), that is, without direction or leadership and with few authentic caregivers.

III. *Jesus' attitude toward the people of today.* So what is Jesus' attitude toward the people we face and live among today, in cities like Los Angeles, Chicago, and Atlanta? Has his attitude changed with the passage of time? No! Jesus' understanding and compassion bridge the time and distance between ancient Galilee and modern Georgia.

Oh, sure, some of the particulars have changed, but the broad, basic needs of society remain—and so does Jesus' compassion. When Jesus sees the crowds cheering at a football game, or searching for food on the empty shelves of a third-world market, or struggling to survive floods in Southeast Asia, he views them with the same sensitivity and care as we read about in Matthew 9:35–36.

IV. *Jesus' timeless message and strategies for meeting people's needs.* Yes, Jesus met the needy people of Galilee with compassion, but that compassion was not static. It was immediately translated into dynamic intervention and loving action. Jesus met the people's needs by compassionately employing three simple but powerful strategies. The record says he came "teaching in their synagogues, preaching the good news of the Kingdom, and healing every disease and sickness" (Matt. 9:35).

Jesus knew just what the people in his day needed: solid, God-based teaching. So he taught them truth that set them free. He preached the Kingdom to them. This was his primary message. He proclaimed his kingship and their freedom to claim rights to it.

His third strategy was to heal all of their diseases. He raised the dead, made the blind see, cast out demons, and freed minds of sin. In fact, Jesus' ministry triggered a dynamic spiritual renaissance in ancient Galilee—something he surely longs to do again today, through us!

V. *Jesus' example: The real test of readiness for meeting people's needs.* There's a crucial lesson for us to learn here from Jesus' example of service. The powerful strategies of teaching, preaching, and healing, as important as they are, are never sufficient by themselves. They must be energized and undergirded by compassion. Every effort we make to bring people to Christ, to involve them in the Church, to hold them for the Kingdom, will fall short of its goal unless energized by authentic Christian compassion.

So the real tests of our readiness for service are (1) Are we motivated by Christ's selfless love? (2) Are we witnessing with the compassionate attitude of Jesus? (3) Are we employing his three dynamic strategies to touch needy lives? and finally, (4) Are we proclaiming the good news that he has come as King and that his kingdom is now available to everyone? If we can answer yes to each of these questions, I suggest that we are ready for service.

VI. *Jesus' call to recruit others to meet people's needs.* There was a problem during Jesus' ministry in Galilee, in the midst of all the success. The response was so great that Jesus couldn't take care of all the people. Being in human form, he depended on his followers to be partners with him in ministry. Be he just didn't have enough people working with him. There was the very real danger that the enormous interest and enthusiasm generated by Christ's ministry would be lost unless Christ could gain additional workers.

So, in the midst of his overwhelming success in Galilee, Jesus made an urgent plea to his disciples: "The harvest is plentiful but the workers are few. Ask the Lord of the harvest, therefore, to send out workers into his harvest field" (Matt. 9:37–38). So the disciples did ask, and also offered themselves in service as apostles (Matt. 10:1, 9–14; Mark 6:6–12).

I believe that Jesus, through this account, is also calling us today to get involved, to pray for, and to recruit others to work alongside him in loving service. But why would he be calling us today? Because we face a situation parallel to that of Jesus' day. Again, there are enormous needs in the world. Again, the masses need compassionate teaching, preaching, and healing. Again, the potential exists for a great harvest. And again, there's a shortage of workers. Let's go to work for the one who has done the ultimate work for us, on the cross of Calvary!—Kenneth B. Stout

ILLUSTRATIONS

SELF-SACRIFICE INCREASES THE IMPACT OF COMPASSION.   Tony Compolo once told the story of being asked to serve as the keynote speaker at a fundraiser sponsored by a group of prosperous people. It was a very worthy and compassionate cause and he was happy to do it. But Compolo surprised the group by challenging them to begin their campaign by opening up their own wallets and purses and donating what they had at the moment. They agreed, but some were a little reluctant because they had quite a large amount of cash on them. They hadn't planned on giving such a sizeable gift. Compolo was testing the depth of their commitment to the fundraiser and the degree to which they would sacrifice themselves to show compassion for others. When all of the money was counted, the group discovered that they had raised their entire goal of $7,000 in a matter of minutes, and even exceeded it by $2,000! They were obviously shocked and pleased at their quick success. In the end, they all realized that compassion, when buttressed with self-sacrifice, can accomplish much more good than mere lip service.—Kenneth B. Stout

PREPAREDNESS.   Every national army, responsible for protecting its people, must be in a constant state of readiness so that it can be effectively employed in a mission against an enemy when needed. To be ready for immediate and effective action, armies require constant training. Soldiers must be outfitted with the proper equipment and repeatedly practice using and maintaining it. Tanks, ships, and missiles must be kept in good repair and constantly tested if they are to function properly when needed. Strategies must be set in place and practiced in what are called maneuvers. This image of readiness or preparedness also applies to Christians. As followers of Christ, we are spiritual soldiers. We must constantly train and test ourselves to see if we are ready to serve our commander, King Jesus; and this is not something that happens by accident. It must be intentional. At this very moment, we are being ordered on a mission into enemy territory. Our goal is to proclaim the gospel to all nations (Matt. 28:19–20) and to bring back and disciple (that is, harvest, Matt. 9:35–10:8) those who respond to the message and escort them safely into the Kingdom. To be ready for the mission, we must constantly be testing ourselves and asking the question, Am I ready to serve my Lord the King?—Kenneth B. Stout

SERMON SUGGESTIONS

Topic: No Laughing Matter

TEXT: Gen. 18:1–15 (21:1–7)

(1) The surprising sovereignty of God (vv. 1–10). (2) Our natural, matter-of-fact skepticism (vv. 11–15). (3) God breaks through our unbelief: (a) in many ordinary, day-to-day blessings of his providence; and (b) in extraordinary extensions of his purposes.

Topic: The Fruits of Justification

TEXT: Rom. 5:1–8

(1) Peace with God. (2) Becoming and receiving what God intends for us through (a) suffering, (b) perseverance, (c) character, and (d) hope.

CONGREGATIONAL MUSIC

1. "Rejoice, Ye Pure in Heart," Edward H. Plumptre (1865)

   MARION, Arthur H. Messiter (1883)

   The upbeat mood of the story of the birth of Isaac (Gen. 21:1–7) as well as the rejoicing motif in the Psalter selection (Ps. 116:1–2) can be echoed in the hearty singing of this hymn of rejoicing.

2. "What Shall I Render to the Lord," Ps. 116:12–19; vers. *Psalter* (1912)

   ROCKINGHAM, *Psalmody in Miniature* (c. 1780); adapt. Edward Mueller (1790)

   Antiphonal singing of this paraphrase of the Psalter reading (Ps. 116:12–19) would be quite biblical. The two singing groups, whether parts of the congregation or entire congregation against choir, could sing in unison on the final stanza.

3. "Alas! And Did My Savior Bleed," Isaac Watts (1707)

   MARTYRDOM, Hugh Wilson (1825)

   As either introduction or response to the Epistle selection (Rom. 5:1–8), the singing of this great hymn on the suffering of Christ would be suitable.

4. "Where Cross the Crowded Ways of Life," Frank M. North (1905)

   GERMANY, W. Gardiner's *Sacred Melodies* (1815)

   The compassion of Jesus for the multitudes (Matt. 9:36) is reflected in this hymn of social concern and mission. This notion is found especially in the fourth stanza, beginning with "O Master, from the Mountainside."—Hugh T. HcElrath

WORSHIP AIDS

CALL TO WORSHIP.   "I love the Lord because he hath heard my voice and my supplications, because he hath inclined his ear unto me; therefore will I call upon him as long as I live" (Ps. 116:1–2).

INVOCATION.   Even now, O Lord, we call upon you and we declare our love for you in worship and renewed dedication.

OFFERTORY SENTENCE.   "But my God shall supply all your needs according to his riches in glory by Christ Jesus" (Phil. 4:19).

OFFERTORY PRAYER.   Our Father, we look to you with our most urgent needs and you give us spiritual strength to face them and deal with them victoriously. Among our needs is daily bread. We pray for that, not only for ourselves but also for others. Let this prayer be answered in part by our sharing of what you have given to us to meet the needs of others.

PRAYER.   Heavenly Father, you have created us and given us the field of the world in which to test and enjoy our freedom. When one door has closed, you have opened another. When temptations have come, you have made a way of escape. When companions have deserted us, you have given us new friends. When suffering has struck, you have taught us what we could never have learned otherwise. When sorrow has visited our homes and hearts, you have opened our eyes to a home eternal in the heavens. How easy it is to acknowledge these truths, but how hard it is to assimilate them. You are patient with us and we are learning, even when we are scarcely aware that anything redemptive is happening. We trust in you, that you will never fail us or forsake us. Grant that we may rejoice in what you have done for us and in what you have promised to do for us yet. Help us in the telling moments of decision always to go your way.

SERMON
Topic: The Challenges of Parenthood (Father's Day)
TEXT: 2 Sam. 18:6–9, 24–33; Mark 5:21–24a, 35–43

Nowhere is it written that fatherhood, or parenthood in general for that matter, is supposed to be easy.

According to the Genesis account, Adam and Eve had to contend with two jealous brothers. The jealousy between them became so great that Cain enticed his brother Abel to go out into the field with him, perhaps under the guise of hunting or some other sport. When Abel's back was turned, Cain rose up against his brother and killed him (Gen. 4). How is that for a parent's nightmare? One son kills the other in cold blood.

Parenthood wasn't easy for Abraham and Sarah either. First of all, they didn't have children until they were nearly one hundred years old. After they finally did have a natural heir, Isaac, Abraham thought God wanted him to sacrifice his son on the altar (Gen. 22). Human sacrifice was thought to be the thing to do in that time and place. So Abraham led his son Isaac up a mountain with a bundle of firewood on his back.

Of course God intervened and stopped him. But the point is, Abraham found it hard to be a father.

We have also read the story of Jairus, another father who faced a challenge that broke his heart. Jairus was a well-known leader of the local synagogue. Jairus's daughter took ill and was even at the point of death. If you, as a parent, have had a child who was very ill, perhaps even at the point of death, you know how Jairus felt. Surely there is no greater challenge in life than losing a child to death or thinking that you might lose your child to death. I honestly don't know how a parent could ever recover from such a thing.

Anyway, Jairus made his way to Jesus, "fell at his feet, and begged him repeatedly, 'My little daughter is at the point of death. Come and lay your hands on her, so that she may be made well and live'" (Mark 5:23). And the story goes that Jesus touched the little girl and caused her to live. What a blessing!

But perhaps the biblical character who faced the greatest challenges of all as a parent was King David. David's family was plagued with one problem after another. Today psychologists would say that David's was a classic case of a dysfunctional family. David's family problems started, of course, when he lusted after and slept with Bathsheba, the wife of Uriah. When David learned that Bathsheba was pregnant with his child, he had Uriah sent to the front lines of battle and killed (2 Sam. 11). From that day forward, David's family was never to live in peace. The challenges of parenthood for David were great and unending.

What are some of the greatest challenges of parenthood today? They really haven't changed much over the centuries: illness (possibly even death) of a child, sibling rivalry, a rebellious and wayward child, trying to set a good example, being a good provider—these are just a few of them.

How do we meet the challenges of parenthood?

I. *We must have faith.* "Only believe," Jesus said to Jairus, whose little daughter was reported to be dead. "Only believe!" Parents must have faith—faith in a loving God who wills good for their children, faith in God's prevenient grace that goes with our children even when we are absent from them, and faith in our children and their ability to make wise choices. Though preacher Henry Bailey lost his sons to accidents, and even homicide, he never gave up his faith.

II. *We must pray.* Parents do well to pray for their children regularly and fervently. The time comes when our children are away from us—at camp, away at school, even in a foreign country—and their well-being is out of our hands. We have no other recourse than prayer and trusting them to the safekeeping of God.

III. *We must love unconditionally.* Our children are our children, regardless of what they might do in life. As John Ciardi has said, "Every parent is at some time the father of the unreturned prodigal, with nothing to do but keep his house open to hope."

The challenges of parenthood are great and many. There comes a time, as it did with the biblical characters of old, when we realize that we cannot go it alone. We realize that we need the help, the grace, and the guidance of God to be the fathers and mothers we ought to be. With God's help and grace we can better meet the challenges of parenthood.—Randy Hammer

SUNDAY, JUNE 23, 2002
Lectionary Message
Topic: Why Our New Life in Christ Is No Hoax
TEXT: Rom. 6:1b–11 NASB
Other Readings: Gen. 21:8–21; Ps. 86:1–10, 16–17; Matt. 10:24–39

All of us generally appreciate things that are new. In our childhood we enjoyed the daily unfolding of new experiences and the budding of our new abilities. I will never forget the wild delight of receiving my first shiny new bicycle at Christmas, or my first fully loaded new Lionel train. And most of us will recall with a rush the new world that opened with our first date, our first car, our first job, and our first paycheck. Even as adults we still enjoy new things: a new baby, a new home, a new computer, a trip to a new part of the world, a new suit, and new friends. All of us, however, have had the experience of being sold something purported to be new and wonderful that, when scrutinized, turned out to be old and useless—and terribly disappointing.

In our passage for today, Romans 6:3–11, those of us who have become followers of Christ are asked to consider the most precious new thing we have ever encountered—the new life that we have in Jesus Christ. Because we sometimes doubt the reality of our new spiritual life—and sometimes even fall back into our old life—we are urged to consider whether or not the new life is authentic and durable, or just our old life puttied up and painted over. After all, how can a new life of purity be possible when, by nature and by birth, sin has been so deeply entrenched in our minds and bodies?

In our text, Paul strongly encourages us to have absolute confidence in the validity and durability of our new life in the Lord. He does this by highlighting and reminding us of the basis for this wonderful new life.

I. *Our new life is based on the fact that we have experienced Christ's death, burial, and Resurrection through baptism.* In Romans 6:3–5, Paul reminds us (along with the ancient believers at Rome) that we can confidently live and trust the dynamic new life that God has given to us because when we were baptized into Christ Jesus we were "substitutionally" (that is, by Christ taking our place) put to death, buried, and raised from the dead, and thus enabled to "walk in newness of life" (Rom. 6:3–4 NASB). Christ's eternal, resurrected life is ours to experience now. We can now start over and begin living a life of purity by the indwelling presence of the Resurrected Christ (Col. 1:27).

This is not to suggest that there is anything magical about the rite (or sacrament) of water baptism in itself, or that it is a direct means of salvation; rather, by being baptized, we are expressing that we are so united with Jesus (v. 5) in faith and experience that, just as he died literally, we died spiritually; just as he was buried literally, we were buried spiritually; and just as he was raised literally, we have now been raised spiritually to an exciting new life of pure and victorious living (6:3–6). The clear imagery of this passage, especially when added to verse 8, also points forward to our future literal resurrection, should we experience death before Jesus' second coming (see 1 Cor. 15:12–17, 51–55).

It appears that Paul was concerned that some of us (and some of the Romans) would forget the fundamental truth about the new life we have in Christ and either get discouraged by doubting its authentic power and reality, or simply become confused about how to handle it. In fact, when Paul shared this wonderful truth, some who had been baptized and had received God's grace were already trying to turn back and live like they used to during their old lives of sin (6:1–2), apparently thinking that their new life of grace gave them not only freedom *from* sin but also freedom *to* sin, even more freely than before. But Paul says of this idea, "May it never be!" (vv. 1–2).

II. *Our new life is based on the fact that our old life no longer exists and that we are now totally free from sin's control.* In verses 6–8, Paul continues to drive home the truth that Christ's death on the cross gives us a marvelous new life by again explaining that Christ's death destroyed our old, sinful life. In doing this, Paul urges us to embrace the reality that our new life in Christ is the only thing that is authentic. He claims that our "old self" (v. 6) was crucified at the time of Christ's own crucifixion and that this had to happen so that our "body of sin" would be done away with (v. 6). As one commentator puts it, this body of sin, or old self, refers to the self in its pre-Christian state, when we were dominated by sin. These terms, then, are figurative expressions intended to person- ify our life before conversion.

But here (vv. 6–8) Paul adds another basis for us to have confidence in the validity and durability of our new life in Christ. With the new life comes the reality that we are set free from sin's control. Paul first says that in this new life we will "no longer be slaves of sin" (v. 6); then he adds that in this new life we are "freed from sin" (v. 7). This is tremendous news! For the first time we have real control over our lives. We are free to choose God and to live the way he wants us to. In this new life in Christ, our will is no longer captive to the evil will of another power. We can shout, "Free at last!"

III. *Our new life is based on the sufficiency of Christ's one-time death, and his everlasting, resurrected life.* In the final portion of the passage (vv. 9–11), Paul proclaims that Christ's death and Resurrection mean that he gained complete mastery over death and that he will "never . . . die again" (v. 9). He doesn't need to! For by his one-time death he has fully accomplished his task. He has paid the ultimate penalty for sin, conquered death (his own and ours), destroyed sin's power over his earthly children, revealed his (and his Father's) lov- ing character, and given each of us a new life—dramatically altering our destiny from eter- nal death to eternal life.

Paul restates, and puts in neon letters, as it were, the fact and importance of the one-time nature of Christ's death: "He died to sin once for all" (v. 10). One commentator has appro- priately said of Jesus: "His death broke the judicial link between sin and death, and he passed forever from the sphere of sin's reign." Yes, Jesus' one-time death was indeed sufficient pay- ment to meet the requirements of universal justice. No other payment will ever be required to save and secure sinners. And because of this payment, Paul can say in Romans 6:8, "Con- sider yourselves to be dead to sin but alive to God in Christ Jesus."

No, our new life in Christ is no hoax. It is an unbelievably precious gift, for which we should be eternally grateful!—Kenneth B. Stout

ILLUSTRATIONS

FREEDOM.   We have to choose acts in which those who see them can find a reflection of God and learn thereby to love him. Freedom helps to achieve this. Without freedom it would not be possible. Again, it is obvious that freedom can never be absurd. All things are lawful, but before undertaking anything, in recognition of our unworthiness and need for pardon, and also of the fact that we shall be pardoned, we have to put the question: Is this to God's glory? Can I honestly believe that this act that I am about to do will bring glory to God? These are the specifications of the freedom that is effectively given to us.— Jacques Ellul[1]

---

[1] *The Ethics of Freedom*

BURIED IN BAPTISM.   Commonly baptism was by total immersion and that practice lent itself to a symbolism to which sprinkling does not so readily lend itself. When a man descended into the water and the water closed over his head, it was like being buried. When he emerged from the water, it was like rising from the grave. Baptism was symbolically like dying and rising again. The man died to one kind of life and rose to another; he died to the old life of sin and rose to the new life of grace.—William Barclay[2]

SERMON SUGGESTIONS

Topic: God's Other People
TEXT: Gen. 21:8–21
(1) God has a purpose for all people of the earth. (2) God has a Savior for those outside his special covenant. (3) Christians have a duty to share the message of Christ with all people.

Topic: Paying the Price
TEXT: Matt. 10:24–39
(1) Jesus has set the example for our discipleship (vv. 24–26). (2) With God's help we can dare face the worst that people might do to us (vv. 26–31). (3) We might face opposition where we would least expect it (vv. 34–37). (4) There is a price to pay (vv. 38–39).

CONGREGATIONAL MUSIC
1. "We Know That Christ Is Raised," John B. Geyer (1967)
   ENGELBERG, C. H. Standford (1904)
   The author of this meaningful contemporary hymn had as his controlling thought the Epistle lesson (Rom. 6:1–11) in which the apostle teaches that in baptism we are united with Christ in his Resurrection. This is the basis of our new life in Christ, which calls forth our alleluias in adoring worship. Geyer's text, with the ENGELBERG tune for which it was written, could well set the tone of this day's worship as an opening paean of praise.
2. "Take Up Your Cross," Charles W. Everest (1833)
   QUEBEC, Henry Baker (1854)
   Relating to the cross principle that Jesus expounded many times and exemplified in his life and death, this great American hymn would be appropriate as a response to the Gospel reading (Matt. 10:24–39) and especially to verse 38, in which Jesus asserts that those who do not take up their crosses and follow him are not worthy of him.
3. "God Is So Good," Traditional
   GOD IS SO GOOD, Traditional
   This simple song echoes in its four stanzas the very spirit of the Psalter reading (Ps. 86:1–10, 16–17). It relates especially to verses 5 and 17b and thus would be either a meaningful response or an appropriate introduction to the Psalter selection.
4. "Wherever He Leads I'll Go," B. B. McKinney (1936)
   FALLS CREEK, B. B. McKinney (1936)
   The first stanza of this gospel hymn relates to the Gospel lesson and its general tenor is

---

[2]*The Letter to the Romans*

consonant with the apostle's teaching in the Epistle selection. The refrain could well be delayed until after all the stanzas have been sung.—Hugh T. McElrath

WORSHIP AIDS

CALL TO WORSHIP.   "Give ear, O Lord, unto my prayer, and attend to the voice of my supplications. In the day of my trouble I will call upon thee: for thou wilt answer me" (Ps. 86:6–7).

INVOCATION.   Some of us are peaceful, O Lord, but some of us have troubles known only to us. In either case, we need you and pray that you will meet our present need, whether to bring calm to troubled hearts or to stir up to creative action those who are unruffled by the needs of others.

OFFERTORY SENTENCE.   "You are so rich in everything—in faith, speech, knowledge, and diligence of every kind, as well as in the love you have for us—that you should surely show yourselves equally lavish in this generous service" (2 Cor. 8:7 REB).

OFFERTORY PRAYER.   Now we bring these tokens of devotion to you and these expressions of love for your causes at home and abroad. We bring them because we have been blessed already. Now bless us again in these moments, gracious Father.

PRAYER.   Father in heaven, we come boldly to your throne of grace because you are our Father, but sometimes we come more readily because of the urgency of our need. Yet we come to you nonetheless, for you have invited us, yes, commanded us to come. We would not rush into your presence as if we did not recognize who you are—not only our Father but also the Creator of the heavens and the Earth, the true ruler of all the kingdoms of this world. We come with reverence; we do not presume that we are worthy, so we confess our sins. Yet here we are—some of us trembling, perhaps, because we have been disobedient to you or because we have wronged someone else or because we have not measured up to what we know we can be or do. We are here with the promise and assurance that you put behind you and us our failures, our misdeeds, our sins—atoned for by the blood of our Lord and Savior. We as your own people would uphold your name among one another and before all the world. Give us hearts that turn like the pointer of a compass straight to you, so we may quietly and surely give direction to the thoughts and lives of others, who may learn both to reverence and to love you because of what they have seen and shared in us.

SERMON
Topic: Forever New to Life
TEXT: 2 Cor. 5:17–21

Second Corinthians 5:17–21 gives us the happy promise that the Christian believer will be forever new to life. "If anyone is in Christ, he is a new creation." Faith is the key. If we have a vital faith in Christ as our Savior and commit our lives to him as our Lord, we are refreshed by the fountain of living waters that continually make life fresh and new. Our vital relationship with the Living Lord fills our days with the energy that comes from the power of God working within us. This is the Bible promise—we are renewed through faith!

Life takes on new dignity and our days take on a new glory as we receive from God the high commission of witnessing to his love, for which he has entrusted to us the message of reconciliation. We are renewed in hope as we look to Christ as our Redeemer. This is a special orientation, for we look to God, not to ourselves. Our natural tendency is to place our hope in ourselves, in the things we can accomplish. But when we place our trust in the redemptive mercies of Christ, suddenly all our horizons are lighted with hope. We have the high honor of being ambassadors for Christ, with God making his appeal through us. The mighty deed on Calvary opens new vistas for our lives. "For our sake he made him to be sin who knew no sin, so that in him we might become the righteousness of God." We are included in the working out of God's purposes, and the future glows bright with hope. Through his saving mercies, we are promised a new life, free from the old selfishness and sin. Examples are more convincing than explanations, and to those who are in Christ is given the happy hope that they may be examples to the world of the righteousness of God. Renewed in hope, we find that doing God's will is more exhilarating than anything else in all the world, and we rejoice in the newness of life that only Christ can give.

Looking to Christ, not only are we renewed through faith and renewed in hope, but we are also renewed to service. The finest expression of Christian faith and Christian hope is Christian love, the unselfish and constructive and compassionate serving that brings the healing grace of the Heavenly Father to the places of the world's hurt and need. The witness of Christianity is unique among world religions in that it looks on every human person with love. There is nothing like it in any other religion. The God who so loved the world that he gave his Son to save it touches our hearts and teaches us to care, to help, to serve. With Christ as our guide and our strength, we are able to be loving servants of our fellow man without becoming weary in well-doing. When we give God a chance to work through our lives, we release into the world untold energies for good that come from God, the source of all good. Renewed through faith, renewed in hope, and renewed for service, we greet the future with happy hearts, knowing we can be forever new to life because we are in Christ, through whose grace we are a new creation.

Second Corinthians 9:24–27 gives a glimpse of athletes in the Corinthian games as it illustrates our most urgent problem: the problem of meaning. St. Paul describes the single-minded earnestness of the successful runner: He does not run aimlessly, but with concentrated purpose, determined to reach the finish line a victor in the race. Likewise, the successful boxer is intent on making his blows tell, not beating the air. If the runner has no sense of purpose and thinks, "What does it matter?" the race will have no meaning for him and he will probably lose it. If the boxer does not concentrate on his purpose to overcome his opponent but thinks, "What's the use?" the boxing match will lose its meaning and become an exercise in futility. In every experience God has placed a golden heart of meaning, and it is the adventure of life to seek out that heart. To cease to ask the meaning of life is to abandon all hope of living the life that is truly human. Without a sense of meaning, life loses point and spirit. Robert Browning believed that the struggle to believe in life's meaning was a struggle for the foundations of faith and the good life.

> This world's no blot for us nor blank
> It means intensely and it means good.
> To find its meaning is my meat and drink.[3]

The Christian believer faces forward with faith that God means good. We see opportunities where the doubter sees only obstacles. When facts are grim, we know that attitudes are more important than facts, and with the attitude of faith we see that in all things God is working for good. We know that what happens to us is not as important as how we respond to what happens to us. Our faith in God tells us that life means intensely and it means good, and in every experience we eagerly seek out the meaning and the blessing that God has placed there.

Nothing contributes more quickly to loss of grasp and failure of nerve than despair of life's meaning. Psychiatrists converge on this point. Rollo May finds emptiness to be the malady of modern man. Carl Jung traces mental illness to spiritual causes: "It is only the meaningful that sets us free." Viktor Frankl writes out of the harrowing experience of a Nazi deathcamp: "Everything can be taken from a man but one thing, the last of the human freedoms—to choose one's attitude in any given set of circumstances. . . . It is this spiritual freedom—which cannot be taken away—that makes life meaningful and purposeful." Following the war, Frankl established a school of "logo-therapy," according to which "the striving to find a meaning in one's life is the primary motivational force in man."

We discover life's meaning, we do not invent it. Our life is given its definitive meaning by that which is above, not by that which is below. As Augustine said, "O God, thou hast made us for thyself, and our souls are restless until they find their rest in thee." When we look into the eyes of Christ, we see mirrored there the person we are meant to be. In the struggle to rise from what we are to what Christ intends us to be, the soul wakes and grows.

In one of those strangely thoughtful flippancies that make *Alice in Wonderland* so delightful, the Mock Turtle says, "No wise fish would travel without a porpoise." "Don't you mean 'purpose'?" replies Alice. To travel life's way with a purpose means to have a destination in view. Heaven is our destination, and it heartens and illumines us in our daily life if we consciously face heavenward in all we do. We need the dimension of eternity for purposeful living in this world of time. Fear and frustration, anxiety and guilt call for an eternal hope beyond the dimensions of mortality. People of faith have found glory begun below. The touch of the eternal gives glory to life on Earth.

What do we see ahead—future or futility? The answer lies in our grasp of life's meaning. We are all called to be spiritual athletes, running to win the imperishable wreath, fighting the good fight so that we may be more than conquerors through him who loved us. In God we find the answer to the problem of life's meaning. With him we can never fail; without him we can never succeed. We never look to him without feeling within us the eagerness and the energy of new hope!—Lowell M. Atkinson[4]

---

[3]Fra Lippo Lippi
[4]*Apples of Gold*

SUNDAY, JUNE 30, 2002
Lectionary Message

Topic: The Great Test
TEXT: Gen. 22:1–14 NASB
Other Readings: Ps. 13; Rom. 6:12–23; Matt. 10:40–42

Life is full of tests. From childhood to the grave we face them. For example, we take various scholastic tests to determine our ability to learn crucial information progressively and navigate a successful life in the academic arena. We face tests of practical skills that show our ability to succeed in specialized jobs and careers. We face social tests of how we get along with others. And we face those tests of life—most important of all—which show our moral character and spiritual depth. Passing life's tests in each of these areas requires investing significant time and effort—intentionally! Success does not come by chance.

In our passage for today, Genesis 22:1–14, we find the incredible story of Abraham, who faced the ultimate test of his faith in God. None of us has ever faced a greater test than that highlighted in this powerful narrative. Because Abraham successfully passed this supreme test, he is considered one of the greatest men in the entire Bible (Gen. 26:5; Heb. 11:8–10).

Let's examine the three phases of Abraham's test. Perhaps by studying how Abraham successfully negotiated his great test of faith, we can learn how to be men, women, and youth of greater faith.

I. *The shocking request.* The narrative begins with God approaching Abraham with the specific purpose of testing him, by asking him to do the unthinkable: to sacrifice his beloved son, Isaac, as a burnt offering to the Lord (Gen. 22:1–2). This request must have just blown Abraham away! Why? First, because Isaac was Abraham's only true son and heir. Second, because he was a son whom Abraham loved more than life itself. Third, because Isaac was the embodiment of a promise given long ago, assuring Abraham that he would have a long line of prosperous descendants who would possess the land and bless the entire Earth (Gen. 15:1–8; 17:1–8, 19). Finally, because it was a request that seems foreign to the very nature of the God whom Abraham had come to trust.

Now, it's important to keep in mind that Abraham was no doubt familiar with the custom of sacrificing children to a god. It was common among the people of that time and place, who worshiped many pagan gods and felt they either had to purchase the gods' favor or appease their anger by making great, sometimes awful sacrifices. While Abraham believed his God to be very different from these gods, he became convinced that his God was now speaking to him and requiring this painful act as a test of his trust.

Perhaps the best case to be made about why the Lord commanded Abraham to take the life of his son Isaac is that ultimately he wanted to test Abraham's faith in the resurrection. In other words, the real question Abraham faced was, Can the God who has already performed a miracle in the *birth* of Isaac in Abraham's old age now perform a miracle in Isaac's *rebirth,* by restoring him to life after he is slain as a sacrifice? The fact that this is a key consideration is borne out in Hebrews 11:17–19, where it is said of Abraham, "By faith Abraham, when he was tested, offered up Isaac. . . . He considered that God is able to raise people even from the dead."

II. *The obedient response.* According to the record (Gen. 22:3–10), Abraham got up early in the morning and began obeying God's command. There is no specific, written indication of protests, doubts, or even struggles. It seems certain, however, that—being a real, human father—Abraham went through an agonizing struggle with his aching heart. Perhaps he cried out loudly to God for another test, or pled that *his* life be taken instead of his son's.

Surely Abraham must have questioned his own sanity, wondered if it was all just a very bad dream, and been tempted to think that slaying his son was simply the evil suggestion of an unseen, demonic power. But in the end, God made it clear that he really was asking Abraham to do this thing, as an ultimate test of faith, and Abraham knew he could not avoid it. So, early in the morning, he woke up Isaac and two of his servants, saddled his donkey, split wood for the sacrificial fire, and headed on a three-day journey toward the place God had told him about (v. 3), carrying out the Lord's command with dispatch and detail.

After arriving at the sight together, father and son built the altar and placed the wood in it (v. 9). Then somehow Abraham explained to his son that he, the son, was the sacrifice God had ordained. Imagine the scene! In shock and fear the son must have at first questioned and groped for understanding. But in the end, the strong, young Isaac submitted himself to the Lord's will, and to his Father's aged hand, to be bound and laid on the altar. This fact powerfully illustrates that this was a test of faith not only for Abraham, but also for Isaac (who becomes a symbol of Christ).

Imagine the scene: father and son hug and say good-bye. Abraham then takes the knife and, lifting it, prepares to plunge it into his son—when suddenly, something totally unexpected happens: an angel's voice cries out, "Abraham, Abraham! Do not stretch out your hand against the lad, and do nothing to him; for now I know that you fear God, since you have not withheld your son, your only son, from me" (22:11–12).

III. *The joyful result.* At the very last moment, God stayed the hand of Abraham, because he determined that Abraham had fulfilled the divine request to sacrifice his only, beloved son, and thus had passed the ultimate test of faith. He had held nothing back from the Lord!

Notice the results as they quickly fall into place: First, Isaac is spared and quickly cut free. Next, the Lord draws Abraham's attention to a sacrificial ram caught in a thicket, and the ram is quickly slain and placed on the altar as a substitute burnt offering for Isaac (v. 13). And then the Lord's angel proclaims with the voice of a heavenly trumpet, "Abraham . . . because you have done this thing and have not withheld your son, your only son, indeed I will greatly bless you, and I will greatly multiply your seed as the stars of the heavens and as the sand which is on the seashore; and your seed shall possess the gate of their enemies (vv. 16–17)." Finally, notice that Abraham is told, "In your seed all the nations of the Earth shall be blessed" (v. 18).

Don't miss why the blessings finally fell on Abraham in the story. They came because, according to God, Abraham "obeyed my voice" (v. 18). Today, if we are as faithful and obedient to God in our great tests of life as Abraham was in his great test, we too will experience the same result: the many joyous blessings and promises that Abraham received (Gal. 3:9), the sons (and daughters) he counted (Gal. 3:7), and ultimately Jesus Christ! (Gal. 3:29).—Kenneth B. Stout

ILLUSTRATION

RESURRECTION FAITH.　　On April 1, 1999, my twenty-one-year-old daughter, Jody, was killed in a tragic bus accident in Taiwan. At the time she was serving as a student missionary, teaching the Bible and English to Taiwanese students. The accident occurred on the way back from a spring holiday break, when the speeding bus driver came around a sharp, wet curve, lost control, and hit a four-foot high concrete median barrier, causing the bus to roll over, end over end. My lovely, one and only, beloved daughter, at the peak of her life, was instantly killed when she was thrown partially out of a bus window and caught underneath when the bus rolled over on its side as it came to rest. I cannot adequately describe the depth of the heartache and terrible sense of loss that my wife and I experienced after learning of her death, and the open wound of grief that we experience to this very day. It has been the greatest trial we've ever had to deal with. But the Lord has given us great encouragement that we will see our daughter again on the great resurrection morning, at the return of Jesus! Jody loved Jesus, believed in his resurrection power, and had committed her life to his service. Jody's faith in the resurrection and our own faith in Christ's power to raise the dead have been sources of tremendous hope and anticipation as we face the future. I now realize, that to some degree, each of us must, with Abraham, have faith in God's ability to raise our loved ones and friends who have preceded us in death if we are to continue loving and serving the Lord with joy in this sinful, tragedy-filled world.—Kenneth B. Stout

SERMON SUGGESTIONS

Topic: Slavery Redefined

TEXT: Rom. 6:12–23

(1) The old slavery: characterized by (a) bondage to sin, and (b) the wages of sin: death. (2) The new slavery: characterized by (a) freedom from sin's power and penalty, and (b) the benefit of a special life in God with eternal dimensions.

Topic: Minidiscipleship

TEXT: Matt. 10:40–42

Service to Christ is within reach of everyone—strong and talented or not. We all can (1) encourage those who speak for God, (2) encourage all who attempt to live a good life, (3) give very special, practical attention to the neediest and most vulnerable of Christ's followers.

CONGREGATIONAL MUSIC

1. "I Will Sing of the Mercies," James H. Fillmore (c. 1960)

    FILMORE, James H. Filmore (c. 1960)

    This early praise chorus would be useful at the beginning of worship. It relates to many of the psalms and could appropriately follow the quoting of Psalm 13:6 at the opening of worship.

2. "Where Cross the Crowded Ways of Life," Frank M. North (1905)

    GERMANY, W. Gardiner's *Sacred Melodies* (1815)

    Stanza 3, which begins, "The cup of water given for you," relates directly to Matthew 10:42. This hymn would therefore be suitable for use in connection with the Gospel lesson.

3. "O Jesus, I Have Promised," John E. Bode (1869)

    ANDEL'S STORY, Arthur H. Mann (1881)

    As a response to the Epistle lesson (Rom. 6:12–23), in which the apostle Paul exhorts his readers to use their lives as instruments of righteousness, the singing of this hymn of commitment and consecration would be appropriate.

4. "Day by Day and with Each Passing Moment," Carolina Sandell Berg (1865)

BLOTT EN DAG, Oscar Ahnfelt (1872)

Today's worshippers can relate to the testing of Abraham in the Old Testament lesson through their own trials and tribulations. This heartwarming hymn would be an appropriate response to the Genesis reading.—Hugh T. McElrath

WORSHIP AIDS

CALL TO WORSHIP.   "But I have trusted in thy mercy; my heart shall rejoice in thy salvation. I will sing unto the Lord, because he hath dealt bountifully with me" (Ps. 13:5–6).

INVOCATION.   Beyond our wildest imaginings and sometimes beyond the grim realities of our lives in this world of pain, you have blessed us, O Lord. This we affirm, but we pray for the faith to embrace unreservedly the love that embraces us, whether we feel it or not.

OFFERTORY SENTENCE.   "Bear ye one another's burdens, and so fulfill the law of Christ" (Gal. 6:2).

OFFERTORY PRAYER.   Now, O Lord, we bring to you our offerings, that we may help one another in this community of faith in the ways we minister to one another, and that these offerings may bless others also in their material and spiritual needs.

PRAYER.   We beseech of thee, our heavenly Father, that thou wilt remember those who are absent from us, scattered across the Earth—some on the sea, some in distant lands, and others suffering in the wilderness. Be near to all of them, and this day grant that messages of mercy may be sent by the Holy Spirit to each heart—the consolation of faith and hope in Jesus Christ. Draw near to all who are detained by sickness at home and whose thoughts come wistfully this way. Wilt thou, O God! Sanctify their sufferings and their deprivations. Grant, O Lord, that they may see thy hand in these providences and submit themselves to thy will. May they be comforted in their souls. And if their sickness in any case is appointed unto death, O Lord Jesus Christ, be near to them and prepare them for dying and for translation into the Kingdom of thy glory.

We pray that thou wilt draw near to those who are suffering in poverty and neglect, to strangers who wander without helpers, to all who are neglected, to the outcast, to those who have fallen into the snares of vice and into crimes. We beseech of thee that they may yet have a power from on high, a gospel of hope, by which they shall be saved.—Henry Ward Beecher

SERMON
Topic: Becoming Believers in God
TEXT: Acts 16:16–34

Becoming believers in God. I took this morning's sermon title from the last line of our Scripture reading, in which the prison guard is transformed in faith and practice. Think back to the images placed before us in the many weeks of this liturgical season: there's the empty tomb and the appearance of the angels; there's the visitation of Christ Resurrected on the road to Emmaus; then there's Thomas's doubt and renewed belief. Each of these scenes—

just to name a few—reminds us of the love of God in our midst, of God's living and guiding presence that comes often when it's least expected.

That's what happens in today's story, too. The recounting of Paul and Silas in prison gives us a view into the mysterious and awe-inspiring ways God works in our world, even—and perhaps most of all—when things seem to be at their worst. The guard locked up Paul and Silas with the other criminals and returned to his station at the end of the cell block. So far it was business as usual.

But then two things happened that made this more than an ordinary workday. First, the new prisoners began to sing and pray; and second, an earthquake struck. Taken separately, these events may seem merely strange; but coupled, they form a cohesive whole that is enough to change this guard's life. Let's look closely at how this happens.

First, the singing. Have you ever found yourself in a place or circumstance that had you so far down you thought you'd never get out? Have you been in a depressed mood or atmosphere you just couldn't shake? Then someone came along who witnessed to another way, giving you hope and making you smile, if only deep inside. You saw someone else who made it through some tough breaks and it made room for the possibility that things might change for you, too.

I think that's what might have been happening in the jail that day: Paul and Silas, from the strength of their faith and convictions, gave witness to the possibility of another way. Their singing and praying to God in front of the other prisoners and the guard pointed to a new source of love and hope, one beyond those prison doors and shackle chains. Although the other people may not have joined in on the chorus of the hymns, at that very moment they saw the possibility of rising above their current circumstances in faith and hope.

Then came the earthquake. Was it a miracle? This earthquake can represent for us those life-shaking moments when all we've lived and prepared for seems to be for naught—those times when things are so bad you think nothing else can go wrong. Then *boom!* You're hit with some unforeseen event that makes all your previous troubles seem like nothing.

In this passage, the earthquake was just that: the last dreadful straw. Remember that I'm looking at this story from the perspective of the guard right now. For the prisoners, the earthquake had to be a dream come true; it was their means to freedom, after all. But for the jail keeper that morning, it seemed to be his worst nightmare. When he saw the doors of the cells opened by the Earth's shaking, his first response was to raise his sword to kill himself. He wanted to die by his own hand rather than be executed under Herod's command, as had happened to two of his colleagues when Peter escaped just four chapters earlier. In pride and desperation, this guard chose to remain in control, even if it meant losing his life forever.

But suddenly he heard a voice. Down the corridor, through the rubble and ruin, Paul cried out, "Don't do it! Don't hurt yourself! We're all here!" Seeing that this was true, the guard fell down, grateful and trembling and transformed. In that moment, he became a believer in God.

What a conversion story! What a great example of change, of hope and faith found in the middle of darkness and desperation. Most of all, what a witness to the mysterious workings of God's majestic love in the least-expected places.

Can we believe it? Dare we take from this account any solace or inspiration for our very own lives?

I think we can. I think we may both believe it and be inspired by it. There is an underlying theme in this passage that not only transfers to our current place in history but that is also highly relevant to the personal challenges we may be facing in our own lives today. Seeing how this nameless, faceless jail keeper responded to the presence of these faithful men can lead us to become deeper and truer believers in God ourselves.

For example, I think we may do well to be inspired by the timing and placement of the events in this passage. On the one hand, it's easy to think that this guard was merely at the wrong place at the wrong time; yet being where he was put him in the unique position to witness faith and service in action. Paul and Silas's songs and prayers may have seemed innocuous (and perhaps even irritating) at first, but in the end they moved this man to fall to his knees and ask, "What must I do to be saved?" He may well have added, "I want the peace and compassion that you have. What must I do to live in the love of your God?"

Like the guard in our passage, we are always offered the chance to turn to hope and salvation in troubled times, to witness courageous and faith-filled actions that can strengthen our spirits rather than deplete all our energy. This is the most important lesson we can take from these final verses, I believe.

The realization that occurred for the jail keeper, quite by happenstance, is what I hope will happen to us, in times of everyday as well as exceptional challenge. I pray that we may be alert and open to the abiding love of God, as it is present in us and as we sometimes witness it in the lives of those around us.

Keeping God at the heart of our days is not always easy, I know. There are so many challenges and temptations that keep Christ at bay, even when things are going well. C. S. Lewis writes about this reality in *The Problem of Pain:* "Everyone has noticed how hard it is to turn our thoughts to God when everything is going well. . . . As St. Augustine says somewhere, 'God wants to give us something, but cannot, because our hands are full—there's nowhere for Him to put it.' Or as a friend of mine said, 'We regard God as an airman regards his parachute; it's there for emergencies but he hopes he'll never have to use it.'"

Lewis's observation shows that God's seeming absence in our lives has more to do with us than it does with God. We are the ones who are distracted, turning in another direction, to look at or listen to something or someone else. We may often choose to cram our schedules too full, leaving little room for a faithful walk with Jesus. As Lewis's words and the Scripture reading remind us this morning, God is present in the dungeons of our days, waiting patiently for us to turn to and find the love and hope of Christ. That is what conversion means, after all, in Greek: to turn. God waits for us to turn—our attention, our time, our gifts and treasures—to a new and loving way. God is there, or even better, God is *here,* waiting patiently for us, extending hope and salvation through Christ.—Lael P. Murphy

SUNDAY, JULY 7, 2002
Lectionary Message

Topic: Rest, Not Relaxation
TEXT: Matt. 11:16–19, 25–30
Other Readings: Gen. 24:34–38, 42–49, 58–67; Ps. 45:10–17; Rom. 7:15–25a

During July, a person traveling around Sweden sees a particular sign over and over again. Regardless of whether you go to a restaurant, real estate office, candy store, or factory, the sign may be found. It isn't a sign for Coca-Cola, or for a public telephone, or even one that indicates where the restroom is located. The sign says *Semesterstängt,* which can be translated "closed for vacation." It is nothing less than amazing that during the height of the tourist season, so many people and companies opt for time off rather than cashing in on the extra trade. Sweden has one of the highest standards of living in the world, and they take pride in their *semesterstängt* placards—signs that they can afford a month of leisure time.

In the United States, closing a business for a month's vacation is almost unheard of, but like the Swedes, we have ways of advertising or celebrating our idleness. Vacation homes and retiring at age fifty-five or younger are two obvious examples of leisure as a mark of status. But the burgeoning number of restaurants, amusement parks, and video rental stores, and the demand for bigger and bigger televisions and for recliner chairs with a built-in massage mechanism, drink cooler, and telephone also suggest that exerting as little effort as possible is a laudable goal. Given these values, it is small wonder that the last few verses of this morning's Gospel reading are usually taken out of context and used to legitimize the desire to bless inactivity.

I. *What kind of invitation is this?* When I picture Jesus speaking the words of verses 28–30, the image that comes to mind is one of those delightful and somewhat sentimental depictions of Jesus with arms outstretched. He might be cuddling some children or receiving a prodigal son home; in any case, it is a warm, welcoming image of the Savior. In truth, however, there is nothing cuddly about the people to whom the invitation was issued. The word *choose* might almost be substituted for *come,* because Jesus was placing a choice before the crowds listening to him. They could choose to acknowledge the authority claimed by Jesus, or they could reject it. They could receive the testimony of John the Baptist about Jesus, or they could ignore it. They could remain in bondage to the yoke of the Law, or they could accept the yoke of Christ instead. Far from being an invitation to relax and take it easy, the invitation of Jesus is urgent and inevitable. It has connotations of divine judgment and eternal consequences. It requires alertness and attention, not idleness.

II. *What kind of rest is it?* Is it gentle, easy, and light—all words found in the passage? The answer is paradoxical: both yes and no. Jesus spoke of "rest for your souls," and we should attend to his choice of words, which point to the inner state of a person more than to simple physical relaxation. The Pharisees of Jesus' time were preoccupied with obeying the Law—the divine governance of the inner person that found outward expression in one's activities, words, and so on. Rabbis spoke of the yoke of the Law, using the imagery of the harness fitted on oxen and used by the owner to direct the oxen in labor. By Jesus' day, the Law had evolved into a complex and lengthy set of rules and interpretations of rules. No human being was able to follow them all exactly, though some people exhausted themselves trying. What is more, some Pharisees misused the Law, competing with others to see who appeared to be most righteous, or quoting the Law in arguments with Jesus in attempts to trip him up. Now, Jesus represented the fulfillment of the Law. He modeled perfect obedience to the divine will because, to use his own words, "I and the Father are one" (John 10:30). The rest that Jesus offers is to rely on him, to receive a righteousness that is not generated by our own efforts but is given by him. It is a rest that frees us *from* striving toward something we will never reach, and *for* identification with Christ's person and purpose. This rest is simultaneously more demanding and more rewarding than what the Pharisees exemplified.

III. *What kind of model is it?* It is not easy for us to envision this kind of rest, is it? We are accustomed to thinking of rest as refraining from effort, or as the luxury of consuming without producing.

We may find the means for the rest of which Jesus spoke by looking at the shape of his statements in verses 25–30. Jesus' pronouncement starts with words of thanksgiving to God. He gives thanks that who he is (the Messiah, the Savior) has been revealed according to God's gracious will, but that this identity is hidden from those who trust in their own wisdom. Our rest begins by thanking and praising God for making himself known to us in Jesus Christ. We thank God not only because the Lord is worthy of our gratitude but also because praise brings us into God's presence and aligns us with his will. Jesus continues with an allusion to what is being revealed: his relationship to the Father and to humanity. For us, trust in the source of our rest is reinforced when we remind ourselves and others who Jesus is. In corporate worship, we do this through hymns, through preaching, and through recitation of the creeds. Jesus' pronouncement concludes with the oft-quoted invitation, "Come unto me, all who labor and are heavy-laden, and I will give you rest." Those who follow Jesus, who rest and are justified in him, are entrusted with issuing his invitation to the world. It isn't enough to enjoy sweet fellowship with him; we must also extend his summons to others, so that they too may find rest from the futility of trying to earn their salvation through human effort.— Carol M. Norén

ILLUSTRATIONS

OUTSIDE POWER.   I've had the opportunity to fill in as organist in several old country churches. Some of them have had pump organs, where you have to pump the bellows with your feet while playing in order to get any sound. Playing a long hymn can be an exhausting exercise, and of course your feet are not playing musical notes simultaneously with your hands. After playing such an organ, it is a relief to go to another church that has an electric bellows. The wind power is supplied by another source. That doesn't mean I don't have to switch the organ on, or that I don't have to put my hands on the keyboard. It does mean that because I'm supported by a power outside myself, I am freed to make more beautiful music in praise of God. When we answer Jesus' invitation to "come, and I will give you rest," we are freed to serve him more excellently, because it is the Holy Spirit's power that supports us.—Carol M. Norén

REAL REST.   Several years ago, a well-meaning Christian friend quoted Psalm 37:4 to me: "Take delight in the Lord, and he will give you the desires of your heart." The friend was trying to tell me that if I delighted in the Lord, God would give me all the other things and relationships for which I longed. I'm convinced that this verse is misquoted and misunderstood as much as Matthew 11:28–30. I believe that if my *delight* is in the Lord, my *desire* is for the Lord. God isn't promising exciting bonus prizes for delighting in him; he's promising himself. And in Matthew 11:28–30, Jesus is not offering rest in the sense that we often mean it: inactivity, lethargy, or sleep. Instead, his rest involves movement ("come"), obedience ("learn from me"), and purposeful activity ("take my yoke upon you"). And this is better than any other rest we could imagine.—Carol M. Norén

SERMON SUGGESTIONS

Topic: Finding a Wife

TEXT: Gen. 24:34–38, 42–49, 58–67

(1) Isaac required help (vv. 34–48). (2) Providence played an active role (vv. 42–49). (3) The matter was concluded with the full consent of Rebekah (vv. 58–67).

Topic: On Doing What Is Right

TEXT: Rom. 7:15–25a

(1) It is impossible for us to solve our sin problem by looking to the Law to save us (vv. 15–23).

(2) God through Jesus Christ meets our deepest needs (v. 25a).

CONGREGATIONAL MUSIC

1. "I Praise the King with All My Verses," Marie J. Post (1985) and Bert Polman (1986)

    O DASS ICH TAUSEND, Johann B. Konig (1738)

    The last two stanzas of this modern paraphrase of Psalm 45 parallel the assigned reading from the Psalter. If this tune is unfamiliar to the congregation, it could be sung by choir or soloist.

2. "Jesus, What a Friend for Sinners," J. Wilbur Chapman (1910)

    HYFRYDOL, Rowland H. Prichard (c. 1830)

    God as guide and helper in life's decisions is one lesson of the Old Testament passages concerning the leading of Rebekah to become Isaac's wife, and Jesus as the friend of common people and sinners is the message of the Gospel lesson. Both ideas are covered in the five stanzas of this long hymn of praise. The stanzas could be alternately sung and read by the congregation.

3. "I Heard the Voice of Jesus Say," Horatius Bonar (1846)

    VOX DILECTI, John B. Dykes (1868), or RESTING PLACE, H. Vander Werp (1911)

    This two-part hymn begins with the invitation of Jesus in the Gospel lesson (Matt. 11:28) but goes on in subsequent stanzas to refer to other gracious sayings of our Lord. This hymn would be effective sung antiphonally between two sections of the congregation, with one group singing the first half of each stanza and the second group singing the reassuring message in the last half of each stanza.

4. "In the Hour of Trial," James Montgomery (1834)

    PENITENCE, Spencer Lane (1879)

    The fine hymn by James Montgomery, "the prince of lay hymn writers," deals with the struggles and trials spoken of by the apostle Paul (Rom. 7:15–25a). The hymn could suitably follow the reading of the Epistle lesson.—Hugh T. McElrath

WORSHIP AIDS

CALL TO WORSHIP.   "Listen! I am standing at the door knocking; if you hear my voice and open the door, I will come in to you and eat with you, and you with me" (Rev. 3:20 NRSV).

INVOCATION.   Almighty God, hear our simple prayer, that we may all leave here today radiating the presence of Christ, willing to mediate it through the power of the Holy Spirit to others in need.—E. Lee Phillips

OFFERTORY SENTENCE.   "But remember: anyone who sows sparsely will reap sparsely— and anyone who sows generously will reap generously as well" (2 Cor. 9:6 NJB).

OFFERTORY PRAYER.   Let our reaping be generous, O Lord, not so much for ourselves but for your glory, as the seed of the gospel is sown to the ends of the Earth.

PRAYER.   O God, creator of the universe and our Father, thy greatness overwhelms us. We press to the outer limits of human knowledge and at last stand before thee alone. Before the mountains were brought forth, or before thou hadst formed the Earth and the world, even from everlasting to everlasting, thou art God. We profess to know nothing of thee but that which thou hast revealed. We trace thy works in the things thou hast made, and stand amazed before thy wisdom and thy power. We see in the manifold acts of thy providence, especially in the gift of thy Son, our Lord and Savior, thy righteousness and thy loving kindness. Yet thou hast hidden so much from our sight and hast challenged our hearts with so many mysteries that we must walk by faith and not by sight. When we cannot understand, help us to trust. When we cannot feel, help us to go on believing. And grant that our wilderness wanderings may at last be rewarded with new strength of character and greater ability to bless others with the very graces that we ourselves have received from thee.

SERMON
Topic: And What If God Were Like That?
TEXT: Luke 15:4–7

Almost from the outset I'm struck by the preposterous nature of this parable. Granted, it couldn't possibly have the same immediate impact on us twentieth-century and technologically sophisticated people as it had on those first-century farmers, field hands, and fishermen. No doubt it would have had its greatest impact on the shepherds who stood, staff in hand, listening to our Lord.

Maybe we would simply shrug our shoulders, thinking nothing of the suggestion that a shepherd might leave the unguarded majority of the flock to search out some simpleton of a sheep who had somehow gotten lost. But I would imagine that the shepherds who were among Jesus' first audience would have broken out in thunderous laughter.

After all, in their stock and trade, any shepherd worth his salt would not risk the well-being of an entire flock just to chase after one crackpot sheep lost in the wilds. It just wouldn't make sense, would it? Why go after one sheep that was so stupid it wandered from the flock in the first place?

And what about us? Well, maybe we still don't get it. So how about this: A diamond merchant in center city Philadelphia one day discovers that a rather small diamond ring is missing from its case. He leaves the store, unlocked and unguarded, and combs the streets of the city searching for the lost piece of jewelry.

I mean, who really acts that way? Let's suppose that it was your farm and your flock. Now, you hired this shepherd, even though you'd heard some rumors that he was a bit quirky. So one night you decide to pay him an unannounced visit.

When you get out there in the wilds, you find the entire flock meandering about in an open field, susceptible to the elements and beasts. Suddenly, and from the shadows of darkness, the shepherd emerges with one ewe lamb draped over his shoulders. Now tell me, do you rejoice or do you rush over and shove a pink slip into his pocket?

Can't you just see those shepherds scratching their heads, leaning on their staffs in laughter, whispering to others in the crowd that this parable is a farce and the rabbi from Nazareth is foolish? And the crowd might agree, were it not for the nagging feeling that somehow they all needed to be found. What would it mean to belong to someone who loved like that shepherd? Someone willing to risk looking ludicrous for any and every expression of love? And what if God were like that?

Jesus said of this shepherd that he went out after the one that was lost until he found it. Until he found it! Doesn't that imply persistence? Of course it does. This shepherd searched high and low, day and night, over hill and dale, scratching his way through briars and bush until he found that one lost sheep.

Maybe it does seem like a ludicrous thing to do. Perhaps it would not win him the Shepherd of the Year award. It didn't seem to matter, did it? What seemed to matter to this shepherd was that each and every lamb was loved, thought to be of infinite value, and worthy to be saved. And what if God were like that?

And then, when this shepherd returned home with the lamb draped over his shoulders, he decided to throw a big bash to celebrate—what? Surely the party fixings would cost more than the value of one crummy lamb. So why bother? Simply bring the silly creature into the corral and then get some well-deserved sleep.

Not this shepherd! He wanted to party! Perhaps because there was nothing in the world of greater value to him than each and all of his silly sheep. Maybe he cared for nothing so much as he did for the life of one single lamb. And perhaps nothing gave him greater pleasure than finding one of his "little ones" who was lost in the wilds of the world. And what if God were like that?

Look at the guest list to that party! The parable tells us that the shepherd sent out his gold-embossed invitations to "friends and neighbors." And while I can't speak for any and all of you, it doesn't seem to me a sensible thing to do, to invite friends *and* neighbors.

Neighbors might as well have been strangers to the shepherd, right? Sure, we might hold some polite chit-chat while cleaning up grass clippings, but I don't make it a point to party with my neighbors. Do you? Especially a party to celebrate something in your personal life? But apparently this shepherd's idea of a good time was to have everyone share in his joy in loving, losing, and finding one little ewe lamb. And what if God were like that?

But somewhere, at some point, they would have remembered. It's found in the prophet Ezekiel. The voice is that of the Lord God: "I myself will search for my sheep, and will seek them out. As shepherds seek out their flocks when they are among their scattered sheep, so I will seek out my sheep. . . . I will rescue them . . . I will bring them [back] . . . I will feed them . . . I will seek the lost; and I will bring back the strayed, and I will bind up the injured, and I will strengthen the weak." God *is* like that!—Albert J. D. Walsh

SUNDAY, JULY 14, 2002

Lectionary Message

Topic: The Road Home or a Dead End?

TEXT: Rom. 8:1–11

Other Readings: Gen. 25:19–34; Ps. 119:105–112; Matt. 13:1–9, 18–23

It had rained most of the day. At times the downpour had been so heavy that I could see only three or four car-lengths ahead of me, but now it had slowed to a drizzle. As I drove east on a four-lane road, I was puzzled by the brake lights going on ahead of me. I slowed down and finally stopped. Rolling down the window, I looked ahead to see what the problem might be.

I saw some cars making U-turns in the middle of the road and then heading west. Other cars turned off onto a side street entering a small subdivision. There was no ambulance on the scene, no signs of a wreck. What was the problem? As the car crawled further down the road, I saw that the obstruction was neither an accident nor a freight train at a standstill. The road was flooded and no one could get through. I had to make a decision: I could change course and go a way I had not planned to at the beginning of the day, I could sit there and get nowhere, I could try to drive through the flood, or I could forget about going home and drive somewhere else. There was nothing bad about the road I was on, but it would only take me so far.

I. *Living for the flesh: A dead end.* The image of that flooded road was helpful to me as I thought about today's passage from Romans 8. The poet Robert Frost wrote about "the road less traveled" as a metaphor for decisions made and lifestyles pursued. Living in the flesh might be one road, and living in the spirit, another. Recent years have seen much controversy about Paul's writing and his understanding of the body. A comedy routine by Peter Cook and Dudley Moore introduced the book of Ephesians as written by "St. Paul, the Killjoy," and indeed that is how Pauline literature is often interpreted. Paul has been accused of being against marriage because of 1 Corinthians 7. The debate about homosexuality that threatens to divide our churches is based in part on how we understand Romans 1. Feminists have selectively quoted Paul's writing, affirming Galatians 3:28 but railing against Ephesians 5 and 1 Timothy 2:9–12. A popular consensus is that Paul had all kinds of hang-ups about sex, that he pitted the flesh against the spirit, and that anything he wrote about the body cannot be taken literally. After all, his dualistic mind-set was a product of his culture. Today we understand a great deal more about sexuality, personality, and integration than a first-century misogynist prude understood.

But suppose our sexually obsessed, self-indulgent culture has misunderstood what the apostle Paul is trying to say here. What if the problem is not denial of the body but "reader competence," as biblical scholar Christopher Seitz puts it? Suppose Paul's teaching in Romans 8 is based not on his own neuroses but on core Christian beliefs about the death and Resurrection of Jesus Christ?

Like his contemporaries, Paul witnessed executions and saw people dying of other causes. He would have seen the bodies of the crucified left to rot, the carcasses left for scavengers and birds of prey. The disintegration of the body was not remote from common experience as it is today, when public health laws, embalming, and makeup shield us from harsh realities. Paul knew that no matter how a body is pampered or indulged, no matter what choice food it enjoys, it is not immortal. Paul proclaimed the truth, that flesh and blood cannot inherit the Kingdom of God (1 Cor. 15:50), and that those for whom satisfying the desires of the flesh was primary, "whose god is their belly" (Phil. 3:19), could not be delivered by God from death. On the contrary, pursuit of bodily pleasure leads quickly to a dead end. Going down that road is a mistake, because it can't take you where you want to go. Our earthly bodies are finite and perishable.

II. *Paul knew which road leads home.* Paul was on the road to Damascus when the Risen Christ intervened and set him in another direction. Yes, he continued into the city, but his life was altered radically: he became a disciple of Jesus Christ. He was baptized and filled with the Holy Spirit. He was able to say, "I have been crucified with Christ; it is no longer I who live but Christ who lives in me; and the life I now live in the flesh I live by faith in the Son of God, who loved me and gave himself for me" (Gal. 2:20). By the power of the Holy Spirit at work in him, Paul became heir to a life that is eternal and imperishable, to be clothed eventually in a new, resurrection body.

What did that mean for his attitude toward his present, earthly body? He did not despise it, but neither did he cherish it unduly. In his letter to the Philippians he wrote, "for me to live is Christ, and to die is gain"; he was content either to have plenty or to be in want, to continue in this earthly life or to depart and be with Christ (Phil. 1:19–24). Paul submitted his body to the dominion of Christ rather than to his personal appetites (Rom. 12:1–2), and in so doing he experienced joy and peace. Directed by the Spirit, Paul was confident that the road he was on led home—to everlasting life through Christ, the one who broke the chains of death in his own Resurrection.

Which road are you on? If you're headed toward a dead end, will you change course at the Spirit's direction and discover the way home, or will you continue stubbornly on your own route and plunge headlong into a flood of destruction? The choice is yours.—Carol M. Norén

ILLUSTRATIONS

SELF-DECEPTION.   Our human capacity for self-deception is almost infinite, but it does not change reality. My friend Jane and I were visiting a European country where I had friends. When we visited one of them, she repeatedly called Jane "June" and commented on her charming British accent. (Jane is from west Texas!) I gently reminded the friend of Jane's correct name and origin, but it made no difference. She said, "But she *looks* like a June to me. I'm going to call her June. And I do think she sounds British." Of course, that didn't alter the facts. In a similar vein, we cannot have our minds on "the things of the flesh," writing our own rules as seems good to us, and expect to please God or inherit the promises made to those who have their minds "set on the Spirit."—Carol M. Norén

RENUNCIATION.   In the Orthodox rite of baptism, one of the four acts that take place prior to the actual baptism is the renunciation. The candidate faces west and, with arms upraised, three times renounces Satan, all his works, his angels, his worship, and his pomp. The candidate confirms the renunciation, and then blows and spits as an expression of contempt for all that has been renounced. The candidate then does an about-face and, facing east, makes a profession of faith using the words of the Nicene-Constantinopolitan Creed. The physical movement and acts that accompany the rite underscore the dramatic difference between one who is baptized into Christ and becomes "a new creature" and one who is not baptized. One's whole life takes on a different orientation and direction.—Carol M. Norén

SERMON SUGGESTIONS

Topic: A Bad Deal
TEXT: Gen. 25:19–34; see also Heb. 12:16
(1) The story: In a minor crisis of desperation Esau bargained away his most important possession. (2) The application: All of us have personal assets—spiritual and otherwise—that we can lose by foolish and impulsive decisions: (a) reputation, (b) character, (c) fellowship with God.

Topic: A Mystery of Hearing Explained

TEXT: Matt. 13:1–9, 18–23

(1) Jesus' parable of the sower. (2) Jesus' explanation of the parable. (3) Specific contemporary applications.

CONGREGATIONAL MUSIC

1. "Come, Labor On," Jane L. Borthwick (1863)

    ORA LABORA, T. Tertius Noble (1918)

    This compelling hymn would be a natural response to the Gospel lesson about the sower and the seed. Alternately singing and speaking the stanzas could be meaningful and effective.
2. "Blest Are the Uncorrupt in Heart," Fred R. Anderson (1986)

    RICHMOND, Thomas Haweis (c. 1792)

    Though this modern version of a portion of Psalm 119 does not paraphrase the particular verses of the Psalter reading, singing it would be a suitable introduction or response to that reading.
3. "Jesus Lives! And So Shall I," Christian F. Gellert (1757); trans. John D. Long (1826)

    JESUS MEINE ZUVERSICHT, Johann Crüger (1668)

    This exuberant hymn receives its spiritual impetus from Romans 8:11, where the Spirit that raised Jesus from the dead is declared to be the power behind the believer's life. Because it relates especially to the last verse of the reading, this hymn is a natural worship response.
4. "Thy Word Is a Lamp," Amy Grant (1984)

    THY WORD, Michael W. Smith (1984)

    This Scripture chorus relates directly to the Psalter reading and thus could be used as a sort of antiphon both preceding and following the reading from Psalm 119.—Hugh T. McElrath

WORSHIP AIDS

CALL TO WORSHIP.   "Thy testimonies have I taken as a heritage forever: for they are the rejoicing of my heart" (Ps. 119:111).

INVOCATION.   Blessed Lord, let the quietness of this place, the symbolism and beauty and serenity of our worship, issue into moral fiber and ethical stability and strong justice that change our world because God demands no less (Isa. 56:1, 2).—E. Lee Phillips

OFFERTORY SENTENCE.   "Therefore, as opportunity offers, let us work for the good of all, especially members of the household of faith" (Gal. 6:10 REB).

OFFERTORY PRAYER.   Gifts and tithes we bring in faith, Father. Let them be endowed with your power and used to accomplish holy ends, we pray in Jesus' name.—Henry Fields

PRAYER.   Lord, you have been our dwelling place in all generations. Before the mountains were brought forth, or you had formed the Earth and the world, from everlasting to everlasting, you are God.

In the scheme of things—in the stretches of eternity—it seems presumptuous, if not preposterous, to come before you with our little times and our petty concerns, but here we are, as we have been many times before, pleading our case before you. And we come in the confidence that whoever we are and whatever our need, you will not turn aside from us, and that we are embraced in the everlasting arms of your love. In every day, in each moment, in every heartbeat, in each breath we draw, in every experience, in each relationship, in any eventuality, we are kept by you. What is so amazing in life's adventure is not our hold on you but your hold on us.

For our journey may we hear afresh Jesus' assurance as he prays for his disciples in the upper room and in turn for his followers in every generation: "Father, keep them in thy name, which thou hast given me, that they may be one, even as we are one . . . and that they may have my joy fulfilled in themselves."

We are tempted to anxiety, but grant to us as persons and a people the poise of faith that confesses we do not know what the future holds and affirms, but we do know who holds the future.

Through faith and love and trust may we all be open to embrace the new thing that you are doing in our day.

"God of grace, God of glory, on thy people pour thy power; Crown thine ancient Church's story; bring its bud to glorious flower." Through him who is the Lord of the Church and teaches us to pray as with one voice!—John Thompson

SERMON
Topic: Requited Love
TEXT: Luke 7:36–50

Unrequited love is never comfortable. I imagine we've all experienced it in some form or another, whether from the giving or receiving end. Either way, it's a sad state of affairs when love that wells up naturally in one person just isn't returned by the other.

Unrequited love isn't limited to our interactions with each other as human beings. I believe that feelings of hurt and rejection abound in the area of our spiritual experience as well, not only as we wonder where God is in some of our more down and dire periods, but also as God may wonder where *we* are in the moments of our day-to-day lives. As in his admonishment of the Hebrew people in the Book of Isaiah, God might well be saying to us today, "I was ready to be sought out by those who did not ask, to be found by those who did not seek me. I said, 'Here I am, here I am' to a nation that did not call on my name" (Isa. 65:1).

In study Bibles, this passage is assigned the heading "A Sinful Woman Forgiven." Certainly that's what occurred in this tender scene. The nameless woman barged in on the private gathering and, in an act of seemingly deep and sincere repentance, she was rewarded with the comforting words, "Your sins are forgiven; go in peace."

But is that all that happened? Yes, her sins were forgiven; but don't we witness more than a moment of absolution here?

If I were to title this passage in Luke, I'd call it "Jesus' Love Returned," or even more concisely, "Requited Love." That's what I see going on here: God's love being recognized and returned in the humblest and most sincere way. How did this woman know Jesus? And what kind of transformation did she undergo to bring her to this pivotal moment in her life?

It's natural to assume that this woman had heard Jesus, had witnessed the power of his ministry as it had been going on around her. Unlike the Pharisees in the story, and the countless others in Galilee at the same time, this particular woman was deeply touched by what she witnessed. Hearing Jesus' words and experiencing God's Spirit in them, her very soul was pierced. She was changed, and in that moment she was moved to humble devotion.

We all know that love is a two-way street. To be healthy and mature in any form, it needs to possess mutuality and respect, care and the willingness to reveal oneself to the other in deepening degrees of honesty and vulnerability. The give and take of love is ongoing, as anyone who is a spouse or partner, parent or friend, can testify. As captured by Amy Carmichael, "You can give without loving, but you cannot love without giving."

So often we *think* of God's love as abiding and unconditional but in a distant, formal way, so we need to remember that we also possess the ability to *feel* this love, deeply and personally.

In our mainline Protestant tradition, we may sometimes assume that first and foremost we're called to actions of justice and peacemaking. We may constantly remind ourselves and others of the oppression in the world, of the hunger and despair and seemingly endless pain that needs fixing—and often we're the ones out helping things get fixed. But as this passage helps us to remember, God's call is not simply for us to bring peace and prosperity to this broken world; it's not for us to live according to a set code of behavior; it's not even for us to become active, giving members of a church.

In his work addressing spiritual living in a secular world, Henri Nouwen shares that in order for us to grow spiritually, we must first open ourselves to the power of being loved by God. Nouwen recognizes our deep need to embrace our *chosenness*—not so that we may feel superior to or set apart from others, but so that we can live in the peace and hope that God extends to us and to all people. As the cherished beloved, we remember that God loves us— loves us as we are, where we are, how we are. In that remembering, we come to be fed by God's life-sustaining Spirit.

This is the heart of the Christian life—quite literally. In our devoted listening and through the Spirit of grace, God's love fills the very core of our beings, transforming us inwardly and then outwardly. That's the good news Jesus brought two thousand years ago and brings this very day: he brings the invitation to receive the unconditional love that reconciles us with God, with our deepest selves, and with each other. He has shown how this love changes us, one by one, person by person. Salvation through tradition and heritage are gone. Through Christ we have come to know redemption on the most personal, intimate basis.

Think back to that woman at the dinner party, the sinner forgiven. It can't get much more personal than that, as she kisses Jesus' dusty feet and washes them with her tears. She doesn't care that she's not welcomed by the host not only because of her implied profession but also because she is a woman. She doesn't consider how she brings the insult of bad hospitality to the righteous Pharisee. She simply comes forward to offer her gratitude and devotion, showing Christ that she loves him back, that she has heard the good news of forgiveness he's offering and claims it as her own.

We all are indebted to God. Like this penitent woman, we all have our sins, no matter how great or small—that's our confession as we live as Christians and it's the example given to us in Jesus' parable of the debtors. But these sins need not keep us from knowing God's love, from experiencing deep transformation in Christ's holy and abiding Spirit. If anything, they might even help us to recognize our need for God's redeeming and sustaining grace.

Sin is what takes us away from God and each other, making it seem impossible to claim God's love as our own.

It's never too late to turn, to move beyond being consumed by self toward the freedom and love offered by God. That's what Jesus and the woman teach us this morning: that we may claim God's love and then requite it—return and repay it—simply, truly, and humbly.—Lael P. Murphy

SUNDAY, JULY 21, 2002
Lectionary Message

Topic: Not Just Any Dream Will Do

TEXT: Gen. 28:10–19a

Other Readings: Ps. 139:1–12; Rom. 8:12–25; Matt. 13:24–30, 36–43

Joseph and the Amazing Technicolor Dreamcoat, by Tim Rice and Andrew Lloyd Webber, has been a perennial favorite since its first performance in 1968. The songs are catchy, the lyrics are clever, and the image of Joseph's coat of many colors is familiar to many. There are two things I find remarkable about the musical, however. First, there is almost no reference to God in the songs. Second, in the final solo and chorus, "Any Dream Will Do," Joseph sings fondly about his dreams and the almost magical qualities of his coat. The line sung over and over is, "Any dream will do," as though having any dream or vision of the future will see you through present difficulties.

I. *Dreams as a medium of self-expression.* In ancient, biblical culture and in our own time, people like to talk about their dreams. Joseph got into trouble with his brothers for speaking about his dreams, and he also got *out* of trouble by using his gift for interpreting the dreams of others. Jacob dreamed of angels ascending and descending a ladder. The prophet Joel foretold a time when "your young men shall see visions and your old men shall dream dreams." An angel spoke through dreams to Joseph, the husband of Mary, telling him not to be afraid to take Mary as his wife, and later telling him to flee to Egypt. In many of the transforming experiences recorded in the Bible, it is unclear whether the subject is having a dream or a vision, or some combination of the two. According to ancient belief, oracles could be received through dreams. Heeding the dream, and interpreting it rightly, could change the course of an individual's life or a nation's.

In the contemporary world, dreams are regarded more subjectively than they were in biblical times, but they are no less important to the dreamer. Psychotherapists and spiritual directors look for symbols and themes in dreams in order to help their clients achieve growth and wholeness. In conversation, saying that something "was like a dream" is understood to mean either it was unreal or it was so ideal as to strain credulity. When Martin Luther King gave his famous "I Have a Dream" speech, few took it to be literally what he had dreamt the night before. The dream was heard as the summary of aspirations for which King was spokesperson.

II. *What did Jacob's dream do?* In studying today's passage from Genesis 28, it is evident that Jacob's dream was more like the other dreams recorded in the Bible and not so much like dreams as we speak of them today. When Jacob had this experience, he was estranged from his brother Esau and, in a sense, in exile from his family and home. He was on his way to look for a wife among the daughters of Laban, his kinsman, but he lacked shelter and family when he went to sleep that night. The first thing the dream did was reconnect Jacob with his family. Verse 15 records God as saying, "I am the Lord, the God of Abraham your father and the God of Isaac; the land on which you lie I will give to you and to your descendants. . . . By you and your descendants shall all the families of the Earth bless themselves." Far from setting Jacob in isolation, the dream connected him to his people in the past and his descendants in the future: a faith community. There was a promise of restoration.

A second thing the dream did was fill Jacob with a sense of awe, not toward the dream but toward God. He said, "Surely the Lord is in this place; and I did not know it." Jacob recognized the Lord's presence where he had not seen it before.

Third, Jacob responded by setting apart the place and his possessions for God. The stone pillar was a sign that he would worship God always, and he pledged that he would give a tenth of all with which God had blessed him. Reconciliation, recognition of God's presence, and dedication: these rather than the angels on the ladder are the important aspects of Jacob's dream.

III. *Dreams from God will do.* People in the Bible had God-given dreams for different purposes, according to their circumstances and God's will for them at the time. Jacob's dream at Bethel offers us a useful model for considering our own dreams and discerning whether they are divine messages or the result of indigestion. Like Jacob, we may recognize God at work in our dreams when they work toward reconciliation with God and with others. In this respect, Peter's dream or trance in Acts 10 is similar to Genesis 28. Dreams from God contain an element of promise; they look toward the future God would have for us. And dreams from God evoke a faith-filled response: reverence, praise, godly action, and so on.

The dreams God sends are in fact remarkably like the Son God sent into the world. Our faith is not in the details of our experience but in the one from whom the experience came. The world will recognize our dreams—and our Lord—when our response authenticates what we claim has happened to us.—Carol M. Norén

ILLUSTRATIONS

GOD'S PURPOSE.   A tablet at Yale University commemorates the Yale students who died in World War I. The tablet is inscribed with part of a poem by Brian Hooker (1880–1946):

> O youth foregone, foregoing!
> O dream unseen, unsought!
> God give you joy of knowing
> What life your death has bought!

Hooker's wish was that those who died on the battlefields of Europe would come to realize, in some sense, that their sacrifice had not been in vain. When God speaks to us in dreams, we may be commanded to do something we do not fully understand. Trusting God's purpose, however, we may act on the divine mandate, confident that our Lord has a plan greater than we may now understand.—Carol M. Norén

DREAMS.   Listening to dreams and interpreting them is part of the New Age influence in popular culture. People may consider them signs, though without a proper frame of reference the signs may as well be in a foreign language. A woman cutting my hair a few years ago told me she dreamed that her grandfather had died. A day or two later her mother phoned and said the old man had suffered a heart attack, though he wasn't dead. The hairdresser said that now she was afraid to go to sleep at night, for fear of what else she might dream—as though the dream had *caused* her grandfather's heart attack. Without getting into a lengthy discussion of paranormal phenomena, I assured her that the dream was almost certainly not a warning from God but simply a coincidence. When she asked how I was sure, I said that if it were from God, it would have prepared her for the future rather than filling her with fear. I did express the belief that God could nonetheless *use* the dream if it resulted in her praying for her grandfather and drawing closer to her family and the Lord.—Carol M. Norén

SERMON SUGGESTIONS

Topic: Labor Pains

TEXT: Rom. 8:12–25

(1) The suffering of all creation (v. 22). (2) The suffering of believers (v. 23). (3) The ultimate purpose: (a) for creation (v. 21), (b) for believers (vv. 23b-25).

Topic: The Weeds of the Field

TEXT: Matt. 13:24–30, 36–43

(1) The good seed: faithful believers. (2) The weeds: doers of evil. (3) The day of reckoning: end of the age. (4) The destiny: (a) of the unrighteous, (b) of the believers.

CONGREGATIONAL MUSIC

1. "How Blessed Is This Place," Ernest E. Ryden (1958)

   SOLOTHURN, trad. Swiss (1826)

   This twentieth-century hymn captures the spirit of Jacob, who woke from his dream and declared the place he was in to be none other than the house of God and the gate of heaven. It could admirably serve as the opening hymn of worship.

2. "Search Me, O God," J. Edwin Orr (1936)

   ELLERS, Edward J. Hopkins (1869)

   The first stanza of this very personal hymn is a paraphrase of Psalm 119:23 and would therefore appropriately follow the Psalter lesson.

3. "Simply Trusting Every Day," Edgar P. Stites (1876)

   TRUSTING JESUS, Ira D. Sankey (1876)

   "It is the Spirit himself bearing witness with our spirit that we are children of God" (Rom. 8:16). The second stanza of this gospel hymn, in particular, echoes this verse. This song could effectively be sung in connection with the Epistle lesson.

4. "Come, Ye Thankful People, Come," Henry Alford (1844)

   ST. GEORGE'S WINDSOR, George J. Elvey (1858)

   The first line of this fine hymn is misleading. "Come, Ye Thankful People" is not basically a harvest thanksgiving hymn but rather a commentary on the parable of the tares and the wheat that Jesus told, as recorded in the Gospel lesson (Matt. 13:24–30, 36–43). Use it in this connection.—Hugh T. McElrath

WORSHIP AIDS

CALL TO WORSHIP.   "Search me, O God, and know my heart: try me, and know my thoughts, and see if there be any wicked way in me, and lead me in the way everlasting" (Ps. 139:23–24).

INVOCATION.   We confess, gracious Lord, that we are often tempted to go away from your paths. Let this service of worship be a time of self-examination, when we know that you indeed will help us to see the way that is true and right, and give us the power to follow it.

OFFERTORY SENTENCE.   "From everyone to whom much has been given, much will be required: and from the one to whom much has been entrusted, even more will be demanded" (Luke 12:48b NRSV).

OFFERTORY PRAYER.   O God, we have been given so much—your mercy and grace first of all—but our many treasures of your precious providence are too numerous to count, though we do not recognize them. Make us faithful stewards of all that we claim as ours, that everything may rebound to your glory.

PRAYER.   Father, this morning we enter your presence through this door of prayer, grateful for your creative genius, which has endowed us with the ability to imagine and create in your likeness and after your fashion. Thank you for faith to ensure that we can be more than our limitations, more than our self-imposed boundaries, when we release ourselves into your keeping and allow your Spirit to work in us.

When doubt clouds the horizons of life, remind us anew of whose we are, that we might be able to see beyond the dark moments to the glory of what is yet to come. Keep us aware that the devastating events of life on this Earth are momentary, that they come to pass and that we will triumph over them as we face them in your strength and power. Turn our vision toward the eternities so that we might not be overcome by the temporary circumstances with which we are surrounded.

When fear paralyzes us and we feel so alone in the midst of some overwhelming event, visit us with the calming presence of your Spirit and give us the direction we need to take to get beyond the grip of fear.

When loneliness comes upon us like a smothering blanket and we find no comfort in others and see no hope for escape from its burden, create in us an island of assurance that will harbor us. In the swirling sea of loneliness, make us aware of divine comfort, so that eternal friendship may be born and our feet may be placed on the path that leads away from devastating loneliness and to wholeness again.

When we are lost amid the forest of our sins, even while we love our sinning, and especially when we are so sin-sick that we despair, come to us with your saving grace to convict and redeem us, that we may not perish. O Father, how we need today to be brought face to face with our sins and evils, individually and collectively, that we might see them for what they are, understand the sorrow and pain they bring to us and others, and turn from them before they do more damage to the world. Give us this morning a vision of what we can yet be in Christ, and grant us the faith and courage to rise up and follow him, so that the vision may become reality. This we pray in Jesus' name.—Henry Fields

SERMON

Topic: How to Get What Belongs to You

TEXT: Luke 16:1–13

The Bible suggests two possible ways for us to get what belongs to us, two kinds of wisdom from which to choose, each of which takes a different approach to the problem. There is the wisdom of this world and there is the wisdom that comes to us from God. And sooner or later each of us follows one or the other in our quest to get what belongs to us.

That brings us to the most puzzling of all Christ's parables, that of the unjust steward. He was a man who set out to get what belonged to him. We can identify with him because we have the same desires, and because we too are stewards, meaning that we have been given areas over which we have responsibilities and dominion. The Bible indicates that the Lord has given the Earth to mankind, to have dominion over it; and each of us has some little area of that Earth in which we rule. But we need to come to grips with what Jesus is saying as he tells this enigmatic story about one man and his pursuit of happiness.

I. *One man's venture.* This particular man had a rather good job. He was in charge of an extensive estate owned by a very wealthy man. In his desire to get what he felt belonged to him, he drifted into dishonesty. We are not told the circumstances that led him to that point; perhaps he began merely by taking home things from the estate to use for his own needs. Maybe he carried home tools that really belonged in the workshop of the master. At any rate, the final result was that he began to juggle the books, to embezzle money from his employer. It was easy at first because, after all, he was the person in charge of everything.

But as always happens, the truth found him out. His employer confronted him and demanded an audit. Realizing he was about to lose everything, he quickly looked over his options. He certainly did not look forward to becoming a common laborer again. He was too old for that. He also detested the sight of beggars, so that was no option. The only thing he could think of was to use his position to quickly feather his nest as best he could. He chose to settle with some of his employer's debtors at a ridiculously low price. Later he would hunt for them and collect their gratitude in one form or another. They would owe him.

But here we have the puzzling part of this parable: Our Lord "commended the unjust steward because he had dealt shrewdly. For the sons of this world are more shrewd in their generation than the sons of light" (Luke 16:8). If the Lord is really suggesting that we all follow the pattern of this particular man's quest for getting what belonged to him, then all we've been taught about the gospel is null and void. If we take this commendation at face value, then we are all saints with no effort at all.

The commendation of our Lord for this man is not a suggestion that we go and do likewise. He still called him a "scoundrel." What he commended him for was being consistent with his goals and values. He had chosen the wisdom of the world by which to pattern his life, and he had remained consistent with the wisdom he chose. He had been wise, astute, alert, energetic, and resourceful. He had no doubt lain awake all night for several nights, planning just what he would do.

Why won't Christians lie awake at night, planning how they can mean more to the Kingdom of God, as worldlings lie awake at night dreaming of how they can increase power and money, their chosen gods.

II. *Your own venture.* Our Lord did not commend the wisdom of the world that the dishonest steward had adopted, but the whole parable brings up the issue of our own approach to getting what belongs to us. In contrast to those who follow the pattern of the dishonest employee stand those who are "children of light." Jesus uses this terminology to speak of those who believe in him, who have been touched by the light of his presence.

The world gives us its brand of truth, which says that we should live selfishly. But the Lord gives us a totally different kind of truth, as found in Christ, which suggests that we live for him. But sometimes we have a great deal of difficulty seeing that.

The gospel suggests an approach to getting what belongs to us, an approach that follows a totally different set of values and goals than the approach of the dishonest employee. Right up front, it is the wisdom that sees Jesus Christ as Lord. The basic choice in life, as presented by Christ, is that we can worship God or we can worship money, but we cannot do both (Luke 16:13). We cannot serve two masters. But we will seek his lordship in the way we pursue it, and spend it.

Because of our basic sinful nature, we begin life in bondage to our selfishness, and therefore in bondage to what money can do for us. Until we learn to break free from money's power over us, through making Christ Lord, we shall not be in a position to follow the wisdom of God.

We could learn a great deal from the apostle Paul because he discovered how to carry money lightly, using it merely to accomplish God's work. He was able to escape bondage to it. He could say, "I know what it is to be in need and I know what it is to have plenty," and he could explain, "I have learned the secret of being content in any and every situation" (Phil. 4:12). I doubt if any of us has arrived at that level in our own life, but we should determine to work in that direction. We should be able to say that the one thing we have to have is Christ, to say that if there were only one thing in the world we could have, we recognize that it must be Christ.

Now, if Christ is indeed the one we worship instead of money, then we will recognize that our own quest to get what belongs to us must be marked by faithfulness to Christ in the very smallest of matters. Our Lord said, "He who is faithful in what is least is faithful also in much; and he who is unjust in what is least is unjust also in much. Therefore, if you have not been faithful in the righteous mammon [money], who will commit to your trust the true riches? And if you have not been faithful in what is another man's, who will give you what is your own?" (16:10–12).

Here is the key to how a Christian must pursue what is his. Notice that our Lord suggested that there is one way to get what is your own. That way is very simple. It is to be faithful in the very least of things. It is to be faithful and honest in your dealings with what belongs to others. Only then will God give to you what really belongs to you, what he has for you. Only then will you really receive in this life all the blessings that God wants to give to you. Honesty in the matter of money is the training ground for discipleship, and only as we dare to be faithful in the very smallest matters will God give us opportunity to be faithful in the largest matters.

If you listen carefully to Christ, you cannot help but be aware that the true riches are those that grow out of an obedient relationship with Christ that is marked by love and that is open to his transforming grace. The true riches are a faith that envelops all of life, a hope that goes beyond the grave, a peace that can exist in the midst of the storms of life, and a forgiveness that lifts all the burdens of guilt. True riches are found in the knowledge that one's life is counting for something, that one is useful in the Kingdom of God. These are riches that carry no dollar value; they are riches you cannot count and deposit and spend. But they are also riches that no one in this world can take from you. They are riches that will still be yours when the stars have all fallen.

Someday, none of us knows when, the Lord will say to us that our lease is up and we are to bring him our books. The divine audit will take place, and what is written there will have our name on it, our calling card. The wisdom by which we have lived and who has been our God will be apparent to all the ages. Are you ready for that moment?—Bob Woods

SUNDAY, JULY 28, 2002
Lectionary Message

Topic: The Kingdom of Heaven
TEXT: Matt. 13:31–33, 44–52
Other Readings: Gen. 29:15–28; Ps. 105:1–11, 45b; Rom. 8:26–39

The author of the Gospel of Matthew was probably a Christian with a Jewish background. He wrote to the Jewish Christians who were dealing with how Jesus' message related to the Scriptures, and with how the transition from the old to the new can take form. Matthew referred many times to different events and writings from the Scriptures and thus demonstrated how the Scriptures are fulfilled through Jesus.

He did this by dividing his Gospel into five main segments. Today's text is from a segment that contains seven parables, all of which talk about what happens when the gospel is preached, and when and how the kingdom of heaven is manifested.

I. *The kingdom starts out small but becomes great.* In the first two parables, Jesus hinted about the essence of the kingdom of heaven. Two illustrations were made about something that is small becoming larger. The mustard seed is the smallest of seeds, but from this little seed grows a tree so large that birds can make nests in its branches. This tree that gives birds a home and shelter is a familiar picture from the Old Testament. Such is the kingdom of heaven and what God intended: a refuge for all people. This is what this particular parable is about. People from all around the world will flock to the kingdom, which is on its way.

The parable about the yeast is similar. A small portion of yeast works its way through the dough, making it rise, to be made into bread later on. The point is that the kingdom of heaven requires only a small amount of power to be effective.

II. *The kingdom is worth more than anything.* The following two parables, in verses 44–46, also have their similarities. They describe the kingdom of heaven's ability to capture a person and hold onto him or her so strongly that everything else becomes less important. The kingdom of heaven is compared with the most valuable thing a poor farmer could hope to find: treasure hidden in a field. Or with a rich merchant who found a pearl of great value. Just as the farmer and merchant were filled with joy and sold all they had to purchase the hidden treasure and pearl, so should Christ's disciples give up everything to possess the kingdom of heaven. The visual language of the hidden treasure and the pearl simplifies for us God's wisdom in the Old Testament (see Prov. 2:4; 8:18; 3:15).

III. *The kingdom is for "whosoever will."* The last parable is taken from the parable of the fish, which is acted out by the sea of Galilee. It is about a fisherman who cast his net into the sea and caught fish of every kind. He put the good fish into baskets and threw out the bad. This parable reflects the disciples' mission to spread the good news to everyone. It illustrates the final judgment, and challenges and urges people to make a commitment to Jesus.

The conclusion of these parables is in verses 51–52 where the main focus is on the kingdom of heaven's closeness to Jesus. The Good News is completed through Jesus. The kingdom of heaven is like a man who can use both the old and the new. The gospel is something new but at the same time is a confirmation of the old.—Inga Johansson

ILLUSTRATIONS

JESUS IN US.   What is constant throughout these parables are the descriptions of events in everyday lives. It is in such events that the kingdom of heaven can break through. In our everyday life we experience both happiness and pain, and even there lies hidden the kingdom of heaven. Many times we are expected to have a strong faith in God, but faith begins like a little seed that sprouts up and grows strong, giving life to every person.

Today people are searching for answers. They are searching everywhere. How can we help these people meet Jesus? When they see Jesus in *us,* the hidden becomes evident.—Inga Johansson

THE CHURCH.   The Church is the kingdom of heaven's manifestation on Earth. But the kingdom of heaven is not the same as the Church. We live in a world of good and evil. As individual Christians and as a Church, we have before us the task of proclaiming the good news to all humanity: to both the good and the wicked.—Inga Johansson

SERMON SUGGESTIONS

Topic: Why Praise the Lord?

TEXT: Ps. 105

(1) Because of his wonderful works (vv. 1–2). (2) Because he is holy—different and special (v. 3). (3) Because of his available presence and power (v. 4). (4) Because he is faithful to his promises (vv. 7–11).

Topic: If God Is for Us

TEXT: Rom. 8:26–39, especially vv. 31–37

(1) He will give everything we truly need (v. 32). (2) He will stand with us and for us against our adversaries (v. 33). (3) He will honor the living Christ's unceasing intercession for us (v. 34). (4) He will make us more than conquerors through Christ (v. 36).

CONGREGATIONAL MUSIC

1. "We Know That God Works Things for Good," Rom. 8:28–39; vers. Calvin Seerveld (1985)
   LESTER, Calvin Seerveld (1985)

   This lovely Bible song accurately paraphrases most of the Epistle lesson in Romans 8 and thus could be sung in place of the reading.
2. "The Kingdom of God," Gracia Grindal (1985)
   MUSTARD SEED, Austin C. Lovelace (1985)

The parable of the mustard seed recorded in Matthew 13:31–32 is beautifully set forth in this modern hymn. Suggestion: Have the choir sing the words of the stanzas and the congregation join in on the refrain.

3. "This Is the Time to Remember," Bryan Jeffery Leech (1982)
   DUDLEY, Bryan D. Smith (1984)

"Remember the wonderful works that he has done" (Ps. 105:5) is the basis for this new but simple hymn of remembrance. It would fit well with the Psalter reading.

4. "O Love, How Deep, How Broad, How High," Anon.; Latin; trans. Benjamin Webb (1854)
   PUER NOBIS, Trier Melody (fifteenth century); adapt. Michael Praetorius (1609)

This ancient hymn expounds on the dimensions of the love of God set forth in Romans 9:39 and would be appropriately sung following the Epistle reading.—Hugh T. McElrath

WORSHIP AIDS

CALL TO WORSHIP.   "Oh, give thanks to the Lord! Call upon his name; make known his deeds among the peoples. Sing to him, sing psalms to him; talk of all his wondrous works" (Ps. 105:1–2 NKJV).

INVOCATION.   O God, make us a thankful people. Make us a praying people. Make us a sharing people, telling of your grace and salvation available to all. And may we praise you this hour and forever.

OFFERTORY SENTENCE.   "It is not that you ought to relieve other people's needs and leave yourselves in hardship, but that there should be a fair balance—your surplus at present may fill their deficit, and another time their surplus may fill your deficit" (2 Cor. 8:13–14a NJB).

OFFERTORY PRAYER.   Make us, O Lord, fair and honest stewards of your blessings, that we might know your joy and grace in what we are and what we do.

PRAYER.   Accept, O Lord, our thanks and praise for all that you have done for us. We thank you for the splendor of the whole creation, for the beauty of this world, for the wonder of life, and for the mystery of love.

We thank you for the blessing of family and friends, and for the loving care that surrounds us on every side.

We thank you for setting us at tasks that demand our best efforts, and for leading us to accomplishments that satisfy and delight us.

We thank you also for those disappointments and failures that lead us to acknowledge our dependence on you alone.

Above all, we thank you for your Son Jesus Christ; for the truth of his Word and the example of his life; for his steadfast obedience, by which he overcame temptation; for his dying, through which he overcame death; and for his rising to life again, in which we are raised to the life of your Kingdom.

Grant us the gift of your Spirit, that we may know him and make him known; and that through him, at all times and in all places, we may give thanks to you in all things.—*Book of Common Prayer*

SERMON
Topic: Micah?
TEXT: Mic. 6:1–8

Microsoft thinks that the question of life is, "Where do you want to go?"—as if life is a highway and each of us gets to pick our directions. There are those who see the Super Bowl as a metaphor for life: Life is a great contest and there is only one winner. But you and I are here because we understand that life is a gift and we are to use the gift to bring joy to the giver. Life is a gift to us from God and we are to live in such a way as to bring joy and honor and praise to God. But even that doesn't get us very far, for there is still the question, "How do you do that anyway?" What kind of things should we be doing to honor and bring joy to God?

A man named Simeon Stylites was convinced that the best way to honor the holiness and purity of God was to avoid as much of life as one can. The Buddhist tend to think along the same lines. The less you want and need, the purer you become and the more holy and faithful your life will be. Simeon lived in Antioch in the fourth century. He lived in seclusion for ten years, in a cell where he prayed, meditated, and read scriptures; but his feet still touched the ground and he feared he was contaminated by the ground. So he built a pillar four feet square and six feet high, and he lived on that pillar with heavy chains around his neck to mortify the flesh. He claimed that he spent his time in adoration and intercession for others. Finally, he increased the height of his pillar until it was sixty feet off the ground, and there he lived for thirty years. Simeon Stylites said that the best way to use the gift of life is to have as little as possible to do with the things of Earth. "Turn your eyes upon Jesus, look full in his wonderful face, and the things of Earth shall grow strangely dim, in the light of his glory and grace." Harvey Cox, who when I was in seminary made a big splash about God and the new urban sprawl, suggested that God's Incarnation in Jesus Christ shows that God does not find offensive the normal messy stuff of human life. We who seek to honor God with our lives ought not be too quick to claim that places and parts of creations are unclean. We are not to attempt to avoid the blood, guts, grime, and gristle of human life; we are invited to live in its midst and redeem it.

There are some who think they want to be like Mike—Michael Jordan or Michael Jackson—but there is a deeper need for us to be like Micah. Micah! Back there in the Old Testament part of the Bible. Micah, who lived and worshipped in the 700s B.C.; Micah, who had watched those around him seek their own form of purity and holiness by faithfully offering sacrifices and rituals; Micah, who knew those who believed that our responsibility was to keep the law, to do what we have been told, to obey the Torah and keep the covenant. This was the same Micah who had watched those who were dedicated to purity refuse to get involved with helping others; the same Micah who had watched as those who kept the Law found ways to make it work for their enrichment; the same Micah who became convinced that the way for us to live our lives to the glory of God and in gratitude for the gift God has given to us is for us to do justice, to love kindness, and to walk humbly with God.

It has been suggested that the only provable doctrine of the Christian faith, the only one of our faith claims that can be demonstrated, is the reality of sin, and Micah said that in this kind of world, we serve God best by working for justice for all. One of the universal claims of the postmodern debate is that all truth is conditioned by self-interest. Micah knew that even in the eighth century, and he suggested that if we are to give glory and honor to God with our lives, we need to seek to do justice for others. The description of life in Micah's community does not sound very strange. The poor were becoming poorer. The rich kept getting richer. People were cheating one another, lying to one another, conning one another in a steady stream of political, social, and economic injustices. Who is conning whom when almost every repair person I can remember talking to begins his explanation for why it will cost so much to fix whatever is broken with the statement that the person who put this in the first time did not do a very good job? Micah had his bankers repossessing the homes of the widows so those homes could be acquired by the banker to sell again. These homes were sold on the courthouse steps for taxes so the sharp real estate people could turn a profit. And best yet, it was all legal.

Micah knew about savings and loan schemes in which the rich sell property back and forth to each other with the loans insured by the taxpayer until the price becomes so unrelated to the market that one of the people simply walks away from the loan and the savings and loan takes a hit and collapses. It was a clever use of the system. It's hard to prove that it was fraud, but no one would call it just.

We live our lives in honor and praise of God by living and doing justice with our actions. We are not able to put down in a few rules or doctrines what justice requires. Justice requires that we consider with equal intensity the reality and needs of others. The demands of justice do not stay the same. When leaders of this community have sat down to talk about what is good for this county, it has been a great step toward justice to include white leaders and black leaders together, but that will not be justice in this county now. Justice means we need to bring into the same meeting the leaders of the ever-growing Hispanic community. Justice means having at the table all those who will be affected by the decisions. The best example of justice I can think of is the process by which two children split a piece of cake. One gets to cut, the other gets to choose. All the interested parties are at the table and the procedure is designed so that the interests of both are the concern of both. But justice can be done without liking each other.

Yet of course justice is not all there is. Justice is not the last word. Justice is only the foundation. Justice is the requirement and the means by which we are able then to love mercy. Justice comes before mercy because respect comes before compassion or else compassion is pity. We honor God first by doing justice, that is, by granting the other party's needs and wants equal status with our own, and in that kind of community, where there is justice and dignity, we then find that we may indeed love to be forgiving and merciful where there has been failure and neglect. We do justice, and then as we deal with others at the table, we may discover their hurts, needs, pains, struggles, and sorrows, and we may find that we do have a great desire to show mercy, to give a kindness that is beyond obligation.

Do justice, and where justice is developed, there we may discover the humanity of each other, which leads to sharing and caring that are merciful. Micah suggested that when we are able to consider the needs of others as important as our own, to share and listen to the common humanity of others so that their pain and suffering are as real as ours, and to forgive them as we are to forgive ourselves, then we have begun to develop a kind of humility and style of living that bring glory and praise to God and all creation.

To do justice: We don't have to like it, but we have to try to give the needs of others an equal place at the table of power. To discover in that justice a relationship, a human face, a sense of sameness, and that the poor put on their clothing just like we do—which opens us to a compassion that gives kindness and mercy to others—is to find ourselves walking humbly with God and in step with creation.—Rick Brand

SUNDAY, AUGUST 4, 2002
Lectionary Message

Topic: Saving Passion
TEXT: Rom. 9:1–5
Other Readings: Gen. 32:22–31; Ps. 17:1–7, 15; Matt. 14:13–21

Through this text we get a good, hard look at the heart of Saul of Tarsus, now known as the apostle Paul. We see Paul's passion—a passion that drove him through hardships, over difficult terrain, during years of concentrated effort in his attempt to lead persons of various races, nationalities, and social groups to salvation in Christ Jesus. In this story we also have a mirror in which we can evaluate our own evangelistic passion.

I. *Paul's passion was sincere.* Paul stated his concern "in Christ." As a Christian, being in Christ was the central fact of Paul's existence, the place where truth lived for him. He went on with his oath in a way that was almost redundant. He said, "I am speaking the truth—I am not lying." He could hardly have been more clear. And then he brought in the big guns: "My conscience is witnessing together with me in the Holy Spirit." Because his tone of voice, face, and body language were necessarily absent from the writing, Paul claimed in as many ways as he could that this passion of his was sincere.

II. *Paul's passion was intense.* He could even utter a wishful prayer that he be anathema, that is, separated for eternity from Christ. He ended chapter 8 with the assurance that nothing "in all creation will be able to separate us from the love of God in Christ Jesus our Lord." Here he indicated his willingness to suffer such separation—and here's the big *if*—if it could be done for the sake of his people, the children of Israel.

III. *Paul's passion was reasonable.* The Israelites were not only his kinfolk, they were also God's specially chosen people. They had been adopted as God's children. They had experienced the glory of God's presence. They had been given a whole series of covenants by which they were designated and commissioned to special roles in God's strategy for redeeming the human race. They had been graced with the law of God through Moses. They had enjoyed the privilege of worshipping God as he instructed. They had the ongoing promise of God's presence and ultimate victory. They also had the tremendous tradition of the fathers and mothers of their faith. And to cap it all off, they had the honor of giving birth to the anointed one of God—the one who was sent to accomplish the salvation of the world.

So Paul's passion was reasonable. He was concerned about a people who not only were his kin but also were specially marked and blessed by the God he served. It was reasonable that he was in anguish over their rejection of his message.

IV. *Paul's passion was goal oriented.* His overarching goal in life was to bring glory to the Christ "who is over all, God blessed forever." He was so dedicated to the Lord Jesus Christ that he worked day and night to lead others to glorify Christ, too. He described this process in 2 Corinthians 4:15: "Yes, everything is for your sake, so that grace, as it extends to more and more people, may increase thanksgiving, to the glory of God." It seems that he could visualize people offering praise and thanksgiving to God all over the world, and he was watching that multitude of worshippers grow as people responded to the gospel he preached. That's the goal toward which Paul's passion drove him.

What goal drives your passion? Do you see the worshipping throng around the throne of God? Do you see it growing as you and other believers spread the word about Jesus? To help people visualize the scene, we have the book of Revelation in our Bible. Read it. Meditate on it. Don't get bogged down in mysterious details, but see the images of worship there and let that goal drive your passion.

What reason guides your passion? How well do you understand the people around you— your relatives, neighbors, friends, coworkers? Do you see them as God sees them? Do you recognize how God has blessed them—how God has worked in their lives to prepare them to hear about his Son Jesus? Do you recall when you are with them that they are people whom God loves, individuals for whom Christ died? Think about it. We have more than enough reasons to share our Savior with our neighbors.

How intense is your passion? Here's where most of us fail as witnesses for Christ. We just don't care enough. Somehow we miss the depth of God's concern for creation. Somehow John 3:16 doesn't register very often with us. If God so loved the world that he gave his Son, should we not share that love and deepen our concern for those who are indifferent to him?

Perhaps what is missing is prayer. Paul prayed with great intensity for God's people. He echoed the prayer of Moses, "But now, if you will only forgive their sin—but if not, blot me out of the book that you have written" (Exod. 32:32). Until our passion is so deep that we would be willing to lose our own salvation to save others, we cannot match the intensity of Paul's passion.

How sincere is your passion? Are you ready to take an oath, on the basis of your conscience and in tune with the Holy Spirit, that you have an intense, reasonable, goal-oriented passion for God's rebellious people? The early Christians who translated the words of our faith into Latin chose the term *sacramentum* to refer to the Lord's Supper. In Roman use, *sacramentum* was the oath of loyalty taken by inductees into the army. Each time we partake of Holy Communion, we testify to the sincerity of our passionate loyalty to Christ. This oath should never be limited to our personal, individual relationship with God; it should also reflect the loyalty of Paul, whose love of Christ included his loving concern for the whole human race.—Bruce E. Shields

ILLUSTRATIONS

HEART AGLOW.   W. H. Griffith Thomas wrote, "And so Paul loves, and longs, and prays, and strives, and writes, and works for Israel's salvation. Have we these marks of a soul-winner? What a rebuke they are to our dullness, dryness, and deadness. A clergyman once asked a friend to find him a Curate, and said that he wanted a man 'whose heart was aglow with the love of souls.' Such was the Apostle, and such ought we to be. If we are not, shall we not seek to 'abound in this grace also?'"[1]—Bruce E. Shields

---

[1]W. H. Griffith Thomas, *St. Paul's Epistle to the Romans: A Devotional Commentary* (Grand Rapids, Mich.: Eerdmans, 1956), p. 248.

HE SILENCED THE DEVIL.   If you find yourself getting very miserly, begin to scatter, like a wealthy farmer in New York state I heard of. He was a noted miser, but he was converted. Soon after, a poor man who had been burned out and had no provisions came to him for help. The farmer thought he would be liberal and give the man a ham from his smokehouse. On his way to get the ham, the tempter whispered to him, "Give him the smallest one you have."

He struggled over whether he would give a large or a small ham, but finally he took down the largest he could find.

"You are a fool," the devil said.

"If you don't keep still," the farmer replied, "I will give him every ham I have in the smokehouse."—D. L. Moody

SERMON SUGGESTIONS

Topic: Wrestling with God

TEXT: Gen. 32:22–31

(1) The strange story of Jacob wrestling with God. (2) Our experience of wrestling with God: (a) in the matter of conversion, (b) in painful moral decisions, (c) in critical vocational choices, (d) in the anguish of doubt. (3) The aftermath: (a) the blessing of God, (b) the recognition of God in retrospect.

Topic: The Compassion of Jesus

TEXT: Matt. 14:13–21

(1) Jesus' deep concern for people attracted crowds to him: (a) he ignored his own grief (v. 12) and met the crowds, (b) he helped those with the most pressing needs (v. 14), (c) he ministered to the basic needs of the crowds (vv. 15–21; see also Matt. 6:11). (2) The church today has a mandate in the example of Jesus: (a) to attract people with the good news of salvation in Jesus Christ, (b) to minister to the multitudes in the variety of their pressing human needs.

CONGREGATIONAL MUSIC

1. "Come, O Thou Traveler Unknown," Charles Wesley (1742)

     SURREY, Henry Cary (1723)

     One of Charles Wesley's most memorable hymns, "Come, O Thou Traveler Unknown" is a recital of Jacob's experience wrestling with the unknown angel in terms of Wesley's own conversion. It can be either read or sung in connection with the Old Testament reading.

2. "Your Hands, O God, in Days of Old," Edward H. Plumptre (1866)

     ST. MICHAEL'S, Gawler's *Hymns and Psalms* (1789)

     This hymn would be a suitable response to the Gospel lesson on the feeding of the five thousand. The four regular phrases per stanza would make alternate antiphonal singing feasible and effective.

3. "Lord, Listen to Your Children Praying," Ken Medema (1973)

     CHILDREN PRAYING, Medema (1973)

     The petitionary mood of the Psalter reading finds a contemporary echo in this miniature hymn. It could be interspersed at various points in the reading of the lesson.

4. "Lord, Listen to My Righteous Plea," Ps. 17; vers. Helen Otte (1982)

BERNARD, J. M. Grotenhuis (1983)

Alternate reading of the verses of Psalm 17 with the parallel stanzas of this modern paraphrase, as follows, would be not only interesting but enlightening: vv. 1–5, stanza 1; vv. 6–8, stanza 2; vv. 14–15, stanza 5.—Hugh T. McElrath

WORSHIP AIDS

CALL TO WORSHIP.   "God, I call upon you, for you will answer me. Bend down your ear to me; listen to my words" (Ps. 17:6 REB).

INVOCATION.   Compassionate God, help us to catch a vision of you in your love for us and for all humankind, and mold us after that image so that your best, even Jesus Christ your Son, will be reflected in what we are and what we do. To that end, give us grace to respond to the challenge of your Word to us today.

OFFERTORY SENTENCE.   "On the first day of every week, each of you is to put aside and save whatever extra you earn, so that collections need not be taken when I come" (1 Cor. 16:2 NRSV).

OFFERTORY PRAYER.   We bring to you today, O God, what we have methodically put aside for your service, as well as what our hearts tell us to give this very day. Bless all that we bring, that your name may be glorified in the uses to which these offerings may be directed.

PRAYER.   In all ages you call men and women, youth, and boys and girls to serve through the life of the Church. We praise you for the life of this congregation in which we share. We are also thankful for the great Church that embraces the faithful of all places and times in the communion of saints. For the gospel that has brought the Church into being and that continues its life through the centuries, we give you thanks. We are grateful for Jesus who, as your anointed one, is the head of the Church and our Lord and Savior.

O You who "desires truth in the inward parts," may we approach worship with integrity, for we know that only the pure in heart—only those who give themselves wholeheartedly—shall see you. Help us to go deeper into ourselves to discover your Kingdom within, for we are created in your image. May these moments in worship be an experience to challenge the mind, enlarge the heart, and quicken the spirit.

As in this congregation we seek to foster a community of faith, a laboratory for spiritual maturing, and a fellowship of Christian love, grant to us, your servants, an eagerness for learning, a readiness for discipline, and a concern that makes for true comradeship.

O you who through the Church declares a love for all people, grant to us a love that is God-like and that goes forth to all persons without prejudice or partiality. In the life of our families, grant love that listens to the other with insight and understanding as we celebrate your presence in all the relationships of the home. As we mourn the death of loved ones and friends, encourage us with a lively hope. Where the flames of hatred, prejudice, and fear rage in war, we pray for reconciliation and a just peace.

Alert us to our ministry so that "we fail not man nor Thee."—John Thompson

SERMON
Topic: Living at Peace with the Environment
TEXT: Ps. 19:1–5; Rom. 8:19–22; Rev. 21:1; 22:1–2

What does all this discussion about ecology, the environment, and pollution have to do with the Church, Christians, and the Bible? It's an interesting question. Questions sometimes can help us get to the truth.

I. *Is the Church responsible for the environmental crisis?* We need to ask some questions about the whole problem with the environment, pollution, and ecology. The first question is this: Do churches and Christians have any responsibility for the crises in which we find ourselves today?

II. *The Hebrew concept of nature.* The Greeks had the notion that the human body and nature were evil. There was nothing inside of man and woman that was pure or good but the soul. The Hebrews did not have that attitude toward life. The body was seen not as corrupt but as good. They saw humankind as being one with God, and people as linked to one another and also to creation itself. In fact, when you read the Scriptures, you discover that the Hebrews had a high concept of nature. They saw nature as alive with God's creation. The marvelous passage from Psalm 19 declares that the heavens and the Earth disclose God to us. The Hebrews saw nature not as evil but as good and as part of God's wonderful creation. A special covenant had been made with them by the great God of the universe. William Blake, the poet, expressed the truth this way:

> To see a World in a Grain of Sand
> And a Heaven in a Wild Flower
> Hold Infinity in the palm of your hand
> And Eternity in an hour.

III. *Nature reveals God.* In the biblical perspective of creation, human beings should be able to look at the wonder of creation and see it disclose God to us. The natural world is not God, but the Creator is revealed through it. When we have eyes to see, we should be able to see God in a rooster, a bird, an animal, a flower, or whatever—something of the awesome mystery of God in his wonderful creation.

IV. *Unfulfilled creation.* Something, however, has gone wrong with God's creation. Sin is a part of creation and we are not quite able to understand what happened in God's good world. One of the things the Scriptures tell us is that creation is good, but it is not perfect. Paul tells us in the eighth chapter of Romans that creation is in travail and is moving toward being fulfilled. Creation itself will be redeemed by God. One day there will be a new heaven and a new Earth. Creation itself will be fully redeemed by God's glorious grace. Creation is moving toward fulfilling what it was created to be. Humankind has the responsibility of living in harmony with and not in opposition to nature.

V. *The prodigal way of humanity.* What, then, is the nature of our responsibility? Humankind has been like the prodigal son. We have taken all the blessings God has given us and have wasted them in riotous living, sometimes in excessive living. We have received the bounty of God's creation and have exploited and sometimes ruined it. I wish I could stand in this pulpit today and tell you that all of our rivers and streams are pure, that our air is pure, and that the water we drink is fine. But no person can truthfully tell you that today.

Suppose someone told you that you have a bank account with enough money in it to take care of you all your life, if you don't overspend. If you spend carefully and wisely, you will always have enough in your account. You don't know the exact amount in your account and you are never going to be told that. But you do know that if you just spend wisely you will always have enough. You would be very careful, wouldn't you?

Our environment is that way. We can't just keep on abusing and destroying rainforests and other parts of the natural world without bringing devastation on ourselves and our world.

VI. *Caretakers of our planet.* As Christian people we have a responsibility. What is that responsibility? Our responsibility is to be stewards and caretakers of God's universe. The Genesis story doesn't tell us that we are to devour the Earth or that we can do anything we want with nature. God placed Adam and Eve in the garden to take care of it. They were to be caretakers and "to tend the Earth." We are to work with nature and learn how to live in harmony with creation. All of God's creation is our home, and it is a beautiful home.

The scientist Teilhard de Chardin reminds us that "the Age of Nations is past. The task before us now, if we will not perish, is to build the Earth." We are all responsible for our planet. We can't pass the responsibility to others.

Nobody can say that he or she can do anything he or she wants to our planet—dump anything into our streams, spew anything into the air. You and I have a responsibility as Christian persons to do our part in trying to make this world a better place to live.—William Powell Tuck

SUNDAY, AUGUST 11, 2002
Lectionary Message

Topic: Saving Words
TEXT: Rom. 10:5–15
Other Readings: Gen. 37:1–4, 12–28; Matt. 14:22–33

Our text from Romans 10 contains the most important words a human being can hear. They are saving words—words that speak about God's work of salvation for the human race, words by which we may respond to God's faithfulness, words by which God promises to respond to our faith.

For this reason, the author of the words of our text, the apostle Paul, embedded his words in a speech by the greatest hero, leader, teacher, and prophet of his people: Moses. Not only did Paul choose Moses as a vehicle for his saving words, but he also chose the words Moses spoke to the people of Israel the last time they saw him. It was the deathbed statement of Moses, so to speak. Deuteronomy 29 describes the scene as Moses summoned the people and gave them their final instructions, preparing them to move into the Promised Land. These words of Moses were held in great respect by all of Israel, and now Paul was using them to frame some of his most important words to his fellow Christians. Paul told about the saving words we preach, hear, and confess, as well as the saving words we can expect to hear from our Lord.

I. *We preach saving words.* For most of us, our Christian faith started when we heard somebody speak about Jesus. There might be a few who were converted by reading, and that indicates that writing is also an evangelistic activity; but for most of us, it was words we heard that turned us toward Christ. Knowing this, it seems strange that we tend to be so quiet about our faith in Christ Jesus. We tend to leave the preaching to the professionals—to the preachers who rarely have access to the people who need to hear the saving words. The Church has become a community of specialists, while the world needs to see the consistency of a community of generalists—a community of people all of whom are ready to bring the world the good news of salvation in Jesus Christ.

The saving words we preach need not be fancy words; they need only be clear. They need not be technical; they need only be understood. They need not be beautiful; they need only speak to people's hearts. When people hear and understand words in plain brown wrappers about Jesus' death and Resurrection for human sin, they will recognize them as saving words from God.

II. *We hear saving words.* Later in Romans 10, Paul says, "Faith comes by hearing." When we hear words about the grace of God in Christ, and the claims of that gracious Lord on our lives—when we hear such words and are ready to act on them, we come to faith. That step might be our first step in the direction of heaven, or it could be another in a long line of steps in that direction. Wherever we are in the journey toward God, "faith comes by hearing."

Each time we respond positively to saving words, our faith grows another notch. We can hear those words in many ways. They come to us in sermons and lessons in church, certainly; but they also come in the hymns and choruses we sing, in prayers, in our participation in the Lord's Supper, as well as in our private times of Bible reading and prayer. They sometimes surprise us in casual conversations and walks in the woods. In short, saving words are all around us, and we can hear them if we pay attention—if we "listen up."

III. *We confess saving words.* When we hear saving words, it is time to confess them to others. Does it seem that I am talking in circles here? Well, I am. People speak saving words so that other people will hear them, so that they, too, can speak them to others. Conversation is like that, you know. Lively conversations rarely proceed in an orderly fashion from start to finish. They more likely go round and round, with one person's statement stimulating another's response.

The saving words of the good news about Jesus should proceed in the same way—like a normal conversation. We hear, respond, speak, listen, hear, respond, and speak again. Faith grows in such exchanges, and lives are changed. In other words, salvation happens.

IV. *God speaks saving words.* The mystery of saving words is how God gets involved in the process. Here is where understanding stops and faith takes over. In some mysterious way, when we human beings use our all-too-human language to speak saving words, God steps in and speaks the critical words: righteousness and salvation. Verse 10 of our text reads, "For one believes with the heart and so is justified, and one confesses with the mouth and so is saved." When Paul says a person is justified, he means that God graces that person with divine righteousness—a goodness we can't attain or earn on our own. And when Paul says a person is saved, he means that God marks that person to spend eternity in God's own presence. The final word is always God's word, and for us who have come to faith in Christ, God promises that the final word will be a saving word; for as the prophet Joel put it, "Everyone who calls on the name of the Lord shall be saved."—Bruce E. Shields

ILLUSTRATIONS

THE FRUIT OF A LIFE.   St. John the Evangelist caught the depth of Christ because he had lived with him so long. We do not know exactly who St. John was, and as long as people read the New Testament, his identity will be a moot question. There is no way of telling precisely, beyond a shadow of a doubt, who wrote the fourth Gospel, but the tradition is that he was an old man, and everything in the Gospel confirms that tradition. For the picture that John gives us of Christ could only be drawn by someone who not only had lived with him as a companion, walking with him over the dusty roads of Judea, but who in some way lived *in* him the way a man's body lives in the air. So John lived in Christ decade after decade. He walked in his light through all the dark ways of his own personal existence. He gloried in his love, and came to see that among all the traits that compose the character of Christ, this is the essential one, and that the one thing that would distinguish the disciples of this man is their love for one another. He gloried in this love, he lived in it, he breathed it the way we breathe air. He lived on Christ's life the way we live on meat and drink. What he wrote, therefore, was the fruit of this lifelong association.—Theodore Parker Ferris[2]

GUIDING LIGHT.   When Bunyan wrote his immortal allegory, he started out by telling of a man who wanted something very earnestly but did not know which way to go to find it. Evangelist found him wandering about in a field and, pointing his finger, asked him, "Do you see yonder wicket gate?" The man answered, "No." "Do you see yonder shining light?" He said, "I think I do." Then said Evangelist, "Keep that light in your eye, and go up directly thereto; so shalt thou see the gate." So the goal of a good life may seem inaccessible, but by keeping the light in the eye, one can really get to the place for which he longs.—Frederick Keller Stamm[3]

SERMON SUGGESTIONS

Topic: Human Schemes and Divine Plans, Part I
TEXT: Gen. 37:1–4, 12–28
(1) The crowning provocation (v. 2b). (2) The confirming evidence (vv. 3–4). (3) The concoctions of envy (vv. 12–28).

Topic: Unexpected Blessing
TEXT: Matt. 14:22–33, especially v. 27
(1) Like the disciples, we encounter many disturbing situations in life. (2) Such situations are especially disturbing when we fear that the hand of God is against us. (3) Faith triumphs when we realize, despite all appearances, our living Lord is with us and we do not have to be afraid.

CONGREGATIONAL MUSIC

1. "Out of Need and out of Custom," Ken Medema (1972)
   GATHERING, Medema (1972)

---

[2]*The New Life*
[3]*Seeing the Multitudes*

This contemporary hymn of gathering is refreshing in its honesty and freedom from pretense. Sung at the beginning of worship, it has the possibility of making the transforming presence of God palpable.

2. "Jesus, Thou Joy of Loving Hearts," Latin (twelfth century); trans. Ray Palmer (1858)

QUEBEC, Henry Baker (1854)

All who call on the name of the Lord shall be saved (Rom. 10:13). This glorious truth is affirmed particularly in stanza 2 of this fine hymn from the Latin. It could be sung as an introduction to the Epistle lesson for this day.

3. "Trumpet the Name! Praise Be to Our Lord!" Ps. 105; vers. Calvin Seerveld (1983)

GENEVAN 105, *Genevan Psalter* (1862)

Stanzas 5 and 6 of this excellent metrical paraphrase of Psalm 105 recounts the story of Joseph that is related in this day's Old Testament lesson. Alternating the selected verses with the stanzas, as follows, would be an effective presentation of the Psalter lesson: vv. 1–3, stanza 1; vv. 4–6, stanza 2; vv. 16–20, stanza 5; vv. 21–24, stanza 6.

4. "I Sought the Lord, and Afterward I Knew," Anon. (1878)

FINDLANDIA, Jean Sibelius (1899)

The second stanza of this anonymous hymn refers to Peter's attempt to walk on the stormy sea and Jesus' reaching out to save him. The spiritual interpretation is that, though we seek God for help, it is God who takes the initiative in offering us help. This hymn would be ideal as a response to the Gospel lesson or a sermon.—Hugh T. McElrath

WORSHIP AIDS

CALL TO WORSHIP. "O give thanks unto the Lord; call upon his name; make known his deeds among the people" (Ps. 105:11).

INVOCATION. For your love for us, as shown in your gift of Christ to us, we thank you, O God. Help us in every way to pass along that reality, so that others may come to know the Christ whom we have come to trust and love.

OFFERTORY SENTENCE. "It is required of stewards that they be found trustworthy" (1 Cor. 4:2 NRSV).

OFFERTORY PRAYER. You, O God, have given us a stewardship that is widely encompassing and profoundly challenging. Grant us the grace to be faithful to your expectations of us, and the joy that can be ours when we are faithful.

PRAYER. O God, whose Spirit searches all things and whose love bears all things, come with truth and mercy to us today. We are often blind to the ways that lead to the hearts and needs of others and to thy throne. Give thy light, O God, and take away our darkness. But when we see ourselves as we are, leave us not to stand confused and helpless in our guilt. Give us thy grace, O God, to take away our fears and to strengthen our laggard hearts. Grant, O Lord, that thy Word may give us increased understanding of the scope of our task as servants of Jesus Christ. May we be encouraged to seek new depths of dedication. May we be inspired to take more seriously our opportunities for preparation for the task of witnessing to thy truth to the ends of the Earth.

SERMON

Topic: When a Person Goes to Church

TEXT: Isa. 6:1–8

Churchgoing has been the practice of multitudes of people for centuries. Some go to church to be seen by others. Others go for social and economical reasons. A few go to worship the living God, Creator of heaven and Earth.

Here is what Isaiah said should happen when a person goes to church:

I. *He should see the holiness of God.* The greatest tragedy of our day may well be that we have lost a sense of the holiness of God. Let us seek to recapture an awareness of his presence. We need not see a preacher, be reminded of a church, or even hear a sermon to worship. We need to catch a vision of the glory of a holy God who created this world and all that dwells therein, who is still in control of that which he created, and who gave his only Son to redeem us through the blood he shed on Calvary's cross.

The object of worship is to see God. Oh, that we could see God as Isaiah saw him—"sitting upon a throne," exalted, his presence filling the place of worship. Oh, that we could see God, "holy, holy, holy," with his glory filling the entire Earth.

II. *He should see his own true nature.* Immediately upon seeing the glory of a Holy God, Isaiah caught a vision of how man's nature compares with the nature of God. Then he cried out, "Woe is me!" Isaiah saw that man was corporately unclean as he said, "I dwell in the midst of a people of unclean lips." He also saw that he was personally unclean as he confessed, "I am a man of unclean lips."

Authentic worship makes us painfully aware that we have "all sinned and come short of the glory of God." This kind of worship also makes us aware that "the wages of sin is death." How sinful we must appear before a holy, righteous God!

III. *He should see the necessity and availability of cleansing.* When we realize our own inadequacy, we will be ready to cast ourselves on the righteousness of Jesus Christ, "who knew no sin, that we might be made the righteousness of God in him" (2 Cor. 5:21). Isaiah was cleansed from sin and his iniquity was taken away.

Authentic worship will not occur until we confess our sins and accept the cleansing and forgiveness offered to us by God through Jesus Christ.

IV. *He should see God's will for his life.* Have you ever wondered why God doesn't zap us and take us to heaven as soon as we trust him? Heaven is a better place than this Earth. Christ has gone there to prepare a place for us. If worship is no more than gathering together to exalt God, we could do a better job in his presence. God has created us for a purpose, and he has left us here for a purpose.

Isaiah heard God ask, "Whom shall I send and who will go for us?" That's God's universal question: "Who will go for us?" The Great Commission which Jesus gave his disciples states, "Go ye therefore, and teach all nations, baptizing them in the name of the Father, and of the Son, and of the Holy Ghost; teaching them to observe all things whatsoever I have commanded you; and lo, I am with you always, even unto the end of the world" (Matt. 28:19–20).

At his Ascension, Christ implied that he would leave when he said, "But ye shall receive power; after that the Holy Spirit will come upon you, and ye shall be witnesses unto me both in Jerusalem and in Judea, and in Samaria, and unto the uttermost part of the Earth" (Acts 1:8).

You can't spell *God* without *go*. You can't spell *gospel* without *go*. And you can't really worship without feeling compelled to *go!*

V. *He should see his own level of commitment.* Isaiah responded to God's call to go with a genuine commitment: "Here am I, Lord, send me." Will you respond in the same way? If our worship is authentic, our commitment will also be authentic, for it will grow out of that worship experience.

The true purpose of worship is that, on seeing the holiness of God, we might grow dissatisfied with ourselves, become cleansed for service, spring into action, and go tell others what God has done to redeem the world in Christ.—Edward D. Johnson

SUNDAY, AUGUST 18, 2002
Lectionary Message

Topic: Saving Grace
TEXT: Rom. 11:1–2a, 29–32
Other Readings: Gen. 45:1–15; Matt. 15:(10–20) 21–28

We saw how Paul, in Romans 9, used several different means of convincing his readers of his passion for the salvation of his people. We then saw how in Romans 10 he used the final speech of Moses to Israel as an authoritative framework in which to highlight the words of salvation. In today's text, from Romans 11, we hear Paul quoting various texts from the Hebrew Bible to demonstrate God's saving grace. Paul is careful here to quote from all three divisions of the Scriptures: the Law, the Prophets, and the Writings, to show that God's mercy is revealed throughout the Bible. In the process, Paul shows us several aspects of God's saving grace.

I. *God's saving grace is active.* The best way to impress people with the reality of God's grace is with personal testimony. That's what Paul did in our text. In answer to the question, "Has God rejected his people?" the apostle replied by pointing to himself. He was one of those "people of God," an Israelite through and through. He was living in the saving grace of God.

Note that there is no heavy theology at this point. Paul could certainly have turned on the theology, but he chose not to here. He merely pointed to his own relationship with God through Christ as exhibit 1 in his argument that God had not rejected Israel.

Whether we intend it or not, our lives—our personal testimonies—are the most important element in our communication of God's grace to others. There is a place for theological reasoning. There is a place for argumentation. There is a place also for study of the Scriptures. But none of these can replace our example as testimony to the grace of God. Scripture can put that grace in its historical context and surround it with additional information. Argument can break down rational barriers to faith. Theology can help people to systematize their faith. But none of these apart from the example of the life of a believer can show God's grace in action. The "I myself" of your testimony, when you use it to point to how God has blessed you, is the primary way your friends and neighbors will come to experience the grace of God themselves.

II. *God's saving grace is irrevocable.* Too often we hear from somebody we are speaking with about Christ that it's too late for them. People actually believe that they can resist God's call long enough to cause God to turn against them. Paul said that wasn't even true for the

Israelites who had rejected their Messiah. A person might continue to reject God, to resist God's call; but God never quits reaching out to every human being. The gracious calling of the Lord is, in Paul's words, irrevocable.

God has spoken saving grace into existence, and no sin, no injustice, no rebellion on our part can cause him to take it back. Oh, God usually won't overpower a person with his gifts and call, but that call to grace is always there.

III. *God's saving grace is surprising.* Paul's whole argument in Romans 11 seems strange to us today. He says there was a remnant of Israel that had accepted Christ. In fact, of course, all the earliest Christians were Jewish. Paul indicates that these were the elect and that the others had been hardened. He then says they had stumbled, but ultimately had not fallen.

At this point he warns the Gentiles, and warns that most of his readers are Gentiles, not to be proud, but to be careful, because God can cut us off quite easily. In other words, Paul reminds us that we are not saved by any means of our own, nor by any aspect of who we are. We are saved only by the grace of God. At the end of his argument here, Paul expresses his conviction that Israel's general rejection of Christianity is part of God's gracious plan, and that eventually "all Israel will be saved."

Can we follow Paul's reasoning here: that it was God's strategy all along to use the rejection of the Israelites to send the gospel to the Gentiles and to use the faith of the Gentiles to make possible the salvation of all Israel? It does sound strange, doesn't it? But is this much stranger than the way God's grace works in your life? Look at yourself. Look at those around you. Could you have dreamed a few years ago how God would be working in you and through you today? Isn't God's grace astounding?

We human beings can never really understand fully the strategies of God, because we think more in terms of law than of grace. God as the waiting father in Jesus' parable of the prodigal son is always ready to receive us. God as the good shepherd is always in search of his lost sheep. God's grace took him to a cross for us. God's grace is so surprising that we, like Paul, can do nothing more than break into a doxology. That's just what Paul does in Romans 11:33, and his praise is a fitting ending for us today: "O the depth of the riches and wisdom and knowledge of God! How unsearchable are his judgments and how inscrutable his ways! For who has known the mind of the Lord? Or who has been his counselor? Or who has given a gift to him, to receive a gift in return? For from him and through him and to him are all things. To him be the glory forever. Amen."—Bruce E. Shields

ILLUSTRATIONS

THE FOUNDATION.   That the Word of God is a foundation that lies beneath the zone where the storms rage and provides us with a place of shelter is shown by the fact that there is not a single stage in our life where we will be obliged to abandon it because it is not relevant. We can have the greatest respect for Goethe's *Faust* and Shakespeare's plays, and they may have set off some grand and stimulating storms in our life. But would you read these things to cancer patients in a hospital ward? Would these works be suitable in the spiritual climate of a crowd of refugees or the mass burials after the great bombing raids? Obviously, these are words for the peaks and pinnacles of the house of life; but they cannot be the foundations that will sustain and preserve us in the storms of meaninglessness, mass deaths, hunger, and the frantic fear of life and the future.

But the Word of the Lord—and Jesus Christ himself *is* this Word—is relevant at every station of life.—Helmut Thielicke[4]

MYSTICS.   Every man is a mystic because every man at one time or another experiences in the thick of his joy or his pain the power out of the depths of his life to bless him. I do not believe that it matters greatly what name you call this power—the Spirit of God is only one of its names—but what I think does matter, vastly, is that we open ourselves to receive it; that we address it and let ourselves be addressed by it; that we move in the direction that it seeks to move us, the direction of fuller communion with itself and with one another. Indeed, I believe that for our sakes this Spirit beneath our spirits will makes Christs of us before we are done, or, for our sakes, it will destroy us.—Frederick Buechner[5]

SERMON SUGGESTIONS

Topic: Human Schemes and Divine Plans, Part II
TEXT: Gen. 45:1–15
(1) The astonishing revelation (vv. 1–3). (2) The theological explanation (vv. 4–8). (3) The loving reconciliation (vv. 9–15).

Topic: Great Faith
TEXT: Matt. 15:28
(1) Seen in a heathen. (2) Attended by great humility (see Luke 13) and producing perseverance (see Luke 18:7). (3) Recognized and rewarded by him who knows the heart (see John 2:24–25).—John A. Broadus

CONGREGATIONAL MUSIC

1. "Christian Hearts in Love United," N. L. von Zinzendorf (1723)
   O DU MEINE LIEBE, Moravian (1735)
   The brotherly (and sisterly) love extolled in the psalm for this day is echoed in this fine Moravian hymn of Christian fellowship. It could be used for opening worship or in connection with the Psalter reading.
2. "There's a Wideness in God's Mercy," Frederick F. Faber (1802)
   WELLESLEY, Lizzie S. Tourjee (1878)
   This hymn proclaiming God's mercy, love, and grace would be useful in connection with the Epistle reading on the mercy of God. The first two stanzas could precede the reading, with the last two stanzas following it.
3. "Heal Us, Immanuel, Hear Our Prayer," William Cowper (1779)
   BEATITUDO, John B. Dykes (1875)
   This hymn of confession and petition for God's healing and mercy could naturally follow the Gospel lesson on Jesus' bringing relief to the demon-possessed daughter. Though it doesn't refer specifically to this incident, the hymn recalls other individuals in Scripture who in faith called for healing and were made whole.

---

[4]*Life Can Begin Again*
[5]*The Magnificent Defeat*

4. "May the Grace of Christ Our Savior," John Newton (1799)
    OMNI DEI, Corner's *Gesangbuch*
    This short benedictory hymn would be suitable at the end of a service of worship in which unity, communion, and fellowship were embraced. The second stanza in particular stresses the joy of "sweet communion."—Hugh T. McElrath

WORSHIP AIDS

CALL TO WORSHIP.   "How very good and pleasant it is when kindred live together in unity!" (Ps. 133:1 NRSV).

INVOCATION.   We thank you, O God, for the unity we have as Christian brothers and sisters in our Lord Jesus Christ. Grant, O Lord, that what is true in the depths of our relationships to one another may become more and more a visible reality as we grow in the grace that you have given to us all.

OFFERTORY SENTENCE.   "I will freely sacrifice unto thee: I will praise thy name, O Lord; for it is good" (Ps. 54:6).

OFFERTORY PRAYER.   O Lord, our God, receive our praises and prayers, and these our offerings, which we present before thee, and with them ourselves, our souls and our bodies, a living sacrifice, holy and acceptable to thee; through Jesus Christ our Lord.—Compiled by Ernest A. Payne, Stephen F. Winward, and James W. Cox.[6]

PRAYER.
    "Dear Lord and Father of mankind,
    Forgive our foolish ways;
    Reclothe us in our rightful minds,
    In purer love Thy service find,
    In deeper reverence, praise."—John G. Whittier (1807–1892)

How foolish are our ways when we do not think your thoughts—when we do not do your deeds. "As the heavens are high above the Earth, so are your thoughts higher than our thoughts and your ways higher than our ways." How foolish we are to draw a circle to shut people out when your love draws a circle to take them in.

Forgive us for our religion that makes us bigoted, self-righteous, and exclusive when your love goes out to all persons without partiality—for you make the sun to shine on the good and the evil and you send rain on the just and the unjust alike. How often our lives are controlled by a fear of others rather than motivated by your love that embraces all. We have been more successful as builders of walls, partitions, and fences than of the bridges your love engineers. As one of our playwrights discerns, "Hell is other people" without your love that forgives, reconciles, and heals spanning the gulfs that separate us.

Our hope is that you have not given up on us. Keep the pressure of your Holy Spirit upon us. Tempt us with a vision of wholeness that your love inspires.

[6]*Minister's Worship Manual* (Chicago: World, 1969), p. 93.

Through him who teaches men and women everywhere to pray as your children: [Lord's Prayer].—John Thompson

SERMON
Topic: Your Own Picture Gallery
TEXT: Ezek. 8:12

In his scintillating Grifford Lectures, McNiele Dixon has this to say: "It is by imagination that men have lived; imagination rules all our lives. The human mind is not, as philosophers would have you think, a debating hall, but a picture gallery. . . . The prophets, the poets, the leaders of men are all of them masters of imagery, and by imagery they capture the human soul."

And this, after all, was the method of the prince of preachers, Jesus himself. He threw brilliant parables and simple pictures on the screen of men's minds, making his way to the will and conscience through the imagination. No wonder the common people heard him gladly!

Imagination rules all our lives—for good or ill, creatively or destructively. It is a wonderful gift of God and a perilous one to handle. We see it at its best in the writings of men like Robert Louis Stevenson, A. A. Milne, and C. S. Lewis; in superb movies like *Mary Poppins* and *The Sound of Music*; in the architect's plans for an imposing building or a lovely bridge.

But there is danger lurking in this room of pictures. Ezekiel saw this with acute perception. In a sickening vision of the city's hidden sins, he saw what the elders of Israel were doing in the dark: feasting their eyes on all manner of repulsive idols, hideous pictures, and evil suggestions. Outwardly all was respectable; inwardly all was rotten. "Son of man, have you seen what the elders of the house of Israel are doing in the dark, every man in his room of pictures?"

Here is a theme that speaks with the utmost relevance to our condition. We all have our own picture gallery, and the pictures we persistently hang there have a dynamic influence on the kind of people we are, and will become.

I. *Consider the powerful effect of this picture gallery on our physical lives.* It is our plain duty not only as rational beings but as Christians to preserve our bodies in the best possible health. Beyond doubt, this is the will of God. Christianity, as C. S. Lewis pointed out, is almost the only one of the great religions that thoroughly approves of the body, that believes that matter is good and goes on to proclaim that God himself once took on a human body. "The Word became flesh and dwelt among us." Paul spoke of the body in the highest terms when he said, "Do you not know that your body is a temple of the Holy Spirit?" (1 Cor. 6:19). As such, it must be reverenced, disciplined, and maintained at peak fitness to the glory of God.

The fears and anxieties that haunt and harass us should be cast as burdens on the God who has declared himself to be our Father, caring for each one of us and promising to sustain us in every experience.

II. *Consider further the powerful effect of this picture gallery on our social obligations.* "None of us lives to himself," say the Scriptures. "No man is an island," says the poet. We are members one of another, bound up together in the bundle of life—not independent people, but interdependent.

We are under obligation to live together in unity and peace. This frightfully difficult business of personal relationships is our shrinking world's number one problem. It glares at us in the home, the community, the Church, the nation. It is so easy to be critical of another's faults and failings, attitudes and actions, but so much harder to try to understand why he is as he is. Imagination is the lubricant that oils the wheels of human relationships and makes for unity and peace.

We are also under obligation to bear one another's burdens. This is the law of Christ, the law of love.

In a memorable phrase, Ezekiel summarizes his own preparation for a ministry of encouragement to his people: "I sat where they sat" (3:15 KJV).

III. *Consider the powerful effect of this picture gallery on our moral struggles.* The prophet knew well enough that the elders of the house of Israel, gluttonously feasting their imaginations on what was lewd and lustful, were committing moral suicide.

There is no sin in temptation itself; everyone is tempted. Jesus himself, declares the New Testament, "was tempted as we are, yet without sinning" (Heb. 4:15). The sin begins when a temptation is welcomed, given hospitality, played with. The only safe way to deal with the barest thought of evil is to throttle it at birth. We must not be vague here. At least two tremendously practical things are demanded of us in this connection. One is sustained vigilance. We must watch our reading, the plays and films we attend, the television programs we view. The other demand is for positive action, a deliberate policy of hanging clean, morally antiseptic pictures on the walls of the mind, thinking, as Paul said, about whatever is true, honest, just, pure, lovely, of good report. Nature abhors a vacuum, and so does the mind of man.

IV. *Consider the powerful effect of this picture gallery on our spiritual loyalties.* Here we take the highest ground of all. How loyal are we to the spiritual vows we once solemnly made? The pictures we hang in our minds are equally as decisive here. Let me put the matter in the form of two questions:

(1) *What is your image of Christ?* Suppose you keep always before you a picture of one who for us and our salvation came into the pit of history and the ugly mess of the sins and miseries of the world and was crucified on two rough, blood-clotted beams out of sheer love for us, who rose again and lives today, active and abroad in our world, to do the work that once he did in the days of his earthly ministry. Suppose you keep looking at such a picture. Could you in the light of it continue to give him a shoddy half-commitment, the odd dollar or two, the leftovers of your time and energy?

(2) *What is your image of the Church?* You can think of the Church as a very human institution, of the Earth, earthy, and in a sense you would be right. It is all that—sometimes quarrelsome, petty, desperately dull, and stubbornly reactionary, always frail and fallible. But there is another side to the Church. You can think of it as a divine institution, the body of Christ, his eyes and hands and feet and voice in the world today. That is the image I choose to dwell on. I love the Church, believe in the Church, give the one life I have to the Church, because I try to see it as God intends it to be: his worshiping, witnessing, working community.

"Son of man, have you seen what the elders of the house of Israel are doing in the dark, every man in his room of pictures?" What are you doing? "Imagination rules all our lives," says the philosopher. What kind of rule is it exercising over your life? The only safe thing to do is to let Jesus Christ rule your life. Crown him Lord of all! The secret of imagination-control is Christ-control.—John N. Gladstone[7]

---

[7]*The Valley of the Verdict*

SUNDAY, AUGUST 25, 2001

Lectionary Message

Topic: Saving Life

Text: Rom. 12:1–8

Other Readings: Exod. 1:8–2:10; Matt. 16:13–20

The eleven chapters that precede our Romans text describe from many angles the saving grace of God. God's mercy, as the psalmist says, "shall follow me all the days of my life" (Ps. 23:6). Paul has shown God's mercy in ancient history and in Jesus and the Church. He has shown God's mercy to the Jew and also to the Greek. He has shown God's mercy to the sinner as well as the righteous. He has proclaimed God's mercy to the hopeless, to the helpless, even to those who don't know they need it. He has quoted God's statement to Moses (Exod. 33:19), "I will have mercy on whom I have mercy, and I will have compassion on whom I have compassion" (9:15).

And now Paul opens chapter 12 with an appeal—an exhortation—on the basis of the mercy of God. Not only does our eternal salvation depend on God's mercy, but the Christian life also grows out of that mercy. As we heard in an earlier sermon, God's grace remains active in the lives of people like us who have received it. So Paul's exhortation is for us to live a life that is appropriate to our status as recipients of the mercy of God—to live a saving life.

I. *The saving life is offered to God.* If everything we are and everything we have is a gift of God, then the most appropriate action we can take is to offer all of it back to God. That is precisely Paul's opening exhortation—"to present your bodies as a . . . sacrifice." This is, of course, a call not for suicide but for consecration, as the rest of the verse shows. Paul describes our sacrifice as "living, holy, and acceptable to God."

The familiar hymn words penned by Frances Havergal after a wonderful experience of God's mercy moving in the lives of people around her spell out the life offered to God:

> Take my life and let it be
> consecrated, Lord, to Thee.
> Take my moments and my days;
> let them flow in ceaseless praise.
> Take my hands, and let them move
> at the impulse of Thy love.
> Take my feet, and let them be
> swift and beautiful for Thee.
> Take my voice, and let me sing
> always, only, for my King.
> Take my lips, and let them be
> filled with messages from Thee.
> Take my silver and my gold;
> not a mite would I withhold.
> Take my intellect, and use
> every power as Thou shalt choose.
> Take my will, and make it Thine;
> it shall be no longer mine.

Take my heart, it is Thine own;
it shall be Thy royal throne.
Take my love, my Lord, I pour
at Thy feet its treasure store.
Take myself, and I will be
ever, only, all for Thee.

Have you ever made a list of aspects of your life that you have offered to God? Maybe it's time for you to do that. Is there a part you have guarded from the altar? Some of your moments or days, perhaps? Some things your hands do or places your feet take you? Words that cross your lips? Money through your bank account? It's time for each of us to pray, "Take my love, my Lord, I pour at Thy feet its treasure store. Take myself, and I will be ever, only, all for Thee."

II. *The saving life is formed by God.* What determines the form of your life—that life you have offered to God? Can you evaluate the power of the various influences in your life? How about the influence of your family or your education or your status in the community? Where does the Church fit in? The primary question, according to our text, is the origin of the formative influences. "Do not be conformed to this world" is the negative side of Paul's exhortation. The term Paul uses here for *world* is *aeon*. Don't let this age, whatever its primary influences may be, force you into its mold. Oh, it tries hard enough and succeeds all too often. We are surrounded by images and sounds that try to form us—pictures on billboards, on television, on our computer screens, in our newspapers and magazines—images trying to convince us to buy a product or a service. The sounds of music and speech come at us from all directions, trying to form us in mind, body, and spirit. From the seemingly harmless ads for stuff to give us the best-looking lawn in the neighborhood to the invitations to immorality, this age of ours is trying to get us to conform to its standards.

But the primary influence for us as Christians should come from a source outside our era. We are to be transformed by the renewing of our minds. Such renewal can be done only by God's Holy Spirit. This means that we are not left to our own willpower or our own self-discipline to accomplish the saving life. God is ready and eager to work it out for us. Once again, it's a matter of turning life over to God. As we offer life to God, we invite the Holy Spirit to work in us to renew our lives beginning with our minds.

III. *The saving life is oriented to God.* When our minds are renewed, we have a new way to orient our lives. The mind of this age is oriented to the things, the stuff, of our world. That means we give most of our attention to the accumulation of stuff. The mind renewed by the Holy Spirit is oriented to the reality of God in the world. That means that things and services offered by our world play a secondary role in our lives. Our primary attention is given to the eternal reality that is God.

This is what Paul means when he writes, "so that you may discern what is the will of God—what is good and acceptable and perfect." Most people are disgusted from time to time with the immorality or uncaring attitude of other people, but we rarely know what to do about it. In a world like ours, it seems impossible even to know "what is good and acceptable and perfect," let alone to be able to do it. Yet the Christian promise—the good news—is that God's work of renewal in our minds leads us to that discernment and way of life, because it leads us to focus our lives on the reality of God in the world.

IV. *The saving life reflects God's grace.* That new orientation results in a different kind of life—a life that reflects the grace of God. Paul exhorts us to live that life and does so "by the grace given to [him]." Toward the end of his exhortation he points out, "We have gifts that differ according to the grace given to us." We would do well to read carefully the rest of chapter 12 and go on through chapters 13, 14, and 15 to see how Paul describes the life of the believer whose mind has been renewed by God's Spirit. In this description, we see humility and respect for others. We see eagerness to serve others. We see people who are peacemakers, people who overcome evil with good, people who obey the law, people who are tolerant of those whose opinions differ from theirs. In other words, here we see the people we would like to have living in our neighborhoods. They are also the people our neighbors would like living near them.

Does your life show the grace of God to your neighbors or to the people you work with, study with, play with? Does your life attract people to the saving grace of God? It is high time for each of us to let go of this age and let God lead us to be the people we really want to be. Lay your life on God's altar and let God make the necessary alterations.—Bruce E. Shields

ILLUSTRATION

STRENGTH TO CARRY ON.   God is not merely the Creator of all things, but He is the Sustainer of all things as well. In writing to the Colossians, Paul writes, "By Him all things are created." And he goes on to say, "He is before all things, and in Him all things consist" (Col. 1:16–17). This is very important, for at some times during history God has been characterized by philosophers as a "cosmic watchmaker" who has created the world and then abandoned it to its own devices, to tick away the moments until it runs out of time. That's not the God of the Bible. After creation, He is intimately involved with the work of His hands, holding it all together. If, even for a moment, He were to remove His hand from this universe, it wouldn't tick happily away like a watch in the grass; it would all fly apart into oblivion. But our God doesn't do that. Instead, He continues to sustain us. He creates and He sustains.

On that day when your journey brings you to a bend in the road, you'll be filled with an unaccustomed sense of helplessness. You'll cry out, "Lord, I need help!" In your moment of deep anxiety, remember this: The One to whom you are praying is the One who made heaven and earth. He is the Creator God. I don't know what kind of problem you may be facing—in the weariness of the journey, I'm certain it can seem all but insurmountable. But take a deep breath and a new look, in the perspective of the One who created and sustains every atom of the universe. He's up to the challenge, don't you think?

That thought renews our strength to carry on.—David Jeremiah[8]

SERMON SUGGESTIONS

Topic: When God Has the Last Word
TEXT: Exod. 1:8–2:10
(1) *The situation:* (a) the growth of the Israelites in Egypt, (b) the fear of the Pharaoh. (2) *The complication:* (a) forced labor, (b) threat of male infanticide. (3) *The resolution:* (a) the birth of Moses, (b) the role of Pharaoh's daughter, (c) the overarching providence of God.

---

[8]*A Bend in the Road: Experiencing God When Your World Caves In* (Nashville: Word, 2000), p. 65.

Topic: Christ Building His Church

Text: Matt. 16:13–20

(1) The spiritual Church of Christ includes all real Christians. (2) Christ himself builds his Church, using his apostles as foundation, and all who believe in him through their words (John 17:20) as materials. (3) Christ guarantees that his spiritual Church shall never cease to exist—there will always be true Christians on Earth.—John A. Broadus

CONGREGATIONAL MUSIC

1. "Built on the Rock," Nikolai Grundtvig (1854)

   KIRKEN, Ludwig M. Lindeman (1840)

   This strong hymn magnifying the establishment of the Church on Peter's confession of Jesus as the Christ could be sung following the Gospel reading. Alternate singing of the phrases between choir and congregation would be effective, with all coming together in the last phrase.

2. "If God the Lord Were Not Our Constant Help," Ps. 124; vers. C. Seerveld (1981)

   GENEVAN 124, *Genevan Psalter* (1551)

   Alternating the reading of the Psalter lesson with the singing of this modern metrical paraphrase as follows may make more relevant the meaning of the psalm's message: vv. 1–5, stanza 1; vv. 6–8, stanza 2.

3. "As Sons of the Day and Daughters of Light," Christopher Idle (1975)

   LAUDATE DOMINUM, C. H. Parry (1894)

   The second stanza of this new hymn relates directly to Romans 12:5, in which the apostle Paul affirms differing gifts for the edification of the body of Christ. Thus it could be used as a response to the reading of the Epistle lesson.

4. "Take My Life and Let It Be Consecrated," Frances R. Havergal (1874)

   HENDON, Henri A. Cesar Malan (1827)

   This gospel hymn of consecration can naturally follow the reading of Romans 12:1. Alternatively, the singing of the entire hymn could introduce the Epistle reading.—Hugh T. McElrath

WORSHIP AIDS

CALL TO WORSHIP.   "Our help is in the name of the Lord, who made heaven and Earth" (Ps. 124:8).

INVOCATION.   Where do we have to go but to you, Lord? You have the final answers. Open our eyes to see past all the dazzling and sometimes destructive glare of this world, so that our vision of what is around us may become real and redemptive. To this end, use our prayers, our hymns, and your Word to prepare us for living victoriously.

OFFERTORY SENTENCE.   "For wherever your treasure is, there will your heart be also" (Matt. 6:21 NJB).

OFFERTORY PRAYER.   We give as an act of faith, Father. Our faith in Christ calls us to give without question. We give as we have been called to do in the faith that our offerings and gifts will enhance Kingdom enterprises across the world. Accept our gifts this morning and strengthen our faith through their use to meet needs everywhere; we pray, in Jesus' name.—Henry Fields

PRAYER.   Ours is a broken world, ours is a needy world, yet ours is also a world of beauty, Father. We bring it to you this morning asking that you mend its brokenness. We see the relationships of nations, families, and beloved persons torn asunder by the sins of greed and hatred and lust—so twisted and broken that all the king's horses and men of this world seemingly cannot put them together again. We have tried, Father, how much we have tried; but human power is so ineffective and helpless. And we will go on trying, doing what we can to mend the brokenness of life, soothe the mountainous hurts, bind up the massive wounds. Yet we know that our little bit can mean something only when it is joined with your mighty caring, healing, and love. So we pray that you will take our little efforts, work through them and apart from them, and mend the brokenness of life as only you can.

So we bring you our needy world, Father. We know that you have already given all we humans need to meet every situation—food aplenty, healing balms in abundance, knowledge sufficient, goods in overabundance; they are already here. When we are honest, we know that it is our selfishness and our inability to use rightly what is here that cause so many of the problems of need. Some of us hoard too much while our brothers and sisters live in want. Some of us grab power at the expense of weaker human family members. Some of us choose disdain over acceptance of those with less ability, less privilege, less standing in the eyes of the world. Ours is the sin that so often causes the need. Awaken us to attitudes that need to be discarded, habits that need to change, spirits that need to be regenerated by the coming of your Spirit to abide in us. Then will we turn our energies, eyes, and attitudes toward meeting the spiritual, emotional, and physical needs of our brothers and sisters in humanity.

We thank you for the world of beauty, Father. Gratitude wells up in us for the beautiful things that grace life with unending rhythm—sunsets, chilly nights, smiles, warm handshakes, small gifts of gratitude, words of appreciation, caring in tragedy and loss, and love. These and so much more combine to create beauty. Help us to add to beauty so that one day soon its power will transform this world into what you would have it be for endless generations yet to come. Fill us in this hour with the beauty and wonder of the Spirit of Christ, that we, like him, may strive to bring beauty and hope to all people.—Henry Fields

SERMON
Topic: Life with Prayer in It
TEXT: Job 21:15

Have you ever felt like that? I'm speaking of a moment when, under stress of some personal tragedy, or perhaps just out of the blue, you questioned the validity of your religion. You began to think the unthinkable. Who is this God I claim to believe in? The man upstairs? A childhood memory like Santa Claus? Or some nebulous force that sometimes seems to be there and sometimes not? And in what sense could my life be described as serving him? Then, what about these prayers that I have sent out in that direction? What good did they do? And why is this God not answering right now, when I am beginning to question his existence?

Nearly everyone in this country has been raised with some kind of belief in God, and a poll would show that a vast majority are in favor of prayer whether they practice it themselves or not.

Yet chances are that you have had, or are having, your moments of doubt about the God you think you believe in, and even more, about the usefulness of your prayers. "What is the Almighty that we should serve him? And what profit should we have if we pray unto him?" In times of great distress you may have even wondered if it would make any real difference to your life if you gave up worrying about God and stopped praying altogether. If that has ever happened to you, you are not alone. Some of the most sturdy Christians who ever lived have confessed to this temptation.

The man who wrote the book of Job saw the problem as clearly as any of us. Yet we wouldn't be hearing his voice after all these centuries if he had not come through to an even deeper belief than he had before and a radiant confidence in a life with prayer in it. Neither would those Christians I have mentioned. So let me turn the page and look at the other picture: life with prayer in it.

First, I would claim that life with prayer in it is satisfying to the mind and spirit. It corresponds to our unique nature as human beings. It takes account of the mystery with which we are surrounded. It allows for the strange events that are inexplicable to the mind, and the dreams and visions that cannot be psychoanalyzed away. If prayer is our opening into the mystery, our contact with a realm that lies beyond the calculations of the mind or the range of technology, then surely a life with no prayer in it leaves us cabined, cribbed, confined, unsatisfied at the very center of our being. Isn't this what the psalmist felt when he came through his time of trial and sang, "Thou has set my feet in a large room." Life with prayer in it is living in a large room that gets larger the more we pray.

Next, I would say that everything in my experience, what I have observed in men and women of prayer, and all I have learned from Christ, leads me to believe that this is the source of hope and joy—two qualities that are in short supply at the present time. To have hope for humanity, or for ourselves, while living in a world that has no access to the realm of the Spirit, no contact with that better way that Jesus called the Realm of God, must be hard going. We know the fearful threats under which we live, and there are fewer and fewer now who believe that the human race can extricate itself from them and move toward a hopeful and happier future without what has been called some "invisible means of support."

"What profit should we have, if we pray unto him?" This sounds like the answer. I believe it is the ultimate answer, but I can hear someone saying, "It hasn't always worked for me. Often when I pray desperately, nothing seems to happen. I don't find hope and joy flooding in, in answer to my prayers." This is where we come up against what seems to us the terrible silence of God. We expect God to respond on our terms and give us what we want. But his very silence on occasion should remind us that we are in touch with one who says, "My thoughts are not your thoughts, neither are my ways your ways." Does that mean that we should not make specific requests in our prayers? What did Jesus say? "Ask, and you will receive." He set no limitations. I sometimes think that sermons and books on prayer are always telling us that we should think of prayer not as asking but as trying to conform to the will of God. Sure, he taught us to pray "Thy will be done," but he also taught us to ask for our daily bread, and what could be more down-to-earth than that? We are told we shouldn't just be beggars. But first and foremost we *are* beggars.

So I see life with prayer in it as the developing of a conviction that the Realm of God surrounds us, pressing in on all we think and say and do, so we begin to live in that large room where anything can happen through God's answering love. This used to be called "the practice of the presence of God," whereby we come to refer every detail, every decision, every relationship to him. But I see it also as a life that is punctuated by specific moments when we actively and consciously pray. This is how it was with our Lord in the record of his earthly life. As no one else has, he lived in that large room. The realm of God was near him, within him, all the time. His life had prayer in it from the moment of rising to the moment of sleep, and God was in his dreams. Yet he felt the need for regular times to be alone to pray. Unlike us, the busier he was, the more time he sought for prayer.

It is Jesus who answers the mocking question of our text: "What is the Almighty that we should serve him?" "My Father," answers Jesus, thus giving to his Church the first article of our creed, "I believe in God the Father Almighty." He is the one who cares for us with a parental love, willing what is best for us with an almighty wisdom that surpasses our understanding. He knew what it was to have a request refused. "O my Father, if it be possible, let this cup pass from me." A few hours later he had to drain that cup. He knew what it was to experience the terrible silence of God when he cried from the cross, "My God, my God, why hast thou forsaken me?" It is because he knew all this that this same cross became the door of hope for all who have met him as their Risen Lord. And this supreme life with prayer in it was crowned with a radiant and infectious joy. To all who are groping toward such a life he says, "These things have I spoken unto you, that my joy might remain in you and that your joy might be full."—David H. C. Read

SUNDAY, SEPTEMBER 1, 2002
Lectionary Message

Topic: A Set Face
TEXT: Matt. 16:21–28
Other Readings: Exod. 3:1–15; Rom. 12:9–21

I. *The story.*

(a) It was a point of change for Jesus and his disciples, staged in Caesarea Philippi, far from Jerusalem. Jesus had asked his disciples about his identity: "Who do people say that the Son of Man is?" The answers were varied and ranged from John the Baptist to Jeremiah, Elijah to "one of the prophets." Jesus pressed the issue with the follow-up question, "But what about you? Who do you say I am?" Typically, Peter spoke up: "You are the Christ, the Son of the living God!" After Peter's answer, Jesus made a rather terse statement about him, his future, and his role in the emerging kingdom of heaven. This salute to Peter's grasp of the situation prompted Jesus to warn the disciples "not to tell anyone that he was the Christ." Immediately Jesus gave an early prediction of his Passion. When Peter heard the shocking prediction, he took Jesus aside and "began to rebuke him. . . . Never, Lord . . . this will never happen." At this dramatic juncture, Jesus turned on Peter as one who was very angry and rebuked him, saying, "Get behind me, Satan! You are a stumbling block to me; you have in mind not the things of God but the things of men!" So, just following some rather elevating and complementary words to Peter, Jesus spoke with force, anger, and resolve about his future Passion and about Peter's obvious failure to understand. Subsequently, Jesus challenged the disciples about the cost of discipleship and about the apocalyptic nature of the appearance of the Son of Man and the coming of the Kingdom. This appearance, he announced, would occur even before some who were then living would experience death. How totally confounded must the disciples have been by this revelation and confrontation. Yet the drama deepens as Matthew then tells us that Jesus took Peter, James, and John "up a high mountain by themselves"—the Transfiguration.

(b) These events of revelation and confrontation encapsulate a radical departure in the life and ministry of Jesus. Luke's interpretation of these same events is presented with the words, "As the time approached for him to be taken up to heaven, Jesus resolutely set his face like a flint toward Jerusalem" (Luke 9:51). So, how does someone living now hear this lection? Underneath the posing of the initial question lies the very mind of Christ. It was decision time for Jesus, and hence for his followers. The die was cast; he had passed the point of no return. It was time to fish or cut bait, so to speak. There was no turning back. It was a time of resolute dedication: "he set his face like a flint toward Jerusalem." The Crucifixion loomed on the horizon. There was mounting evidence of conflict with the elders, chief priests, and teachers of the law. Jesus indicated that the ultimate confrontation would come in Jerusalem and that he would "suffer many things." This prediction the disciples did not understand. It was new information to his audience. No one had said or done the things he had said and done. His uniqueness was ratified by demons, Nicodemus, and crowds of people, because "he taught as one having authority, not as the scribes and the Pharisees." But his self-paradox was that the commonly held view of the Messiah did not include crucifixion, and certainly not crucifixion at the hands of his own people, or Romans. The Messiah was to usher in an unbridled period of peace. The Jews could not get it—this suffering servant who turned aside from their narrow and exclusivist interpretations of the Torah and spoke of crucifixion. Yet even his inner circle could not get it either. This strategic movement toward Jerusalem was a narrowing of numbers. There were at first the large crowds of four and five thousand who followed him and were fed. Then there were the "seventy-two-by-two," and subsequently the twelve, with whom he spent most of his time, instilling the ethic of the Kingdom. Along with Jesus' question and Peter's erudite answer at Caesarea Philippi, Peter, James, and John emerge as the inner circle, the big three. Yet by the time of the Crucifixion, even Peter fails to grasp the meaning of crucifixion in the completion of Jesus' messiahship. So, Jesus is left alone, in despair and pain, crying out, "Why hast thou forsaken me?"

II. *The meaning.*

(a) To be a follower of Jesus means being an informed disciple. A disciple is a "humble learner." This passage would seem to warn us that from time to time we can actually speak the words of Satan, as shocking as that is. Yes, God does rebuke his followers, yet his words of discipline position us back in line, so to speak. Peter needed an attitude adjustment, and so do we from time to time. Just as Peter had to be further informed, so we must seek the "mind of Christ," because Christ is, in fact, "in us, the hope of glory." Peter's education continued with many lessons, even one on a rooftop when he was again rebuked by the Lord for calling "what God had cleansed, unclean." The tradition that says that Peter asked to be crucified upside down is not inconsistent with his informed encounter with the Christ.

(b) The continuous nature of the crucifixion in us and in the life of the Church is an ever-challenging reality. Self-crucifixion is integral to discipleship and is an ongoing and daily event. Selflessness and obedience are a constant challenge. Inner death or crucifixion is a loss of limited and selfish constraints. To embrace Christ is to embrace crucifixion. With each change in our life situation, we have an opportunity to experience another aspect of crucifixion. Human ways are not the ways of crucifixion. As Bonhoeffer reminds us, "We are called to be crucified" (see Gal. 2:20).

(c) To be a disciple is to be ripped out of our comfort zones of self-indulgence, materialism, and "affluenza." We are not called to swim in the safe and shallow water where we may tap our toes on the bottom. We are called to swim in a bottomless deep. On one occasion, a ship I was on spent the night dead in the water just off the Island of Mindoro in the Philippines. As was the custom, when the ship was seemingly motionless in quiet water, many would fish. It was time to fish! In this case, when I saw a Filipino chief petty officer fishing, I asked about his success, and he told me he was "bottom fishing, and it was really hard to do." As I walked away from him I heard laughter and I realized that we were gently situated over the Mindanao Deep, the deepest water in the world. So it is when God calls us into the deep water of faith to do our fishing, where it is awesome and fearful. As Albert Schweitzer reminds us, "He still calls us to follow him," to go fishing with him and be "fishers of men." We human fishermen are frustrated from time to time, yet Christ tells us to "let down our nets." When we follow in obedience, our nets overflow. So be it! May God ever call us as individuals and as the Church to a deeper and ever challenging faith with a set face.—Dave Hunsicker

ILLUSTRATIONS

A LITTLE BLOW.   I was just a week short of twenty when I was finally discharged after months of compiling AWOL and VD reports and other somewhat less than vital statistics, and once again I missed my chance to be a hero. We were lined up in alphabetical order, ready to march into the Army chapel where the discharge ceremony was to take place when I was called aside by the officer in charge. I might have noticed, he explained in an undertone, that the man at the head of the line was black, and would I mind, therefore, taking my place in front of him as unobtrusively as possible so that the ceremony could proceed with proper decorum. Accustomed as we all were in those days to accepting such things as simply the way the world worked, I probably did not even consider protesting any more than I had protested the behavior of the bartender at the Nassau Tavern. But even if I had considered it, I doubt I would have protested for fear that it might somehow endanger my own getting out of the Army then and there. So I went and stood where I had been told and within moments stepped out of the chapel as free a man as it is possible to be in a country where not everybody is free. But the memory has haunted me ever since, and with it the thought of the pathetic but who knows how telling little blow I might have struck for common decency.—Frederick Buechner[1]

MARTYRDOM.   Bonhoeffer's witness turned into its own kind of leadership. He called upon his fellow ministers to speak up and out—to refuse the authority of Nazism, to take it on as the enemy. He refused for himself any number of convenient exits, refuges—he said

---

[1]*The Sacred Journey*

no to a gangster regime, even if death was to be his certain fate, so he knew as he took the measure of a lawless state determined to kill by the hundreds of thousands its own citizens. An intellectual's life, a theologian's, gradually became a daily embrace of a faith (as it had to be, for him) worked into remarks, friendships, and deeds of various kinds—all elements of a growing martyrdom unselfconsciously assumed.—Robert Coles[2]

SERMON SUGGESTIONS

Topic: The God Who Called Moses

TEXT: Exod. 3:1–15

(1) The God who initiates and seeks a new leader (vv. 1–5). (2) The God who relates redemptively to those he seeks (v. 6a). (3) The God who calls and equips his new leader (vv. 7–12). (4) The God of mystery, grace, love, and power (vv. 13–15).

Topic: How to Survive and Do Something Meaningful

TEXT: Rom. 12:9–21, especially v. 21

(1) Through genuine love (vv. 9–10). (2) Through zealous service (v. 11). (3) Through persistent hope (v. 12). (4) Through unprejudiced outreach to both saints and strangers (v. 13).

CONGREGATIONAL MUSIC

1. "To God Be the Glory," Fanny J. Crosby (1875)

   TO GOD BE THE GLORY, W. J. Doane (1875)

   The great things God has done that are celebrated in the Psalter reading find a general but enthusiastic echo in this hymn, possibly the finest of all Fanny Crosby's praise hymns. Sing it to introduce Psalm 105.

2. "Go Down, Moses," African American Spiritual

   TUBMAN SPIRITUAL; arr. W. F. Smith (1986)

   This poignant spiritual would be a natural accompaniment to the Old Testament lesson recounting Moses' call to lead the Israelites out of Egypt. It could be sung by soloist and congregation.

3. "Take Up Thy Cross," Charles W. Everest (1833)

   GERMANY, Gardiner's *Sacred Melodies* (1815)

   This vibrant call to follow Jesus by taking up one's cross can be appropriately used with the Gospel lesson. This fine American hymn expands on the meaning of Jesus' call to discipleship in Matthew 16:24–25.

4. "Help Us Accept Each Other," Fred Kaan (1975)

   BECK, John Ness Beck (1977)

   The apostle Paul's instructions about loving one another and living Christian lives in both thought and action are reflected in the general spirit of this contemporary hymn. The choir could introduce it by performing the first two stanzas before asking the congregation to come in on the remainder of the hymn.—Hugh T. McElrath

---

[2]*Lives of Moral Leadership*

WORSHIP AIDS

CALL TO WORSHIP.   "O give thanks unto the Lord; call upon his name; make known his deeds among the people" (Ps. 105:1).

INVOCATION.   Gracious Lord, help us to realize that we, in our place and time, can make a difference in this world, that your wonderful works take place in our very ordinary lives.

OFFERTORY SENTENCE.   "And God, who supplies seed for the sower and bread to eat, will also supply you with all the seed you need and make it grow, to produce a rich harvest from your generosity" (2 Cor. 9:10 TEV).

OFFERTORY PRAYER.   Generous God, our loving Father, magnify the importance of our humble gifts and glorify your majestic name in our offering of our resources for your service.

PRAYER.   Today we turn our thoughts to labor, Father, and give thanks for jobs that allow us to provide for the needs of family, for the betterment of the community, and for the work of the Lord in the world. We thank you for the strength given daily that enables us to do work in an efficient manner. We are grateful for a strong economy that provides jobs so that laborers in every field of work are not left idle. Thank you for laws that enhance the joy of working and limit the excessive demands that were made on laborers in other times.

Lead those of us who work to be aware of the necessity to do our jobs well. Deliver us from sloth and inspire us to give an honest day's work for the wage to which we have agreed. Then lead us to do the little more that expresses appreciation for the opportunity afforded us in the workplace. Thank you for those who have taken risks that we might have a place to labor. Across the years may we indeed be laborers worthy of our hire, and through our labor may benefits come to those for whom we work as well as for ourselves.

We pray this morning for those who cannot work for various reasons. Show us how to help them as they face the daily needs of life. Wherever legitimate reason exists that hinders another's effort to be a good and honest laborer, may that reason be acknowledged by everyone as we do our part on their behalf. And for those who because of ignorance and lack of skills are denied opportunities to earn a living or to advance in their work field, may we give energy, time, and skills to help them prepare themselves, that they might gain a better opportunity in their tomorrows.

We ask now that you bless this sacred hour with your presence, your Spirit. Lead us to Christ, that in him we may find healing for our diseases, comfort for our sorrows, guidance for our futures, salvation from our sins, and restoration in love and grace to the Father and to one another. And out of this hour may we go to live with renewed power in the days through which we shall walk before we meet again in your presence. For this we pray in Jesus' name.—Henry Fields

SERMON

Topic: Labor Day: Putting Work into Life Under God
TEXT: 2 Tim. 2:15

He was an active member of the church. In fact, he taught Sunday school and served on the finance committee. He also owned a department store and paid some of the lowest wages in town. The working conditions at his department store were far from ideal. It was even known that some of the business deals he made were quite shady. There was a gap between what he professed to believe and the way he ran his department store. One day someone mentioned that to him. He said simply, "What I believe has nothing to do with the way I run my business. Church is church and business is business. Religion should keep its nose out of people's work. It has no business being there."

Is that right? Should faith be divorced from the other areas of our life, like work or play or school? Does faith deal only with spiritual matters and with spiritual things, heaven and not Earth? Does it matter what we do with our lives if we are Christians?

The Bible is not on the side of divorcing faith from life. It's not on the side of laziness either. The Bible deals with a Christ who came to be the Redeemer of all life, not part of it. Jesus is Lord of all life: our work, our play, our home, or anything else we do with it. If what we believe does not spill over in how we live our lives, then we have vastly misunderstood faith.

Our faith ought to make a difference in our work.

Paul wrote to Timothy, a young man entering the ministry, about his work. He gave some good advice to Timothy. If he remembered what Paul said, Timothy's work would be alive, not boring and routine. Let us see what Paul told Timothy and realize what we can do to reveal our faith in our work.

I. *What we do reveals what we believe.* Timothy went into a profession that would be pleasing to God. He was going into the ministry to "rightly" divide "the word of truth" (KJV). He was going to preach. He would not be ashamed of that. He would be doing something honorable. What Timothy did would be a testimony to everybody that here was someone whose beliefs were deep and rich. He did what was pleasing to God.

There are a lot of honorable professions in our world. Our work ought to be something we feel called to. It should be what God wants us to do and where God wants us to be.

II. *Why we do our work can reveal our faith.* "Do your best to present yourself to God as . . . a workman who has no need to be ashamed." Timothy did what was honorable, but why did he do it? He did it because of his response to the grace of God in his life. He did it because he saw in it an opportunity to serve God, to bring others into the joy of the Kingdom that he knew. To serve God, to serve others—that was the reason Timothy did what he did.

Why are we doing what we're doing? Just to make money? Just to survive? If that's the reason, then our work will be dull, tedious, and agonizing. We ought to see our work as an opportunity to serve God and others. Our work ought to be an offering to God. What we do should make this world a better place. If our work is not trying to help others to become better than they are, if our work is not contributing to the development of this life we live, then we need to reexamine what we do and why we do it.

Is this what we say about our work: I clean the house, or I fix or make cars, or I serve on ships, or I sell merchandise, or I cook food, or I teach, and I offer what I do as service to God?

III. *The way we do our work reveals what we believe.* "Do your best . . . rightly handling the word of truth." That's what Timothy was told: Do your best! Timothy would make mistakes. He would not be a perfect preacher. Sometimes he would preach and nobody would listen. He would say and do the wrong thing and probably make some people mad. That would be all right because they would be honest mistakes, made because Timothy was an imperfect human being. Timothy was not asked to be perfect. He was asked to do his best.

If there's anyone who ought to be giving an honest day's work for an honest day's pay it's those of us who bear the name *Christian*. We ought to work hard. We ought to do the best we can. We ought never attempt less than our best. Christians ought to do their best.

Too many of us have divorced faith from life. What we believe in church on Sunday we don't live on Monday. That may be the reason our lives are not as full as we want them to be, that we struggle through life with discouragement and disappointment, not with joy and confidence. We have kept God boxed up in a building and not let him into the world where we live. Our work ought to be under God. We must realize that *what* we do, *why* we do it, and *how* we do it are our testimony to whether or not we believe God is indeed Lord of all life.—Hugh Litchfield[3]

SUNDAY, SEPTEMBER 8, 2002
Lectionary Message

Topic: A Magna Charta from Christ
TEXT: Matt. 18:15–20
Other Readings: Exod. 12:1–14; Rom. 13:8–14

On the one hand, English common law made a bold step forward when it stated the principle of due process in the Magna Charta. On the other hand, human relationships were given an even bolder step forward, a Magna Charta if you please, when Jesus spoke the words of Matthew 18:15–20. The American Constitution included the provision of due process in the Fifth Amendment, stating, "No person shall be deprived of life, liberty, or property without due process of law." Matthew 18:15–20 may well be a Magna Charta from Christ. No single body of Scripture appears more often in the rubrics of church order than this Scripture. It is usually found in the section on discipline. Indeed, these words of Christ constitute a basic principle of human relationships that is integral: the right of a person to hear a charge of "ought" or wrongdoing directly from the person who believes they have been wronged. This simple procedure could be replicated in every personnel or policy manual in any organization. The only change required would be the substitution of the various levels of review beyond the two persons primarily involved. Certainly if it were rigorously applied in the life of the church, much hurt and discord could be averted. The stories are legion regarding charges that have been brought to the church prefaced with "They said" or "We heard." Proceeding beyond the personal level and carrying the matter to the leadership of the church before speaking to the individual would seem to indicate that due process has been obliterated.

I. *Among the Jews, the principle of due process involved the testimony of two witnesses* (see Deut. 19:15–20). This tradition was alive during the ministry of Jesus and during Paul's ministry at Corinth (see John 8:17; 2 Cor. 13:1). The witness or accusation of a single person should not humiliate another person. The words of two people would lift the charge to a different level and protect an individual from an unfair public accusation. The Dead Seas Scrolls indicate that this principle of due process operated in the Qumran community as well. As

---

[3]*Sermons on Those Other Special Days*

noted, this due process concept was operative at Corinth. However, as one traces out the process in Corinth, one can see how Paul began with a categorical condemnation of the immoral person (see 1 Cor. 5:1–5), yet by the end of the Corinthian letters Paul tempered his judgment with mercy and compassion. In the process, Paul also noted the influence of such an immoral person on the community (see 1 Cor. 12:26). No one sins in isolation. Sin has community implications.

II. *These words of Christ reported by Matthew come just as Christ was setting forth the principle of ministry toward "lost sheep."* Is it coincidental that he moved from the thought of the lost sheep to the matter of human straying? One would think not. Upon reflection, one is prompted to ask, How many of the flock who have strayed have had the benefit of due process according to Jesus? Rushing to judgment, kangaroo courts, and a lynch mob mentality have too many times characterized the life of the Church. Why does the Church shoot its wounded? Many a person's reputation has been irreparably damaged by the lack of the application of due process, according to Jesus. The U.S. Marine Corps follows rigorously a procedure called *request mast,* by which the lowest ranking Marine can take his case to the top of the chain of command, even to the commandant, if need be, to protect due process. Interestingly, the rest of the lection, Matthew 18:18–20, gives us a follow-up thought about binding and loosing. Now, on the one hand, such binding has been noticed in as varied church applications as the Roman Catholic concept of excommunication or the Mennonite concept of shunning. Many believe that shunning is a cruel and merciless procedure of discipline. These actions would seem to follow a literal or severe interpretation of Matthew 18:17: "Treat him as a pagan or a tax collector." Well, other words of Christ tell us how to treat a pagan or a tax collector. It's not that excommunication, if believed, is any less cruel than shunning. In either case, many others in Christendom have had difficulty with this kind of judgment over the requirement to forgive "seventy times seven," or the conditional forgiveness concept of Matthew 6:14–15, or the basic concept of "judge not" found in Matthew 7:1.

III. *Somewhere between mercy and judgment, between the fold and the lost sheep, the truth of the Kingdom can be found.* If Jesus' due process had been applied early and with love, many of the premature judgments that too often have resulted could have been settled at a minimal level. Many fires that have destroyed great buildings or forests could have been put out if firefighters could have gotten there early enough with a shovel of sand or a small amount of water. In too many cases, an unsubstantiated accusation has been enough to ruin the ministry of many a church leader from every church tradition. There is enough guilt in this regard for all of us, regrettably. However, since the offending person is spoken of as a "brother," these words of judgment may imply that after due process there is a limit to the evil that the Church can endure. The use of the word *church* is troublesome if in fact the Church did not exist when Jesus spoke these words. However, A. B. Bruce indicates that a nucleus of the Church was present among the twelve. Further, taking one's case to God as the righteous judge is hinted at in Matthew 18:18–20. These words would seem to admonish the Church toward unity in prayer and unity in purpose. The word used for *agree* is *sumpheo,* which refers to a symphony of instruments in unity even when they are not identical. How many Church difficulties could have been averted if "my people who are called by my name will humble themselves and pray?" (2 Chron. 7:14). In the high priestly prayer of Jesus in John 17 we find direct and intense prayer to the Father that the Church may be one—a symphony of prayer. How does one get oil and water to mix? When they are heated up sufficiently they come together! How many times has the Church seen unity come not by organizational structures or arbitrary conventions but by the intensity or the heat of common prayer? Most of the spiritual awakenings that America has experienced have been the result of direct and intense prayer. If, as the early church found, society is in fact shipwrecked and adrift, then God's people have a common sense of unity in the need both to "tend the sheep" and to see that all of God's people are treated to due process as well as to the love and mercy of the Lord Jesus. Through intense prayer that is done in agreement comes unity in service and mission. This is the very unity that Jesus prayed for and that will bring in the Kingdom early. We are all in need of the Magna Charta from Jesus.—Dave Hunsicker

ILLUSTRATIONS

POSITIVE GOODNESS.   The difference in the two techniques—pulling up the weed or planting good seed—is illustrated in the ancient story of the Greeks: Ulysses, returning from the siege of Troy, wished to hear the Sirens who sang in the sea, tempting many a sailor to his doom. Ulysses put wax in the ears of his sailors and strapped himself to the mast of the ship—so that even if he wished to answer the appeal of the Sirens, he would be saved from doing so. Some years later, Orpheus, the divine musician, passed through the same sea; but he refused to plug up his sailors' ears or to bind himself to a mast. Instead, he played his harp so beautifully that the song of the Sirens was drowned out.

A positive and not a negative goodness is the Christian ideal.—Fulton J. Sheen[4]

TRUE LOVE.   You will have noticed the stern streaks in Jesus' character, the warnings, the woes and the hard sayings. "Woe unto you Scribes and Pharisees, hypocrites! For ye compass sea and land to make one proselyte and when he is become so, ye make him twofold more a son of hell than yourselves." All that and more in the week before he went to his Cross, dying out of love for man and love for God, but not loving to the point of weakness. There is love, but there is judgment. There is mercy, but there is truth.

It is not surprising then that for all the mention of love in the Bible there is no use of *Eros* as a word anywhere at all. Instead the word *agape* is used, meaning love which considers the object of its love. Love which is not self-centered, nor selfish, nor grasping, but love which seeks to give, to strengthen and to help. To love a man as God loves a man may at times call for rebuking the man; it certainly calls for a clear statement of where we stand. A man who loves as God loves is never putty in the hands of sentiment. True love is not unprincipled. Perhaps that is the lesson we need to learn today. Love can be unprincipled. We can love to the point of weakness, and then it is not love.—D. W. Cleverley Ford[5]

SERMON SUGGESTIONS

Topic: A Day of Remembrance
TEXT: Exod. 12:1–14, especially vv. 7 and 13
(1) The Passover as a day of remembrance. (2) The Lord's Supper as a day of remembrance.

---

[4]*On Being Human*
[5]*A Pastoral Preacher's Notebook*

Topic: When Love Is Real

TEXT: Rom. 13:8–14

(1) We will keep God's commandments. (2) Our concern for others will even exceed the letter of the Law. (3) The urgency of God's timetable for world events and our personal affairs will demand self-denying commitment.

CONGREGATIONAL MUSIC

1. "Sing Praise to the Lord," *Psalter* (1912)

   LAUDATE DOMINUM, C. H. Parry (1915)

   This grand paraphrase of Psalm 149 makes a fine hymn for the opening of worship. A faithful version of the psalm, the hymn could well be used in place of reading the Psalter lesson.

2. "The Lord Is Here!" Timothy Dudley-Smith (1985)

   CRIMOND, Jessie S. Irvine (1871)

   This new hymn that affirms the truth of Matthew 18:20, that God is present in the midst of two or three gathered in his name, would be quite usefully sung before the Gospel reading.

3. "Wake, Awake, for Night Is Flying," P. Nicolai (1599)

   WACHET AUF, Hans Sachs (1513); adapt. P. Nicolai (1599)

   Although this grand chorale is usually sung during Advent, its basic message fits the spirit of the apostle Paul's instruction in Romans 13:11–12. It would be appropriate, therefore, to use it in connection with the Epistle lesson for this day.

4. "Jesus, Thy Blood and Righteousness," N. L. von Zinzendorf (1739)

   GERMANY, Gardiner's *Sacred Melodies*

   The Passover story in the Old Testament lesson depicts the saving power of blood. It foreshadows the redemptive power of the blood shed by Jesus on the cross—a thought celebrated in this venerable hymn.—Hugh T. McElrath

WORSHIP AIDS

CALL TO WORSHIP.   "Praise the Lord. Sing to the Lord a new song, and his praise in the congregation of saints" (Ps. 149:1 NKJV).

INVOCATION.   Bring our hearts together, O Lord, as we pray and sing to you in worship. And bring our hands together in service as we hear your word, live it, and proclaim it by lip and life.

OFFERTORY SENTENCE.   "Each of you is to bring such a gift as he can in proportion to the blessing that the Lord your God has given you" (Deut. 16:17 REB).

OFFERTORY PRAYER.   We ask you now, O God, to give us clear eyes and willing hearts to see what you have done for us and to attempt to measure out our service, our love, and our offerings accordingly.

PRAYER.   Thou, O Lord, art the searcher of the spirit. Thou knowest the heart altogether. We do not know thee, but thou knowest us. Naked and open are we before him with whom we have to do. And yet we are commanded to come boldly before thee. Thy knowledge is not for our condemnation. Thy thoughts are thoughts of mercy, and thy knowledge is for our salvation. We beseech thee that we may from day to day draw near with boldness and simplicity, with sincere penitence, with earnest desires, that we may be Godly, living above this present world while living in it, with purer motives, with nobler aims, with a better endeavor than other men. Because we are called by thy name, may we have thy spirit, walk in thy footsteps, bear out thy precious example, and be, according to the measure of our knowledge and our strength, to others what thou art to us. Forgive the deficiency of our past lives. Forgive the outright sins we have committed. Our forgetfulness, our heedlessness, our infirmities—we beseech thee, not only that thou wilt pass them by, but that thou wilt give us strength in time to come. For we desire not so much to remove pain and penalty as to remove impurity and selfishness and pride. It is not so much joy that we seek as that we may have a better manhood, nobler thoughts, truer purposes, and purer hearts, and be more gracious and generous and beneficent, as thou art. And we beseech of thee that thou wilt grant us that we may grow in grace and in the knowledge of our Lord and Savior Jesus Christ, and to thy name shall be the praise, Father, Son, and Spirit.—Henry Ward Beecher

SERMON
Topic: A Plea for Patience
TEXT: Matt. 24:13; Luke 8:15

There are times when we can be in too much of a hurry. Patience is not a virtue greatly coveted in these exciting days. Who wants to wait for anything? Under the impact of a mechanical culture we have been schooled to demand things at once. Delays, detours, and even disciplines tend to irritate us.

Whatever the world in general may think of it, patience occupies a high place in the New Testament list of virtues. And Christian patience is not a dull, negative passivity, waiting for something to turn up. Far from it! It is a strong, active virtue. It is more like what we mean by endurance and perseverance. It means holding on tenaciously when the going is tough, plodding doggedly on while others are giving up the game and the outlook seems hopeless.

It is good to be enthusiastic, eager, forceful, visionary. It is better when we add to these admirable qualities the equally admirable but less romantic quality of patience.

I. *Are you patient with yourself?* The hardest battle on the hands of most of us is the battle with ourselves. Much of our irritation and impatience with others is a projection of our own feeling about ourselves. Listen to someone who is always criticizing and condemning his fellows and notice what he habitually aims at: You may get a clue to the nature of his own inward struggles. We tend to give ourselves a lift by dragging someone else down.

The committed Christian is as acutely aware of this fight as the uncommitted good man or woman, often more so. What disappoints us in our moments of ruthlessly honest self-examination is the slowness of our growth in character, in grace, in faith, in love.

What we have to understand is that the Christian life demands patience—a steady, unwavering perseverance. There is no such thing as instant sanctity, any more than there is instant culture.

Listen to Paul, after years of living and serving in Christ: "Not that I have already obtained this or am already perfect; but I press on to make it my own, because Christ Jesus has made me his own. Brethren, I do not consider that I have made it my own; but one thing I do: forgetting what lies behind and straining forward to what lies ahead, I press on toward the goal for the prize of the upward call of God in Christ Jesus" (Phil. 3:12–14).

Are you patient with yourself? There is no limit to the heights of character we can reach, no limit to the victories we can achieve, if we will wait patiently and walk humbly with God.

II. *Are you patient with the Church?* It is fashionable to be impatient with anything institutional today, and not least the Church. A favorite pastime of rebel priests, radical theologians, and sundry other ecclesiastical morticians is that of belittling the Church, exposing with great delight its many faults and failings and pronouncing with monumental dogmatism that the days of the Church are numbered. There is nothing specially new about this, of course. Impatience with the Church is as old as the Church. The radicals and the reformers have always been in evidence in every age. And rightly so! One shudders to think how impossibly corrupt the Church would be without their costly efforts. The Church must always stand under the judgment of the Word of God. It must be constantly prodded by its own ideals. It must be continually reformed and renewed. But the posture of protest should never be adopted without the patience of love. Robert Frost, the poet, wanted engraved on his tombstone these words: "I had a lover's quarrel with the world." He rebuked and criticized the world out of his tremendous love for it, his longing to see its rich possibilities fulfilled. Shouldn't we have a lover's quarrel with the Church, remembering that love is patient?

The most foolish of all myths is the myth of perfectionism. As someone else has said, we frequently ruin our chances of happiness and usefulness by expecting too much from our relationships. We expect too much from our marriage, our children, our schools, our church. We overlook the fact that God builds the Church out of the rough material of human nature. It is to the Church's glory, not its shame, that it welcomes sinful, struggling, weak, slow, ungracious people. The Body of Christ consists of an unpredictable and often unattractive mixture of fallible but believing hearts. The Head of the Body alone is perfect, and it is he who invites us: "Come unto me, all who labor and are heavy-laden, and I will give you rest." "Follow me, and I will make you. . . ." All the fitness he requires is that we should feel our need of him. I am a member of the Church only because of his grace. Is it not so with you?

We must be patient with the Church's traditions. An institution as old as the Church has inevitably gathered around itself powerful traditions, creeds, ceremonies, customs. There are ways of thinking, worshipping, and serving that, having been accepted as agreeable to the Word of God and having proved themselves in experience, have been passed on from one generation to another. Moreover, the Church is the guardian of a historic revelation. A vital part of our mission is to preserve and proclaim the once-for-all acts of God in Christ "for us men and for our salvation." This gospel is always relevant to all people, at all times, in all places. It must be made known by the hymns, the prayers, the sermons, and the sacraments of the Church. It is the same yesterday, today, and forever. There is, of course, nothing sacrosanct about some of the traditions of the Church. A new and changing day demands new methods, new images. Old traditions may well be inadequate. Different patterns must evolve. The point is that such adjustment is always a slow and painful process. There is an ingrained tendency in human nature to fear, resist, and delay the new and untried. Emotion rules rather than reason, and the past is venerated with fierce devotion. Tradition hardens into traditionalism. Change must certainly come—but how can it come effectively except as a reward to the patience of love?

III. *Are you patient with God?* Many of us are wrestling with God, baffled by his reticence, impatient with his slowness. We are in a hurry, and God isn't. So we bombard heaven with our passionate prayers and complain that God does nothing. Why doesn't he intervene dramatically and decisively? Why doesn't he answer our prayers when and how we desire? Why doesn't he smash the vicious circle of evil and compel the allegiance of men? If God is God, he should get a move on!

We must have patience with the patience of God, for if that patience should ever grow weary, we would be lost indeed!

Christian patience is rooted in the conviction that God's time is always the best time, the right time, the only time. No one who believes in him will ever be disappointed.—John N. Gladstone[6]

SUNDAY, SEPTEMBER 15, 2002
Lectionary Message

Topic: Costly Forgiveness
TEXT: Matt. 18:21–35
Other Readings: Exod. 14:19–31; Rom. 14:1–12

Conditional forgiveness seems easy enough on the surface. If one has been forgiven, then one is forgiving. However, in real-life situations it doesn't seem to work out that easily. The words of the Lord's Prayer exist to prod us toward the full cycle of forgiveness: "Forgive us our debts as we forgive our debtors." From Peter's question at the outset, to the parable of the steward's inconsistency, one is gently moved toward a conclusion. The trajectory of the parable is revealed in the impact of the conclusion in verse 35: "This is how my heavenly Father will treat each of you unless you forgive your brother from your heart."

This section on forgiveness follows from the previous lessons on the ethic of the kingdom in chapter 18. The first lesson was one of valuing the "greatest in the kingdom." The kingdom person must reflect the weakness not only of a child but also of a weak brother, or even a lost or strayed sheep. The kingdom disciple is expected to act differently than a pagan, simply put. This point is made explicitly in 1 John 4:8, 11, 20–21. This regarding or valuing of other people drives the point straight back to the essential motivation of the kingdom person. Such a person is defined by his own redemption. His entrance into the kingdom is brought about by his redemption from sin. His growth in the application of the ethic of conditional forgiveness—heart forgiveness—is validated in his own forgiveness of others' sins.

If a person has been shown mercy, then that person's mercy should flow to others. Jesus illustrates forgiveness with reconciliation in the parable of the unmerciful servant. The words "the kingdom of heaven may be compared to" build on the prior story. As in the life of the Church, so now the kingdom ethic is applied to one's personal heart attitude. This lection may properly be called "Costly Forgiveness: From the Heart in Three Acts." For in reality, Jesus carefully crafted a three-act drama of costly forgiveness from the heart.

Act I. There is an implicit warning in this story about an unmerciful servant. The basic

---

[6]*A Magnificent Faith*

setting of the story is clearly intended to awaken the kingdom person to the sheer terror of incomplete or heartless application of mercy. The opening has dramatic impact: the servant is in debt beyond his ability to repay. The arithmetic of Jesus' answer to Peter—seventy times seven—and the enormity of the debt incurred by the servant—ten thousand talents (150,000 years' wages)—is contrasted with the heart mercy that the king expressed. The use of the term *king* is consistent with its use by Isaiah (6:5), Jeremiah (46:18; 48:15), and the psalmist (5:2; 24:7). This opening act clearly establishes the principle of grace on the part of the king: "The servant's master took pity on him, cancelled the debt, and let him go." Is this not a clear statement of amazing grace on the part of a merciful God? The enormity of the debt corresponds with the enormity of the mercy.

Act II. The second act of the drama moves to the actions of the servant toward one who is indebted to him. In contrast to the action of the king, the servant is heartless and unmerciful. The contrast is clear and unequivocal. This kingdom person is acting totally inconsistently with the heart mercy shown to him by the righteous king. Clearly this parable establishes God as having a heart of mercy. By contrast, the penetration of this heart mercy into the life of the kingdom person is not easy or automatic. The difficulty of the penetration of the gospel ethic into the heart is unmistakable. God's accounting and our accounting are contrasted here. The plain truth of our spiritual formation can be noted in the difference between the head and the heart. The unmerciful servant processed the transaction with his head only. Forgiveness from the heart is a different matter. What a sober measure of our spiritual progress is suggested here. Sanctification is an unending process, a "pressing forward," as Paul notes in Philippians 3:14. Our progress is "from one degree of glory to another," little by little, as we find in 2 Corinthians 3:18–20.

Act III. Divine actions and human actions are contrasted in this final act. It is not so much that we had better forgive or God will get us. Rather, Jesus says that God's wrath will come on those who do not forgive their brothers or sisters from their hearts. This final summation gently reminds us that kingdom people can get out of sync, so to speak. We can become disassociated. Do we not have here the classic condition of "the divided self" described by William James? Again, the penetration of God's mercy into the heart is the issue. There is no equivocation here. One cannot serve two masters. Is this not the "double-mindedness" noted by James (1:7–8)? Is not the corrective to this situation what Kierkegaard called "purity of heart"?

In sum, this parable has both personal and community implications, as does the whole of chapter 18. The kingdom person must process the impact of mercy and forgiveness in such a way as to see it acted out in the most dramatic of circumstances.—Dave Hunsicker

ILLUSTRATIONS

MERCY.   Burt owned a small leather business that had fallen on hard times due to the flood of cheap goods from overseas. Bankruptcy was his only alternative. His integrity and personal sense of duty was so strong that all of those to whom he owed money were prompted to get together and agree that such a good man should not go under. They all agreed on a settlement plan that would keep him in business. When they told him of their action, he wept openly. Shortly after they came to him and told him of their mercy, he applied for and received a contract that subsequently produced millions of dollars of profit. Burt never forgot his desperate situation and the heart-based mercy that was extended to him. Until his death, his tithe and offerings were certain and dependable.—Dave Hunsicker

REMEMBERING.   Muhammad Ali is reported to have given one of the most memorable baccalaureate addresses ever given at Harvard. He simply noted that many of the graduates would probably become doctors, lawyers, and possible senators, and even possibly one would become president of the United States. He told them that in his mind one of the worst things human beings can do is "forget where they came from." He noted that he constantly goes back to the west end of Louisville, Kentucky, where his family still lives, and each trip reminds him of where he came from. It was a simple speech, but some said it was one of the best.—Dave Hunsicker

SERMON SUGGESTIONS

Topic: The Event That Changed the World

TEXT: Exod. 14:19–31

Introduction: The Exodus story. (1) The presence of God in the tumult of events. (2) God's use of natural means to accomplish his purpose. (3) The subsequent fear of God and faith in God, and confirmation of the leadership of Moses.

Topic: The Strong and the Weak

TEXT: Rom. 14:1–12

(1) If we are strong in faith and solid in our convictions, it's easy to judge or reject others who are weak or unsure. (2) We have a duty: (a) to try to understand those who differ from us, (b) to help them if we can, (c) to accept them in any event. (3) We can be powerfully motivated when we remember that God is *our* judge and that we must give account of ourselves to God.

CONGREGATIONAL MUSIC

1. "When Israel Fled from Egypt Land," Ps. 114; vers. H. Ten Harmel (1895)
   ANDRE, William B. Bradbury (c. 1800)
   This modern paraphrase of Psalm 114 relates to both the Psalter reading and the Old Testament lesson about the delivery of the Israelites from the armies of the Pharaoh at the Red Sea. It could therefore be sung in connection with either reading.
2. "Forgive Our Sins as We Forgive," Rosamond E. Herklots (1969)
   DUNFERMLINE, *Scottish Psalter* (1615)
   This recently written hymn on forgiveness relates beautifully to the Gospel lesson. If the tune is unfamiliar, it would be not only interesting but functional to have a soloist act as precentor and sing a stanza or two for the congregation.
3. "Lord, Speak to Me," Frances R. Havergal (1872)
   CANONBURY, Robert Schumann (1839)
   This simple prayer hymn elaborates on the teaching in Romans 14:7 that none of us lives to himself. Consequently, it would be appropriately sung in connection with the Epistle lesson. The stanzas could be sung alternately between the choir and the congregation.
4. "When We Are Livin'," Anon.; trans. Elsie S. Eslinger (1983)
   SOMOS DEL SENOR, trad. Spanish
   This Scripture song translated from the Spanish quotes Romans 14:8. It would therefore be quite appropriate and effective as a response to the reading of the Epistle lesson.—Hugh T. McElrath

WORSHIP AIDS

CALL TO WORSHIP.   "Earth, dance at the presence of the Lord, at the presence of the God of Jacob, who turned the rock into a pool of water, the flinty cliff into a welling spring" (Ps. 114:7–8 REB).

INVOCATION.   You, O God, can do mighty things, and we now pray that you will do such among us today, turning our hardness of heart, our indifference, and our selfishness into forgiveness, love, and service as we contemplate your grace freely bestowed upon us, through our Lord Jesus Christ, who loved us and gave himself for us.

OFFERTORY SENTENCE.   "Offer to God a sacrifice of thanksgiving, and pay your vows to the Most High. Call on me in the day of trouble; I will deliver you, and you shall glorify me" (Ps. 50:14–15).

OFFERTORY PRAYER.   Help us to find new joys in giving, whether in church or outside, for we have so much to be thankful for and so much we can share with the world, which needs our love and caring.

PRAYER.   O God, most holy and most gracious, never could we climb up to you by any ladder of our own making; therefore, in pity you have sent your Son into the world to show us the way to you. You have set the glory of your omnipotence in heaven and on Earth. If you were only an infinitude of might, our hearts would faint within us. But now in Jesus Christ you have veiled your power and come forth in the strength of your gentleness to live our life and die our death, that you might win us to sonship and eternal life. O God, we know not the meaning of Gethsemane and the cross. If we seek to grasp it, too often we but darken counsel with words of ignorance. We can only praise you for your grace and lift up a cry of penitence and trust.

Living Father! We thank you for our life with its unspeakable privilege and dread responsibility. You have given it to us so that through it may throb the mighty tide of your life, that in it may be revealed some aspect of your being and beauty. You have beset us behind and before. You make us to sorrow for our sins. You stir us with a divine discontent, and we forget the things that are behind and reach forth unto the things that are before. We rejoice that you have set our life amid gracious opportunities, whereby you would train us to truer vision and larger understanding of you and of ourselves.—Adapted from Samuel McComb[7]

SERMON
Topic: Spiritual Growth
TEXT: Luke 2:52

Paul used a phrase in Philippians 2:12 that has always intrigued me. He said to "work out your salvation with fear and trembling." Because I always thought that salvation was something we were to receive rather than work out, I was interested in understanding what that phrase meant. I received help from a Roman historian named Strabo. Strabo lived in the first century before

---

[7]*A Book of Prayers* (New York: Dodd, Mead, 1912), p. 81.

Christ and wrote in Greek. In his writings he gave an account of the once-famous silver mines of Spain. He referred to the "working out of the mines" and used the exact word that Paul used in Philippians 2:12. When Strabo said they were working out of the mines, he meant they were getting the utmost value out of what was already securely in their possession.

The word was also used in Paul's day to refer to the working out of a field so as to get the greatest harvest possible from it.

The Greek word actually means "to carry out to the goal, to carry something to its ultimate conclusion."

Paul meant that when we become Christian, God plants a tremendous potential in our lives and he wants us to realize that potential to its fullest. To work out our salvation means to experience all the dimensions of his grace that came to us in Jesus Christ. To work out our salvation means to grow up spiritually.

In the descriptive statement in Luke 2:52, the Gospel writer says, "And Jesus increased in wisdom and stature and in favor with God and man." Jesus increased in wisdom, Luke says: that is intellectual growth. Then Luke says that Jesus increased in stature: that is physical growth. But notice the third phrase Luke uses. He says that Jesus increased in favor with God: that is spiritual growth, and it is another vital dimension of growing up.

I. *A decision.* Spiritual growth begins with a decision. It begins with a decision to accept Jesus Christ as your personal Lord and Savior, because the Bible says that when you call on the Lord, you will be saved (Rom. 10:13).

Now, you can know about the Lord and not be saved. You can sing about the Lord and not be saved. You can read books about the Lord and not be saved. You can know a lot about the Bible and not be saved. You can attend Sunday school and church and not be saved. But this one thing you cannot do: You cannot call upon his name and not be saved, for if you call on the Lord, you will be saved. God will do something to your heart and life. Spiritual growth begins with that decision.

II. *Discipline.* Spiritual growth continues with discipline.

The Christian life does not end with the decision of faith. That is where it begins. When you accept Jesus Christ and turn the reins of your life over to him, you become a new creature in Jesus Christ. But being a Christian does not end there. Rather, the Christian life is an event followed by a process, an experience followed by a relationship, an act of faith followed by a daily walk with him.

What are the disciplines that lead to spiritual growth?

(1) *Corporate worship.* There is no way you can live as a real disciple of Jesus Christ if you isolate yourself from his people in the Church.

(2) *Daily prayer.* Prayer is not some magical mumbo jumbo that brings instant protection and abundant blessings. It is a daily quiet time with God when we share with him out of the depth of our soul and then listen to him speak to our heart. There is no spiritual growth without that.

(3) *Bible study.* In the history of the Church, wherever there has been renewal, there has been renewal in the study of the Bible.

(4) *Service.* Growth comes not just by what we take in but by what we give out.

(5) *Witnessing.* You talk about growing in the Lord. If you talk to someone about Christ and then see that person begin a new life in Christ because of your witness, it will cause your spiritual life to blossom.

There is nothing glamorous about these five disciplines. They will not always make you feel good. They will not always make you happy. But they are the disciplines that will lead to spiritual growth.

III. *A direction.* Spiritual growth begins with a decision; it continues with discipline. Then spiritual growth has direction.

Romans 8:29 says, "For whom God foreknew, he also predestined to become conformed to the image of his son."

The Bible says that God's purpose and desire are to form each and every one of us into the image of Jesus Christ, to make us like him.

IV. *A destination.* Finally, spiritual growth moves toward a destination.

Where will you go when you die? The answer to that question is determined by what you do with Christ when you live. What happens when you die will be determined by what you do now. A decision for Jesus now will ensure that you will be with him then.—Brian L. Harbour

SUNDAY, SEPTEMBER 22, 2002
Lectionary Message

Topic: Fairness and the Justice of God

TEXT: Matt. 20:1–16

Other Readings: Exod. 16:2–15; Phil. 1:21–30

Fairness is a big word in the dictionary of modern thought. Some writers think the simple lessons learned in kindergarten capture the essence of Christian thought about justice, or they unthinkingly accept contemporary notions of justice that emphasize punishment for wrongs committed or compensation for past sleights or injuries.

Jesus' story of the laborers in the vineyard helps to address both points of view. The story about God's righteousness is drawn from everyday life. A wealthy landowner hired several men to work in his vineyards. The first group agreed on the "fair market price" for a wage of about a dime (denarius) a day. Other men were hired at different intervals. The last group was hired about one hour before quitting time. But when time for the day's pay came around, the last hired were paid first, and they all received the standard pay for a day's work, a fact not missed by those who had worked all day. They complained about the unfairness of it all, believing that their long hours of hard work should claim a greater reward than was given to those who had been in the field so short a time.

Jesus made a simple point in a straightforward way. There is nothing unfair about this arrangement. Those who contracted early in the day got exactly what they agreed to and the landowner was entitled to pay other laborers as he saw fit. For those who had worked fewer hours, the pay was generous, far beyond anything they had any reason to expect.

Several truths stand out in this story.

I. *Christian thought turns on the centrality of grace, not fairness.* Fairness looks at the balance that obtains in a system of rewards and punishments. It is an important measure of equity in the marketplace. Unions insist on it and workers embrace it as one way to measure the worth of work in the world of business.

Fairness is also at issue in a debate among some Christians. Is it really fair that one can be saved on one's death bed when others have served the Lord all their lives? Do they get the same reward in heaven? Peter's question in 9:27 reflects this concern. Jesus assured him that the long-suffering faithful will "receive a hundredfold and inherit eternal life" (29). Even so, it is also true that some latecomers will be even more richly blessed than those of long standing: "Many that are first will be last, and the last, first."

God's grace is not measured by human standards of fairness. It is not a doctrine of preferential treatment based on years of faithful work. That would be salvation by works. Grace is God's free and undeserved mercy and love. Grace is also not reserved for those who see themselves as righteous or pious followers of God. Jesus pointed out that "it rains on the righteous and the unrighteous." God's gracious actions are not doled out only to those who deserve it most. It is needed by everyone and thus is experienced by even the most undeserving.

II. *All people are recipients of God's grace and all have different attitudes.*

(a) One group is composed of complainers who are jealous and critical. They believe they have special claims on God and should receive more blessings than others. Some Christians construe their relationship with God in terms of a contract. They believe they are owed riches or the good life or successful children because of signing on with God.

(b) Another group understands that grace is reason enough for pure joy. The later groups of workers never asked how much they would be rewarded. They left it to the owner, whose wisdom and goodness could be trusted. What they received was the measure of the master's beneficence, not of their just desserts. Grace (*karis*) is both gift and mercy. It translates and captures the Hebrew notion of *hesed,* the overflowing, unmeasurable, unmerited favor of God.

(c) Christians know that human spiritual bankruptcy leaves us as dependent on the grace of God as the last ones hired were dependent on the generosity of the owner. Economically, laborers were among the most vulnerable in society. Slaves and servants had connections that assured both social stability and economic security. But these laborers were dependent on the vagaries of the marketplace. Had they not been hired at the last minute, they would have been desperate for food and shelter when the rainy season hit. Recipients of grace should be among the most appreciative of people. They should neither be complainers nor believe they should be blessed more than others.

III. *This story helps clarify the Christian understanding of the relation of grace to justice.* Those who say they want not justice but grace from God either have not read or have failed to understand the nature of God's justice. God's justice is also God's *hesed.* Righteousness (*tsedeqah*) and mercy, love, and grace (*hesed*) are related. They are two sides of the divine nature. Too many interpreters project the secular notion of retributive justice onto God. Retribution imposes punishment appropriate to the crime or wrongdoing committed. But God's justice is defined by radically different standards. The Christian belief is that God relates to people on the basis of grace, not retribution or even punishment in kind. Grace defines the justice of God, not some secular theory that tends to portray God as a fiend rather than as the divine friend Jesus portrayed.

Christian support for economic justice is informed by Jesus' portrayal of God's grace toward the poor. There is no Christian economic system or theory of governance, but some practices are preferable because they are more humane and committed to human rights in the marketplace.—Paul D. Simmons

ILLUSTRATIONS

DISCRIMINATION.   Irenaeus read this passage allegorically. The early workers were the Patriarchs, and those who came later were the followers of Jesus. Some Jews resented the inclusion of Gentiles, as if the Mosaic covenant gave them exclusive membership.

The market notion of differential reward holds that it is ethical to pay a lower wage to certain people who do the same work as others. The idea reverses Jesus' story and thus justifies discrimination, not equal treatment.

One TV preacher speaks of prayer and contributions (to him) as if they bind God to a promise to make them rich. He calls it "seed money" but promises that God is thus bound to deliver for those who sign on.—Paul D. Simmons

WORKING WOMEN.   *Quadragesimo Anno* (1931) held that women working outside the home was an "intolerable abuse" that should "be abolished at all costs." Women's role was predetermined by God's created order. Differential reward was supported as a way to ensure that the woman's job would be only supplementary to the income of her husband. The bottom line was that it was morally acceptable to pay women less than men.—Paul D. Simmons

SERMON SUGGESTIONS

Topic: Food for the Undeserving

TEXT: Exod. 16:2–15

(1) The complainers (vv. 2–3). (2) The gracious Provider (v. 4). (3) The belated recognition (vv. 12, 15).

Topic: When Living Is Christ

TEXT: Phil. 1:21–30

(1) We can anticipate a far better life with Christ hereafter (v. 21). (2) However, God has important work for us to do here and now (vv. 22a, 24). (3) To do that work, it is essential (a) to live worthily (v. 27a), (b) to stand firmly in unity (v. 27b), and (c) to suffer willingly (v. 29).

CONGREGATIONAL MUSIC

1. "Guide Me, O Thou Great Jehovah," William Williams (1772)

    CWM RHONDDA, John Hughes (1907)

    Based on the imagery of the pilgrimage of the Israelites, this noble hymn relates closely to the Old Testament lesson.

2. "O Jesus, When I Think of Thee," George W. Bethune (1847)

    CAPEL, English carol melody

    The final stanza of this little-known hymn quotes Philippians 1:21 and would be effective either sung or read in connection with the Epistle reading.

3. "Hark, the Voice of Jesus Calling," Daniel March (1868)

    ELLESDIE, Leavitt's *Christian Lyre* (1833)

    This gospel hymn is inspired by the parable of the laborers in the vineyard (Matt. 20:1–16). It could be effectively sung by a soloist following the reading of the Gospel.

4. "O Day of God, Draw Nigh," Robert Scott (1939)

    ST MICHAEL, *Genevan Psalter* (1551)

A delineation of God's just acts and judgments on the Earth, this twentieth-century hymn, based in part on Psalm 105:7, could be appropriately used with the Psalter reading.—Hugh T. McElrath

WORSHIP AIDS

CALL TO WORSHIP.   "Look to the Lord and be strong; at all times seek his presence" (Ps. 105:4 REB).

INVOCATION.   We believe that you are with us even now, O Lord, even as we look to you for your grace and blessing. Strengthen us in our awareness of the presence of the living God—Father, Son, and Holy Spirit.

OFFERTORY SENTENCE.   "One who is kindly will be blessed, for he shares his food with the poor" (Prov. 22:9 REB).

OFFERTORY PRAYER.   As we pray for our daily bread, O God, may we at the same time remember those who have no bread at all, and may we be aware of the many who need even more the Bread of Life. Grant us loving and willing hearts always to share your many good gifts with others.

PRAYER.   Gracious Lord, in Jesus you taught us that you are among us as one who serves; and in your Son Jesus, you whom the stars obey set aside your crown and took up a towel and washed the disciples' feet.

Teach us to set aside our crowns: our crowns of fear and our crowns of pride, our crowns of knowledge and uncentered busyness, our crowning arguments, even our crowns of knowing just what is needed, and our crowns of despair; that we may take up a towel and do what we can, and be all we can be, trusting in your promise and leaving it there—leaving the outcome to the clarity and mystery of your love.

And in all things make us your glad disciples, in harmony with you: your life and ministry, your death, your new life.—Peter Fribley

SERMON
Topic: Which Way Is Up?
Text: Matt. 20:17–28

In those moments when you wish upon a star, what is it you're really asking for? When you allow your fantasies to run loose, what do you see yourself being and doing? If you could wave a magic wand and have what you want, what would you want? If you are making progress in your own life, what are you progressing toward? And if you feel you are not making progress, what is it you're not progressing toward?

Everyone wants to climb the ladder to success, but now and then we need to stop and ask ourselves, "Which way is up?" What is progress? What is success? In Matthew 20:21, James and John, along with their mother, pulled Jesus aside to ask a favor. Our Lord asked them, "What do you want me to do for you?" Suppose he asked you that question this morning: What do you really want God to do for you?

I. *In whose eyes?* Before we know whether or not we are making progress, or what we really want to strive toward, we have to sort out some basic definitions of greatness and success. If we are going to make it to the top, we have to decide what top we are talking about.

Men of the world, operating by their own value judgments, see the top as a place where one is able to sit in the seat of power, to reign over some portion of this world, and thereby lord it over those under one.

When that becomes your concept of where greatness and success lie, you reach it by the quickest means possible. If there are shortcuts, you take them. If you can arrive at that point through who you know, you seize the opportunity. If you can receive an appointment that lifts you immediately above others, you grab it. In one way or another, you try to get the jump on everyone else. That's what James and John were trying to do, particularly with regard to Simon Peter. The three of them were on the Mount of Transfiguration when Jesus talked with Moses and Elijah. They were the inner circle. But James and John, perhaps encouraged by their mother, pulled Jesus aside in an effort to get a jump on Peter and the other disciples. They wanted to ask a small favor. They wanted the seats of power and privilege when Jesus set up his Kingdom.

The Kingdom of God presents a different view of greatness, and therefore shows a different way as the "way up." The Lord has a way of turning all our values and priorities upside down. He said that the way up is in reality the way down. Listen to him: "You know that the princes of the Gentiles exercise dominion over them, and that they who are great exercise authority upon them. But it shall not be so among you: but whosoever will be great among you, let him be your minister; and whosoever will be chief among you, let him be your servant" (Matt. 20:25–27). There is no greater possible contrast between two concepts of success than that which Jesus presents here. Greatness is not to be found in arriving at the top, where one sits on a throne, ruling like a little god over his own little kingdom. Rather, greatness and success are to be found in servanthood, in the willingness to involve oneself in the world of people, as a servant of God. Greatness is to be found in being willing to serve rather than in being served.

We often assume, without any serious consideration, that any promotion is another step on the way up. We seldom contemplate the fact that rather than a step up, it could be a step out. It could be a step away from the kind of success the Lord wants us to have.

Now, of course God does not call everyone to be a preacher. I believe every vocation is a gift from God and must be lived out within the role of servanthood—subservient to the laws and will of God. I believe that every vocation is a means of bearing witness, of serving humanity, of touching the lives of those who are struggling, in the name of Christ. You cannot live the role of a servant of God while climbing over the heads of others who are also struggling with life. Keep in mind that the Lord does not condemn ambition, nor the desire to be great. But he does redefine the great as those who are the most willing to give themselves as servants. They never get beyond the awareness that regardless of their accomplishments or possessions, they are servants of God. In that awareness they find their meaning and purpose. And even if they find themselves sitting on a throne, they use it not as a place of power but as a place of service.

II. *The process of arriving.* When Christ asked James and John what he could do for them, they replied that he could appoint them to places of greatness and authority. Jesus' reply was, "You do not know what you ask. . . . To sit at my right hand and at my left is not mine to give, but it shall be given to them for whom it is prepared by my Father" (Matt. 20:23). Jesus was saying that greatness in the Kingdom is not achieved by favoritism or appointment. Those who become great in the Kingdom of God arrive at that greatness through the process of daily servanthood. One does not climb to greatness in the Kingdom by taking huge steps up some shining ladder, above the crowd, but rather finds greatness by climbing down the ladder into the crowd, where one lives as a servant of Christ. Greatness is not found through positions that elevate a person above the obligations laid on ordinary folks. True greatness understands that whatever throne one may sit upon is to be used for the Lord, and that one never gets beyond needing to be reminded that one is but a human being in the eyes of God. No one has a place of authority, nor is anyone exempt from the daily obligations and responsibilities that fall from God upon everyone else. There is no place of privilege and favoritism in the Kingdom of God. One never arrives at the point where one need no longer concern oneself with being a servant of Christ.

Jesus tried to explain to James and John, and to their mother, that greatness in his Kingdom involves living as a servant and can best be understood in terms of a cup and a baptism. He asked them, "Are you able to drink of the cup that I shall drink of, and to be baptized with the baptism that I am baptized with?" (Matt. 20:22). To accept a cup, in Hebrew thought, was to accept a God-given destiny. Jesus had recognized that his destiny was a cup of suffering, and he knew that the same kind of suffering would await his disciples. He had just tried once more to explain to them that his mission was to die on a cross, and they had refused once more to hear him. There would be a cross for them as well, and for everyone throughout the centuries who would dare to follow Christ.

As he talked to the disciples about their willingness to take the cup and to experience that kind of baptism, he was in effect saying, "Can you two dare to offer your lives as I'm about to offer mine?" He was trying to help them understand that the price of greatness was to be found in that area: in the willingness to minister. The word *minister* means to get down into the dust so that one's travel leaves a trail of dust. The word *servant* literally means a bond slave. It means to belong totally to another person. Greatness is the willingness to give one's life in service to the Lord. One arrives at greatness by way of the cross lived out in one's own life.—Bob Woods

SUNDAY, SEPTEMBER 29, 2002
Lectionary Message

Topic: A Tale of Two Sons
TEXT: Matt. 21:23–32
Other Readings: Phil. 2:1–13; Exod. 17:1–9

Few things are more perplexing than piety that is blind to issues of justice and truth. The problem is especially prominent among people of faith. Religious leaders embody the requirements they think are important to God. But they have often been found emphasizing the wrong things. Not only is their list of sins or virtues sometimes too short, but sometimes they are the wrong lists altogether.

The story of the two sons touches the memory centers of every family. What parent cannot think of similar encounters with children? Different children may have adopted predictable patterns of behavior: one may be polite and seemingly cooperative, another may be a bit rebellious but eventually gets the job done. With which child is the parent most pleased? One could say neither, but Jesus made a point that every parent understands: It is the child who gets the job done. There is nothing worse than the frustration of getting nice promises but never seeing the task get done. "I go sir," sounds good, but it has a ring of mockery and insolence.

I. *Social graces and pious postures are no substitute for the moral commitments God requires.* Jesus' story portrays those around him who are most identifiably religious as those who are a major problem for God. Publicly, they make a display of their good intentions toward God. They have mastered all the forms of piety: prayer, benevolence, quoting Scripture, engaging in religious discussions, frequenting holy places, and attending to the details of ceremonial law. But they are oblivious to the true demands of God's righteousness. They just don't get it. God does not want a lot of pious rhetoric and ceremonial formality that becomes a substitute for love and justice toward one's neighbor. What really counts is not formal declaration but ethical action.

Jesus shows profound insight into the blindness that accompanies religious zealotry and into the evil designs of which religious leaders are capable. The irony is that the very trappings of religion tend to beguile its adherents. Piety makes certain demands if one is to be a leader in a certain culture. The form of obedience gets confused for the content of genuine faith. The tragedy is that the confusion has an ultimate dimension. Life in God's Kingdom is forsaken for life in an alien land. Mistakenly assuming they know what God's demands are all about, religious leaders may never consider that they could be wrong. Few things are worse than spiritual blindness. It's little wonder that "even the publicans and sinners go in before you."

II. *Jesus' central agenda is the true standard for participating in God's Kingdom.* The danger for religious leaders is a false trust in religious entrapments and organizational power. God has no more difficult job than getting through to those who work with religion. Because they work with and handle holy things, because they preach and say wonderful things about the Bible, they assume they are exempt from God's call to Kingdom standards. The measure of righteousness is not found in liturgical duties but in the work of the Kingdom. We are to be people of repentance, justice, and mercy. We cannot lie, cheat, and steal and claim that it is all for the sake of God's Kingdom.

The sheer brilliance of Jesus' teaching style and his perceptions of the plots of those who meant to do him harm becomes obvious. He had been confronted with the question of authority. He was not part of the religious establishment. The question was about credentials. By controlling the process of induction into ministry, Jesus' questioners could control the prophetic temper of their critics. They would approve only those whose religious perspectives were orthodox, that is, like theirs. Totalitarian thinkers do not allow dissent within the system and thus will never be confronted with the prophetic word.

Jesus refused to engage in debate; his interrogators' question was an open attempt to entrap him and change the subject. Instead, he went on the offensive by posing the question about John's authority for baptizing the repentant. The scribes and Pharisees were trapped. If they said John's authority was from heaven, then why were they not baptized? If they said it was only human, they feared the reaction of the crowd, who thought of John as a prophet.

Jesus thus shifted the emphasis to the basic issue. The central question was about human action and involvement in matters pertaining to God's Kingdom. Many things are important, but God's priorities are a constant challenge to human perspectives that tend to stress order, decorum, politeness, obedience to authority, and cooperation with the central powers.

Jesus' tale of two sons drove the point home. Which son did the will of his father? The obvious answer was the one who actually did the work. A parent will overlook or dismiss a rebellious attitude and decide whether in fact the son did the will of the father.

III. *The story has a disturbing moral: that tax collectors and harlots are more sensitive to the life God wills than those who are educated and molded to be religious leaders.* How could it be that people of such careless morals would enter God's Kingdom before certain religious leaders? Three features of the sinners' situation may explain why they may hear and do what God requires: (a) they may be intensely aware of their moral shortcomings, (b) they may not be inclined toward judgmentalism and exclusivism, and (c) their isolation may have sensitized them to those who are rejected and shunned.

Jesus seemed to portray publicans and prostitutes as people keenly aware of their moral failings who thus may also be best prepared and eager to hear God's Word of forgiveness and grace. These souls are able to know genuine remorse and repentance, for their sins are ever before them. Their hearts are ready for God's message of love and mercy. Further, they know what God's people should be all about on the basis of their bitter experience of humiliation and deprivation. They are the ones shunned by people who claim to be God's representatives: The pious are in, all others are to be scorned and rejected.

Jesus insisted that the Kingdom of God is not a matter of privilege of birth, gender, ethnicity, or religion. It is a commitment of heart and mind to God's rule in the human heart and larger society. Those who portray themselves as keepers of God's truth are tempted to believe they are not saved by grace. God must find it as hard to bear the prudery and arrogance of the self-righteous as to deal with the effrontery and resistance by those who mock religion. Many are kept from the Kingdom by the arrogant ugliness of the pious (Matt. 23:13).—Paul D. Simmons

ILLUSTRATION

THE REAL PROBLEM.   Gandhi's most critical comment about Christianity followed his attempt to worship in South Africa. Ushers blocked his entry until they were told who he was. They rushed to him with an open invitation to services. He refused, saying, "I love your Christ but I cannot stand your Christianity."

Bonhoeffer traced Hitler's rise to power and the devastation that followed to the fact that "the Church . . . was silent when it should have cried out because the blood of the innocent was crying aloud to heaven. . . . It has stood by while violence and wrong were being committed under cover of . . . the name of Jesus Christ. It is guilty of the deaths of the weakest and most defenseless [the Jews]."[8]

Hair was a raucous, ill-mannered, and immoral rock musical. Actors shouted profanities, simulated sex, glorified drugs, parodied dogma, and mocked organized religion. But it was also a shocking protest against religious support for the Vietnam War and indifference

---

[8]Cited by Eberhard Bethge, *Costly Grace* (San Francisco: HarperCollins, 1979), p. 112.

toward its victims. Claude, who was drafted into an immoral war, symbolized the helplessness of the GI.

Martin L. King Jr. once gently dealt with racism by saying, "The problem is not that people are bad, but that they are blind."—Paul D. Simmons

SERMON SUGGESTIONS

Topic: The Story That Must Be Told

TEXT: Ps. 78:1–4, 19–16, 38–39

(1) A story of mysteries and miracles (vv. 1–4). (2) A story of disobedience and forgetfulness (vv. 9–16). (3) A story of compassion and forgiveness (vv. 38–39).

Topic: Have This Attitude

TEXT: Phil. 2:1–13 NIV

(1) Its definition: being of the same mind (v. 2). (2) Its example: the self-emptying of Christ Jesus (vv. 5–8). (3) Its reward: God's approval (vv. 9–11). (4) Its empowerment: God at work in us (vv. 12–13).

CONGREGATIONAL MUSIC

1. "Lord, Enthroned in Heavenly Splendor," G. H. Bourne (1874)

    ST. HELENA, G. W. Martin (1889)

    This is designated a Lord's Supper hymn because it Christianizes the daily manna and the water from the rock received by the Israelites (Exod. 17:1–9) into the body and blood of Christ. Because all worship includes remembering the glorious deeds of the Lord, this hymn, either read or sung, would be appropriate used in connection with the Exodus reading.

2. "Let the Children Hear the Mighty Deeds," Ps. 78:1–7; vers. Isaac Watts (1719)

    WEYMOUTH, Theodore P. Ferris (1941)

    This comparatively simple childlike song based on the first verse of Psalm 78 would be ideal as both introduction and response to the Psalter reading. The first stanza, possibly sung by a children's choir, could precede the reading, with the second stanza sung after the reading.

3. "King of the Universe," Michael Saward (1970)

    RUSSIAN HYMN, F. Lvov (1833)

    The priests and elders did not recognize Jesus' authority (Matt. 21:23–32), but Christian worshippers can in a majestic hymn like this. It would be appropriate as an opening hymn.

4. "All Praise to Christ," F. Bland Tucker (1970)

    ENGELBERG, C. V. Stanford (1904)

    The great self-emptying passage in Philippians 2 finds a modern echo in this majestic hymn. The stanzas could be alternately sung and read, as follows, because none should be left out: stanza 1, sung; stanza 4, read; stanza 2, read; stanza 5, sung; stanza 3, sung.—Hugh T. McElrath

WORSHIP AIDS

CALL TO WORSHIP.   "If then there is any encouragement in Christ, any consolation from love, any sharing in the Spirit, any compassion and sympathy, make my joy complete: be of the same mind, having the same love, being in full accord and of one mind" (Phil. 2:1–2 NRSV).

INVOCATION.   Help us, O Lord, to rise to the challenge of truth as we find our love for you, and consequently for one another, growing deeper and broader and higher, through Jesus Christ, who loved us and gave himself for us.

OFFERTORY SENTENCE.   "He will always make you rich enough to be generous at all times, so that many will thank God for your gifts through us" (2 Cor. 9:11 TEV).

OFFERTORY PRAYER.   Give us eyes to see, O God, that we may always have something to give to you, whether money or time or service. Receive now our gifts, whatever they are, for the glory of your name and the spreading of the good news of your salvation in Christ.

PRAYER.   Father, help us throughout today to remember that a very real portion of your Kingdom has been placed in our hands for keeping and for use in your world. Teach us therefore to love you with all our hearts, that we may love those whom you love—people from all walks of life, all stages of the economy, all levels of learning, and all stations of understanding. Fill us today, Father, with your compassion and mercy, that we may labor rightly in the Kingdom.

Teach us to love you with all our souls, that we may seek fresh ways in which your divine power may surge through our commonplace routine from morning till night.

Teach us to love you with all our strength, that our hands may not grow weak and may do the works of him who sent us, that our energy may be poured out for the needs of your family, until all we own or earn or gain may be spent in a stewardship of loving kindness.

Teach us to love you with all our minds, that we may think thoughts after yours from moment to moment, making beautiful and significant each expenditure, always placing you first, that your Kingdom may come through our caring, our sharing, and our daring, we pray in Jesus' name.—Henry Fields

SERMON
Topic: What Is Truth?
TEXT: John 18:33–38

This Sunday we are back at the last days of the life of Jesus. The story of Jesus before Pilate focuses for us the question of which of these two kingdoms endures. Whose kingdom is stronger? Whose kingdom do we really want to be in? Who rules over all creation and will come to judge the quick and the dead? Pilate's kingdom of the military-industrial-religious complex seems at the moment to have the upper hand. Pilate is in charge of these proceedings. Jesus is in chains. Jesus is being questioned by Pilate. Jesus is the one whose power does not seem able to match the power, might, authority, and command of Pilate.

So Pilate enters into the praetorium and asks Jesus a question. Jesus is on the hot seat. "Are you the King of the Jews?" Are you a subversive element? The House Committee of Un-American Activities used to ask all kinds of people if they were members of the Communist party. "Are you claiming to be the King of the Jews?" Jesus does not play his part very well. He puts a question back to Pilate. He is on equal footing. "Are you asking me that question because you believe it or because you have listened to some other people?"

Pilate snaps back, "Do I look like a Jew? I am the one who is in charge here, and your own people have brought you here. They claim that you're a troublemaker. What have you done to get them so angry?" Jesus then tells Pilate, "My Kingdom is not of this world." Pilate jumps at this, "So you are a king?" Jesus says, "Well, you said it. I have just come to bear witness to the truth. Everyone who is of the truth hears my voice." Pilate ends the discussion with his great question, "Ah, what is truth?"

The verbal wrestling and jousting between Jesus and Pilate has centered on this claim that Jesus is a king. If Jesus claims to be a king, it validates a charge of treason. But Jesus keeps trying to push Pilate to make his own decision. "Do you say that yourself? Is that your statement? You say that I am a king. That is your term. Is that what you believe about me? I have only come to bear witness to truth, and those who share the truth respond to my voice." Pilate tries to slip away from having to decide by throwing out the old philosophical chestnut, "What is truth?"—a question that has entertained and fascinated the great sages for centuries.

Jesus asks for a response from Pilate: "Who do you say that I am? What is your opinion? How would you describe me? Speak your own verdict." When pushed and put on the spot, Pilate bails out with his great perplexing mystery question, "What is truth?"

Pilate throws this question out there as a kind of answer that seems to me to reflect the attitude that because we cannot answer the great question of what truth is, because we cannot give a general, precise, and technical answer to this question, there are no truths.

It is currently the attitude that because all absolutes are now considered conditional, because all truths are said to be culturally conditioned, because all values are relative, because all standards are provisional, there must not be any absolutes, truths, or values. What is truth? Well, because you cannot answer what truth is in the abstract, there must not be any truths that really matter. What is justice but the outcome of the best lawyer? What is goodness but what I want at the moment? What is beauty but what I happen to like to look at for the time being? What is love but temporary satisfaction of my pleasure? What is truth? Pilate seems to suggest our mood. If you can't answer that question, then there must be no truth. Everything is relative.

Jesus kept asking Pilate what his decision was: "Do you say that?" Maybe the abstract philosophical discussion of truth is complicated, but you have to have some truths by which you live. You have to make some decisions about the truths you will claim as the foundations of your life. "Pilate, what do you say?"

Some of you may remember the great debate that Bill Cosby had with his girlfriend. She was a philosophy major and Bill said she was always going around asking such questions as, "Why is there air?" She never could find an answer that satisfied her. Bill said he knew why there is air. You have to have air to blow up volleyballs. Jesus says he is a witness to truth— a truth lived, a view of life, a kind of hope, a spirit of love, a power of grace—and those who share that vision, desire that love, live in that kind of hope, know that power, and seek that joy respond to that witness. They seek the life of Jesus and they say yes. "What do you say, Pilate?" They see it, they claim it. They live in it. They affirm it themselves. They commit themselves to that kind of life. "Do you call me a king on your own, Pilate?" Pilate avoids answering by trying to suggest that because we cannot answer all the great philosophical questions, we don't have to make a commitment. Jesus says we always have to make a commitment, to some voice, some witness, some truth as our truth.

Pilate wanted to avoid making a decision because once you decide, there are consequences. There are actions. To decide is to become involved. To answer Jesus' questions is to be pushed to either side of the fence and on each side of the fence there is grass to be mowed, there are duties to be carried out, there are obligations and responsibilities to be shouldered. Pilate hides in his great question and goes out and says that as far as he can see, this Jesus really hasn't broken any statutes and "I could let him go if you wanted me to use that Passover exemption I have." And the people said, "We would rather have Barabbas."

What is economic justice in our world? This is one of those big questions that we would just as soon stay away from because it might force us to look long and hard at the fact that we, such a tiny percentage of the world's population, continue to use up so much of the world's resources, consume so much of the world's productions, and produce so much of the world's waste. And once we have looked at the question of economic justice in the world and at the witness to truth in Jesus, how could we ever continue to live as we had before?

Pilate throws out this big question because it gives him some space so he does not have to decide, and not deciding means he does not have to do anything on the basis of this decision.

What is truth? We like to hide behind that kind of big question because it enables us to claim that because we can't answer that question, there are no truths, so there is nothing to contradict or undermine our position, our attitude, or our behavior. If we accepted for ourselves that there were truths by which we could live, it would lead us to action, and it might lead us to change the way we see, feel, think, and talk about others.

What is truth? *Consumer Reports* did research on steel-belted radial tires for cars. They ranked them for safety and for cost and gave their standard best-buy recommendation. A woman saw the report and noticed that the tires her husband had been buying for the last thirty years were at the very bottom of the list. She showed him the list and showed him the tires that were rated number one. The husband shrugged his shoulders—and went out and bought the same tires he had been buying for thirty years.

What is truth? If there is an answer to that question, then we try to pretend that there are no answers to any questions. The new woman in the work pool was snubbed, insulted, and treated rudely by the other women in the work pool because the others believed that the new woman was the reason the old beloved secretary got fired, that the old secretary had been fired so they could hire a young one at half the cost. The manager's explanation was that the old beloved secretary had begun to think she owned the place. She had been refusing to work overtime. She had refused to use the new computer program for her reports and had thought her seniority entitled her to exemptions from the general rules of office behavior. No matter how many times and how many ways management attempted to explain the dismissal of the old beloved secretary, the current office staff refused to change its mind about how shabbily the old beloved secretary had been treated, and continued to blame the new secretary for getting the old secretary fired.

What is truth? We like to play this big card because it provides such protection from having to deal with our own truth and its consequences.

D. T. Niles was one of the great Christian apologists of the 1950s and 1960s. Born in India, he was converted by missionaries and became an international witness for the truth in life of Jesus Christ. Dr. Niles was on campus at Davidson College and was talking about the claims of the Christian faith and the consequences of following the truth that Jesus reveals. One of the students, attempting to show his ecumenical spirit, said, "Dr. Niles, you have made a strong case for the truth to which Jesus bears testimony, but what about the Moslems, the Hindus, and the Buddhists?" Dr. Niles said, "I am sorry, I did not know you were a Buddhist."

The student said, "Well, no, I am not a Buddhist." "Oh, you are a Moslem?" "No, I'm not a Moslem." "So you are a Hindu?" "No, I am not a Hindu either; I am a Christian." "Well, then," said Dr. Niles, "I was right. You do not need to decide for the Hindu. You have to decide about the Christ you claim to follow."

What is truth? That question is too big for most of us, and most of the time we use it as a shield to protect ourselves from having to answer the other question. The question Jesus puts to each of us, as he did to Pilate, is, Do you think I am a witness pointing to the truth for your life?—Rick Brand

SUNDAY, OCTOBER 6, 2002
Lectionary Message
Topic: Ten Words as a Guide for Living in Covenant
TEXT: Exod. 20:1–4, 7–9, 12–20
Other Readings: Ps. 19; Phil. 3:4b–14; Matt. 21:33–46

I. *The content and significance of the Ten Commandments for Israel.* Among scholars, the Ten Commandments are never described specifically as law, but rather as "the Ten Words." At Mount Sinai, Yahweh gave these Ten Words directly to the people of Israel, with the expectation of obedience. However, contemporary views of the Ten Commandments as necessary prerequisites for salvation are inaccurate. They embody Yahweh's direct offer of salvation in the covenant he made with the people of Israel at Mount Sinai. They are part of the gift of salvation offered by Yahweh, and it is Israel's acceptance of this gift that confronts them with the response of obedience.

This response of obedience is an integral part of Israel's covenant with Yahweh. The Ten Commandments are meant as guidelines for living as the people of God. The direct revelation of these Commandments to the people of Israel was the unique result of Moses assuming the role of mediator at the request of the people. The Commandments are not rules to test individuals toward exclusion from the covenant. They are guides to instruct the whole people of Israel about the boundaries of the covenant of Yahweh's divine will for justice. Within the bounds of these Commandments, Israel could live in covenant and assume the identity of the people of God. By keeping the Commandments, Israel not only responded to Yahweh's gift of covenant, but was also recognized as God's people. The Ten Commandments were given to Israel as a brief and memorable introduction to the Book of Covenant and the more detailed Torah for daily living and worship practices. The ten brief prescriptions—no more than the fingers of both hands—are significant as a usable guide for the people of Israel. They remind Israel of their covenant with Yahweh and of their identity as the people of God, while at the same time offering a guide for seeking justice and dignity in relationships among God's people.

The Ten Commandments are often described as being in two sections or tablets. The first tablet contains the first through fourth commandments, the second tablet contains the fifth through the tenth commandments. The first tablet speaks generally about expectations for Israel's relationship with Yahweh, while the second tablet provides guidelines for relations among the people of Israel. The guidelines given in the second tablet regarding neighborly duties find their impetus in the first tablet. Relations with neighbors are based in the people's relationship with God. It is the people's relationship with Yahweh that defines their relationships with one another. The interconnection of Israel's relationship with Yahweh to the relationships among its people demonstrates the fragility of the covenant that seeks God's divine justice in human relationships. Through the Ten Commandments, a foundation is laid for a society in which right relationship is pursued with Yahweh and the well-being of the people of Israel is preserved.

II. *The significance of the Ten Commandments for the contemporary Church.* The importance of the Ten Commandments, and of the Old Testament in general, in communities of faith is often overlooked. In Matthew (17–18), Jesus is described reminding the disciples that he came not to abolish the law and the prophets but to fulfill them. The life and ministry of Jesus Christ do not negate the significance of the Old Testament or the Ten Commandments, but build on them, encouraging our love of God and neighbor.

Similar to Yahweh's gift of salvation to Israel on Mount Sinai in the covenant introduced by the Ten Commandments is Jesus' continuation of God's invitation to reconciliation and salvation in his historic presence on Earth, recorded in the Gospels. In Jesus Christ, God offers the gift of salvation and covenant to all peoples. Similar to the event on Mt. Sinai, God's gift of grace in Jesus Christ does not require obedience as a prerequisite to reconciliation and relationship with God. Rather, God's love and mercy offered in Jesus Christ confront persons with the inevitable response of obedience. The Ten Commandments are not superseded as guidelines for living out obedience to God, but rather are restated in Jesus' command to love God and one another (Matt. 22:34–40). This command mirrors the two-dimensional nature of the Ten Commandments tablets that address the people of Israel's relationship with both God and one another. Jesus instructs his followers to love God, and from that relationship arises the impetus to serve one's neighbor, as a response to God's salvific work.

Through our decision to follow Jesus Christ in response to God's gift of salvation, we enter into relationship with God, to which the first tablet of the Ten Commandments remains applicable. Additionally, we are given the responsibility of working toward justice for and with our neighbors. The second tablet of the Ten Commandments provides a foundation on which Jesus' ministry and parables build. In responding to Jesus' invitation to salvation, we are offered wholeness in relationship with God that invites our response to love and serve our neighbors. Through our two-dimensional response to the love of God, our words and actions can witness to God's invitation to all peoples. As we respond to God's gift of salvation and enter into relationship with God through Jesus Christ in the power of the Holy Spirit, our identity as the body of Christ will be recognizable as the people of God grafted onto the covenant given to Israel. As the world recognizes us as the body of Christ, others will also hear the invitation to enter into relationship with God and with one another as brothers and sisters.—Laceye Warner

ILLUSTRATIONS

THE CROSS.   The symbol of the cross is a reminder of the two-dimensional character of our relationship with God. Through Jesus Christ's death on the cross and his Resurrection, God offers reconciliation and forgiveness from our sins in the gift of salvation. The vertical portion of the cross represents God's gift of forgiveness and salvation in Jesus Christ. Our response to this gift elicits our response of gratitude to God that is also demonstrated in love and service to our neighbors. The horizontal portion of the cross demonstrates this love and service for and with our neighbors. In looking at the cross, we remember Jesus' death and Resurrection and are reminded of our response that is embodied in our relationship with God and one another.—Laceye Warner

PARAPHRASED QUOTE FROM GANDHI.   Gandhi stated that he would have become a Christian if he had ever met one. Gandhi's observation is poignant to our lives as Christians. Although as humans we all fall short and succumb to sin, our response to God's great gift of forgiveness and salvation in Jesus Christ cannot be compartmentalized or isolated from our daily lives in the world in relationship with one another. Our acceptance of God's forgiveness and salvation in Jesus Christ necessitates a response of gratitude that must in part be embodied in our relationships with one another and in our struggle for justice in service to our neighbors.—Laceye Warner

SERMON SUGGESTIONS

Topic: Profit and Loss

TEXT: Phil. 3:4b–14

(1) The supreme profit of knowing Christ Jesus. (2) The superiority of the righteousness based on faith. (3) The priceless value of identifying with Christ both in his suffering and his Resurrection. (4) The humble necessity of pressing on toward the goal and its prize.

Topic: The Cornerstone

TEXT: Matt. 21:33–46

(1) The parable of the wicked tenants. (2) The meaning of the parable: The treatment of Jesus, God's Son, is the touchstone of obedience to God: (a) in prospect—through the prophets; (b) in the days of his flesh—as the incarnate Word; (c) in the age of the Holy Spirit—as God present in the Living Christ among us. (3) The application: (a) Christ is the cornerstone of the household of faith; (b) to reject him is to do so at one's own peril.

CONGREGATIONAL MUSIC

1. "My Soul, Recall with Reverent Wonder," Exod. 20:1–17; vers. Dewey Westra
   LES COMMANDEMENS, *Genevan Psalter* (1547)
   This setting of the Ten Commandments could be alternately sung and read in place of the Old Testament reading. Suggestion: sing stanzas 1, 3, 5, 7, and 9; read stanzas 2, 4, 6, 8.
2. "The Spacious Firmament on High," Joseph Addison (1712)
   CREATION, Franz Josef Haydn (1797)
   This eighteenth-century hymn has the stateliness and awe-inspiring spirit of the psalmist who contemplates the sweep of creation in adoring wonder. Set to Haydn's great, exhilarating tune from his oratorio *The Creation*, this hymn is a great favorite for use in connection with the Psalter reading.
3. "We Sing the Praise of Him Who Died," Thomas Kelly (1815)
   WINDHAM, Daniel Read (1785)
   Philippians 3:8 is beautifully reflected in this Kelly hymn. Its use is indicated as a response to the Epistle lesson (Phil. 3:4b–14).
4. "Christ Is Made the Sure Foundation," Latin (seventh century); trans. J. M. Neale (1851)
   WESTMINSTER ABBEY, Henry Purcell (c. 1692)

This majestic hymn that focuses on Matthew 21:42 would be an appropriate response to the Gospel reading (Matt. 21:33–46). It would also serve well as an opening hymn for corporate worship.—Hugh T. McElrath

WORSHIP AIDS

CALL TO WORSHIP.   "The heavens declare the glory of God; and the firmament shows his handiwork. Day unto day utters speech, and night unto night reveals knowledge" (Ps. 19:1–2 NKJV).

INVOCATION.   Wherever we turn, O God, you confront us. In the many-splendored creation we see the tracery of your powerful and gracious hand, but in your nearness in our worship we know you in the intimacy of your parental care of us, and we call you Father. Grant that in this relationship we shall increasingly understand that we who worship you are brothers and sisters and can serve you when we love and serve one another.

OFFERTORY SENTENCE.   "Verily, verily, I say unto you: he that believeth on me, the works that I do shall he do also; and greater works than these shall he do, because I go unto my Father" (John 14:12).

OFFERTORY PRAYER.   Receive these offerings, O God, as part of the works we do in the name of Jesus Christ, and bless them, as only you can do, multiplying them as your Word is taught and proclaimed and lived.

PRAYER.   Sometimes, Father, in the midst of our busyness, we find ourselves swamped with feelings of aloneness. Family and friends surround us. Familiar tasks beckon us. Well-known coworkers stand beside us, yet in the center of our souls we experience that emptiness that longs to be filled. Then it is that we discover our need to be for something beyond ourselves. Indeed, our hearts are restless because they do not rest in you.

This morning, we ask that you come into our dwelling place and make your abode with us.

Comforter of all comforters, abide among us and do not leave us comfortless, but fill our sadness with your eternal joy.

Rushing mighty wind of God blow through us to stir up and quicken and cleanse us, and fill our souls with your breath of life.

Holy flame of fire, burn up the evil that is within us, kindle our coldness and enlighten our darkness.

Giver of holy, convicting voices, teach us to speak to others in the language of their own hearts, using the gifts of wisdom and understanding.

Spirit of truth, dwell with us and guide us into all truth, that we may worship nothing but him who is of the highest holiness.

Spirit of remembrance, stay with us to keep our hearts and minds fixed on the things of worth that are the foundation stones of the Kingdom of Christ, lest we fall away from them.

Eternal dove of peace, descend upon us to still our restlessness, quell our fears, and fortify our souls, now and evermore, we pray in Jesus' name.—Henry Fields

SERMON
Topic: The Peril of Sin
TEXT: Gen. 4:3–9

At this point in the history of the world, we are at the place where sin entered into humanity through the disobedience of Adam and Eve. And this sin drove a wedge between God and humanity. It separated us from a loving God, and the only reconciliation possible would be through Jesus Christ at some point in the future. We are focusing on the two sons of Adam and Eve—Cain and Abel. Cain was a farmer and he brought an offering of fruit of the ground. Abel brought the firstborn of his flock.

The way in which God related to the offering suggests that he was trying to teach something about the sacrificial system that was to be in place for hundreds of years until Jesus would come. God preferred Abel's offering because, as we are told in Hebrews 11:4, it was a more excellent sacrifice because it was offered through faith.

Cain's demeanor had turned sour, and God said, "Why are you angry and why has your countenance fallen? . . . If you do well, you will be accepted." If you do not, sin is at the door like a wild animal. Anger is just beneath the surface in many of us. It is just waiting for the opportunity to come out.

Cain's attitude was brought on by jealousy toward his brother. This same scenario has been played out time and again throughout the ages. Many of you understand what it is like to compete during the growing-up years. Remember that Cain was firstborn, and under the Jewish law, to be developed later, he was entitled to more of an inheritance than the secondborn.

Cain knew he had been first on the scene and he was angry about his offering not being accorded priority with God. The sin of pride had entered into his heart. That is often the case with us. We have our rights, you know. Nobody can get ahead of us. No one has a greater need than we do. Take a good look at yourself. But you know there was someone who denied himself, and when we look at Jesus Christ, pride takes on an entirely different meaning.

The life and death of our Lord Jesus Christ are a standing rebuke to every form of pride we experience.

The Jesus we know gave up his place as the firstborn to die on the cross to save you and me. Cain was mad because God did not accept his offering. He was also mad because he wanted first place. He didn't know much about God's order, did he? The last shall be first and the first shall be last. If God wants to go against established practice, he will do it. If he wants to change the rules, he will do it. He'll turn the whole system upside down.

If he prefers Jacob over Esau, then that is God's business, even though Esau was born first. You cannot put God in a straightjacket. If he wants to raise up Joseph to high stature in Egypt and have him save his family, then he will. God has a purpose for everything he does. We cannot always see his purpose, but we must yield to it.

God was trying to teach something in these verses. It was something about the sacrificial system. He expected the best of the flock, the firstborn. He preferred Abel's offering because that is what God desired. It is also implied here that God had previously taught them what was acceptable as an offering. It is not that he disliked what Cain had done or did not appreciate his labors in the soil and what he had produced; he just preferred what Abel had offered because it was in line with what God desired.

We may be proud and puffed up about what we have done or accomplished, but God may not like it. He may not like the way we went about doing what we did or he may not like the attitude of our hearts when we did what we did. Were you doing it for the right reasons? It cannot be said often enough: You have to get your heart right or you will not please God. "All our righteousnesses are like filthy rags" before him (Isa. 64:6).

In verse 4:7, sin is lying or crouching at the door. Sin is pictured as a wild animal ready to attack and devour you. It will overtake and consume you. Yet you have the power within you to resist it. If you don't have that ability to resist evil, then our theological system is in error. Our theological system is based on free will. We have a choice to make as to whether to commit an act that the Bible and society say is wrong. You have the power within yourself to say no! And if you are a Christian, you have the Holy Spirit to help you.

This Scripture shows us that God notices all of our sinful passions. He knows what we are capable of and what kind of trouble we can get into if we fail to control our anger. Cain was angry without a cause and God was trying to show him that. He was trying to bring him back to his right mind once again, asking him to stand back and take a good look at himself.

I believe in Satan, but we give him too much power. You have within you the ability to resist. First Corinthians 10:13 says, "No temptation has overtaken you except such as is common to man; but God is faithful, who will not allow you to be tempted beyond what you are able, but with the temptation will also make the way of escape, that you may be able to bear it." Don't say it was Satan that made you do it. Remember the comedian, Flip Wilson, who said, "The devil made me do it"? You give the devil too much credit and don't take any responsibility for yourself. Most of the time the devil didn't make you do it. It was your own lust and desires that made you do it. Satan may have provided the opportunity and the atmosphere for you to sin. "But each one is tempted when he is drawn away by his own desires and enticed. Then, when desire has conceived, it gives birth to sin, and sin, when it is full-grown, brings forth death" (James 1:14–15).

Sin is pictured as a wild animal crouching at the door. Think of Satan as riding on the back of this wild animal called sin. Scripture says that if you resist him he will flee from you. Remember, sin is at the door. It is not inside yet. It is up to you whether or not you let it inside. If you let it inside, you allow sin to entice your lusts and passions. Satan loves that. For then he rides on the back of the animal sin and can take over the whole house, your body. You open the door a crack. You allow yourself that sexual fantasy. You allow yourself to look at that pornographic magazine. Then Satan, riding on the back of your sin and lust, can take over your mind completely. Then you are serving Satan. You cannot serve two masters, else you will hate the one and despise the other. When you serve Satan, you hate God. Make up your mind each day whom you are going to serve.

God said to Cain in verse 6, "Why are you angry?" God is sovereign, which means he can prefer one person over another or one offering over another. We have no right to question God, regardless of whether we think our offering is better, our work is better, or we have a better pedigree or a more upstanding family. The Lord said, "Do what is right and you will be accepted." I may prefer another type of offering because that is the system I want to set up. But that is not any of your business. Do not make my business your business. Be satisfied with what you have.

The last part of verse 7 says, "Its desire is for you, but you should rule over it." This definitely raises the question that you can overcome your sin problem and the way you react to things that happen to you in life. There are some things that happen that you cannot do anything about. You do not have the power. You do not have the position. Perhaps you do not have the ability. Someone in authority over you has spoken, or God has spoken; you have to suck it up and go on about your life.

Furthermore, you have the greater possibility of overcoming sin if you are a Christian. God says right here in Scripture that you can overcome. And if you have the Holy Spirit within you—and you do if you know Jesus as your Savior—then you have the power to overcome. The sin can be left at the door. The door does not even have to be opened to let it in. And Satan can take over the whole house.

Character is important here. We know that Cain went out and killed his brother and then lied about it. Sin was crouching at the door, and he was forewarned by God. But he let it in anyway. And Satan came in and took over the whole house. God looks at the heart of man. It seems as if God is continually asking questions: Are you obedient? Can you be trusted? Are you trustworthy? When God finds out that you can be trusted, then he can use you. If your past behavior shows you to be untrustworthy, then God has doubts.

The origin of Cain's anger was in God's preference for his brother's offering over his own. He should have been angry with God, not his brother. God can take it, if you want to be angry with God. Jealousy and pride were the cause of the first murder in the Bible. The jealousy was fueled by anger against Abel.

So, what is my purpose in talking about these matters this morning? I want you to understand how sin operates on you. Temptation is presented. We can either resist or allow this temptation to appeal to our lustful desires. And I am not just talking about sexual sins. I am also talking about the sins of anger, jealousy, pride, and so on. When we do not control our desires, then sin becomes full-blown within us. Don't say the devil made me do it! That is failure to take responsibility. That is making the devil a scapegoat. You make him too powerful. God said you have it within you to resist temptation. And if you are a Christian, you have the Holy Spirit to give you added power to resist. I urge you to become a Christian today, if you are not already.

But don't do it unless you are committed to living the Christian life. This involves studying to make yourself a workman approved, as Paul says. Don't be half-hearted about following Jesus. Unless you intend to work on your character and make some changes in your life, don't even take the step. I have seen people come forward to accept Christ as their Savior. They look like genuine converts. There are often tears. But there is a difference between sorrow for your sins and repentance. Repentance means turning away from sin and turning to God. It means a life spent in devotion to the Lord, not just a one-time affair.—Robert L. Poff

SUNDAY, OCTOBER 13, 2002
Lectionary Message

Topic: A Shrunken Imagination

TEXT: Exod. 32:1–14

Other Readings: Ps. 106:1–6, 19–23; Phil. 4:1–9; Matt. 22:1–14

"Holy Cow!" is a phrase that some folks use frivolously to denote being awestruck. It rolls so loosely from their tongues, yet where did it originate? Some say that "Holy Cow!" originates from Harry Caray, the historic broadcaster for the Chicago Cubs baseball team. Harry would use the expression after a Cub hit a home run—although after a careful reading of Exodus 32, you can imagine it was uttered long before it was used by Harry Caray.

I. *Idolatry warps reality.* When nothing existed, God spoke creation into being, and it was very good. Then, from the dust of the Earth, God molded and designed human beings in the divine image and breathed into them the breath of life. But in a travesty of this creation story, the stiff-necked Israelites molded and fashioned gold dust into a god, a golden calf. Their attempt to reverse the divine and human positions became a bitter experience. Out of no *thing* God created the mystery of life. From many *things* humanity's idolatrous creativity produces lifelessness, both figuratively and literally.

When Moses went up the mountain for a conversation with God, he received this Word: "You shall not make for yourselves a graven image, or any likeness of anything that is in heaven above, or that is in the Earth beneath, or that is in the water under the Earth; you shall not bow down to them or serve them" (Exod. 20:4 RSV). God's people were to follow this Word, not only because it was the law, but also because people are so easily intrigued by their own creativity that they begin to imagine themselves God's equal.

II. *The gods we create come from a shrunken imagination.* Moses was a visible reminder of God's presence to the wandering Israelites. But after Moses had spent forty days on the mountain, the people became impatient in their leader's absence. They became restless and easily distracted from their new covenant relationship with God. Convinced that Moses was not returning, they wanted a visible replacement for him, so they assumed their creativity could produce a god worth worshiping and honoring with trust and festivals.

This familiar Old Testament story is one of many that depict our temporal desire for a god who can ultimately be controlled and supervised. Idolatry is the ever-present sin of shrinking our imagination of God to the size of human manageability. You can picture it: that shiny gold calf with a big old ring in its nose. It is a devilish temptation to want a god we can lead around, a god who will serve our narcissistic cravings. We want to hold the reins on the Sovereign, but God does not have a nose ring, nor has God created us with nose rings. He simply gives us holy commands for guidance and a promise of fidelity. And the God who is unseen, but not overseen, calls us to trust that covenant relationship.

More than ever, we are being culturally conditioned to a visual and tactile orientation. When we cannot see or touch God, we feel an urge to construct such an experience. We make excuses and justify making for ourselves a god that is functional. Objectifying God for our purposes and using him as a tool for human comfort and pleasure could be a description of the idolatry within the Church today. It is not difficult to see that culturally shaped gods exist in the community of faith. Actually, if we are not careful, the Church itself can be the idol. When we give most of our energy to preserving the institution rather than following the living Spirit of a God who calls us forward into a holy reign of justice and righteousness, we are falling before the secular gods that undo us and leave us lifeless. It is easy to be seduced into believing that the Church exists to serve our own agendas, to meet our social expectations and desires, to offer a place of comfort and eternal security, to entertain us, and to place no real demands on our lives. Basically, then, God becomes a commodity within our fellowships. When the faithfulness of the Church is judged by its ability to meet the needs of its participants rather than by being a visible sign and instrument of God's reign, we have made for ourselves nothing more than a golden calf.

III. *When our fidelity to God fails, God remembers the covenant and remains faithful.* Living by faith in God's covenant calls for our willingness and ability to imagine a reality outside the given of this world. Some people think it doesn't matter what you believe as long as you are sincere, but our relationship with God is not a matter of how we feel. What we believe in shapes our lives and images; therefore, what we believe in matters. The purpose of the law and covenant is to empower us to be holy as God is holy. So, Christian faithfulness is not tested by whether it feels right but by our fidelity to God's covenant. The third verse of *Come Thou Fount of Every Blessing* says it well: "O to grace how great a debtor daily I'm constrained to be! Let thy goodness, like a fetter, bind my wandering heart to thee. Prone to wander, Lord, I feel it, prone to leave the God I love; here's my heart, O take and seal it, seal it for thy courts above."

When our love and faith fail, God's love and fidelity and promise remain steadfast. When we forget God, God continues to remember us. This Sovereign God calls us to root our hope and life in the Holy Covenant and to stand firm in the Lord.

"Holy Cow!" is one of those utterances that has been around for a while, but there are no holy cows—unless, of course, its those we imagine kneeling beside the manger of the Christ Child Jesus, Immanuel, God with us, Word made flesh.—Lisa A. Stone

ILLUSTRATIONS

REAL FAITH.   Faith, real faith, is keeping alive the tension between the God we know and the God beyond our knowing. It is the tension between the God who is as real as a guilty conscience calling for forgiveness and the warm embrace of reconciliation and the God who does not answer when we call out in the dark night of our soul. It is the tension between the God who is as real as the beauty and promise of a brilliant dawn and the God who seems to hide the future from us or whisper the divine word for our time in a voice so low that we cannot hear it. It is the tension between our doctrines—revealed in the sacred Scriptures, refined in the fires of history, and forged on the anvil of the Church's experience—and our theological explorations—rising out of new frontiers where old answers do not always fit the new questions and where each generation must follow the ever-moving footprints of the Transcendent One.—Kenneth L. Carder[1]

TRUTH AND REALITY.   In faith, we imagine ourselves whole, imagine ourselves in love with our neighbors, imagine ourselves bathed and fed by God, imagine creation at peace, imagine the breath of God coinciding with our own, imagine the heart of God beating at the heart of the world. It is a vision of the kingdom, but is it true or false, fact or fiction? That is the question God continues to ask us: What is real to us, what is true, and what do we intend to do about it?—Barbara Brown Taylor[2]

SERMON SUGGESTIONS

Topic: The Lord Is Near

TEXT: Phil. 4:4–7, especially v. 5b

(1) Rejoice (v. 4). (2) Be gentle (v. 5a). (3) Don't be anxious—pray (v. 6)! (4) Therefore, expect the peace of God (v. 7).—Edward Schweizer[3]

---

[1]*Sermons on United Methodist Beliefs* (Nashville: Abingdon Press, 1991), p. 77.

[2]*The Preaching Life* (Boston: Cowley, 1993), p. 50.

[3]*God's Inescapable Nearness*

Topic: God's Nevertheless

Text: Ps. 106

(1) *Situation:* God's love and grace toward his people were unfailing (vv. 1–5). (2) *Complication:* However, these same people sinned and suffered the consequences (vv. 6–7, 13–42). (3) *Resolution:* Nevertheless, God delivered them, answered their prayers, and showed compassion toward them (vv. 8–12, 43–46).

CONGREGATIONAL MUSIC

1. "Rejoice in the Lord Always," Phil. 4:4

   REJOICE, Anon.

   This round based on Philippians 4:4 could be used as an antiphon before, during, and after the Epistle lesson. The reading could be interspersed with the round as follows: singing of the round, reading of Phil. 4:1–4, singing of the round, reading of Phil. 4:5–7, singing of the round, reading of Phil. 4:8–9, singing of the round.

2. "Rejoice, Ye Pure in Heart," Edward H. Plumptre (1865)

   MARION, Arthur H. Messiter (1883)

   In those situations in which singing a round would not be appropriate, this fine hymn focusing on the Philippian passage's theme of rejoicing could be used. It would also be a good selection for the beginning of worship.

3. "The Kingdom of God Is Justice and Joy," Bryn Austin Rees (1973)

   HANOVER, William Croft (1708)

   These twentieth-century lyrics relate admirably to the parable of the Kingdom found in the Gospel lesson for this day.

4. "O Praise the Lord, for He Is Good," Ps. 106; vers. Marie Post (1987)

   SEDGWICK, Lee Hastings Bristol (1951)

   The stanzas of this long metrical version of Psalm 106 that would relate specifically to the selected verses in the Psalter reading would be 1, 2, and 4. The praise motif of the beginning would also make it suitable for the opening of worship.—Hugh T. McElrath

WORSHIP AIDS

CALL TO WORSHIP.   "Praise the Lord. Give thanks to the Lord, for he is good; his love endures forever" (Ps. 106:1 NIV).

INVOCATION.   We are here to praise you, O Lord, and to come to clearer understandings of your love and care for us. Give us the faith to keep seeking until we see that your mighty acts include us, our lives, and our salvation.

OFFERTORY SENTENCE.   "We then who are strong ought to bear the infirmities of the weak, and not to please ourselves" (Rom. 15:1).

OFFERTORY PRAYER.   We confess that many motives drive us, Lord, as we bring our offerings to you. Help us, as we come to these moments, to remember that we can often do what others cannot do, and so grant that we may give even in their names.

PRAYER.   O Lord our God, make our hearts obedient to your divine will; turn our eyes away from vain things, that, free from the world's attraction, they may always look on your glorious beauty. For you are our God, the God of compassion and salvation, and we glorify you, Father, Son, and Holy Spirit, now and for ever, to the ages of ages. Amen.—Eastern Orthodox Church

SERMON
Topic: Does God Hear Us When We Pray?
Text: Mark 11:20–24

Every once in a while you meet a person who had prayed all his life; he was brought up to pray, he had prayed regularly and naturally, and then gradually he stopped praying—because he thought God did not hear him when he prayed.

Our question this morning is, Does God really hear us when we pray? The answer, let it be said at once, is yes, he does. "When I was in trouble, I called unto the Lord and he heard me." But it is not as simple as that, and it is not enough simply to say that and nothing more.

One of the reasons that you wonder from time to time whether God hears you when you pray is that it is almost impossible for you to visualize it. Isn't that true? You can't picture it. You may have a picture of God as a great man, a magnified man. I don't mean a man with a gray beard; you outgrew that image long ago. But nevertheless you picture God in human terms—the great Cosmic Executive with the management of the universe in his hands. Then you go on to picture him getting calls from all over the inhabited world.

When you stop to think of the number of people in the world and of the vast variety of requests they make to the God of the universe, and of the calls that cancel out each other, the whole thing seems fantastic.

You may have a less personal picture of God. Your image of God, as you think of him either consciously or unconsciously, is the God of the sun and the planets, the great cosmic God who keeps the universe going. And if you have that sort of picture of God, you can hardly imagine him being interested in the likes of you and your rather unimportant needs and desires.

You know that the sun shines graciously and gloriously on everybody and you can praise the sun; you can expose yourself to the light and warmth of it, but it never occurs to you to think that the sun singles you out for special attention. You can worship God, but you can't expect him to single you out for special attention.

Whatever your picture of God may be, it becomes increasingly difficult for you to visualize that God hears you individually, so you may come to the conclusion that he doesn't hear you at all, and if he doesn't hear you, there isn't much use in praying.

Just two or three suggestions: First, because you are a human being, you are bound to visualize; you will never get away entirely from pictures, and the deeper the thing is that you are thinking about, the more you will depend on pictures.

I think you are on safer ground with the picture of the big cosmic God than you are with the picture of the Senior Executive. Both pictures have drawbacks and dangers, but the larger picture is more likely to be the better one.

As you grow, your picture of God ought to grow, and as your imagination, understanding, and depth of perception increase, you ought to reach out to greater depths of understanding the nature of God, until God becomes vaster, more wonderful, and more majestic than he was when you were a child. After all, that is how it happens in the Bible. God appears in the opening chapters of Genesis in very human terms, as a God walking in the garden in the cool of the day, and in the last chapters of Revelation as the great cosmic energy of love who is making all things new. This growth in man's picture of God is right; it is natural.

This suggestion may help. Think of God not as someone at the other end of a long-distance telephone call, but as a living spirit within you. In other words, try to think of your prayer not as a long-distance call by which you are trying to reach someone way out there hundreds of miles away, but as an intensely local call, communing with someone who is already with you.

St. Paul talked about the body being the temple of the Spirit of God. But I came across a line in his Epistle to the Romans. It was a line that was made clear to me for the first time when I read J. B. Phillips's translation of the Epistle. This is the line: "We do not know how to pray worthily as sons of God, but his Spirit within us is actually praying for us in those agonizing longings which never find words." In other words, St. Paul is saying that the longings you have in you, the reaching upward of desires that you may never know how to express, are the Spirit of God in you praying for you. This may help you to overcome the feeling that God is far away.

And remember, finally, that there are things you cannot visualize yet you know they are true.

There is another more practical reason that you sometimes wonder whether God hears you and that is that you don't get an answer. No answer, no one home.

But not *quite* so. The situations are not altogether comparable. In the first place, you don't expect a verbal answer to prayer as you would expect an answer to a letter or a telephone call or a conversation. The answers to prayer come in the course of events, in the things that happen to you. If things don't happen the way you want them to, you assume that you've not gotten an answer. If you ask God to make you well when you are sick and you get well, you say your prayer was answered. But if you don't get well but get worse, you say your prayer was not answered. There is another possibility, of course, and that is that the answer was no, that God heard you but his answer was no, or "Not yet."

Even though it is hard to take no for an answer from anybody, let alone from God, we know—and we know beyond the shadow of a doubt if we have lived very long—that we are not always going to get everything we ask for in prayer.

When Jesus went up to Jerusalem with his close friends, two of them, James and John, asked him to give them places of priority on either side of him in his Kingdom. Do you remember what Jesus' answer was? "You don't know what you are asking. You may be able to drink of my cup and be baptized with the baptism that I am baptized with, but to give you places on either side of me, this is not for me to give; they will be given to those for whom they have been prepared." Jesus was saying point-blank that there were some things he couldn't give them no matter how often they asked for them or how much they wanted them. Nor could God. Jesus was saying in the first instance that when you pray, you pray with the simple trust and confidence of a child. He was saying in the second instance that you also pray with the humility of a child, knowing that everything you want and ask of your Father will not be given to you.

You know that even Jesus did not get everything he asked for. On the very last night of his life he asked to be spared from the agony of death. He wasn't spared. He was given the strength to meet and face the ordeal and to go through it in such a way as to save the world.

When we ask for things in absolute confidence and trust, as he taught us to ask, we also ask with humility, always adding to our prayer, "Nevertheless, not my will but thine be done."

Shorthouse had the boldness to put into a single line in *John Inglesant,* "Only the infinite Pity is sufficient for the infinite pathos of human life."—Theodore Parker Ferris[4]

SUNDAY, OCTOBER 20, 2002
Lectionary Message

Topic: Fairness Under God

TEXT: Matt. 22:15–22

Other Readings: Exod. 33:12–23; Ps. 99; 1 Thess. 1:1–10

I. Can you imagine a political leader in America who was considered so great a danger that a group of George W. Bush Republicans would unite with Albert Gore Jr. Democrats to attack him? In a sense it was that kind of diverse crowd that Jesus faced one day. There were the devout, law-oriented Pharisees who wanted to get rid of Jesus. Then there were the Herodians, who also wanted to ruin Jesus, but they were members of the political party that supported King Herod and Roman rule. Here were strange companions who had only one thing in common: their desire to destroy Jesus.

The Pharisees and Herodians decided to use a church-state question to bait their trap: Is it lawful to pay taxes to the emperor, or not? If Jesus had answered, "Yes, pay the tax," he could have been accused of being a Roman collaborator and might have disillusioned his followers. If he had answered, "No, don't pay it," he would have been charged with inciting insurrection. After asking his questioners for a coin and having them concede that it bore an idolatrous image of Caesar, Jesus said, "Give therefore to the emperor the things that are the emperor's and to God the things that are God's." That was very practical advice, then, and still is now. Jesus knew that God's people live in the world, with its various political and governmental structures. That was and is reality, and the issue is simple: What is the relationship between a disciple of Jesus and the government?

During every modern-day election campaign, religion inevitably surfaces and the great debate between church and state goes on. On the liberal or left side of the aisle there are fears of a grand right-wing Christian conspiracy that wants to force our nation into a conservative, Christian straightjacket. On the conservative or right side of the aisle there is continual complaining that the clergy and leaders of mainline Protestant denominations lean toward the left and are always pushing the agenda of the Democratic Party.

II. Even as political wars have raged within the religious community, Christians living in the western democracies have been conditioned to believe that we are very lucky to be living in nations where freedom of religion is written into our laws. If religious persecution exists at all, it lives more as general public indifference to church life and things spiritual. The state may not be persecuting Christians in our part of the world, but there are means of keeping Christians in place. In ancient days, martyrdom was one way; in these modern days of runaway secularism, trivialization of religion is another.

---

[4]*Selected Sermons*

If one is to believe Hollywood, the only active believers remaining are African Americans who sing in the choir and aging priests who solve crimes or perform exorcisms. Faithful people in all religious communities must beware lest we be shunted aside as irrelevant and outdated. There is a spiritual yearning in our nation. We need to be actively involved in sharing the gospel of Christ, witnessing to God's love through faithful words and loving actions.

III. But we are also to be good citizens. We pay taxes to support a government that is charged with keeping order and defending the people, yet cheating on their tax returns by U.S. taxpayers exceeds an estimated $1 billion a year. Students have defaulted on 14 percent of federal educational loans. On election day, a large percentage of the population does not bother to vote. Some of us do not render to Caesar.

Jesus quickly added, to the astonishment of his hearers, "and give to God the things that are God's." Not only do some people cheat their government, but some Christians also cheat their God by offering back too little out of all their blessings. When volunteers are needed for some task in the church, many members scrunch down behind the folks in the front pews. When a church committee meeting conflicts with Monday night football or *E.R.*, some of us have God-denying priorities. How many of us tithe or place in the offering plate a financial gift that is honest and proportionate? Is there a bequest for the mission of the church in our wills? Sacagewea's image on the gold dollar coin may not apply to the second part of Jesus' teaching, but Genesis teaches that we are created in God's image, that the divine image is stamped on us. Therefore, we should all the more "give to God the things that are God's."

IV. Jesus' point is clear: the Christian holds dual citizenship and lives in two kingdoms. To live under the earthly government is one kingdom, to live in one's heart in the Kingdom of God is the other. Each kingdom is a gift from God. Martin Luther said that God's right hand rules through the kingdom of grace and the left rules through the civil government. Ultimately, God reigns over both. Each kingdom is a necessity, but one is the rule of law while the other is the rule of love. The baptized people of God are responsible to both arenas of God's rule. In the arena on the left, the believers vote and pay taxes to support the civil government and the societal infrastructure. In the arena on the right, we worship, feed on God's Word, and live out Christ's call to serve others in love.

To render or give to Caesar what is Caesar's steals nothing away from God. Why? The powers claimed by governments are always God-given; and that which we are to render to God—the full love of heart, soul, and mind—has never been Caesar's and cannot be demanded by him. The truth is that God does not always approve of what political leaders or modern governments do, but the authority to govern is given by God. Elected officials cannot take this authority with them when they die or leave office. Someone else then assumes that authority. The final authority is God's, loaned only for a time.

The motive for accepting the responsibilities of dual-citizenship comes out of the word meaning "to give" or "to render." The Creator has given us government and church, law and gospel, obedience and grace. Therefore, we return to God what is proper in both realms—to Caesar's what is Caesar's and to God what is God's. Jesus put to silence those who asked the loaded question. May Jesus' answer also put us to silence, allowing us to reflect deeply on giving faithfully all that we can to God and to society. To whom does this coin belong? The government. Toss it in the tax chest. To whom does your mind, soul, and heart belong? To your Creator. Offer them up to God with thanksgiving and service. Amen.—Dennis K. Hagstrom

ILLUSTRATIONS

DISCUSSION.   On June 19, 2000, the U.S. Supreme Court ruled six to three that student-led prayers in the public schools were unconstitutional. The ruling struck down a Texas school board's policy of allowing students to decide, by majority vote, whether to have a student-led "invocation" at football games, graduations, and other school gatherings. Justice John Paul Stevens wrote for the majority, "The religious liberty protected by the Constitution is abridged when the state affirmatively sponsors the particular religious practice of prayer. School sponsorship of a religious message is impermissible, [transmitting the] message to members of the audience who are nonadherents that they are outsiders, not full members of the political community, and an accompanying message to adherents that they are insiders, favored members of the political community." For some, the Supreme Court decision marks the end of the discussion. Others are challenged to find creative ways to battle for prayer in the public schools.[5]

DISBELIEF.   In his much-discussed book, *The Culture of Disbelief,* Yale University law professor Stephen L. Carter writes, "In a sensible zeal to keep religion from dominating our politics, we have created a political and legal culture that presses the religiously faithful to be other than themselves, to act . . . as though their faith does not matter to them." To treat "religious beliefs as arbitrary and unimportant." To imply "that there is something wrong with religious devotion."[6]

SERMON SUGGESTIONS

Topic: Serving God
TEXT: Exod. 33:17–23
(1) We can see God in his gracious works on our behalf (vv. 17–19). (2) However, we cannot see God in the totality of his being (vv. 20–23). (3) Nevertheless, what we can only partially realize now, we can anticipate experiencing completely in the blessed future (see 1 Cor. 13:9–10, 12).

Topic: An Odyssey of Imitation
TEXT: 1 Thess. 1:1–10, especially v. 6
Paul, Silas, and Timothy proved to be worthy examples for the Thessalonian believers: (1) in service (v. 3), (2) in depth of experience (vv. 4–5), (3) in unfettered joy despite suffering persecution (vv. 6–7), (4) in decisive rejection of idols (vv. 8–9), and (5) in expectant and patient anticipation of the completion of the plan of God in a glorious future (v. 10).

CONGREGATIONAL MUSIC

1. "The Lord God Reigns in Majesty," Ps. 99; vers. *Psalter* (1912)
   ELLACOMBE, *Gesangbuch,* Wittenberg (1784)
   Sing this paraphrase of Psalm 99 in alternation with the reading of the text, as follows:

---

[5]*The Denver Post,* June 20, 2000.
[6]*The Culture of Disbelief: How American Law and Politics Trivialize Religious Devotion* (Waxhaw, N.C.: Anchor, 1994), pp. 3–6.

vv. 1–3, stanza 1, vv. 4–5, stanza 2, vv. 6–9, stanza 3. If this suggestion is not suitable, then sing the hymn entirely in place of the psalm.

2. "Lo, God Is Here! Let Us Adore," Gerhard Tersteegen (1920); trans. John Wesley (1778)

ST. CATHERINE, Henry F. Hemy (1864)

This reverent hymn breathes the spirit of the Old Testament lesson. We "bow before the hidden face" in John Wesley's translation just as Moses saw God's glory but not face to face. It also makes an excellent call to worship.

3. "A Spendthrift Lover Is the Lord," Thomas H. Troeger (1985)

BEACH HAVEN, Alfred V. Fedak (1990)

This unusual contemporary hymn could be sung or read as a response to Jesus' challenge, recorded in the Gospel lesson, to "render unto God the things that are God's."

4. "Stand Up and Bless the Lord," James Montgomery (1824)

ST. THOMAS, Aaron Williams (1763)

A fine hymn for the opening of worship, "Stand Up and Bless the Lord" would also serve well as a response to the heartening words of the apostle Paul to the Thessalonian church (1 Thess. 1:1–10).—Hugh T. McElrath

WORSHIP AIDS

CALL TO WORSHIP.   "The Lord by wisdom hath founded the Earth; by understanding hath he established the heavens. By his knowledge the depths are broken up, and the clouds drop down the dew" (Prov. 3:19, 20).

INVOCATION.   O God, we would escape from ourselves this hour, from our little and partial selves, from our mean and selfish selves. We would escape from our fragmentary and broken selves into thy greatness. Teach us once again the everlasting mystery that only as we lose ourselves in something higher than ourselves can we find ourselves.—Harry Emerson Fosdick

OFFERTORY SENTENCE.   "I have shewed you all things, how that so laboring ye ought to support the weak, and to remember the words of the Lord Jesus, how he said, 'It is more blessed to give than to receive'" (Acts 20:35).

OFFERTORY PRAYER.   Lord, grant to our giving sustenance, to our intent holiness, and to the result the glory due your name.—E. Lee Phillips

PRAYER.   Father, we know that you are able to give light that will make it possible for us to see in the darkness through which we so often have to walk. We know that you give life that causes us to rejoice amid the gloom of despair. We know that you give peace that brings quietness to our troubled spirits.

We know that most of the darkness and despair and unrest we encounter are of our own making. We get busy seeking those treasures that moth and rust corrupt, and satisfying our self-centered drives, and do not take the time to engage in those enterprises that will glorify your name and bring good to everyone. So we come asking forgiveness for our lack of sensitivity to our truth, and to follow your leadership as we walk through each day. Arrest us this morning with some word fitly spoken, some thought rightly placed, some visions timely delivered, so that we can begin the walk along the road that will lead us to where you would have us be and allow us to do the deeds you have called us to do. O Father, deliver us from continuing to center all our energies on your demands, so we can follow your commands.

And before you this morning we also bring the many sufferers of our congregation, community, country, and continents. Our feeble efforts seem so small beside the massive pains of others. This morning, be with those who care for the wounded, those who wait through hours of anxiety, and those who endure afflictions. Somehow, in the murkiness of disease and pain, make your powerful presence known as you come with healing in your wings to minister to the sufferers. Now we commit the hour to you even as we commit ourselves to your care and keeping.—Henry Fields

SERMON

Topic: We Are Not Alone

TEXT: Matt. 13:31–33, 44–53; Rom. 8:26–28

In this passage in Romans, Paul begins with the recognition of our weakness: "The Spirit helps us in our weakness, for we do not know how to pray as we ought, but the Spirit himself intercedes for us with sighs too deep for words" (8:26–27). At the heart of life, he says, there is this Achilles' heel. Not one of us in this room does not have some kind of vulnerability, some kind of weakness. It may be hereditary or sociological. Backs hurt. Hearts break. The black dog of depression just won't go away. Sometimes it's a job, a child, no child. It's a marriage, no marriage. It's a bad lab report. It could be a parent or a grief, or just the realization that for us and ours or somebody we love, life is just unfair. So when Paul wrote to the Christians in Rome, he wrote in very realistic terms. He wrote about the world they lived in. The treasure, he says again and again, always comes in some flawed vessel.

The old King James Version translates the words, "The Spirit helps us in our infirmities." Henri Nouwen, brilliant Roman Catholic devotional writer, called our afflictions "wounds." One of his great books was *The Wounded Healer.* Taking the words from Jeremiah and from Carl Jung, he said, "Only the wounded can truly heal." For you see, we are to use our wounds and our vulnerabilities to help somebody else.

We are all vulnerable to changing circumstances. A plane on the way to a wedding misses its course and a promising young man and his wife and her sister are gone forever. Once again, a family must make do and pick up the pieces and try to find life again and go on. But it's hard—so very hard. We are all beset with infirmities, wounds, weaknesses, and vulnerabilities.

So Paul addresses these concerns.

The Spirit helps us in our weakness, he says. He begins with the human condition: weakness, despair, immobility,—depression. Beside these he writes, "The Spirit is here, helping us in our weakness." And this is the sermon: We are not alone—none of us. The Spirit is here. Paul says the Spirit comes as helper, as enabler, to stand by us—not to do our work but to let us know we don't stand alone.

I have a grandchild named Libby who is as independent as anybody I have ever met. "I can do it myself!"—whatever it is. Then two minutes later she will come by and say, "Granddaddy, could you help me?" We all do that. Paul says the Spirit helps us in our weakness—even when we have said, "I can do it all myself."

Paul says we don't know how to pray as we ought. I don't know how many people I have seen through the years who have confessed to me, "You know, I just don't know how to pray." We've been working on that here. But some of these people are activists, and they say, "I just don't think I have the temperament for this. I'm just not the meditative type."

Paul says the Spirit intercedes for us with sighs too deep for words. The word *intercede* is found only here. It means that the Spirit translates the things we have brought and laid on the doorstep. The Spirit translates the mystery and the meaning.

The Spirit stands with us and takes the consonants and the vowels of our lives, the gibberish, and somehow works out some kind of meaning. John Fulton is an artist who at one time was commissioned to do a piece for the window of the American Bible Society in New York City. He took the stuff of people's lives—the ugly stuff, mostly: whiskey bottles, an empty rice bowl, brass knuckles, bullets, barbed wire, dollar bills, playing cards, poker chips, crutches, a smashed automobile headlight, a dirty magazine, a cast for a broken leg—and he formed all these into a sculptured cross that was seven feet high. He called it, "Christ Makes All Things New." He takes the broken, ugly, wounded stuff and somehow makes it all right. So the Spirit takes the sighs of our lives and carves them into something that is healthy and life-giving. Nothing is left out, everything is transformed. This is truly the alphabet of grace.

Paul ends his meditation with some of the strongest words he ever wrote: *"Everything works together for good to those who love him, who are called according to his purpose"* (8:28). The King James Version has it wrong. Everything does *not* work together for good. Plane crashes, child abuse, the ticking of a clock within our bodies, trouble at work—not everything works together for good. Where did we get that? The Revised Standard Version says, "We know that *in* everything God works." Do you see the difference? It's not that everything is just going to be fine and it's wonderful. It isn't. Moffatt's translation says, "In everything God cooperates for good." In all things, whatever they are, God really is there—which means that evil does not have the last word. Which means that God is stronger than the wrongness of life, that nothing can separate us from the love of God.

We say, "I can't pray. I don't know how to pray." We say, "Life is just too hard. I don't know what to do." Then the gospel comes to us from the book of Romans, saying "The Spirit helps us in our weakness; for we do not know how to pray as we ought, but the Spirit himself intercedes for us with sighs too deep for words. And he who searches the heart knows what is the mind of the Spirit, because the Spirit intercedes for the saints according to the will of God." And then the old promise: "We know that in everything God works for good with those who love him, who are called according to his purpose."—Roger Lovette

SUNDAY, OCTOBER 27, 2002
Lectionary Message

Topic: Face to Face
TEXT: Deut. 34:1–12
Other Readings: Ps. 90:1–6, 13–17; 1 Thess. 2:1–8; Matt. 22:34–46

Moses had a face-to-face relationship with God. But of course Moses was one of the biblical superheroes. You and I could never have a relationship like that—could we? How could we be good enough, with the garbage in our past lives and our stubborn sinfulness in the present? A look at the character of Moses may just surprise us, and offer hope that invites even the likes of us to draw near to God.

Very early in the book of Exodus, after learning about Moses' unusual early years, we learn that he murdered a man and fled for his life—a rather unlikely candidate for someone about whom our text says, "Never since has there risen a prophet in Israel like Moses, whom the Lord knew face to face." Yet this murderer is the man with whom God initiated what became an intimate, face-to-face relationship. One would expect that with a past like his, Moses would want to hide his face from God—which is exactly what he did! Do you remember the response of Moses when God first appeared to him in a flame of fire and spoke to him out of a burning bush? It wasn't a face-to-face response. Exodus 2:6 tells us, "Moses hid his face, for he was afraid to look at God."

Face-to-face relationships involve the following:

I. *Ongoing engagement of both parties.* Neither God nor Moses pulled back. God continued engaging Moses and told him his plans to deliver his people, and he called Moses to be the leader of this project. In the conversation that followed, Moses also stayed engaged; he raised objection after objection, and God patiently answered each one. This went on for a while, and when Moses' excuses continued and got out of hand, God became rather ticked off, if not downright angry (Exod. 4:14). But they continued to negotiate, and God suggested a compromise of sorts: Moses would lead but his brother Aaron would be the spokesperson. Notice that this face-to-face relationship between a flawed man and a Holy God developed and was sustained as both continued to engage and neither turned away or ignored the other.

II. *The outpouring of all negative and positive emotions to God.* When Moses was upset or frustrated or angry, he didn't turn away from God and try to work things out on his own. Rather, he poured out his frustration and anger to God many times in their life together. In 5:22, the negotiations with Pharaoh were not going well and Moses complained, "Oh Lord, why have you mistreated this people? Why did you ever send me? Since I first came to Pharaoh . . . you have done nothing at all to deliver your people!" Was this the way to address a Holy God? Did God zap him dead on the spot for disrespect? No, there was no scolding. God replied with strong assurance (chapter 6) that he would come through for them (see Num. 11:11–15 for another similar interaction).

III. *Obedience on the part of the one who isn't God.* The response of Moses to God's directives was also significant in this developing face-to-face relationship. We read in chapter 7, verse 6, that Moses did just as the Lord commanded him to do. Obedience to God's directives was a pattern in Moses' life and is a necessary ingredient in loving intimacy with God. Several times in John, chapter 15, Jesus said, "If you love me, keep my commandments." If you glance at Exodus 40, you will see expressed a number of times the idea that "Moses did everything just as the Lord had commanded him." Even in intimate relationships, God is still Lord and we are not.

IV. *Fervent and honest speaking and listening to God (prayer).* Another almost humorous look at this face-to-face (or we might even say "in-your-face") relationship between Moses and God is recorded in Exodus 32. Moses had been up on the mountain with God, receiving the Ten Commandments. He had been away for forty days, and while he was gone the people got into trouble and made golden calf idols to worship. The conversation sounds like one parent saying to another, "You'd better go down there and see what *your* kids are doing; I've had it with them!" And the other parent responding, "Why are you so angry with *your* kids?

It will make *you* look bad if you are too severe with them." Moses asked God to change his mind, and the text tells us the Lord did change it. Amazing! Yet throughout the history of God's dealings with humankind, for whatever reason God seems to choose to act in response to the prayers of his people. Would your prayer life and mine indicate that we truly believe that? It is part of a face-to-face relationship with God.

V. *The desire to know God.* It is clear that God did not honor Moses with a face-to-face relationship because Moses had never done anything seriously wrong or because he was compliant and quick to say, "Yes, sir!" But one important characteristic we do see in Moses was his intense desire to know God. Exodus 33:13 portrays Moses as saying, "Show me your ways so that I may know you and find favor in your sight," and a little further on, "Show me your glory"—and God did. Earlier in the same chapter, we read, "Thus the Lord used to speak to Moses face-to-face, as one speaks to a friend" (33:11). Psalm 103:7 tells us that God did make his ways known to Moses, as Moses had asked.

A line in an old hymn speaks of "you who are longing to see his face." Do you, too, long to see God's face? Then learn from Moses that God welcomes you to pour out your heart and your praise, but also your fears, your complaints, and your anger. God is big enough to handle them. God is a refuge for us. But he is still God and asks for our loving obedience. When life is difficult and frustrating, stay engaged with God, the source of help and peace. Wait for him to act on your behalf, as you and I wait for the day when we will see God not dimly but face-to-face (1 John 3:2; 1 Cor. 13:12).—Martha Berg

ILLUSTRATIONS

JUST ANSWER.   Does it seem unlikely that a fearful, stubborn, former murderer could have an intimate relationship with God? I heard of someone else like that. This guy had committed adultery as well as murder, and he used to be depressed and angry and wish that God would kill his enemies. But that person, David, the Scriptures tell us, was "a man after God's own heart." The Psalms give an intimate look at the heart of David, who, like Moses, poured out his anger, frustration, and depression to God, as well as his praise. Can you think of something Moses and David had in common? Both of them stayed engaged with God in their down times as well as in their good times. They talked with God about what was on their hearts, and they waited for God to respond. The result for both of them was a deeply satisfying relationship with God. Moses wrote in Psalm 90, "Lord, you have been our dwelling place." Home is being in God. David wrote in Psalm 63, "Your loving kindness is better than life. . . . My soul is satisfied with a rich feast . . . for you have been my help, and in the shadow of your wings I sing for joy." That sort of relationship is available even to you and me, as we come to God just as we are and allow him to work in us.—Martha Berg

TURNING TO GOD.   How do you feel when someone ignores you or, if you know they're upset with you, brings their complaints to everyone else except you? I hate being ignored, especially when it involves close friends and relations; I would by far prefer that they tell me what they are thinking and feeling rather than ignore me. But I wonder how often you and I do that with God? We experience trying times and frustrations and disappointment, and then, rather than turn to God, we turn inward or spew out our frustration on the nearest person. Nothing is resolved and God seems distant besides. I suspect God hates being ignored by us, when we act as though he's not there. I have found that healing and help and nearness to

God come in turning to God—in bringing the pain and anger to him, trusting that he is able to deal with me as well as with whatever is causing my distress.—Martha Berg

SERMON SUGGESTIONS

Topic: In Spite of Opposition

TEXT: 1 Thess. 2:1–8

(1) Those who stand for God's truth will sooner or later encounter opposition: (a) sometimes it is the fault of the messenger; (b) usually it is the fault of the hearer. (2) Therefore, it is urgent that the messenger do self-examinations: (a) to avoid deceitful motives and methods, (b) to be gentle in all circumstances, (c) to be self-giving in the spirit of one who cares.

Topic: A Redeeming Contrast

TEXT: Ps. 90:1–6, 13–17

(1) A grim view of life (vv. 1–6). (2) The difference God can make (vv. 13–17).

CONGREGATIONAL MUSIC

1. "O God, Our Help in Ages Past," Isaac Watts (1719)
   ST. ANNE, William Croft (1708)
   Isaac Watts's great paraphrase of Psalm 90 would be a good opener for worship. It could naturally also be used in connection with the Psalter reading.
2. "Spirit of God, Descend upon My Heart," George Croly (1867)
   MORECAMBE, Frederick C. Atkinson (1870)
   The Golden Rule enunciated by Jesus in this day's Gospel lesson could be responded to devotionally with many hymns and gospel songs. This prayer to "love thee as I ought to love" (stanza 4) could be one of these, sung immediately after the reading in Matthew (22:24–46).
3. "The God of Abraham Praise," Thomas Oliver (c. 1770)
   LEONI, Meyer Lyon (c. 1770)
   A fine hymn for opening worship, this paeon of praise relates generally to the Old Testament reading on the death of Moses (Deut. 34:1–12). It can forge connections in joint worship services involving Jews and Christians.
4. "Eternal God, Whose Power Upholds," Henry Hallam Tweedy (1929)
   FOREST GREEN, English folk song; arr. Ralph Vaughn Williams (1906)
   This modern hymn relates in some way to all the Scripture readings for the day, with the exception of the reading from Deuteronomy. It echoes particularly Psalm 90:2. It lends itself to line-by-line antiphonal performance between two groups of singers.—Hugh T. McElrath

WORSHIP AIDS

CALL TO WORSHIP.   "O satisfy us early with they mercy, that we may rejoice and be glad all our days" (Ps. 90:14).

INVOCATION.   Here we are, O Lord, because of your many mercies. Help us to know that fact and to understand it in the most difficult circumstances. Then we can rejoice and praise you from the depths of our hearts. Let this service of worship increase our knowledge of you and your ways, that we may rejoice and be truly glad.

OFFERTORY SENTENCE.   "The angel said, 'Your prayers and acts of charity have gone up to heaven to speak for you before God'" (Acts 10:4b REB).

OFFERTORY PRAYER.   What an act of worship our offerings can be—tokens of our love for you, O Lord, and of our love for those whose lives will be blessed because of what we give of our very selves and our material possessions. Receive these offerings, we pray, and help us to know the joy of worship and sharing.

PRAYER.   Father, we ask this morning that you be with those who have sorrows to bear that are even greater than the sorrow of the death of a loved one. Bring light to their situations and flood their souls with the assurance of your presence in the midst of their sorrow.

We ask that you bring hope to hopeless situations. Come down into the human heart that has been crushed by life's events and mend the broken cords of hope that they may vibrate once more.

We ask that our ignorance be removed as truth and knowledge of Christ are imparted to help us manage life. Here, in this sacred place, let some word be fitly spoken that will give guidance and set folks' feet on lofty places.

We ask especially that hearts be touched here today and find the Savior of our souls. Let the Holy Spirit move mightily among us, mending a relationship here, strengthening a marriage there, sealing faith in a needy life, convincing a soul of the need to let Christ be Lord for all life and eternity.

Make this a mighty hour, an hour to be long remembered, Father, as we wait in expectancy before you, worshiping and praying in Jesus' name.—Henry Fields

SERMON
Topic: Balm in Gilead
Text: Matt. 4:23–25; 8:14–17

Gilead was known for the production of a healing ointment exported to surrounding cultures and tied to national pride. When Jeremiah mourned the spiritual sickness that had infected his people, he raised the question, "Is there no balm in Gilead? Is there no physician there? Why then has the health of my poor people not been restored?" The African American spiritual emerged from the agony of slavery with the gospel of Christ to answer Jeremiah: "There is a balm in Gilead to heal the sin-sick soul." The question of Jeremiah is still relevant: Where is the medicine to heal and sustain God's people?

Matthew set the stage for the ministry of Jesus. Jesus came teaching, preaching, and healing. Douglas Hare compares Matthew with Mark and notes that Matthew's Jesus is always the teacher whose deeds are servant to his words. Hare imagines a conversation in which Matthew tells Mark, "Miracles do not certify teaching; it is the other way around! In themselves miracles are ambiguous events. It is the authenticity of Jesus' teaching that renders his miracles significant. He is Messiah of Word before he is Messiah of Deed." What do you think?

I. *Is there a balm in Gilead?* We cannot begin to understand Jesus apart from his work. The miracles of the New Testament are not optional. They are central to the identity of the Christ. The healing ministry of Jesus is more than a miracle that demonstrates the power of

God at work in Christ. The healing work of Jesus addresses the nature of our disease and the compassion of Christ for all human suffering.

John Newport regularly reminded his students in the philosophy of religion that the Bible is *prescientific.* This rather obvious observation is a simple key to understanding the Bible. In brief, we cannot read the Bible as if it were written in the shade of computers, space shuttles, and modern hospitals. We have to understand the radical difference in thinking that has come with the modern era in which we live. The Bible observes the world as it appears to the unaided eye—flat, small, and moved by mystical powers. The analogy of the wind in the conversation between Jesus and Nicodemus loses something of its mystique in a study of meteorology, and the healing miracles of Jesus are confusing when the diagnosis is demon possession. The abandonment of the healing mission of Jesus has been supported by a new understanding of the world in the application of a valid principle of biblical interpretation.

C. S. Lewis, in *The Problem of Pain,* observed that the great religions were "first preached and long practiced in a world without chloroform." When the only available healing was faith healing, the clinical role of the Church in life was central to existence. However, in a few short centuries the center of healing shifted from the Church to the hospital, and the healing ministry of Jesus and the early Christians was set aside as an artifact of an antiquated understanding of the world. Thus, the epileptic boy needed drugs or surgery rather than exorcism of demons, and the man born blind needed surgery rather than a saliva mudpie on his eyes and a ritual washing in the Pool of Siloam. We cannot know enough to prescribe cures for the diseases described in the Bible.

The question is closer to home. With a new urgency and a new sense of discovery, spiritual healing is finding a new level of importance in the whole picture of human suffering. You have probably seen the reports—on television newscasts, no less—about the therapeutic application of meditation and prayer to supplement the administration of drugs and surgery. Billy Williams came back from radiation treatment in the Harvard medical community with a book by Herbert Benson, M.D., *Timeless Healing: The Power and Biology of Belief,* and I have just finished reading a book by Larry Dossey, M.D., *Healing Words.* There is a growing body of literature based on statistical, scientific study that suggests that faith and prayer have a significant place in the art of healing. Dr. Dossey is so impressed with the effectiveness of prayer in healing that he envisions a day when prayer will become the standard in scientific medical practice, and the failure to use prayer will be viewed as malpractice.

II. *God is involved in human suffering.* I must confess my discomfort with some so-called scientific analysis of faith and healing. God does not fit too well under our microscopes or into our computers. To speak of using faith or prayer like we would use surgery or drugs has a taint of manipulation that does not fit into my understanding of God. I recall a sarcastic snort by Paul Scherer to the sentimental cliché, "When all else fails, try God." Scherer replied, "Why not try aspirin?" Indeed, we cannot even perceive, much less exhaust, the mystery of God. God is by nature beyond our feeble instruments of measure and evaluation. Despite the hype, God does not fit into our prescription bottles or our over-the-counter products.

Following his teaching in Matthew's Sermon on the Mount, Jesus plunges into a series of healing events, and Matthew alone offers the explanation from Isaiah: "He took our infirmities and bore our diseases." I always read the passage with the vicarious suffering of Jesus in mind. He bore on the cross the sin of the world. He was smitten by God and afflicted, punished for my iniquities, for my failures; but Matthew gives us a new context. The Messiah came to absorb our sickness into himself. In other words, the healing mission of Jesus was more than demonstration of divine power and more than acts of eradicating human disease. I have heard the victory shout that smallpox is no longer a threat in the modern world, and we are rapidly approaching the eradication of polio. Matthew suggests a cost in the act of healing that we often overlook. Jesus was not a charlatan who threw crutches away and declared sight to the blind. Matthew suggests that Jesus was so involved in the suffering of this world that he took on the burden of human illness.

In *A History of God,* Karen Armstrong tells of a group of Jews during the Holocaust who decided to put God on trial. They created their court and held their mock trial with all of the rules of evidence and the allowance for reasonable doubt that any system of justice would require. They then concluded that God was guilty as charged. The rabbi declared the conviction of God and passed a sentence of death. Then, as if nothing had occurred, he called the community to their evening prayers.

The trial goes on. Something inside us cries, "Injustice!" in the face of the human suffering all around us. Without defense or explanation, God continues to be present to us, and Christ continues to bear our pain for us and with us.—Larry Dipboye

SUNDAY, NOVEMBER 3, 2002
Lectionary Message

Topic: People of the Lie
TEXT: Matt. 23:1–12
Other Readings: Josh. 3:7–17; Ps. 107:1–7, 33–37; 1 Thess. 2:9–13

This passage is part of a much larger setting of confrontations between Jesus and the Jewish leaders that begin with the question of John's authority (Matt. 21:23–27) and climax with his precrucifixion discourses. The Pharisees are consistently depicted through this Gospel as standing in opposition to Jesus' message.

I. *The religion of the Pharisees had become a religion of "show."* At the heart of this religion was the Pharisees' desire to dress and act in such a way as to draw attention to themselves. This was, of course, in conflict with the Christian notion that one should "die to self" so that people may see one's good deeds and glorify God. Any religion that nurtures pride in the heart is a false religion, because it places self above God.

Jesus warned his disciples of the dangers not only of a Pharisaic lifestyle but also of Pharisaic teachings. Yet this was the only time that Jesus specifically instructed his followers to give heed to the instruction of his opponents. He recognized that the Pharisees were worthy of being heard, so far as they upheld the Mosaic Law. It was their practices that were to be avoided.

These practices included requirements and countless rules that, in effect, made following the Law intolerable for ordinary people. In addition, the Pharisees did nothing to relieve the burden of their decrees. They did nothing to empower the faithful to fulfill the Law. The people found themselves enslaved by the Law. When religion enslaves, it ceases to be true religion. St. Paul wrote, "Now, before faith came, we were confined under the Law, kept under restraint until faith should be revealed. So the Law was our custodian until Christ came, that we might be justified by faith. But now that faith has come, we are no longer under a custodian, for in Christ you are all sons of God, through faith" (Gal. 3:23–26).

II. *The focus of this passage is hypocrisy—the chasm between the teachings of the Pharisees and their conduct.* Their passion for the Law was evident. The fruits of that passion were not evident. This discrepency is echoed in the Epistle of James (2:17), where it is written that "faith without works is dead." There can be no true faith if there is no evidence to prove that faith. The Pharisees were, in fact, "people of the lie."

In his book *People of the Lie,* M. Scott Peck wrote,

> Utterly dedicated to preserving their self-image of perfection, they are unceasingly engaged in the effort to maintain the appearance of moral purity. They worry about this a great deal. They are acutely sensitive to social norms and what others might think of them. . . . They outwardly seem to live lives that are above reproach. The words *image, appearance,* and *outwardly* are crucial to understanding the morality of evil. While they seem to lack any motivation to be good, they intensely desire to appear good. Their "goodness" is all on the level of pretense. It is, in effect, a lie. That is why they are the "people of the lie."

We are warned that religious privilege and position involve great responsibility. Proud claims of spiritual leadership and the performance of religious rites do not establish one as truly belonging to God. Faithful service to God's children is inspired by a pastoral heart.

III. *At the heart of this passage is the Christian ethic of humility and service.* We have already heard Jesus speak to this in the Gospel of Matthew. The teachings of the Savior are clear: "Whoever humbles himself . . . is the greatest in the Kingdom of Heaven" (Matt. 18:4), and "Whoever would be great among you must be your servant" (Matt. 20:26b). These proclamations forcefully stand against the Pharisaic practices of his day.

Jesus often took the logic of the day and turned it upside down. That is the case here. The humble one is always exalted and the servant is always the greatest. Unlike the Pharisees, we are called to be servants, not superiors. We are called to lift the burdens of others instead of oppressing them further. As disciples of our Lord and Savior, we can find greatness through servant-hood and experience exaltation through humility.

Of course, we are given the model in Jesus Christ himself. All we need to do is turn to that oldest of Christian hymns found in Paul's letter to the church in Philippi, where we read, "Do nothing from selfishness or conceit, but in humility count others better than yourselves. Let each of you look not only to his own interests, but also to the interests of others. Have this mind among yourselves, which is yours in Christ Jesus, who, though he was in the form of God, did not count equality with God a thing to be grasped, but emptied himself, taking the form of a servant, being born in the likeness of men. And being found in human form, he humbled himself and became obedient unto death, even death on a cross. Therefore, God has highly exalted him and bestowed on him the name which is above every name, that at the name of Jesus every knee should bow . . . and every tongue confess that Jesus Christ is Lord" (Phil. 2:3–11).

As people of the lie, the Pharisees could not emulate the model of Christ, for "the Word became flesh and dwelt among us, full of grace and truth . . . for the law was given through Moses; grace and truth came through Jesus Christ" (John 1:14a, 17). It is for us to follow the example of Jesus Christ. He is "the way, the truth and the life" (John 14:6) and it is through Jesus Christ, and not Pharisaic law, that we come to the Father. To believe anything else would be a lie.—Clark Sherman

ILLUSTRATION

TWO MONKS.   Two monks on a pilgrimage came to the ford of a river. There they saw a girl dressed in all her finery, obviously not knowing what to do since the river was high and she did not want to spoil her clothes. Without more ado, one of the monks took her on his back, carried her across and put her down on dry ground on the other side.

Then the monks continued on their way. But the other monk, after an hour, started complaining, "Surely it is not right to touch a woman; it is against the commandments to have close contact with women. How could you go against the rules of monks?"

The monk who had carried the girl walked along silently, but finally he remarked, "I set her down by the river an hour ago. Why are you still carrying her?"—Irmgard Schloegl[1]

SERMON SUGGESTIONS

Topic: Certification
TEXT: Josh. 3:7–17
(1) God promises Moses recognized leadership (vv. 7–8). (2) God promises his people a sign of his presence with them (vv. 10–11). (3) God uses a dramatic incident to certify Moses' leadership and to reassure his people of his continuing providence (vv. 12–17).

Topic: Toward the Bottom Line
TEXT: 1 Thess. 2:9–13
(1) Ethical support (v. 9). (2) Reliable example (v. 10). (3) Paternal love and concern (vv. 11–12). (4) The result: unhindered reception of God's true message through the faithful messenger (v. 13).

CONGREGATIONAL MUSIC

1. "Thanks to God Whose Word Has Spoken," R. T. Brooks (1954)
   WYLDE GREEN, Peter Cutts (c. 1955)
   The Thessalonians received the words of the apostle Paul as the Word of God. This contemporary hymn voices thanksgiving for that Word and thus would be appropriately used in connection with the Epistle lesson.
2. "Redeemed, How I Love to Proclaim It," Fanny J. Crosby (1882)
   ADA, Aubrey L. Butler (1966)
   Psalm 107:2 invites "the redeemed of the Lord to say so." This gospel hymn furnishes a vehicle for this to be accomplished.
3. "He Leadeth Me, O Blessed Thought," Joseph H. Gilmore (1862)
   HE LEADETH ME, William B. Bradbury (1864)
   This hymn offering God's leadership and guidance "by waters calm o'er troubled sea" could appropriately accompany the Old Testament lesson about Joshua leading the Israelites on dry ground over the Jordan river.
4. "Come Down, O Love Divine!" Bianco da Siena (fifteenth century); trans. R. F. Littledale (1867)
   DOWN AMPNEY, Ralph Vaughn Williams

---

[1]*Chicken Soup for the Soul*

The third stanza of this fifteenth-century hymn expresses the spirit of humility that Jesus calls for in the Gospel lesson. The excellent tune by the finest British composer of the twentieth century, if unfamiliar, could be sung by a soloist or a choir. The congregation could then be invited to sing the final two stanzas.—Hugh T. McElrath

WORSHIP AIDS

CALL TO WORSHIP.   "Happy are those whose way is blameless, who walk in the law of the Lord. Happy are those who keep his decrees, who seek him with their whole heart" (Ps. 119:1–2 NRSV).

INVOCATION.   Today, O Lord, teach us again that the way to true happiness lies in doing your will, not halfheartedly, but with our whole being. We look to you for grace and help to enable us to do what you expect us to do for our highest happiness.

OFFERTORY SENTENCE.   "Very truly, I tell you, the one who believes in me will also do the works that I do and, in fact, will do greater works than these, because I am going to the Father" (John 14:12 NRSV).

OFFERTORY PRAYER.   We know, our Father, that the greater works that Jesus spoke of are actually accomplished by his presence in our lives and by the power of his presence working through us. Even in these moments, as we give our offerings, we reflect his love and self-giving.

PRAYER.   God of refuge, be a strong refuge for the strugglers of life who are battered and worn. God of comfort, be the present comforter for those who face all the questions of the unknown and sense loss larger than they can comprehend. God of healing, in gentleness touch the ill folks suffering from the many maladies of life, spirit, soul, and heart so that wholeness may be realized and health may be real. God of salvation, let the searching light of your truth and presence penetrate the darkness of our lostness so that we may be guided into the brightness of redemption. God of hope, fill the crevices of hopelessness with the sunshine of hope. God of faith, remind us of your faith in us, that we might hold faith in you and have faith in others. God of joy, visit the joyless places of life with the wonder of your presence, which to abide in is life's greatest joy. God of love, impart your love to us so that we might love genuinely, helpfully, powerfully, and eternally all whom we are called to love. God of eternity, make transparent the eternal dimension of life so that we may meet life in all its different phases without fear or dread, but with assurance and great expectation.

Throughout this hour, surprise us with your presence, reveal to us your truth, bathe us in your love, assure us of your salvation, and fit us for the living of life as it opens before us throughout all the days to come, we pray in Jesus' name.—Henry Fields

SERMON
Topic: God's Unchanging Mind?
TEXT: Exod. 32:14

What is a poor teacher to do? It was right there in his lesson about the political end of Saul as King. Do you remember that the prophet Samuel had been used by God to pick Saul to be the first king over Israel? Well, now, here was Saul, later, and he had let his power and position go to his head. God had told Saul to destroy all the Amalekites, but Saul had thought it would be better if the army got to keep some of the livestock and the best of the spoils. To the victor go the spoils.

Then Samuel said to Saul, "The Lord has rejected you from being king over Israel." God had picked Saul; now God was rejecting Saul. But the story makes it even harder. When Saul tried to grab hold of Samuel to explain his position, Saul tore Samuel's jacket and Samuel said, "The Lord has torn the kingdom of Israel from you this day and has given it to a neighbor of yours who is better than you. For the God of Israel will not lie or repent." Samuel said that God does not repent or change his mind when God had just changed his mind about Saul.

It was not a very happy class. They did not want to talk about the idea that God changes his mind. What would happen if it sounded like God makes mistakes and has to change his actions? What kind of God would we worship if God is not always the same—yesterday, today, and forever?

Yet the Old Testament is full of stories that describe God as a partner in an ongoing discussion with his people, as a participant and a responder to the deeds and actions of his children. God is always faithful in his love for his people, but when they act, their actions have consequences, and God has to respond to those actions. What are we to make of this magnificent story of God's involvement with the children of Israel and their little golden bull? Like so many of the stories in the Bible, it becomes so quickly our story. It is a story about people. It is a story from which most of us can take great comfort. It is a boost of confidence for all of us who long for the coming of the promised Kingdom of God.

Moses had been gone too long. Suddenly the religious security blanket of Moses was gone, and the people got frantic. We human beings are always so fickle. We don't want to mention God or talk about prayer while things are good, but when evil strikes at Columbine High School, we have religious services all over the place. Just let the president get through a state of the union address without mentioning any theology and at the end we still want to hear, "God bless the United States of America." We want God to be close at hand so we can grab him when we need him.

Moses was gone. What will happen when Billy Graham is dead and is no longer available to pray over new presidents? Where would we be if the Rev. Jesse Jackson wasn't always available to come visit when a tragedy happens? Moses had been gone too long. The people did not have their religious comforter.

They asked the priest to make them a god they could hold on to. Make us a god we can carry, they said. We make the Bible our god so we can carry it about; make Jesus on the cross our god so we can wear it around our neck. Make us a god we can channel through New Age prayers. Make us a god we can see and touch.

The priest had no problem accommodating their desires. We priests are always happy to try to be of service. Most of us go into the ministry because we want to help people, and if you need a blessing on your new condo, we will do that. If you want somebody to make you feel less guilty, we will be happy to help. The *Wall Street Journal* published a very perceptive article titled, "To Hell with Sin." The author suggested that the new priests have gladly created churches that care more about feelings than about truth. "Largely drained of doctrine, they are little more than a club for good works." We want everybody to come; everybody gets a vote, everybody is welcomed, and nobody is asked to be obedient to anything. The new priests focus on affirming, consoling, and accepting others for exactly who they are. They are more concerned with having something for everybody than with having everybody understand the same truth about the grace and justice of God. They want a God who will make you feel comfortable by making it possible for you to see God; they will make you a God-bull that you can come and touch, like the Clemson football team touching the rock and running down the hill before each home game.

Aaron was willing to do whatever the people wanted. We ministers are supposed to please the people. But of course, God was not a happy camper with what he saw. After all, he had done so much for them up to that point, but because Moses had been gone for a few days, the children of Israel rejected God. I don't know how to describe God's anger. Most of the thoughts that come to my mind are expressions that you would not think are appropriate in worship. God immediately started planning his destruction of this rebellious, snotty little group of wimps. He would wipe them from the face of the Earth. God said to Moses, "Moses, I'm going to take them out. Not you—I'll keep you and let you be the recipient of all the blessings I have planned for them. But they are history."

This was perhaps a moment of temptation for Moses. He could be free from those whining, constantly complaining, stiff-necked people and get all of the Promised Land for himself. But the temptation passed in a hurry. Moses saw the flaw in the temptation. If God would not keep his promises to the children of Israel, what hope did Moses have that God would keep the promises God had made to him? That is the reason this story is so important to us as well. Would God wipe out his people and destroy them as he had decided to do, or would he change his mind again and stay with them? God told Moses, "Get out of my way and leave me alone, for there is going to be some chaos made."

But Moses would not back off. God was not the only one involved in this enterprise. Moses had something important to say and he would be heard. Moses was a significant player in this discussion. You and I are called by God to be his children and to be significant players in our care for all creation and for one another. In the Scriptures, God always seems to respect and respond to human beings who believe they are important enough to God to speak back to him. Moses gets right back in the face of God and says, "If you wiped them out, that would really be stupid. How smart do you think you would look if, after going through all of the plagues, the pillar of fire and cloud by day, the parting of the Red Sea, the manna and doves, and the water from the rocks to save these people, you just turned around and killed them?" Moses believed that God was the kind of God who considered such information important.

Moses moved to his second point: God, your reputation as a dependable God will be over. Just what do you think the people who worship Baal will say, or those who worship Re in Egypt? Yahweh, the God who promised to take care of the children of Israel, is not a very reliable God. You made a lot of noise declaring that these are your people and you will take care of them, and then they die out in the wilderness. You are not able to preserve your people. Just who do you think you would be able to convince to follow you in the future if you cannot protect and preserve these people now? You wipe out these people and you will look like a silly investor who spent a lot of effort on a project only to abandon it. How wasteful! You will look like a God who was powerless and unable to keep and protect his people; and not only will your power and your wisdom look pretty feeble, but your integrity will not get you a cup of coffee, because you promised to protect these people. You gave your word; you swore an oath on the integrity of who you are that the descendants of these people would be as many as the stars in the sky, more than the grains of sand on the beach; if you kill them now, where will that promise be?

Well, look what happened when Moses confronted God with the consequences of God's proposed actions. God did not strike Moses dead for being too assertive or uppity. He listened to Moses and recognized that Moses had spoken truth. God cannot do whatever God wants to do whenever God wants to do it and still be God. Even God must be limited by what God has done and said in the past. God's commitments in the past limit God's options in the future. God's vision and plans for the future have helped to shape God's work in the past, and that work is the foundation for the future.

Moses stood in the presence of God and spoke straightforwardly, honestly, and without fear, and God responded. Intercessory prayer matters. God is responsive to human actions as his anger burns, and he is tempted to destroy what he has done, but God was moved by Moses and responded. Human petitions are heard. Human prayer is listened to. Intercession on the part and on behalf of others will be considered.

And then, the stories say, God repented of the evil he had planned. God changed his mind. It says so in the Bible. God decided to swallow his anger and endure his disappointment and disgust with his people in order to be faithful to his promises.

Did you notice that nothing Moses said was about the children of Israel? About what good people they were and how hard they were trying to get along? Moses did not try to excuse them or defend them. They'd had a bad childhood. They'd been overly indulged as teenagers. They hadn't had all the technological advantages of the Egyptian people. Moses' hope for saving his people was based in the personality and integrity of God. Our hope for our own salvation is not in ourselves but in the grace and promises of God. This is a story of the great good news of the Bible. Our hope is in the promise that God will be with us: "Lo I am with you always, even to the close of the age." Our future is built on the promises of this God and on our faith that God is able and faithful to his promises. This story bears testimony that God listens and hears the prayers and petitions of his people. He will consider our presentations, and even God will change his mind rather than betray his promises. That is such good news to us because our hope, too, rests on the promises of God made to us in Jesus Christ. Thanks be to God, who gives us the victory through Jesus Christ our Lord.—Rick Brand

SUNDAY, NOVEMBER 10, 2002
Lectionary Message

Topic: Almighty God Amid the Gods
TEXT: Josh. 24:1–3, 14–25
Other Readings: Ps. 78:1–7; 1 Thess. 4:13–18; Matt. 25:1–13

Evidently, the people of Israel had left God somewhere back yonder in an unmarked grave. For that reason, in this celebrated text Joshua calls on the people to "put away the strange gods that are among you and incline your hearts unto the Lord God of Israel" (v. 23).

We who believe in the Almighty may be reluctant to say it but, to tell the truth, God has, at least on the surface, never fared too well in competition with the gods our hands have made. Carlyle Marney put it succinctly: "The Temple is always downtown." Joshua is aware that the God who delivered Israel "from the house of bondage" has receded into the background of the people's daily concerns and consciousness, and now other forces power their thoughts and actions. The people of God had forgotten the stones set up for a memorial on this side of the Jordan to commemorate their passage across the river on dry land (4:22–24). They had sworn never to forget. I ran across an ad in a trade magazine headlined with the words, "There is no expiration date for memory." But the memory of what God had done for them had expired for Israel. The memorial would be remembered most for its short shelf life. So often for me, too, my tormentor for the day is myself left over from yesterday. Time is a relentless solvent of memory.

The world of Joshua is portable. Although our popular culture considers the supernatural irrelevant, it offers a steady stream of redeemers. We encounter daily a towering pantheon of man-made gods, all the way from the gross national product to Viagra, offering redemption from our ills. In this world of pluralism, where we seek absolute security or an object around which to organize our lives, that object becomes the "god of this world" (2 Cor. 4:4) for us as it did for Israel.

To understand better the dynamics of Israel's infidelity, and the alleged demise of the supernatural in our own culture, we must ask, How does a worldview in which God is so central to Israel's experience collapse? How could this have happened? They were the people of God, blessed with the mission of "being a blessing to every nation," yet they had forsaken the very God who called them into existence and upon whom their very existence depended. Now their worship was laced with a mixture of devotion to "strange gods."

Likely, the plates of Earth did not suddenly shift under their theology, as they don't under ours. From a veritable smorgasbord of would-be deities to be forsaken, Joshua singled out "the gods of the Amorites in whose land you dwell" (v. 15). In these words we may find a clue to what has gone on. As the Israelites leaned over the back fence to visit with their Amorite neighbors, or worked with them in the fields, or hung out with them around the watering holes, their distinctive beliefs, values, and lifestyles began to mingle. Soon "a common grayness silvered everything." Assumptions geared to this world—assumptions on which the Amorites' world operated—began to seem more plausible to the Israelites than the Commandments of Moses. The signals from the guidance systems of the culture seemed almost irresistible.

Although modern people may possess a degree of resistance to a scorched-earth aggression that seeks to dislodge belief in whatever has been elevated to the eminence of the divine, it appears that we are pushovers for the gentle persuasions that nudge and rub off. Gradually, the unyielding antagonism of the world (James 4:4) undermines the old certainties of faith in God. Theological crises rarely consummate in a precipitous moment; more likely, inch by inch a nation, a people, or a religion moves away from the God once worshiped and served. No time or culture is exempt from creeping doubt.

Is there some antidote for the corrosive effects of the gods of this world on belief in a supernatural power? The battle will be uphill for us because a desire persists to adjust religious tradition to philosophical truth and to free all religious language from supernatural notions. It wasn't easy for the people in Joshua's time either. But he found the reinforcement secret in the word *serve*. "Reverence the Lord, and serve him in sincerity and truth" was Joshua's formula for recovery of faith (24:14).

Get used to it. Belief in God deviates from the norms of the culture, and because we live in the teeth of antagonistic assumptions about reality, it is necessary to have a countercommunity in which the plausibility of a deviant knowledge can be affirmed and cultivated. In this light, there is a delicious relevance to the passage in Hebrews in which the writer enjoins readers to "forsake not the assembling of themselves together" (Heb. 10:24–25). The logic is that what is known of God has been imparted by others, and only as others help reinforce and encourage the plausibility of what is believed can faith be maintained and enriched.

Also, for faith in God to be kept alive it must be shared. This was the very life and breath of Judaism (Deut. 4:10). To go everywhere preaching the gospel is the pulse of the New Testament (Mark 16:20; Acts 8:4). The good news is that God ultimately prevails over the strange gods of any culture (Rev. 11:15); and finally, "every knee shall bow [in humble adoration] and every tongue shall confess that Jesus Christ is Lord" and master of all human destiny (Phil. 2:11). At last, "every high [false] thing that exalts itself against the knowledge of God" shall be defeated (2 Cor. 10:4). "Let us ponder anew what the Almighty can do, when with his love he befriends us." Yes, the good in good news is in the telling of it.

Therefore, if you are present in worship with others when this is read, do not think of the time as spent unwisely, but rather think of a "building fitly joined and strengthened by that which every joint [person] supplies" (Eph. 4:16; 2:21). In the last words of his valedictory, Joshua promised, "As for me and my house, we will serve the Lord," because "hast thou not seen how thy desires e'er have been granted in what he ordaineth?"—John C. Huffman

ILLUSTRATIONS

RESTORATION.   In London after World War II, I went to see the Metropolitan Tabernacle, where the noted Charles Spurgeon preached. Only the basement of the structure had survived the bombing. Upon entering, I noticed a black bust of the preacher sitting on a table. An usher explained that it was the fires that had blackened it. Farther into the building, I saw another precisely like it, only it was a beautiful white marble. Brandishing my American aptitude for advice, I suggested that the black one should be cleaned up and the pair exhibited together. The usher explained that they had tried this very thing. They had sought the efforts of rocksmiths, but to no avail. Finally they were told that burying the charred statue in the heart of the Earth from which it had originally been dug and leaving it there might restore it, but no known human artistry could accomplish it. It was then that I thought of how sin had blackened me and that I had to be carried back to the heart of God from whence I had come and there plunged beneath a cleansing flood.

> "There is a fountain fill'd with blood,
> Drawn from Immanuel's veins,
> And sinners plunged beneath that flood
> Lose all their guilty stains."

--John C. Huffman

CAPRICIOUS WINDS.   During the Second World War I worked at Camp Tyson, a barrage balloon training base. Here men were trained in the skilled technique of lofting over London the balloons that would snare the propellers of the German planes. Each balloon had strands of cable hanging from it to discourage the strafing of the city. Great care was required to keep the large cable that moored the balloon to its control below from kinking and thus breaking. One day I saw a balloon get away and I thought, "Goody, now it's free!" Was it really? I watched with fascination as the "free" balloon frolicked in the sky, somersaulting amid the clouds and driven by every subtle pressure. Finally, however, it reached a height where it exploded. More soberly now, I watched the collapsed bag float helplessly back to Earth. This event reminded me of the social pressures that "carry us about with every wind of doctrine" (Eph. 4:14) unless we are moored to a control that is more powerful than we are.—John C. Huffman

SERMON SUGGESTIONS

Topic: Comfort for the Bereaved
TEXT: 1 Thess. 4:13–18
(1) Faith in Jesus' death and Resurrection as the basis of the future life of believers. (2) The blessed priority of those who have died in Christ. (3) The reunion forever of all believers when the Lord returns.

Topic: On the Alert
TEXT: Matt. 25:1–13
(1) Life provides us with an open door to the future. (2) We are tempted to take the immediately easy, pleasant path, while a more difficult but more promising way is an option. (3) The time of accounting comes and reveals at last whether we were wise or foolish.

CONGREGATIONAL MUSIC

1. "Rejoice, Believers, Rejoice," Laurentius Laurenti (1700); trans. Sarah Findlater (1854)
   GREENLAND; attr. J. Michael Haydn (1737)
   The parable of the wise and foolish virgins is recounted in this old hymn that draws the worshippers into the drama of the story. This would be a fine hymn to begin worship after the initial recognition of the presence of God.
2. "How Great Thou Art," Stuart K. Hine (1949)
   O STORE GUD, Swedish folk song
   The choice of this popular favorite would be on the basis of the strength of its fourth stanza, which contemplates the sense of joy and liberation accompanying the second coming of Christ. Because this is the theme of the Epistle lesson, this hymn could be an appropriate response to that reading.
3. "Let the Children Hear the Mighty Deeds," Ps. 78:1–7; vers. Isaac Watts
   WEYMOUTH, Theodore P. Ferris (1942)
   This excellent children's hymn is Isaac Watts's version of the Psalter reading (Ps. 78:1–7). The first stanza could be sung before the reading and the second stanza afterward. If the tune is not familiar, it could be taught to a children's choir.
4. "Once to Every Man and Nation," James Russell Lowell (1844)
   EBENEZER, Thomas J. Williams (1890)
   Use this hymn on making the choice for God in connection with the Old Testament reading in which Joshua declares that he and his family will serve the Lord.—Hugh T. McElrath

WORSHIP AIDS

CALL TO WORSHIP.   "But the hour cometh and now is when the true worshippers shall worship the Father in spirit and in truth: for the Father seeketh such to worship him" (John 4:23).

INVOCATION.   As we come to worship you, our Father, cleanse our motives of anything that would dim our vision of your glory. Enable us to worship you in spirit and in truth.

OFFERTORY SENTENCE.   "Therefore, my beloved, be steadfast, immovable, always excelling in the work of the Lord, because you know that in the Lord your labor is not in vain."

OFFERTORY PRAYER.   As we bring our offerings before you, O Lord, strengthen our desire to follow these gifts with prayer and willing service in the many ways that honor you and help others.

PRAYER.   Almighty God, thou dost lead us by ways that we have not known and have not always wanted, for by our short vision and selfish heart we have not always known the ways that make for our peace nor the paths that lead to our best ends. We rejoice and give thanks for the paths that have brought us to this place and to this day. Lead us forth, O Mighty Love—you who are full of grace and wisdom, full of tenderness and eager to bring us all to the full joy and glory that are ours in obedience to thy will and purpose. We thank thee for all that has blessed, sustained, and entertained us on our journey; for the goodness of sleep upon the way; for the challenges of work before us so that we know the satisfaction of physical exhaustion and the deep contentment of completion of our work; for those who make the visions and for those who keep urging us on to be more and to do better; for those who have loved us despite our slowness; for those who have shared the journey as friends, as coworkers, and as family. O Gracious God, we thank thee for the gift of time, from the dream time to the work time to the waiting time to the time of rest. We thank thee for the gift of life, and for the times when life has been fun and has contained as much joy as we could receive.

Keep us now in thy mercy, O gracious God. Reveal thyself to us in all ways. May we not lose sight of thy grace as it leads us into the testing. May we immerse ourselves in the words of Scripture, wrap around us the music of our hymns, and drive down our foundations into the comfort of the worship; and may the traditions of the saints who have gone before us speak to us guidance and encouragement. May our whole lives be lifted up in the mystery of thy providence and presence, that we may feel the infinite joy in thee that is the beginning of our deepest worship. May the mystery keep us in tender communion with each other and may our prayer and presence bless those who have been in pain, who have faced illness, who have broken their bones or had surgery, who have discovered that their bodies can no longer serve them as they once did, and who have had their journey of grace changed by the death of one who meant so much to them on the road.

Bless all those who are in places of decision and responsibility, that their primary concern may be how to make our common life together better, stronger, and healthier for all, for we pray in Christ's name.—Rick Brand

SERMON
Topic: The Stewardship of Life
TEXT: Gen. 1:2; 2:2, 18

Our church is once again engaged in its annual stewardship campaign. The focus on under-writing a new operating budget by pledging financial gifts may cause some members to assume that stewardship applies only to money, whereas in the Bible it applies to the entirety of life. In Scripture, stewardship is the way in which we take responsibility for the totality of the time, space, and energy entrusted to us.

The first chapters of Genesis provide a foundation for the biblical understanding of life. In these chapters we confront three curious questions, but in searching for answers we dis-cover crucial insights that help us to unify sacred and secular, values and vocation, spiritu-ality and work, in an overarching stewardship of life.

I. *Why did God take so long to create the Earth?* The book of Genesis begins with a sce-nario of creation in six days, on each of which God called into being some major part of our universe. Ever since the evolutionary hypothesis of Charles Darwin gained favor with scien-tists a century ago, we have debated whether this account in Genesis depicts creation as hap-pening in too short a time—in only six days instead of millions or billions of years. Such issues are difficult if not impossible to resolve because we were not present in the beginning, but this scientific debate misses the deeper spiritual question of why creation should have taken any time at all. Obviously the author of Genesis knew nothing about our modern sci-entific theories, but he was insistent that God toiled day after day to make the world as we know it.

Why should that be? If God is all-knowing and all-powerful, could he not easily have con-ceived of the world he wanted and called it into being with a single sovereign word? Gene-sis stresses how, on each of the six days, God merely said, "Let there be . . . and there was. . . ." Why give a whole day to each stage of the process? Why not just say on the first day, "Let there be the world that I want" and be done with it? Some scientists speculate that the universe may have started with a "big bang," and it seems as if an instantaneous creation would have been the simplest and most impressive way for God to do his work.

The mystery deepens once we move further into the Bible. For even though creation was viewed as completed in Genesis 2:1–2, the remainder of the Hebrew Scriptures, particularly the Psalms, are full of references to God continuing to sustain and renew his creation. In the Gospel of John, Jesus says plainly, "My Father is working still" (5:17). The Jewish rabbis agreed that divine providence remained active, even on the Sabbath day of rest. The first-century philosopher Philo said, "For God never ceases creating, but as it is the property of fire to burn and of snow to chill, so it is the property of God to create."[2] What the Bible is trying to tell us is that our world is an unfinished work in progress.

The laborious accounts of creation in Genesis suggest that God worked day after day on his project in order to show us that getting our world right is slow business, even for him. But once God got it right, his world still had to be serviced, requiring what we might call

---

[2]*Allegorical Interpretation of Genesis II-III*, Book 1.5.

maintenance and repairs. By making the world in this way, God was inviting us to enter into a partnership with him, to work together on this unfinished agenda. As Jesus put it in the verse just cited, "My Father is working still, and I am working" (John 5:17). If God had simply made a perfect universe from the beginning, there would be no need for us to protect and improve it, which means that finally we would feel no responsibility for it. Without accepting the mandate "to have dominion" (Gen. 1:26, 28), we would never develop our own creativity and ingenuity. At first it might seem that to be handed a perfect world would be wonderful, but such a world would only pamper us and leave us without any resourcefulness. Instead, God "blessed" us with the daunting challenge to "be fruitful and multiply, and fill the Earth and subdue it" (Gen. 1:28).

God made a world that needs human involvement because our freedom to accept responsibility is extremely important to him. If the world were perfect, there would be no need for either faith or works. We would be reduced to religious robots who never have to make any decisions. So God built freedom into the created order just as he did into the human heart. What the six-day sequence of Genesis suggests is that things need to be made to fit, to harmonize, to work together. In other words, everything that was created became part of a complex interlocking process that requires its own sequence, arrangement, and order. The true meaning of ecology is that we have to figure out how to use one part of the world in ways that will not damage or destroy other parts of the world. Otherwise, we become not caretakers but plunderers of God's magnificent creation, which he entrusted to us stewards.

To summarize what we have learned in answering the first question: From the beginning, God revealed himself to be a worker who toiled long and hard to make this world and he has never given up on making it better. But he has done it in such a way that each of us plays a meaningful part in becoming, as the apostle Paul put it, "laborers together with God" (1 Cor. 3:9). So, why do we work? Not just to make a living but to make a better world, to build on what God began, to curb the chaos that ever seeks to regain its sway and plunge the world into darkness (Gen. 1:2). Think of all that has already been done to build dams that prevent floods, to build bridges that span rivers, to build homes that shelter families. Yet there is still so much that needs to be done if all of God's world is to become livable for all of God's children. Genesis told the beginning of the story, but the rest of the story is waiting for us to write.

II. *Why did God rest on the seventh day?* The climax of the creation story in Genesis emphasizes that God rested from his labors on the seventh day (Gen. 2:2–3). On the face of it, that seems like a strange thing for God to do. If he is all-powerful, why would he get tired after only a few days of toil? The story of the six preceding days emphasizes that God did his work simply by speaking a word: "Let there be. . . ." In other words, we have no hint of any unusual exertions that would have exhausted God and left him spent, which makes the word *rest* a peculiar term to be attributed to God. Indeed, if, as we have seen, the world continued to need so much work done on it even after it was created, then why would God take a day off? If he is the source of all energy, why did he not draw on it to work straight through without a break so as to make faster progress on the job before him?

We have already seen that God took six separate steps to create the world as a way of showing that he wants to involve us in an ongoing partnership. Now we see that God also built a day of Sabbath rest into the weekly cycle because it meets our need far more than his. The Sabbath is God's way of saying to us, "If I pause from my work to take a day of rest even though I am almighty, how much more do you need to take a day of rest because you are finite? As important as I have made work, it is not everything. If you are to become my partner, you must learn the deeper meaning both of working on six days and of not working on the seventh day." What is the significance of the Sabbath for us?

Notice first that it was to be a day of *rest*. That is, work is inherently tiring; it produces deep fatigue. Even Jesus was often exhausted from his daily labors. So God is saying, "I know that I have given you a seemingly endless task, but I have provided a way in which it will not wear you out before it is completed." For all of our previous efforts, the primeval chaos still lurks on the margins of life. We see its fury in tornadoes, avalanches, volcanic eruptions, and a host of other disasters. It is no easy job to subdue this kind of world (Gen. 1:28). We must learn to pace ourselves or we will soon succumb to weariness and fatigue. God first gave work dignity by deciding to work himself, but that did not make work any less demanding. Because God knew that our labors could be arduous, even punishing, he said, "Take a regular day of rest, or work will soon break your body."

If we do not learn how to say no to work on at least one day of the week, it can finally become an addiction that sometimes goes by the name *workaholism*. Its characteristics are a conscientiousness that becomes indifferent to other legitimate claims, a compulsiveness that drives us to unnecessary extremes, and a competitiveness that makes us hostile to the success of others. Somehow we must use the Sabbath to break the tyranny of *should* and *ought* and *must* or we will lose the very freedom that God has made a hallmark of human life. On at least one day of the week we are not to worship the clock or the dollar or the company but are to pursue other goals in life.

This does not mean that Sabbath rest is an invitation to laziness. The suspension of daily toil provides the opportunity for another kind of creativity, the chance to build an inner world of the spirit as spacious and beautiful as the outer world we seek to enhance during the work week. This is a day to let the soul catch up with the body, to stop and smell the roses, to be gripped by the wonder of life itself. Because this day is built into the rhythm of the calendar, it is a chance to bring closure to the failures of the past week, to negotiate a sense of ending to those things we need to put behind us, while at the same time offering a chance to start all over and walk "in the land of beginning again."

When we describe the Sabbath as a day of worship, we mean that it is a day to discover the beauty, truth, and goodness of God. Beauty may involve taking time to read great literature, listen to great music, or ponder great art. Truth may mean clearing the mind of clutter, listening to the voice of conscience, opening the heart to Scripture. Goodness may involve sharing our core values with others of like conviction so that we will find the reinforcement and encouragement sufficient to withstand the seductions that await life at every turn. It is a day for introspection, for looking closely and clearly in the mirror at who we really are. It is a day to ponder the deeper *why* questions of life.

But most of all, it is a day to celebrate the grace that lies at the bedrock of our existence. What are the forces that keep even our tallest building earthbound? Who created such a remarkable profusion of raw materials that we never stop devising new combinations? Why are the so-called laws of science so dependable? Behind everything we touch is a gift we call grace—not just the grace of forgiveness but the grace of gravity, the grace of penicillin, the grace of never-ending discoveries that enrich life in ways that we never dreamed were possible. Only as we celebrate this grace do we learn gratitude and generosity and humility.

Without this grace to make us gracious, we become arrogant, abrasive, and finally abusive. Without grace we try to compete, conquer, and control, and when we fail, it leads to anger, retaliation, and revenge—a sure formula for making life miserable. A Sabbath day of rest is God's antidote to the terrible tyranny of work as an end in itself.

III. *Why did God save the creation of woman for last?* In Genesis 1, the creation of humanity comes at the conclusion of the six-day sequence. The summary verse lumps together male and female as if both genders were fashioned simultaneously (Gen. 1:27). But Genesis 2 elaborates this single phrase into an entire paragraph (Gen. 2:18–25) rich with significance for our understanding of stewardship. Here we see that woman was the climax and crown of creation, as if God saved the best for last. But why should this be? Obviously both male and female were needed from the outset to propagate the human race. Woman can hardly have been an accidental afterthought on the part of God. So what unique place was she assigned within the divine purpose to make us custodians of an unfinished world?

The first clue is provided by the description of man as "alone" (Gen. 2:18). Adam could not reach his full potential in solitude but needed a responsible relationship to bring him to maturity. In other words, any thought of self-sufficiency is not good. Instead, God knew that what Adam needed most was to learn to share so completely with another that he and his partner would become a single entity. To say that they were to "become one flesh" did not mean simply that they were to be physically intimate. Rather, it meant that they were to coexist in solidarity with each other, that a unity was to underlie their duality, that their pairing of life in togetherness was to transcend the separateness of their two lives apart. Just as a piece of paper, by its very nature, cannot have only one side, so humanity, by God's design, is two-sided, complementary, made not just for autonomy but also for reciprocity. The word *Eve* in Hebrew means "one who answers," which suggests that man without woman is like a question without an answer.

A second clue is found in the strange procedure by which woman was created—from a bone taken out of the protective cage around man's heart. At first it seems as if Adam had been invaded, wounded, and robbed of his rib, but paradoxically, this very vulnerability left him enhanced and enlarged to enjoy the companionship of another life. Now man was less than he had been before the divine surgery, but the resulting humanity was more than it had been before that surgery. Pain and sacrifice were essential prerequisites to the fashioning of a meaningful life together.

Most important, notice that Eve was to be a unique "helper" in the work of creation (Gen. 2:18). As God prepared to step back and let Adam share responsibility with him, he paraded all of the creatures of Earth before Adam as if to say, "You decide who you will need to help get the job done," but none of them proved worthy (Gen. 2:20). Then, after woman was created, God brought her to man as well for a decision (v. 22). Once Adam accepted personal responsibility for his relationship with Eve, God stepped aside and delegated the care of the Earth to this new couple.

Why, we must ask, was Eve so indispensable to the work that humanity had been assigned in Creation? It is because only when we learn to care for another, to share so fully that the boundary is obliterated between "what is mine and what is thine," do we learn the deepest meaning of partnership. In a very real sense, the home is a laboratory where we learn in a unique one-on-one relationship how to overcome every egocentric impulse on the spectrum from self-centeredness to self-pity. Here we learn the kind of give-and-take that is essential to teamwork whether in the home or in the workplace. To become one with another person is to learn how to work together in partnership rather than in isolation, to cooperate rather than to compete, to accept diversity rather than to insist on uniformity. Work in the business world becomes effective only as employees learn to share a common mission and vision, but if we cannot become one in relation to those with whom we live, it is doubtful that we will learn to become a true team player within our vocational structures.

Here, then, are the earliest answers ever given to the question of why we are called to stewardship of life: to partner with God in making a better world in which to live, to learn what a great gift we have been given so that we will take time to celebrate the graciousness of the Giver, and to express in our work the kind of sharing we experience most deeply in the oneness of our homes.

This understanding of stewardship is a powerful corrective to the prevailing understanding of life as entitlement, for it defines life in terms of what we can give rather than what we can get. It honors persons as creators rather than denigrating them merely as consumers. It strikes at the heart of the something-for-nothing culture being promoted today by rampant gambling. It calls us to a life of hard work in the world punctuated by interludes of Sabbath rest for inner renewal, a life in which sharing with others at the most intimate level triumphs over grabbing from others at the most impersonal level.

What are our marching orders from the first pages of Holy Scripture? Work hard! Rest well! Give freely! It is a way of life that will quickly underwrite any church budget. But much more, it is God's way for us to underwrite the finest fulfillment that life has to offer.—William E. Hull

SUNDAY, NOVEMBER 17, 2002
Lectionary Message

Topic: Using or Losing?
TEXT: Matt. 25:14–30
Other Readings: Judg. 4:1–7; Ps. 123; 1 Thess. 5:1–11

In a sermon on this text, a pastor tells of a visit to his grandparents when he and his sister were each given a package of chewing gum. Immediately his sister chewed all of hers. He, being more frugal, chewed one piece and put the rest away. Much later he found the forgotten cache, but to his dismay the chewing gum had hardened and gone stale. His sister had enjoyed hers while it was fresh, when she could derive the most pleasure from it. He had hidden his away, and lost it for all practical purposes.

Jesus told an engaging story about this very thing. Before going away for a time, a man gave his slaves some money to invest while he was gone. He gave one man five amounts, to another two amounts, and to a third only one amount. The first slave began immediately to invest and to seek to multiply what he had been given. So did the second slave. But the third one hid his in the ground lest something bad happen to it. After a while the master of these slaves returned. He called for his servants to account for what they had done with his possessions. Each of the first two reported that he had doubled the investment. The master of these two found their stewardship worthy of praise, and both received the same commendation.

Many of us may identify with the poor third slave. He was afraid of making a mistake. Immobilized by anxiety, he hid that which was entrusted to him. Also, like some of us, he located the problem outside himself—the fault was the master's disposition. Consequently, he didn't do anything with what he had been given. His master excoriated him as a "wicked and slothful servant." That was not all, however. He lost out all around; even what he had was taken away.

This story is one of those that Jesus used to emphasize the urgency of spiritual preparedness. It is aimed at giving more precision to what it means to watch and be ready for the unexpected. There will be no alerting sign or calamitous events signalling Jesus' coming back to Earth. Period. Also, in the opinion of some, Jesus was warning against spiritual laxity during "what deceptively may appear to be a pause in the progress of salvation history when the gospel is to be proclaimed to the nations."[3]

Common to these stories is an interval of time—"the bridegroom tarries" or "a man makes his journey into a far country," and so on. This interval likely represents the lapse of time between Jesus' departure and the end of time, during which the kingdom of heaven or the reign of God operates in the lives of the believers. The point is how believers will respond to this governance of God in their lives during this window of opportunity. It presses the reader with the question, How am I using this intervening period? Jesus urges us not "to light a candle and put it under a bushel, but on a candlestick" (Matt. 5:15). Paul instructed Timothy, and us, to "do the work of an evangelist" (2 Tim. 4:5), beseeching others in Christ's stead to be reconciled to God (2 Cor. 5:20), to "study to show oneself approved by God" (2 Tim. 2:15), and "to grow up in him in all things . . . even Christ" (Eph. 4:15). The Scriptures assume that during this interval the believer will grow in knowledge of God, expand the soul with increasing sensibility to reality, and be prepared for whatever happens. If so, then the believer can say with the current television ad for the Hartford Insurance Company, "Whatever life brings, bring it on!" Implicit in the story is that troublesome preoccupation with *when* that leads one astray from the primary tasks of the here and now. To endure means more than to survive; it means to remain faithful—and fruitful.

The master in the story made an *investment* in his servants. Despite claims that the parables provide particular wisdom regarding historical events, one may generalize and say that God has invested himself in this world. One author has said, "The incredible has happened. History has become the vehicle of the eternal. The absolute was clothed in flesh and blood. . . . This world has become the scene of a divine drama."[4] In many places, Scripture affirms this statement with words like these: "For the law was given by Moses, but grace and truth came by Jesus Christ" (John 1:17).

Beyond this word is the scandalous fact that God bestows his gifts on persons who have done nothing to deserve them (Eph. 2:8–10). "The well have no need of a physician," Jesus said. "I have come to call sinners to repentance" (Matt. 9:12, 13) and to be known as "a friend of publicans and sinners." His gift is a right relationship with him, "even the righteousness of God which is by faith of Jesus Christ unto all that believe" (Rom. 3:22).

---

[3] David E. Garland, *Reading Matthew* (New York: Crossroad, 1993), p. 240.
[4] C. H. Dodd, *The Parables of Jesus* (London: 1935), p. 297.

As in the story, God expects an increase in his investment. "But how can I add to what God has already done for my salvation?" you ask. Unfortunately, there are some who believe they can, but there is no such thing as merit in the sight of God. What is implied here is the question, What will I do with God's gift of salvation now that I have received it? Will I hide it under a bushel? Or will I allow it to be a city of light set on a hill?

Salvation implies, among other things, healing, newness, joy, and a sharpening of one's spiritual perception that apprehends the presence of God in daily life. This may be the meaning of what Jesus said to Nicodemus about a benefit of "being born from above" (John 3:3). As one lives the Christian life, one should experience an increase and enhancement of skills with which to serve the Lord.

In light of the preceding, there is in Revelation a delightful or disturbing passage, depending on one's point of view, that says, "Blessed are the dead who die in the Lord from henceforth: yea, saith the Spirit, that they may rest from their labors, and their works do follow them" (14:13). The word that is translated by our English word *works* is the word from which we also get our word *energy*. Energy is the dynamic or force that enables one to work. So, the intention seems to be that our capacity to work, not necessarily our deeds, will follow us. An enlarged capacity for spiritual things, a keener sense with which to perceive the presence of the Almighty, and an expanded appetite for the joys of the Lord are some of the increase God expects from his children. No wonder the master never said to the servant who buried his one talent, "Enter into the joy of your Lord" (v. 23). Is our reward, then, to be based on our ability and capacity to receive and enjoy, which we develop here during this window of opportunity?

Even now, some people work with five or two talents, and there are the one-talent persons; all are precious in the sight of God. He, too, distributes according to our ability to be responsible. Like the slaves with five or two talents, we can increase our Master's investment 100 percent, or like the slave with one talent, we can be afraid and hide the investment in self-centered caution. This parable causes me to hear the haunting line of an old song, "Must I empty-handed go?" Will you answer with me: Absolutely not!—John C. Huffman

ILLUSTRATIONS

WORK.   There is a perennial nobleness, and even sacredness, in work. Were he ever so benighted, forgetful of his high calling, there is always hope in a man that actually and earnestly works. In idleness alone is there perpetual despair.

The latest gospel in this world is, *Know thy work and do it.* It has been written, "An endless significance lies in work." A man perfects himself by working. Foul jungles are cleared away, fair seed-fields rise instead, and stately cities. . . .

Blessed is he who has found his work; let him ask no other blessedness. He has a work, a life purpose; he has found it, and will follow it. . . . *Labor is life.*—Thomas Carlyle

VALUES.   If we work on marble, it will perish; if we work on bronze, time will efface it; if we build temples, they will crumble into dust; but if we work on immortal souls, if we imbue them with just principles of action, with fear of wrong and love of right, we engrave on those tables something which no time can obliterate, and which will brighten and brighten through all eternity.—Daniel Webster

SERMON SUGGESTIONS

Topic: Beyond Our Control

TEXT: Ps. 123

(1) Unmanageable situations: (a) the contempt of the self-satisfied and proud, (b) the lies of the envious and jealous, (c) rejection by those misled about us. (2) Remedial response: (a) prayer, (b) expectation of sympathy and response from God, (c) concrete graciousness of God in empowering us to deal with our situation.

Topic: To Encourage One Another

TEXT: 1 Thess. 5:1–11

In view of the inevitable day of the Lord: (1) Be alert. (2) Protect yourself: (a) with faith, (b) with love, (c) with expectation of salvation. (3) Reassure yourself and fellow believers with the provision for our salvation in the death and Resurrection of our Lord Jesus Christ.

CONGREGATIONAL MUSIC

1. "Sing, Deborah, Sing!" Luiza Cruz (1973); trans. Gertrude C. Suppe (1987)
   DEBORA, Luiza Cruz (1973)

   This popular song of Deborah that celebrates the Lord's victory over Sisera (Judg. 4:1–7) was originally written in Portugese. Its translated version is a fine contemporary vehicle for general praise and thanksgiving. A soloist, possible accompanied by piano, guitar, and string bass, could sing the stanzas, with the congregation responding with the joyous refrain.

2. "To You, O Lord, I Lift My Eyes," Ps. 123; vers. *Psalter* (1912)
   SARAH, Hughes M. Huffman (1976)

   An easily learned setting of Psalm 123; this hymn could be used in place of the Psalter reading.

3. "As Sons of the Day and Daughters of Light," Christopher Idle (1975)
   LAUDATE DOMINUM, C. Hubert Parry (1894)

   This fresh, new hymn relates to part of the Epistle reading for this day, especially 1 Thessalonians 5:8–11. It is appropriately set to a bright, positive tune for encouraging one another in the Christian walk.

4. "We Give Thee but Thine Own," William W. How (1858)
   SCHUMANN, Mason and Webb's *Cantica Laudis* (1850)

   This good stewardship hymn would fit as a response to the Gospel reading about the parable of the talents.—Hugh T. McElrath

WORSHIP AIDS

CALL TO WORSHIP.   "To you I lift up my eyes, O you who are enthroned in the heavens! As the eyes of servants look to the hand of their master, as the eyes of a maid look to the hand of her mistress, so our eyes look to the Lord our God, until he has mercy on us" (Ps. 123:1–2 NRSV).

INVOCATION.   We are completely dependent on you, O God, to show us the way in our worship, our work, and our witness. Touch our hearts as we worship, strengthen our hands as we work, and anoint our speech as we share your Word.

OFFERTORY SENTENCE.   "Keep your lives free from the love of money, and be satisfied with what you have. For God has said, 'I will never leave you; I will never abandon you'" (Heb. 13:5 TEV).

OFFERTORY PRAYER.   Father, we look to you for our daily bread and you care for us. Some of us have unusual abilities and can earn large sums of money that we can use creatively to help others. Purify our motives, bless what we do with what we have, and bless what we give.

PRAYER.   O God, who hast sent us to school in this strange life of ours and hast set us tasks that test all our courage, trust, and fidelity, may we not spend our days complaining at circumstance or fretting at discipline, but give ourselves to learn about life and to profit from every experience. Make us strong to endure.

We pray that when trials come upon us we may not shirk the issue or lose our faith in thy goodness, but committing our souls unto thee, who knowest the way we take, come forth as gold tried in the fire.

Grant by thy grace that we may not be found wanting in the hour of crisis. When the battle is set, may we know on which side we ought to be, and when the day goes hard, cowards steal from the field, and heroes fall around the standard, may our place be found where the fight is fiercest. If we faint, may we not be faithless; if we fall, may it be while facing the foe.—W. E. Orchard[5]

SERMON
Topic: The End of the World
Text: Mark 13:1–8

In our Gospel lesson for today, Jesus hears some people talking about the beauty and grandeur of the Temple, which is as grand and beautiful as our own Trinity Church, and in response Jesus predicts a catastrophe.

That's quite a blast coming as he nears the end of his ministry. These predictions of a terrifying end time are part of what we call the apocalyptic writings of the Old and New Testaments. The word *apocalypse* means "something that has been revealed," and passages such as these come from people who believe that the end of the world is near and that it has been revealed to them what the end is going to be like.

Jesus preached this way sometimes—of the sun and moon falling, of cataclysmic wars, of the heavens shaking, and of the Son of Man coming to judge the world. He seemed to have especially liked using this sort of language in places like Trinity Church—where things seemed to be decent and in good order, where his hearers were well-composed and seemed to be managing things pretty well. If you think you've got things pinned down, he would say, don't be so sure.

Since then, there have been people in Christianity who have looked for the end. St. Paul,

[5]*The Temple*

at least in his early years, thought it could happen any day, and for that reason he didn't think marriage was important and didn't seem to worry very much about such societal evils as slavery. But of course the end didn't come as so many early Christians expected, and in the New Testament we can even see the focus shifting to the long haul.

Still, down through the centuries countless Christian groups have read these texts literally, anticipated the end, calculated the exact date it would happen, and gone to a mountaintop to wait.

The sticking point is that the much anticipated end has never come, and so even though we say in our creeds every week, "And he shall come again in glory to judge the living and the dead," we don't give all this wild talk a great deal of thought. Of course, scientists are predicting a number of scenarios that might spell the end of our world—from the final expansion, cooling, and dying of the universe over billions of years to the collapse of the universe in a big bang as noisy as the first—but the time horizons for these scenarios are pretty far off. I doubt that many of us are going to cancel our pension plans based on any of them. But this strange, ancient text says that the end time could happen at any moment.

In the last two decades, we in America have experienced the collapse of any sense of living in a firm, secure world. We are living in the time of postmodernity, in which just about every certitude on which the structure of our society has been built has been rolled away as if it was scenery on a stage.

We were once clear that human beings were children of God capable of evil but made for grandeur; now we have become a society of consumers looking for a few images to help us look good and feel good, at least for the moment. We are living in the time of what someone has called "the empty self."

We once thought that there were clear moral absolutes. Now the prevailing ethic is that if it works for you and it doesn't hurt someone else, then it must be fine. It's carnival time in America; few hard questions are being asked about what our new ways of living are doing to our souls, our neighborhoods, our children, and our larger society.

We once believed in a coherent story about our lives—about a good America with a Manifest Destiny to spread freedom across the world. Now we know how many people have been left out of that story. We are also learning that our American and Christian stories have been too small. The grand structure had to break so that a new, deeper, truer structure could emerge.

"There will be great earthquakes, and in various places famines and plagues; and there will be dreadful portends and great signs from heaven," Jesus says in the Gospel. It is as if a great earthquake has shaken Western society.

But apocalypse is often deeply personal as well. Breast cancer, prostate cancer, AIDS, divorce, job loss—they are part of life around this congregation. And when they come, the Earth shakes, the towers dissolve. Everything we thought was certain seems to vanish before our eyes.

You see, our experience isn't so different from that of the earliest followers of Christ. We know what it means for the Earth to shake, for the stones to begin to tumble. Luke's Gospel helps us to see that and name it for what it is.

But he also does something much more. He gives us a way to see God's hand in all this. "When you hear of wars and insurrections," Jesus says, "do not be terrified. . . . I will give you words and a wisdom that none of your opponents will be able to contradict. . . . By your endurance you will gain your souls."

Jesus is saying that when the world we know collapses on us, we can still take heart. Worlds will come and go. Finally, the world every one of us here has composed will teeter and collapse in death. But behind the fragile world we have created is a God who is holding us. The end of the world in the New Testament is always the beginning of a new world. When things are at their worst, Christ comes to build things again.

The shattering of our proud, confident Christian and American worldview had to happen. We have much to learn about what really does matter as so many certainties are called into question. Reality is bigger than that. Christ wants to build something deeper and stronger and stranger in us and in our churches.

Christian faith is, after all, ultimately a comedy with a happy ending. And it says to us that we too can lighten up and, of all things, relax a little. Because even when the stones tumble and the Earth shakes, there is still a safe place to stand, and even when we can hardly imagine it, Christ will come.—Samuel T. Lloyd III

SUNDAY, NOVEMBER 24, 2002

Lectionary Message

Topic: Seek and Serve Christ in All Persons (Christ the King)

TEXT: Matt. 25:31–46

Other Readings: Ezek. 34:11–16, 20–24; Ps. 100; Eph. 1:15–23

In most Christian traditions, today is proclaimed Christ the King Sunday. It is a day when we look back over the season of Pentecost to the Ascension of our Lord and forward to the glorious time of his return as King of Kings and Lord of Lords. It is a day of celebration, power, and joy.

I. This is one of the most sobering parables ever told by our Lord and its message is clear and to the point: Christ the King will judge us in accordance with our response to human need. In this parable, Jesus used an image common to the people of his day: a shepherd and his flock. At the end of the day, the shepherd could be seen in the field separating the sheep and the goats. The sheep, who were quite sturdy, would be allowed to weather the night out in the fields while the less hardy goats would be taken in and sheltered from the night. The image of the loving and caring shepherd as the leader of the faithful had long existed in Hebrew literature. And this image is, of course, quite prevalent in Christian art and literature today.

As the shepherd divides the beasts into two groups, the sheep find themselves in the position of honor, at the shepherd's right hand. It is clear that they represent the chosen or saved. It is here, as he addresses the two groups, that the shepherd is identified as the King. The King proclaims to those on his right, the righteous, that they are "blessed by my Father" (v. 34). They are identified as such because of the righteousness found in their caring for others who were in need. They seem astonished to learn that in doing this they have actually provided care for the King.

The King then turns to the unrighteous and pronounces judgment: "Depart from me into the eternal fire prepared for the devil and his angels" (v. 41). These animals, too, seem surprised to learn that they have failed to care for the King when they have not responded to the needs of others. This powerful scene of judgment suggests a conviction toward the principle and practice of caring for the needy; it also suggests that Christ the King is cared for, or neglected, when others are cared for or neglected.

This parable comes after several other sayings of Jesus that deal with the coming of the Kingdom of God. Matthew presents the community with the importance of preparing for that day, and with the idea that being prepared means living faithfully as followers of a loving and caring shepherd. Living faithfully means being prepared and willing to give aid to those in need—seeking and serving Christ in all persons.

II. Wonderfully, this parable tells us much about the aid we are to give. First, we must help with ordinary things. The examples Jesus uses are simple things that are easily accomplished—providing food for the hungry and drink for the thirsty, welcoming a stranger, caring for the sick, and visiting those in prison. We are called to give simple aid to people we meet every day.

Second, the help we give must be uncalculated and without thought of gain. A loving heart responds out of compassion. Such a response is natural, instinctive, and from the heart. Neither group in the parable knew they were addressing our Lord when they responded to need. Therefore, the help that meets with the King's approval is that which is given without thought of gain; it is help for the sake of helping.

Last, we are told that the help we give to others is in fact given to our Lord. Conversely, that which is withheld from others is withheld from our Lord. When we help someone, even in the simplest of things, without thought of gain, we discover the joy of helping Christ himself. Simply put, we are to seek and serve Christ in all persons.

III. Many people throughout the history of the Church have discovered this joy. Martin of Tours and Francis of Asissi are two such people. Their stories serve as examples to us today. Martin was a Roman soldier and a Christian. One winter day, as he entered the city, a beggar stopped him and asked for alms. Martin had no money to give the man, who was nearly frozen from the cold, so he gave him what he had—his soldier's coat. He cut the coat into two pieces and shared one with the beggar. Later that night, Martin dreamed that he saw Jesus in the heavens, surrounded by angels and wearing half of a Roman soldier's winter coat. He heard one of the angels ask the Lord, "Master, why are you wearing that battered old cloak? Who gave it to you?" And Jesus replied, "My servant Martin gave it to me."

Francis was born a wealthy Italian nobleman who could not find happiness and fulfillment in riches and power. His life was incomplete. Then one day, he was out riding and met a leper, repulsive from the effects of the disease. Something moved Francis to dismount and embrace the deformed and wretched man. In Francis's arms, the face of the leper changed into the likeness of Christ.

As we await the coming of Christ our King, let us not wait passively. Rather, let us await his coming faithfully and actively. Let us seek and serve Christ in all persons. In doing so, we may find that we have found our Lord already here.—Clark Sherman

ILLUSTRATIONS

A CHURCH WITHOUT WORKS.   I was naked and you questioned my lack of modesty in my appearance. I was imprisoned and you debated the legal aspects of interference.

I was penniless and you discussed tax-deductible donations from your wealth. I was sick and you thanked the Lord for the blessings of your health.

I was hungry and you formed a club to study malnutrition. I was homeless and you said God's love was shelter under any condition.

I was lonely and you left me by myself while you and your friend prayed. You seemed so holy and close to God, yet I'm still sick and alone and afraid!—Ruth M. Walsh

AN INSPIRED COMPLAINER.   November 8 marks the anniversary of the birth of Dorothy Day, uncanonized saint of the homeless. She was also one of America's most inspired complainers. For most of her life she kept saying that things aren't the way they should be, and that it would be a far less cruel world if those who went to church cared for the poor half as well as they took care of their Bibles.

For six years Dorothy looked for a way to connect her social conscience with her religious conversion, a search that gave birth to the Catholic Worker movement in May 1933. Originally, the *Catholic Worker* was just a newspaper, but within weeks of its publication, the first house of hospitality—Dorothy's apartment—came into being simply because she couldn't turn away a homeless woman who had seen the paper and came asking for help. Today there are nearly 175 Catholic Worker houses of hospitality, not to mention the many more places of welcome that wouldn't exist had it not been for Dorothy Day's struggle to live the gospel with directness and simplicity.

At the core of her life was her experience of ultimate beauty—Christ's face hidden in the faces of America's human castoffs. "Those who cannot see the face of Christ in the poor," she used to say, "are atheists indeed."—Jim Forrest[6]

SERMON SUGGESTIONS

Topic: Better Than the Prophet Dreamed

TEXT: Ezek. 34:11–16, 20–24

Ezekiel saw victory for Israel among the nations, a prophecy that has its ideal fulfillment in Jesus Christ of the line of David. (1) God is unrelenting in his quest for his lost and scattered flock (vv. 11–12). (2) God's purpose is to lead his people into an abundant life (vv. 13–16; see also John 10:10). (3) God has anointed Jesus Christ as the Supreme Shepherd to unite, protect, judge, and defend his people (vv. 20–24; see also Rev. 11:15–16).

Topic: When Our Eyes Are Opened

TEXT: Eph. 1:15–23 NEB

We can appreciate (1) the hope to which we are called (v. 18a), (2) the wealth and glory of our heritage (v. 18b), (3) the vastness of power open to us who trust in him (v. 19).

CONGREGATIONAL MUSIC

1. "The King Shall Come When Morning Dawns," Greek; trans. John Brownlie (1907)
    MORNING SONG, Wyeth's *Repository of Sacred Music* (1813)
    This hymn would be suitable as a response to the Gospel reading. It also relates to the general theme for this Christ the King Sunday and could well be used for the opening of worship.

---

[6]"An Inspired Complainer," *Sojourners*, Nov.–Dec. 1997.

2. "All People That on Earth Do Dwell," Ps. 100; vers. William Kethe (1560)

OLD HUNDREDTH, *Genevan Psalter* (1551), Louis Bourgeois

Alternating the singing of this venerable paraphrase with the verses of the Psalm 100, as follows, would be effective: vv. 1–2, stanza 1; v. 3, stanza 2; v. 4, stanza 3; v. 5, stanza 4.

3. "For the Fruit of All Creation," Fred Pratt Green (1970)

AR HYD Y NOS, Welsh melody (c. 1784)

Because it is appropriate both for the Thanksgiving season and because of its concern for the hungry of the world, this contemporary hymn is suggested for use in connection with the Gospel lesson on the Last Judgment.

4. "He Is King of Kings," African American Spiritual

HE IS KING, African American Spiritual; adapt. Melva Costen (1989)

This spiritual is eminently appropriate for Christ the King Sunday. Its call-and-response pattern would make logical the use of a soloist on the stanzas with the congregation joining in singing the refrain.—Hugh T. McElrath

WORSHIP AIDS

CALL TO WORSHIP.   "Make a joyful noise unto the Lord, all ye lands. Serve the Lord with gladness; come before his presence with singing" (Ps. 100:1–2).

INVOCATION.   Because of you, O Lord, we have much to rejoice about. Even in the midst of difficulties, we can sing your praises. You have promised never to leave us or forsake us, and your presence is our strength, our hope, and our joy. We are yours and we worship you.

OFFERTORY SENTENCE.   "Blessed be the Lord, who daily loadeth us with benefits, even the God of our salvation" (Ps. 68:19).

OFFERTORY PRAYER.   As you bear the burden of our constant need, our Father, you make us partners in your concern for others. We dedicate our individual and family offerings to you for the benefit of individuals in special need and for the advancement of your causes in all the world.

PRAYER.   O Thou who art from everlasting to everlasting, whose glory is not dimmed by time or change, we thy children, swept by all the storms of this mortal life, beseech thee to steady us in this shifting scene and grant us a new vision of eternal things, that we may take hold and press forward. Refresh us by thy Holy Spirit and renew a right mind within us, that we may know beyond the peradventure of a doubt that thou art our salvation, and that nothing on Earth can shake the sure repose of thine everlasting arms. Deepen us down past all the thin and painted charms of this world's mock securities, until we stand on that rock of ages more firm than Earth itself, trusting in thee beyond all human sight and at peace with time and travail such as mortal man must suffer. In Christ therefore we lift up our eyes to hope.—Samuel H. Miller[7]

---

[7]*Prayers for Daily Use*

SERMON

Topic: Foolishness or Power?

TEXT: 1 Cor. 2:1–2

There was a day when the cross of our Lord and Savior, Jesus Christ, meant something to the Church. People could not speak of it without a catch in their throat and a mist in their eyes.

I am persuaded, however, that for too many of us who say the name of Christ in this day, the cross is not "the power of God unto salvation" that once wrought conviction in the hearts of sinners. Instead, it has become mere foolishness to a vast segment of the world's people.

It had meaning once. It still has meaning for those with eyes to see. The message is so plain.

I. *The cross is a vivid picture of sin.*

(a) Sins come from that sinful disposition the Bible calls sin. God becomes suspect in our minds. That is what the old-time preachers meant when they preached about the cross and sought to convince their hearers that the listeners' sin had placed Christ there. What the preachers were attempting to say was this: there is that disposition in you which, given long enough to grow and develop in your life, ultimately will do to God what those who crucified him did to Jesus.

(b) This is what James spoke of when he said, "Lust, when it conceives, brings forth sin, and sin, when it is finished, brings forth death" (James 1:15). When is sin finished? Sin will not be finished until time shall be no more.

Whose death? My death, to be sure, but the death of God is also implied. Sin, when it has finished its work, produces a disposition that could attempt to kill God!

II. *The cross is a picture of salvation.*

(a) God created man with the power of contrary choice. He made the human race one, but in the cross of his only begotten Son we see him acting in justice on rebellion and in love that pays the price for all sin. Now, God can be just, and the justifier of those who believe. This is what the apostle Paul spoke of in 2 Corinthians 5:21.

(b) The cross opens a way not only for forgiveness but also for a new life to be granted to all who by faith receive it. No man need ever be separated from God because of an inherited disposition. Those who are seeking him may now find him. The barrier has been broken down. The curse has been removed. A way has been opened and whosoever will may freely come.

III. *The cross is a picture of service.*

(a) The cross says to each of us, "God may do with his sons what he did with his Son." This is the principle of the cross in the life of believers. Luke 9:23 might be freely translated as, "If any man would come after me, let him deny his right to himself and take up the cross resulting from this and follow me." This is the meaning of service. Some are seeking strange experiences these days. Others claim that none may come into true service unless they come by way of some ecstatic experience. Not so! There are no shortcuts now, nor were there then, into Christian service. All must deny their rights to themselves and march under sealed orders to a destination not known to them.

(b) So many problems of the ministry would be solved by this commitment. Our dependence on the rearrangement of circumstances would be laid aside if we had truly given up our rights to ourselves. Our running away from life's tough experiences and our resulting lack of spiritual development would somehow cease if we could give up our rights to ourselves.—Carl E. Bates

SUNDAY, DECEMBER 1, 2002
Lectionary Message

Topic: Watching and Waiting
TEXT: Mark 13:24–37

I. *It is appropriate that we begin Advent with a reading from Mark 13, or "the Little Apocalypse."* As we prepare to celebrate the birth of Jesus, it is all too easy to approach Christmas as nothing more than Jesus' birthday. It is indeed that, but isolated from the rest of God's salvation story, Christmas becomes merely the commemoration of a historical event 2002 years ago. Its hope is confined to the honoring of newborn babes and the promise of each new human life before it experiences the pain and disappointment of growing up. Certainly there is value in those elements of Christmas that people of any faith (or no faith at all) can share. Mark 13, however, reminds us that there is something about the story of Christmas that cannot be affirmed by any but those who recognize Christ as Lord. A star rises and obediently leads the Wise Men to the one whose second advent will cause the stars to fall. Angels herald his arrival to shepherds who dwell on the edge of civilization in anticipation of their duty to gather the elect from the four winds when he comes again.

II. *The things that scare us most are the things we do not know.* Have you ever waited in fear and dread for something to happen and been relieved when it finally does? One of the hardest things for those who go into the hospital for tests is waiting for the results. If the news is bad, they can deal with it. They can start planning with the doctor how to treat the cancer or the heart disease or the infection. That doesn't minimize the grief and the pain of bad news, but knowing what to expect takes away some of the paralyzing fear.

(a) *That is why Jesus, just before his crucifixion, described what it is going to be like before he comes again.* He described wars, earthquakes, famines, and persecutions. He did not describe his coming again in order to instill terror. He told about it in order to relieve fear. If you know what to expect, you will not live in dread. If you know that even the end of the world is something over which God has control, then how can you be afraid of anything else?

(b) *If God holds the course of the heavens and the Earth in his hands, how can we think the things that trouble us are too big for God?* When the prophet Isaiah felt God's absence in his life, when sickness and evil and despair seemed to have the upper hand, he did not tremble in fear. He cried out to God. He trusted that God was there even if he was hidden. "O that you would tear open the heavens and come down so that the mountains would quake at your presence," he pleaded (Isa. 64:1). And that is our cry when we are overcome by all the fears that paralyze us: "O that you would tear open the heavens and come down—to heal my body, to restore my marriage, to lift me out of despair. O that you would come down to bring peace to the Middle East, to put an end to killer earthquakes, to keep babies from dying of hunger."

(c) *It is not too much for God, who orders the stars, to come down and order our chaotic lives.* That is why Jesus gave this vivid description of the course of the universe just before going to the cross. He was telling us who he is. The same one who throws galaxies at each other is the same one who went into a twelve-year-old girl's room with her parents, spoke gently to her, and told her to get up from her death bed. He is the same one who called some fishermen from their boats and gave them a part in his eternal plan of calling people to eternal life. He is the one who fed the hungry, gave sight to the blind, and cleansed the lepers; the same one who experienced life just as we do, except without sin; the same one who submitted himself to the brunt of evil on the cross. He is the same one who watches the stars burst forth, and the one who set aside all the glory and majesty of the galaxies and came to us in Bethlehem.

III. *So Jesus told us to watch and wait until he returns.* But waiting and watching does not mean counting the days until the end.

(a) *Watching and waiting does not mean trying to correlate the book of Revelation to an earthquake in Turkey or reading the predictions of Nostradamus in a supermarket tabloid.* Jesus compared our waiting to that of servants whose master went on a long trip. Each servant of the household had a job to do until the master returned. If the servants spent all their time looking out the window and trying to guess when the master would get back, the house would be a mess when he arrived. Proper waiting means keeping the house in order so that when the Master does show up, things will be ready. Waiting, for us, means showing the world that in Christ we have nothing to fear.

(b) *Anyone can see that the universe is a vast and complex place.* You can go to the Hubbell Observatory Web site and download thousands of pictures that make your jaw drop with awe at the vastness of outer space. But only by faith can we know the one who is behind it all. In Jesus we know that everything, from the infinite vastness of the cosmos to the intricate secrets of our hearts, belongs to God. We do not have to fear anything. Jesus may not come according to our timetable, but he will come. And he will be right on time.—Stephens G. Lytch

ILLUSTRATIONS

EXPLANATION.   *Bedtime for Frances* is a children's book about a little girl who has a hard time falling asleep. Lying in bed she sees a large shape looming in the corner of her room. The longer she looks at it, the more menacing it becomes. In fact, she thinks she sees it move. So she bolts out of bed and into the living room, where her mother and father are watching TV, and cries, "There's a tiger in my room." Her father goes back to her room with her, turns on the light, and shows her that what she had seen was a pile of clothes—clothes that should have been put away in her closet. Her father leaves and turns off the light. Frances tries again to fall asleep but hears something bumping against her window. The longer she lies there the more menacing it sounds, so she bounds out of bed into her parents' bedroom, where her father is brushing his teeth. "There's someone trying to break into my room!" Her father goes with her to her room, walks with her to the window, and shows her the branch bumping against the panes. Everything that terrifies Frances loses its grip on her when her father shows her what is really happening.[1]

Fear thrives on the unknown, on our sense of being out of control. The things that scare us most are the things we do not know.—Stephens G. Lytch

---

[1]Russell Hoban, *Bedtime for Frances* (New York: HarperCollins, 1960).

GOOD NEWS.   *The New York Times* carried a front-page photograph from the Hubbell Space Telescope.[2] Called "Things That Go Bump in the Night," it was a picture of two galaxies in the constellation Canis Major streaming gas, dust, and stars and colliding with each other. Each of the galaxies is 100,000 light years across. That means that it would take a beam of light travelling at 186,000 miles per second 100,000 years to go from one end of one of these galaxies to the other end of the same galaxy. It took millions of years for those two galaxies to pass through each other. Because it took the light from those galaxies millions of years to reach the Earth, they have probably already collided with each other in a cataclysm that is beyond description. What we see in a time delay of several million years, God sees in real time. God sees us looking for the first time at something God finished millions of years ago.

Looking at that photograph from the Hubbell telescope, Jesus' words in the Little Apocalypse of Mark do not sound so far-fetched: "The sun will be darkened and the moon will not give its light, and the stars will be falling from heaven and the powers in the heavens will be shaken." Astrophysics has shown us that such events are probably happening somewhere in the universe all the time. But Jesus' point was not that he knew something it has taken astronomers two thousand years to discover. His point was that nothing is outside of God's domain. Even when those things we count on for stability start to fall apart, when the moon and the sun and the stars run their course, the one who made them is still in charge. The end of the world as we know it is approaching, but that is not bad news. It is good news. God's plan is running its course. Jesus will restore the universe to how it is supposed to be—a place where there is no such thing as greed or anger or hatred or suffering.—Stephens G. Lytch

SERMON SUGGESTIONS

Topic: Are You Listening, Lord?

Text: Isa. 64:1–12

(1) *Attention:* Sometimes we face situations in which we bitterly believe that God has forgotten us (v. 11). (2) *Need:* We need reassurance that we and God are in business together (v. 12). (3) *Satisfaction:* We could be reassured if (a) God gave some dramatic or even some modest token of his caring (vv. 1–3); (b) we could remember how God acted sooner or later on behalf of those who waited for him (vv. 4–5). (4) *Visualization:* Otherwise, we can remain smitten with a sense of guilt and hopelessness (vv. 6–7). (5) *Action:* Our best strategy is to face our situation with faith and decisive obedience.

Topic: Reassurance

Text: 1 Cor. 1:3–9

(1) *The basis*—grace and peace from God the Father and Jesus Christ. (2) *The gift*—enrichment: (a) knowledge, (b) full expression of this knowledge, and (c) therefore, confirmation of genuine experience. (3) *The promise*—eternal security.

CONGREGATIONAL MUSIC

1. "Not So in Haste, My Heart!" Bradford Torrey (c. 1875)
   DOLOMITE CHANT, Austrian; harm. J. T. Cooper (1879)

---

[2]*New York Times,* Nov. 9, 1999, p. A1.

The exhortation of the apostle Paul (1 Cor. 1:3–9) to wait for the revealing of the Lord finds a powerful echo in this nineteenth-century hymn. After a soloist or choir sings prayerfully the first stanza or two, the congregation could join in the singing.

2. "My Lord, What a Morning," African American Spiritual

BURLEIGH, African American Spiritual; arr. William F. Smith (1987)

The Gospel lesson describes the apocalyptic events attending the coming of the Son of Man. Mark 13:25 speaks specifically of the stars falling from heaven, which is the recurring theme of this spiritual. It could be sung immediately after the Gospel reading.

3. "Hear Us, O Shepherd of Your Chosen Race," Ps. 80; vers. Bert Polman (1987)

YORKSHIRE, John Wainwright (1750)

Stanzas 1, 2, and 5 of this modern paraphrase of Psalm 80 relate to the verses selected for the Psalter reading. For some the tune will have significant association with Advent and Christmas.

4. "Have Thine Own Way, Lord," Adelaide A. Pollard (1902)

ADELAIDE, George C. Stebbins (1907)

This familiar hymn of submission and consecration reflects Isaiah 64:8 in its vivid image of the potter and the clay. Its could well be sung to introduce the Old Testament lesson.— Hugh T. McElrath

WORSHIP AIDS

CALL TO WORSHIP. "Turn us again, O God, and cause they face to shine, and we shall be saved" (Ps. 80:3).

INVOCATION. Because things can and do go wrong for us, our Father, we implore your forgiveness and your corrective guidance where we are at fault. Cleanse our hands and purify our hearts, that we may worship you and do your will.

OFFERTORY SENTENCE. "The Lord is good to all, and his tender mercies are over all his works" (Ps. 145:9).

OFFERTORY PRAYER. You have richly blessed us, O God, and now we would honor and thank you with these tokens of our gratitude. You have blessed us with the ability to bring these offerings, and now we pray that your Kingdom may grow and that many will turn their hearts to you because of our stewardship.

PRAYER. We can only stand in awe, Father, when we recall the many ways you have come into our lives this past week. Indeed, your Advent has been for us not something that happened long ago but a recent experience taking place right down in the middle of life. We have faced unknown situations and felt frightened and alone. Then, in a moment of given strength, we were able to face the situation and not be defeated by it. We have heard heartbreaking bad news and, in that moment, wildly wondered where you were, only to discover you right in the midst of life, bearing our burdens and feeling our tears. We have stood in the presence of death asking long questions to which there are no short answers, and we have despaired that we could do nothing to prevent death's arrival. In the depths of our despair we have found hope and encouragement about life because you came to us bringing light to our darkness and eternity to our finiteness. We have walked a while with pain, praying that its power over us would cease. In a moment of relinquishment to you, we have been able to bear it and function rather than be destroyed by it. We have cried out from the lostness of misunderstandings, wanting to renew broken relationships, and have found solution through your Word fitly spoken of old and now spoken again. We have watched as beloved people have made dangerous and destructive choices, wanting with all our hearts to protect them from the ultimate end of their choices. Yielding them to you, we have found ways to help them and found rest for our own troubled souls. We have met temptation with all its glamour and would have been overcome by its power but for the remembrance of your love and grace and strength. Yes, Lord, you have come to us this week and, because of your constancy, your caring, and your presence with us, we have been redeemed and our week has been made meaningful and strong.

Thank you for Advent, Father—for that first time you made yourself known in human form to us when you came to Bethlehem, and for the multitudes of other times you have come to us in our moments of need. Now we worship you, first as the child of Advent, then as the ever-present helper in every time of need. Accept our worship we pray.—Henry Fields

SERMON
Topic: Four Imperatives for Advent
Text: Various

In 1659, the Massachusetts Bay Colony passed a law forbidding the observance of Christmas. What they really wanted to forbid was the wrong kind of observance of Christmas. The struggle to keep Christmas Christian goes on. Christmas is a happy holiday of glittering delight, but its true beauty is in its truth, not in its tinsel. We will not be ready for Christmas until we are ready in spiritual understanding. Here the lectionary helps us, for it is a springboard from which we dive into God's Word and experience afresh the wonders of his truth.

Here are four guideposts to help us: *know, go, grow,* and *glow.*

I. *The glory of Christmas is in the truth that God has given for us to know.* Luke 2:1–20 is the classic Bible statement telling of the first Christmas. It is centered in the message from God given by the angel, "Be not afraid, for behold, I bring you good news." God is revealing to man a heavenly truth of definitive importance: "to you is born this day, in the city of David, a Savior who is Christ the Lord." This is indeed "good news of a great joy that will come to all the people." It is the foundation of Christian faith. Without it there would be no Christian religion. With it, believers live in the light of an unquenchable hope.

The truth was given to Joseph in the days of Mary's pregnancy: "Do not fear to take Mary as your wife, for that which is conceived in her is of the Holy Spirit; she will bear a son, and you shall call his name Jesus, for he will save his people from their sins" (Matt. 1:20–21). So Joseph was prepared for that first Christmas by knowing the central truth that a Savior was to be born, and because he knew, he believed.

The truth of Christmas finds theological expression in John 1: "The Word became flesh and dwelt among us, full of grace and truth; we have beheld his glory—glory as of the only Son from the Father." This is the basis of the fundamental Christian truth on which we build our confidence—the doctrine of the Incarnation. It echoes through the New Testament. "In this the love of God was made manifest among us, that God sent his only Son into the world so that we might live through him" (1 John 4:9). To know this glorious truth is indeed to enter into life. Titus 2:11 says it again: "For the grace of God has appeared for the salvation of all men." This is the great thing we know. It gives Christmas its meaning; there is no Christmas for us unless we do know it.

Luke tells of the heavenly chorus, the angelic song of joy and praise: "Glory to God in the highest, and on Earth peace among men with whom he is pleased." Why did the angels sing? They sang because they knew! Angels have knowledge where we have only faith. Because they knew what God was doing in that first Christmas—giving mankind his Son in love and mercy to reclaim a lost race—they sang! And when we know the truth of Christmas, our hearts, too, will sing.

II. *Let us go.* The response of the shepherds to the angelic announcement of the good news that a Savior was born was to turn faith into action. Whenever we have a glorious spiritual experience, we need to do something about it. Vision must be translated into venture, creed into deed. The joy and wonder of Christmas find their proper consequence when we say, "Let us go."

The shepherds did go to Bethlehem, and faith became experience. They not only went; they found! When vision becomes action, we find the blessings God has for us. The shepherds found the Holy Family—"Mary and Joseph and the babe lying in a manger." So their faith found its reward in their experience that the announcement of the angel was true—that what God promises he performs!

In the joy of experienced truth, the shepherds became witnesses. Happily they told of their wonderful experience—how the heavens burst asunder and there was glory all around, how they had trembled in fear, how the angel had promised them good and allayed their fears, and how they had heard the wonderful tidings that a Savior was born in Bethlehem, as a babe lying in a manger. They told of the heavenly chorus praising God, and of how they had come to Bethlehem and found the Christ child, even as the angel had said. So we can validate our faith in experience, if we go.

III. *The truth of Christmas is so great, we must grow into it.* Christmas is not only a cheery holiday, for as we grow in understanding, we focus on the great centralities—"to you is born a Saviour" (Luke 2:11); "his name shall be called Immanuel" (Matt. 1:23); "when the time had fully come, God sent forth his Son" (Gal. 4:4). The shepherds grew from fear to faith because of the good news God gave.

St. Paul vividly pictured the growing of the believer from slave to son: "When we were children, we were slaves to the elemental spirits of the universe. But when the time had fully come, God sent forth his Son, born of woman, born under the Law, to redeem those who were under the Law, so that we might receive adoption as sons. And because we are sons, God has sent the Spirit of his Son into our hearts, crying, 'Abba! Father!' So through God we are no longer slaves but sons, and if sons, then heirs" (Gal. 4:3–7). What a graphic account of Christian growth! From slavery to freedom, sonship, and the privileges of being sons—and these were made possible by God's gift of Christmas!

The Bible challenges us to grow in understanding of Christmas—God's great deed of love, the sending of a Savior. If it is only a holiday, Christmas will be a hollow day.

A little girl assembling the Christmas creche was happily naming the figures she found: "Here is Mary. Here is Joseph. Here are the shepherds. Here are the Wise Men." Suddenly, her voice faltered and she cried out in alarm, "But where is Jesus? I can't find him. We've lost the Baby Jesus!" Already the little girl had grown in her understanding of Christmas. There was no Christmas in the world until Christ came. There can be no Christmas now if we have lost the Baby Jesus!

IV. *Christmas makes our hearts glow.* After seeing Jesus, the shepherds were different persons when they returned to their flocks. "Glorifying and praising God," they were radiant with the glow that only God can give. They had acted on God's revelation and had found his promise to be true. They had grown from fear to faith, from faith to experience, from experience to witness, from the commonplace to the glorious. If we go in faith to the holy manger, we too shall find in the Savior the light of our seeing, the hope of all our being, the glorious radiance of hope and meaning. The joy-giving fact of the Incarnation, once experienced in faith and devotion, sets our life aglow. We join the shepherds in glorifying and praising God because we too have come to know the glory of Christmas, and because we know, we glow!

The Christian's secret of a happy life is found in praise. The life of praise is turned toward God. All our experience is lighted by his goodness and love. Glory fills our days. We have power to cope.

Isaiah 61 tells of "the year of the Lord's favor." To live in the favor of God is to find all life aglow. In a cascade of happy expressions, Isaiah 61 (2–3, 10) tells about it:

> To comfort all who mourn;
> to grant to those who mourn in Zion—
> to give them a garland instead of ashes,
> the oil of gladness instead of mourning,
> the mantle of praise instead of a faint spirit;
> that they may be called oaks of righteousness,
> the planting of the Lord, that he may be glorified. . . .
> I will greatly rejoice in the Lord,
> my soul shall exult in my God.

The shepherds went back to the old life but as new men. They wore the mantle of praise instead of a faint spirit!

In a world so dominated by bad news, the good news of Christmas heartens us. It tells of the wonderful character of our God, who cares for us with saving concern, lights our lives with hope, and sets our spirits aglow. The believer knows that there is good news today, and every day, because the universe is sound at heart and loving in purpose. This had been made known to us, and this is the heart of the meaning of Christmas. Because we know and because we go, we will grow and we will glow, and this is of God, to whom we give grateful and happy praise.

"I will greatly rejoice in the Lord, my soul shall exult in my God."—Lowell M. Atkinson[3]

---

[3]*Apples of Gold*

SUNDAY, DECEMBER 8, 2002
Lectionary Message

Topic: The Wilderness

TEXT: Mark 1:1–8

Other Readings: Isa. 40:1–11; Ps. 85:1–2, 8–13; 2 Pet. 3:8–15a

I. Some may think that, compared to the other Gospels, the beginning of Mark's Gospel is pedestrian.

(a) Luke begins his Gospel with angels announcing a miraculous birth. Matthew begins with the mysterious Wise Men bearing precious gifts of gold, frankincense, and myrrh. The Gospel of John starts with resounding words that place his story in the context of eternity.

(b) Mark begins with crowds of people—ordinary people who are responding not to a decree from the heavens but to a very human longing from deep within their hearts. The first proclamation in Mark is not the angelic chorus of "peace on Earth, good will to all," but a call to repent from sin, given by a hermit dressed in camel's hair who lived off locusts and honey.

II. *The beginning of Mark's Gospel is never reenacted in Christmas pageants, but perhaps it should be.* Unless we hear what Mark tells us as he begins his Gospel of Jesus Christ, the Son of God, the angels of Luke and the Wise Men of Matthew and the eternal Word of John will be for us just seasonal stories that may warm our hearts but will not change them. To receive the Holy One who was born at Christmas, we have to begin where Mark does. We have to prepare.

III. *And how do we prepare for Jesus?*

(a) It is not as though Jesus is waiting in the wings for us to be prepared before he arrives. Just as Christmas comes whether we are ready or not, Jesus comes into our lives every day whether or not we are prepared. The question is whether we are ready for him. Do we know where to look for him? Do we know how to recognize him when he comes?

(b) Isaiah talks about preparing. He says to "make straight in the desert a highway for our God. Every valley shall be lifted up and every mountain and hill be made low; the uneven ground shall become level and the rough places a plain." Deserts, uneven ground, rough places—these are where John the Baptist prepared for Jesus. He called people out into the wilderness to get ready for Jesus' arrival in their lives.

IV. *Sometimes, in order to prepare for Jesus, we have to find those wildernesses in our lives.*

(a) Like the people who went out to hear John the Baptist, we have to go to those places that are destitute and abandoned, that challenge us most, the places we try so hard to ignore. If you look at your life as a vast and varied country, parts of it are full and joyous like Zion, the holy city where blessings overflow. Other parts are ordinary, like the suburbs of Bethany, where there is orderliness and ordinariness that bring the comfort of what is expected. There are also wild, scary, uncharted areas where we do not have control—the wilderness.

(b) Many of us are blessed that the landscapes of our lives include wilderness areas around which we can skirt. They are so small that we do not have to spend much time there. But John the Baptist invites us to go out into the wilderness to prepare for Christ because it is in the wilderness that we are confronted with our need for him. It is in the wilderness that we recognize what sustains us in the places of fullness and joy. If we can strip away all those things that distract us when life is going well, those things for which we recklessly take credit without ever recognizing God, then we return to that manageable terrain having met the one who sustains us. We can find joy in the things we have rather than resentment because of the things we lack.

V. *That is why there is something different about the way we prepare for Christmas in church.* Our preparations lack some of the giddiness of the mall. There is a place for the effervescent joy of Santa Claus, the sparkling trill of brass choirs on street corners, and the warmth and celebration of our Christmas parties. Nevertheless, during these weeks of Advent we remind ourselves that there is still wilderness in this world, and it is in the wilderness that we prepare to meet Christ. The color of the season is purple, the same as Lent. We sing the plaintive strains of "O Come, O Come, Emmanuel." We remember at the Lord's table that it is only by dying with Christ to sin that we are raised with him to eternal life.

VI. *The first step in welcoming Jesus is recognizing that we need his grace.* This is not a once in a lifetime revelation. It is something we have to confront every day. Mark begins his Gospel by inviting us to enter the wilderness that we try so hard to avoid. We want to look the other way. We want to pretend that everything is just fine, that we do not need a Savior. Mark invites us to go to the wilderness unafraid and confident that we will meet Jesus Christ, the Son of God.—Stephens G. Lytch

ILLUSTRATIONS

WHERE CHRIST AWAITS US.   John the Baptist called people into the wilderness to prepare to meet Jesus. The wilderness is different for different people. There is a woman for whom this will be the first Christmas in forty-five years without her beloved husband. The Christmas carols sound flat for her this year; the lights just make her more aware of the darkness that has pervaded her life in the months since her husband died. She knows what it means to be in the wilderness, where you do not have the resources to make it on your own.

There is a young man who made some reckless business decisions over the last six months. He had always relied on himself to get through, but now he does not know what the future holds for him. The dreams he had nine months ago have crashed and his life is like a trackless wilderness.

There is the high school girl who feels she is in the wilderness every day at lunch. Everyone else seems to have friends and be included, but she feels like a social leper whom no one likes. The feelings of loneliness and isolation are overwhelming.

There is the new mother who loves her baby more than she can say, but after a week of getting up three times in the night and paying constant attention to the demands of her child, she feels totally depleted of any strength and joy—and guilty because she is so drained.

Each of these people is living in the wilderness this Advent. Christ is waiting for them there.—Stephens G. Lytch

CONTAGIOUS COURAGE.   We are tempted to avoid the wilderness. We want to look the other way and pretend that everything is just fine, that we do not need a Savior. Those who are not afraid of the wilderness but go there to meet Christ are like the people on a crowded street who see an assault take place. Our inclination is to turn the other way and not get involved. It is the victim's business and why should we take a risk? But social scientists have proved that if one person goes to the aid of a victim of an assault, if one person notices an evil being done and tries to stop it, then others will also respond. It takes one person to take the initiative, to confront evil honestly, and others will have the courage to do what they know is right.—Stephens G. Lytch

SERMON SUGGESTIONS

Topic: The Word the World Needs

TEXT: Isa. 40:1–11

(1) A word of forgiveness (v. 2). (2) A word of promise (vv. 3–4). (3) A word of embrace (v. 5). (4) A word of realism (vv. 6–8a). (5) A word of ultimate comfort (vv. 8b–11).

Topic: God's Timetable

TEXT: 2 Pet. 3:8–15a

(1) God's timetable is not like ours (v. 8). (2) It is in our favor (v. 9): (a) It does include a negative aspect (vv. 10–12; see also Amos 5:18–20). (b) However, the bottom line is salvation (vv. 13, 15c). (c) Yet this implies our being at peace with the Lord and living ethically responsible lives (v. 14).

CONGREGATIONAL MUSIC

1. "Comfort, Comfort, Now My People," Isa. 40:1–5; vers. J. G. Olearius (1671); trans. Catherine Winkworth (1863)

    GENEVAN 42, Louis Bourgeois (1551)

    This fine musical rendering of the Isaiah 40 prophecy would be quite appropriate for the beginning of worship.

2. "O Zion (Christians), Haste," Mary A. Thomson (1868)

    TIDINGS, James Walch (1875)

    This excellent hymn on mission would be suitable as a response to the Epistle lesson, especially 2 Peter 3:9.

3. "On Jordan's Bank the Baptist's Cry," Charles Coffin (1736)

    PUER NOBIS Trier MS (fifteenth century); adapt. M. Praetorius (1609)

    This old hymn relates specifically to the Gospel lesson about John the Baptist. It is an excellent selection for Advent worship.

4. "Lord, You Have Lavished on Your Land," Ps. 85; vers. Marie K. Post (1985)

    NEW 113TH, William Hayes (1774)

    Stanzas 1, 3, and 4 of this metrical version of Psalm 85 parallel the verses selected for this day's Psalter reading. The length of this metrical psalm might make quoting rather than reading stanza 3 appropriate.—Hugh T. McElrath

WORSHIP AIDS

CALL TO WORSHIP.   "For thus saith the high and lofty one who inhabiteth eternity, whose name is Holy: I dwell in the high and holy place, with him also that is of a contrite and humble spirit, to revive the spirit of the humble, and to revive the heart of the contrite ones" (Isa. 57:15).

INVOCATION.   We know that you are with us now, O God, and that your reaching down does not compromise your majesty. Indeed, it is of your glory that you dwell with us, sinful though we are, forgiving us, strengthening us, and making us your useful servants.

OFFERTORY SENTENCE.   "As a piece of willing service, this is not only a contribution toward the needs of God's people; more than that, it overflows in a flood of thanksgiving to God" (2 Cor. 9:12 REB).

OFFERTORY PRAYER.   Because of what we do now, O Lord, the gospel may be received by some who have never heard it, and the lives of others may be blessed by ministries to their own special needs. Let what we do from gratitude for your grace to us be the occasion of many thanksgivings to you from many grateful hearts.

PRAYER.   How strange, O Father, is your amazing grace that we should have the privilege of knowing the name that is above every name when there are so many who do not.

We thank you for parents, Sunday school teachers, youth counselors, ministers, and friends who have lovingly and faithfully shared the gospel with us.

We praise you for congregations that have sounded your call, nurtured us, and sent us forth. For guiding us to this household of faith where our hearts are strangely warmed with your love, where our minds are challenged with fresh thoughts of the newness that is in Christ, and where we are called to mission that embraces the world and all its people, we are grateful.

We thank you, too, O Father, for those guardian angels who, when we have been threatened with shipwreck, have ridden out the storm with us, encouraging and supporting us, believing in us when we could not even believe in ourselves. Because of all your goodness and mercy in times past, may we be confident of your providence for today and for any future. Grant us wisdom, faithfulness, and hopefulness to plant trees in the shade of which we may never sit.

Having heard your Word, your call in Christ, may we respond with an eagerness to share your healing grace with all others. For this calling, pour out your Holy Spirit upon us, purifying our motives so that we may seek only the good of the other, whoever that other may be.

For any brokenness among us—illness of body, infirmity of age, depression of spirit, loneliness of heart—we pray for your health and wholeness. For all of us passing through the valley of the shadow of death, we pray for the assurance that "life is ever lord of death and love can never lose its own."

For our leaders who have the power to turn the tide from war to peace, we pray for a change of mind and heart to accept the new age of the coming of your Kingdom in Christ—the world community—that we will no longer squander the rich resources of this planet on implements of death when there are so many who need food and clothing and shelter for life.

We pray for leaders in our government and in other nations who seek conciliation and reconciliation rather than pursue attitudes and policies that can only foment mistrust and hostility.

And now, O God, grant us the courage to live as we have prayed, through him in whom word and deed are one and who teaches us to pray and live: [Lord's Prayer].—John Thompson

SERMON
Topic: Feeling Our Pain—Those for Whom Jesus Wept
TEXT: John 11:17–36

People aren't much to count on. We frequently don't care as we should about the pain and plight of others, and the few of us who actually know how to care and who take time to care without assessing a fee are rare gems. We are blessed with several of these truly caring types in this congregation; still, most of us know how hard it is to find someone who really cares about us out there in the big wide world.

But God is another story. We want to be able to count on God no matter what, and we want to know that God understands what we're going through and that God cares about us as we endure some difficulty or hardship. We want and need to know that God feels our pain. As Elie Wiesel said, "Better an unjust God than an indifferent one."

In Christian tradition, we have claimed that if God were human, he would act toward people the way Jesus of Nazareth acted. If that is true, then we have some very strong evidence that God not only cares about us but cares deeply. And God would not have any of us suffer.

Why doesn't God keep innocent people—at least the innocent people—from suffering tragedy?

What I want to remind you of today is that God is with us through every experience in our lives to which we invite him; in the most turbulent storms, we are never alone unless we choose to be. As to the other question, God doesn't build any protective shields around anyone that would keep her or him from experiencing precisely what all humans experience. Random tragedy for no good reason at all as well as the inevitable consequences of our bad choices bring catastrophe to us and others connected to us. God isn't any less God and not a bit less loving for allowing us to be human in a world where both randomness in nature and human free choice prevail.

Sometimes divine healing can occur. Sometimes divine intervention can prevent certain kinds of tragedy. Every time, as a matter of fact, there can be healing or restoration of life, or tragedy can be averted; God sees to these, every single time. But human freedom prevails, often even when we choose to do what hurts others—such as parents who blow cigarette smoke into their babies' faces, or drinkers who drive drunk and plow into the autos of innocent people who just happened to be out driving at the same time the drunk decided to get back on the highway.

Whoever told us that when bad things happen to us and to those we love God is behind it, these people were dead wrong! What we need to know above all else is that God loves us, and when we are in pain God feels that pain with us—every bit of it!

Having been brought up in the Church, there has never been a time when I haven't turned, almost reflexively, to God when the burdens have been heavy. I'm not sure what else one would do.

Despite our otherwise often very bad theology, some of us have still somehow believed the scriptural admonition that gently invites, "Cast all your anxiety on [God], because [God] cares for you" (1 Pet. 5:7 NRSV). But sometimes I fear that we may believe this only academically, and not in a way that actually changes the way we live, and especially the way we carry around our concerns.

Despite all the burdens Jesus bore with and for others, we have only one direct indication that he cried in the face of others' pain. Because the Gospels are so brief, it is certainly more than likely that they are, among other things, trying to give us examples of how Jesus lived; thus Jesus likely cried many more times than we know about as he sat with the oppressed and the bereaved and the alienated and the poor. But we look to the one story of such tears that is available to us.

The story centers around Jesus' very close friends: Mary, Martha, and Lazarus. They were siblings and very close to one another. Lazarus died. Mary and Martha lost their brother and naturally they were bereaved. Their bereavement, as is often the case, was intensified by their frustration. He had been sick. They'd done everything they knew they could do for him, and had done for him everything they knew to have done. No doubt he had been taken to the best medical people they could find. They had carefully and painstakingly attended to every one of his needs.

When things didn't begin to look better, they called on their friends to pray for their dear brother, and when the end seemed at hand, they called on their friends to come in person to pray for Lazarus and to comfort him. Nothing worked and Lazarus died.

Mary and Martha wept, and they asked themselves and each other, between their sobs of loss, "If we had only done more, if we had only known more to do, do you think our dear brother would still be alive?"

One of those for whom they had sent, and maybe, in their minds, the most important friend for whom they'd sent, was Jesus. Strikingly, to them, Jesus hadn't shown up. Either he hadn't received their message or he hadn't dropped everything and come to them. Thus the very first thing Martha wanted to know from Jesus was, "Did you not get our message in time?"

Jesus said, "Yes, I got the message a few days ago."

And Martha angrily asked, "You couldn't make it a lousy two miles in time to save the life of this man you claim to have loved? What kind of friend are you?"

After a little while, Mary, too, saw Jesus, and her questions were similar: "Jesus, if you'd been here, he'd still be alive; we'd still have our brother. Why didn't you come to us when we called for you?"

Jesus wept. He was shedding tears that God also shed. Why? Because he cared deeply—as God does—about the pain people like us must bear. Jesus wept because his friends misunderstood God. He wept because his friends misunderstood him, because his friends were in pain, because his dear, dear friend was dead and he wasn't sure how God would lead him to respond.

No, I think Jesus didn't interfere with the natural order of things, and until he arrived in Bethany and consulted with God in prayer about what the right response would be, I don't think he knew for sure if this was a situation in which using his healing powers would be appropriate. Remember that Jesus healed only a small number of the sick and dying people with whom he came into contact. In this case, by God's power, Jesus raised Lazarus from the dead.

Being children of God, being followers of Jesus, does not and will not keep us from pain; but such commitments and associations will keep us from having to feel alienated, from feeling, as Elie Wiesel described it, that God is "indifferent." God is not indifferent. God is loving, God is compassionate, God is empathetic, and God feels our pain. God feels *your* pain, and when you hurt, God weeps. That won't fix everything the way we'd prefer all the time, but because our pain is magnified when we feel forgotten, God's great care for each of us is healing.—David Albert Farmer

SUNDAY, DECEMBER 15, 2002
Lectionary Message

Topic: We Can Rejoice

TEXT: 1 Thess. 5:16–24

Other Readings: Isa. 61:1–4, 8–11; Ps. 126; John 6:8, 19–28

I. *The early Christians were wise to put Christmas where they did.*

(a) The Bible does not give us the date of Jesus' birth, but sometime in the early centuries of the Church, December 25 was selected as the date to celebrate the Nativity. It happened to be the date of an ancient pagan festival that marked the return of the sun. After six months of ever-shorter days and longer nights, the ancients noticed that around December 25 the sun starts to work its way back toward the north. Little by little the days grow longer. Even though the worst of winter is still ahead, that reversal of the disappearing sun gave hope that warmth and life would eventually return to the Earth.

(b) It says something about what we believe that we celebrate the birth of our Savior when we do, that we sing carols of joy in the gloomiest days of the year, knowing that snow and ice, flu and colds await us in the months ahead. On these darkest of nights we light up our houses and trees. While the Earth is frozen over and nothing can grow, we hang evergreens on our doors as proof that there is still something the frost has not killed. All of this is our way of affirming that nothing can overcome the hope and joy that are ours through the one who was born at Christmas.

II. *The life of each of us is a mixture of happiness and sadness.*

(a) All of us live through tragedies as well as triumphs. Paul's words to the Thessalonians remind us of the joy that nothing can overcome—a joy that is ours in Christ. He wrote, "Rejoice always. Give thanks in all circumstances."

(b) If Paul had been a person to whom nothing bad ever happened, we could dismiss him as an unrealistic optimist. From someone who had never suffered, his advice would sound like empty fluff. Paul, however, had been beaten and jailed. He had some kind of physical ailment, his "thorn in the flesh." He had been run out of Thessalonica by his enemies, and the people to whom he wrote were being persecuted for their faith. Some of the Thessalonians had hoped that believing in Jesus would save them from pain and hardship, but they were discovering what Paul knew well—that sometimes those who believe in Christ face more hardship than anyone else.

(c) Paul reminded the Thessalonians that God had promised to overcome everything that harmed them. He reminded them that God is faithful and keeps promises. We read some of those promises in Isaiah 61: God binds up the brokenhearted and frees the prisoners. God comforts those who mourn and restores whatever has been devastated, even human hearts. Thessalonians reminds us that even when the fulfillment of those promises is hard to see, there is something more going on than what we comprehend. The direction the world is headed has already been decided. Regardless of how things look, God has already done something that affects the future. Isaiah describes it like this: "For as the Earth brings forth its shoots, and as a garden causes what is sown in it to spring up, so the Lord God will cause righteousness and praise to spring up before all the nations" (61:11)

III. *Because of the promise that God will triumph, we can face whatever we encounter in life.*

(a) We can confront our own fears and weakness, our failures, even our death. We do not have to pretend that we are invincible or perfect or immortal, because we know that someone stronger than ourselves holds the future.

(b) That is why Christians can go out of their way to confront suffering and pain. That hope and joy is what gives missionaries the confidence to give up the comforts of home and country and go to far-off places to confront disease and illiteracy and hopelessness. That is what gives churches the confidence to establish soup kitchens, literacy centers, mentoring programs, and other ministries that face intractable problems with the boldness of a hope beyond sight.

(c) When Christ sends us out into a broken and hurting world, he does not send us out without contact with the source of our joy and hope. We are not like astronauts on the far side of the moon, cut off from home. That is why Paul reminded the Thessalonians to "pray without ceasing." Prayer is what sustains our joy. In prayer we can acknowledge to God our fears and sadness. When we are overwhelmed with what looks like the futility of it all, prayer keeps us in touch with the one who is in charge.

(d) There are plenty of problems we cannot solve. We can sit with a terminally ill friend, but as badly as we want to do it, we cannot cure his disease. We can comfort a grieving widow, but we cannot stand between her and her pain. We cannot always make everything right for ourselves or for the people about whom we care, but prayer can open channels for God to do what we are unable to do. Prayer can help us find the pulse of God's promise that is always there.

IV. *Whether things go well or whether they go badly, we can always rejoice.* Sometimes our joy is the kind that makes us want to dance and sing. Sometimes it is more subdued and gets us through difficult times with the hope that keeps us from giving up altogether. But our joy in Christ is always there. Every year, just when it is darkest and nature is preparing to give us its worst, we celebrate Jesus' birth and remember that he lives. Whatever happens, that is reason enough to rejoice.—Stephens G. Lytch

ILLUSTRATION

THE PROMISE.   In the middle of December, a garden is bare and empty. It is not able to sustain any life, not even a dandelion. But something is happening that the gardener cannot see. She planted bulbs in October, confident that by late February her garden would be bright with snowdrops and crocuses. She is certain that in March there will be daffodils, and that by April the garden will be ablaze with tulips.

Sometimes we are tempted to ignore the harsh realities of life—the things that bring us sadness and pain. There are days when we do not want to read the newspaper, with its reports of yet another murder or scandal. We can sympathize with the man who puts off seeing the doctor about his stomach pain because he does not want to hear the bad news that he has an ulcer. We can understand the couple who will not write a will because they do not want to admit that one day they are going to die.

We know what God has in store for us, so we face pain and sadness squarely. In Jesus, God has the last word about what is going on. In Christ, God came among us, stands beside us, lifts us up, and gives us strength to meet whatever happens. God promises that a time is coming when there will be no more crying or pain. That promise is underneath everything that happens to us, like a heartbeat you rarely notice but that is always there, sustaining us with its pulse.—Stephens G. Lytch

SERMON SUGGESTIONS

Topic: Agenda for the Messiah

TEXT: Isa. 61:1–4, 8–11

(1) Good news. (2) Healing. (3) Freedom. (4) Proclamation of grace and judgment. (5) Comfort. (6) Reconstruction. (9) Reward. (See Luke 4:16–21.)

Topic: The Witness

TEXT: John 1:6–8, 19–28

(1) John the Baptist had a tremendous responsibility (v. 7). (2) His responsibility required him to take a secondary role (v. 8). (3) Even John's secondary role led to difficulties with the religious leaders (vv. 19–25). (4) Nevertheless, John was steadfast in affirming the Christ.

CONGREGATIONAL MUSIC

1. "Hark, the Glad Sound! The Savior Comes," Philip Doddridge (1735)
   RICHMOND, Thomas Haweis (1792)

   This eighteenth-century classic based on Isaiah 61:1–2 is a natural hymn for the opening of Advent worship. Its joyous, celebrative character could be enhanced by adding a descant to the singing of the last stanza.
2. "When God Brought Zion's Remnant Band," Ps. 126; vers. Calvin Seerveld (1985)
   MAG ICH UNGLEUCK, J. Klug's *Geistliche Lieder* (1535)

   This imaginative metrical rendering of the psalm for this day could well replace the Psalter reading. The first stanza could be sung by a soloist, with the congregation coming in on the second stanza.
3. "Go Forth for God," John R. Peacey (1968)
   WOODLANDS, Walter Greatorex (1916)

   This contemporary hymn that echoes many of the exhortations of the apostle Paul in the Epistle lesson should be sung in response to the reading of that lesson.
4. "Savior of the Nations, Come," Ambrose (fourth century), M. Luther (1523)
   NUN KOMM DER HEIDEN HEILAND, *Enchiridia* Erfurt (1524)

   The prologue to John's Gospel is echoed in Martin Luther's Advent hymn. Alternating between singing and reading, as follows, would add variety to its use: stanza 1, sung; stanza 2, read; stanza 3, sung; stanza 4, read; stanza 5, sung.—Hugh T. McElrath

WORSHIP AIDS

CALL TO WORSHIP.   "They that sow in tears shall reap in joy. He that goeth forth and weepeth, bearing precious seed, shall doubtless come again with rejoicing, bringing his sheaves with him" (Ps. 126:5–6).

INVOCATION.   You care for us, O God, with an indescribable love, a love that suffers with compassion as did the Christ of the cross. Help us to learn, even as we worship now, to emulate your love in fresh resolves that anticipate joy and success in service.

OFFERTORY SENTENCE.   "Bless the Lord, O my soul, and forget not all his benefits" (Ps. 103:2).

OFFERTORY PRAYER.   We can hardly name the many benefits of your providence, O Lord, yet we would begin with the gift of your Son, our Savior and Redeemer, and from there forever bless you for all the good things that have come our way. Let our offerings now be a token of our everlasting gratitude.

PRAYER.   O God of all truth and love, our prayer in this Advent season is for this redeeming Lord to live anew among us and become the conscience of all humankind. Let us, with your help, turn from making tinsel and holly ends in themselves and see rather the meaning in the glow of a star that leads us to who he is and where we too can be. Let us, by your grace, make the love of the company around each evergreen tree a forecast of that holy family of all people who will hail him when he comes again to reign. Let us, through the urgings of your will, cause the cheerful tones of the bells at Christmas to ring out the end of wrong and ring in the new age of righteousness and peace. Prepare us, we pray, to see in this happy festival the wonder and mystery of God with us, and in the spirit of our common hope may we make our daily cry, "O come, O come, Emmanuel."—Donald Macleod

SERMON
Topic: The Cloverleaf and the Cross
TEXT: John 19:17–22; Acts 18:1–5

The symbol of American culture is the cloverleaf—shuttling the traffic of America to her cities, where the people are, where the culture-shapers are, where the economic power structures have their home offices.

Harvey Cox, in *The Secular City,* mentions the highway cloverleaf and the telephone switchboard as the symbols of this new life. And then, for good measure, he tells us what they mean: mobility and anonymity—the two characteristic components of urban life.

To the switchboard and the cloverleaf I would add another element of urban life. It is what I would call profanity—the loss of the sense of the sacred. This is not altogether bad. There are some sacred cows that deserve to die. But age and the reverence given in the past are not reasons enough to cast down old landmarks. We must be more discerning than that. We must ask ourselves if that which we would scuttle as unnecessary ballast may not help us keep our equilibrium when the going is heavy.

I. *Embodiment.* Ralph Bunche once said, "To get an idea across, wrap it up in a person." And that is exactly what God has done. The meaning of Bethlehem, Nazareth, and Golgotha is this: God has wrapped up his concern, his love, his redemptive initiative in a person—Jesus of Nazareth. When Jesus said, "He that hath seen me hath seen the Father" (John 14:9), he was saying in effect, "God has wrapped himself up in my person. If you want to know what God is, look at me. If you want to know what concerns God, observe what concerns me." "I and the Father are one" (John 10:30). Jesus is the means by which we know God.

Jesus himself faced the question of his retirement from Earth's scene and spoke of it to his disciples: "I tell you most solemnly, whoever believes in me will perform the same works as I do myself; he will perform even greater works, because I am going to the Father" (John 14:12–13, Jerusalem Bible). And Jesus speaks of, even promises, to send his Spirit into the hearts of men. Just as Jesus came so that men might know God, so the Spirit comes that men may experience God. God is still in the business of wrapping himself up in persons— you and me, or any Christian—and we express that reality in the quality of our relationships with our brethren.

II. *Involvement.* This, of course, is the means by which we serve. We would be altogether wrong were we to conclude that the essence of Christianity is to withdraw from the world into splendid isolation. God became involved with the pain of the world—even the pangs of death—in Jesus Christ. The symbol of our faith—the cross—was not raised in a cathedral between two candles, but on a hill just outside a city, between two thieves. A road passed by that cross, a road so cosmopolitan that Pilate had the inscription written above the head of our Lord in three languages: Hebrew, Latin, and Greek. Below and around the cross were the kinds of people God loves, the kind for whom Christ died. The cynics talked smut, the thieves cursed, and the soldiers gambled for Jesus' robe. That is where Jesus was. That is where he died.

And those were the kind for whom Jesus died.

This is a cue for us. We come together to worship, and we must. But that is not the end of our Christian involvement; it is only the beginning. We go from there to "raise the cross in the marketplace," as George Macleod said.

The most incisive incursion into the real world that I know of was Jesus, who challenged the assumptions of the men who sat in the seats of power in his day, and paid for his daring with his life on a cross.

III. *Implementation.* And now I have an action word: *implementation.* How do you implement the God whose Spirit is in you in practical ways?

Your answer to this question will be as brilliant and surprising as your own drive, initiative, and intelligence. It will be in your sphere of action, where you make the scene.

But there may be more—there is more—than one sphere. There is the sphere in which you work, the sphere in which you make your home with your family, and the sphere of your church and its denominational outreach.

The symbol of our culture is the expressway cloverleaf. Christians have another symbol, however—a symbol that characterizes a unique lifestyle. That lifestyle moves in and through the culture (whatever it is) in time to its own beat. The symbol of that lifestyle is the cross. To most serious students of our society, it is obvious that what we need, more than anything else, is to come more completely under the influence of the cross. The ethic of the cross, the love of the cross, the concern of the cross, the involvement of the cross—these need to penetrate our society in meaningful and personal ways.—Ralph L. Murray[4]

---

[4]*Christ and the City* (Nashville: Broadman Press, 1970), pp. 11–20.

SUNDAY, DECEMBER 22, 2002
Lectionary Message

Topic: Mystery and Surprise
TEXT: Luke 1:26–38
Other Readings: 2 Sam. 7:1–11, 16; Luke 1:47–55; Rom. 16:25–27

I. *These are the days of expectation, planning, and getting ready.*

(a) Traveling grandparents have bags to pack and presents to wrap before the long trip. Pastors and choir members have extra services to prepare. Homemakers, flogged on by magazines and holiday specials, try frantically to create "the merriest Christmas ever." How will Christmas ever get here if we are not ready for it? How can we enjoy it unless the house is cleaned, the tree is trimmed, and everyone's favorite once-a-year dish is fixed just right?

(b) Sometimes it feels like we are setting an elaborate trap to capture memories we can pull out in the years to come. We weave a net of lights and cookies and cards and wrapping paper so we can grab the Christmas we have always dreamed of while it whisks by, and it speeds by more quickly each year than it did the year before.

II. *One way people survive in an increasingly complex world is by detaching themselves from it.*

(a) They put themselves above anything that calls for commitment or faith or complexity and give life a dismissive laugh when it gets too heavy. Life cannot hurt us if we are not engaged in it too deeply. The tragedy is that if you are not willing to risk the possibility that someone may give you something with no hidden agenda other than love, if you are not willing to be vulnerable to the possibility that things may happen for no reason other than the grace of God, then you are going to live a pretty dull life that is confined to your cynical expectations. There is no room for anything other than what fits your perception of how things are.

(b) What a shame it would be to prepare so hard for Christmas by doing all the things we are told we are supposed to do, and then to miss out on what God has prepared for us. How sad to be so preoccupied with getting ready for what we expect that we do not notice unexpected blessings when they fall right into our laps.

III. *God is always showering us with blessings for which we never asked, but a gift even greater than God's blessing is the faith to receive that blessing.*

(a) It is a gift to be able to see God's hand in life's pains and joys, knowing that they are not merely random events. Someone has wondered if there were other women the angel Gabriel approached before he went to Mary and said, "Greetings, favored one! The Lord is with you." If there were, did they look at Gabriel with a smirk and reply, "Yeah, right"?

(b) Who can imagine a virgin having a baby? It is humanly impossible, but then who can imagine creating a universe out of nothing? That is humanly inconceivable. Mary could accept the blessing God gave her because she believed what the angel told her: "Nothing will be impossible with God." God can make galaxies, so why could God not make a virgin a mother? Mary expected God to give blessings beyond human imagination.

(c) Consider how all Mary's plans and preparations were interrupted by God. History has idealized Mary as someone to admire from a distance, someone superhuman with whom we ordinary people do not have that much in common. Mary was an ordinary Jewish girl, preparing to marry an ordinary carpenter named Joseph. She was probably concerned with whatever it was girls engaged to be married were concerned with in those days.

(d) Mary had the gift of being able to accept something mysterious and incomprehensible. She had faith that there is more going on around us than we can possibly understand. So often it is in the ordinary that God comes to us in these days of preparation. God comes in the twinkle of a child's eye, in the quietness of a church, by the bedside of an elderly resident of the nursing home. Christmas is all about the spectacular showing up in unexpected places, like mangers on a winter's night.

IV. *On this third day before Christmas, remember that not even Mary was prepared for the perfect Christmas.* She was nowhere near a midwife, and the nursery was not prepared. Instead of bundling her baby into a brand new sleeper, she wrapped him in bands of cloth.

(a) Of course, preparing is part of the fun of the season. If Christmas just sneaked up on us and we did nothing to get ready for it, it would hardly be the same. Today's lectionary passages remind us that no matter how well we prepare, God can always surprise us. No matter how much we are on top of our holiday gift lists, there is still room in the middle of it all for God to astonish us with God's gifts. Even if you start preparing for it in January, even if you repeat the same traditions year after year, God has a way of breaking into all those expectations and doing something brand new and totally unexpected.

(b) For many people, these days of preparation are a time of excitement and joy. But if things get a little too intense and panic starts to set in, look around for some unexpected blessings—beautiful lights, a child's innocent eyes, a Christmas carol that unwraps a memory of some special joy from long ago. Sometimes the best gifts of Christmas are the ones we do not expect, the ones that come to us only when what we are prepared for is a surprise from God.—Stephens G. Lytch

ILLUSTRATIONS

FUTILE PLANNING.   Sometimes the plans we make are just not the right ones. In the former Soviet Union, the central planners had objectives for everything, whether they made sense or not. One large shoe factory consistently exceeded the production quotas the planners gave it. The manager was awarded a medal for meeting the plan so well. Only later did someone discover that the plant made shoes that were all the same size and all for the left foot. During Advent, it would be a shame to prepare so hard for all the wrong things.—Stephens G. Lytch

AMBIVALENCE.   *The Best Christmas Pageant Ever* by Barbara Robinson is one of the most popular Christmas novels ever. It is narrated by a girl whose mother is directing a Christmas pageant at their church. There is a scene in it that captures some of the ambivalence we have about Mary, who was probably as surprised at what happened to her nine months before Christmas as you or I would be if something similar happened to us.

The director of the pageant is reading the story of Christmas to the children who will be in the pageant, including the "horrible Herdmans," the worst kids in town, who had never heard the story before. The Herdmans listen more intently than anyone wished they had as the pageant director began reading:

"Joseph and Mary, his espoused wife, being great with child—"

"Pregnant!" yelled Ralph Herdman.

Well, that stirred things up. All the big kids began to giggle, and all the little kids wanted to know what was so funny, and Mother had to hammer on the floor with a blackboard pointer. "That's enough Ralph," she said, and went on with the story.

"I don't think it's very nice to say Mary was pregnant," Alice Wendleken whispered to me.

"But she was," I pointed out. In a way, though, I agreed with her. It sounded so ordinary. Anybody could be pregnant. "Great with child" sounded better for Mary.[5]

SERMON SUGGESTIONS

Topic: The Predecessor

TEXT: 2 Sam. 7:1–11, 16

(1) David's concern about an appropriate house for God (v. 2). (2) God's concern about a house for David (v. 11). (3) The ultimate, best house of all (v. 16; see also John 1:14).

Topic: The Remarkable Gospel

TEXT: Rom. 16:25–27

(1) What was a mystery is now manifest. (2) What was focused is now universal.

CONGREGATIONAL MUSIC

1. "Tell Out, My Soul," Luke 1:46–55; para. Timothy Dudley-Smith (1961)

   WOODLANDS, Walter Greatorex

   Based on the Song of Mary found in the New English Bible, this hymn is an excellent paraphrase of the Magnificat. It is further strengthened by the vibrant tune and would make a good beginning to a service of Advent worship.

2. "For Ages Women Hoped and Prayed," Jane Parker Huber (1986)

   VOX DILECTI, John B. Dykes (1868)

   This new hymn gives a woman's view of the Virgin Mary's experience. It could be sung in connection with the reading of the Annunciation story from either of the two lessons drawn from Luke 1.

3. "Long Ago, Prophets Knew," Fred Pratt Green (1970)

   PERSONET HODIE, *Piae Cantiones* (1582)

   This fine contemporary Advent hymn could be used in connection with the Old Testament reading from 2 Samuel 7 or the Epistle lesson in Romans 16:25–27. Its festive tune helps voice the mood of glad welcome expressed for the coming of the God-man, Jesus.

4. "To a Virgin Meek and Mild," Vigleik E. Boe and Oscar Overby (1935)

   LO DESEMBRE CONGELAT, Spanish carol; arr. D. P. Hustad

   This Advent carol focuses on the visit of the angel Gabriel to the Virgin Mary. It would therefore be a good response to the Gospel lesson in Luke 1:26–38.—Hugh T. McElrath

---

[5]*The Best Christmas Pageant Ever* (New York: Avon, 1972), p. 41.

WORSHIP AIDS

CALL TO WORSHIP.   "And I heard a great voice out of heaven saying, Behold, the tabernacle of God is with men, and he will dwell with them, and they shall be his people, and God himself shall be with them and be their God" (Rev. 21:3).

INVOCATION.   Because you make your home with us, O God, here and hereafter, we do not have to plead with you to be with us, for you are here. But we ask for a deepening awareness of what that means in our worship of you and in our fellowship with fellow Christians now.

OFFERTORY SENTENCE.   "And when they were come into the house, they saw the young child with Mary his mother and fell down and worshipped him: and when they had opened their treasures, they presented unto him gifts: gold and frankincense and myrrh" (Matt. 2:11).

OFFERTORY PRAYER.   Heavenly Father, we pray that in our giving and in our receiving, during this season and throughout the year, we might become instruments of your Spirit. We pray also that through our acceptance of the greatest gift, your son Jesus Christ, you are more clearly and perfectly revealed to each of us. Help us in turn to reflect the light of that gift throughout the world.—Kenneth M. Cox

PRAYER.   O thou everlasting God from whom all blessings flow, hear our prayer as again we call to remembrance the birth of thy Son, the Prince of Peace. We thank thee for his coming among us as a little child and his making for himself a place among the diverse peoples of the Earth where he could love and be loved. We think especially of the signs of his coming that the ages and sages set before us: thy sustaining providence through all the years as an ancient people awaited deliverance, the voices of prophets foretelling the direction and goal of human history, the shining star and the angel song in the heavens, and the wonder of that holy night when the whole creation hailed him in whom our human redemption had come near. With true believers everywhere, we rise today to sing, "Joy to the world! the Lord is come: let Earth receive her king."—Donald Macleod[6]

SERMON
Topic: Wisdom, Wonder, and Worship
Text: Matt. 1:18–2:12

When the Wise Men came to visit the Christ child centuries ago, they most probably did not come on the very day of the birth of Christ. Some scholars have speculated that they may have arrived several years later, because the Scriptures depict the Wise Men finding the young child with his mother in a house. No one can know for certain. I wonder if the Wise Men were ever the same after they invested so much of themselves to find the Christ Child. And do

---

[6]*Princeton Pulpit Prayers*

you think the shepherds went back to their sheep and did not look at themselves and life differently after their visit to the manger? Was there not something radically different in their attitude then?

When men and women encounter the power of the living Christ, their lives should be different because of it. When the apostle Paul met Christ, his life was never the same again. When an American reporter went to interview Albert Schweitzer and saw his ministry in Africa, the reporter's life was never the same again. When you and I kneel down and worship before the Christ in this Christmas season, I hope that our lives will not be the same again. We should not be able to live our lives in the same routine. He will have turned our face and feet to a new path. Christ challenges all of our old ways and directs us to a new way—his way. He opens us to more of the wonder, mystery, and grace of God than we have ever seen before. We cannot turn back to the old way. We move forward into his new way of love and service.

In a small town there had been a family of four, but now there were only three because the young son had died. The family members were having a difficult time adjusting to their grief. The father was the superintendent of the local post office. A few days before Christmas he was looking at some of the mail in the "what do you do with it" pile and noticed that several letters were addressed to Santa Claus. The handwriting on one of the letters was very familiar to him. He recognized that it was a letter from his own daughter. He opened it and read it. It said, "Dear Santa, Our family was once so happy till my little brother died. Mommy and Daddy are not like they used to be, and when I ask Daddy about it, he says that only eternity will ever change it. I don't know what eternity is, but if you have any extra eternities, would you leave one of them at our house on Christmas Eve?" From his small child the father sensed what had happened to him and his family. When he went home that day, he was different. His daughter noticed that her father had received his present of eternity early. In Jesus Christ, God has opened the doors of eternity and has revealed to us his presence, love, and grace. Let us respond to it. We shall be different because of it. Kneel down in wonder and awe before the Incarnate Christ whose birth we celebrate.

O God of mystery, God of wonder, God of light, and God of love, encircle us this Christmas season in the greatness of your grace as we kneel down before your Son.—William Powell Tuck

SUNDAY, DECEMBER 29, 2002
Lectionary Message

Topic: God's Inbreak
TEXT: Luke 2:22–40
Other Readings: Isa. 61:10–62:3; Ps. 148; Gal. 4:4–7

I. *The Gospels tell us very little about Jesus' life as a child.*

(a) Matthew and Luke are the only two Gospels that mention Jesus' life before the age of thirty, and their descriptions are sparing. We do not know what life was like around the carpenter shop in Nazareth or who Jesus' playmates were. In fact, the Gospels seem to be more interested in telling us about the reactions of those who encountered the boy Jesus than in describing his childhood. These reactions are surprisingly few and far between.

(b) Hundreds of people must have met Jesus before he started his public ministry, yet only a handful ever knew that the one they encountered was the Son of God. On the night Jesus was born, Bethlehem was packed with people who had gathered for the census, yet it was only the rude, uncouth, and probably irreligious shepherds who saw the angel chorus and paid homage to the baby. The Magi could not have been the only people to see the star that heralded Jesus' birth, yet these foreigners were the only ones to recognize it as a sign that the King of Kings had been born. The Temple was surely crowded when Mary and Joseph brought their two-month-old son for his dedication, yet it was only Simeon and Anna who recognized him as the Messiah. These occasions make one wonder how many people today encounter Christ right before their eyes but do not recognize him in the midst of the commonplace affairs of life.

II. *Simeon and Anna looked at a baby boy in the arms of a poor couple from the hinterlands and saw the ruler of creation.* They can give us guidance as we look for the Holy One in the events of our lives.

(a) Simeon and Anna belonged to a group of people who lived around the Temple in Jerusalem. Like many others of their day, they were hoping that God would send someone to reestablish the halcyon days of David's kingdom, when Israel was among the greatest of all nations. They were not religious professionals like the priests and scribes, who made their living performing rituals and teaching Scripture to devout Jews. Simeon and Anna were poor. They probably had little formal education. They stayed around the Temple so they could worship every time the doors opened. They passed their days watching the people come and go, talking about religion with anyone who would take the time, doing chores for the priests, and perhaps doing a little begging on the side to help make ends meet.

(b) Simeon and Anna had seen many people go in and out the Temple gates. Anna was eighty-four. She had lived around the Temple ever since she was widowed at the age of nineteen. Simeon was no youngster either, but he was convinced that God was going to send the Messiah before he died. Simeon and Anna were the sort of people who blended into the landscape of the Temple, the ones an average visitor would barely notice while hurrying by on the way to the important business that lay inside the sanctuary.

III. *There was nothing unusual about Mary and Joseph and their son that would have made anyone notice them over all the other faithful who came to the Temple that day, but something inside Simeon and Anna told them this was no ordinary family.*

(a) Something told them that here was the one for whom they had been waiting all those years. How did they know? At least the shepherds had heard angels and the Wise Men had seen a star. What had these elderly Temple-dwellers seen except the same sight everyone else in Jerusalem saw over and over, day after day: an ordinary family bringing their humble offering to perform their religious duty?

(b) Simeon and Anna recognized Jesus because they expected to see God at work even in the commonplace events of their poor lives. Looking for God, they were ready to see him when he appeared. There was still an element of mystery in their discovery. Not everyone who was devout and expectant recognized the Messiah. The Holy Spirit chose to show Simeon and Anna who Jesus was. It was not something they deduced for themselves. Nevertheless, Simeon and Anna were prepared when the Spirit revealed Jesus to them.

IV. *When we expect to see God moving in our lives, we can begin to make sense out of where we have been and where we are going.*

(a) Knowing that God came among us as a poor baby and entered the lives of people like Simeon and Anna, we can look back over our own lives and find evidence that God has had a part in them. If, like that faithful pair, we look for God to work in his creation, we can trust that God is always moving through human history in spite of our greed and shortcomings, showing himself to whomever will see.

(b) As Christians, we look at things differently. We see every event that happens as an arena in which God can work. Paul told his friends the Colossians to "let the peace of Christ rule in your hearts. . . . Whatever you do in word or deed, do everything in the name of the Lord Jesus, giving thanks to God the Father through him." When we let Christ rule in our hearts, we attune ourselves to see God at work in our lives. Our perspective becomes more like God's perspective. We expect to see God's hand in every part of his world, even that tiny part we inhabit. When Christ is the one who guides, we can recognize the Eternal One when he breaks into our lives, just as he did so unobtrusively for Simeon and Anna.—Stephens G. Lytch

ILLUSTRATION

GOD SPEAKING.   Her husband had just come out of the operating room after life-threatening surgery. He was in serious but stable condition. Because he was still under the effects of the anesthesia, she could not talk with him, and it would be hours before the doctors would have anything to report about the results of the lab tests. When she left the hospital late in the afternoon, she was anxious, worried, and deeply concerned about what the future held in store. It had been raining that day, but as she drove home it began to clear. In the distance, over a field, she saw a rainbow. It was a breathtaking sight, though not an unusual one following a summer storm. But this was more than a rainbow. All of a sudden she felt absolutely assured that everything would be all right. Something told her that God was with her. She had nothing about which to worry. The rainbow was, for her, a message from God. No one else she talked to later had even noticed it. We were all too busy doing other things. But through that common late summer event she had felt God, the eternal Creator of the universe, speaking directly to her.—Stephens G. Lytch

SERMON SUGGESTIONS

Topic: Fulfillment in Jesus the Christ
TEXT: Isa. 61:10–62:3
(1) The growth of the Church (61:10–11). (2) The message of the Church (62:1–2). (3) The glory of the Church (62:3).

Topic: Our New Status
TEXT: Gal. 4:4–7
(1) It came in God's good time. (2) It made us sons—children with special standing and privilege. (3) It opened our hearts to the Spirit of Jesus, with a sense of belonging and security.

CONGREGATIONAL MUSIC

1. "Sing Praise to the Lord," Pss. 148, 150; Henry W. Parker (1875)
   LAUDATE DOMINUM, C. Hubert Parry (1894)
   The celebrative spirit of the Psalter reading finds exuberant expression in this free paraphrase set in the declamatory style of the Parry tune.

2. "Now May Your Servant, Lord," Luke 2:29–32; vers. Dewey Westra (1931)

NUNC DIMITTIS, Louis Bourgeois (1551)

The Gospel lesson includes the Song of Simeon, the righteous and devout man who blessed God that he had finally seen the Lord's Christ. This canticle set to a venerable psalm tune could follow the reading of the Gospel.

3. "Because He Lives," Gloria and William J. Gaither (1971)

RESURRECTION, William J. Gaither (1971)

The Galatian passage speaks of God sending his Son in the fullness of time to redeem the world. This modern gospel hymn would be a good response, therefore, to the Gospel lesson.

4. "Jesus, Thy Blood and Righteousness," Nicholaus L. V. Zinzendorf (1739); trans. John Wesley (1740)

The prophecy of Isaiah describes the rejoicing that comes when the Lord clothes one with the garments of salvation (Isa. 61:10). This great Moravian song Christianizes that thought through exulting praise of Jesus' blood and righteousness that metaphorically clothe the believer.—Hugh T. McElrath

WORSHIP AIDS

CALL TO WORSHIP.   "But thanks be to God, who gives us the victory through our Lord Jesus Christ" (1 Cor. 15:57 NKJV).

INVOCATION.   We thank you, blessed Father, that we never have to be defeated amid life's challenges and struggles, for you give us victory through our Lord Jesus Christ. Let your strength course through our lives today as we lift our hearts to you in faith and praise, that we may be more than conquerors through him who loved us and gave himself for us.

OFFERTORY SENTENCE.   "For God is not unjust to forget your work and labor of love which you have shown toward his name, in that you have ministered to the saints, and do minister" (Heb. 6:10 NKJV).

OFFERTORY PRAYER.   Lord, we know that we cannot buy your favor, for you first loved us, undeserving as we are. But we are assured that you do not forget what we do for the advancement of your Kingdom, and we now receive with thanksgiving the privilege of giving, and we seek the joy of faithful stewardship.

PRAYER.   O God, whose throne of grace is hymned with continual praise and thanksgiving, we add our voices to those of all the saints and angels, saying, "Thank you, Lord, for your love and mercy and power that flow constantly into our universe, filling it with hope and energy and redemption!" There is nothing in us that deserves your gifts, yet you have chosen to share yourself with the very least of us and to send your bounty upon us even when our hearts have not been turned in your direction. Help us to turn our thoughts and lives to you in recognition and gratitude, and to align ourselves with your hopes and vision for our world. Use us as instruments for loving your little ones in all the Earth—for seeing that they are fed and clothed and educated, that they receive the medical and technical aid they need, and that, with all of this, they hear the good news of your Kingdom in Jesus Christ. Bless with your mercy in this holiday season all children who are away from home, all students who travel on the highways, all the elderly who languish in pain or loneliness, all patients in hospitals and inmates in prisons, all ministers and teachers of the gospel, and all servants of society. Let the hope that was born at the coming of Christ continue to flower among us, leading us to new heights of commitment and new depths of love for one another. For yours are the kingdom and the power and the glory forever.—John Killinger

SERMON
Topic: What Is Your Life Expectancy?
TEXT: Isa. 55; Matt. 13:53–58

"The whole creation is on tiptoe to see the wonderful sight of the children of God coming into their own" (Rom. 8:19 JBP). "Nothing to look backward to with pride. Nothing to look forward to with hope" (Robert Frost).

What is your life expectancy? As someone has put it, rather cynically, "What is the good of a longer life expectancy with nothing to expect?"

Life for many of us will never be any different, for we do not expect it to be different. We would probably be disappointed if it did turn out differently. Many a life is plagued by self-fulfilling prophecies. We find in life what we look for. If we fear the worst, the worst has a way of catching up with us. Life is as big as you make it, or as little.

Is this not the mood that our New Testament lesson addresses? It is the familiar story of Jesus returning to his hometown of Nazareth in the early days of his ministry. It seems natural enough that he would want to share the good news of the coming of the Kingdom of God with his compatriots. But they were not expecting the long-promised Messiah to appear as one of them. They objected, "This fellow can't be the Messiah. We know him. He is one of us. He is Joseph's and Mary's boy." Because they didn't expect God to raise up the Messiah from among them, they missed their day of visitation. Through the centuries, the epitaph has stood over that sleepy little town of Nazareth, "He could do no mighty works there because of their unbelief"—their lack of expectancy.

But let us not too quickly condemn the Nazarenes for their unbelief, for their blindness. Do we not often miss the coming of the Kingdom in the common, everyday events of our humdrum lives because we are not expecting God to draw so near—not in the familiar, not to our mess? This is the real tragedy: that we miss our day of visitation!

The opposite of unbelief is belief, or faith; the opposite of nonexpectancy is expectancy, or hope. Whatever else the call of the gospel is, it is a call to faith and hope. In the biblical text, the apostle Paul challenges us to live by hope: "Live life on tiptoe to see the wonderful fulfillment of the children of God." This is the expectancy that faith in the living God excites—to get up on our toes in anticipation of the coming of the Kingdom to us and to the whole creation.

Even in later years, life is calling us to be so much more than we are—than we have been.

Do I need to remind anyone that Church membership must never be interpreted as the end of one's pilgrimage, but as the beginning. We are to "grow and grow and grow in the grace and knowledge of our Lord and Savior Jesus Christ."

In one of Charles Schulz's cartoons of the Peanuts characters, Charlie Brown comes downstairs for breakfast, sleepily rubbing his eyes, trying to get them open, and exclaims to his mother, "I think I've discovered my trouble in getting out of bed; I'm allergic to morning!"

There are persons who develop an allergy to morning, but the real tragedy is when one develops an allergy to life. Life is not the paltry thing in which many of us are engaged.

John, in his Gospel, warns that there are those who love the darkness rather than the light. They are allergic to morning—the dawning of God's new day. The call of the gospel to every generation is, "Awake all you who sleep, and Christ shall give you life."

Most of us are familiar with the aphorism, "As long as there is life, there is hope." But it is our thesis that as long as there is hope, there is life. Life can be forestalled by our unbelief.

Fear or faith—there is no dilemma so full of consequence.

To live with expectancy—to get off our heels and onto our toes, to live with hope—is to choose to live by faith in the living God—the God who raised Jesus from the dead. When we discover ourselves low on hope, could it be that we are living on the wrong side of Easter?

The issue, it seems to me, is not whether God is available, but are we available? God is present to us in the greatest way he can be. As the apostle Paul declares in the chapter from which our text is taken, "He who spared not his own son but delivered him up for us all, how shall he not with him freely give us all things?"

A grace freely given is the theme of our Old Testament lesson, too. God speaking through the prophet Isaiah invites us to "come, buy and eat! Come, buy wine and milk without money and without price." What a graphic image of God's grace so freely given. God continues: "Listen to me and eat what is good, and delight yourselves in fatness. Incline your ear, and come to me; hear, that your soul may live; and I will make you an everlasting covenant, my steadfast sure love for David."—John Thompson

MESSAGES FOR COMMUNION SERVICES

SERMON SUGGESTIONS

Topic: The Lord's Supper

TEXT: Luke 22:14–20; 1 Cor. 11:23ff

It seems as though our nation has had a lapse of memory in regard to the sacred. Life seems more expendable today than it ever did before. Children are less courteous, senior adults are less patient, the church is less vocal, and people are less hopeful. All these things can be attributed to loss of memory. Just as people lose their ability to recollect things when they get older, a nation, it seems, can have the same problem. The idea of remembrance is at the heart of the Christian faith and is found specifically in the Lord's Supper. Jesus commanded, "Do this and remember me." Many churches continue to take the Lord's Supper on a regular basis, but it seems as though everyone has forgotten the Lord who commanded the action. A closer look at the institution of and regulations regarding the Lord's Supper will perhaps allow us to reassess our memory loss and redefine our priorities.

I. *It was Jesus' plan* (Luke 22:14–18). The first thing that is seen clearly is that it was Jesus' idea to take Communion. Why? He wanted the disciples to make a habit of remembering who he was and what he did. He broke his body, he shed his blood, and he offered them free salvation and an abundant life. Some things in life are better left forgotten; however, the suffering of Christ should never be overlooked. Why should we remember? Well, at least a couple of reasons can be given. First, remembering reminds us of God's great love shown to us in the sacrifice of Christ on the cross. It was the ultimate expression of love. Second, remembering reminds us how seriously God takes sin. One need not think that simply because one has been forgiven God does not take one's sin seriously. Dietrich Bonhoeffer noted, in *The Cost of Discipleship*, that although grace is free to all who believe, it is not cheap. The Lord's Supper recalls the love of God toward sinners and the wrath of God against all sin.

II. *It was for his purpose* (Luke 22:19–20). Although God made it clear that he owes nothing to any human, it is quite obvious that humankind owes much to God. Communion is one event that is based on the assumption that we owe a great debt to our Lord.

The observance of Communion is multifaceted. First, it commemorates the Lord's sacrifice. Second, it celebrates our salvation. Third, it allows us to contemplate our sin and the seriousness of that sin. Finally, it challenges us to reevaluate our lifestyle. Through the acts of commemoration, celebration, contemplation, and reevaluation, the Lord's Supper becomes an important and effective aspect of the Christian life. Through the remembrance of the Lord's sacrifice, we believers become more committed to our missions and more serious about our holiness as well as about God's glory.

III. *It was by his rules* (1 Cor. 11:23–32). The Church wasted no time in desecrating this wonderful practice that was modeled, performed, and commanded by our Lord. The Church at Corinth had many problems. Its members were gluttonous, greedy, competitive, and unloving. The priority of remembrance was demonstrated in their idea of Communion, which consisted of both feast and famine, drunkenness and thirst. Paul noted that many were full and some were hungry, many were drunk and some had nothing to drink at all. He exclaimed, "This is not the Lord's Supper!" He then described exactly what the Lord's Supper is: It is a time of remembrance. The very words "Do this in remembrance of me" were at the heart of Paul's explanation. We are to remember the physical sacrifice of Jesus and recall God's wrath against our sin. Because of the seriousness of the sacrament, Paul commanded the people to examine themselves. If they did not, they would be accused of drinking in an unworthy manner, and therefore "drink judgment against themselves" (v. 29 NRSV).

IV. *Conclusion.* To summarize, the Lord's Supper can be a time of glorious remembrance, of praise and worship, or a time of obstinate rebellion and condemnation. The result comes in the dual revelation of God's holiness and humankind's sinfulness. It is during this time and for this purpose, then, that we take Communion. Therefore let us begin in prayer to give honor to God and to ask the mandatory questions of self-examination.

Dear God, you are almighty in your ways and your knowledge is unreachable. You are the only true God, who gives and takes life at your discretion. However, you are also our Savior. You are both the standard for holiness and the avenue to holiness. Your sacrifice of mercy leads us, as your children, to confess our sins to you. Cleanse us of our impurities, forgive us our unholy thoughts and actions. Lord, take this as your time; speak to us, convict us by your Holy Spirit, and lead us into your will. In Christ's name, Amen.—Jeffrey D. Brown

Topic: Communion Sunday—Understanding the Supper, Knowing Its Names
TEXT: 2 Cor. 11:23–26

Do you understand the meaning of the Lord's Supper? Unfortunately there is a lot of misunderstanding about it. Down through the years, arguments over this particular celebration has been a bone of contention among religious groups. It has led to furious debates and fractured fellowships. It is a tragedy that what God intended to be a reminder of what we have in common has often been a reminder of what separates us.

Do we understand it? If someone came up to you and asked you to explain the meaning and significance of the Lord's Supper, what would you tell them? Who is it for? What does it mean? What is supposed to happen to us because we go through it? Can you answer those questions? We need to understand what we do when we celebrate it in our worship experience. What I want to do is help us understand its meaning by sharing with you the four names by which it is known. Knowing these names will help us as we seek to explain the meaning of this practice to others.

I. *It is known as the Lord's Supper.* This is the name I prefer and use more than any other. I like it because it reminds us, for one thing, that it is the *Lord's* Supper. He is the one who brought this practice into being. It was on the night in the upper room, after they had eaten the Passover meal that celebrated their deliverance from slavery in Egypt, that Jesus added this part: He took the bread, he took the cup, and he said, "Do this in remembrance of me." This supper was not the creation of any church. It was not the idea of any man or denomination. It was created by Christ for every one of us. He is the one who started it. He is the one who invited us to it.

That is why I do not believe in what is often called "closed Communion," which means that only those who are members of a particular local church can celebrate in the Communion. It is not the church's supper, it is Christ's. He is the one who does the inviting and his invitation is to whosoever will believe. This supper is for all who believe in Christ as Savior and Lord. All believers are invited to come and participate.

The Lord's Supper is also a symbol of what he has done for us. He said, "Do this in remembrance of me." That's a key phrase in our understanding of the Lord's Supper. He set this meal apart to aid our memory because it would be easy to forget, with all that goes on in life, exactly what the heart of the gospel is. The Lord's Supper is meant to remind us what Christ did. It is a symbol, a signpost, something that prods our imagination and causes us to think of another reality. The danger is that the symbol sometimes comes to be identified with the reality, and it must not be. The flag is a symbol of our country. It points to the reality of our country, but it is not our country. We must not worship the flag; we must serve the United States. The Bible is a signpost that points beyond itself to Christ. We must not fall into the habit of worshiping the Bible. Instead, we must make sure we worship the Christ to which the Bible points us. The elements of the Lord's Supper are symbols: the bread that symbolizes his body broken on the cross, and the cup that symbolizes his blood shed for us on the cross. They are symbols that point to the Crucifixion and Resurrection of Christ. They remind us that God loves us so much that he was willing to die on our behalf to give us love we don't deserve, forgiveness we desperately need, and hope for eternal life that we must have. He died on a cross to bring about these things. Remember, the cross is empty. This reminds us that Christ is risen. He died on a cross and conquered it. Our sins can be forgiven, love can be known and known forever, and each one of us can be part of the Kingdom of God because Christ loved us so much he was willing to have his body broken and his blood shed for each one of us.

When we come to this table, we are to remember that Christ, who died for us, also rose for us because he loves us. The heart of our gospel is the death and Resurrection symbolized in the Lord's Supper.

II. *It is called Eucharist.* This is a strange word to us. It's how our Catholic friends refer to their celebration of the Lord's Supper. It's a good word. It means "to give thanks." To celebrate the Eucharist is an act of thanksgiving to God for what he has done.

Surely this is what we ought to be doing, too, as we remember all that Christ has done for us. We ought to be filled with the spirit of thanksgiving and joy when we participate. It is a way of thanking God, for he has saved us from our sins and our lostness. In a movie called *Family Life,* a daughter, Jan, feels alienated from her parents. Her parents are decent people, but somehow their relationship has fractured. They cannot communicate, cannot get together. The picture portrays Jan's misery and frustration. At one point she and her boyfriend put paint all over the garden. They break expensive furniture all through the house, showing that the daughter is not happy, that she feels lost and cut off.[1]

This is how we feel when we have cut ourselves off from God: frustrated, miserable, and empty inside. No matter what we do to numb that emptiness, it doesn't happen, because we're cut off from the one with whom we need to be at home. What Christ has done is to remove all the barriers that keep us from going home, all the barriers that keep us from being

---

[1]Alec Gilmore, *Tomorrow's Pulpit* (Valley Forge, Pa.: Judson Press, 1975), p. 33.

at one with our heavenly Parent. Each one of us can go home again. Christ has made it possible. No one needs to be cut off from God, because Christ has taken care of our rebellion and its consequences. If we want to go home to God, we can.

To remember this ought to cause us to offer praise to God, to offer thanks. That's what we do by our participation in this. We thank God for his willingness to offer us a chance to be his children again.

III. *It is called Communion,* or the Communion service. The word *communion* means "to experience another" and "to have close union with another." When we commune with nature, we experience nature. When we commune with a friend, we experience friendship. When we commune with God, we experience God. We do not remember and celebrate what a dead person did. We celebrate a living presence. Because Christ rose from the dead, he is alive, and the hope of our celebration is that we will experience the presence of God in a new way inside us.

The Scripture tells us that where two or three are gathered, God is with us (Matt. 18:20). We are two or three; therefore, the presence of God is indeed with us in this experience of worship. The hope of our worship is that we will experience Christ as really here in our Communion, as really speaking to us through the bread and the cup.

A woman went to a worship service and the preacher was preaching about Christ. The woman said, "It got so that I felt Christ had come right down the aisle and looked at me and said, 'Here am I.'" It is my belief, faith, and hope that we can experience his presence in what we do. As we remember and give thanks for what he has done, he is here reaching out to us with the same love and forgiveness he offered then. We can know it again.

IV. *It is called Sacrament.* The word *sacrament* scares us, but it should not, because it's a good word. It means "oath of allegiance." It originally meant the oath that a Roman soldier swore at the beginning of his military service. He swore that he would serve the emperor to his own death. Every now and then throughout his career, the soldier would be asked to renew his sacrament, his oath of allegiance, his pledge of loyalty.

In this sacrament, we remember Christ's sacrament to us. He pledged his loyalty to us to the death. He pledged to God that he would do whatever was needed to bring us a chance at salvation. He kept that pledge, all the way through death, and beyond.

When we remember all of this, we will hopefully renew our sacrament, our pledge of allegiance, our oath of loyalty. We made this pledge, didn't we? When we became Christians, we were full of all sorts of promises and pledges. We were going to be this and we were going to do that. Sometimes, in the rush and busyness of life, we forget the promises we have made. But we can renew them! The experience of celebrating this sacrament is supposed to do that for us. As we participate, remember, give thanks, and open ourselves up to Christ's presence, the result will hopefully be that we will renew the pledges, the commitments, and the loyalties we offered him. We will do what we said we would do: serve him to the end.

Sometimes a couple comes and wants to renew their vows. They made them at the beginning of their marriage, but sometimes promises made at the beginning of marriage get broken or forgotten. So some couples come to me and say, "We need to renew our vows." We enter a sanctuary, where they speak their vows to one another again, renewing their commitment to keep the promises of love. In the same sense, when we participate in this sacrament, it is our way of renewing our promises of commitment and love that we have made to the Lord.

So, we come to celebrate the Lord's Supper. He invites us to do that, to remember the sacrifice he made on our behalf. We celebrate this Eucharist by giving thanks to God for doing what he did for us. We celebrate this Communion as we open ourselves up to the living presence of Christ, who is here even now. We celebrate this sacrament as we renew our pledge of loyalty, devotion, and commitment to the Christ who committed himself to us.

There's something about the celebration of the Lord's Supper that speaks to us. It is the gospel not only of the word but of the eye. It does remind us; it opens us up to all that Christ did and was and all that he wants to be. One woman said, "Every time I celebrate the Supper, it makes me want to love him more." I hope so, because we can't love him too much. We need to love him more. To remember and celebrate will lead us to do just that. Let us remember and celebrate!—Hugh Litchfield[2]

Topic: God Is Love
TEXT: 1 John 4:7–21

I. According to George Gallup, the past fifty years of U.S. polls have consistently shown that 95 percent of Americans believe in God or some higher power. Only one in twenty Americans could be called atheist or agnostic. More than 90 percent want their children to have a religious education, while about four out of five adults acknowledge their need for spiritual growth and think seriously about their relationship with God. We are a nation of believers. It would seem that we have come of age, that there is little left to be done in the work of religion in America; but the practice of faith does not match the expression of opinions and beliefs.

Only one-third of the people claim to have had a life-changing religious experience. That experience is identified by Gallup as "evangelicalism," but the issue here is more than which brand of church you happen to prefer. What possible difference could it make that you believe in God if you have no experience of God in your life? Although two-thirds of people affirm the need for church in society, 44 percent of Americans are unchurched. Although 40 percent claim to attend church regularly, the facts do not support the claim. People exaggerate their actual involvement in church either because they are dishonest or because they do not see the connection between faith and practice.

A few generations before polls became popular, the Epistle writer James (2:19) questioned the importance of faith without works: "You believe that God is one; you do well. Even the demons believe—and shudder." James challenged the Church to practice faith. The Christian religion is not a head exercise completed in the opinion polls. Religion, for James, was a matter of practice (1:27): "to care for orphans and widows in their distress, and to keep oneself unstained by the world." The harsh words of Jesus for the Pharisees focused not on their love of the Law or their religious beliefs; the word he used was *hypocrisy*—the dissociation of faith and life. That was and is the practical issue of the "great commandment" to love both God and neighbor.

People are more than bodies. We are connected to God at the spiritual center of ourselves. You cannot explain the nature of a person simply through biology or chemistry. The mystery of love is directly connected to the mystery of God. John said that we ought to love one

---

[2]*Sermons on Those Other Special Days* (Nashville: Broadman Press, 1990), pp. 128–133.

another. Obviously that would solve our problems of conflict and violence in this world. It is like telling our children to "play nice." They need a little more to go on than our assumption that they know what it means to be nice.

John anchors the call to love one another in the nature of God, for "God is love." Love stands at the center of the nature of God. Our puny understanding of human psychology and biology does not define love. The nature, the character, of God determines the meaning of love.

II. *Love is experience in life.* In an attempt to explain the task of translating and interpreting the Bible, Bill Hull said that words have uses rather than meanings. Dictionaries do not last. They are based on the practice and use of terms and therefore have to be rewritten periodically. The Bible needs to be retranslated periodically because human language keeps changing. The words of our faith are rooted in the practices of the people of God. We are reminded that the Word spoken by God to the world was more than words, certainly more than ink on paper. In Christ, "the Word became flesh." In Christians, the Word must be expressed in action.

Love has a downside. People who hate, whose behavior is destructive, give evidence of the absence of God in their lives. Giving people, who live with compassion toward others, give evidence of the presence of God. We have a problem in our society that we cannot ignore. Each week about one in five households experiences an act of violence. Spousal-abuse shelters have cropped up all over the country to protect women and children from men who speak words of love but perform acts of anger and injury. Shall we believe the words or the actions? It gets into the Church. John had harsh words for people who claim to love God while expressing hatred toward their siblings.

Love is the practice of the presence of God in our lives. You can understand the meaning of love only as you watch the acts of God through the ages, especially the act of God in Christ. Jesus said, "There is no greater love than this, to lay down one's life for one's friends." There is good evidence that the Twelve did not have the foggiest notion of what Jesus was about. They were always asking the wrong question or giving the wrong answer. The evidence of a God of love comes through in action. The apostles saw people who had been hopelessly shut out from the rest of society welcomed into the fellowship of the Kingdom. The lame walked, the blind saw, the lepers were healed, the prostitute was cleansed, the mentally ill were made whole, and criminals became philanthropists. Hearing the abstract Word that we ought to love our enemies did not "take" until the apostles heard Christ pray from the cross for the forgiveness of his executioners.

Your religious opinions and even your theological positions on the major issues of our faith are of secondary importance to the faith you live. Let the words of our mouths and the meditations of our hearts be acceptable to you, O Lord our God, and let your love be known through our acts. Amen.—Larry Dipboye

Topic: Coming Down from the Mountain
TEXT: Luke 9:28–36

Sometime after World War I, the box camera became a basic instrument for recording significant family events. The ability to capture the sight of a newborn child, a proud graduate, a family vacation, or a final visit with elderly relatives opened new doors for tracing family history and forced us to distinguish the important from the ordinary in our lives. We continue to make statements of value when we come together and pull out our cameras. The Gospels are like that. The four albums of the ministry of Jesus reflect the interests and commitments of the ones who gathered them. When Matthew, Mark, and Luke agree on the significance of an event—such as the Transfiguration of Jesus—we need to pay special attention, even if we have trouble understanding.

Nothing in our experience compares with the changes that took place in the face and clothing of Jesus while he was praying on the mountain with Peter, James, and John. Some believe that this event belongs in the Easter revelations at the end of the Gospels; that like a misplaced photo, it was pasted into the wrong page of the album. It was certainly a unique event. Most of the visionary experience in the Gospels is limited to Jesus' birth and Resurrection. The Transfiguration must have been a significant moment; it must have been more than just another vision. Yet the change that took place in Christ and the appearance of Elijah and Moses flowed out of the ordinary. Nothing mystical is reported to have happened during the climb up the mountain or in the pause to rest and pray; yet the Transfiguration of Christ and the appearance of Elijah and Moses seem to have come in the twilight of sleep for the three followers of Christ.

This was a pivotal moment in the life of Christ. The confession of Peter at Casarea Philippi was the watershed event in the Gospels. From that point on, every passage was a way to the cross. The glory of God shining in the face of Jesus was a statement about the place of Christ in the work of God, and preparation for the confusion and contradiction that Christians encounter in the cross. The Transfiguration of Christ was almost certainly described with the mountaintop experience of Moses in mind. The cloud that descended on Moses was a symbol of the presence of God. From the cloud Moses received authority and detailed directions for the life of the nation. A cloud descended on Jesus at the Transfiguration, and the disciples heard a voice from the cloud saying, "This is my Son, my chosen; listen to him!" Elijah and Moses—prophets of messianic significance—appeared with Jesus. Only Luke records that the visitors' conversation was about Jesus' departure—perhaps about his death, or even his exodus.

Rudolf Schnackenburg declares that the Transfiguration was the "manifestation of his hidden glory despite his imminent death, and even more, vindication of Jesus' way of death and divine authentication of his words." Two significant revelations prepared the disciples for this moment: (1) Peter confessed that Jesus was the Messiah of God, and (2) Jesus predicted his own suffering and death. Here was a photographic moment that signaled a turn of events toward the cross. Whether or not it is a misplaced Resurrection appearance, it is a call to follow Christ all the way to the cross.

The vision of the eternal glory of God carries us through the devastation of human tragedy. The Transfiguration falls at the right point in the Gospel—exactly where the disciples need a vision of divine authority and presence to keep them going. Matthew specifically calls what the disciples saw "a vision." A vision is sometimes a peek into the future, but this event was more than a forecast. The Transfiguration was a revelation of the glory of God. To call it an inspiration sounds too much like singing birds and beautiful sunsets. The description in this Gospel is an indelible mental picture of the divine presence in the life of Christ that dominates the meaning of his death. We need vision to see beyond the devastating prospect of the cross.

Peter, James, and John came down from the mountain with a vision of the glory of God in the face of Jesus. When the cross came, with all of its horror, they had a vision of an eternal God greater than the moment, a vision of an unspeakable glory of God greater than the evil of the cross.—Larry Dipboye

Topic: Inescapable
TEXT: Gen. 3:8–9; Ps. 139:7–12

God could have abandoned Adam and Eve in the Garden of Eden after the Fall. He could have given up on them because of their sin. But he came seeking, searching, and asking, "Adam, where are you?" This was not a question about location. It was a question about divine love. God knew where Adam was physically. What God wanted was to lead Adam to take responsibility for his actions.

Jesus said of himself, "For the Son of Man came to seek and to save the lost" (Luke 19:10). Luke 15 contains three of Jesus' parables: the lost sheep, the lost coin, and the lost boys. Each of these memorable stories depicts God as one who seeks the lost.

The Lord's presence is inescapable. In the biblical story of Jonah we find a nationalistic prophet. Jonah was a superpatriot who resented God's universal love of all nations. When the Lord called him to prophesy in Nineveh, he did not want to—but not because he feared failure. Rather, he was afraid he might succeed. If he preached and they repented, God would forgive and spare the people of Nineveh. Jonah preferred to see them blasted!

In an effort to escape the call of God to go and preach in Nineveh, Jonah took a ship to Spain, at the far end of the Mediterranean world. As we all know, his escape was rudely intercepted by a great fish.

In this experience, Jonah learned that God cared for all people and nations, not simply his own. There was also the gospel of a second chance in Jonah's experience. When he repented and prayed, he was forgiven and given another opportunity. He eventually went to Nineveh, preached, and saw his message received. The greatest lesson for Jonah was that the Lord's presence is inescapable.

Now consider the message found in Psalm 139. The divine presence is real in heaven, on Earth, and even in Sheol (the grave or the abode of the dead). The poet sang, "If I take the wings of the morning. . . ." Flying from the United States to Europe, one spends the shortest night of one's life. One is going toward the sunrise. Day breaks about 2:00 A.M., New York time.

The psalmist also sang, "If I . . . dwell in the uttermost parts of the sea, even there . . . thy right hand shall hold me." I served as a member of an ordination council. The minister being examined gave his testimony to the examining group. He had felt the call of God to the ministry when he was a young man. But he was not interested in preaching. Instead, he joined the U.S. Navy. This did not, however, enable him to escape the call. To his amazement, the divine presence was equally as strong on the far side of the Earth as it had been at home, and the sense of call was as insistent as ever. Finally he gave into it and became a minister.

The poet concluded that even the darkness is not dark to God. We may go through dark days of doubt, failure, guilt, or grief. But our Heavenly Father is always with us. We can count on his presence and help.

The Lord's presence is inescapable. Saul tried to evade it and kicked "against the pricks" (Acts 9:5 KJV). However, he eventually had to confront the Lord and faith's claim. He became the missionary apostle Paul.

Francis Thompson ran from the Lord and his calling. He was a religious man who grew up in a Christian home. He studied for the Christian ministry. Giving up on that, he studied for medicine. Failing at that, he became a drug addict. Thompson came to the point where he had absolutely nothing left except his love of poetry. A publisher found him in a pathetic and bereft condition, a ragged beggar with no shirt on his back and bare feet. The publisher rescued Francis Thompson, who then began to write. This time he wrote his most famous poem, "The Hound of Heaven."

Francis Thompson learned that the Lord's presence is inescapable. He pursues us not simply to hound us but to help us. He pursues us not like some special agent or bounty hunter. Rather, he pursues us in love, calling us to faith and to follow.

The Lord's presence is inescapable. Adam and Eve learned it in the garden, Jonah learned it in the belly of a great fish, the psalmist learned it in his despair, Francis Thompson learned it when he fell so low he had to reach up to touch bottom, and we may learn it at the Lord's table. The Lord's presence is inescapable. He is here. His presence is symbolized by broken bread and poured-out fruit of the vine. This observance calls us to remember that we never escape the divine presence. In fact, we come now to meet him at the Lord's table.—Alton McEachern[3]

Topic: Lost in Your Own Backyard
TEXT: Luke 15:11–23

Yesterday's experience can never meet today's need! If you have lost what you once held precious in faith because the freshness has gone out of it by neglect, you may find it again, no matter how far back in the past it may be buried. When the prodigal son returned from the far country, he made the same mistake as his elder brother in thinking that his father's love was based on his worthiness as a son.

In the pigpen, he decided to go home and ask for a servant's position on the farm, for at least there he would be well fed. He felt he had lost all rights to his sonship because of his unworthy behavior. He determined to return and say, "Father, I am not worthy to be called your son: make me as one of your hired servants" (Luke 15:18–20). But his father rushed out to kiss and caress him and welcomed him home as a son who had been lost but was now found, who had been dead but was alive again.

"You were always my son," he said. "You were my son in the far-off country, and you were my son down among the pigs—a disobedient son, but still my son! You have now repented and returned, and the fellowship that was broken can be restored. It was your communion with me that you lost, son. Your union with me, as a son with his father, remains. You can break our family fellowship by disobedience, but you cannot break the family relationship!"

If there is a change in your position with God, who moved? You can be so far away from the Father in faith and in fellowship, so plundered by pride, envy, selfishness, and neglect,

---

[3]*The Lord's Presence* (Nashville: Broadman Press, 1986), pp. 13–16.

so far down among the pigs that you may question whether he is still your Father and you are still his child. You may have broken the fellowship and ruined the communion, but if you truly are God's child, the relationship and the family union still stand. Only remembrance, repentance, and return are required for them to be recognized afresh.

You may be off in a far country or you may be just as far away from the Father in the church's own backyard. You may be so busy with the farm that you neglect the essentials of fellowship with God. You may be so self-centered that you do not care for others as you should. You may be jealous and proud, and these sins can rob you of the experience of full faith in your Father. William Cowper wrestled through this kind of experience in well-known words:

> Where is the blessedness I knew,
> When first I saw the Lord?
> Where is the soul-refreshing view
> Of Jesus and his word?
> What peaceful hours I once enjoyed!
> How sweet their memory still!
> But they have left an aching void
> The world can never fill.
> The dearest idol I have known,
> Whate'er that idol be,
> Help me to tear it from the throne
> And worship only thee!
> So shall my walk be close to God,
> Calm and serene my frame;
> So purer light shall mark the road
> That leads me to the Lamb.

—Craig Skinner[4]

ILLUSTRATIONS

THE LORD'S SUPPER.   The words "They sang a hymn and went out" (TEV) are intriguing. As we study the worship patterns of Judaism, we learn that singing was a basic part of the Passover meal. Jews came together to remember that time in their history when God had delivered them from their enemies in Egypt. Passover literally meant the time when the death angel had passed over them and touched the Egyptian babies that died. It was this past punishment or plague that came at the end of a long, tortured struggle that helped to set the people free. So, annually the Jews gathered for Passover celebration—a time of remembering what God had done for them back in Egypt. At every celebration, they sang a hymn. They sang from the Hallel—Psalms 113–118. We now think they sang Psalms 113 to 114 before the meal and Psalms 115 to 118 after the meal. But these were all hymns of praise. They sang out of their rich memories and history to the glory of God.

---

[4]*Back Where You Belong* (Nashville: Broadman Press, 1980), pp. 39–41.

What are we to sing as we leave the Lord's table and go out into the world? Like our spiritual forefathers long ago, we lift up praise to God. We remember, in the singing, his goodness and his love. And like them, we make our way back into the world, peculiarly conscious that we are kept by a love that will not fail.—Roger Lovette[5]

LOVE.   It is not easy to love God with all your heart and soul and might when much of the time you have all but forgotten his name. But to love God is not a goal we have to struggle toward on our own, because what, at its heart, the Gospel is all about is that God himself moves us toward it even when we believe he has forsaken us.

The final secret, I think, is this: that the words "You shall love the Lord your God" become in the end less a command than a promise. And the promise is that, yes, on the weary feet of faith and the fragile wings of hope, we will come to love him at last as from the first he has loved us—loved us even in the wilderness, especially in the wilderness, because he has been in the wilderness with us. He has been acquainted with our grief. And loving him we will come at last to love each other, too.—Frederick Buechner[6]

HE MEETS US.   The breaking of bread at holy Communion can break you right open. Sometimes you can be right in the middle of it when suddenly the tears start rolling down. It is like the gates to your heart have opened and everything you have ever loved comes tumbling out to be missed and praised and mourned and loved some more. It is like being known all the way down. It is like being in the presence of God. One moment you see him and the next you do not. One moment your eyes are opened and you recognize the risen Christ, and the next he vanishes from your sight.

Take heart. This is no ghost. Do not fear. You cannot lose him for good. This is the place he has promised to be, and this is the place to which he returns to meet us again and again. Risen Lord, be known to us in the breaking of the bread.—Barbara Brown Taylor[7]

IN SPITE OF ALL.   The Emmaus story and the Holy Eucharist, which we are now about to celebrate, speak to our hearts, very simply, to us as we are, in all our distress, our sense of being forsaken, and our hopelessness. Don't be afraid! Be at rest—not in a spirit of passive resignation, not as though there were nothing more to hope for, but because, in spite of everything, the hope is still there, living and already fulfilled! Since the cross of Calvary, the hour of fulfillment has dawned for the world. Brothers, it is the last hour.—Helmut Gollwitzer[8]

FOR ME!   When I was about twelve years of age, there came a Communion season, and most of the boys I knew united with the Church. Before we did so, we were told to search our hearts and find out if we loved him. We thought we did; and having answered many questions about what he had done for us, we were received at the Communion table. I had often watched, from our pew, the congregation march slowly up the aisle to the table, singing

[5]In J. E. Hightower Jr. (ed.), *Illustrating the Gospel of Matthew.*
[6]*A Room Called Remember*
[7]*Gospel Medicine*
[8]*The Dying and Living Lord*

the forty-fifth Psalm, verse 13, about how the "King's daughter is all glorious within." At one end of the table stood a hunchbacked elder, dressed in broadcloth, with a grave, friendly face. He took our tokens as we passed to our seats at the table. Then one of the ministers delivered a short discourse, after which, amid profound silence, the elders passed the bread and the wine. There was something overwhelmingly solemn about the service. I felt that I was sitting in the shadow of an awful tragedy and mystery, yet at the same time something inexpressibly sweet and tender. The words that impressed themselves upon me were those pronounced by the minister: "This is my body, broken for you; this do in remembrance of me." That taught me that I had offended God, but this friend had saved me by dying for me, and therefore I must always love him and remember him.—Clarence Edward Macartney[9]

RECONCILIATION.   Courage in the face of creation. The modern aphorism for indifference and inaction is, "If it isn't broken, don't fix it." Saint Paul, never willing to avoid a problem if he could help it, acknowledged that only that which is broken can be fixed. This time it was God, the same God who asked so much of Abraham, who offered his own son on behalf of those who doubted him; thus, by Christ, he reconciled us to himself and to one another. By what is broken, sacrificed, and fractured we are healed and made whole; and not simply are we mended but, as Saint Paul said, "If any one is in Christ, he is a new creation. The old has passed away; behold, the new has come." It is God who repented of his awful testing of Abraham and who, as an act of reconciliation, offered us himself in Jesus Christ in the feast of his Passion, death, and Resurrection. Saint Paul invites us to be reconciled to God, to restore the brokenness in our lives and in our world. In Christ, God has made the first move toward us; he now invites us to respond, to accept what he offers and who he is. This is an act of reconciliation that we can, and now must, make our own.—Peter J. Gomes[10]

---

[9]*Macartney's Illustrations*
[10]*Sermons*

MESSAGES FOR FUNERAL AND BEREAVEMENT

SERMON SUGGESTIONS

Topic: Because He Is My Shepherd

TEXT: Ps. 23

Jesus is the Good Shepherd. It is the identity of the Shepherd that urges us to think of ourselves as his sheep.

Today we have again come into the valley of the shadow. Death is the darkest valley of life through which we must travel. The twenty-third Psalm assures us that God is our shepherd, and because of that we have abundant assurances.

I. *Because the Lord is my shepherd, I shall not want* (vv. 1–3a). Jesus promised that we would never want for food, shelter, clothing, and life's necessities while we put him first. But at this moment you want more than physical items. You want what no store can sell, no merchant can provide. You want confidence, comfort, and cheer.

(a) He provides *comfort.* He has been where we are and he knows how we feel.

(b) He provides *confidence,* even in the crises of life when we have feelings we feel we cannot bear.

(c) He provides good *cheer.* Jesus turned the tears of more than one funeral into shouts of joy. On the day Jesus came back to life, the sounds coming from the cemetery were those of a festival: laughter, delight, excitement, and hope.

II. *Because the Lord is my shepherd, I am led in righteousness* (v. 3b). Any other shepherd might lead me into sin. The very mention of sin at a funeral is enough to dismay us, but not if Jesus is our Shepherd.

(a) He leads us in the way of forgiveness, goodness, and purity.

(b) I may die as a sinner, but I am a sinner who is saved by God's grace. That is an old Christian promise, but it deserves to be retold at the funeral of any Christian.

(c) "For his name's sake," he is righteous, and so are his followers. We share in his righteousness.

III. *Because he is my shepherd, I am not afraid* (vv. 4–5). The shepherd's staff is used to both correct and comfort the sheep. He can use its crook to retrieve a lost lamb from trouble. That same staff becomes a deadly weapon to drive away a hungry wolf or sneaky thief.

(a) His staff is our comfort. It is curious that our faith has come to be symbolized by a cross when a staff would be much more appropriate. Perhaps we should put a shepherd's staff instead of a cross on our church steeples and into our stained glass windows.

(b) With Christ as our shepherd we are not afraid. He defends us from our enemies. The staff frightens them, but the sight of that staff is a comfort to us.

(c) The good shepherd wants to comfort you today, in your own time of grief and loss.

IV. *Because the Lord is my shepherd, I shall dwell with him* (v. 6). The analogy of the psalm changes here. We no longer think of ourselves as sheep following a shepherd, but as house-guests of a generous host. We are accorded all the pleasures of Middle Eastern hospitality.

(a) We dwell in the Lord's house in this life. We exist in his presence. There is comfort in that.

(b) We shall dwell in the Lord's house in the next life. Jesus spoke of his Father's house and its many rooms, with a place for everyone in the family. There is a place there for you.

"And I shall dwell in the house of the Lord forever." This last line of the psalm is as perfect as the first line, "The Lord is my shepherd." I needed those words to be said, especially today.

I need to know that life goes on, beyond the valley of the shadow of death. I need to know that life is good there. I need to know that life is infinite there. But most of all, I need to know that my Good Shepherd, my host, is there. Without Jesus there, heaven would not be heaven. But Jesus is there and he makes heaven heavenly.

The Lord is my shepherd. Because of that truth, this day is one not of tragedy but of comfort, assurance, and victory.—David Beavers

Topic: That Your Days May Be Prolonged
TEXT: Deut. 5:16

How do we measure the quality of a person's life? How do we come to understand a person's life to have been meaningful—particularly as we stand on this side of death and he has passed over that great divide? I believe we can see the meaningfulness and the quality of a person's life most clearly when the measuring device is the Word of God. We can take this great yardstick, lay it across any person's lifespan, and it will reveal the richness or the barrenness, the fruitfulness or the fruitlessness of that person's life.

The Commandments of God form the particular order of the measure of the quality of a life. These words that have thundered over the centuries in the voice that booms "You shall," "You shall not," and "Neither shall you" point us in the direction God would have us take. These words are not meant to frighten us; rather, they are given out of love and concern; they reveal the pathway that leads to life and health, joy and fulfillment. These words oppose all devices we would use to measure the value of a person's life; they call our methods of measurement into question.

We could never measure the quality of R.'s life, as we so often choose to do, by the wealth of his material possessions. He had little in the way of worldly goods. And we could never adequately measure the quality of R.'s life by his many friends and family members. He lived very much to himself. We could not measure the quality of R.'s life by considering the great contributions of talent and energy he left behind for all succeeding generations. He wrote no book, he passed along no great information, he made no contribution to science. These are the values we as humans use.

In the sight of God, R.'s life was of great value and worth. Why? Because he followed the command of God and listened to the voice that would ensure a rich and full life: "Honor your father and mother." This R. did with the greatest sincerity and devotion, with fidelity and love. While we look to the great and glorious accomplishments of a person as the measure of his or her value, the Lord fixes his gaze on the seemingly small and insignificant events, such as caring for and remaining faithful to one's parents even to the point of self-sacrifice. It is to the person who follows this command that God promises "prolonged days" and that all "may go well."

The divine measure, laid across the life of this man, reveals the true quality of his being in the sight of God. His days were prolonged and it went well with R. The promises of God in this one command came to full fruition in R.'s life, and that beyond all else makes his life both meaningful and of great value! Our measurement is temporal, God's is eternal. Our measurement is limited to the material and the practical, God's penetrates to the very depth of human existence, to the heart and soul. Our measurement ends with death, which is the point at which God's measurement of the value of human life begins.

R. has earned his place at the table in the Kingdom of God, not merely through obedience but through grace. We may deem his life small and insignificant, but then the Word of God measures our value judgment through these words of the Lord Jesus himself: "And behold, some who are last will be first, and some who are first will be last."—Albert J. D. Walsh

Topic: She Died, to My Sorrow
TEXT: Gen. 48:7

This text is the lament of a husband for his wife. She died delivering their youngest child during a long journey. After three thousand years, this lament of Jacob for Rachel touches us. In just a few words he spoke volumes.

If anyone ever earned a wife it was Jacob, by working fourteen years for her father, Laban. Yet Jacob felt those years were only a few days when compared to his joy with Rachel. Now their years together had ended.

The Bible says that Jacob loved Rachel. The Scripture also speaks of her beauty of form and face. Such praise of beauty in a woman is rare in the Bible.

The child born as Rachel died was named Benjamin. She had given Jacob another son, his favorite, Joseph. This son would become the great ruler of Egypt. But Rachel would never see that. To Jacob's sorrow, she died.

We find ourselves in complete empathy with Jacob today, because another young wife and mother has died, to our sorrow. Her friends and family speak of her cheerfulness and full life, her potential, her energy and beauty. But she died, to our sorrow.

What are you feeling right now? And what can you do about that? There are many ways you can react to this death. What is right?

I. *You can have bitterness.* You can blame God. You can speak of his harsh action, without realizing that God will always do what is best for us—and that there are worse things than death.

(a) The one thing you must remember is that God loves you. He is not mean or careless with human life.

(b) Please know that we may never know why she died. But God is not to be blamed or to be the object of our bitterness.

(c) Rather, reach out to God for comfort and guidance in this crisis.

II. *You might be defeated.* Death is an intruder. It barges into our lives to disturb the order of things, taking those we love. Death has no respect for any of us, not even the young and the healthy. She died to our sorrow. Jacob sorrowed but was not defeated.

(a) You can say, "What is the use?" and allow death to make you its doormat.

(b) Death does that to some. Will you be crushed and defeated?

III. *You can go on with your life.* Jacob still had a journey to complete. He had a new son to rear and the rest of his family to care for. He had the Lord's mission to finish. So Jacob mourned Rachel, then buried her in Bethlehem and went on with his life.

(a) If we believe that Jesus told us the truth about death, we can face the death of our loved ones with confidence.

(b) We can accept that death is only temporary and that there is life beyond the grave.

(c) We can be comforted by the knowledge that Jesus will return to resurrect us. We can trust that our bodies will be resurrected, just as Jesus was raised from death.

(d) We believe in eternal life—not just a long life, a few thousand years, or even a million years, but eternal life.

This funeral occasion is essentially a time of decision for you. You will decide now on a course of bitterness or defeat or to live your life to its best advantage. Will you be so defeated by death that you will fear your own death and not enjoy life?

I want you to express your sorrow here. It is not only normal, it is good and healthy. And then, like Jacob, take up your journey through life.—David Beavers

Topic: The Dark Valley
TEXT: Ps. 23

A Christian sorely bereaved wrote to an older pilgrim who shared his grief: "Together we travel this dark valley. As Christian, shrouded in darkness, heard Faithful singing ahead of him, so I hear you singing a song of faith and hope. I thank you for that song, and I shall take heart." Bunyan's pilgrim found the valley full of terrors—a ditch on one side of the path, a quagmire on the other, the very mouth of hell in the midst of the valley, with flames, hideous noises, and a company of fiends.

Evidently, as David himself said, there are dangers in the valley of the shadow. What are some of these dangers?

1. There is the temptation to rebel. "I cannot stand it!" one sometimes cries. Yet we must stand it. "How can God be good and let this happen?" demands another. Yet God is good, and this sorrow, which may be due to accident or human ignorance, or even to wickedness, is not beyond his power to bring good out of evil.
2. There is the temptation to be bitter, which may ruin the rest of one's days.
3. There is the temptation of sharp self-condemnation, passing the bounds of true humility, forgetting God's mercy and forgiveness.
4. There is the voice of despair—refusing to learn the lessons that lie in every grief.
5. There is the whine of self-pity, which is just selfishness.

But there is a path in the valley. Sometimes, because of shock and confusion, we do not see it. Yet always some plain duty lies before our dim eyes. We take that one step, perhaps mechanically, and there is another step before us. Presently we find we are following a path, a path that we can see and that leads toward the light.

There are springs in the dark valley—the spring of memory, rich in comfort unless we poison it with resistance, crying, "How can I give up all that?" and the spring of mercy in the present hour. There is always some circumstance to be thankful for—either the privilege of ministering to the last moment, with perhaps a glimpse of heaven in the parting, or else the suddenness of the going, which has spared the loved one pain and sorrow. We know that death must be, yet in each case we lament the fact: "So young, such promise of a beautiful life!" "So useful and busy; how can this life be spared?" "So full of rich wisdom and inspiration for us all; we hoped for years yet." Surely we are unreasonable. Nothing could be so sad as to be willing to give them up. Let us turn it around, and be thankful for mercies in the midst of grief.

There is also the spring of hope. Surely the world, even the Christian world, is wrong in the verb tenses used in time of sorrow. "I loved her so!" Then love her still. "She was so good and kind!" She still is. "He was such a blessing to me!" He may still be.

The spring of human sympathy lies close. Few, indeed, are the griefs one must bear alone, and we can help each other. Often when the sharing is more widespread or more tender than we had dreamed, there is sweetness beyond words, and exaltation of spirit akin to joy.

The Shepherd is here in the valley. No matter how close is the companionship of loved ones in sorrow, there is an inner experience none but the Good Shepherd can know. Sometime his conscious presence makes us see as God sees, and "none of these things move" us. How simply the psalmist says it: "I will fear no evil; for thou art with me." But sometimes we long in vain for this consciousness. We cannot see his face or hear his voice. What then do we do? The Shepherd's staff beyond the corner of a rock, his rod protecting us—may not these mean providences unexpected but vital, the sure tokens of his presence, on which the heart may rest till a stronger faith brings him clearly before us?

There is light. "After the dark valley, does he make it light again?" asked a four-year-old child, discussing this verse with his mother. She agreed, and the little boy added, "He wouldn't let it be too dark; he made the light!"

May not the change of figure in the next verse be the writer's instinctive expression of the same feelings? "After the dark valley, he makes it light again." And isn't the last verse gratitude for guidance through the valley and beyond—all the way home?—Ella Broadus Robertson

Topic: Don't Let Your Heart Be Troubled
Text: Various

I. *Introduction.* The reason that brings us all together is a grim one. The loss of a loved one is never an easy event to handle. Although our faith helps us in times like these, our grief is still very real. That is why Paul told the church at Thessalonica to mourn, but not to mourn like those who have no hope (1 Thess. 4:13).

So today we attempt to understand the loss we have encountered through the lens of Scripture. It is only in this way that we can be given an eternal perspective and begin the much-needed healing process. As a foundation, we must understand that Jesus had great experience with loss and death. His reaction when hearing of John the Baptist's death is essential to understanding how, even when the answers are known, one can grieve the loss of someone one loved.

Jesus, in the Gospel of John, revealed to the disciples that he would soon be leaving them. Here, during the most difficult time of his disciples' life, our Lord offered some useful advice in regard to sorrow. The disciples, troubled and confused, sought some amount of guidance.

It is within this context that we find that the words of John 14–16 are even more applicable to our specific situation.

II. The disciples, in distress, took the news of Christ's soon-coming departure very hard. Even more troubling was the realization that they would abandon him. However, Jesus stated clearly, "Don't let your hearts be troubled." What an unusual request. In the midst of all this troubling reality, Jesus wanted them to have a happy heart? Why? The reason was threefold.

First, Jesus explained, "You believe in God; believe also in me. In my father's house are many mansions." Simply stated, they should keep their faith, because it would ensure their eternal dwelling in God's heaven. Jesus encouraged them by revealing that he was leaving to prepare a place for his followers. He also promised to return for them. Therefore, if they believed in Christ, they would have nothing to fear. This explains why Paul addressed deceased Christians as those "who have fallen asleep." For a believer, death is not permanent.

Jesus made a second promise: that he would send the Holy Spirit (the Comforter) to assist them in their daily discipleship. The Holy Spirit would assist them in their endeavors to remain in Christ. If they remained in him, Christ promised, their lives would be fruitful. Because of this, as well as other realities, Jesus went so far as to say that his departure would be a good thing, so that the Spirit could come.

Finally, once again, Christ gave a strange command to the disciples. The command followed, however, an even more bizarre promise: "In this world you will have tribulation." This promise is one that all believers could identify with and about which the disciples could give many testimonies. Life is hard. Jesus knew this. Losing someone because of death is difficult as well. Jesus understood this, too. The reality, for the disciples, was that even though Jesus would leave physically, he would never forsake them and would never really leave them, because the Spirit would come and testify about the Lord's person, ministry, and gospel. If Christians would remain in Christ, their lives would model a consistency that is remarkable. They would possess a peace that passes understanding, a confidence that supercedes their level of education or training, and a hope that cannot be quenched, even in the greatest periods of mourning and loss.

With this in mind, the conclusion of the matter remains a clear result of a solid faith in Christ. He commanded that although troubles would come, they should "take heart" because he had "overcome the world." Jesus began his last sermon to his followers by stating, "Don't let your heart be troubled" and ended it by exhorting, "Take heart." The presence of Jesus in one's life makes all the difference. Whether one is fighting illness or depression or is struggling with sin, Jesus gives victory. Scripture is clear that not only does Jesus give victory in life, he also offers victory in death. Once again, the taunting question is asked, "O death, where is your victory? O grave, where is your sting?" The answer, "They have been swallowed up in sweet victory."

III. *Conclusion.* Please, do not feel that you cannot grieve because of your faith; instead, take confidence in the fact that you can grieve as a person with hope. The difference is twofold. First, we have a Savior who has conquered death through his Resurrection. Second, we have the Holy Spirit, who gives us comfort, guidance, power, and discernment in all matters of living. With this understanding of life and death, we echo the words of Romans 8, noting that we are persuaded that neither death nor life is able to separate us from the love of God found in Jesus Christ. The conclusion? We are more than conquerors through him who loves us.—Jeffrey D. Brown

Topic: In Thanksgiving for Stephen Christopher Norman
August 12, 1964–April 12, 2000
Based on remarks by Ralph Norman, Stephen's father, for the Memorial Service at St. John's Cathedral, Knoxville, Tennessee, April 15, 2000

Our business and privilege this day is to rejoice and give thanks for the life of Stephen Christopher Norman.

There will be time later—too much time, in the long dark watches of the night or in the unexpected and unwelcome crevices of the busy day—to think about what we should have done, what we could have said, what we wanted to do. Our privilege today—all of us who knew him and loved him, and whom he knew and loved—is to give thanks. My own special privilege is to remind you of one or two things about him that I have come to know fully only in these last days.

Stephen was born in Hamilton, Ohio, in the hot summer days of August 1964. When I first met him, he did not seem especially happy to have come into our world. He seemed awfully fragile and frail to me, and I asked the doctor, Benjamin Layman, who had delivered him, "Dr. Layman, do you think he will be all right?"

Standing at the elevator door, Dr. Layman said, "He'll be a bigger man than you are."

This prediction seemed unlikely at the time, but I took Dr. Layman at his word, and indeed it came to pass. Stephen was a bigger man than I.

But what the doctor did not know and could not say was that Stephen would not have as long a lifespan as I. And what he could not know and did not say was that Stephen would have a larger world, that he would make for himself and his countless friends a larger space for kindness and for love than I ever would or could.

For some years I have been wrestling in my writing with questions about reconciliation and forgiveness that came to me about the time Nelson Mandela was released from prison in South Africa. How can one make sense of this possibility that people can forgive each other and live with each other after devastating losses and rifts and betrayals and disjunctions? How is it possible that the world can be healed? How will that happen? I turned these questions over and over, first one way and then the other way, then from side to side, and then from front to back and back to front, and I have concluded at least this much: that it's not about globalization and it's not about treaties and it's not about mergers.

The more I looked at it, the more it seemed to be about, well, about *music*. About *listening* and *attending* and *hearing*, and about *waiting*. It seemed to be about *friendship*. It seemed to be about finding people whom the philosopher Aristotle would call the "great hearted."

As I pondered and wrote about these things, my study would from time to time be interrupted by telephone calls or unexpected visits from my beloved son. He would call to ask about some game show question or the spelling or meaning of a word, or to remind me to get new batteries for the smoke detector, to be sure to bolt the basement door, to remember to get in touch with some old friends his mother and I had been neglecting lately, to offer to do something for us, to propose that we work on some task in the yard or in the house together, to strategize about a birthday or Christmas gift for Connie or Emily or Jonathan or David or Carrie, to check on whether we old folks were all right, or just to share indirectly but with great pride some wonderful new aspect of life with Julie.

The agenda was always open and vast and unpredictable. It would be in midmorning or midafternoon, in the early evening or at midnight; and at whatever hour and for however long or short a time we would talk, it would be, I now see, the best of all good fellowship, the very best that two men who are father and son can ever hope to have with each other, and it is only in these last days that I can see that *he* was the one who would teach *me* the central lesson about great hearts and about how the world will heal. For I was by no means the sole recipient of such visits and calls. This would be the way in which he was a bigger man than I.

Not long after Stephen was born, at his christening, the Reverend William Hawley took our son in his arms and walked up and down the center aisle of Holy Trinity Church in Oxford, Ohio, and declared in his strong and definitive voice to the congregation, "This is Stephen Christopher Norman. He is now a member of our family, and you have promised to be with him always, to support him and protect him. Stephen, here is your family."

Twelve years later, after we moved to Knoxville, Stephen was confirmed here at St. John's, in a class that Dan Matthews brought before the Bishop, and in due time Stephen was head-long into the life of the EYC, doing his very best to keep up with Emily and David and Brad and Danny and the Burdettes and the Frederickson girls and so many others who in the early and mid-seventies were working out for themselves what it was like to be a circle of true friends. During those years, he was to enjoy also the gift of certain very special persons of an older generation, men who were to be, what? *Mentors* is the wrong word, and so is *role models;* the right word is *presences*—who were to be presences in his young life. So many presences: Stan Lusby and Glen Claiborne and Richard Marius and Charles Hoglan and Harry Scott and Rod Townsend and, yes, Bob Bonich of Demopolis, Alabama.

And in this same church, at this same altar, Stephen would take Julie Ann Bonich to be his wife, swearing before God and Father John Ross and Canon Laura England and the whole company here assembled that he would love and honor and cherish her and keep himself only unto her, for richer and for poorer, in sickness and in health, from that day forward.

You know, the funny thing that got into his head is that that's what it's all about. It isn't about what the world wants or expects or cares about. What got into his head somehow, which he learned in your company, is that the Church is the visible representation of a far larger company—that who we are to be is in and for each other, so that if you know someone is sick, you go to them; if you know someone has suffered a loss, you call and comfort them; if you know someone has a child, you go and love that child and rejoice in it and lift it up and give it cherry bellies as if it were your own. You spend the time, you take the time, you make the time to be there.

I'll add one more modest item to this unspoken credo: If you are served a meal in a restaurant, you and your server are not just in a business transaction, and you are certainly not to think of yourselves as superior and inferior but as partners and as parties to yet another of those unassuming sacraments that the Lord has prepared for us. Though Stephen never to my knowledge ever quite put it this way, it was as if for him the tip were the outward and visible sign of an inward and spiritual grace at any meal anywhere—whether at Sarge's or Macalester's or the University Club or Pizza Kitchen. A generous and unbegrudging tip, 20 percent at the very least, was to be given and received as token of a bond between those who serve and those who are served—a bond that runs from the table or the counter clear to heaven and back. That is who you are and where you are: always in the presence of some fellow member of the beloved community.

Jesus' words from the Gospel of John keep coming to my mind: "My peace I give to you; my peace I leave with you. Not as the world gives, give I."

Not as the world gives. The world knows many fine things, which Stephen wanted as much as the next person, yet the world knows next to nothing about the one central thing. But Stephen did, and does. All these years it is what he was teaching me. We are all stronger for his presence.

"My peace I leave with you, my peace I give to you. . . . Let not your heart be troubled, neither let it be afraid. . . . You believe in God; believe also in me."

Thanks be to God for our dearly beloved son.

ILLUSTRATIONS

DOING DEATH.   I trust that with God's grace I will increasingly see death for what Christ our Lord made it. Not a horribly painful event at the close of life, but that unique moment when the yes I have said to God all my life reaches its climax. Not something I endure, but something I do. Not a tragedy to be avoided at all costs, but the extraordinary experience when the Christ who is life, who has been my life, fashions me finally to his life, in his image. The moment when my journey reaches not its nadir but its high point. The day when, for all the human loss it entails, I can confidently cry with Christ, "Father, into your hands I commit my spirit."—Walter J. Burghardt, S.J.[1]

FINDING CONSOLATION.   Time would fail us if we should attempt to track the Master in his glorious pathway after his resurrection. Let it suffice us briefly to observe that, having led his disciples out onto a mountain, where he had delighted often to commune with them, he was suddenly taken up from them, and a cloud received him out of their sight. We think we may conjecture, by the help of Scripture, what transpired after that cloud had covered him. Did not the angels

> Bring his chariot from on high
> To bear him to his throne,
> Clap their triumphant wings and cry,
> His glorious work is done?

Do you not see him, as he mounts his triumphal chariot,

> And angels chant the solemn lay,
> Lift up your heads, ye golden gates,
> Ye everlasting doors give way?

Behold angels gazing from the battlements of heaven, replying to their comrades who escort the ascending Son of Man. "Who is the King of Glory?" And this time, those who accompany the Master sing more sweetly and more loudly than before, while they cry, "The

[1]*Grace on Crutches*

Lord strong and mighty, the Lord mighty in battle! Lift up your heads, O ye gates, and be ye lifted up, ye everlasting doors, that the King of Glory may come in." And not the doors

> Loose all their bars of massy light,
> And wide unfold the radiant scene.

And he enters. "He claims those mansions as his right," and all the angels rise to "receive the King of Glory in." Behold him, as he rides in triumph through heaven's streets; see death and hell bound at his chariot wheels. Hark to the "hosannas" of the spirits of the just made perfect! Hear how cherubim and seraphim roll out in thunder their everlasting song—"Glory be unto thee; glory be unto thee, thou Son of God, for thou wast slain and thou hast redeemed the world by thy blood." See him as he mounts his throne and near his Father sits. Behold the benign complacency of the paternal Deity. Hear him as he accepts him and gives him a name which is above every name. And I say, my brethren, in the midst of your tremblings, and doubtings, and fearings, anticipate the joy which you shall have, when you shall share in this triumph, for know you not that you ascended up on high in him? He went not up to heaven alone, but as the representative of all the blood-bought throng. You rode in that triumphal chariot with him; you were exalted on high and made to sit far above principalities and powers in him; for we are risen in him, we are exalted in Christ. Even at this very day in Christ that psalm is true—"Thou hast put all things under his feet; thou madest him to have dominion over all the works of thy hands." Come, poor trembler, thou art little in thine own esteem, and but a worm and no man! Rise I say, to the height of thy nobility; for thou art in Christ greater than angels be, more magnified and glorified by far. God give you grace, ye who have faith, that ye may now, in the fact of Jesus Christ's exaltation, find consolation for yourself!—C. H. Spurgeon[2]

CERTAINTY.   When the Holy Spirit witnesses with our spirit, and when our lives are fulfilled within the will of God, then we become possessed with a certainty that needs neither external defense nor internal justification. Though we know in part, we nevertheless know that we know and, more importantly, we are fully known.

This world is looking for certainty to make it free and secure. Certainty can be had, but only at the price of doing God's will. Within that will are quietness and confidence. Within that will are peace and power. Within that will are both rest and creative satisfaction.

As we live ourselves into it and are lived by God, false certainties and false uncertainties alike begin to fall away and we earn the right to say with Paul, "I am sure." "I am sure that he who began a good work in you will bring it to completion."—Nels F. S. Ferré[3]

JOY IN BELIEVING.   From a half century of people-watching, I am persuaded that the most effective sign we can raise to unbelievers is our joy in believing. The German philosopher Nietzsche was so correct in his caustic critique of Christians: We do not look redeemed. There is indeed a discouraging amount of death in our world; and like God, we take no

---

[2]*Metropolitan Tabernacle Pulpit*
[3]*God's New Age*

delight in death. But the message of our sending is life, the breathtaking promise of Christ the night before he died: "I live, and you shall live" (John 14:19). If *we*, the sent, show no joy in being alive with the life of the risen Christ, why should anyone believe us when we proclaim without passion "Christ is risen"?—Walter J. Burghardt[4]

BEYOND THE STORM.   When mists have hung low over the hills and the day has been dark with intermittent showers, at length great clouds begin to hurry across the sky, the wind rises, and the rain comes pouring down; then we look out and exclaim, "Why, this is the clearing-up shower." And when the floods have spent themselves, the clouds part to let the blue sky tremble through them, and the west wind bears them away seaward, and though they are yet black and threatening, we see their silver edges as they pass and know that just behind them are singing birds and glittering dewdrops; and lo! while yet we look, the sun bursts forth and lights them up in the eastern heaven with the glory of the rainbow.

Now, to the Christian whose life has been dark with brooding cares that would not lift themselves, and on whom chilling rains of sorrow have fallen at intervals through all his years, death, with its sudden blast and storm, is but the clearing-up shower; and just behind it are the songs of angels, and the serenity and glory of heaven.—Henry Ward Beecher

A NEW PERSON.   Suppose you want to be a better person. Imagine that I say to you, "I know how you can have the Spirit of Jesus." This is not beyond you. This is a possibility. The New Testament clearly states, "If any man be in Christ, he is a new creature: old things are passed away; behold all things are become new" (2 Cor. 5:17). This promise I do offer, not because of what I can do but because of what Christ has already done.

Once, in the midst of a storm that threatened to overturn his ship, a rough, cursing, self-willed sailor knelt and prayed for the first time in his life. Later on, John Newton was to call that experience his conversion, and he spent over forty years of his life thereafter preaching the gospel of Christ.

When he died, Newton had this epitaph put on a stone in the church he had served in London:

> John Newton, Clerk
> Once an Infidel and Libertine,
> A servant of Slaves in Africa,
> Was by the rich mercy of our
> Lord and Savior Jesus Christ,
> Preserved, Restored, and Pardoned,
> And Appointed to Preach the Faith
> He Had Long Labored to Destroy.

> —Ralph L. Murray[5]

---

[4]*Still Proclaiming Your Wonders*
[5]*Plumb Lines and Fruit Baskets*

LENTEN AND EASTER PREACHING

SERMON SUGGESTIONS

Topic: Wrestling with God

TEXT: Gen. 32:22–32

The Jabbok is a twisting, turbulent stream that cuts its way through the hills of Gilead as if they had been hewn with a mighty ax.[1] As it rushes westward to join the Jordan River near Jericho, the great gorge narrows into an even deeper ravine whose high walls cast shadows by day and cover the chasm with gloom by night. The word *Jabbok* in Hebrew contains the root of the verb "to wrestle" (*'abaq*), suggesting that this raging torrent was a "struggler" because of the difficulty with which it made its tortuous way through obstructing rock.

Our story opens where the canyon walls widen at Penuel, spreading the waters enough so that travelers may safely ford on their journey from Gilead to Canaan. A solitary figure stands beside the restless stream, shrouded in utter darkness (Gen. 32:24a). It is our ancestral patriarch, Jacob, caught up in the greatest crisis of his life. As he listens to the wild roar of the waters, they seem to echo the writhing of his own heart. Before the night is over, Jacob will, like Jabbok, become "the wrestler." But more, his struggle anticipates the dark night of the soul through which we, too, must pass before we are ready, with him, to enter the Promised Land.

I. *Anxiety.* On that fateful evening, Jacob was hemmed in by more than the high walls of the *Wadi Zerqa* formed by the Jabbok. For twenty years he had worked for his uncle Laban (Gen. 31:38), marrying two of his daughters, Leah and Rachel. After cheating their father out of an entire herd through a breeding scam (Gen. 30:25–43), Jacob gathered up all of his family and flocks and fled from Haran while Laban was away shearing sheep (Gen. 31:19–21). Enraged by this deceptive departure, and by the fact that treasured religious icons had been stolen, Laban hotly pursued Jacob until he caught up with him in the hill country of Gilead, where he bitterly upbraided him for carrying off his daughters and grandchildren without so much as a farewell kiss (Gen. 31:25–32). When a careful search failed to turn up the missing household gods—because Rachel had hidden them under her skirts (Gen. 31:33–35)—Jacob was able to lodge a self-righteous protest of his own (Gen. 31:36–42) and pressure Laban to accept a "covenant" that amounted to little more than a nonaggression pact designed to keep the family members from each other's throats (Gen. 31:43–55).

The bad blood between Jacob and Laban, however, was nothing compared to the rift between Jacob and Esau. Years earlier, Jacob had tricked his brother into squandering his birthright for a bowl of soup (Gen. 25:29–34), then later had cheated him out of the deathbed

---

[1]This description is suggested by Nelson Glueck, *The River Jordan* (Philadelphia: Westminster, 1946), p. 127.

blessing of their father, by which Isaac designated his chosen successor as head of the family (Gen. 27:1–29). Seething with hatred of Jacob for twice supplanting his rights as firstborn (Gen. 27:36), Esau determined to kill his brother as soon as Isaac was dead, a plot that was thwarted by Jacob's hasty flight to Haran (Gen. 27:41–45). But the death vow had never been revoked, and now Esau was approaching with four hundred men (Gen. 32:6). Jacob was utterly defenseless, able to meet this veritable army with nothing but women, children, and livestock. Cold terror clutched at his heart as he contemplated the prospect of a massacre in which Esau "may come and kill us all" (Gen. 32:11).

Outwardly, Jacob was alone in the inky darkness, his back to the wall, with nowhere to hide, relentlessly pursued by threats both behind him and before him. Inwardly it seemed as if the sins of a lifetime had finally caught up with him, despite the legendary cunning that had served him so well. All of us know those who seem to cut corners without ever stumbling, who dance down the sidelines of life without once stepping out of bounds, who bend every rule and exploit every weakness to get their way, only to make a fatal mistake when all of their cleverness catches up with them, when their success is seen to be leveraged by promissory notes that cannot be paid, when smoke and mirrors can no longer conceal a lack of bedrock character.

Jacob had always been a quick study, a fast-start artist who, at midlife, should have been reaping the rewards of patient labor but instead found himself not empty-handed but empty-hearted. His ill-gotten gain was worthless to buy him a good night's sleep beside the surging Jabbok. We join Jacob at the moment of his greatest vulnerability, on that fateful evening when he knew that the next day he might lose it all. Now there was nothing to keep his conscience company but rampant anguish over what another day might bring. To be sure, he had already launched a last-ditch effort to blunt Esau's raw and violent rage with extravagant gifts that amounted to a bribe; but in the suffocating darkness, Jacob had no way of knowing whether this ploy would suffice to outsmart his brother one more time. No wonder that some of the early Jewish commentators supposed that Jacob had stayed behind on the other side of Jabbok in order to flee in case his peace offering failed to placate Esau's wrath.

But precisely here, during the desperate hours, when Jacob was frantic with fear, when his pain was as palpable as the darkness, when every vestige of security had been shattered, God came to Jacob in the depths of his ordeal, and Jacob bound himself tightly to his predicament and entered fully into the abyss of his wretchedness.[2] My pastor often likes to pray that God will "meet us at the point of our deepest need." Believe me, we have now reached that point in Jacob's life when we discover that God will come to us when we feel utterly alone, when all is darkness, when life seems like nothing but an endless struggle. Call it, if you will, the ministry of the midnight watch, which means that when we have *nothing*—absolutely nothing but emptiness and fretfulness and weariness—it is precisely then that we also have God!

II. *Adversity.* But how can God help those who are rendered helpless by their own pride and self-sufficiency? All of his life Jacob had practiced salvation by shrewdness and seduction. He always thought he could be saved by his wits, but now he was at his wit's end. What

---

[2]Terrence E. Fretheim, "The Book of Genesis," in Leander E. Keck (ed.), *The New Interpreter's Bible,* Vol. 1 (Nashville: Abingdon Press, 1994), p. 567.

Jacob needed to learn more than anything else was that ingenuity is no substitute for integrity, that he did not always have to win at any cost, that the best things in life come from the goodness of God rather than from one's own selfish grasping. How could God help Jacob discover that divine grace cannot be won by human guile? The incredible answer of our text is that he would do it *by wrestling with him!* Jacob had always been able to run from his problems, but now he would have to engage in hand-to-hand combat, entwined in a tortured embrace of body with body. Especially when he had secured Isaac's blessing, Jacob had been able to camouflage himself, but now he would feel fingers dig into his flesh, reaching for the bone.[3] Jacob had just prayed his favorite prayer for the blessings of peace and prosperity (Gen. 32:9–12), but God decided that what he really needed was to be shaken to the very core of his being.

He began by giving "The Trickster" a taste of his own medicine. Suddenly, out of the darkness, the defenseless Jacob felt himself blindsided by a hostile intruder who attacked without warning and refused to identify himself. If the primitive superstitions of that time were to be believed, Jacob might well have supposed that the local river god had sent a night demon to thwart his crossing of the Jabbok at dawn. But he quickly realized that this was no nightmare of his imagination, for he was fighting his own kind, "a man" (Gen. 32:24b). Was it Laban, determined to exact secret revenge before returning to Mesopotamia? Or even more plausibly, was it Esau, whose army could easily destroy Jacob's family at sunrise after the hairy hunter had first taken care of his supplanter in the night? As the fight continued and Jacob began to realize that his opponent was not intent on slaughter, he may have supposed, as did the prophet Hosea many years later (Hosea 12:2–4), that his striving was with an angel such as one he had encountered at Bethel during another anxious moment in his life (Gen. 28:10–17). But when the titanic struggle neared its end at daybreak, it finally dawned on Jacob that he had in fact been wrestling with God himself (Gen. 32:30).

This discovery was slow in coming because of the remarkable way in which God condescended to meet Jacob. Not only did he assume human form, but he limited himself to human strength. Here the Sovereign of the universe, who had flung a world into space, who had sent floods to cover the earth and fire to demolish Sodom and Gomorrah, decided not only to fight Jacob but to fight him on even terms, to risk a draw or even a defeat. As hard as it is to picture God grunting and sweating and groveling in the dirt, it is even harder to conceive of him with his shoulders pinned to the ground or with his arms held in a hammerlock by a mere mortal. But Jacob needed to learn his limits, to find out what he could do without the benefit of pretense or subterfuge. So God set the ground rules for this midnight wrestling match: "Pick on somebody your own size!" and "May the best man win!"

Let us admit that we are hardly prepared for the confrontational theology lurking in this little story. We want God to come in the sunshine and give us peace, to offer the blessings of comfort and strength and so make us feel good about ourselves. But there are times when God decides instead to come in the darkness, not to pat us on the back but to pick a fight. Sometimes we must contend with God when we do not realize that it is God with whom we

---

[3]For a meditation on the intimacy of wrestling, see Gordon Dalbey, "Fingers on the Flesh, Touched to the Bone: Wrestling with God for New Life," *Preaching*, July-Aug. 1988, pp. 24-26. Based on a prize-winning sermon in the Billings contest at Harvard Divinity School.

struggle, when we conjecture that we are being hounded by a host of sinister forces or earthly enemies. Often it is after the fact, when the crisis has run its course, that we realize that neither demons nor angels nor humans but God himself has been forcing us to test our limits and plumb our depths as never before. Such is the hiddenness of the *Deus absconditus,* the God incognito who condescends to deal with our true condition by ambushing us when we least expect it.

Many years ago, the congregation in Louisville to which our family belonged offered a series of Sunday evening services in which selected members recounted their pilgrimage of faith. After several weeks I began to notice a consistent pattern according to which those giving testimony always located God in the good times of life. Almost as a refrain, one person after another affirmed the reality of God in terms of the success and happiness, the fulfillment and usefulness they had experienced as a Christian. While our text does not discount for a moment the value of such blessings, it balances them with the reminder that God can also be found in our torments, our anguish, and our struggles. If Jacob had contributed to that series, he might well have said, "God came to me—and here are the battle scars to prove it!" Ministers sometimes decline a challenging job because they cannot get a sense of peace about the offer. Jacob did not find a sense of God's peace in his Jabbok ordeal, but he found instead what God felt Jacob needed even more: a good dose of Kierkegaardian fear and trembling.

We have tried so hard to tame God and keep him on a leash, but our story will not have it. Can we not, with Jacob, learn to look for God in our doubts, in our fears, in our struggles, in all the senseless tragedies that threaten to engulf us? According to the text, God gives us permission to wrestle with him because he first decided to wrestle with us. It is permissible for us to beat our fists against the silent vault of heaven when prayers go unanswered, to argue with God when the riddles of human existence seem insoluble, to accuse God when he seems to have stacked the deck against us. Carlyle Marney had wise counsel for a young friend broken by tragedy when he said, in effect, "Don't repress your bitterness and hostility just because it is God with whom you are frustrated. Go ahead and have at it with the Almighty. God has much to answer for, but he can take care of himself." Whatever the issue, it is far better to fight *with* God than it is to throw in the towel and run *from* God!

III. *Ambiguity.* The only thing as strange as the combatants in this struggle was its outcome. Wrestling is so strenuous, and even dangerous, that we usually look for a verdict in a matter of minutes, but this fight lasted throughout the night, as if it would never end. Who would finally prevail—the mighty God, willing to hold his divine power in check and fight like a man; or the wily Jacob, trying desperately to survive? In this awful conflict, there was no winner and no loser. In one sense, God and Jacob fought to a draw, each needing what only the other could give, both prevailing because neither prevailed. In another sense, both won something and both lost something as the fearful encounter took its toll. Jacob's victories were at God's expense and God's victories were at Jacob's expense, yet both wrestlers emerged from the fray enhanced rather than diminished. Let us look more closely to see how this could be.

As night wore on toward morning, the stranger sought to leave before sunrise, only to find himself snared in Jacob's frantic grasp (Gen. 32:25a, 26a). Even though he had succeeded in throwing Jacob's hip out of joint as they wrestled, the wounded warrior refused to release his nocturnal assailant without receiving a blessing (Gen. 32:25b, 26b). Here is one of the profoundest expressions of the tenacity of faith in all of Scripture. If Jacob did not give God his freedom, it might prove fatal, for no one could look directly on God in the full light of day and live (Exod. 33:20). But Jacob now had God so tightly in his grip that he was willing to risk that fearful possibility rather than miss the blessing that only God could bestow. By this desperate strategy, he declared he would rather die than forfeit God's favor.[4] At last Jacob's ultimate priorities had been defined in life-and-death terms: better not to live another day, better not to face his brother Esau, better not to enter the Promised Land unless he could do so in the strength of God's grace.

Wonder of wonders, as Jacob held on to God for dear life, his audacious request was granted. But first he was asked to disclose his name (Gen. 32:27). *Jacob* meant "the supplanter," the one who grabs from behind to get ahead of others, who does whatever it takes to end up on top. But now Jacob was given a new name. Henceforth he would be known as *Israel,* which meant "the struggler," the one who must strive for what he gets, who must pay the price of pain in order to prevail. The change of name signaled not only a new identity but a new destiny as well. Now Jacob would become, as Israel, the namesake of a nation, the patriarch of a people who would perpetuate through the centuries his contentious struggle with God, wrestling with the demands of prophets and priests, yet clinging in hope to the covenant of blessing. At the moment, Jacob may have wished for more tangible tokens of divine protection, such as a battalion of soldiers with whom to fight Esau's army; but instead he was given only a promise: that he would now embody a new people called Israel and they would forever embody what he had learned in his jousting with God beside the Jabbok.

This does not mean that Jacob got all he wanted by grappling tenaciously with God. Even though he had met God in a face-to-face encounter (Gen. 32:30), he could not penetrate the mystery of his antagonist. God could learn his name, and even change it, but he could not learn God's name (Gen. 32:39) or change it. Jacob could scratch and claw for all he was worth, but only God had the power to bless. God could give him a whole new future, but he could not give God anything. This means that Jacob prevailed in securing from God what Jacob needed to receive, but God prevailed in offering to Jacob what he wanted to give.

Furthermore, remember that Jacob gained that blessing only at the cost of becoming a cripple. Wrestling is not a very nice way to negotiate differences, and this was obviously a no-holds-barred fight to the finish. God seemed to get in a lick below the belt, a punch to the groin that, as Jacob fought on with reckless abandon, threw his hip out of joint (Gen. 32:25b). Another thing that Jacob learned from his Jabbok ordeal is that if you push God to the limit, he will leave you with a limp. Ironically, the very ferocity with which Jacob fought earned him both a blessing and a curse. From now on he would be a new man, Israel, but he would also be hobbled in the hip. His successors, the Israelites, would forever remember the high price that Jacob paid to prevail by refusing to eat the meat of the high muscle that God had damaged in the fray (Gen. 32:32).

We dislike indecisive outcomes, but does this ambiguity not speak to our true condition? On the one hand, we find here an incredible expression of the hidden motions of grace. We, like Jacob, have the chance to prevail because God allows himself to be prevailed upon, to

---

[4]Clyde T. Francisco, "Genesis," in Clifton J. Allen (ed.), *Broadman Bible Commentary,* Vol. 1, rev. ed. (Nashville: Broadman, 1973), p. 226.

be badgered and begged, even to be coerced and, in a sense, captured by our desperate assaults on his mercy. When Walker Percy was asked why he was religious, he replied, "I take it as axiomatic that one should settle for nothing less than the infinite mystery and the infinite delight [that is] God. In fact I demand it. I refuse to settle for anything less. I don't see why anyone should settle for less than Jacob, who actually grabbed ahold of God and wouldn't let go until God . . . blessed him." When pressed to account for his faith as a gift from God, Percy persisted in saying, "The only answer I can give is that I asked for it, in fact demanded it."[5]

On the other hand, this determination to force the hand of God is dangerous business indeed. Isn't that what Jesus learned in the agony of Gethsemene and in the terror of Calvary, that even when he was rescued by God's Resurrection, the scars of defeat were still visible for all to see? Paul pushed his calling to the breaking point, and it got him the stigmata, or marks of the Master, branded on his body (Gal. 6:17). So it is with us: Wrestle with the deepest truths of Scripture and the encounter will leave your mind with a limp. Wrestle with the mandate of God for a worldwide mission, and the encounter will leave your will with a limp. Wrestle with the scandal of an apathetic church, and the match will leave your heart with a limp. Paradoxically, it is when we take hold of God by faith and try to wrest from him the greatest blessings that we also receive the deepest wounds. What our text is whispering to us between the lines is that we will never get the best of God without becoming utterly vulnerable in the process.

So, is the prize worth the price? Are you willing to demand the best that God has to offer if, by the very act, your self-sufficiency is forever lost? Are you willing to do it God's way, as Israel the struggler, if that means you can no longer do it your way as Jacob the supplanter? The deeper point of the story is that we cannot avoid the choice, because God may decide at any time to jump us in the dark and insist that we struggle with the deepest issues of our destiny until we decide what really matters most. When the long night is nearly over and we must confront the claims of our self-centeredness, we will either let go of God and run for cover in a frantic effort to save our skin one more time, or we will bet everything on his blessing and head for the Promised Land, confident that God will not let us be destroyed by the foolish mistakes we have made. What did Jacob do with his Jabbok experience? Let us see how the story ends.

When the long ordeal of the night was over, we are told, as he passed Peneul "the sun rose upon him" (Gen. 32:31)—that shaft of light after so much darkness, the omen of a better day. Jacob's story is not of a long day's journey into night but of a long night's journey into day! He crossed the Jabbok, seemingly alone again, yet God's signature was upon him, for he walked with a limp. The meeting with Esau no longer held any terrors for Jacob, even with the gimpy hip, because he had now fought with God and lived to tell about it. Granted, he was no longer cocky and self-assured, but to know that he had claimed God's blessing was enough. Renamed and yet lamed, defined and yet diminished, he set out to claim the Promised Land, dragging his leg behind him like a trophy from heaven.

Years before, Jacob had met God at Bethel as friend. Now he had met him at Peneul as enemy—the enemy of his whole bag of tricks, of his shortcuts and deceptions, of his invin-

---

[5]From a self-interview in *Esquire,* reprinted in *Context,* Feb. 1, 1978, p. 5.

cible self-sufficiency. But when Jacob received that blessed limp, God became what Frederick Buechner called his "beloved enemy."[6] And if we, like Jacob, go not only to Bethel but to Peneul as well, we can know the magnificent defeat that comes only when we wrestle with God.—William E. Hull

Topic: The Three Loves
TEXT: Mark 12:30–31

Love is at once the most desired reality in human experience and yet the most difficult to express. More than anything else, we want to love and be loved, for love sets the heart singing with an ecstasy sublime. In paying tribute to 1 Corinthians 13, Henry Drummond called love "the greatest thing in the world,"[7] and his verdict has been affirmed by universal acclamation. Yet how hard it is to love in a mature and sustained fashion. The most intimate of human devotions are often wrecked by divorce, and we see tender affection become angry bitterness, as if love and hatred coexist side by side as Siamese twins. Even our highest religious affections often prove fickle when we are seduced by the allure of careless trifles. How may we protect true love from the pathologies that so easily beset it?

Jesus set love at the center of his understanding of life and made it the hallmark of true religion. When asked to identify the core convictions of his ancestral faith, he responded with twin commandments that unify the three great loves in triadic fashion: (1) the upward love of God, (2) the outward love of others, and (3) the inward love of self (Mark 12:30–31). As we prioritize, balance, and relate these three expressions of love so that each shapes and reinforces the others, we learn to live the life of love in all its splendor and fullness. Let us examine each of these loves in turn, with that goal before us.

I. *Love of God.* Jesus was certain that love must begin with an undivided adoration of the one true God that claims the whole person. The imperative of loving God that is implied by the command "Thou shalt!" is based on a radical decision to renounce all unworthy infatuations—such as with materialism, the rapacious desire for earthly gain (Matt. 6:24)—or with egotism—the use of even religion to seek the vainglory of human adulation (Matt. 6:1–2). In uncompromising fashion, Jesus insisted that to love God is to exist for him exclusively, to value him supremely, and to make his sovereignty the compelling aspiration of one's life.[8] The totality of this commitment is expressed in the fourfold "all" of heart, soul, mind, and strength (Mark 12:30) which Eugene Peterson translates as loving God with "all your passion and prayer and intelligence and energy."[9]

Why did Jesus stress that love of God must always be first and foremost, the essential prerequisite to other loves? Because God is the only one who never uses our love to his own advantage. All of us know how selfish, manipulative, and exploitive love can become, as

---

[6]Frederick Buechner, *The Magnificent Defeat* (New York: Seabury, 1968), p. 18.

[7]Henry Drummond, *The Greatest Thing in the World*, Centennial Edition (Birmingham, Ala.: Samford University Press, 1997).

[8]Ethelbert Stanffer, "Agape," in Gerhard Kittel (ed.), *Theological Dictionary of the New Testament*, Vol. 1 (Grand Rapids, Mich.: Eerdmans, 1964), p. 45.

[9]Eugene H. Peterson, *The Message: The New Testament in Contemporary English* (Colorado Springs: Navpress, 1993), p. 102.

when teenagers whisper in the moonlight, "I love you, I love you," but really mean, "I love me and I want you!" Even parents or spouses can use love to smother or control the beloved, but no matter how intensely we love God, he never makes unfair use of our affections. Loving God never leaves us vulnerable to abuse, because God is utterly free of fickleness. Thus we begin by offering him our unworthy human love, that it may be purified and enriched before we offer it to anyone else. Until we offer all of our love to God, we will never learn what it means for passion to be guided by purpose, for devotion to be infused with discipline, for impulsiveness to be based on integrity.

Here we reach the heart of the matter: the mortal enemy of love is self-centeredness, but try as we may, we cannot rid even our most exalted efforts to love of this deadly virus. Because we are mortal, insecurity lurks on the edge of our existence, suddenly asserting itself as a self-preservation instinct that clamors for the kind of power and prestige that are incompatible with love. But God is sovereign, and therefore not insecure; he is the one and only utterly unselfish person in the universe (Mark 12:29), and we can love him without fear of having our affections misused to bolster his troubled ego. By definition, love seeks the best for the beloved, but only God can define the highest good without a trace of self-aggrandizement. When we begin by loving others, we are immediately drawn into the many little games that love plays in seeking its own advantage. But when we begin by loving God, we immediately confront one who plays none of our little games but rather bids us forget these subtle strategies and love him with all the abandon of which we are capable. Only in the divine-human relationship do we discover the true nature of single-minded love that cleanses our duplicity.

So, how far have you gone in loving God with every fiber of your being? A Jesuit priest, Father Edward Collins Vacek, has noticed how "many contemporary Christians subscribe to Jesus' second great commandment, but not to his first." That is, "almost all of them talk approvingly about love for others, some talk confidently about God's love for us, but few are willing to talk about their love for God."[10] We often try to compliment God by emphasizing his great love for us, as if he never wants or needs our love for him. But the Bible pictures God yearning to receive our love, reciprocating our love with his forgiveness, and suffering to win our uncoerced love as the tragic cost of human freedom. By adopting the language of family and friendship, Scripture tells us that God is not a self-sufficient deity content to live in splendid isolation. Indeed, the pathos of Jesus weeping over Jerusalem mirrored the anguish of his unrequited love.[11]

II. *Love others.* When asked to identify the one commandment that is greatest of all, Jesus replied by citing *two* commandments, one from Deuteronomy 6:5 and the other from Leviticus 19:18. Although these two verses were not normally connected, Jesus fused them together as a unity, making each inseparable from the other. To identify the latter as "second" (Mark 12:31) did not mean that it was of secondary importance. Rather, both commandments taken together were set over against all the other requirements in the Law as constituting the

---

[10]Edward Collins Vacek, S. J., in *America,* Mar. 9, 1996, cited by Martin E. Marty in *Context,* June 1, 1996, p. 6; and in *Christian Century,* Dec. 18-25, 1996, p. 1271.
[11]Stephen G. Post, *A Theory of Agape: On the Meaning of Christian Love* (Lewisburg, Pa.: Bucknell University Press, 1990), pp. 52-66.

essence of true religion. Here the two parts were not being ranked in value but were being listed in sequence as components of equal importance.[12] By concluding (Mark 12:31b) that "there is no other commandment greater than these," Jesus was clearly distinguishing between love in two very different relationships, yet holding both of them to be integral parts of a larger whole.[13]

Why are this linkage and sequence so crucial? Because the act of first loving God completely redefines how we are then to love others. In Luke's version of our text, the admonition to love neighbor prompts the further question, "But who is my neighbor?" (Luke 10:29). Originally, the injunction in Leviticus (19:18) was directed toward one's "own people," that is, fellow Israelites—exactly the kind of folks we prefer to love today. But Jesus responded by telling the story of the Good Samaritan (Luke 10:30–37), which shifted the issue from the question, "Who is my neighbor?" to the question, "How can I be a neighbor?" Love for others is based no longer on the social status of the one to be loved but on the concrete actions by which we express our love. In revolutionary fashion, Jesus radically redefined *love* in terms not of its object but of his subject, and *neighbor* in terms not of kinship or friendship but of anyone in need who is near enough for us to help.

Now we see why the second commandment is bound so tightly to the first. Only in relation to God do we learn to lavish our love without calculation, with no trace of self-interest, no trading of favors, no hint of possessiveness. But God created every person with whom I will ever come in contact, and he seeks the best for each of them as his children. So, says Jesus, love them all—not as you love God, for they are certainly not godlike, but as God loves them, which is utterly without partiality. As nature itself discloses, "he makes his sun to rise on the evil and on the good, and sends rain on the just and on the unjust" (Matt. 5:25). But as the gospel of forgiveness reveals even more deeply, God relates to us all with a pardoning love for the many rather than a preferential love for the few. So we are not merely to love those who love us in order to win their approval (Matt. 5:46a), but to love those whom God loves in order to meet their needs.

The Jews, Greeks, and Romans alike all had elaborate definitions of friend and enemy that fixed a gulf between the two groups "as though the relations of enmity was natural and permanent."[14] But Jesus transcended this dichotomy by including enemies among the neighbors we are to love. After all, "if you salute only your brethren, what more are you doing than others? Do not even the Gentiles do the same?" (Matt. 5:47). Love of enemy was the most daring advance that Jesus made over the prevailing ethic of antiquity—an incredible breakthrough that he accomplished by grounding the second commandment in the first. Eugene Peterson nicely captures the thrust of Jesus' thought in the climactic Matthew 5:48: "In a word, *grow up!* Now that you are subjects of the King, express your God-given identity by living as generously and graciously toward others as God does toward you."[15]

Here we see even more clearly just how dangerous it is to love God with the totality of our being. For only in the fateful embrace do we grasp just how indiscriminately God loves

---

[12]Victor Paul Furnish, *The Love Command in the New Testament* (Nashville: Abingdon Press, 1972), pp. 25-28.

[13]Ceslaus Spicq, *Agape in the New Testament,* Vol. 1 (St. Louis, Mo.: Herder, 1963), p. 64.

[14]Lionel Pearson, *Popular Ethics in Ancient Greece* (Stanford, Calif.: Stanford University Press, 1962), p. 87. For a survey of the evidence, see Furnish, pp. 46-47, 65-66.

[15]Adapted from Peterson, *The Message,* p. 19.

every person. After all, God has no "neighbors" defined as his "own kind." If he loved only his equals, he would not have anyone on Earth to love, for we all stand in need of his boundless mercies. So God changed the ground rules by which we are accustomed to love: he loves not those who *deserve* him but those who *need* him.

Now comes the question that cannot be avoided: how can we love a God like that with all our being and not love others as he does? Indeed, in the parable of the last judgment (Matt. 25:31–46), Jesus taught that loving needy neighbors—not our "own kind" but those who are hungry, thirsty, lonely, naked, sick, and imprisoned—is precisely how we must love God himself (v. 40)!

III. *Love of self.* The deeper we dig into our text, the more dangerous it becomes. We began on the safe side by being told to love a God who will never take advantage of our affections. But then we were told to love all of those nearby (the root meaning of *neighbor*), even if they are enemies who may slap our faces or sue us for the coat on our backs or demand that we carry their burdens an extra mile (Matt. 5:39–41). Jesus loved his enemies and look what it got him: the cross! So are we setting ourselves up for grief by following what appear to be counsels of perfection? I think of two groups with whom I have struggled endlessly over this dilemma.

The first group is drawn from my fellow clergy—what one psychotherapist has called "the overhelpers." They give themselves so relentlessly to serving others that they seek nothing for themselves. As one analyst put it, "These people are pathological givers . . . and they can even be good at it, to a degree, but they become impoverished after a while. They have given so much that they finally run out of spiritual and nervous energy, and what remains is the underlying resentment. You find a great deal of resentment and sourness among the clergy" behind a facade of benevolence and contentment.[16] Why? Because they are so into loving God and loving neighbor that they have forgotten how to love themselves.

The second group are devout Christians who struggle so long with hostile relationships, particularly within the family circle, that they themselves are broken by the very problems they are trying desperately to solve. I shall never forget a luncheon date that lasted all afternoon with one of the finest church leaders it has been my privilege to know, a deacon who for years had been attempting to pacify the furies of an utterly egotistical wife. Hour after hour we reviewed the extraordinary lengths to which he had gone to meet her exorbitant demands, only to be rewarded with screaming fits of rage that threatened his very sanity and had clearly driven him to the brink. At no point in this grim recital did he seek to justify himself or to convince me that he deserved a divorce. Quite the opposite, his whole purpose was to find out if I could possibly think of anything else he might do to save his marriage, even when it was obvious that the relationship had long been shattered beyond repair and that further efforts in that hell of hopelessness might shatter his own life as well.

All of us can multiply stories like this that illustrate how many deeply religious people risk the destruction of their own selfhood in an attempt to love God and others ever more completely. Indeed, there is a very strong tradition in Christian ethics that insists on defining love exclusively in terms of self-denial, self-sacrifice, self-renunciation, and self-crucifixion. In its extreme form, the demand is that love be so radically free of any form of self-interest that

---

[16]Thomas Maeder, "Wounded Healers," cited by Martin E. Marty, *Context*, Mar. 1, 1989, pp. 3-4.

one would even be willing to be damned if it were for the glory of God.[17] In the most prominent theology of love written in the twentieth century, Anders Nygren argued that any notion of self-love "is alien to the New Testament commandment of love. . . . Self-love is man's natural condition, and also the reason for the perversity of his will. . . . So far is neighborly love from including self-love that it actually excludes and overcomes it."[18]

But notice in our text (v. 31) how Jesus addressed this issue. After pairing the two commandments in careful sequence, it would have seemed logical for him to say, "Love others *as you love God*," or even better, "Love others *as God loves them*." But instead he stuck to the formulation in Leviticus and said, "Love others *as you love yourself*." Does this final phrase somehow compromise the dual love commandment by corrupting it with self-interest? No, for it is impossible to love one's self in a selfish fashion if that self has first loved God with utter abandon and then has then loved others with sacrificial service. Elsewhere Jesus clearly taught us to renounce self-centeredness (Mark 9:35; 10:43–44), but here he is being completely consistent in teaching us to love self as well as others because we, like they, are both made in the image of God. Just as love impels us to meet the needs of others, so it also impels us to meet the needs of self for growth, enrichment, and the fulfillment of all that God meant us to be.

Why did Jesus make this Old Testament emphasis the hallmark of his ethics? Because he understood love in relational terms, as the building of true communion through the reciprocity of sharing. We not only need to love, we also need to *be* loved. We grow in godliness as we *give* love, but we also grow in godliness as we *receive* love because God made us for mutuality, with a will to belong. To renounce all concern for self in the name of love, as if my selfhood had no intrinsic value or inalienable rights, comes perilously close to implying that God cares for everyone in the universe but me. Moreover, it gives a blank check to the enemies I am seeking to love and allows them to trample on my most cherished values without fear of protest, which is not good for them or for me.

For us to love the self that first loves God and others is the most unselfish thing we can do, for such love values the self as God values it, builds the kind of self-respect that merits the respect of others, and takes seriously the development of the self's highest potential. Conversely, to neglect or reject the self in the name of love is to depreciate the image of God with a low self-image, to divorce love from faith and hope and so risk depression or despair, and to view love as a source of personal weakness rather than strength. Eric Hoffer, the longshoreman philosopher, observed, "The remarkable thing is that we really love our neighbor as ourselves: we do unto others as we do unto ourselves. We hate others when we hate ourselves. We are tolerant toward others when we tolerate ourselves. We forgive others when we forgive ourselves. It is not love of self but hatred of self that is at the root of the troubles that afflict our world."[19]

---

[17]The view of love as "disinterested benevolence," advanced by Samuel Hopkins, with its "willingness to be damned" theory of conversion, was popular during the Second Great Awakening early in the nineteenth century and may be traced back to the *resignatio ad infernum* of the medieval mystics. For details, see Post, *A Theory of Agape*, pp. 36-51.

[18]Anders Nygren, *Agape and Eros* (London: S.P.C.K., 1954), pp. 100-101. This negative attitude toward self-love, which is prominent in the Lutheran tradition, owes much to Søren Kierkegaard, *Works of Love* (Princeton, N.J.: Princeton University Press, 1949), pp. 15-20. See also Rudolf Bultmann, *Jesus and the Word* (New York: Scribner's, 1958), pp. 115-116; Günther Bornkamm, *Jesus of Nazareth* (London: Hodder and Stoughton, 1960), pp. 111-114.

[19]Eric Hoffer, *The Passionate State of Mind*, cited in *Reader's Digest*, July 1994, p. 149.

What have we learned from this engagement with the teaching of Jesus? That true love is trilateral, with upward, outward, and inward dimensions that need, most of all, to be kept in balance. Some love only God as the source of every blessing, feeling inviolable within the divine caress, but their spirituality becomes otherworldly and finally irrelevant. Some love only others, feeling that the best chance for security this side of heaven is to scratch every back and please every friend. Some love only themselves and are content to live like a sponge, soaking up all they can from those around them. But Jesus calls us beyond a narrow focus on love, whether it be God-centered, other-centered, or self-centered. When each of the three loves extends and enriches the other two, we begin to attain that moral maturity perfectly expressed by the God who loves each one of us and himself with the fullness of his being (Matt. 5:48).—William E. Hull

Topic: Cheer Up! The Worst Is Yet to Come
TEXT: Jer. 12:5

As a new millennium dawns, we are caught in the terrible tension between a hopeful future and a horrible past. One the one hand, the twenty-first century finds our nation in a dominant position as the world's only superpower. The stock market has roared to new highs, offering the promise of almost boundless prosperity. Technology is rushing to invent marvels that would make Buck Rogers blush, while medical science is learning to alter our genetic makeup so we will live longer to enjoy these dazzling prospects. No wonder we set off fireworks around the globe to celebrate the advent of a new era, unspoiled by hardly a single Y2K computer glitch.

On the other hand, over this bright horizon the twentieth century casts a dark shadow drenched in blood. We remember that it began a hundred years ago with almost invincible optimism. Victorian splendor soon gave way to the Edwardian opulence of the Gilded Age. Theodore Roosevelt summoned our country to exercise its burgeoning power on a world stage. Christianity talked grandly about winning the world to its cause in a single generation. But soon these millennial anticipations went up in the flames of two world wars. A succession of despots ravaged the planet with unbridled butchery: Hitler, Mussolini, Stalin, Mao. Nuclear threats lurked behind iron curtains where the balance of terror was maintained by a world armed to the teeth. More recently, tribal genocide has erupted in the name of ethnic cleansing. Thoughtful people must wonder if we can move from this midnight madness to millennial euphoria simply by flipping a single page of the calendar.

Clearly one of our greatest needs is for guidance in the titanic struggle between dark heritage and bright hope. Is the appropriate mood of the new millennium one of bleak pessimism or buoyant optimism? Is humanity inching toward the abyss or away from it? More than 2,500 years ago, the prophet Jeremiah wrestled with this dilemma as his nation was poised between triumph and tragedy. Musing on the bewilderments of life, he burst into God's presence, hot and angry, stunned by the cruel usages of life. Unfair! he cried, as frowningly he looked into the face of the Almighty and framed his accusations in a series of questions:[20] "Righteous art thou, O Lord, when I complain to thee; yet I would plead my case before thee. Why do the wicked prosper? Who do all who are treacherous thrive?" (Jer. 12:1).

---

[20]Arthur John Gossip, "But When Life Tumbles In, What Then?" Andrew Watterson Blackwood (ed.), *The Protestant Pulpit* (Nashville: Abingdon Press, 1947), p. 198.

To this protest the prophet received a disturbing reply that was not so much an answer as it was a challenge: "If you have raced with men on foot and they have wearied you, how will you compete with horses? And if on a level field you fall down, how will you manage in the jungle of the Jordan?" (Jer. 12:5). Let us probe this strange imagery for an understanding of how God would have us face a new millennium that is rich with both promise and peril.

I. Jeremiah had recently been having a great deal of trouble. Here his struggle was likened to a race, or perhaps better, to a chase. In his battles on behalf of God he had frequently been beaten. His enemies had always seemed to outrun him, leaving him far behind. Now, trouble had arisen even in his relatively obscure hometown of Anathoth. In the supposed safety of his native countryside, he had narrowly escaped assassination at the hands of his own kinsmen, forcing him to flee for safety.

But did God instruct Jeremiah to go back and work with his countrymen, confident of success? Is there here any hint of the assurance, "You will come out on top, you will win them over to you, everything will be fine?" No. God said, rather, "It is true that your little contests and skirmishes have been failures. But there are even harder races out before you, with competition that is even stronger. You have raced on almost even terms with men on foot. Now what will you do if I send you to vie with horses?" As Demosthenes put it, "If they cannot face the candle, what will they do when they see the sun?"[21]

Then God went a step further by asking, "How will you fare in the jungle of the Jordan?" As the river twists and winds its way down the backbone of Palestine, it is surrounded on either side by dense vegetation. This forest is tropical and, for the most part, lush with growth. Its foliage is rank; thorns and thistles grow shoulder high. It is covered with almost impenetrable thickets of oleander, cane, tangled bushes, vines, willows, poplars, and twisted tamarisks. Thus it is well called the "Jungle of the Jordan." The name was doubly appropriate, for lions once had their lairs there (Jer. 49:19; 50:44; Zech. 11:3), until the time of the Crusades. Even to this day it is haunted by jackals and wolves.[22]

Moreover, this gorge cut by the river could be exceedingly treacherous. Rising out of the rocks and forests of the Lebanon Mountains, the Jordan flows in a zigzag course through a serpentine rift and at last empties into the Dead Sea. In the summer it is harmless and may be forded in many places on foot. A child can throw a rock across it with ease. But when the rainy seasons come, the waters quickly begin to rise. Soon they break over the narrow banks and the once placid Jordan becomes a raging torrent. Cattle flee from the advancing waters, and even the lions are driven from their jungle lairs. Nothing can withstand the devastating flood that covers the surrounding plains. Thus the Jungle of the Jordan was a vivid picture of desperate danger, and it was toward such a threat that Jeremiah was pointed by God. Naturally, God's answer did not mean that Jeremiah would soon race against actual horses or that he would have to cope with the physical dangers of Jordan's dense thickets. Rather, these were vivid pictures of extreme danger and difficulty. God was not saying that all of Jeremiah's problems would soon be over, as in a dream. Rather, he was saying that Jeremiah's troubles had just begun: "If a few footmen have worn you down in your race on

---

[21]Cited by Stanley Romaine Hopper, "The Book of Jeremiah: Exposition," in George Arthur Buttrick (ed.), *The Interpreter's Bible*, Vol. 5 (Nashville: Abingdon Press, 1956), p. 916.
[22]Nelson Glueck, *The River Jordan* (Philadelphia: Westminster Press, 1946), pp. 62-63.

my behalf, what will you do when you come up against thoroughbreds? If you fell flat on your face when contending for me on level ground, how will you fare when the swollen angry waters burst their banks and rush down to engulf you?" "Cheer up, Jeremiah," said God, "the worst is yet to come!"

Nor was this a novel answer given only to Jeremiah. It reflects the attitude of the entire Bible. James and John, for example, came to Jesus seeking to arrange places of prominence for themselves in the coming Kingdom of God. Having endured the harassments of the Galilean ministry, they were now ready for their reward. Instead they received the reply, "Are ye able to drink the cup of tragedy that I will drain to its dregs, and be baptized with the baptism of rejection that will soon overwhelm me?" (Mark 10:38). Jesus gave no soothing answers to his troubled disciples. Instead, he pictured the Christian life as one that would be blessed, not when it basked in the sunshine of success but rather when "men revile you and persecute you and utter all kinds of evil against you falsely on my account" (Matt. 5:12).

The early Christians found this prediction of struggle and rejection to be realistic. Paul prayed repeatedly that his "thorn" would be removed, but the petition was not answered. Much earlier, God had revealed to Ananias a glimpse of Paul's future now that he had become a Christian. It would be no stunning success. Rather, "I will show him how much he must suffer for the sake of my name" (Acts 9:16). Paul would later summarize just how literally that fearful prophecy was played out in his life:

> with far greater labors, far more imprisonments, with countless beatings, and often near death. Five times I have received at the hands of the Jews the forty lashes less one. Three times I have been beaten with rods; once I was stoned. Three times I have been shipwrecked; a night and a day I have been adrift at sea; on frequent journeys, in danger from rivers, danger from robbers, danger from my own people, danger from Gentiles, danger in the city, danger in the wilderness, danger at sea, danger from false brethren; in toil and hardship, through many a sleepless night, in hunger and thirst, often without food, in cold and exposure [2 Cor. 11:23b-27].

There is no need to multiply examples further. The point is plain: we are promised that the bad may be but a foretaste of the worse that is yet to come. Real religion may not get us out of trouble, but it may get us into even deeper trouble! Any soul serenity that God gives us is like the calm in the eye of a storm, safety in the midst of swirling dangers. But if in our faith, of all places, we can find no peace, might we not just as well give in to despair? If in claiming God we find no escape from the world's problems, then surely there must be none available. But no, in the reply of God to Jeremiah there lurks an answer, not only for his life but for ours as well.

II. Jeremiah had known success in the first eighteen years of his prophetic career, as the throne smiled on his ministry. But the benevolent Josiah was succeeded by the treacherous Jehoikim, and Jeremiah became an unpopular fugitive. With courage he sought the security of his own village, only to be "led as a lamb to the slaughter" by his kinsmen. In his distress he was confronted by God with a shattering word that became his salvation. Harris E. Kirk has explained it like this:

> God hit this man a tremendous blow. The hammer came crashing down through all the mush sentimentality until it struck the anvil underneath. And when Jeremiah heard the clang of good

steel beneath all the softness, he said to himself: "O my God, I did not know I had that in me. I did not know that under all this complaining there was something hard and strong and steel-like!" He stood up, and one can imagine him growing in stature—gathering his strength, girding his loins, and going obediently out of that obscure little village where he was born and brought up. . . . For the first time Jeremiah realized this: that the function of an iron pillar is not to stand in some splendid museum, to be admired by all observers, but to carry loads . . . and thus he learned what God meant by living dangerously.[23]

God was saying to Jeremiah, "You have had sufferings that were relatively minor. Instead of removing them, I will let them be your preparation for the even greater battles that are yet to come. I believe in you. Thus I have given you an elementary course in conflict so that I may promote you to a more difficult field of battle."

What God is saying to us is that our sufferings will equip us for even more challenging adventures. But he will not throw us out to contend with horses until we have first had training with the footmen. Every struggle of life that we overcome fits us more fully to face the testing of yet greater crises. Consider it a compliment when you graduate from the minor skirmishes of the daily round and are ready to take on the really great battles that decide the major issues of life.

This truth is proved over and over again. From the furnace of affliction comes finely tempered steel. Cripple a man and you grow a Franklin Roosevelt. Put him in a prison cell and you produce a John Bunyan. Bury him in the snows of Valley Forge and you get a George Washington. Let him be born in abject poverty and he becomes an Abraham Lincoln. Load him with bitter racial prejudice and a Martin Luther King emerges. Make him play second fiddle in an obscure South American orchestra and he matures into Auturo Toscanini. Our muscles are not trained so that we may rest at ease, but rather so that we may fight a bigger fight. History records no examples of greatness that come without testing and challenge. God may be hammering out a strong soul of steel in your life on the anvil of conflict.

We have already seen that few have ever faced a life of trial and tribulation as did the apostle Paul. How did he learn in whatever state he found himself, whether abased or abounding, to be content? (Phil. 4:11–12). The secret of his serenity is disclosed in this testimony: "A thorn was given me in the flesh, a messenger of Satan, to harass me, to keep me from being too elated. Three times I besought the Lord about this, that it should leave me; but he said to me, 'My grace is sufficient for you, for my power is made perfect in weakness.' I will all the more gladly boast of my weaknesses, that the power of Christ may rest upon me. For the sake of Christ, then, I am content with weaknesses, insults, hardships, persecutions, and calamities; for when I am weak, then I am strong" (2 Cor. 12:7b–10).

The less Paul was able to do by his own strength, the more Christ had a chance to do things through him. The less he could depend on himself, the more he was forced to depend on Christ. "Grace," as Samuel Rutherford said, "grows best in winter."[24]

Every human failure provides an opportunity for the power of God to work in human life. A biologist tells how he watched an ant dragging a piece of straw that seemed almost too

---

[23]Harris E. Kirk, "The Hammer and the Anvil," *Interpretation, 1,* p. 37.
[24]*Gossip,* "But When Life Tumbles In, What Then?" p. 201.

heavy to be carried. The ant came to a crack in the ground that proved too wide to cross. The ant stopped for a time, as if perplexed. Then it put the straw across the crack and walked over it. Would that we were as wise as that ant who converted its burden into a bridge. We think of burdens as bearing us down. Why not see them as bearing us up to the inexhaustible power of God?

To return to the question with which we began: In what mood shall we face the new millennium that is coming, ready or not? At first it seems that our text urges pessimism, but that is only because we associate pessimism with things getting worse and optimism with things getting better. If the future is anything like the past, it will be marked by the ebb and flow of advance and decline, progress and retrogression, steps forward and steps backward. If we tie our mood to the swings of history's pendulum, we condemn ourselves to the endless ups and downs of success and failure, for we can do little to change the human heart, with its enormous potential to visit both good and evil on the lives of others. Left to our own devices, life will always be an endless seesaw of bane and blessing, no matter how many millennia we may celebrate.

With Jeremiah we are brought to the threshold of a new insight—namely, that our emotional equilibrium need not be determined by outward circumstances, whether fair or foul. God's bracing challenge to a troubled prophet hints at a truth confirmed in the lives of Jesus and Paul: the paradox of strength made perfect in weakness, of success made perfect in failure, of growth made perfect in struggle. The great Good News of our text is that as the situation in which we find ourselves becomes more pessimistic, we can actually become more optimistic in the confidence that God has prepared us to face even greater challenges and will be with us through thick and thin until victory is won.—William E. Hull

Topic: The Mysterious Fact of Resurrection
TEXT: John 1:4–5

"In him was life; and the life was the light of me. And the light shineth in darkness; and the darkness has never put it out." These are two verses from the grand prologue to St. John's Gospel (1:4, 5). He began his Gospel by setting the background of the story he was about to tell, the story of Jesus of Nazareth. But the setting was not the events that were taking place in Rome and Jerusalem, not the names of emperors, kings, and governors who were in power at the time of the action. The setting was eternity. If it were ever set to music, the direction would be *maestoso,* with majesty.

"In him was life; and the life was the light of me." There are different kinds of light. There is the natural light of the sun by which the world around us comes back to life every morning, almost miraculously, each object resuming its shape, and the color we thought the darkness had drained out of it is once again bright. By this light we know where we are and we can see where we are going. Sometimes the way is beautiful and sometimes it is ugly.

There is also the natural light of the moon. It is not as powerful as the light of the sun, and if clouds come across it we can't see it at all. But when we can see it, we sometimes see a beauty that is almost unearthly, particularly if the moon is full and the night is clear.

Then there is what we might call "artificial" light, which may have begun with a candle set in the middle of a room to make at least a center of light so that the family could see what they were eating. Then came the gas lamp, and finally the incandescent bulb. Now, with electricity, we can light our cities so they are sometimes brighter at midnight than they are at midday—alas, too bright for some of us. And by this artificial light, signals start and stop the trains and the automobiles, and warn the pilots on their flights.

But there is another kind of light: the light of a life. Picture a room at night, already well lit. Into it steps a person. The minute he enters the room, it is brilliant as it wasn't before. His presence makes it bright. It's the light of the person's life. Less dramatically, imagine that, if you are anything like me, you are having trouble with a math problem. You can't make the figures go the way they are supposed to go. They don't come out right; they never do. They don't make sense and you have almost given up. You are developing a definite dislike for figures. Then a teacher works with you. It is as though a light were turned on. He knows exactly what to do, how to approach your antimathematical mind so that you even come to enjoy the figures and can make sense of them; you can add, subtract, and even multiply them.

Still more significantly, you meet a man—perhaps not face-to-face but only on the printed page. Even so, in his life there is light. I have met both men and women who have done that for me, but I will speak of one because he did it to such an extraordinary degree. He was the French novelist and essayist Albert Camus. He made no pretense of being a Christian, not even a theist. He was an avowed atheist. It was in the fifties and I found myself in some of the corners of the world that I had never faced before. They were the dark areas of a troubled world. It was increasingly an unbelieving world, in which we were beginning to hear about "the absurd" and "the meaninglessness of meaning." I was lost in it, and Camus helped me find my way. His sensitivity, his kindness, his brilliant intellectual power, everything about him, everything he did, shed light. In his life there was light—the way he accepted the poverty of his boyhood and the tuberculosis of his manhood; his exuberant response to the sun and the sea; his moral response to the Nazi crimes and the part he played in the French underground; his novels, his essays, and his notebooks; and particularly his address to the Dominican monks in 1948. He was more Christian in spirit than many church people I have known, and he helped me find my way through some of the immemorial problems of the human race.

This is the kind of light that Jesus is. The light that was in his life was the light of men. He lived simply, but he lived intensely. At times he burned with a white heat. His life overflowed, so to speak; he could not contain it. Everything he touched became more alive. He gave sight to the blind—not only to the blind who couldn't see because their eyes were gone, but to the others, many more in number, who couldn't see because they were "in the dark."

They were in the dark about so many things: about themselves—they didn't quite know who they were, especially in the presence of God. Jesus said to them, you are not servants; you don't need to bow and scrape in the presence of God. You are his friends, his children. Stand up! They were in the dark about their mistakes, about their violations of the law, or more often, I am sorry to say, about the violations that someone else had made. And Jesus always implied—though I think it was never recorded that he said it, but I can hear him say it when people were criticizing others for violating the law—Which law? One of the relatively unimportant ceremonial laws or one of the basic laws like "Thou shalt not kill"? More often it was one of the less important laws.

They were in the dark about their neighbors. Who were they? Jesus tried to tell them. Your neighbor, he said, is not the one you like the most, not necessarily the one who lives next door to you, or the one who agrees with you. You have a natural affinity with those people, but your neighbor is the one who needs you the most. They were in the dark about failure. They thought that failure was a disgrace. It is now in the eyes of many people. If a son drops out of college or fails to pass, it is seen as a disgrace brought on the family. It is sad, because it may be largely the son's fault. But Jesus says, don't forget that failure—failure of a certain kind—may be the way to let the light through. And suffering—so many people were (and are) in the dark about suffering. They thought it was something sent to them, directed to them personally, by God, and usually as punishment for something they had done or not done. By his own suffering, Jesus showed them that suffering is the price you pay for being the person you are. If you are any kind of person at all, you will suffer, and the way you do it may be something like the light that was in him. *In him was life; and the life was the light of men.*

It is what follows that statement that captivates our attention today: "and the light shineth in the darkness and the darkness has never put it out." If you are familiar with the Authorized Version, you expect to hear, "and the darkness comprehended it not." William Temple gave me the ground for saying that the verb used here can mean either "to comprehend" or "to overcome." In this case, the latter was chosen. The darkness has never overcome the light that was in Christ. The darkness has never put it out.

Not the darkness of ignorance through the long night of barbarian darkness that came down like tidal waves from northern Europe in the fifth, sixth, seventh, eighth, and ninth centuries. That darkness, you would think, would have extinguished any light that Jesus might once have lit, but there were groups of monks here and there who kept it burning. It was dim, but it didn't go out.

Not the darkness of wealth and power in the thirteenth century. The church of Europe was so drenched in wealth and power that it almost forgot what it was there for. But even that darkness didn't put out the light entirely, because there was a little Italian who went up and down singing about the Lord Jesus. He possessed nothing, yet he had all things. Thousands of men and women were drawn to his light. He asked them to do only two things: to give away everything they had and to be cheerful. In eighteenth-century England, the established church was in almost total darkness. But John Wesley rode up and down the land, and wherever he went, the light began to shine!

What is more surprising, perhaps, is that even now—in this secular, materialistic, violent, cynical age in which we live, and in which every value that a Christian holds dear has been attacked, challenged, or just ignored—in this age of rapid, revolutionary change, there is *Jesus Christ Superstar* on records, and now on the stage; and *Godspell.* Some of you who know me know that I am not particularly drawn to either of them, but I am drawn by the spirit that animates them, by the incentive that leads the young people in the cast to perform them and that draws people to the theater to see them. I do not see in them my picture of Jesus; but no two eras have exactly the same picture of Jesus. They never do. For in Jesus every generation sees, to some degree, a reflection of itself; and this age sees violence, ugliness, and failure. There are also the Jesus Movement and the Jesus Freaks. I am sure that a great deal of both movements would not draw me and will not last long. But this I know: there is a life in Jesus that is light, and the young will not let it go.

This is something we can see and understand, but what we are celebrating today we can't always see and we may never understand it. This is it: not even the darkness of the tomb or the darkness of death could put out that light. This is the key sentence of the sermon: *The Resurrection of Jesus remains the most mysterious fact in human history.* How could it happen? How *did* it happen? Did it actually happen? Or was it an event that took place in the inspired imagination of devout followers? Was it the fulfillment of an extravagant desire?

In other years we have probed the Resurrection narratives in the Gospels and the references to the Resurrection in the letters and the rest of the New Testament. It is a fascinating subject for any student, or for anyone who has a shred of intellectual curiosity. To see where they coincide, where they contradict one another, and at what point they diverge is a fascinating exercise. But for the person who meets the risen Lord on his way to work, or as he sits by the deathbed of someone he loves, or as he waits for his first child to be born, that study doesn't help much; in fact, I would say it is almost completely irrelevant.

What is relevant in the New Testament is the men and women who walk through its pages—Peter, Paul, John, Barnabas, Mark, and Luke. A slave like Onesimus, do you know anything about him? Or about a couple like Priscilla and Aquilla? A young girl like Rhoda, so excited that she didn't even let Peter in when he knocked at the door until she had gone to tell her family that he was there, just out of prison? And the prison guards in Rome—do you remember what happened to them?

One thing they all had in common, different as they were, was that they were all once "in the dark," and they were now in the light. And the light was not a brighter sun or better weather or even a better government, better schools, or a more adequately administered welfare program. The light was the light that was in Christ, that not even the darkness of death could put out and that now shone across their way.

But you may say, I have never met the risen Lord on my way to work, or in any other place for that matter. Neither have I. If you mean a person walking up the street with pierced hands and feet, I've never met him. Some have, but I never have. But if you mean the life that takes hold of a person and changes him from a self-centered brat into a companionable, loving human being, I've seen him. Or if you mean the life that gradually developed an overgrown, spoiled teenager into one of the most sensitive, competent professionals in his field, I've seen him. Or if you mean a middle-aged person whose life had gone down the drain with alcohol, or something worse, who suddenly begins to live, to stand up, throw back his head, have a job, and be glad to be alive—if you mean that, I've seen him.

I have met that life. In fact, I think if it weren't for him I'd give up. For the darkness of life is deep and powerful. I cannot face it alone. I can face it because I know that in him is life, and that that life is the light of men. And the light shines in the darkness and the darkness has never yet been able to put it out. In fact, it is shining here now!

Thanks be to thee, O God, for the life that is in Jesus, and for the light that comes to us from him and guides us on our way and makes sense of life, that gives us a better direction. Steady us, Lord, for the way we have to go. Save us from unnecessary mistakes; and when we make them, help us to remember that thou art not only our Judge, but also our Father. Amen.—Theodore Parker Ferris[25]

ILLUSTRATIONS

THE CENTER.   Let us depend on this: Whatever happened on that day became, was, and remained the center round which everything else revolves, the point from which everything

---

[25]*Selected Sermons*

else comes at first and to which it is hurrying in the end. There are many real and many apparent, many bright and many dim lights, but this one will burn longest, even when all the rest have had their day and are once more put out. For anything lasts its time, but the love of God, which was at work and found expression in the raising of Jesus Christ from the dead, lasts forever. Because this once happened, there is therefore no reason for despair, and there is every reason for hope—even as we read the newspaper, with all its confusing and frightening news; even in the story uncannily reflecting so many colors, which we call world history.—Karl Barth[26]

THE MESSAGE.   But here is the stumbling block of the world. It may admit that, by the power of God, Christ rose from the tomb, but it will not admit that the power of the Risen Christ continues beyond the tomb. It sees the Church on its human side, made up of weak, frail creatures, and therefore thinks it something to be ignored. It makes the same mistake Mary Magdalene made the first Easter morning. She mistook the Risen Savior for the gardener—that is, for but a human thing. The world, too, sees the Risen Christ in his Mystical Body, the Church, and takes it to be the gardener—something human and not divine. But divinity is there as it was in the garden the first Easter, and only that same Divinity can give hope to a hopeless world. We may yet attain our peace if we but seek—not the political and the economic, but the new life of the Kingdom of God. For such is the message of Easter Day: the resurrection of the dead, the triumph of the defeated, the finding of the lost, the springtime of the Earth, the waking of life, the trumpet of resurrection blowing over the land of the living.—Bishop Fulton J. Sheen[27]

---

[26]*Call for God*
[27]*On Being Human*

SECTION VI

MESSAGES FOR ADVENT AND CHRISTMAS

SERMON SUGGESTIONS

Topic: Jesus Christ: His Birth

TEXT: Various

The birth of Jesus was a powerful event. It divides history. From the Christian point of view, all that went before that event is B.C., and all that came after it is A.D. We never write a letter, check a date on a calendar, observe a birthday, sign a legal document, or celebrate a national event without doing it in relation to that faraway event.

No life has had an impact on our world and history the way Jesus of Nazareth has. His shadow lies across the landscape of our modern world, to say nothing of his living presence among us. He is alive! That is the great exclamation of the Christian gospel.

The earliest literary account of the birth of Jesus is not from the Gospels but from Paul. That has always interested me. In Galatians, Paul wrote, "But when the time had fully come, God sent for his Son, born of woman, born under the law, to redeem those who were under the law, so that we might receive adoption as sons" (Gal. 4:4–5).

While Matthew and Luke began their Gospels with the birth of Jesus, Mark skipped over his birth, bringing him abruptly onto the stage of history when he was a grown man: "The beginning of the gospel of Jesus Christ, the Son of God" (Mark 1:1).

I believe that in thinking about the birth of Jesus we should keep five things in mind.

I. *His preexistence.* John went back to eternity, to the beginning, to the preexistence of Christ. He existed before he became a historical person. "In the beginning was the Word, and the Word was with God, and the Word was God. He was in the beginning with God" (John 1:1–2).

Not only did Christ preexist but he was the agent of creation: "All things were made through him, and without him was not anything made that was made" (John 1:3).

Paul developed the same idea in his letter to the Colossians: "He is the image of the invisible God, the firstborn of all creation; for in him all things were created, in heaven and on Earth, visible and invisible, whether thrones or dominions or principalities or authorities—all things were created through him and for him" (Col. 1:15–16).

Then this preexistent Word who was with God from the beginning took a nosedive into our world and history: "And the Word became flesh and dwelt among us, full of grace and truth" (John 1:14).

Here is the doctrine of the incarnation. God came down to us and became enfleshed. He took upon himself our frail and fragile form.

I once heard a well-known theologian say, "Christianity is a religion of Incarnation." That statement excited me and I've never forgotten it.

II. *Jesus was conceived of the Holy Spirit and born of a virgin.* Both Matthew and Luke speak of the divine conception.

"When his mother Mary had been betrothed to Joseph," Matthew wrote, "before they came together she was found to be with child of the Holy Spirit. . . . An angel of the Lord appeared to him in a dream, saying, 'Joseph, son of David, do not fear to take Mary as your wife, for that which is conceived in her is of the Holy Spirit; she will bear a son and you shall call his name Jesus, for he will save his people from their sins'" (Matt. 1:18, 20–21; see also Luke 1:30–31, 34–35).

These accounts have been very important because their purpose was to affirm the divinity and uniqueness of Jesus. "Therefore the child to be born will be called holy, the Son of God" (Luke 1:35b).

III. *Jesus was born of a woman.* This is the way Paul put it: "But when the time had fully come, God sent forth his Son, born of a woman" (Gal. 4:4). Luke tells about Mary bringing forth her firstborn son.

It was a real birth. Mary knew the pain of childbirth. The baby was no spiritual phantom. He was real and human.

If conception by the Holy Spirit speaks of Jesus' divinity, then being born of a woman tells of his humanity.

On that first Christmas, the Shepherds and Wise Men no doubt asked how they would know the child. Two signs were given: swaddling clothes and a manger (Luke 2:12), and the light of a star (Matt. 2:9). The swaddling clothes were coarsely woven wool. They were of the Earth. The child would be human, of which these clothes would be a sign. But that was not all. He would be a baby with the light of a star in his face. He could only be fully known by a sign from heaven. He would be divine.

IV. *His birth was a historical event.* Jesus was born into our history. We know where and when he was born. The Christmas angels announced, "For to you is born this day, in the city of David, a Savior who is Christ the Lord" (Luke 2:11). Where was he born? In heaven, in some etheral realm? No, in Bethlehem, the city of David, which was not far away. This is very important because Christianity is a historical religion. God reveals himself, speaks to us, and tells us who he is, not from the celestial realms but along the common ways of life, in the Bethlehems of our world. He does not jar the Earth with his mighty power or address us with a cosmic voice. No, he speaks to us in much more modest ways. There is a kind of everydayness in the way he speaks.

V. *His birth tells of God's radical action.* God entered our world in a strange new way in Christ. In some basic sense he clothed himself in our flesh and came among us. That is what John says he did. Or to put it in a different way, he sent a Savior into the world. That is what the angel announced. God took the world seriously. He knew how sick, lost, and alienated it was. And God took himself seriously. He knew that only he could redeem men and women and save the world.—Chevis E. Horne[1]

Topic: Christmas as Homecoming
Text: John 1:1–13

There is something warm and intimate about Christmas. Jesus was not born into an unfamiliar place, among strange people. He came into a world that had his imprimatur on it. He

---

[1]*Preaching the Great Themes of the Bible*

had made it, and he came among his own people. John tells us, "He came to his own home" (1:11). It was a kind of homecoming for Jesus.

I. *The world is Christ's creation.* Jesus came into his own created order. Mark introduces Jesus as a grown man making his entrance onto the stage of history. Matthew and Luke begin with his birth, both telling lovely stories about him. Luke's story is exquisitely beautiful. Someone has said that Luke gave us Christmas. But John goes all the way back to a time before time. He tells of the preexistent Christ who was from eternity. John begins his prologue like this: "In the beginning was the Word, and the Word was with God, and the Word was God" (v. 1). Christ was the Word.

John made the startling claim that Christ was the Creator of our world: "All things were made through him, and without him was not anything made that was made" (v. 3).

Christ came into the world order he had created, and having created it, he did not leave it but stayed in it. He did not abandon it like a skipper leaving his ship. Phillips' translation puts it like this: "He came into the world—the world he had created—and the world failed to recognize him" (John 1:1). He was the light enlightening every man as he came into the world, but the world in its alienation and blindness cast a shadow over his face so they could not recognize him.

While Christ's human creation was hostile to him, nature was not. Nature was kind and generous. We see him standing on the prow of a boat that was about to sink, and with a hand lifted above the waves he commanded, "Peace, be still" (Mark 4:39), and there was a great calm.

Jesus rode a donkey on Palm Sunday through the streets of Jerusalem. The animal was obedient and submissive.

Jesus appreciated nature and felt kin to it. He spoke of the lilies of the field and said that they were not matched by Solomon in all his glory. He spoke of the birds of the air about whom God cared.

Jesus enjoyed nature. He delighted to look on dawns and sunsets and starry nights; he enjoyed feeling the puff of fresh air on his hot face on a summer's day, the sifting of loamy soil through his fingers, and the feel of cool grass beneath his bare feet.

Ecological crises like ours would grieve Jesus, would probably outrage him. He knows nature is our home. To love nature is to love ourselves, to destroy nature is to destroy ourselves. He would hate to see our streams polluted, our air made unclean, our soil poisoned, nature's beauty marred, and her wealth squandered on easy profits. He would warn us that sooner or later nature in wrath would stand on her feet to destroy us.

II. *We are his people.* Christ did a more significant thing than entering his created order; he came to his own people. "He came to his own home and his own people received him not."

Jesus was not born in Athens or Rome. He was born in Bethlehem. He was a Jew born to Jews. These were his people—bone of his bone, flesh of his flesh, life of his life. He belonged to them and they belonged to him.

Jesus took pride in his people, believing they were God's people. To them had been given the oracles and revelation of God. They were a light to the people of Earth.

Jesus exulted in the religion of the Jews. He knew their great stories, such as the Exodus; he was conversant with the heroes of their history, and his mind was saturated with their Holy Scriptures.

Jesus was especially devoted to the synagogue, which was a school and a place of worship. It was the center of the community's life. There he worshiped with his family and neighbors every Sabbath.

He rejoiced in their monotheistic faith that claimed Yahweh is God and that beside him there are no other gods. He loved their hymnal, the Psalms. His mind was furnished with the imagery of the psalms, and their melodies sang in his heart.

Yet, irony of ironies, his own people rejected him. He came unto his own people and they did not receive him. This is the shadow side of Christmas. It was his own people who put him to death.

Why did Jesus' own people reject him? There was light in his eyes that uncovered the darkness of their minds; there was truth in his mind that judged their falseness; there was serenity about him that exposed their fear and anxiety; there was purity about his life that made them uncomfortable with the lust in their hearts; and there was love in his heart that belied their lovelessness. Beyond that, he, as the Messiah, was caught in the fierceness of their narrow nationalism and their frenzied patriotism. They wanted a political messiah.

III. *He came to give us life.* He was rejected by his own people, yet not totally. All was not lost. "But to all who received him, who believed in his name, he gave power to become children of God; who were born, not of blood nor of the will of the flesh nor of the will of man, but of God" (John 1:12–13).

Jesus did a wonderful thing: he gave new life with new dignity to people. The human heart cries out for both. We want new life as well as dignity.

Jesus told Nicodemus, a well-known jurist who was the flowering of the best in his religion and culture, that Nicodemus must be born again. The new life would come from above. It would be mysterious, like the blowing of the wind. You can hear the sound of it but cannot tell from whence it comes or where it goes. So is the person born of the Spirit.

Christ gives a new dignity. "He gave power to become children of God." He makes us the sons and daughters of God. Nothing is so elevating as the power of Christ. He takes people who do not love themselves and whom the world does not love and assures them that they are dearly loved by God.

Peter, looking out on the early Christians with their poor background, said to them, "Once you were no people, but now you are God's people; once you had not received mercy, but now you have received mercy" (1 Pet. 2:10). They had been people with no identity; they had not known who they were, but now they knew. They were God's people.

No one escaped the elevating influence of Christ, not even slaves. In the Church, slaves found the most accepting and affirming atmosphere anywhere. They often became outstanding leaders in the Church.

There are so many people in our world like that. They feel useless, empty, and worthless. They see no goodness, beauty, or value in their lives. They have no purpose for life.

The Church is to continue Christ's affirmation of people. Is not the Church his body? The Church should be Christ present in our world.

The Church, when it is authentic, takes the poorest, weakest, most illiterate and most nonproductive and says to them, "We could not be who we are without you. You are indispensable." I remember the day this truth broke into my mind. I said to myself that, if for no other reason, I would want to belong to the Church because of what it can do for unlikely people.

It will all happen again this Christmas. Christ will still come to his own, and many will still reject him. But as many as receive him he will make the children of God.—Chevis E. Horne[2]

Topic: Finding Signs of Christmas
TEXT: Isa. 7:10–14; Luke 2:8–14

Yes, there are signs of Christmas all around us today. But centuries ago there were not many signs. Shepherds were keeping their flock on a hillside. Suddenly they were interrupted by angels, who told them they had for them a sign from God that their deliverer had come. What was the sign? The sign was a baby lying in a manger. "Go and see it," they were instructed. "For unto you is born this day, in the City of David, a savior who is Christ the Lord." What a strange sign for God to send to his people.

Notice *when* the sign was given. It was given at night. We are told that the shepherds were watching their flocks at night. The Wise Men traveled in search of Bethlehem and the baby's place of birth by a star that guided them at night. The shepherds heard the angels at night and went to the manger at night. Night has always played a significant role in the Christmas season. Christmas Eve services, midnight masses, and candles symbolize that Christ is the light that came into the world to shatter the darkness that surrounds us.

There is still much darkness in the world. Some of us have darkness within our own lives.

In this Christmas season, we affirm again that God came into a dark world to bring light.

Notice *who* the angel said would come. It would be a savior. The Savior is Christ the Lord, the Anointed of God, the Messiah, the Christ of God. He is the Deliverer, the one who came to free his people from their sin, their disease, their bondage, and their captivity. He is the Savior who has come into the world to deliver us from our captivity to sin. That is a word we still need today because no matter who we are, sin still captivates our life. Sin binds us up, pulls us down, and seeks to destroy us. But Christ comes into our life to give us hope and freedom.

It is a shame to come into the Christmas season and not know the freedom, victory, joy, and wonder that Christ gives to our lives.

God's spirit came at night and he came as a savior. But *how* did he come? He came as a baby. God did not choose to come through the might of a military warrior. He did not come to the royal palace of Caesar Augustus or some other high Roman official, nor to the high priest in his temple or to another member of the religious establishment. The incarnate God made his entrance into the world as a tiny baby. It is astounding when we think about it— how humbly, modestly, gently, quietly, lovingly God's Spirit entered the world.

It is difficult for us to understand this beginning because we live in an age where the emphasis is on the powerful, the rich, the prestigious, and those who have political, military, or monetary powers. But Jesus came in manger power, which is so radically different that often the world does not understand its quiet and unpretentious way.

When God chose to come into the world, he came in the form of a baby at Christmas time. In helpless infancy, God came to bring us help. In human frailty, he revealed his divinity.

---

[2]*Basic Bible Sermons on Christmas*

Through this gentle beginning, this baby would later unleash a revolution like the world had never seen before.

Notice *where* he came. He came to a manger. He did not come to the bustling marketplace, nor to the temple, nor to the throne room, nor to the military base. When Jesus was born, he was placed in a manger, and a manger, remember, is a feeding trough for animals. The manger in a cattle stall indicated the lowly state of the birth of this child, and the humble conditions surrounding his birth. Here, in this place of simplicity, God surprised the world with his unexpected appearance. God chose to come among us with humble shepherds, a lowly maiden, and an ordinary cattle stall.

But this is so like God. He has always identified himself, down through the centuries, with the outcast, the lowly, the poor, the ill, the blind, the deaf, the ordinary people, and the needy. And those of us who belong to the wealthy part of society, and that includes all of us here, must remember that God is always concerned with the lowly, the needy, and the hurting people. The one who came into the world in a manger introduced a new kind of power into our life. The power of the manger is paradoxical. This same Jesus would show that the foolishness of God is wiser than man, that the weakness of love is stronger than the force of hate, that the spiritual will outlast the material, that his narrow way leads to the wideness of authentic life, and that his peace sustains in the midst of the worst circumstances.

In this Christmas season, the gift you receive is not the most important thing. It is whether or not you have experienced love. Some of us need to get our hands out of our pockets and reach over and embrace those who mean so much to us and say to them quietly and gently, "I love you and you mean a great deal to me."

In the sight of God, all of us are on the same level. The message of Christ comes to both the poor and the rich, the famous and the obscure, those who are known and those who are unknown. It comes to each one of us because in God's eyes we are all the same. When we stand before him, whether we are the president of the world or the king of the universe, we are still poor, and we need his grace and love. We all have needs, hopes, dreams, and longings. We are all sinners he came to save and make whole.

Notice *what* they received. They received joy. The shepherds' hearts were filled with joy when the angel of God made the announcement about Christ's coming. The angelic chorus began to sing, "We bring you good tidings of great joy." Our joy is that God is with us. Spread the joy of Christmas: Christ has come. He has come to set us free from our sins and to enable us to experience real, genuine life. Experience that joy and share it with others.—William Powell Tuck

Topic: The Wonder of Christmas
TEXT: Isa. 52:7–10; John 1:1–2, 14

I. *Christmas is an exciting time.* What does Christmas mean to you? Well, for me it is an exciting time. Excitement fills the air! Sometimes the days before Christmas are not just exciting but hectic. We become almost frantic when we think of everything we anticipated doing for Christmas and wonder if we can get it done in time.

But don't you think there was a feeling of excitement at the first Christmas—for Mary and Joseph; for the shepherds as they heard the angelic message, and even for the angels as they sang the message; and for the Wise Men who traveled, following a star in anticipation of finding the newborn King? It was an exciting time.

II. *Christmas is a time of wonder.* It is also a wonderful time. Isaiah said, "His name shall be called Wonderful." The shepherds wondered at what the angels had told them. Look at the wonder of Jesus Christ. People down through the ages have wondered at his birth. They have wondered at his teachings. We sing, "Wonderful words of life" as we reflect on his words. The teachings of a man who came into the world without benefit of scholarly training or education, who lived in an obscure part of the world, have been studied and examined by some of the world's best minds. His words continue to penetrate the lives of people centuries after they were spoken. Think of the wonder of his miracles. Lives were changed by his touch and were never the same again. Think of the wonder of his life. It uniquely revealed the presence of God. Think of the wonder of his death and Resurrection.

At Christmastime there is a great sense of wonderment about God. An air of mystery hangs over the birth, life, and death of Jesus. I think it is tragic if we ever lose that marvelous sense of mystery at Christmastime. We touch the edge of a mystery that can never be fully known or explained.

Think of the difference it would make if Christ had never come. Think of the difference! It is hard to imagine. Christmastime is wonderful because it reminds us of the difference Jesus Christ has made in the world.

III. *Christmas is a unique time.* Matthew and Luke began their Gospels by dating them with Roman emperors and high priests. But John reached back into eternity, into the bosom of God, and wrote, "In the beginning. . . . In the source of all things." His Gospel bursts forth with a song—a hymn—that has resounded through the ages like a symphonic overture. Then John wrote a sentence that is the most pronounced sentence in all of his Gospel and that reflects the purpose of his Gospel: "And the Word became flesh." He leaps from eternity to a time, place, and person, and bursts forth with a tremendous claim. The great God of the universe came uniquely into our world through Jesus Christ. He "tabernacled" among us. He "pitched his tent," and we are able to see something of the nature of God through him. The doctrine of the Incarnation points to the real humanity of God. God was in Christ.

John wrote, "And we beheld his glory, glory as of the only begotten of the Father, full of grace and truth." He was filled with grace—the unmerited favor or gift of God. We see that he was full of truth—the embodiment of truth, the example of truth—and that he was the communicator of the words of truth.

IV. *Christmas is a time of giving.* It is a time when we exchange gifts with those we love, as we seek in some small way to give them the message that they are special and meaningful to us. But sometimes we forget that Christmas itself is a gift. John wrote, "For God so loved the world that he gave. . . ." Paul said, "Thanks be to God for his unspeakable gift." Christmas itself is God's gift to us. Christmas is the gift of God's Son, who came into the world in a manger, in a cattle stall, at Christmastime. Remember, you can never buy Christmas. You can never earn it. You can never merit it. You receive it. God's gift of his love was given to us at Christmastime.—William Powell Tuck

Topic: For Christmas Day
TEXT: Luke 1:39–56

About fifty years ago, in my Sunday School days in Rochester, New York, Christmastime always triggered a minor debate among the kids looking forward to the annual children's

Christmas pageant. I suspect that some of the adults in the church talked about this particular issue as well; in any case, it did cause speculation and whispers among us boys—but even more so, among the girls. And what was our momentous question? What compelled kids to await breathlessly a word from on high? The question grabbing our adolescent attention was, Who was going to play Mary in the pageant? Oh, of course we wondered whether the latest baby born into the church family or just a cheap rubbery doll would lie in the manger. But the real question was, Who among the high school fellowship would get the call for Mary? She played center stage. The sheep, the cows, the shepherds, the magi, the angels gathered around *her*. Spotlights focused on *her*. She got the best solos. It usually turned out that she was one of the most beautiful girls we adolescent male clowns could conceive of. She also possessed a gorgeous voice, and sometimes—though I do not want to be a cynic about it— she may well have been the favorite of the director of christian education. Believe it or not, Mary's position in our church's Christmas pageant was as jealously coveted as were the limited slots on what was then an all-female high school cheerleading squad.

As I look back on it, that was OK. The whole scene reflected the culture of the time. Motherhood still bore a sort of mystical, iconic place in our cultural and religious pantheon. The Madonna and child that permeated classical art, and the tradition of Roman Catholic veneration of Mary—respecting her as a model of what were then considered the virtues of femininity—all of this and much more conspired to present us with an image of grace, loveliness, and modesty.

There is only one problem: that picture—as it was in the 1950s and whatever it may be these days—is inaccurate. Even a loose reading of Mary's response to being chosen from on high, as rendered by Luke, throws our romantic images of Mary into a cocked hat. We read that response known as The Magnificat just a moment ago. Remember? First of all, Mary thanked heaven that a marvelous savior was about to come upon the human scene. She expressed wonder that she was to have any part in the whole affair, and then, instead of pealing off the virtues of what some people in some quarters these days might call family values, she launched into what is perforce among the scariest and most revolutionary of political statements to be found anywhere in Scripture, in Tom Paine, in Karl Marx—anywhere! In anticipating the vocation of her newborn child, she sang:

> The arrogant of heart and mind he has put to rout.
> He has brought down monarchs from their thrones,
> But the humble have been lifted high.
> The hungry he has satisfied with good things.
> The rich sent empty away.

What is this? Surely not the language of your friendly neighborhood pageant. This is the language of a world turned upside down. This is the perspective of one who could not care less if the most beautiful girl with the finest voice plays Mary. For what really counts in the birth of this pending babe is that those of low estate, those starving in this world, those who are lost or discouraged, those who are lonely or in despair, those who are broken and defeated—that these people be healed and redeemed. Oh, Mary makes promises to those who wield political power all right. She promises that they will fall on their faces. To those who seek to rule the world, she promises only a new definition of what is worth ruling, and the virtues—grace, compassion, empathy—found in true royalty. She promises that this newborn will shame and subvert the little empires that most of us build.

Mary, you see, may be to some degree a Rembrandt Madonna, but that is not all of her. Could she be a revolutionary? The harbinger of a new way of living together and treating one another? Indeed, that is what she is about. That is what her Son is about. And that is why we celebrate Christmas.—James W. Crawford

ILLUSTRATIONS

A NEW COMMUNITY.   In John the Baptist, an outsider crashes into our routine. An undomesticated, indescribable, anarchic figure breaks into our ordered systems, confronts our military, political, commercial, and church establishments and cries, "Stop! Reverse! Turn around! There's a new world coming!" The old arrangements, your previous agendas, your vaunted pecking orders collapse. A human community rooted no longer in the survival of the fittest, a human community in which wealth or genes or residence or fire power no longer determines who is valuable and who is not; a human community released from the obsession of looking out for number one—this new community now becomes the order of the day.

You see, this new era signaled by that ultimate outsider, John the Baptist, heralds the world's true character.—James W. Crawford

AT HOME WITH JESUS.   People are at home with Jesus—afraid and yet deeply at home. We must never pretend that the heavens were emptied when he came. He does not resolve or dissolve the mystery of God: he reveals God. But could any answer better satisfy our longing to "behold the face of God" than the event of Christ—at our corner of the road? Then have it so, venturing life!—George A. Buttrick[3]

THE HUMAN AND THE DIVINE.   Now, we might ask, On which side of the gulf does Jesus stand? Is he on the human or the divine side of the gulf, on ours or on God's?

The answer is that Jesus is on *both* sides of the gulf. He is certainly on *our* side of it, for he is a real man, a figure in history at a particular time and place, in which he lived a completely human life. So we can take him as our example of how human life ought to be lived in this world. As we read the Gospels, we ought to try to see him as he was, in all his humanity, so that we can follow him. We can, as it were, stand beside him and hear him praying to God, and we can pray with him and through him. He stands beside us, facing God across the gulf.

Yes, but it is also true to say that he stands facing us from the other side of the gulf, the divine side, and we can hear him say (as in the New Testament), "He that has seen me has seen the Father." So, as we look across the gulf, we can, as it were, look into the eyes of Jesus Christ, and through his eyes God looks at us, and through his lips God speaks to us. So, as we look at Jesus, we can say (in the words of St. Thomas the apostle), "My Lord and my God."—D. M. Baillie[4]

PILGRIMAGE TO GOD.   As all-encompassing as God's love is, it does not become operative in a human being's life in the New Testament sense until that person complies with the

---

[3]*Sermons Preached in a University Church*
[4]*Out of Nazareth*

basic requirements laid down by the gospel. The first of these is a *sense of need*. No one can be helped until he or she realizes that help is needed. This means that we must see our own lives in all of their sinfulness and shabbiness, and we are able to do this by comparing ourselves not with other people but with Jesus Christ. It is like the contrast between a candle flame and a sunrise, or between the pop art of a comic strip and a painting by Titian or Tintoretto. We are shamed and overwhelmed by our selfishness, our wrongdoing, our moral cowardice, and our colossal human failure. We know we need a savior! This is the beginning of any person's pilgrimage to God.—Earl G. Hunt Jr.[5]

OUR GIFT.   When John Killinger was pastor in Lynchburg, Virginia, a young woman named Betty Jo Kendall was called as the christian education director at the church. Her first Christmas at the church, she directed a Christmas pageant with angels, shepherds, the Wise Men, and the other familiar figures. Each child who represented the angels was to bring a gift to the Christ child. Some decided to bring toys or stuffed teddy bears as their presents. One of the young girls, Sallie Baldwin, was reluctant to say what she was going to bring to the Christ child. Finally she stated in an embarrassed way, "I want to bring Jesus a kiss." When the parents gathered for the pageant, the other children dressed as small angels walked over to the manger and put their toys down beside it. At this point, Sallie leaned over the manger and kissed the Christ child. When she did, a sigh went through the congregation.[6]

Maybe the greatest gift we can give to express our love to another is a kiss, a hug, or an embrace. Our presence may communicate the best gift we could possibly give. This is the greatest gift we have experienced from God. Let's share this gift with others. It's time to begin.—William Powell Tuck

---

[5]*I Have Believed*
[6]John Killinger, *Christmas Is Spoken Here* (Nashville, Tenn.: Broadman Press, 1989), pp. 86-87.

SECTION VII

EVANGELISM AND WORLD MISSIONS

SERMON SUGGESTIONS

Topic: The Power of the Gospel

TEXT: Rom. 1:16; 1 Cor. 15:1–4

If someone caught you today and said, "Please, tell me what the gospel is," could you do it? The gospel is the reason we build our churches; it is the reason we call our pastors, educators, and musicians; it is the only hope of this lost world. But can you really say what it is?

The Greek word for *gospel* means "good news." From it we get our words *evangel* and *evangelist*. The gospel is literally the best news this sinful world ever heard. And if we have heard it a thousand times, it is ever new.

I. *The gospel is good news about what God has done.* Most of the news in the newspapers is about human beings—and most of it is bad. But in the gospel, humanity stands back, for God is at work. The gospel really begins in the eternal heart of God, and it is expressed in his boundless love, which broke forth in the creation of humanity for fellowship with God.

For the gospel is the overwhelming news that in the Judean village of Bethlehem, God came bodily into the human race through the Virgin of Galilee. What incredible news!

The very heart of the gospel hinges on this fact: *God was in Christ*; the divine Word became flesh and dwelt among us. The Incarnation is the very foundation of the gospel message.

II. *But what does this mean for you?* These are just words—unless they mean something to you. Here is what they mean: they mean that you are not alone in your struggle in this world. We do not worship a God who is far away. Our God has *come to us*. Only Christianity makes the audacious claim that the living God entered into our human flesh, shared our human lot, and died our human death—and triumphed over it. If man was ever to be saved, it had to be this way. Man could not lift himself up by his own bootstraps; he had to wait for God. He became flesh and dwelt among us. *Immanuel*—God with us—is the Christian gospel. If it is true, as we believe it is, then it is the point from which everything else takes its meaning. If it is not true, then Christianity is nothing at all. About this every individual must make his or her own decision. Have you made yours?

III. But the gospel is more: it is the Good News that God was in Christ on Calvary's cross, offering up his incarnate life for sinners like you and like me. The living Lord of the universe entered into this human vale of sin and suffering and bore my guilt and stain on that bloody cross. How could he love me so? He died for all, yet he did it just for me!

IV. But every Christian knows that the gospel does not end on Calvary. Some people exalt the crucifix—and this cross is rightly central. But the climax is this: on that third morning, in Joseph's garden, there was an empty tomb. He arose! Death could not hold its prey; the grave could not defeat his love. Redeeming love triumphed over all. Ten thousand times ten thousand little men have tried to bury this one and his followers. But he lives, and one day he shall reign from shore to shore and from sea to sea.—Wayne E. Ward

Topic: Born Again?

TEXT: John 3:1–7

There has been a tremendous surge of interest in the phenomenon known as being "born again." Think with me about this, and as we do, consider the question, "Am I born again?" Jesus is speaking here of an experience that is central to being a genuine Christian and his disciple.

I. *The new birth is a spiritual birth.* What Jesus is speaking of in John 3:1–7 is a spiritual and moral transformation wrought in the heart of a person as he listens to and believes in the gospel. This vital, efficacious work is the result of the Holy Spirit's mighty transforming power. He—that is, God's Spirit—effects belief and faith in the heart of the hearer, producing such concern for sin, trust in Christ, and consequential spiritual reorientation that it may only be justly called a "birth."

(a) One of my favorite texts for sharing the gospel with persons is John 1:12: "And to as many as received him . . . to them he gave the power to become the children of God." But let us not forget the conclusion of John's thought in verse 13: "who were born, not of blood, nor of the will of the flesh nor of the will of man, but of God." Is your trust in Christ, your faith in him, genuine? Is it the product of heartfelt conviction? Is it the consequence of the Holy Spirit's convincing work in you upon your hearing the claims of Christ? Has it resulted in lasting faith and a continued assurance of hope in the power of Christ to save?

(b) We have so diminished this element in the Christian experience that people think they are genuine believers simply because they've been baptized or catechized, because they've walked down an aisle or learned a creed, because they were born in a nominally religious country, or because they've never committed a serious crime. This is nonbiblical thinking. This is contrary to what Jesus was telling Nicodemus. In fact, Jesus' words *be born again* may well have been translated "be born from above." Be transformed by hearing the Gospel message, "Christ died for our sins!" Be converted by putting your rebellion against God behind you. Be made new by receiving that life of the Spirit that can be infused only through the work of God's Holy Spirit through faith in Christ.

II. *The spiritual birth Jesus spoke of here is a "second" or a "new" birth.* It is an introduction into a new way of life. The Scriptures are clear that life outside God's forgiveness and grace is a life of frustration and failure—spiritually, morally, and in terms of usefulness to God.

(a) Once a weathered evangelist was asked, "Preacher, do you believe that conversion is the end of salvation?" "Yes!" came the reply. "It is the front end!" I've often wondered about those who claim an experience of God's grace and forgiveness and yet demonstrate no change in their lives that in any way mirrors the life of Jesus. That is not biblical conversion. No! The new birth changes our wills—to serve Christ and not ourselves. It changes our values—to glory in the things of God, Christ, and the cross and not in earthly achievement or material possessions. It changes our affections—to be filled with love for God and other persons and not to be trapped in suicidal narcissism. We're speaking here of an experience and state so radically life-altering that it cannot be spoken of as a new beginning, as self-improvement, as a point of renewed efforts or earnestness, but only as Jesus said it—as a birth!

(b) Let me ask: As a consequence of any or all religious experiences that you might have had, what has changed in your life consequently? Is there the witness of God's Spirit in your heart that you are a child of God? Is Christ central to your life—indeed, Master and Lord of it?

Has your behavior been altered so that what you do is controlled by what Christ would want you to do? This is what the new birth produces. It is the introduction and subsequent fruit of a life centered on the will and purposes of God as we know them in Christ. There was a saying among the Puritans that when a man was born again, so great was the subsequent change in his life that not only did he notice it, but his wife noticed it; and not only did she notice it, but his friends noticed it; and not only did his friends notice it, but *his horse noticed it!*

III. *The new birth is also a saving birth.* Notice that Jesus said to Nicodemus, "You must be born again" (v. 7). Jesus did not lightly suggest such an action. He did not merely recommend it as helpful in order to enter God's Kingdom. He was doubly emphatic—"Verily, verily" or "Truly, truly"—in stating that the new birth was imperative to being counted as a child of God. It seems clear above all things in Scripture that one must experience awareness of God's grace, turn in faith to Christ, repent of sin, and own Jesus Christ as one's Lord and Savior in order to be counted in God's Kingdom. I lived three and a half years in England. Do you realize that in the course of that time not once was I ever invited to have tea with the queen at Buckingham Palace? In fact, whenever I walked past the grand residence, the gates were always locked and guards were posted and ever careful that no uninvited guest be allowed entrance. Why was I not allowed to enter? Because I was a commoner, an alien, and no relation to the Royal Family. But Prince Charles! What about him? When he arrived at the palace, the gates swung open and the guards snapped to attention.

He was home. Why? Because he was born a child of the monarch, a member of the Royal Family. Have you been born into the Royal Family? Have you the earnestness and certainty that sins are forgiven? That the Spirit of God resides in you? That Christ is your Lord? That's what it means to be born again. The invitation is out. The news is to be proclaimed and pressed that the Word of God says, "The Spirit and the Bride say, 'Come.' And let him who hears say, 'Come.' And let him who is thirsty come, let him who desires take the water of life without price."—R. Phillip Roberts

Topic: On Making the Wilderness Fruitful
TEXT: Mark 4:1–20

Probably all of us have heard of Johnny Appleseed, the gentle wanderer who roved the countryside planting apple seeds in remote places. He believed that God had given him a mission to preach the gospel of love in the wilderness and to plant apple seeds that would produce orchards for the benefit of men and women and children. Johnny Appleseed's whole life was devoted to making the wilderness fruitful, whether that wilderness was geographical or spiritual.

This was Jesus' mission, too: to be a sower of seeds in order to make the wilderness wanderings of our lives spiritually fruitful. As he sowed, Jesus gave a challenge: "He who has ears to hear, let him hear." This is a parable on hearing and heeding God's Word.

I. *Hearing and heeding God's Word can penetrate the shell of the hard heart* (Mark 4:15).

(a) The habit and routine of sin harden the spiritual heart.

(b) Persons with a hardened spiritual heart do not want to do anything to change for the good.

(c) The gospel of Jesus Christ can soften a hard heart, change a life of sinful habits, and give you meaning and understanding.

II. *Hearing and heeding God's Word can overcome the fears of the shallow heart* (Mark 4:16–17).

(a) The shallow-hearted person makes a quick and ready response to God, but he falls away just as quickly.

(b) The shallow-hearted person's spiritual life is planted in the soil of wishy-washiness that does not count the cost of following Christ.

(c) "The same heat that killed this plant would have made it flourish if it had had deeper roots" (Halford Luccock).

III. *Hearing and heeding God's Word can destroy the lukewarmness of the distracted heart* (Mark 4:18–19).

(a) The person with a distracted heart hears and responds to the gospel, but his life ceases to be fruitful.

(b) The person with a distracted heart has too many activities of lesser priority growing in his soil.

(c) God deserves our undivided allegiance.

IV. *Hearing and heeding God's Word can cause a new heart full of abundant faith to grow in your life* (Mark 4:20).

(a) Planting the gospel seed may at first seem to be hopeless and futile.

(b) But Jesus sees the bumper crop at the harvest.

(c) This encourages us not to be fainthearted in our labors.

Jesus still calls Johnny Appleseeds like you and me to sow the gospel message in the wilderness of this world where people are hurting and without God. All who have ears, hear and heed this message on making the wilderness fruitful.—Ronnie R. Blankenship

Topic: Inescapable Summons
TEXT: Luke 16:1–8

I. The branch office manager played fast and loose with his company's money. His department went into the red. His boss was aware of the situation, cornered him, and gave him a thirty-day notice. The manager was shaken. He had been drifting along, making some bad deals, wasting money on expense accounts, but he had figured that his company was so large no one would notice. After all, the company could not make profits in every area and it would be able to write off his division as a tax deduction. Now, suddenly, the branch office manager's future was in jeopardy. His pipe dreams were shattered. All his ambitions for promotion were scuttled. He faced the great crisis of his business career. So he sat down in his swivel chair, stunned. He made a swift assessment of his alternatives: he could accept failure, close the books, and pack up the office. So he contemplated construction work, checked his biceps, and decided that would not do. Then he thought of selling pencils on the sidewalk and his pride overtook him. Another alternative that had not been obvious broke into his awareness. He could act boldly and quickly in the face of impending ruin. He could choose to act with dispatch. So he became a one-man collection agency, singled out the big accounts, reduced them sharply, and turned dead accounts into cash. His hope was that the customers would be so pleased with his action on their part that they would either give him a job or at least a place to sleep.

Then the boss showed up a second time, found out what the branch office manager had

been up to, and applauded his actions! He did not commend him for his previous misman-
agement but for his bold wheeling and dealing.

II. It is very likely that Jesus refashioned a story that had been gossiped in the streets, a
secular story that he used for religious purposes. It is not that Jesus wants us to go and mis-
manage. It is not that he wants us to copy this man's slippery morals. Yet, in daring fashion,
Jesus was willing to use an ambiguous situation about a dishonest character because there
was one thing about this man's actions that was right. When he faced a crisis, when he was
in a jam, and when he assessed the alternatives, he saw the necessity of bold, right action
while there was time. It is bold action that Jesus wished to commend in this story.

(a) As we first come upon this branch office manager, this steward, he is indeed in a desperate plight. He has been caught red-handed, in either poor business tactics or dishonest
business activities. This happens when Christ invades our lives today. When Christ invades
our daily routines, our flimsy excuses and moral standards do not meet his expectations.
When God comes in Jesus Christ, threatening our way of living and calling our lives into
question, he will not allow us the luxury of a sidelong glance at some obvious sinner to bolster our personal pride.

(b) In this parable, we see how Christ brings us, in a moment of truth, to a desperate
plight and allows us to see reality as it really is. Not only is a desperate plight portrayed in
the parable, but an inescapable summons is implied throughout. For Christ tosses a challenge
into our laps. Like the dishonest businessman, we must decide.

Indeed, as is the case with him, so it is with us. Evasion of decision is not possible. There
is a great feeling of urgency surging through the parable. This sense of urgency coursing
through the story demands some kind of resolution to the crisis.

And is there not need among Christians today to have some sense of urgency about the
gospel? Some of us were drawn into the Church by a sense of urgency. Is it not true in many
instances that people have been drawn into the preaching ministry, into mission, into concern for social problems through a burning sense of urgency that the gospel really matters
enough for them to become concerned and to care?

Is there not in this Christian sense of urgency a creative spinoff? If indeed Christ brings a
sense of urgency to life, and if indeed the gospel places a sense of urgency on our lives, there is
then some meaning to human existence. Then indeed there is a quality of living and of life that
is worth living and worth having. So many people in our times, and surely within our congregation, do not, on occasion, recall any good reason for staying alive or for engaging in any significant purpose in life. It is helpful for us, in the light of that fact, to be recalled by this unusual
parable to the reality that meaning is given to us in the gospel of Christ, that life itself has a
pulsating quality about it. We have a God who cares about the salesman struggling to make a
living, about the teenager who may be disappointed, and about a diplomat looking for life.

The parable dramatizes an inescapable summons to say yes, to say no, to make some kind
of response.—Peter Rhea Jones

Topic: A Letter to God
TEXT: Matt. 28:16–20

Jesus told a parable about a landowner who had gone away and left his servant in charge
of his kingdom. We understand the servant to be us. As believers of Jesus' gospel, we are

stewards of his property, his creation, his people, and his mission. Imagine if he were to ask, as always happens at work, the general or the shepherd to report on what has been happening. What if one of us here were to write a letter to God about what has happened since he left, giving detailed explanation of our activities and of our efforts toward the fulfillment of his stated goals? Unfortunately, it might look something like a letter from summer camp. We all sent them, and as parents we have mixed feelings about receiving them. On one side, we are happy to hear from our children and grateful that they took time to write. However, on the opposite end of the spectrum is our fear of what is actually going on at camp. We worry about the food they eat, the sleep they don't get, what they did with the snake they saw, what happened to their counselor, and so on. When we receive such reports, we wonder what in the world our children were supposed to achieve on their camping "mission."

What if one of us here were appointed to write a letter to God about what has happened since he left? Unfortunately, such a letter might look something like a confused and perhaps exaggerated letter from a child at camp rather than a report from a soldier to the leader of the army. The words might be a little too informal, the tone might be much too relaxed, and the content would probably be very unflattering to "His Majesty." One thing is for certain, there would be much to write to our Lord about the activities, or lack thereof, within his Church. However, the mission on which we would undoubtedly have to report first would be what Jesus commanded last: the fulfillment of the Great Commission found in Matthew 28:16–20.

I. *All authority belongs to Christ* (Matt. 28:16–18). Many who have attempted to summarize the commitment of American evangelicals to reach the lost have referred to this Great Commission as the "Great Omission." Unfortunately, most churches have done nothing to prove that that insult is unfounded. When I was a child, my mother would leave a list of things for me to do every time she left; when she was ready to exit, she would repeat the most important things last. Why? For emphasis, so that I would understand her expectations and adjust my work accordingly. The spreading of the gospel within the ministry of Christ had a similar emphasis, which he commanded throughout and here reemphasizes directly before his ascension. We are expected to adjust our priorities to reflect the Lord's emphasis.

What is important to note is the position of authority. It is not given to the disciples, but it is clearly the possession of Christ. The result of Christ's authority is the call of his disciples. So, what is to be our response to the Lord's possession of all authority? We are commanded to go! It is within the going that he judges the faithfulness of his people.

II. *All action belongs to us* (Matt. 28:19–20). The action for which Christ calls is far more difficult than winning a person to the Kingdom through their repentance and acceptance of the gospel. It involves discipleship. The difference between a church that practices evangelism without discipleship and a church that makes discipleship a priority for each believer is unmistakable. The difference is similar to the difference between training someone for a temporary position and training someone for a full-time career. The commitment level of learning and performance is clearly defined in each situation. The acceptance of Christ is a full-time, lifelong commitment—that is why Christ insists on discipleship.

The reaction to Christ's possession of all authority is simply to go. It is not just to add numbers to the congregation but to make disciples of all nations. Notice the use of *all* within this text. His call is comprehensive and complete. He expects boldness from his disciples and obedience from his new converts. Our response, as believers, should be consistent with that.

Perhaps then our letter to God would seek further instruction and a replenishing of boldness and strength rather than seeking repentance for avoiding what we know we are called to do.

III. *Conclusion.* Think for a minute: What do campers do? They learn how to "rough it," right? Well if listening to CD players and watching battery-operated TVs are considered roughing it, that is exactly what campers today do. Camp doesn't always turn out the way it is supposed to. Instead of learning to build a fire, we start destructive fires. Instead of living off the land, we destroy the land. Instead of helping and training one another, we criticize one another. This type of misapplication and practice sounds very similar to the attitudes and conviction within the Church. When is the last time we were upset over something more serious than a misunderstanding, disagreement, or harsh word? When is the last time our unholiness devastated us and our sins were seriously confessed?

Write Christ a letter. Tell him who you have shared your faith with, or why you have failed to do so. Let him know if you have been a good steward of his money, of his time, of the privileges that have been afforded to you. "To whom much has been given, much will be required."—Jeffrey D. Brown

ILLUSTRATIONS

PROCRASTINATION.   A man was filling out an application for a job in a factory. He puzzled for some time over this question, "Person to notify in case of accident?" Finally he wrote down, "Anybody in sight." When there is a real crisis, never mind the fine points; go right to the heart of the problem. We do not always have time to debate, and the man who must always postpone will find that the events pass him by. There is a time for decision, and to do nothing is to fail.—Gerald Kennedy[1]

REPENTANCE.   The preaching of Jesus follows directly upon that of John. It is a call to repent (to be converted) in view of the coming reign of God. The time is fulfilled, the reign of God is at hand; repent and believe the good news. The repentance, the conversion, is in view of the good news. It is as though someone were to say that the person you are waiting for is coming but you cannot see him unless you turn around and look the other way. Conversion, then, means being turned around in order to recognize and participate in the dawning reality of God's reign. But this inward turning immediately and intrinsically involves both a pattern of conduct and a visible companionship. It involves membership in a community and a decision to act in certain ways.—Leslie Newbigin[2]

STRENGTH IN GOD.   Do you know that a man is as strong as the thing to which he commits himself? If I commit myself to a paper box in which to cross the Atlantic Ocean, as soon as the paper box gets wet and goes to pieces and goes down, I go with it. I am no stronger than the thing to which I commit myself.

But if I get into that grand old ocean steamer, all the strength in her, all the power of her boiler, all the comforts of her cabin are mine, and I shall never go down till she goes down. If I commit myself to the arm of flesh, I am no stronger than the arm to which I commit

---

[1]*Fresh Every Morning*
[2]*The Finality of Christ*

myself. But if I commit myself to God, I shall never go down until God goes down, blessed be his holy name.—Sam P. Jones[3]

WORK AND GRACE.   Several years ago, the children of a certain church invited their pastor in one morning to talk to them about what it meant to be a Christian after many years as a disciple. Gordon Cosby thought for a few minutes and then told them, "The Christian life, as you go along, gets harder and harder and better and better."

This was what Paul had discovered, in the middle of his conflict with Corinth, years before. . . .

Paul knew that life, for him, became harder and harder and better and better. Salvation, then, is not work or grace; it is work and grace. Through the tension of the two great concepts, heart and hands, something great emerges. Paul's challenge to Philippi is a word to the divided camps in the Church today: "Work out your salvation with fear and trembling; for God is at work in you, both to will and to work for his good pleasure."—Roger Lovette[4]

RULES AND LOVE.   Here is a daughter going to Canada, let us say, for a year. She and her mother are devoted to each other. From one point of view it would be much easier for the girl, perhaps, if her mother gave her a list of twenty rules to keep if she was to be a dutiful daughter, pleasing to her mother. That would leave the girl quite free to do anything she liked outside the ground covered by the twenty rules. But love is more binding than that. The mother gives her no rules, yet in the girl's mind and heart there is a consciousness of what would please her mother and what would not. This knowledge is inconvenient, for it covers the whole of life, both the known and the unknown situations, both the present and the future. Because she loves her mother, she will always find the challenge and standard for her actions. She will live under love and not under law.

So it is with the Christian life. Our main purpose, put quite simply, is to please God; or to put it in a more specifically Christian way, to please Christ. That is an enormous task; there is no end to it and there is no escape from it, if we really love him.—Bryan Green[5]

---

[3]*Sam Jones' Revival Sermons*
[4]*Journey Toward Joy*
[5]*Saints Alive!*

PREACHING ON THE TEMPTATIONS OF JESUS

BY WILLIAM P. THOMASON

TEXT: Matt. 3:13–17; 4:1–4

The temptations of Jesus in the wilderness are often taken as models for us to follow as we face temptation in our own lives. On the face of it, this suggestion seems odd and beside the point—odd because (on the face of it) Jesus' temptations are not our temptations, and beside the point (on the face of it) because Jesus, as the Son of God, apparently had resources to draw on that you and I lack.

What sort of connection could there be, then, between these seemingly irrelevant experiences of Jesus, face to face with Satan himself, and our desire to skirt the boundaries of what we know to be right? On the face of it, the answer seems to be, there is no connection, no connection whatsoever.

Yet for all of this oddness and apparent irrelevance, Jesus' wilderness experience says something to us as we struggle with temptation. "The face of it" may be a mask that we would find, if we could only get behind it, has concealed a great and wonderful face, the face of a fully human Jesus who "was in all points tempted as we are, yet without sin" (Heb. 4:15).

If these temptation stories are about Jesus' humanity, then it follows that they are also relevant to us as we struggle with temptation, because the best excuse we have for yielding to temptation is, "I'm only human." I am only human and you are only human and Jesus was only human, too—yet human without sinning. If one human being lived a fully human life without yielding to temptation, then we have lost our best excuse for yielding to temptation. In a way, that is discouraging.

But so is yielding to temptation. Deep down inside, I believe, we all want to be better than we are, we all feel a sense of loss when we fail to live up to the best we know we can be. Yielding to temptation is more discouraging in the long run than losing our excuses, because yielding, in the long run, is a violation of our best selves.

So, in Jesus we have an example of one human being who knew temptation with all the force you and I experience, but without giving in to it. Jesus opened up a path for us to go down and set an example for us to follow. But Jesus is more than just an example; if we believe in him, he also empowers us when we are tempted. The power that was at work in Jesus when he resisted temptation in the wilderness, the power that raised him from the dead, is a power he makes available to us, too. So, if we believe in him, when we face temptation we begin to find that what we cannot do on our own—say no—we can begin to do with Jesus' help.

I. *Baptism.* Jesus' wilderness temptations came immediately after his baptism by John the Baptist—a baptism that John proclaimed for the repentance of sins. John proclaimed the need

367

for repentance because God's rule in the world was about to begin, and unless the people repented, they would not be a part of that new order. The sign of their repentance was baptism—stepping into the Jordan River and allowing John to dip them beneath its muddy waters.

Despite his off-putting appearance, harsh message, and uncouth ways, John drew the crowds, including Jesus, who came like the rest, asking for baptism. At first John refused, saying, "I have need to be baptized by you." But Jesus insisted, saying that he had to be baptized in order to "fulfill all righteousness." We, like John, may be puzzled by Jesus' insistence on being baptized; baptism is for sinners who are repenting, and Jesus had nothing of which to repent. How, then, did Jesus' baptism fulfill God's righteousness?

The answer, I think, is this: Jesus was to be the one who would inaugurate God's rule on Earth. But God's rule is not forced on us as was Caesar's rule over Palestine. It is instead a new way of living in the world, which we are free to accept or reject. This new way of living is the way of peace and justice and self-giving love, the way of setting right the things that have gone wrong. God wants us to freely choose this way, so instead of appearing in the fullness of divine glory and power, God appeared among us in human form. This human being who incarnated God was like us in every way, except that he was fully human—that is, he was what we were supposed to be but have fallen short of because of our sin.

For Jesus to be an appealing example, he had to identify with us in every way, and his divinity (at first, at least) had to be masked by his humanity. By insisting that John baptize him, Jesus insisted on identifying completely with us and our humanity, including identifying with our sinfulness. So, Jesus was baptized by John the Baptist with the baptism of repentance (of which he had no need) in order to identify with us completely. He had no need of such baptism, but we do. As our example, by voluntarily submitting to the baptism of repentance he showed us exactly what we need.

He is an example for us to follow. But more that that, his human life opened up a path down which we can walk, whose destination is the real, full humanity we crave in our deepest selves. He "who knew no sin" was "made sin for us" so that we who know sin may know it no more and start down the path that leads to life.

II. *Wilderness.* How odd and disturbing was the sequel to Jesus' baptism! When he came up out of the Jordan River, the Spirit of God descended on him in the form of a dove, and a voice form heaven declared, "This is my Son, my beloved." Then that same Spirit sent Jesus into the wilderness, utterly alone, where he was tempted by the devil. The wilderness is a place where one can lose one's way; it is a place that can bewilder one. It is a place where wild animals dwell and where wild things can happen. It is dangerous. One misstep can cause death. It has no nourishment to sustain one.

The Spirit led Jesus to this place, according to Matthew and Luke. According to Mark, however, the Spirit *drove* Jesus there, which implies that he was not entirely willing to go.

Given the hostile nature of the wilderness, we have to ask, Why did Jesus go there? Why did the Spirit drive him to such a place? The wilderness would give Jesus the solitude to think through the implications of his baptism, but Jesus would not have chosen on his own to go there.

Perhaps the Spirit drove Jesus there because Jesus was so naturally attuned to God that he would not have experienced the full force of temptation (as you and I do) had he not gone, alone and vulnerable, to that place. In the wilderness, temptation was the strongest because wilderness also represents the experience of being abandoned by God, the experience of being in a place where God is not.

Jesus went from the profound experience of God's presence at his baptism to the experience of abandonment by God in the wilderness. This movement was a paradigm of our own experience: We encounter God in what seems to be an unmistakable way, then things begin to go wrong and we are tempted to doubt the reality of our encounter with God. Why do we go suddenly from clarity and certainty to ambiguity and doubt? Why are we now facing temptation without a strong sense of God's presence with us to sustain us?

Perhaps this is the real reason that Jesus was driven into the wilderness. If he was to know temptation as we know it, then he had to experience the sense of God's abandonment that comes so swiftly on the heels of God's presence.

Jesus' wilderness experience must have been terrifying and perplexing to him, because of this sense of God's abandonment. This may be why he taught us to pray, "Lead us not into temptation"—that is, lead us not into the wilderness, where we are alone and vulnerable without God. The wilderness, then, is another link between the temptations of Jesus and our experience of temptation. The wilderness is where we all find ourselves when temptation is strongest and God seems farthest from us.

III. *Bread.* Jesus' first temptation came after he had been fasting in the wilderness for forty days and forty nights. The number forty is symbolic and not to be taken literally. It is a way of signifying the completion of some purpose of God's. During this wilderness period, Jesus became clear about what God wanted him to do and how God wanted him to do it. He was ready to begin his divinely appointed task, but Satan appeared and tempted him to turn stones into bread. The wilderness is Satan's domain, so there was no way for Jesus to hide or escape. He had to face this challenge.

One of the strongest aspects of this temptation is seeing why it is a temptation. Jesus had been fasting, that is, engaging in a physical discipline for the sake of his spirit. This period was now over, and the number forty indicates that he had successfully accomplished his purpose. He now had to go out and live among others, to eat, drink, and sleep—all necessary activities for him to accomplish God's will.

He was hungry ("famished," according to Matthew), so why would it be wrong for him to turn stones into bread? Is there anything wrong with providing for physical necessities like food?

Furthermore, the tempter suggested that Jesus could use his powers not only for his own good but also for the good of others. "Are you the Messiah?" Satan seemed to be saying. "Then do something about hunger, do something about the appalling social conditions of poverty and economic injustice under which most people live." Why didn't Jesus turn stones into bread, then, for his own sake, and later in his ministry, for the poor, the starving, the homeless?

Jesus could accomplish some very good things by turning stones into bread, so why did he resist the tempter's suggestion? Why did he answer Satan, "It is written, 'We shall not live by bread alone but by every word that proceeds from the mouth of God'"? Jesus saw in this temptation an implication he knew to be false—the implication that all we really need in order to live are physical things, symbolized here by bread. It is easy to fall into the trap of thinking that because we all need bread to live, that bread is all we need to live. To provide food for the hungry is good, but not if it denies something even better and more important—the nourishment of our spirits. We do not live by bread alone, but also by every word that comes to us from God.

Furthermore, Satan was appealing to the very human desire to achieve absolute material security—complete freedom from material want and need. Satan was saying to Jesus, "You can be completely free from worry about the material necessities of life; after all, you can turn stones into bread."

Jesus did have this power, but if he exercised it he would be separating himself from the rest of us, who do worry about our daily bread. He would be, in effect, denying his full humanity, his identification with us, which he had accepted in being baptized. But if he denied his full humanity by turning stones into bread, we would find ourselves saying, "He doesn't really know what it's like to be human. Why should we believe him when he asks us to give up everything for the sake of the Kingdom?"

For Jesus to have turned stones into bread would have meant that he couldn't really know the power of the temptations we feel about material things, and that would mean that we can't really trust him. And if we can't trust him, then he can't save us. So Jesus would have denied his main purpose in coming to us if he were to have turned stones into bread.

We are not literally in the wilderness and we are not literally tempted to turn stones into bread, but we do live in twenty-first–century America, probably the most materialistic society ever in human history. Some people like to call us a "Christian nation," but the real god we worship collectively in this country is the false god the Bible calls "mammon." "In God We Trust" is inscribed on our money, and this truly is a case of the medium being the message. The god we trust in is our money, of which we all want more and more.

The god mammon is a false god because it cannot satisfy our real needs. It says to us, "If you only had that new job or that raise or that second (or third) car or that vacation home in the Smokies; if you could only win the lottery." Fill in whatever it is you don't have now that you think, if you did have it, would make your life complete and beautiful. The problem is that if we do get that job or raise or new vehicle, we find we're not happy; our old longings have been replaced by new ones, and the cycle of desire and frustration starts again.

Mammon is a god that cannot satisfy us, because we cannot turn stones into bread. As a bumper sticker I saw recently put it, "The best things in life aren't things." And living in a culture that is almost totally dedicated to the futile pursuit of things means that you and I are sorely tempted by bread.

What resources do we have to help us resist this temptation?

We have Jesus' example in the wilderness and his words, "We do not live by bread alone, but by every word that comes from the mouth of God."

There is also the petition Jesus taught us to pray in the prayer he gave us: "Give us this day our daily bread." I think Jesus included this petition because he knew what it was like to be tempted to believe that things are all we need. The proper attitude for one who follows Christ is to be satisfied with what is enough for this day and not to worry about provisions for tomorrow.

How do we keep from putting undue emphasis on material things? By remembering that we do not live by bread alone. By remembering that we are more than our bodies, more than the sum total of our physical needs.

If we can learn to be satisfied with whatever is enough for each day, then we will have learned something very valuable to help us resist this most basic of temptations. We do not live by bread alone, though we do live by bread. We also live by the Word of God, which nourishes and sustains our souls.

Topic: The Pinnacle of the Temple

Text: Ps. 91:1–12; Matt. 4:5–7

I. *The first temptation.* The first temptation, the temptation of bread, occurred at the most basic level of existence, the level of our physical being and material needs. It was a temptation to give priority to the material needs and conditions of life; to say, for example, that when we are hungry there is nothing more important than food.

Jesus, though famished, saw through the first temptation and knew that if he yielded to it he would be denying the importance of our inner reality; he would be denying that we are spirit as well as flesh. Jesus, though famished, resisted the temptation to turn stones into bread because he knew that, though we do live by bread, we do not live by bread alone. We also live by the spiritual nourishment we receive from God.

The first temptation, therefore, failed. So, the tempter tried another tack, shifting the focus of temptation from the material world to the spiritual. It was as if Satan said to himself, "Jesus knows there's more to life than physical well-being. He also recognizes the reality and importance of the spirit. Perhaps I can get him to have a false idea of what spirit is like. Perhaps I can get him to misunderstand what the proper relationship between God and human beings is."

II. *The second temptation.* So, the tempter took Jesus to the highest point of the Temple in Jerusalem and said, "If you are the Son of God, throw yourself down." Why did he want Jesus to do this? Because Scripture (Ps. 91) says that God's angels will always be there to protect God's chosen ones, even when they stumble and fall.

At first blush, this doesn't seem very tempting, does it? It's the kind of thing only an idiot, a fool, or a lunatic might do. Nevertheless, the tempter knew what he was doing. There were two hooks on this fishing line, from either one of which Jesus may have taken the bait and gotten caught. The first hook was, "If you are the Son of God," and the second was, "Scripture says/It is written." Let's examine both.

In the first two wilderness temptations, Satan used a conditional form of argument: If you are the Son of God, turn stones into bread/jump from the Temple without harm. In this second temptation, in particular, I think the tempter was implying that if Jesus did not take the suggested action, then he was denying the condition on which the action was based. The logic of this appeal was, if you are the Son of God, then you will jump from the Temple, and if you don't jump, then you're not the Son of God.

The second hook that might have snagged Jesus was similar: Scripture says that God's angels will take care of you if you start to fall. If you believe Scripture (and of course the Son of God would believe Scripture), then you will jump; and if you don't jump, then you don't really believe Scripture.

Satan was assaulting Jesus' identity, but doing so in a subtle, implicit way. Had he engaged in a frontal assault—"Are you sure you're the Son of God?"—Jesus would have had a ready answer. He would simply have pointed to his baptism, to the descent of the dove, to the voice from heaven, and to the forty days and nights in the wilderness during which he had become clear about God's purposes. A frontal assault would merely have confirmed Jesus' identity as God's beloved and strengthened his resolve to resist temptation. So, the tempter attacked indirectly.

There was another reason this action might have been tempting to Jesus. Diogenes Allen says that there was a tradition that when the Messiah came he would appear on the pinnacle of the Temple as a sign that he was the Messiah. People with spiritual discernment would see this sign and recognize it to be an indication that the Messiah had come. Many would see the sign, but only a few would understand what it meant. Jesus did in fact perform signs in his public ministry, so what would have been wrong with appearing on top of the Temple? Why couldn't this have simply been one more sign Jesus performed that pointed to his Messiahship?

Furthermore, consider that Jesus' purpose in coming into the world was to make disciples, to get people to follow him, to inaugurate us into the new way of being in the world that he called the Kingdom of God. Jesus would achieve this only if he could get us to believe in him. If all he did was appear on top of the Temple, then only a few would believe. But if he were to jump and land unharmed, people would follow him anywhere and do anything he said. This would be a surefire way to get people to follow him. What, then, would have been wrong with performing a sign that would guarantee that people would believe in him?

The full force of this at-first-unpromising temptation is now clear. It was a plausible appeal, employing valid forms of argument. It was (superficially at least) the sort of thing Jesus was going to do anyway. What appeared to be a blunder at first, a temptation that was not at all tempting, emerged as an alluring prospect, something Jesus had to consider.

It's obvious that no person of sound mind would jump off a tall building. But what if you had a working parachute? What if you believed there was a safety net below that would break your fall but not your neck? What if you believed you were the Son of God, the Savior of the world? What if you believed scriptural promises that God would keep you safe from harm? Doesn't it follow that you would be willing to act on that belief? And if you didn't act, wouldn't it follow that you really didn't believe?

III. *Why Jesus resisted.* In spite of the force of this temptation, Jesus resisted. He said to Satan, "It is written, 'You shall not put the Lord your God to the test.'"

This temptation assumed one of the soundest of all religious principles—that religious belief is demonstrated by action. "Not everyone who says 'Lord, Lord' will enter the Kingdom of heaven," Jesus said, "but those who do the will of my Father who is in heaven." "By their fruits ye shall know them," Jesus said, and Satan would agree completely with this central theme of Jesus' preaching and teaching.

Why, then, did Jesus resist? Because the tempter insinuated into this sound principle a false belief about the nature of God and our relationship to God. Satan said that we are to test God by our action; Jesus said we are to trust God in our action. Satan said God is there to serve us; Jesus said we are here to serve God. Satan twisted Psalm 91 to make it say that we have right to force contingencies on God. Jesus correctly saw that Psalm 91 is really a statement of trust that when contingencies come in the ordinary course of life, God will be with us to see us through.

To deliberately set up test conditions for God in order to prove God's care is to get the divine-human relationship backwards. This is one reason that Jesus said no to this temptation. It assumed that we have the right to set the conditions on which we will believe in and serve God.

There is another reason Jesus said no. He saw that such an act would get people to follow him, but such a following would not be a free commitment of faith. Instead, it would represent a calculated decision based on self-interest. "I'll follow Jesus," we would say, "not because he's right or because he's telling the truth about me, but because he knows how to manipulate God. I'll follow Jesus, not because he will be a steadying presence in the contingencies of life, but because he can guarantee my freedom from those contingencies."

What this temptation tempts us to do is to view faith as magic and God as a magical power, always at our beck and call. All we have to do is learn the proper formulas for manipulating God—"abracadabra," "open sesame," "the inerrant, infallible, holy Word of God"—and then repeat them like a mantra. If we master these formulas, then God will have to take care of us, keep us from harm, come to our aid when we need it, and bless us. We can have absolute religious certainty because God is a magical power, and we have the infallible magical formulas for making God jump.

Satan said to Jesus, "Say all the right words—'I believe in God,' 'I believe in Scripture'—and God will have to protect you. Jumping from the Temple to test that belief is the sort of thing you will do."

Jesus responded, "If I really believe in God and in Scripture, if I'm not just mouthing magical formulas, then jumping from the Temple to test that belief is the sort of thing I will not do. God is not a magician at my beck and call. He doesn't have to protect me just because I say I believe. Not even I have the right to set the conditions for God."

Jesus said, "It is written, 'You shall not put the Lord your God to the test.'"

IV. *Our experience of this temptation.* Of the three wilderness temptations, the second one, I think, is the most difficult one to see as somehow relevant to our lives. I understand the temptations that material things can cause, and I understand how power and glory can become temptations. It's more difficult to see how I might be putting God to the test, how I might be laying down conditions for God to meet. Few of us are so crass as to bargain with God: If you do this for me, then I'll do that for you.

But suppose we find that the things that have given us religious satisfaction in the past no longer do so? Suppose we find that our spiritual needs are no longer being met by our usual religious practices? Are we testing God by dropping out, by ceasing to practice our faith through the disciplines of worship, study, and service? Are we setting conditions on God by saying, "I'm going to try something else because my needs are no longer being met?" Judging faith and practice in terms of one's personal needs may be the most significant danger in that amorphous phenomenon called New Age spirituality. It may be the most significant danger to that generation the sociologist Wade Clark Roof has called "seekers."

There seem to be centripetal forces at work—that is, forces tending inward, toward the center. And the center is the lone individual with his or her individual needs. Every religious experience is judged in terms of how well it meets those needs.

Since our needs, or at least our perceptions of our needs, change constantly, we find that what worked yesterday doesn't address where we are today. So we tend to drift from one spiritual phenomenon to the next, because the implicit test for accepting some belief or practice is what we happen to need at the time. Drifting, in turn, sets up a restlessness in our souls that may make us susceptible to any appeal that promises us contact with the absolute truth and absolute security. This restlessness is one of the reasons we have witnessed a resurgence of religious absolutism in the last thirty years or so.

But restlessness may be the way God finally gets through to us. Dissatisfaction with spiritual needs that are not being met may be the way God begins to break back into our lives.

Anne Lamott, in her book *Traveling Mercies,* describes her life up to her late thirties, early forties, as such an aimless, restless wandering, as a search to find the fulfillment of her needs. Her search included drug and alcohol abuse, promiscuous sex with married men, and involvement with a variety of left-wing political causes. Her life began to change, however, when she found herself drawn to a seedy little Presbyterian church across the street from a flea market she would frequent on Sundays, in Marin City, California. It was the singing she heard coming through the doors of that run-down church that drew her at first. She would stand in the doorway and listen, then leave when the sermon began, because sermons are "ridiculous." (She was already in good theological company with that opinion. Paul speaks of the "foolishness of preaching.")

She continued listening to the music on Sundays while her life continued to spiral downward, out of control, until she finally hit bottom. When that happened, she knew she had to choose one of two options: accept what the singing of that poor little congregation pointed to, or accept the death of everything that was still good about her. She knew that if she chose the first option, the reality the singing pointed to would not allow her to set the terms of her acceptance of it.

In the months leading to her conversion, she had been picturing Jesus like a little lost cat, following her everywhere she went and looking expectantly at her every time she entered her front door. The cat wanted in, and "You know how cats are," Lamott wrote; "once you let them in and give them some milk, they never leave." That was the last thing she wanted Jesus to do.

But it was accept that condition or die. Once she was able to accept it and stop insisting on setting the terms herself, she was able finally to say the word to Jesus that would have been, only a few months earlier, an embarrassment even to think about.

"You can come on in," she said.

The centripetal forces in her life reversed and became centrifugal. Instead of centering on herself and her needs, she became centered on something outside herself. And when she was finally able to say to God, "Come on in," she discovered that all the things she'd been looking for were now hers.

There is an important qualification to make about the issue of our religious needs. If we find that our needs are not being met, it may be that we are focusing on ourselves in a way we shouldn't and that the problem is with us. But it may also be that the problem lies in the religious environment we inhabit. Religious communities can be bad for our religious health; they can even be toxic.

When our souls are not being nourished because of an unhealthy environment, we have two options. One is to try to insulate ourselves from the poison of our environment, usually by finding a smaller community within the larger one where we do find nurturance. The other is to leave the environment altogether and search for a better one. Here our spiritual needs are not the primary focus of our concern but rather a sign to us that something is wrong with our environment and we need to act to save ourselves.

V. *Hallowed by thy name.* The temptation of the pinnacle of the Temple is the temptation we feel when we want to put something between us and God, something that becomes a condition of our acceptance of God. It is what we succumb to when we give ourselves the final authority to determine our relationship with God. It is the sin of giving absolute status to ourselves, not God.

Another way to say this is to say that it is the sin of not giving God what is due to God, not recognizing God as the only holy, sacred, ultimate reality. When we commit this sin, we hallow ourselves, not God.

What resources do we have to help us resist this temptation?

We have Jesus' example in the wilderness and his words to the tempter that we are not to put God to the test. We also have the prayer he taught us to pray, the very first words of which, after the address to God, are "Hallowed be thy name." We are to hold as sacred and holy God and God alone. We are to hallow God and not to hallow any other thing. This comes first in the prayer because this is the first thing we must understand about our relationship to God.

If we remember that only God is absolute and only God is to be hallowed, we will have learned something very valuable in resisting this most subtle of temptations.

We are to trust God, not test God.

Topic: The Power and the Glory—Gethsemane
TEXT: Ps. 23; Matt. 4:8–11; 26:36–46

I. *Jesus and the third temptation.* The first two temptations in the wilderness failed, so Satan tried one more time to tempt Jesus to sin, by transporting him to a very high mountain from which they could survey all the kingdoms of the Earth. The power and glory of the world passed before them and Satan said, "You have come to save the world? Well, here it is. It is powerful, it is glorious, it is beautiful, and it can be yours, to do with as you like. It's yours, if you will fall down and worship me."

Anyone who has stood on the observation deck of the Empire State Building surveying New York City below can surely identify with the psychology of this temptation. Above all that wealth and power, who hasn't wondered, What would it be like to have all of this, to be able to do whatever I like with all of this? Who hasn't wondered how much good could be done if only all that power and glory were in the right hands?

That was of course the thought Satan wanted Jesus to think. Whose hands could be more right than those of the Son of God? When we consider the good that could be done if Jesus were the political and economic ruler of the world, we have to ask, What would be wrong with that?

Furthermore, the third temptation (like the first two) was a temptation to do what Jesus intended to do eventually any way. He proclaimed God's rule on Earth, which supersedes all other claims to power. The book of Revelation puts it this way: Jesus is "King of Kings, and Lord of Lords."

Presumably Christ's absolute authority throughout the world would mean that even Satan would be excluded from the world and could no longer work mischief by tempting us to sin. If so, then, paradoxically, by yielding to this temptation, Jesus could have eliminated temptation for the rest of us. What would have been wrong with that?

While we can easily feel the force of this temptation, something about this reasoning to these conclusions should bother us. It doesn't seem quite right to say that Satan would be excluded from the world and would no longer tempt us.

The problem is this: Were Christ to have achieved God's ends by Satan's means, Satan would not have to be present in the world to tempt us, because evil would have already won! By worshipping Satan in order to gain the power and glory of the world (even for the sake of doing good), Christ would have been using Satan's means to achieve God's ends, and in so doing the ends would no longer have been God's.

In the new Kingdom proclaimed by Christ, the way we achieve justice and peace is as important as justice and peace themselves. God's purpose in sending Jesus was to create on Earth a community of people who had freely chosen the way Jesus had laid out for them to follow. For Jesus to have worshiped Satan and thereby have gained the power and glory of the world would have been for Jesus to renounce God's intentions by using worldly means. Instead of freely choosing this way, we would have been forced to do what is right; and Jesus, by worshipping Satan, would have tacitly admitted that human nature responds only to force, and that love is a nice ideal that won't work.

II. *Why Jesus resisted.* The world might indeed be a better place if Jesus had just taken over the power to make us all toe the line. The problem is that we would not be better people for having been forced to be good. God wants a world where peace and love and justice are real. But God wants these ideals to be real because we have chosen the way that leads to them. Such goodness has to come from inside us, because our hearts have been changed, if it is to be our goodness.

The world of peace and justice Jesus would have achieved by worshipping Satan would not be the world of peace and justice intended by God. It would be a world imposed on us, not a world we had created by our free choice of God's way.

So, Jesus rejected this temptation, too. He said to the tempter, "Away with you! For it is written, 'Worship the Lord your God and serve only him.'"

Jesus knew that to achieve a good end by evil means is to compromise the goodness of that end. We are therefore to achieve the good only by using means that are consistent with God's ends, that is, by worshipping and serving God and God alone.

III. *Our experience of this temptation.* Of the three wilderness temptations, this one is probably the one with which we can most easily identify and that we can most easily translate into the terms of our own existence. On a literal level, of course, this temptation is foreign to us. Unless we are megalomaniacs, none of us is tempted to take over the world and its power and glory. But all of us live in worlds particular to us—our jobs, our families, our religious communities, for example—and in these worlds we are often tempted to gain advantage at the expense of others. The job promotion, the salary increase, the upwardly mobile status we could achieve by pulling a few strings or engaging in some shady dealings that might not bear exposure to the light of day—these are the kinds of things we are tempted by on a regular basis, and they are examples of how we experience this temptation.

There is nothing wrong with job promotions, raises, or moving upward in social status. The point is that they easily become occasions for this temptation.

There is a scene in the movie *Jesus of Montreal* that brings home to us forcefully the power of this temptation. A young actor named Daniel has become the rage of Montreal for portraying Jesus in a Passion play sponsored by a Catholic shrine. A lawyer has asked Daniel to lunch at a posh restaurant on top of a Montreal skyscraper to discuss career planning with him—that is, how he can capitalize on his fame as Jesus.

As they walk down a long corridor with floor-to-ceiling windows, the city of Montreal lies forty stories below them in the background. The lawyer says that Daniel could make a lot of money doing the weekend talk shows, giving magazine interviews, exploiting the media. He could publish a book—about his travels, his struggle with drugs or alcohol, anything. Daniel objects that he is not a writer, but the lawyer responds, "I said publish, not write. Publishers all have writers with talent and no money."

They have stopped by one of the floor-to-ceiling windows in the corridor and forty stories below lies one of the main thoroughfares of Montreal, teeming with traffic.

"Do I shock you?" the lawyer says. "I'm just trying to show you that with your talent, this city is yours, if you want it."

Furthermore, the world with its received wisdom makes it easy to believe that there's really nothing wrong with pulling strings to get your way. "It's a dog-eat-dog world," we say. "It's kill or be killed," we say. We intend to do good when we get where we're going, so does it matter if we bloody a few noses to get there or step on a few people on the way up the ladder?

"That's just the way the world is," we say. Doesn't our good end justify our less-than-good means? How else are we to achieve good in the world?

IV. *Some examples.* Jesus wants very badly for the world to hear his message and go down the path that leads to peace and wholeness and justice. He realizes that this can occur only by the free choice of his disciples. His disciples, unfortunately, have not always followed his example and many times have tried to do good by evil means.

No one has portrayed this rejection of Christ by Christians better than Fyodor Dostoevsky in the chilling chapter entitled "The Grand Inquisitor" from his novel *The Brothers Karamazov*. The Grand Inquisitor frankly admits to Jesus in their midnight interview that the Church has made a calculated decision that Jesus' way of freedom and love won't work, so the Church has cast its lot with the devil.

If you think this is just a work of fiction, like a movie not to be taken seriously, let me tell you a story—a true one. Many years ago I sat in the office of a very high-ranking and powerful denominational official who had recently gotten rid of some people who had threatened his position and power. He had done this in a very clever way that minimized the possibility that he would be held accountable.

A friend of mine and I, when we finally learned about what had happened, made an appointment to ask this man why he had taken the action he had. He responded by saying that his primary responsibility was to leave this institution stronger and more viable than it had been at the beginning of his tenure. This, of course, is a good end for which to strive. Next he said that if anyone threatened the institution, he would do whatever was necessary to get rid of the troublemaker.

His actual words were, "If someone hits me, I'm going to hit him back, only harder."

I wish I had had the presence of mind (as well as the courage) to respond, "What about turning the other cheek?" Someone recently told me that this same man once said to him that it is impossible to run a Christian institution on Christian principles.

V. *Thy Kingdom come.* Perhaps the greatest failing of Christians in our witness to the world is our failure to resist the allure of power and glory, our yielding to the temptation to use the world's means to achieve spiritual ends. The world apparently expects more of us than we expect of ourselves, and the world might be more receptive to our message if we consistently practiced what we preach.

We are all tempted to exercise wrongly the power we do have, so what resources do we have to help us resist this most powerful of temptations?

We have Jesus' example in the wilderness, where he recognized that using worldly methods for spiritual ends is really to worship Satan. And we have the prayer he taught us to pray, which includes recognition that we are to achieve God's will in God's way: "Thy kingdom come, thy will be done, on Earth as it is in heaven."

If we remember that the means we use must be consistent with the ends we intend, if we remember that it is God's rule and will on Earth we are trying to achieve, then we will have learned something very valuable in resisting this most powerful of temptations.

VI. *Jesus in Gethsemane.* If Jesus was fully human, he was probably tempted throughout his life, not just on one occasion in the wilderness. Our experience with temptation is that we struggle continuously with it; the same temptations come to us in various guises again and again. So, it seems unlikely that Jesus, "in all points tempted as we are yet without sin," had only the one experience of temptation in the wilderness.

The Gospels do not record any other temptation as such. But if any event they record was indeed a temptation, it was Jesus' struggle in the Garden of Gethsemane to find some way other than the cross.

Jesus' experience in Gethsemane is much closer than the wilderness to what we experience when we are tempted. In Gethsemane, Jesus struggled with an internal conflict over what he really wanted. He wanted two contradictory things: to avoid the cross and to do God's will.

The crisis in Gethsemane occurred in Jesus' prayer: "My father, if it be possible, let this cup pass me by. Yet not as I will but as thou wilt."

All three Synoptic Gospels agree that Jesus used the image of the cup to describe the bitter ordeal he was facing. The cup is a symbol often used in Jewish prayers to indicate what God was giving at a particular moment in life. In Psalm 23, the psalmist proclaimed "my cup runneth over." Here the cup was the cup of blessing, a way of symbolizing something good coming from God.

But there was also the cup of God's wrath (for example, Ps. 11:6). God could offer a cup of poison, and that is how Jesus saw the Cross. He didn't want to drink this cup. I think we sometimes gloss over Jesus' agony in the garden and think that his prayer was perfunctory. The oldest of Christian temptations—to deny that Jesus is fully human—rears its head here.

We must understand Jesus' struggle as real and must therefore consider that the possibility of escape was also real. It is dark. Jesus was on familiar ground, his would-be captors were not. It would have been easy for him to slip away under cover of night, to lie low for awhile, and then to begin again when things had cooled down.

Furthermore, if Jesus were to die then, the future of what he had started seemed pretty dim. The Gospels present the disciples as constantly misunderstanding Jesus. Here, at the most crucial moment of his public life, they fell asleep!

VII. *Why Jesus stayed.* The temptation to escape the cross must have been very strong. Yet Jesus did not give in to it. He stayed in Gethsemane, was arrested, tried, condemned, and executed as a common criminal. Why did he stay?

He stayed because he believed it was God's will for him to face this ordeal. But how could it be God's will for him to die? What kind of God would want that? This God did not seem to be the Father Jesus had addressed in such an intimate way. I am a father and I would never will that my daughter die a horrible death such as this.

Yet if Jesus was to be true to what he had taught his disciples about the power of love, then he could not flee this dangerous moment but had to face it. He had taught his disciples that God's ways are not the ways of the world. He had told those who used the ways of the world in the name of God that they were wrong and needed to repent.

One of the essential aspects of Jesus' teaching was that love is more powerful than brute force. For him to escape in the face of force would have been to admit that force is stronger. God's will was not that he should die but that he should be faithful to the rule of God that he had proclaimed and to the primacy of love. It could have been that in this climactic confrontation, those who ruled the world would finally listen and finally understand the right way of life.

But even if they didn't, Jesus couldn't escape the consequences of the truth he had taught and embodied. For him to flee would have been for him to admit that God's way doesn't really work.

VIII. *The power of love.* The writer of the Song of Songs had written, "Love is as strong as death," which is perhaps as good a summary of the gospel as it is possible to get. The temptation of Gethsemane is the temptation to give up that belief when the choice is between it and our lives. Is the love of God really as strong as death?

Jesus came proclaiming the good news of God's love and grace toward us, which we don't deserve. We can respond to that love and grace in faith and discipleship or we can reject it. If Jesus really believed what he had been preaching, then he had to be willing to trust God's love and care and choose faithfulness to God, even when that faithfulness led him to the unjust, cruel, humiliating death of the cross.

Is God's love this powerful?

The only way we can know is that Jesus resisted the temptation to escape the cross. If God is who Jesus said he is, then not even the cross could destroy that kind of love.

Knowing only that he would die a horrible death, Jesus nevertheless prayed, "Not my will, but yours be done."

IX. *Our experience of Gethsemane.* The most difficult thing we are called to do is to face up to death—our own or that of someone we love. Facing death is difficult partly because it is often painful and sometimes tragic or cruel and unjust. Even death that comes at the end of a long life well lived can be difficult, because it is so often accompanied by the decline of physical and mental abilities.

Perhaps the deepest reason we are tempted to deny God because of death is that no one really knows what happens when we die; no one knows what kind of reality we might have or whether we have any reality at all.

If death is so mysterious and unknown, then why should we trust God to be there to see us through, to keep us safe? When faced with the unknown, our instinctive reaction is to cling to the familiar. And because this life is all the reality we have known, this life is what we are tempted to cling to when death confronts us. This is especially true if we can do something to avoid death.

Probably we will never have to face death for our faith, as Jesus did in Gethsemane, though there are places in the world where we could be put to death for doing what we are doing right now. But there are other ways we may die before we have to face the death of our body. These other ways to die tempt us to lose our faith as much as literal death does.

Have you ever cared for and loved someone else who simply didn't care for you, who was indifferent or perhaps even hostile to your love? When love dies, something within us dies.

Have you ever had a dream die, something worthwhile for which you had worked passionately and sacrificially, only to see it unfulfilled, destroyed by forces over which you had no control? When a dream dies, something within us dies.

Have you ever seen someone you love slowly destroyed by disease, slowly turning into something that's not even a bad caricature of the person he or she had been, the way Alzheimer's disease destroys? Or a young child, full of beauty and promise, destroyed by cystic fibrosis or leukemia? When someone we love dies, something within us dies.

When life confronts us with these unjust cruelties, the tempter is there by our side, suggesting that God is perhaps not so trustworthy, and that perhaps we should rely on something or someone else.

X. *Our Father, Abba.* Why was Jesus able to resist the temptation in Gethsemane to cling to life one more day, to avoid the cross and its humiliation?

I have interpreted the prayer Jesus taught us to pray as a counterpoint to the temptation Jesus experienced. Knowing the power of temptation because of his experience in the wilderness, Jesus taught us this prayer, in part at least, to give us strength when we are tempted. Is there anything in the prayer that indicates he was looking not only backward to the wilderness but also forward to Gethsemane and his Passion?

I think there is one element in the prayer that bears directly on death in all of its guises, and on how we face death. Jesus taught us to pray, "Our Father." The word Jesus actually used was not the formal term, *Father,* but the word *Abba,* the word Jewish children used in the privacy of the home. It is the most intimate word a child can use, and what it conveys is a sense of unconditional trust, a sense that all is well.

Abba conveys the almost naive innocence of a child, before the child has learned by experience about the world's power to hurt. It is the innocence all of us have to give up when we become adults and put away childish things. The loss of childhood innocence is necessary for all of us, because no human parents, even with the best of intentions and resources, will always do what is right by their children.

Yet Jesus taught us to pray, "Abba, who art in heaven." And even in the garden, he called God "Abba."

If any event in Jesus' life had had the power to make him renounce his unconditional trust in God, it would have been Gethsemane and the Passion. Yet in Gethsemane he prayed "Abba."

As we face death in the many ways in which we all die before we die, the tempter says to us, "Do you really believe that God's love is more powerful than even death? Are you really willing to bet everything on that? There's so much evidence that it's not true—all the pain and suffering in the world, all the deaths you die before you die, and then finally the unknown reality of the death of your body. Wouldn't it be more prudent to trust your own resources, follow your own counsel, cling to the life you can see and hear and feel? You can't see or hear God, so how can you be sure that God is there to rely on, especially in the hour of your death?"

The tempter is right: We can't see or hear God. But we can see Jesus in Gethsemane and we can hear him pray, "Abba, not my will but yours be done."

If we believe in Jesus, then that will be enough.

SECTION IX

RESOURCES FOR PREACHING ON ETHICAL ISSUES

BY ALLAN M. PARRENT

Topic: Heavenly Citizenship and Earthly Citizenship
TEXT: Phil. 3:17–4:1

I. *Their glory is in their shame.* We don't have to look far in our culture to find contemporary examples of what Paul was talking about to the Christians of Philippi. Afternoon TV shows are filled with people who glory in telling the world about such accomplishments as seducing the spouses of their sons or daughters. Teenage boys take pride in fathering illegitimate children, and teenage girls take pride in having them. Obscenity as art and the compulsion to shock dominate much of popular culture, as fame and fortune are showered on the purveyors of lyrics that express emotions ranging from sadism to nihilistic rage. And elsewhere in the world, terrorists are lionized for the indiscriminate mass murder of innocent people in crowded public places. Their glory is in their shame.

Why have such phenomena come to have such a prominent place in contemporary culture? Several reasons might be suggested. One reason is the decline in the broad moral consensus that any healthy society requires. As a society we seem to have difficulty agreeing anymore on such basics as what is noble and what is base, what is to be held in esteem and what is to be scorned. Popular entertainment too often honors violence and infidelity and denigrates religion, marriage, and respect for legitimate authority. The virtues of self-discipline, civility, and integrity are often derided, while acquisitiveness and instant gratification are lifted up.

A second reason is found in what Senator Moynihan calls "defining deviancy down." That is, as a society we have come to accept as normal much social behavior that a generation ago was considered alarming. The killing of seven gangsters on the streets of Chicago in 1929 is still remembered as the St. Valentine's Day Massacre. Today, street killings occur somewhere almost daily.

A third reason is that the positive political and cultural changes brought by the civil rights movement, which aimed at liberation from poverty and oppression for the have-nots in society, also promoted a set of values that often wreaked havoc in the lives of those same have-nots for whom help was sought. Just when the hard-won successes of the civil rights movement were removing barriers to opportunities, the virtues that enable people to seize those opportunities—industriousness, sobriety, self-discipline, deferral of gratification—were being subverted by ridicule from many of the cultural elite.

There is, of course, no necessary connection between the gains in political liberty and racial and sexual equality on the one hand, and lack of discipline and moral debasement on the other. Martin Luther King Jr., our most revered advocate of social and racial justice, knew that

381

justice cannot last long in a cultural ethos that denigrates the classical and civic virtues, that calls evil good, that glorifies the shameful. That knowledge came not from his political convictions but from his Christian convictions, from which his political convictions were derived.

II. *Our citizenship is in heaven.* It is those same convictions that caused Paul to make the contrast between those whose "glory is in their shame" and the Christians at Philippi. He reminded them that our primary loyalty is to another community and that the moral norms that govern our actions in our earthly community come from that more ultimate allegiance. Our citizenship in that transcendent community provides the plumb line by which we determine what is in fact shameful or admirable, noble or base. It is not just a matter of opinion, majority rule, or cultural trendiness.

But it is significant that Paul spoke of heavenly citizenship and its moral implications in the same city, Philippi, where he appealed in Acts to the moral implications of his own earthly citizenship, his Roman citizenship, and its requirement of justice. As Christians, we are, like Paul, dual citizens—that is, we are citizens of both the Kingdom of God and one of the kingdoms of the Earth. As Christians, we derive legitimate rights and obligations from both kingdoms. This has been a fundamental insight of Christian political thought for two thousand years.

Not only are we citizens of both "cities," but the two, while distinct, are inextricably intertwined. Some people portray Christians as only "resident aliens" on this planet. Others call us to christianize the social order. Still others, distorting the meaning of separation of church and state, would exclude from deliberations in the public square those whose perspectives on public issues are admittedly informed by Christian convictions.

Paul would have rejected all these options. Instead, he would have encouraged Christians to translate their religiously shaped understanding of justice into culturally understandable terms, and to participate fully with their fellow citizens in the public square to help shape the moral ethos of the earthly community of which they are a part. The task is to create not a Christian society but rather a good, just, and humane society. The effort will be informed by a gospel that gives some distinctive content to those adjectives. Our citizenship is in heaven, yes. But precisely because of that citizenship, we have some guidelines for determining what earthly citizenship means.

III. *Therefore stand firm in the Lord.* The obligations of earthly citizenship put limits on what we as citizens should and should not do. To borrow words from the preamble to the Constitution, we are not free to act in ways that are destructive of domestic tranquility or that would deprive our posterity of the blessings of liberty. The same is true of our heavenly citizenship. It too has implications for how we are to live in the earthly city, and we are to "stand firm in the Lord" as we live out those implications.

Just as Paul warned the Galatian Christians against legalism, against righteousness based on law, so he warned the Philippian Christians against antinomianism, against casting aside all restraints and allowing freedom to degenerate into license, against glorying in that of which we should be ashamed. Just as he told the Galatians to "stand fast" in their Christian freedom and not put themselves under the yoke of slavery to the law, he also told the Philippians to "stand firm" against the abuse of freedom and not to imagine that it means license to sin with impunity, which also leads to slavery.

Today our environmental awareness makes us aware that our assaults on nature can have irreversible effects on our ecology. Similarly, some of our current assaults on the virtues and practices that make community life possible can also have irreversible effects on our moral ecology. It is not natural for individuals to restrain their aggression, to patiently nurture off-spring in marriage, to defer gratification, or to work with discipline. These are learned traits, civic virtues necessary for a life of ordered liberty in the earthly city. But they are also traits that are consonant with some of the Christian virtues Paul commended to citizens of the heavenly city—patience, forbearance, justice, self-control. For Christian citizens of twenty-first-century America, or any other earthly city, our primary citizenship is, by God's grace, in heaven. But that citizenship, when taken seriously, inevitable helps to shape our earthly citizenship and the way our earthly cities order their common life.

Topic: Faith and Works

TEXT: Hab. 1:1–6, 12–13; 2:1–4; Luke 17:5–10

It would be difficult to find Old and New Testament texts that, when held together, carry more of the essence of the Protestant Reformation than these two verses. It would also be difficult to find two texts that, when held together, provide a firmer theological ground for relating Christian faith to the political, economic, and social issues of the day.

The words from Habakkuk, "The righteous shall live by faith," came to be central to Paul's doctrine of justification by grace through faith and later became the rallying cry of the Reformation. Likewise, the words of Christ to his disciples in Luke—"When you have done all that is commanded of you, say, 'We are unworthy servants, we have only done what was our duty'"—speak directly to the central issue of the Reformation, our ability to make ourselves worthy before God through our good works.

Faith and righteousness, faith and works—these two themes are as central to the Christian faith and to moral life today as they were for Paul and for Jesus. Both also have to do with the basic religious question of trust. In whom or what do we put our ultimate trust, and what does that mean for the way we live?

I. In the summer of 1988, the five-hundredth anniversary of Luther's birth, I spent two weeks in what was then East Germany with a group of Lutherans. In addition to Wartburg Castle, Erfurt, Wittenberg, and Eisleben, one of the highlights of the trip was the Kirchentag, the Church Assembly, held in the beautiful city of Dresden. The Assembly's theme was "Dare to Trust." On a warm Sunday afternoon in that then-Communist state I stood with ninety thousand East German Christians and sang that great Lutheran hymn of trust, "Ein Feste Burg." It is a hymn that Habakkuk would have found congenial, especially verse 2.

Habakkuk was concerned about the absence of justice in Judah. He asked the age-old question of why a just God allows the unjust to flourish. He carried on a dialogue with God for a while, but then rather than trying to provide an answer of his own, as we are all tempted to do, he decided to wait for God's answer. When the answer came, however, it at first seemed not to deal with the question of justice at all (2:2–4).

Write the vision? What does that have to do with the prophet's interest in creating a just society? Ultimately, everything. It is our vision that causes us to see the world in a particular way, walk in a particular way, seek to shape public life in a particular way. And it is the writing of our vision, our proclamation of it, our witnessing to it, that assists others to see that way. It is only when people have a proper vision of justice that they can recognize perverted justice as perverted. It is only when they have a clear vision of what a just society should be that they understand what might be done to shape their social environment to be more in keeping with that vision.

And what was the vision revealed to Habakkuk? It came in two parts, and was seemingly simple. First, "He whose soul is not upright in him shall fail." That is, the nation or individual that proceeds with a policy that is not upright and honest will fail. That is the way God made the world; we live in a moral universe. Second, "The righteous shall live by faith." That is, trust in God is the only sure basis of strength and security in this world where evil has not yet been fully overcome. The righteous are those who dare to trust in God regardless of current circumstances. They will be sustained by their faithfulness to the vision of justice and to the promise that it will become a reality.

That reality may be slow in coming, however. Some may therefore seek to bring in an earthly kingdom of their own design, and be willing to use any means to achieve such a supposedly worthy goal. History is filled with examples of such utopian fanaticism, which is at least as destructive as the inaction of those who are devoid of vision. We are not to anticipate God. Even though we work constantly to achieve some degree of proximate justice, as those with vision must, we may never see the results. But faith must be based on something more than visible good results. The only faith by which the righteous can live for very long is faith based not on results but on trust in the author and revealer of the vision itself, and on his promise that the results will come. Habakkuk's own later response affirms exactly that kind of trust (3:17–18). In short, then, justice questions drive us to faith questions.

II. The reverse is also true. Faith questions drive us to justice questions. In the Gospel lesson, the disciples asked Jesus to "increase our faith." But Jesus responded by telling them a story about servants doing their duty, that is, about works, not faith. Servants are supposed to do what is commanded of them and to expect no special reward for doing so. The same is true for God's servants. In God's sight we cannot act more justly than we are required to act, we cannot build up an excess credit or moral brownie points, we cannot give God more than his due today to compensate for yesterday's deficit.

There are two important points here. The first is that works are integrally related to faith. Faithful servants are expected to do justice and good works, to order their lives in accordance with God's commandments. That is God's Word given to us as law, as a lamp unto our feet. The second point, however, is that works are not a substitute for faith. We are justified and made righteous by faith alone, apart from any reliance on good works. That is God's Word to us, his gospel, given for our salvation. The whole of the Christian life then becomes a life of free and grateful response to God's prior saving action toward us, and that response of good works applies to every facet of our private, public, and vocational lives. We perform good works not in order to be justified, but because we already are

III. Habakkuk's concern for social justice, that is, for good works, led him to a crucial insight about faith. The disciples' concern for increased faith led them to a crucial insight about works, about doing what is commanded. These themes can also speak to the Christian community today. Our proper concern for justice must be rooted in a biblical vision, and in trust in the source of that vision, if it is to endure the persistence of injustice. Conversely, our proper concern to increase our faith can never be fully expressed if it does not include concern for our neighbors and for the public policies that affect them, that is, if it does not include actions by obedient servants seeking to be faithful to our duty to obey the commandments of the one in whom we put our ultimate trust.

"The righteous shall live by faith"—but it is a declared righteousness, God's free gift, that becomes not the goal of our obedience but its presupposition. "When you have done all that is commanded of you, say, 'We are unworthy servants; we have only done what was our duty.'" What is commanded is not slavery but service to him in whose service is perfect freedom.

Topic: Power and Responsibility
Text: Gen. 16:1–14

According to Lord Acton's too-often quoted aphorism, "Power corrupts and absolute power corrupts absolutely." A well-known ethics professor used to quote that line and then add the paradoxical addendum, "Yet we need power in order to survive." That truth captures part of the paradox of the Christian moral life, namely, how to use responsibly whatever degree of power we have been given by the grace of God, while knowing that the use of power will inevitably involve us in compromise and sin. As individuals and in our familial, vocational, and institutional relationships, we all have been given some degree of power. We are called to exercise it in ways that will at the same time serve our neighbors' needs, be consonant with our vocational obligations, and be in keeping with our primary identity as followers of Christ. Even with the purest intentions, that is a difficult if not impossible task.

All of us who have a degree of power and influence, regardless of how broad or constricted it may be, will be tempted to misuse it, perhaps solely for selfish purposes or perhaps refusing to use it at all. The text tells us a story about Sarai, Abram, and Hagar that illustrates three of the ways we human beings are tempted to misuse our power. It also points to three of our contemporary illusions about those whom we would entrust with power.

I. The first example is Sarai, who suggested that because she apparently could not have children, her husband should follow the custom of the day and have an heir by Hagar, Sarai's maid. Abram seemed quite willing to take the suggestion. But when Hagar conceived and looked with contempt on her childless mistress, what did Sarai do? First, she blamed Abram for the disrespect she received from Hagar; second, she dealt so harshly with Hagar that Hagar fled into the wilderness. Sarai illustrates the temptation we all have to deny our responsibility for the unforeseen negative consequences of our own exercise of power, and to blame and punish others for those consequences. This first temptation we might call the *buck-passing use of power*.

The second example is Abram. Abram took his wife's suggestion and caused Hagar to conceive. But when he was asked to deal with the unhappy result—to use the power he obviously had in that patriarchal society—to adjudicate the matter, what did Abram do? He abdicated his responsibility. In Pilate-like fashion he proclaimed, "Your maid is in your power; do with her as you please." Whether out of timidity, inadequacy, unconcern, or a desire to maintain the illusion of an above-the-battle moral purity, Abram refused to use his power. In doing so, he illustrated the temptation we all have to relinquish our stewardship of the power given to us, to renounce it or withdraw from it, especially in difficult or morally ambiguous situations. This second temptation we might designate as the *abdication of power*.

The third example is Hagar. As a maid she was obviously one of the powerless in that social setting. She probably had little choice in the matter of surrogate motherhood. But the fact is that in that act her status changed, and with it, her social clout. In a society where barrenness was a social stigma and fertility a social plus, the pregnant Hagar proceeded to show contempt for the barren Sarai. Her new status and power became the occasion for showing a kind of overt proletarian disdain for the once powerful bourgeoisie, to use more contemporary terminology. In doing so, Hagar illustrated the temptation we all have to use newly acquired power to retaliate, to pay back, to get even, to lord it over those who formerly had power over us. This third temptation we might call the *misapplication of power*, especially of newly acquired power.

II. We have in this ancient story, then, three examples of the human temptations of power and its use. Each character tells us something about ourselves as individuals, but each also tells us something about some of our cultural illusions about those whom we would entrust with power. As in many good biblical narratives, some of our favorite oxen get gored in the process.

Sarai might cause us, for example, to question the myth of an innate feminine superiority in matters of peacemaking and conciliation. Ann Ulanov, a professor at Union Seminary who is in the front ranks of feminist theologians, warns us of this illusion. Surely the T-shirt logo that proclaims "a woman's place is in the House, and the Senate"—places where power is wielded—is correct. But that conviction is based on a love-inspired sense of justice and equity, not on a belief that one-half of the human race is by nature necessarily more irenic or conciliatory, or less likely to abuse power, than the other half. Indira Gandhi, Golda Meir, and Margaret Thatcher might be seen as cases in point.

Likewise, Abram should cause us to continue to question that older and dying but still extant myth of masculine superiority in matters of leadership and decision making. The illusion of the take-charge male who gets things done, who coolly analyzes the problem and does what is necessary to solve it, in Rambo style if necessary, is belied by numerous examples in history of bumbling, indecisive, and power-abdicating men, of whom Abram and Pilate were early examples.

Finally, Hagar should cause us to question the contemporary myth that those on the lower rungs of society are somehow innately more morally pure, more discerning, and less infected in their use of power by the human frailties of envy, hatred, and greed than are the rest of humankind. Of course, this basic theological truth about the universality of sin must never become a rationalization for legitimizing an unjust status quo on the fatuous and self-serving grounds that when "they" get power, "they" will only abuse it like "we" do. The empowerment of all persons, especially those who have been denied their rightful share of power, is a moral necessity in every society. But that imperative must be based on the requirements of transcendent love translated into the currency of justice, not on the illusion that those who today are victims of social injustice will somehow be above the temptations of power when they have their rightful share.

III. In the biography of his brother, *Brother to a Dragonfly*, Will Campbell writes of one of his many conversations with his friend, P.D., the local agnostic. P.D. had a way of pressing for simple answers. "Just tell me what this Jesus cat is all about. I'm not too bright but maybe I can get the hang of it. If you would tell me what the hell the Christian faith is all about, maybe I wouldn't make an ass of myself when I'm talking about it. Keep it simple. In ten words or less, what's the Christian message? Let me have it. Ten words." Campbell's response was, "We're all bastards, but God loves us anyway."

Will Campbell would doubtless apply both that label and his point about God's love to you and to me, as well as to Sarai, Abram, and Hagar, and properly so. While I don't think his definition is a direct scriptural quote, it is a fundamental theological truth. It is important to add to it, however, the truth that God not only "loves us anyway," he also empowers us anyway. Just as his grace provides forgiveness for the sins of commission and omission we share with the characters in the biblical story, so does his grace empower us to do his work in the world, however imperfectly we may in fact do it. He calls us to go forth into that world, "rejoicing in the power of the spirit" and seeking unashamedly to be good stewards of the human power allotted to us. As we respond to God's call to use our power responsibly, however, biblical realism also reminds us of the prudential wisdom captured in Reinhold Niebuhr's famous prayer, "God give us the serenity to accept what cannot be changed, the courage to change what should be changed, and the wisdom to distinguish the one from the other."

Topic: Love and Conflict
TEXT: Gen. 25:33; Heb. 13:1

I. The story of Jacob and Esau and the selling of the birthright tells us, with unvarnished biblical realism, something about the darker side of human nature. It illustrates, as does this whole section of Genesis, the inescapable reality of human conflict and deception.

Conflict between the brothers evidently began even before birth. Likewise, parental conflict is revealed in Isaac's love for Esau and Rebekah's love for Jacob, showing the integral relation between love and conflict. There was conflict even between the brothers' professions, lifestyles, and characters. The impulsive Esau gave little thought to the future in the face of his present desire for gratification, while the calculating Jacob left nothing to chance. There was earlier conflict between Abraham and Sarah over Hagar, later conflict between Jacob and Laban, and finally conflict between Jacob and God. There was also deception—deception of Isaac by Jacob and Rebekah, deception of Jacob by Laban, and deception of Laban by Jacob and Rachel. There is certainly no idealizing of national ancestors in this story.

This narrative is in stark contrast to the moral exhortations in Hebrews. There we hear of the gospel of Jesus Christ and its implications for the moral life. The writer calls on those who are mature in the faith to shape their lives in accordance with that faith: Show love to your brothers and sisters, show hospitality to strangers, and honor your marriage vows. Though we recognize that such actions may not always be in keeping with our natural inclinations, we are given the promise that "the Lord is my helper" and the assurance that "Jesus Christ is the same yesterday, today, and forever."

II. These two texts represent two inescapable but contradictory realities of the Christian life—love and conflict. Covenantal love, central to both the Old and New Testaments, implies faithfulness, loyalty, and steadfastness in our various relationships. But an unavoidable feature of covenantal life is conflict—between one's own interests and those of others, including our fellow Christians; arising from our being simultaneously involved in various covenants; and over the just distribution of the benefits and burdens of social life. Because of these conflicts, we must constantly choose among alternate claims, conflicting interests, and contending groups. Simply talking about how we ought to relate to one another in love is not sufficient. We still face decisions about what that means in specific conflicts, knowing both the limits of our own moral wisdom and the temptation to be guided by our more self-regarding tendencies, as well as the danger of unintended consequences. Here are a few examples.

Love presses us as a church and as a society to try to improve the quality of human life. Much of our technological development has been, at least in part, a result of the desire to improve the quality of human existence, to provide greater freedom from want. But that same technology that has produced material resources beyond the dreams of earlier eras has also put us in greater peril from each other than ever before. Technical advances that were seen as harbingers of redemption from various limitations have also often proved to be occasions for a new and more threatening dimension of the perennial problems of human community. This is one of the contradictions of human life.

Love presses us as a church and as a society to support movements toward political freedom. Thus we have encouraged and applauded the historic changes that have taken place since 1989 in Central and Eastern Europe and the former Soviet Union. The gradual expansion of basic freedoms, the pressures for a market economy, and the widespread acknowledgment that Marxism in its actual practice is a failed and morally bankrupt system—all these are welcomed by those who want justice to roll down like waters. Yet from the same movements have come a pogram in Armenia, anti-Semitic incidents in Central Europe, terrible violence arising from ethnic rivalries in the former Yugoslavia, and protests in Bulgaria against religious freedom for Muslims—another of the contradictions of human life.

Love presses us as a church and as a society to show compassion for all people, both in personal relations and in social policy. This extension of the call to love our neighbor undergirds, for example, much of the medical research that seeks cures for ancient and new human ills. But compassion can at times be myopic and even cruel. It can cause us to fail to confront adulterers or racist joke-tellers for fear of causing guilt feelings or appearing judgmental. In the academic world, it can inflate grades, distorting people's self-knowledge and encouraging unrealistic aspirations. It can make the therapeutic ideal of individual self-fulfillment and the church's *summum bonum* replace the gospel itself. This is yet another of the contradictions of human life.

III. As members of both the human community and the Christian community, we live in the midst of a sea of contradictions. To ask the question Lenin asked at the time of the Russian Revolution, "What then is to be done?" The Christian answer to how to overcome the contradictions and conflicts of history is not as simple as Lenin's, which was basically to eliminate those designated as enemies, after which all problems would be solved. Christian faith knows that such all-too-easy solutions to the human predicament are destructive and demonic. In fact, the contradictions of human history cannot be overcome by human actions at all, but only by divine action.

No human action can be totally free of the mixed motivations, the self-interest, or the unanticipated consequences illustrated in the above examples. Even the most just peace is not to be confused with the peace of God that passes all understanding. Even the most just social arrangements are not to be confused with the Kingdom of God. Justice is in fact a concept that assumes conflicts and the continuing need for proper adjudication. We can never, in this life, dispense with the confession that we have left undone those things we ought to have done. There is always "a law in our members that wars with the law in our minds." These are permanent characteristics of human life, not simply the consequences of the malevolence of this person or that nation that we can fully overcome by appropriate human action.

It is only in the life, death, and Resurrection of Jesus Christ that we find an adequate answer to the contradictions of human life. It is there that we find the good news that a transcendent God redeems us, overcoming in his own heart and action that which cannot be overcome by us. It is there that we find the revelation of God as a God of both judgment and mercy, who overcomes the tragic consequences of our contradictions without negating the distinction between good and evil. It is there that it is revealed that, while we are yet sinners, we are justified by grace through faith, freeing us not from our continuing moral obligation of neighborly love but from dependence on its perfect fulfillment. These eternal truths of the gospel are part of our own birthright as Christians, and we dare not sell them.

Topic: "Where Faith and Politics Meet"
TEXT: Isa. 1:10–20; Luke 19:1–10

How do you relate your Christian faith to politics? How is your perspective on government and the political vocation shaped by your Christian convictions? These are questions with which the Christian community has struggled for two thousand years, and to which it has given a variety of answers, from political authority understood as "instituted by God" to the state understood as a "beast from the abyss"; from theocracy to the total withdrawal of Christians from political involvement.

Overall, however, the primary Christian perspective on politics has been and is one of guarded acceptance or even affirmation. While no particular political program, policy, or structure can simply be identified with Christian faith, lest it become an object of idolatry, only a prematurely truncated or privatized faith can look on such programs, policies, and structures as irrelevant for the Christian life. While the task of answering these initial questions may be shaped by one's time and place in history, our two lessons can give us some insights into at least two facets of the subject. One facet is the intersection of faith and politics in worship, the other is the intersection of faith and politics in the political vocation.

I. The Old Testament lesson tells us of a nation that tried to seal off its religion from its politics, to sever its worship from the quality of its public and social life. "Hear the word of the Lord, you rulers of Sodom! Give ear to the teachings of our God, you people of Gomorrah!" It is of course the rulers and people of Israel who were addressed in this Scripture and likened to the people of those sinful cities. Why? Evidently not because of any flagrant sexual licentiousness, overt godlessness, or rampant secularism. There was plenty of religious ceremony going on.

No, the controversy that God was having with his people was fundamentally political, in the fullest meaning of that word. The integral relationship of worship and social justice was a fundamental tenet of Israel's faith, an integral part of the covenant between God and his people. But the prophets saw that that integral connection was being severed and, good traditionalists that they were, tried to call God's people back to living out fully the implications of their covenant with God.

The immorality they saw stemmed in a real sense from Israel's failure to continue to mix religion and politics. "What to me is the multitude of your sacrifices. . . . Bring no more vain offerings. . . . When you spread forth your hands I will hide my eyes from you; even though you make many prayers, I will not listen."

And why does God reject their worship? Because worship that chooses to ignore its own this-worldly implications is not worship. It is "an abomination." Celebrations of God's goodness that do not lead to efforts to reflect that goodness in the structures of communal life are objects of God's contempt. So, "seek justice," Isaiah demands, which means, for those who may be obtuse, "correct oppression, defend the fatherless, plead for the widow."

To seek justice is, of course, the quintessential political task, along with the maintenance of order. And here God is saying, if you would truly worship me, then order your common life in ways that reveal my righteous will for justice (*mishpat*) and righteousness (*sedaqah*) in the social order. This is at least part of God's Word as we seek to answer our contemporary questions about relating faith and politics.

II. But if God is concerned with political structures and their effects on human beings, especially the powerless, he is equally concerned with those who make political structures function justly or unjustly, that is, the powerful. I refer of course to those for whom we pray at every service: "Those who bear the authority of government in this and every land, that they may be led to wise decisions and right actions for the welfare and peace of the world."

Zacchaeus was one of those governmental authorities, a chief tax collector. And he was rich, a fact evidently not unrelated to his use of his official capacity. Though he was also a collaborator, the crowd seemed more concerned about his dishonesty. At least that was the sin of which he repented, and that is significant.

Zacchaeus's desire to see Jesus resulted in a transforming personal encounter with Jesus. We are not told much about what really took place between them, or why Jesus declared that salvation had come. But we are told about the manifestation of that salvation. The chief tax collector became a born-again politician, acknowledged his unjust practices and his abuse of power, and undertook restitution well beyond the requirement of the law. But as far as we know, he did not give up his official position. He did not become one of the Twelve. He did not conclude (nor did Jesus) that tax collecting was an intrinsically evil vocation.

No, Zacchaeus's encounter with the one he called Lord transformed, among other things, his perception of his political vocation and his way of carrying it out. Instead of becoming a former tax collector, he became a just tax collector. He recognized that, at least to the eyes of faith, bringing justice to the social order is the raison d'être of every public position, tax collection included. This is also part of God's Word as we seek to answer our contemporary questions about relating faith and politics.

III. Classical Christianity has always refused to exclude the political arena from God's care and concern, and from the Christian's area of responsibility. The real question, at least for those who refuse to confine God to the religious ghetto, is and has always been not whether but how to relate faith to politics. There is no blueprint for it, and there are dangers in the effort for whoever undertakes it. There is the danger of self-righteousness, of equating group interest with God's will, of making the state more than a good state by using it to coerce the Christianizing of society, or of making the state less than a good state by making it subservient to special interests.

But at least one guideline is clear, according to Isaiah, Luke, and a great cloud of other biblical witnesses. That guideline is justice. Certainly we are called to love, to a higher obligation that transcends justice. But as Reinhold Niebuhr so often reminded us, love is no substitute for justice. Undue emphasis on the higher possibilities of love in personal relations may tempt Christians to let individual acts of charity become substitutes for seeking justice.

Many moral visions of politics vie for attention in the public square. How do we distinguish among them? Not just any old political position deserves to be called religious. We have heard from the prophet Isaiah and from the politician Zacchaeus. They are reinforced by a modern prophet-politician John Danforth, former senator from Missouri and an Episcopal priest: "What is found in Scripture, over and over again, is a boundless concern that justice be done to the needy—the poor, the fatherless, the widow. Like it or not, this message of social justice is at the heart of the biblical standard for political commentary. A political position that does not include serious concern for the plight of the needy may have many interesting aspects, but it simply does not meet the biblical norms, and it should not be labeled religious."

That is the guideline, the plumb line, the central core of the biblical message about politics. We who would respond faithfully to God in Christ and relate faith to political life can give thanks for that guiding lamp unto our feet as we tread across that busy but dimly lit intersection where faith and politics meet.

SECTION X

CHILDREN'S SERMONS

January 6: Worship as Celebration

TEXT: Ps. 150

Object: Paper streamer

Somebody pull this toward them. [*A string of paper breaks off.*] We're going to need some more help. [*Several more paper ribbons are pulled.*] What *is* this stuff? [*Colored paper? Ribbons? Streamers? and other reactions.*] What do we use it for? [*For parties, parades, New Year's Eve.*] That's right, we use this and sometimes paper hats and horns to celebrate. You have named some of the times and places that we celebrate. I wonder why we didn't mention church. The word *celebrate* originally meant "to go in great numbers." When we gather here in great numbers, are we celebrating? (You are shaking your head, Joel; you don't think so?) One of the meanings of *celebrate* is "to honor or praise publicly." Does that sound like what we do here? Who do we honor or praise? That's right, that's really what worship is about, praising and honoring God. Do you think we could do it with paper streamers? Yes! But celebrating could also mean being very quiet when you are thankful you weren't hurt in a family car accident. It could even mean crying for joy when you are safe in your home again. We need both kinds of celebrating, here and at home.

Before you go, would you like to throw this stuff up in the air? One, two, three!

Praise God! Thank you for coming this morning.—Gary D. Stratman

January 13: God Forgives Our Sins

TEXT: 2 Cor. 8:5

Object: Wire coat hanger

Song: "Jesus Loves Me"

Good morning, boys and girls. I'm glad you chose to come to church today and learn about Jesus. [*Hold up coat hanger.*] I think everyone knows what this is. [*Wait for response.*] Yes, you are correct. This is a coat hanger. Can someone tell me the purpose of a coat hanger? Of course, this object is to hang clothes on. We may find them in a closet where we store our shirts, dresses, coats, and other items of clothing.

[*Begin to unwind the wire.*] Now, let me show you something about a coat hanger. This is a piece of wire. As long as it was in the shape that a coat hanger was supposed to be in, you could use it for its intended purpose. In other words, you could hang clothes. Now it's a piece of wire that is irregular in shape. In this shape, it's not really good for much. [*Show the piece of wire.*]

You know, our life can become like this useless piece of wire, but God can make us into something useful. If we give our life to Jesus and ask him to forgive our sins, we can serve him in many ways. I could try to put the hanger back in its original shape, but that would be impossible. God can put our lives back together again. Isn't that wonderful news?

Listen as I read from 2 Corinthians 8:5: "They gave themselves to the Lord" (NIV). [*Lead the congregation in prayer, asking God to help each boy and girl find ways to serve him. Have the pianist play softly "Jesus Loves Me" as the children return to their seats.*]—Carolyn R. Tomlin

January 20: Jesus Prayed Alone
TEXT: Mark 1:35
Object: Yo-yo

Some sports are played in teams, other games are played alone. To play baseball, you must join a league team or gather a group of friends. To play with this yo-yo, all that is needed is one person with a desire to learn some special tricks.

Prayer is a unique spiritual exercise that can be done in a group or alone. When we pray during our church services, we bow our heads together while someone voices a prayer for the whole congregation. The Bible promises that when two or three believers are gathered for prayer, the Lord is with them in a special way. Praying with a group is very important, but praying alone is encouraged by the Bible, too.

Jesus prayed alone. Listen to this verse. Early in the morning, Jesus went to a place all by himself and prayed to God. The disciples noticed that Jesus was missing and impatiently said everybody was looking for him. Months later, Jesus prayed in the garden of Gethsemane late at night after his followers had gone to sleep. Praying alone was very important to Jesus. Whenever Jesus made a crucial decision, he prayed for God's guidance. Jesus emphasized the need for all of us to pray individually. He encouraged believers to go into private places and talk to God from their hearts (Matt. 6:6).

Think about it this way: We enjoy playing baseball when our best friend is on our team. We also enjoy getting to spend time alone with our best friend to watch videos or fish. If we only played team sports with our best friend and never spent quality time with him or her, we would begin to lose our special friendship. God welcomes our congregational prayers at church. He also seeks to hear from us individually when we are willing to commit some quiet time to him. It is good when we pray to our Heavenly Father like Jesus did, in a solitary place.

It is normal to wonder what to ask for while praying alone. We should ask God to be our Savior. That is the first prayer that anyone prays. Then we may ask God for help in making decisions. We can pray for help in school, for protection, and to help our friends who have special needs, like sicknesses. The more we spend time praying alone, the more we feel like praying. As we pray, we are speaking to God, but if we listen, we can also hear his voice. Be sure to take some time to pray alone.—Ken Cox

January 27: We Can Talk to God
TEXT: John 10:27
Object: Extension cord
Song: "Jesus Loves the Little Children"

Hello, boys and girls. I'm glad to see you today. Isn't it great to come to God's house to worship him?

Have you ever seen one of these in your home? [*Hold up an extension cord. Wait for response.*] That's right, it is called an extension cord. But do you know what it is used for?

[*You may get responses such as to plug in a lamp, a TV, a computer, and so on.*] Yes, all those are correct. This cord connects another cord to electricity. When one cord is not long enough to reach, we use another one. By plugging this end into a lamp, a TV, a computer, or another appliance, we get electricity.

As I was thinking this morning about the extension cord, I was also thinking about how we talk to God. When we want to ask him something, we simply pray. When we are afraid, we ask God to keep us safe. When we are lonely, we talk to God as a friend. Isn't it wonderful that we can talk to God ourselves without having to use another person? We don't need an extension cord to talk to God. He is always there. He is always ready to listen.

So the next time you see an extension cord at home, just remember that you can talk to God without having to ask someone to pray for you. You can do it yourself.

Listen as I read from John 10:27: "My sheep listen to my voice; I know them, and they follow me" (NIV). This verse tells us that Jesus hears us. We should listen to what he tells us to do. [*Ask the pianist to play one verse of "Jesus Loves the Little Children" as they return to their seats.*]—Carolyn R. Tomlin

February 3: Bring an Offering

TEXT: 1 Chron. 29:14
Object: Church offering envelope
Song: "Because I Have Been Given Much"

Hello, boys and girls. I'm glad to see you today. I'm going to give each of you something. [*Pass out a church offering envelope to each child.*] Can someone tell me what I gave you? [*Accept any response.*] Yes, this is an envelope. Does the mailman deliver envelopes to your home? What might come inside an envelope? Could a birthday card? What about a bill your parents have to pay? What about an invitation to a party? What about an announcement about a church program? Yes, many things can come to your house in an envelope, and you can send things to others.

But the envelope you are holding is different. Look at the front. Those letters show it is printed for our church. Can you tell me something else about the envelope? Yes, there is a place for your name on it, and there is a space showing the amount of money you are placing inside.

God says we should bring an offering. This offering, which we call *money*, helps support Christ's church. Our church gives a percentage to missions, we support the local church, and we give to our denomination for various programs. Without your financial support, our church could not exist. The next time you see an envelope, think about how you can earn extra money to help support the work of Christ.

Listen as I read from God's Word. "Everything comes from you and we have given you only what comes from your hand" (1 Chron. 29:14 NIV). [*Ask someone to sing one stanza of "Because I Have Been Given Much" as the children return to their seats.*]—Carolyn R. Tomlin

February 10: Nothing Can Separate Us

TEXT: Rom. 8:28
Objects: A metal cookie box and an assortment of refrigerator-door magnets

Good morning! Do you know what I have in my hands this morning? That's right; it is a box, and it is a special kind of box that you see in many places this time of year. It is sometimes called a cookie tin and people make a gift of cookies or candy by putting the goodies into this kind of decorated box. But even after Christmas is over and all the goodies have been eaten, you can still use this box in a special way.

What do we keep in boxes like this one? Treasures! That's right, Ben. I'll bet you would keep Civil War patches in yours. Some of you would have stickers or trading cards. Treasures! I'll remove the lid so you can see what is in my treasure box. What does that look like? Yes, it is a cinnamon roll. Well, its not real but it looks just like what we call sticky buns.

See this one? It is a small plaque that was given to me when I taught a course last summer on the Ten Commandments. It says, "The Ten Commandments are not multiple choice."

Do you know what this treasure is? You remember when we looked at it on another Sunday? It is a sand dollar. You do remember.

Now, let's put these things back in the box. What would happen now if we shook the box up? Would all the treasures smash into each other? Yes, they would! [*Shake the box and then open the box and show the children what happened.*] Why haven't they moved or crashed into each other? Yes, there are magnets you couldn't see on the side of these treasures. We can't always see God's love that holds us secure—like a magnet. That love is stronger than anything else in the whole universe. All the treasures were kept safe. They didn't go flying away from the box or crashing into each other. Keep that picture in your mind, and this thought from God's Word: "Nothing will be able to separate us from the love of God in Christ Jesus our Lord." Amen.—Gary D. Stratman

February 17: Your Own Knob

TEXT: 1 Pet. 3:8–15a

Object: A radio

Good morning, boys and girls. How are you today? Do you have control of yourself? Do you know what I mean when I ask you if you have control? [*Let them answer.*] Jesus and his followers thought that control was very important in being a Christian. There is one part of our body they thought needed more control than almost any other. Do you know what part I am talking about? [*Let them guess.*] We use this part almost more than any other part of our body. Now do you know what I mean? That's right, the tongue. We really need to control it or it gets away from us. Let me show you what I mean.

[*Have the radio plugged in, pre-set at its loudest volume.*] I have a radio with me and I am going to plug it in so we can listen to it. How do you like that for a radio? It's a little hard to hear what you are saying when I have my radio on so loud. That is the reason I don't have it plugged in all the time. It would be nice if I could talk to you and also play my radio, but the radio seems a little loud for me to hear you. I know you feel the same way, but it is all I can do to talk over the radio, let alone listen to you. Do you have any suggestions? [*Wait for someone to turn it down or suggest that you turn it down.*] Did you say turn it down? That's a good idea, but how do I do it? Maybe one of these knobs will work. I suppose you call this a control knob. [*Turn the radio down.*] Now that's what I call control!

Wouldn't it be wonderful if I could have the same kind of control over my tongue? We should be able to if we want to have a happy life. Jesus taught all of his disciples the value of having good control over their tongues, and he argued the same thing for us.

We don't have knobs but we do have minds that tell us when we are talking too much or when we are saying something bad or telling lies. Our minds are all the control we need if we believe in Jesus. So the next time you see a radio and turn it up or down, think about the kind of control you must have over your tongue and be glad that you do, so you can have a happy life.—Wesley T. Runk[1]

February 24: Don't Hide the Truth
TEXT: Ps. 32:3–5
Object: A coffee can

This is a coffee can. Some people who don't trust banks will put their money in a coffee can and bury it in the backyard. They feel that all their money will be safe if it is hidden.

We may try to hide our wrong actions. If we have stolen something, we may act like it never happened. We may conceal the stolen item or destroy the evidence by throwing it in a trash can. Our attempts to conceal the truth don't work because God knows everything. We may be the only human who knows what we have done, but that is one too many. Whenever we remember what we have done, it bothers or worries us. The result is that God isn't happy with us and we are mad at ourselves.

If we never open up and tell the truth about what we have done, we will know that there is a barrier between us and God. Furthermore, the more our thoughts remind us of our deeds, the more unhappy we get. Listen to these verses (vv. 3–4).

The good news is that God will forgive us for our wrongs. To receive God's forgiveness, we tell him in a prayer how bad we feel. This is called a *prayer of confession.* Because of Jesus' death on the cross, all of our sins have been paid for and God will instantly forgive us. We must make restitution for our sins by paying back the person we have wronged. This may seem impossible, but God will make a way for us to set matters right in heaven and on Earth.

The devil doesn't want us to confess our sins to God. Satan knows that as long as we have foul deeds hidden in our hearts, we won't feel close to God. The father of lies also wants us to feel bad about ourselves. So, it is best to confess the truth to God and everybody else. Listen to this verse that describes instant spiritual relief (v. 5).

Don't hide your feelings or actions from God. Confess your faults to God and his love will fill your life. You will also feel better about yourself.—Ken Cox

March 3: Turned On to God
TEXT: Luke 16:1–9
Object: An electric switch in the "on" position

Good morning, everyone. Today we have a very good lesson for boys and girls, and for fathers and mothers. This is such a good lesson because it will help us all week around our house. How many of you know what I have in my hand? [*Show them the switch and let them answer.*] That's right, and where have you seen an electric switch like this? [*Let them answer.*] That's right, in all the rooms in your house. It helps you to do what? [*Let them answer.*] Right

---

[1]*Pass It On*

again. It's this little switch that can turn on some of the most powerful energy we know. One little flip of the switch and it turns on lights all over the house.

Now, I know what the switch can do, but I also know what the switch cannot do. How many of you know what the switch cannot do? [*Let them answer.*] Those are some pretty good ideas, but the one I'm looking for is this one: A switch cannot turn itself off. That's right. When this switch is left in the "on" position, the light burns and burns and burns. It will burn in the day when the sun is out and it will burn during the night when everything outside is dark. The switch cannot turn itself off, so the light burns out much sooner than it should. Why does the light burn out sooner? Because it was wasted. Do you know what I mean? Does anyone ever ask you to turn out the light and you forget? Sure you do, as we all do, and when that happens we waste good bulbs.

There is a story in the Bible that Jesus told about men who do a lot of wasting. If you waste someone else's belongings, they get very unhappy with you. It can even mean that you will lose their friendship if you waste what belongs to them too often. A waster is a very careless person and sometimes that carelessness gets us into a lot of trouble.

There are a lot of people who waste the good things that God gives to them, and they make God angry. They waste the talent he gives them and they waste the land and the happiness of others. God is very disappointed in a waster, and he tells us so. If we are going to waste the good things in this world, then we had better make friends with other wasters, because we are going to have a bad time with the best friend we ever had, our God. God gives us all of the things we need, and then some extras so we will never have to worry; but when we waste them, then we have to look around and take some of the things that belong to other people. When we take the things God gave to other people, then we are in trouble, not only with God but also with the others.

We should be careful with God's gifts and share them, but we should never waste them. Remember how easy it is to burn a light during the day when we don't need it but are too lazy to turn it off? That energy could have helped cook a meal or done something good for somebody who needed it. The same is true with God. Sometimes we waste his love and keep someone else from knowing him the way they would like to. Don't be a waster, but be a sharer, and God and his people will thank you for it.—Wesley T. Runk[2]

March 10: Growing in His love
TEXT: Luke 2:52
Object: Birthday card
Song: "Savior, Teach Me Day by Day"

My, it's good to see all these boys and girls in church. Today we are going to talk about something that is important to all of you. Let me give you some clues: This is a day that comes once a year. Someone usually gives you presents. Perhaps your mother bakes a cake. You may even have a party! Now, who knows what day I'm talking about? Yes, of course: a birthday.

Birthdays are special. That is the day we celebrate the day of your birth. Each year you are one year older. As you grow bigger and taller, your clothes become too little. My mother

[2]*God's Little Beggars*

said that when I was four years old, I thought I couldn't wear any of my clothes I had worn the day before. I was really surprised to find out that the clothes still fit!

As you celebrate your birthday this year, ask yourself, How can I grow to be more like Jesus? How can I know Jesus as my best friend? Can I talk to him about any problems or share any secrets? Just like we become another year older each birthday, we should also grow more Christlike. Wouldn't it be terrible if we never grew from being a baby? Wouldn't it also be terrible if we never grew to be more like Jesus?

When Jesus was a boy, he went to the Temple and heard the teachers speak. Those who heard him were amazed at his understanding and his answers. Luke 2:52 says, "And Jesus grew in wisdom and stature, and in favor with God and men" (NIV). [*Lead the children in one stanza of "Savior, Teach Me Day by Day." Ask the children to quietly return to their seats.*]—Carolyn R. Tomlin

March 17: God Promises to Answer

TEXT: Jer. 33:3
Object: Letters, printed e-mail

These letters are answers to my correspondence. I mailed suggestions or questions to various people and they wrote back to me. This is a printout of some e-mail. I e-mailed some information to a friend, and he sent a thank-you note over the Internet. Whenever someone writes us a letter, we should always send them an answer. Answers to letters and e-mails let folks know that their messages were received and appreciated.

Each of us can write our U.S. Representatives or Senators and expect an answer. Even though these public servants are important and very busy, they will answer the letters from the people who elected them.

Someone more important than a Senator will answer our requests. It's God. Listen to this verse. God has promised that when we call on him, that is, pray to him, he will answer our prayers. The Lord states that he will show us new and great things.

I encourage you to pray to God about your needs. We should not pray only at mealtimes and bedtimes. We should pray whenever we see a need. Instead of being troubled by the problems we see, we should ask God for help. His word guarantees that he hears us and will respond to us.

The Lord doesn't have to answer our prayers with what we ask for. He may respond with something better or different. When we pray, we must trust God to provide the answer that he determines to be best for everyone. We pray with only our own needs in mind; God answers prayers with the interests of the whole world in mind. There is a big difference in the way we see things and the way God sees them. So, don't think that God will not keep his promise if answers to prayers are delayed. God always answers at the right moment and in the perfect way.—Ken Cox

March 24: Living for God's Love

TEXT: 1 John 4:7–16
Objects: Two small Tupperware cups with lids, one with water

Good morning! This morning our Bible reading tells us about love. I wonder what you think of when you hear these words. So I want to begin this morning by asking you, "What is love?"

[*Answers may include kindness and joy, caring, sharing your favorite things.*] Those are very good answers. I have been thinking about when we begin to love others and love God. Our Scripture lesson tells us we love because Christ first loved us. In my bag today I have two objects that look very much alike. What is the difference between them? You are right. This one in my right hand has water in it. Now, as I take off the lids, you can see that the water flows into the once-empty cup. In the same way, when God loves us, we are reminded that we are his children. When we believe that Jesus died for us, we are reminded of how much God loves us. We are filled up, just like this cup. We love because God first loved us. Now we can share God's love with others and help fill them up. [*This is said while pouring the water back and forth between the cups.*] But this doesn't tell us all about God's love, because unlike this cup, when God pours love into us, God does not become empty. God's love is like a fountain. We could all fill up our cups and there would still be plenty of water flowing to us as we fill up again. "We love because he first loved us." You are able to be joyously kind to others today because you are loved with an everlasting love. Praise God!—Gary D. Stratman

March 31: A Sign of the Cross
TEXT: Heb. 12:2
Object: Three toothpicks
Song: "Am I a Solder of the Cross?"

Good morning, boys and girls. I'm glad to see you today. I'm holding three objects in my hand. [*Display three toothpicks.*] These are products from nature. Before they were toothpicks, they were something else. Can you tell me? [*Response.*] Yes, they were trees. Toothpicks were once mighty trees.

Watch as I make some shapes. Raise your hand when you recognize one. [*Using the tooth-picks, make an A, a Z, an I, an F, an H, an X, and a T. Hold up the shapes for the children to recognize. Next, make the sign of a cross with two toothpicks.*] And this is a symbol of the cross. The Scripture tells us that Jesus was crucified on a cross by Pilate, the Roman governor. He was buried and rose again on the third day. The cross is a symbol of Jesus. Can you tell me where you have seen a cross? [*Response.*] On top of a church steeple, on a church alter, and on jewelry are a few places.

Yes, a cross reminds others that this building is a place of worship. A cross we wear shows others that we love Jesus. A cross we wear also reminds us to follow God's rules and to be Christlike in our actions.

Listen as I read from Hebrews 12:2: "Let us fix our eyes on Jesus, the author and perfecter of our faith, who for the joy set before him endured the cross, scorning its shame, and sat down at the right hand of the throne of God" (NIV). Remember, following the cross will lead us to God. [*Lead the children in singing one stanza of "Am I a Solder of the Cross?" Ask them to quietly return to their seats.*]—Carolyn R. Tomlin

April 7: The Worry Sack
TEXT: 1 Pet. 5:6–11
Object: Paper sacks (different sizes); if possible, one for each child

Good morning, boys and girls. I am going to share something with you this morning that will be a help to you all of your life if you use it. I know that it works because I have tried it and

I think it is just great. First, I want to show you what I have and then I will tell you how to use it.

[*Hold up the paper sack.*] This is a paper sack, the same kind you get whenever you go to the grocery. This sack is a lot more important than it looks. I call it my worry sack. This is how I use it. Every night before I go to bed I think about the things that have worried me during the day and about the things that are going to worry me before I fall asleep. I write out my worries and put them in the worry sack. Do you know what I do then? I give my worry sack to God. God gets all of my worries. I sleep so much better without worries that I do this every night. Sometimes I give God the same worry and sometimes he gets a brand new worry.

I saved all of the worries that I had last night so I could show you this morning what a worry sack is like. [*Pull out some slips of paper with worries written on them.*] Here are some things that a lot of people worry about: How shall I pay that bill from the dentist when he wants to be paid? I wonder if my friend John will forgive me for what I said about him to Bill? Have you ever said something about somebody and worried that he might find out and think bad things about you? I have a lot of other worries written down, like the repairs that need to be made on the car and the things I should say at my appointment tomorrow. They are all in the sack. God is going to work on them so I don't have to worry.

I can think of only one thing at a time and when I am worrying I cannot help anyone or do anything that is good for people. I must let God take over my worries and I must do the things God wants me to do. One of the things God does not want me to do is worry, so I put them into a sack and let God take care of them.

This is a wonderful system, and it works. Besides that, I am doing just what the Bible teaches me to do; it tells me to turn all of my worries over to God and he will take care of them. I have a worry sack for each of you. I hope you will take it home and use it. Let God take care of your worries and you take care of the things he has asked you to do.—Wesley T. Runk[3]

April 14: Let Our Light Shine

TEXT: Luke 11:36
Object: Candle and matches
Song: "This Little Light of Mine"

Hello, boys and girls. I'm glad you chose to come to church today. I'm holding in my hand something you may have at home. Can you tell me what it is? [*Allow for response.*] Yes, it is a candle. Now, can someone tell me why we use candles? I hear you saying a candle is used for light in the darkness, a scented candle smells good, and candles are placed on a birthday cake. Do you add one more candle each year?

Now, watch as I strike a match and light the candle. Before, it was pretty, but it didn't do what a candle is supposed to do. Now, with the flame, it burns brightly. Which do you think is best? A candle burning, or one without a flame? Of course, boys and girls should never strike matches. That's a job for adults.

---

[3]*Pass It On*

You know, our lives are like candles. If we don't show others that we love Jesus, we aren't doing what Jesus wants us to do. But if we love Jesus, pray, come to church, obey our parents, and keep God's laws, our lives can burn as brightly as this candle.

Will you do something for me? The next time you see a candle, will you think of ways your life can burn brightly for God? Then will you tell me about how you love Jesus? I would like to hear what you are doing to love him.

Jesus spoke of light in Luke 11:36. "Therefore, if your whole body is full of light, and no part of it is dark, it will be completely lighted, as when the light of a lamp shines on you" (NIV). [*Lead the children in doing the hand motions and singing the familiar song "This Little Light of Mine." Invite the congregation to sing along.*]—Carolyn R. Tomlin

April 21: We Are All Special to God
TEXT: Ps. 100:3
Object: An old teddy bear

This teddy bear has been used a lot. It is almost forty years old. A lot of its fur is gone, and in spots the fabric is visible. If you received a teddy bear in this condition for Christmas, you would feel cheated. A teddy bear like this probably wouldn't bring one dollar in a garage sale. However, this teddy bear is very valuable to the person who owns it. It was slept with, hugged, and carried for years by a child who is now an adult. The reason it has been kept is because of its value. To the owner it is priceless.

If we don't treasure someone or something, we may feel that that person or object is worthless to everyone else. God values us like the owner of this cuddly toy treasures his teddy bear. Because we belong to God we have great value. Listen to this verse. God made us as we are for a reason. That makes us valuable to him and to everyone else. God considers us his sheep. Because we are a part of his flock, we can be sure that he is watching over and protecting us as his special possessions.

It is easy for us to see other human beings and think they don't have much value. This is especially true when we look at the large population of a foreign country. Big crowds cause us to discount the worth of the individual. Yet all people are important to God because they belong to him. There are some countries with millions of people that have never heard the good news of Jesus Christ. Because of their value to God, we are commissioned to take the truth about God's love to them.

If you ever feel unloved or unimportant, remember that God places a very high value on you because you belong to him. God loves us, and we should love ourselves and others because of his love.—Ken Cox

April 28: Thoughts Come Before Actions
TEXT: Matt. 5:21–22a
Object: An egg or picture of an emu

This is a picture of an emu. Emus are huge birds that can't fly, but they can run very fast. Emus weigh about ninety pounds, stand about five feet tall, and can sprint at speeds of up to thirty miles per hour. Regardless of their size, all emus start out as little eggs, just like chickens. Emu eggs are green and look like big avocados. Even though the eggs are large, it is hard to grasp that such a big bird could begin so small.

Each of our actions has a starting place, too. Our actions begin in our thoughts. Jesus taught that evil thoughts are as bad as evil deeds. This surprised some of the people who listened to Jesus. They thought, as we might, that thinking about stealing or killing was not as bad as actually doing it. Jesus corrected them. Listen to this verse.

Crimes begin in our thoughts. When we witness news reports about crime sprees, it is hard to imagine that such suffering and hardship began as improper thoughts. Our thoughts are like seeds that grow into towering redwood trees. Thoughts are the starting points of all bad and good actions. Accordingly, the Bible teaches us to guard our hearts, the beginning place of our thoughts (Prov. 4:23).

To please the Lord, our thoughts must be wholesome and good. It is wrong to allow our minds to be filled with how much we don't like someone. One reason our thoughts ought to be pure is that God knows our thoughts. Bad thoughts are as unpleasant to God as the smell of a skunk is to us. Also, our minds must be pure because our thoughts will become actions. If we continually think about stealing, sooner or later we will. Our thoughts are the beginning of all our deeds.

The positive side of this truth is a wonderful thing. As we let good thoughts fill our minds, we begin to have better lives. We also have peace and joy in our hearts (Phil. 3:8–9). We should think of how good God has been to us. We should dwell on how fortunate we are to live in our homes, eat our food, and enjoy our friends. When our minds are filled with good thoughts, good actions are always the result.

Let's remember that our thoughts are the beginning of our deeds. Thoughts start small, like eggs, but grow big, like this emu. Bad thoughts end up in evil deeds and unhappiness. Good thoughts result in good deeds and contentment.—Ken Cox

May 5: God Bless Our Homes
TEXT: Ps. 128:1 NIV
Object: Magazine picture of a family
Song: "God Give Us Christian Homes"

Hello, boys and girls. I'm glad to see you today. I'm holding a picture. Do you know these people? [*Pause for response.*] Probably not. This picture came from a magazine. Let's say that the people in it represent all families. They may be a family or they may be models that the magazine is using, but I want you to think about your family today.

Did you know that God had a plan when he created families? He planned for mothers, fathers, grandparents, single parents, foster parents, and caregivers to help take care of you.

God wants what is best for each boy and girl listening today. That is why he created homes, so you will have someone to love you. You will have medical care when you are sick. You will get an education so you can learn about the world he created. Food will be provided so your body can grow strong. Just by your being here today, I see that your family realizes the importance of honoring God. Don't you think God's plan for creating families and homes was wonderful?

As part of your family, you have a responsibility. You must obey your parents or the person caring for you. As a member of your family, certain work or chores belong only to you. Remember, being a family is part of God's plan.

Listen as I read from Proverbs 22:6: "Train up a child in the way he should go, and when he is old he will not turn from it." Let us ask God to bless our families. [*Lead the children in one stanza of "God, Give Us Christian Homes." Ask the pianist to continue to play as the children return to their seats.*]—Carolyn R. Tomlin

May 12: God Holds Our Lives Together

TEXT: 2 Cor. 16:13
Object: Clothespin
Song: "A Mighty Fortress Is Our God"

Good morning, boys and girls. I'm happy you chose to come to church today. I'm holding an object that some of you may not recognize. [*Allow time for response.*] This is something your grandmothers used every time they washed clothes. It is called a clothespin. Today, with modern dryers, we may dry our clothes inside instead of hanging them on an outside wire to dry. But you know something, I miss the smell of clothes dried by the sun. A clothespin is used to hold clothes on the line. It can also be used to hang pants or a skirt on a wire clothes hanger. I've seen people keep a bread sack or a potato bag closed with this object. Would you say a clothespin is very strong?

As we learn more about Jesus, we realize that he holds our lives together. When we listen to him and ask him to guide our lives, he helps us keep everything in balance. God is very strong.

Our Scripture verse today is 2 Corinthians 16:13: "Be on your guard; stand firm in the faith; be men of courage; be strong. Do everything in love" (NIV). This is what God wants us to do: to understand right from wrong, to be faithful to his teachings, to be courageous in difficult times, to be strong in our beliefs, and to do these things in a spirit of love.

Our hymn this morning speaks of God's strength and how he wants us to remain faithful. [*Ask the pianist to play two stanzas of "A Mighty Fortress Is Our God" as the children return to their seats.*]—Carolyn R. Tomlin

May 19: Nehemiah Prayed First

TEXT: Neh. 1:11
Object: A picture of a house

Before this house could be built, a foundation had to be laid. The foundation is an area of concrete underneath the house. The foundation provides stability and keeps the lumber from collapsing into a disorganized pile. A house will be only as strong as its foundation.

Foundations are not just for houses. The foundation for every decision is prayer. The Bible describes the heroic actions of a man named Nehemiah. Nehemiah accomplished much in his lifetime because he prayed before he took action. He built his life on the foundation of prayer.

Nehemiah lived in a country far from his home, which was Jerusalem. Israel had been conquered in a war and all the people, including Nehemiah, had been made to move to a place called Babylon. While there, Nehemiah served in the palace of King Artaxerxes. Even though Nehemiah had a good job, he was homesick for Jerusalem. He wanted to return to Jerusalem and take some of his countrymen with him. This was a very unusual desire, because if Nehemiah and the people left, the king would lose their help.

Nehemiah kept thinking about going home to Jerusalem. When the Lord is directing us, he puts a persistent dream or idea in our minds. However, before Nehemiah took any action based on his idea, he prayed. Listen to this verse.

After Nehemiah prayed, he asked the King for permission to return to Jerusalem. The king granted Nehemiah's request. So the adventure of Nehemiah's life began with the foundation of prayer.

We can learn from Nehemiah's example. We will make many decisions in our lives. One day each of you will decide what kind of career to have. Some will choose to be doctors, some teachers, some mechanics, some computer programmers, and some police officers. Before we make an important life decision like that, we need to pray first. When we do pray first, the rest of our life can be put together properly with God's help.

If we don't pray first, we can begin efforts that are not right for us. We may think we know what to do, but we need God's wisdom to guide us. In some life decisions, if we take a few steps, there is no turning back without great difficulty. So, it is good to put first things first and pray for God's permission and guidance. When we pray first, like Nehemiah, we are building our lives on the strong foundation of prayer.—Ken Cox

May 26: Good Habits
TEXT: Luke 4:16–19
Object: A small rubber ball imprinted with a map of the world (sold in toy stores and quite inexpensive)

Who can tell me what a habit is? That's right, it is something you do over and over again until it becomes a part of you. Can you give me some examples of habits? Did you notice that a lot of the habits we thought of this morning were bad habits? They are the kinds of things people want to quit doing. Now, can you think of some good habits? One good habit I know you have is regularly being a part of worship and our "Time for Children." In our Bible story this morning, we learn that Jesus was in the habit of going to a place of worship on the Sabbath. This habit helps us remember who we are and whose we are.

What do I have in my hand? That's right, it is a ball. [*Open your hand.*] What kind of ball? That's right, it looks like our world. In my hand it got all squeezed out of shape, didn't it? Now look at it. It reminds me of the way our lives and the lives of others in the world get pressed and squeezed out of shape by things that happen to us during the week. We need regular times of worship to hear God's Word to us, to pray together, and to let our lives be reshaped by God's love. "God's got the whole world in his hands." [*Lift the reshaped ball in the palm of your hand.*] Thank you for coming; it's a good habit.—Gary D. Stratman

June 2: Stepping Stones
TEXT: Mark 9:38–42
Object: Several flat rocks or smooth stones from a riverbed

What am I pulling out of my bag this morning? You all knew the answer at the same time. They are rocks, sometimes called stones. Now, what are some ways these stones might be used in harmful, hurtful, or frustrating ways? That's right. They could fall on you, or cause you to stumble or fall. Yes, I did not think of that. They could be piled up against a door so you could not get out. That would be frustrating.

Now, can you think of some ways these same rocks could be used for good, to help others? Yes, you could decorate them or give them as gifts. You are much more creative than I am. All your examples are good. It makes it plain to me that these same objects can be either stepping stones or stumbling blocks. These stones can be thrown across a shallow stream or a muddy lawn without getting all yucky. By the same token, they could be scattered across a darkened room and cause us to stumble. Jesus taught that our actions and words are like these flat stones. They can be used to build up God's children or they can be used to trip up God's children.

If someone gives us a cup of cold water when we are thirsty, that person is doing the work of Jesus. They are a stepping stone that leads to Jesus. When we call people names or laugh at them because they are different, we may cause them to stumble on their way to Jesus. You know how you feel when those things are done to you. Think this week about ways you can be a stepping stone for other children of God. Thanks for coming.—Gary D. Stratman

June 9: An Amazing Secret Potion

TEXT: Matt. 7:15–21
Object: A glass of white vinegar

Good morning, boys and girls. This morning I need some volunteers who know how to keep a secret. Anyone who can keep a secret please hold up your hand and I will choose you to help me with the lesson this morning. [*Select some volunteers.*] Now, I must warn you that no matter what happens, you may not give away our secret until I tell you it is all right for everyone to know. Do you understand the conditions? [*Ask each child for his solemn vow.*] That is very good. I now have each person's sacred pledge not to give away the secret.

I have a most secret potion that I brought with me in my very special glass. Some people would try through some very devious means to find out what this is, but I have kept the whole world guessing until now what is in my special glass. I am going to let each of my secret keepers taste this mystery drink in a moment, but first I must have absolute silence and your promise that you will not tell a soul what you taste or what you think you taste. Now, this is a powerful drink, so I am only going to allow you to wet your lips. When your lips are wet, then you can run your tongue over your lips and savor the most amazing taste of my secret drink. Do you understand? Are there any questions? [*Let them ask anything they want to.*] Is there anyone who does not want to try my secret drink? Remember, it must remain a secret until I tell you that you can share it with others. Good. [*Let each child wet his lips with the vinegar.*]

How did you like that wonderful secret drink? Would anyone like to take a large swallow? You wouldn't! Why not? [*Let them answer.*] Would you like to share our secret with the others? What do you think I have for my secret drink? Was it water? Was it a soft drink? Who knows what I gave you to taste? [*See if they can guess.*] It was vinegar, white vinegar. Wasn't that awful? I am so sorry that I tricked you, but I did it for a good reason. Let me tell you why.

The Bible teaches us that we must beware of people who come to us making big promises only to get us away from the teachings of Jesus. Some people make the things Jesus teaches us not to do look like so much fun that they are hard to turn down. The bad things sound so exciting. Some people think these things will make them rich or powerful. The devil is always trying to trick us, just like I tricked you today with the idea that I had something special I wanted you to try. A secret drink and a bad word may be a lot alike if they get you to forget Jesus and follow somebody else. You must be careful and remember never to take a chance with someone who wants you to give up Jesus or the things he teaches. Remember what Jesus says: "Some wolves dress up like sheep so they can fool us." Beware of sheep who look like that.—Wesley T. Runk[4]

June 16: Lot Made a Bad Move
TEXT: Gen. 13:12–13
Object: A collapsed packing box

This flat piece of cardboard is a moving box. When it is necessary to move to another city, a bunch of these boxes are needed to pack dishes, toys, and books. Watch as I put the box together. When these boxes are filled up they are put into a big truck and delivered to a new hometown.

The Bible describes a move by a man named Lot. Lot lived near his uncle Abraham for a long time. In those days, there were no moving vans or cardboard boxes. Lot moved his possessions by packing up his tents and herding his livestock. Lot's relocation was necessary because the pastures were too crowded for the sheep and goats that Abraham and Lot owned.

Lot enjoyed a good life when he lived close to Abraham. Abraham worshipped God and told others about the Lord. He served God through his honesty and righteous life. Abraham refused to associate with evil people (14:22–23). Lot followed the good example of his uncle and was blessed by God.

After Lot moved, the rest of his life was sad. Lot moved to a city called Sodom. The people of Sodom were evil. Listen to these verses. Just as Abraham's upright life helped Lot, the corrupt people of Lot's new home hurt him. Lot began to act like the people he lived near. After Lot moved to Sodom, his life became a sad disaster.

We become like the people around us every day. If we make friends with boys and girls who curse and steal, we will soon begin to talk and shoplift just like them. There is an old saying, "Birds of a feather, flock together." Have you noticed that? Birds of the same kind fly around together. It is the same for humans. If we hang around with the wrong crowd, we become bad, too.

Here's what to do. If you are with some kids and they begin to do wrong things, leave quickly, run if you have to, and go home. Tell your parents your feelings; they will understand and help you. The voice of our conscience warns us when we see others breaking the rules. This voice inside us will lead us to do right, not wrong, things. We must be decisive and move away from troublemakers. Always choose to be around friends who do the right thing and are obedient to God.

As long as Lot stayed close to Abraham, he was happy and blessed. When Lot was around

---

[4]*God's Little Beggars*

evil people, his life was sad. Our lives will be the same way. Let's be sure to move our tents close to people who are pleasing to God.—Ken Cox

June 23: The Ugly and the Beautiful

TEXT: 2 Tim. 3:16
Object: Two pictures: a garbage dump and a beautiful scene
Song: "Jesus Loves Me"

Good morning, boys and girls. I want you to look closely at these two pictures. What can you tell me about these scenes? Are they alike? How are they different? [*Wait for response.*] This one is a picture of a garbage dump filled with rubbish, piles of discards, and throwaways. Would you enjoy looking at this scene? Does it make you feel happy? Now focus your attention on the other scene. I see a beautiful picture that is pleasant to view. When I look at this scene I feel good. It brings pleasant thoughts to my mind.

Which picture represents the way Christ wants us to live our lives? [*Wait for response.*] Now, which picture represents the way the devil wants us to live? [*Wait for response.*] Yes, Christ wants his children to live happy lives that represents what is good and right in the world. If you let Christ into your lives, he will help you to have a beautiful spirit. And when others look at your life, they will know you are following Jesus' commands.

The next time you see a beautiful picture, say to yourself, "Jesus wants my life to be beautiful, too. I will try to have a life that shows others that I love Jesus." Will you remember to do this?

The Bible is our guide for living the kind of life Jesus wants us to live. The Bible is useful for teaching us how to live (2 Tim. 3:16). [*Lead the children in one verse of "Jesus Loves Me." Ask the pianist to softly play another stanza as the children return to their seats.*]—Carolyn R. Tomlin

June 30: Nehemiah Didn't Give Up

TEXT: Neh. 4:8–9
Object: Picture of a walled city

Nehemiah became a hero because he didn't give up. He returned home to Jerusalem after being held captive in Babylon. Nehemiah's dream was to rebuild the wall of the city of Jerusalem. In those days, important cities had walls around them, like the wall in this picture. The wall provided protection against enemy invaders. The wall around Jerusalem had been torn down in a war seventy years before Nehemiah arrived in Jerusalem.

Nehemiah began rebuilding the city wall and ran into opposition. Some men who lived nearby didn't want Jerusalem to become a strong, important city again, so they got together and made plans to discourage the workers. Rebuilding a city wall is very hard work. The heavy, large stones had to be moved up the hillside on which Jerusalem was built. Rebuilding becomes nearly impossible if a hostile group is threatening or robbing the workers. The villains who lived nearby were very powerful and effective in scaring and hindering the workers.

Even though rebuilding the wall was difficult, Nehemiah didn't quit. He persevered and finished building the wall. Listen to these verses.

Nehemiah was able to finish building the wall because he was determined to finish God's plan. He knew he was involved in God's plan because the Lord had made it possible for him to return to Jerusalem. Also, the Lord had provided help from the king. Nehemiah prayed for additional strength and took action. He posted guards to watch for those who were working against him. He worked hard with God's help in spite of the difficulties and finally finished.

Nothing in life that is worthwhile is easy. Even if we pray for God's initial direction, it is not guaranteed that our pathway will be easy. Just because the going gets tough doesn't mean that God has left us. When we pray for God's help, we will discover that he is right there with us. God wants us to depend on him and complete our tasks with his extraordinary assistance. If we quit when the going gets tough, we will never accomplish significant goals. We should follow Nehemiah's example of praying for help and never giving up.—Ken Cox

July 7: God Bless America

TEXT: Ps. 33:12 NIV
Object: Miniature American flags, Bible
Song: "America the Beautiful"

Boys and girls, I'm glad to see you today. I want to show you something that reminds me of our country: an American flag. [*Pass out miniature flags or use one larger flag.*] This flag represents the people of the United States. It reminds us of the brave men and women who gave their life for our country during times of war. When we see this flag, we should show respect and honor. Where do you see the American flag displayed? Do you have a flag like this at home? [*Pause for response.*]

[*Hold up the Bible.*] You know what this is? It is God's Word—the Bible. This book tells us how we should live. It tells of the people who lived during Bible days. The Bible is filled with stories of the brave men and women who believed in Jesus. During the New Testament period, many Christians were persecuted for believing in Jesus.

When you see an American flag and the Bible, remember to show respect. Both represent sacrifices made by many people.

Let us bow our heads and ask God to bless America and to bless Christians all over the world. Pray that Christianity may spread to all nations and that people may come to know Jesus. "Blessed is the nation whose God is the Lord" (Ps. 33:12 NIV). [*Lead the children in one stanza of "America the Beautiful." Ask the pianist to continue to play as the children return to their seats.*]—Carolyn R. Tomlin

July 14: Good and Bad Choices

TEXT: Job 37:14
Object: Empty cartons of junk food, cartons of healthy food
Song: "God Will Take Care of You"

Good morning, boys and girls. Today I have several containers that I want you to see. You are probably familiar with most of these. [*Hold up several and ask the children to identify each.*] These containers represent both good and bad choices in food. Some of them are healthy and nutritious. They keep our body and mind strong. The others may taste good, but they are filled with empty calories and lack the nutrition our bodies need.

What would happen to our bodies if we ate candy and drank soft drinks instead of eating vegetables, fruit, meat, grains, and milk products? [*Pause for response.*] That is right, we would not feel our best.

Just like we make good choices to feed our bodies, we must also make good choices in our actions and behavior. If we obey our parents, follow God's laws, read the Bible, pray, and carefully choose our friends, we will live the kind of life God wants us to enjoy.

In Job 37:14, we read, "Look at the wonderful things God has made" (NIV). Yes, God has made all these wonderful foods to keep us healthy. He wants us to make good choices in what we eat and in how we live our lives. Will you promise me that you will obey God's commands? [*Ask a soloist to sing one verse of "God Will Take Care of You." Have the pianist continue to play as the children return to their seats.*]—Carolyn R. Tomlin

July 21: The Psalms Are Hymns of Praise
TEXT: Ps. 9:1–2
Object: An old hymnal

In this old hymnal are songs we still sing and some that have been replaced by newer songs. About every fifteen years a new and revised version of this hymnal is published. This is not the oldest hymnal, however. An older collection of hymns is the book of Psalms in the Bible. The Psalms are located in the middle of the Bible. There are 150 of them. That makes the Psalter the longest book in the Bible. There are no musical notes in the book of Psalms; the people memorized the tunes and passed them down from generation to generation. The Psalms are songs of praise. Listen to these verses.

Praise is like applause. In the theater, when we like the performance of the actors, we clap our hands. Clapping is a way of thanking and encouraging the actors. When we sing songs of praise, we are applauding God with our voices.

It helps us to sing praises to God. If a person is sad, he or she can choose to sing a type of sad song called the blues. The more someone sings the blues, the sadder they get. On the other hand, when a person sings praises to God, they feel better and better. Singing is important because it makes us focus on the goodness of God. The Bible reports that Paul and Silas sang songs of praise when they were wrongfully thrown into prison. They sang because they didn't want to be saddened by dwelling on the problem of being in jail. The Bible says that the other prisoners listened and later that night the warden was saved (Acts 16:16–34).

There are many kinds of music in the world. There is rap music, country and western, and the blues. The most worthwhile songs are hymns of praise to God. God hears our songs of worship and gratitude to him, and the more we sing praises, the better we feel.—Ken Cox

July 28: A Praying Community
TEXT: James 5:16 NIV
Object: City map
Song: "We've a Story to Tell"

Good morning, boys and girls. I'm glad you chose to come to church today. What do you call this object I'm holding? [*Pause for response as you unfold the map.*] That's right, it is a map.

It is a map of our city [or community]. A map shows the streets, rivers, railroads, airports, and numerous other items. Did you know that the street where you live is listed on this map? If I want to find directions to your house, I can look on the map. This paper tells me the route I must take. It's like a picture of your neighborhood.

All of you have neighbors. Some live next door, others live further away, and some live in other states or even other countries. A friend of mine said, "When I take a daily walk on my street, I pray for the people whose homes I pass. If there is a particular need, I ask God to help the family with this concern." Isn't that a wonderful thing to do? I thought, what a simple yet great way to ask God to help families in my community. So, when I take my daily walk on my street, I remember to pray for my neighbors. I wonder what would happen if everyone developed this habit? Do you think this is something you would like to do?

In James 5:16 we read, "Pray for one another." Prayer is a way of asking God to help our friends. I hope that every time you see a map you will remember to pray for neighbors both near and far away. [*Lead the children in "We've a Story to Tell." Ask the pianist to continue playing as the children return to their seats.*]—Carolyn R. Tomlin

August 4: Understanding God's Word
TEXT: Ps. 119:18 NIV
Object: Pair of eyeglasses
Song: "Open My Eyes, That I May See"

Good morning, boys and girls. I'm holding something that some of you may wear. Or perhaps someone in your family uses these? Yes, these are eyeglasses. Can you tell me why a person might wear glasses? [*Pause for response.*] Of course, to help you see better. Some people use them for close-up work, such as reading. Other people need them to see things at a distance. I think that eyeglasses are a wonderful invention that helps us do and see the things we need to do and see. Without glasses, some people are almost blind.

Just as glasses help us to see, the Bible tells us about God's Word. When we know and understand Scripture, we realize how God wants us to live. Sometimes we can read a Bible verse several times without understanding the words. Then suddenly the meaning becomes clear. We understand. We can apply it to biblical truths and to our lives.

So the next time you see a pair of eyeglasses, think about how God's Word, the Bible, helps us see clearly. Listen as I read from Psalm 119:18: "Open my eyes that I may see wonderful things in your law." [*Ask someone to read the words to the song "Open My Eyes, That I May See." This song was written by Clara H. Scott (1841–1897). Ask the children to listen to how the writer spoke of the wonder of allowing God to use our lives. Ask the pianist to continue to play as the children return to their seats.*]—Carolyn R. Tomlin

August 11: Deborah's Palm Tree and Song
TEXT: Judg. 4:8–9
Object: Picture of a palm tree

This is a picture of a palm tree. A woman named Deborah made a palm tree in Israel a famous landmark. Deborah sat in the shade of the palm tree every day and people came to her for advice. They trusted Deborah to give them the truth of God.

Deborah was very strong. Her strength was not from muscles, riches, or any army, but from doing what pleased God.

One day Deborah delivered God's message of truth to a man named Barak. She told Barak to take ten thousand men and attack an evil man named Sisera. Sisera and his men had abused the people of Israel for many years, and God was about to rescue his people from them. God had chosen Barak to be a leader in redeeming Israel.

Barak was afraid to attempt this great deed. He told Deborah that he would attempt it only if Deborah would go with him. Listen to these verses. So a big strong warrior would not go unless Deborah went, too.

Real strength is not from physical size. Strength comes from always doing the right thing that God commands us to do. When we continually worship God and follow his commands, we become mighty in courage. It is a strength inside of us. It doesn't matter whether we are old or young, male or female; we all can be strong through obedience to God.

God was true to his word. Barak and Deborah led the ill-equipped army to battle. The army of Sisera was very mighty and had nine hundred iron chariots. However, God made it rain on the day of battle. All of those chariots bogged down in the mud, and Barak and Deborah won the battle! After they had won, someone wrote a song that they sang for years and years. The tune was called "The Song of Deborah," and it is in Judges 5.

Remember Deborah. She was strong in the Lord. She made a palm tree famous and they named a song after her.—Ken Cox

August 18: Tell the Good News
Text: Matt. 28:19–20 NIV
Object: Newspaper and a Bible
Song: "So Send I You"

Good morning, boys and girls. Do you know the name of this object? [*Pause for response.*] Of course, it's a newspaper. Many of you have a newspaper delivered to your home each morning or afternoon. Can someone tell me what type of information we find in the newspaper? [*Allow time for answers.*] Yes, we read of news events, the comics, the weather forecast, advertisements, grocery ads, and many other things. The paper keeps us aware of events that happen all over the world. I would say that reading a daily newspaper helps us grow mentally.

Just like the newspaper helps us learn information, the Bible helps us follow God's plan for telling others about Jesus. In Matthew 28:19–20, Jesus said, "Therefore, go and make disciples of all nations, baptizing them in the name of the Father and of the Son and of the Holy Spirit, and teaching them to obey everything I have commanded you. And surely I will be with you always, to the very end of the age." In this Scripture, Jesus commands us to tell others about Christianity. Does this mean just those people who live near you? What about people who are from a different culture or who have different customs? The Bible tells us to tell people of all nations about Jesus. We can do this by praying for our missionaries, sending our love offerings to support missions, and being a person who tells others that Jesus loves them—right in our own neighborhood. [*Lead the congregation in prayer, asking God to help each boy and girl be a missionary in his or her own community. Ask the pianist to play "So Send I You" as the children return to their seats.*]—Carolyn R. Tomlin

August 25: Jesus Has Promised to Return
TEXT: John 14:2–3
Object: A pocketknife

Jesus has promised to return to Earth for those who believe in him. After Jesus ascended into heaven, he wanted his disciples to cherish the promise of his return. He said that when he comes he will take us to be in heaven with him.

This pocketknife is a reminder of a story told about some early settlers in Texas. Over a hundred years ago, a mother, daddy, and their son were very happy living on a farm in Texas. One day the boy's mom was working in the yard and stepped on a nail. The nail went through the mom's shoe and stuck deeply into her foot. In those days there were no tetanus shots and not many doctors. The mother's foot and leg became infected from the rusty nail. The infection spread and the mother died after three weeks. The boy's father was so sad, he couldn't run the farm and take care of his son. So the man left the boy with an aunt and uncle and traveled to work on a ranch in another part of Texas. Before the brokenhearted father left, he gave his son a promise and his best pocketknife. The dad told the boy that he would come back to their farm as soon as possible, and he told him to keep the pocketknife to remember his promise.

There were no telephones in those days and mail service was very poor. The boy never received a letter from his dad. Every night before going to sleep the boy would say his prayers and put the knife on the table by his bed. Right before he blew out the candle on the nightstand, he would see the knife and drift off to sleep remembering his dad's promise. During the day, whenever the boy would take the knife out of his pocket, he would think about his dad.

One day two years later, when the boy was in school, he looked out the window and across the fields and saw a man riding up to the schoolhouse. It was his dad. The father had not forgotten his promise. The boy treasured the knife as a reminder of his dad's promise.

Jesus has done the same thing for us. He has promised in the Bible that he will come back for us. Listen to this verse. One day when the world is not expecting Jesus to return, he will come for us. Let's live for Jesus as though he could come back today. God has never broken a promise. Jesus will keep his promise and come back for us one day.—Ken Cox

September 1: For Labor Day
TEXT: Mark 6:17
Object: Small items associated with various types of work, such as a ruler, chalk, dishrag, wrench, paintbrush

Tomorrow we celebrate a holiday that is not as well known as Thanksgiving or the Fourth of July. That's right, it's Labor Day. I'm not surprised that many of you did not know about this holiday. Labor Day gifts aren't given and there aren't many family celebrations. What does *labor* mean? [*Don't be surprised by an answer having to do with childbirth.*] Labor means to work. This is a time in our country when we give thanks for the good things that come from the work that is done by all kinds of people.

What kind of work might be done with this? Yes, it is a ruler, and you could use it to measure boards for building a Habitat House. Some of your parents are doing that right now.

What about chalk? Your teacher may use it to put a lesson on a chalkboard. God gives us all work to do that uses our gifts and abilities to do what God wants done in the world. We are placing these work tools on the Communion table where we put our offerings each Sunday. Don't you think our work can be an offering to God? Our Scripture this morning says that the people in the town where Jesus grew up were astounded by his teaching. In other words, they didn't think that wisdom and great deeds could come from a carpenter (Mark 6:1–3 NRSV). Never be surprised by the work that Jesus can do through anyone, no matter what their job is. If you offer God whatever your work is, you will be worshipping God through what you do. Maybe these tools on the Communion table will be a reminder of that. Thanks for coming this morning.—Gary D. Stratman

September 8: Talking to Jesus
TEXT: 2 Chron. 7:12
Object: Telephone
Song: "What a Friend We Have in Jesus"

Good morning, boys and girls. It's good to see you today. I'm holding in my hand an object found in almost every home in our country. What is this? [*Pause.*] That's right, this is a telephone. A telephone communicates with someone in another location. In fact, you may have more than one phone in your house. Do you ever try to call a friend and the line is busy? This means they are talking to another person, or perhaps the phone rings and no one answers. Why would no one answer the phone? [*Wait for responses.*] Could it be because they are not home? Or perhaps they didn't hear the phone. Or maybe it is inconvenient for them to talk now. Yes, a phone is nice to have, but sometimes we can't get through to the person we want to talk with.

I'm so glad it is not that way when we talk to Jesus. We have the promise that he hears us when we pray. He is never too busy to listen, and all these other reasons do not apply either when it comes to talking to our friend Jesus.

God's Word tells us that when we pray, he is listening. Listen as I read 2 Chronicles 7:12: "I have heard your prayers. . . ." (NIV). [*Ask the congregation to join with the children as you sing one verse of "What a Friend We Have in Jesus." This song tells us that we can carry our problems to Jesus and he hears us. Isn't that a wonderful feeling! As the pianist continues to play, the children return quietly to their seats.*]—Carolyn R. Tomlin

September 15: You Are the Christ
TEXT: Mark 8:27–35
Object: Some public opinion polls on the president, the top ten teams in football, and any other polls that are used in your newspaper

Good morning, boys and girls. How many of you know anything about the polls that are taken every day to find out what is the most popular TV show or the best football team or things like that? [*Let them answer.*] What would you say is your favorite TV show that is on at night? [*Let them answer.*] Those are pretty popular shows. Most people watch the same kinds of shows that you watch, and people who are called pollsters ask questions about those shows. A lot of people ask questions about the president to find out how people think he is doing. They ask people just like you and me if he is doing a good job, if he is solving problems, if he takes too many vacations, or if he is working too hard. Pollsters ask all kinds of questions, and the answers to their questions are printed in the newspaper. We do the same thing with football teams. Every week coaches and newspapermen are asked to pick the best team in the country, or in the state, and then they print the answer the people gave. People love to take polls, and we must love to read them because our newspapers and magazines are filled with polls.

Of course, this is not brand new. Jesus once took a poll. Did you know that? He asked all of his disciples some questions to find out who the people thought he really was. Jesus said, "Who do the people say that I am?" That was a very good question. He had done some teaching in their church, he had healed some of the people who were deaf, blind, or sick, and he had done some miracles, like walking on water and turning water into wine. Jesus was a pretty famous person, and he wanted to know what the people thought of him, so he took a poll.

The amazing part was that he got different answers from different people. Some of the people thought he was John the Baptist brought back to life, some of the people thought he was the prophet Elijah who had done so many wonderful things many, many years before, some people named other prophets. Jesus reminded them of many good people. That would be pretty special if you were an ordinary person, but Jesus was really different.

So Jesus asked the disciples who they thought he was. Before anyone else could say a word, Peter said, "You are the Christ." That was special, the most special answer that anyone could give. Jesus looked at Peter and told him that what he said could come only from God. No poll could have come up with that answer. Jesus was the Christ and Peter had to listen to God to have such an answer.

The next time you hear about a poll, perhaps you can think about the one that Jesus took, and how he got the real answer from God. Amen.—Wesley T. Runk[5]

September 22: Who Is Number One?

TEXT: Mark 9:30–37

Object: Some roots

Good morning, boys and girls. Have you ever heard of the time that the disciples had a discussion about which one of them was the greatest? [*Let them answer.*] We have heard a lot of people call themselves number one or the greatest, haven't we? But we never thought that the disciples of Jesus were that way. But it's true. One day, when Jesus and the disciples were walking along a road, the disciples began to fall back and get into a little discussion. Every once in a while you could hear one voice get a little louder than the rest, but for the most part they were pretty quiet. Finally, when they arrived at a small village called Capernaum, Jesus asked them what they were talking about, and of course they were a little embarrassed. But Jesus had heard enough of what they had said to figure out why they were embarrassed, so he told them a story. He said that the greatest man is not the one who gets the credit but the one who does the work to help others look great. He called the great-

---

[5]*Let's Share Jesus Together*

est the servant. We don't think of servants as being the most important, but Jesus said that the person who served the others most was the greatest as far as he was concerned.

Let me show you what Jesus was talking about. I have something here that I think is pretty important. [*Show them a root.*] What do you call one of these? [*Let them answer.*] That's right, a root. What does a root do? [*Let them answer.*] Very good: a root feeds a plant and makes it strong. It buries itself deep in the ground and brings water and food to the rest of the plant. Without a strong root, the plant will not grow or stay strong. Do you see the root? When people look at a tree or a flower, do they say, "What wonderful roots that tree or that flower must have?" [*Let them answer.*] I never hear them say anything like that. People think a tree is great because it is strong or beautiful. No one thinks about the root. But I think Jesus would, because he knew that roots were the most important part of big trees or beautiful flowers. The root is the servant. It works hard to make the rest of the tree or flower look great.

I hope that many of you plan to be roots. You will be the greatest if you work hard to make other people look good. We need a lot of roots. If you are working for Jesus, you need to be a good root. Jesus said that his people were servants, that each one was trying to help the other one look better or be better. The next time you look at a tree, think about the kind of roots it has, and then look at the size or beauty of the tree.—Wesley T. Runk[6]

September 29: Jesus Was Different
Text: Matt. 7:28–29; 5:16
Object: A heavily bandaged thumb

First, let me ease your mind: there is nothing wrong with my thumb. I put this big bandage on my thumb to get your attention. You were wondering about it, weren't you? Before the worship service began, several people asked me what had happened to my thumb. There is an old saying, "It sticks out like a sore thumb." A bandaged thumb really does draw attention.

Jesus drew attention by his life, ministry, and power. He was refreshingly different to the people of his day. They were sick of fake religious leaders. When Jesus came and performed miracles and was so genuine, they welcomed the noticeable difference in his testimony and life. They were attracted to him. Listen to these verses [7:28–29]. In his own way, Jesus stuck out like a sore thumb.

Our different lives are to be noticeable, too. We are not to be different in a weird or offensive way. For instance, some church members think it is their job to correct everyone else. People don't like to be corrected. Other churchgoers may consider it their job to be better than everyone else and they look down their noses at those outside the church. In a Ray Steven's comedy video, one of the characters is named "Bertha Better Than You." It is sad when church members stick out like a sore thumb in the wrong way.

When Jesus called his followers to be different, he asked them to shine as lights in a confused and hurting world. Listen to this verse [5:16]. Jesus' followers are to shine light by their upright lives. When his disciples are honest at all times, it is noticeable. When people put others first, it is noticeable. Have you ever had someone let you go in front of them at the

---

[6]*Let's Share Jesus Together*

water fountain? That's conspicuous, isn't it? Kindness, honesty, and goodness are very observable. These good actions draw attention to Jesus in the right way. When people notice the way we live and ask us why, we can tell them it is because we love Jesus and want to be like him. When we intend to witness with our lives, it is OK to stick out like a sore thumb.—Ken Cox

October 6: Wonderful Grace

TEXT: Eph. 1:7 NIV
Object: Picture of Jesus
Song: "Amazing Grace"

Good morning, boys and girls. It's good to see you today. I want us to think about the person in this picture. Can someone tell me his name? [*Pause for response.*] Yes, his name is Jesus. In the Bible he is referred to by other names also. They include Savior, Lord, the King of Kings, the Everlasting Father, the Prince of Peace, the Good Shepherd, and others. But what is so amazing about this man named Jesus is his ability to forgive our sins. He loves you and he loves me so much that his love, which we can call grace, wipes our wrongdoings away. He remembers them no more. I would call that amazing.

When we come to church, we sing about grace. The writers of many Christian hymns refer to this word. We enjoy singing "Wonderful Grace of Jesus," "Grace Greater Than Our Sins," and one of my favorites, "Amazing Grace." The next time you hear someone talk about grace, you will know that it is this wonderful love that Jesus gives to his children.

In Ephesians 1:7 we read, "In him we have redemption through his blood, the forgiveness of sins, in accordance with the riches of God's grace." [*Ask a musician to play all stanzas of "Amazing Grace" on a dulcimer or string instrument. Ask the children to think of the words as they hear the music. Pray that each child will understand more about God's grace. Ask the children to return quietly to their seats after the last stanza of the song.*]—Carolyn R. Tomlin

October 13: Look Up to Find Truth and Strength

TEXT: Ps. 122:1–2
Object: A picture of a mountain

This is a picture of Mount Everest. Mount Everest is 29,028 feet tall and is the tallest mountain in the world. When we look at a mountain, we have a sense of amazement and grandeur.

Jesus lived close to many mountains. In the Bible, mountains are used to describe the greatness of God. In the Scriptures, mountains are a place to go and meet with God, to find truth and strength. Listen to these verses.

In this Psalm, the believer looks up to the hills and envisions the truth and strength of God. Looking up to God is something we must do every day. If we climb a tree and look down from one of the top branches, we are likely to be scared. If we look closely at the world around us, we are likely to be frightened, too. All around us are sickness, people who have broken laws and been arrested, and others without homes or food. If all we do is look down or around, we can become too frightened to live confident lives of faith.

God commands us to look up to him. Like looking up at a magnificent mountain, we must look up to God for strength. The Lord tells us to shift our vision from the things that frighten us and look to things that are true and lovely.

When God gave wanted to give the Ten Commandments to Moses, he told Moses to climb Mount Sinai. On Mount Sinai, Moses received the Ten Commandments and went down to the people to share the truth with them. God spoke to a mighty prophet name Elijah on Mount Sinai, too. Elijah was scared, lonely, and tired when God spoke to him on the mountain. After gaining strength from God on the mountain, Elijah was able to return to the important mission God had given him.

God wants us to look to the mountains, too. We may not have mountains near us, but we can look up to God whenever we pray. Also, we gain strength from on high when we read our Bibles. If all we do is look down and around us, we will be frightened. When we look up to God, we learn the truth and gain strength. So, whenever you see a mountain, think of looking up to God.—Ken Cox

October 20: Jesus Is a True Friend
TEXT: John 15:15 NIV
Object: Empty picture frame
Song: "Jesus, My Friend, Is Great"

Hello, boys and girls. It's good to see you today. I want you to look at something I'm holding. Can someone tell me what is wrong with this picture frame? [*Pause for response.*] That's right, there is no picture inside the frame. Of course we can purchase an artist's illustration, but there are no pictures of what Jesus looked like when he was born, when he was a boy, or when he became a man. I'm sure that in your home there are many pictures of you and your family. Is that right? [*Allow children time to respond.*]

Although we have no true picture of Jesus, we can hold him in our hearts. And how do we know he is there? Because he says he will be. Remember, Jesus never fails to keep a promise. He is watching over you and me when we are afraid and when we are happy, and he is always there for us. Isn't it nice to have a special friend like Jesus?

The Bible tells us many times that Jesus is our friend. We sing songs about this friendship. One verse I like is found in John 15:15, "I have called you friends, for everything I learned from my Father I have made known to you." [*Say a prayer asking God to help each boy and girl make Jesus their special friend. Lead the children in singing "What a Friend We Have in Jesus." Ask the pianist to continue playing as the children return to their seats.*]— Carolyn R. Tomlin

October 27: Don't Be Green with Envy!
TEXT: Prov. 14:30
Object: A green poster

This green piece of paper has one word written on it: *Envy.* When we have envy, we intensely desire the personal qualities and possessions of someone else. If we wish for the handsome or beautiful looks of a friend, we are envious of their physical appearance. When we are envious, we are said to be "green with envy." This means we are so unhappy that our faces turn green as though we are ill.

Envy is the opposite of thankfulness. Envy hurts us physically and spiritually. Listen to this verse.

We are not to be envious because God has made each one of us for a special purpose. The Lord has given us unique personal characteristics so we may fulfill this special calling. If we are envious and want someone else's special characteristics, we will lose sight of our own unique calling. God's will is for us to be thankful for our special qualities. As we express our gratitude to God for who we are, we become aware of what God has for us to do.

One way to be thankful is to count our blessings. The song "Count Your Blessings" includes the lyrics "Count your many blessings, name them one by one, and it will surprise you what the Lord hath done." It is by being grateful for our blessings that we become aware of God's power in our lives. If we are envious, we focus on what we think is missing or needed and we lose sight of God's perfect provision for us. The blessings are there; we just don't notice them.

Seasickness turns people pale and green. The motion of the waves can make someone who is not used to being on a boat feel sick to his or her stomach. It's worse than being carsick. If we are envious, we will always be green and frowning with unhappiness. If we are thankful to God for all he has done for us, we will be satisfied and smiling.—Ken Cox

November 3: Leaning on Jesus
TEXT: Matt. 9:12 NIV
Object: A crutch or a walking stick
Song: "The Great Physician"

Hello, boys and girls. I'm happy to see you today. I'm holding something in my hand that you may have used or that someone in your family may have used. Can you identify this object? [*Pause for response.*] Yes, this is a crutch [or walking stick]. This item is used to help people stand or walk. If you have ever broken your foot or leg, you may have used crutches. Sometimes a person who is ill or elderly may need a walking stick to help him balance when walking. A walking stick or crutches helps our body by offering support. We can lean on this object and place less strain on an injury.

We are told in the Scriptures that Jesus loves us and wants us to depend on him for support. In the Scriptures he is called the Great Physician. How can we learn to depend on Jesus? [*Allow time for each child to respond.*] Yes, we can pray. We can read our Bibles or ask our parents to read from the Bible. We can attend the services of our church. We can join with the congregation when singing hymns. There are many ways we can lean on Jesus to help us live a better life.

So the next time you see a walking stick or a crutch, remember that we need to lean on Jesus for support every day.

Listen as I read from Matthew 9:12: "It is not the healthy who need a doctor but the sick." [*Ask a soloist to sing one verse of "The Great Physician." Ask the pianist to continue playing as the children return to their seats.*]—Carolyn R. Tomlin

November 10: David Respected Other People

TEXT: 2 Sam. 23:16

Object: A glass of water

This is a plain glass of water. How we behave regarding little things, like a glass of water, reveals our inner qualities.

One afternoon, David, the famous and powerful king of Israel, was thirsty. King David and his people were at war with the Philistines. David said to a group of soldiers that he wished for a drink of water from a well in his hometown of Bethlehem. David felt like we do when we are away from home. There is nothing as refreshing as a drink of water at home. In other places, the water tastes different and it makes us wish we were in the comfort of our own home.

There was a problem with David's desire for a drink. The Philistines had conquered Bethlehem and a company of enemy soldiers were headquartered there. David could not travel home and draw some water from his favorite well without being captured or killed.

Three of David's loyal men overheard David's wish for water from Bethlehem. These courageous and strong men loved and respected David so much they made a plan to go to Bethlehem. They broke through the enemy lines, drew water from the special well, and escaped to give the water to David. David did not drink the water. Listen to this verse.

At first, it may sound like David did not appreciate what the three mighty men had accomplished. Actually, he was thankful for the risk they had endured for him. However, David in good conscience could not drink the water. To do so would encourage other rash behavior on the part of his men. David valued his men so highly that he didn't want them taking unnecessary risks for one of his whims. This event was a defining moment for the rest of David's reign. His men realized how much David valued their lives and it made them love and respect him even more.

When we give a glass of water to a thirsty friend, this simple act of kindness reveals our concern for others. Furthermore, the more we share and show simple acts of kindness to others, the more we feel like being charitable. Acts of selfishness tend to make our hearts cold and hard. Good deeds make us feel good inside. The more we practice these defining acts of concern for others, the more we will become genuinely benevolent people.

Let's remember the lesson of the water from the well at Bethlehem and practice small acts of kindness. The small acts add up to something big in God's eyes.—Ken Cox

November 17: The Sign of the Fish

TEXT: Matt. 4:18 NIV

Object: Fish crackers

Song: "Lead Me to Some Soul Today"

Good morning, boys and girls. I'm glad you chose to come to church today. In my hand I'm holding a small cracker in the shape of a fish. I'm also going to pass out fish crackers for you to eat. [*Ask the children to pass around a bag of fish crackers.*] Why do you think I'm offering you a fish cracker today? [*Pause for response.*] During the New Testament period, a fish was the sign of Christianity. It meant that you belonged to a group of people who recognized Jesus as God's Son. Many of these people made their living from the sea, and Jesus often sat on a boat and spoke to groups of people who were on shore.

Today, the fish symbol is often worn as a pin in a man's lapel or on a woman's dress. Do you know what a symbol is? [*Pause for response.*] A symbol stands for something else. The fish stands for Christianity. It symbolizes that this person is a Christian. If we follow God's commandment, we are to become fishers of men. That means we should tell all people about Jesus and his love for them. If they will accept Christ as their Savior, they will have eternal life in heaven with him.

Jesus talks about us leading others to Christ. In Matthew 4:18, he says to Simon Peter and his brother Andrew, "Come, follow me, and I will make you fishers of men." And the men who had been fishermen stopped their work and followed Jesus.

Let us sing one stanza of "Lead Me to Some Soul Today." [*Ask the pianist to continue playing as the children return to their seats.*]—Carolyn R. Tomlin

November 24: We Must Learn to Wait on God

TEXT: Isa. 64:4; Ps. 40:1

Object: Picture of a long waiting line

This photograph is of a crowd waiting to buy tickets for the first showing of a movie. Some fans got to the theater the day before the movie opened and spent the whole night waiting in line.

It's difficult to wait. We would rather get what we want immediately. To ride the roller coaster at some amusement parks, it may be necessary to wait in line for an hour. If you want to enjoy that thrilling roller coaster ride, you have to be willing to wait.

The Bible teaches that we must learn to wait on God. Waiting is required for the promises of God and for our prayers to be answered. Listen to this verse.

The prophet Isaiah described Jesus seven hundred years before he was born. Imagine that. God gives a promise that will be fulfilled one day and expects us to live as though the promise has already come true. No matter how long God's promises take to be fulfilled, God always keeps his promises and expects us to believe in him with all our hearts. As the long days pass until the promise is fulfilled, we "wait on the Lord." While we wait, we live by faith and are fully obedient to all we know God has said.

We also must wait on God for our prayers to be answered. It would be nice if we could ask God for something and receive it immediately. Sometimes we do, but with other prayers we must wait for God to answer us. The Lord expects us to wait on him because he may have to arrange some events over several years. For instance, if you prayed to be a great baseball or softball player, you might have to wait through years of practice and playing games to have your prayer answered. Also, God may give us something different than we asked for. When that happens, we trust and depend on God to do what is best for us. While the time passes, we "wait on the Lord," knowing that God's answer will be perfect when it comes.

Listen to this verse [*read Ps. 40:1*]. We must learn to wait on God because he is worth waiting for.—Ken Cox

December 1: God Came in Jesus

TEXT: John 3:16

I want to tell you a story. This story really did happen when I was the pastor of another church. One Sunday morning, before our worship service was to begin, the custodian told me that there was a bird trapped in the sanctuary trying to fly to freedom. The two of us tried everything we could to convince the bird to escape through an open window. But the bird didn't understand what we were saying. It would wing its way to a bright, colorful light that seemed to be the opening that led to safety. Yet as it flew toward the light, it would time after time crash into one of the great stained glass windows. Can you imagine two grown men running around the sanctuary flapping their arms faster than the bird was moving its wings? We were frantically trying to keep the bird from harming itself and to help it find the way home. If I could have become a bird, I could have made the poor little creature understand and lead the way home. I had heard stories like this before, but it was the first time I was in one! I knew why God became a person: it was the only way we could know what God wanted to say to us and to find our way home. That's really the reason we celebrate Christmas: God came in Jesus. Now God can speak to us through what Jesus said and did. "For God so loved the world, he gave his only Son." That's the truest story I know.—Gary D. Stratman

December 8: The Day of the Lord
TEXT: 1 Thess. 5:2; 4:16
Object: Symbols of special days

We use all sorts of things to celebrate special days. On the Fourth of July we wave flags and pop fireworks. On birthdays we send cards. On New Year's Day we wear silly hats, blow whistles, and throw confetti. We look forward to and remember festive days in unusual ways.

The Bible has promised a future special day that will be unlike any other. It's called the Day of the Lord. Listen to this verse.

The Day of the Lord is when Jesus is coming back. After Jesus was born in Bethlehem, he taught God's Word and performed miracles. Then Jesus died on the cross to pay the penalty for the sins of the world. After three days, he was raised from the dead and ascended into heaven. Jesus has been in heaven ever since the day of his ascension. The Bible promises that he will come back to Earth to take us from this often sad and violent world to enjoy heaven with him forever.

The day of the Lord will be an awesome occasion. We must be ready when that day comes. We can get ready by being obedient to Jesus. As we begin to understand who God is and how much he loves us, we respond to that love with our obedience and honor to him. That means we become the disciples of Jesus. If we live for Jesus, we will be ready when he comes back. We don't have to be afraid of Jesus' return because he loves us and wants the very best for our lives.

Birthdays, the Fourth of July, and Thanksgiving are great days. However, they pale in comparison to that coming day when Jesus will return for us.—Ken Cox

December 15: David Is Chosen to Be King
TEXT: 1 Sam. 16:7
Object: A yardstick

To measure someone's height, a yardstick is used. To gauge thinking capacity, an IQ (intelligence quotient) test is administered. To determine personal wealth, bank accounts are tallied.

These are some of the ways of measuring size, ability, and wealth. However, the Lord uses a different measuring rod to calculate worth.

One day God sent a prophet named Samuel to select a new king for Israel. Samuel went to the home of a man named Jesse. Jesse had eight sons. Samuel's task was to select one of Jesse's boys as king. When the oldest son came into the room, Samuel was impressed with his size and appearance. Samuel thought that this outstanding young man must be the one. The Lord told Samuel that the oldest and strongest was not the one. Seven of the sons paraded before Samuel that day. Some had outstanding characteristics, but the Lord didn't choose any of them. Finally, Samuel asked Jesse if he had any more male children. Jesse replied that there was only one son left; he was a little guy and had been given the job of watching the family's sheep. Jesse sent for the boy, and God chose that boy to be king. His name was David.

God has his own method for determining greatness. The Lord does not use a yardstick, standardized test, or bank book. God is interested with what is in our hearts. Listen to this verse.

With God's measuring techniques, all of us can be great. Though the world selects only a few persons to be celebrities, we can be shining stars for God if our hearts are right with him. Our hearts can be pleasing to God if we devote all of our talents to serve him. The Lord uses everyone who is committed to him in great ways. One afternoon, the Lord used a boy's lunch to feed a whole crowd of hungry people. That little boy had a willing heart, and the Lord was able to bless many people through him.

Only a few select stars make the halls of fame of the sports and entertainment industries. We can all make God's all-star list. When we devote our hearts to serve the Lord, we will be listed with the distinguished faithful of the ages.—Ken Cox

December 22: Angels Proclaim Jesus' Birth
TEXT: Luke 2:14
Object: Angel figurine or statue
Song: "Hark! The Herald Angels Sing"

Hello, boys and girls. I'm holding a small statue in my hand. Can you tell me what this object is? [*Pause for response.*] Yes, it's an angel. Today we see many pictures of angels and objects with angels on them. Did you know that angels are spoken of in the Bible many times? They brought news of events that were to happen.

I especially like the Christmas story in Luke that tells how the angels welcomed the birth of the Christ child. Do you remember hearing your teachers and parents tell the story about Jesus' birth? The angels sang, "Glory to the newborn King!" Can you imagine what it must have been like to have heard the angels singing? And can you imagine how Mary and Joseph must have rejoiced when they heard this heavenly choir?

Luke 2:14 says, "Glory to God in the highest, and on Earth, peace." Let us pray that our world will know peace as God intended.

So the next time you see a statue or figurine of an angel, think about the choir of angels that welcomed the birth of Jesus in Bethlehem. Just as the angels sang praises to God, so should we lift our voices in song. Let us ask the congregation to join us in singing "Hark! The Herald Angels Sing." [*Ask the pianist to continue playing as the children return to their seats.*]—Carolyn R. Tomlin

December 29: What Will You Carry into the New Year
TEXT: Heb. 12:1, 2
Object: Ankle weights

What do I have in my hands? Maybe you would like to hold them. They are heavy, aren't they? People use them when they exercise, when they jog or practice basketball. They are called ankle weights, and some of you have seen your parents or older brothers and sisters use them. But let's imagine for a moment that you are going to run a race. It is very important for you to run this race. You know that you can win it if you run as fast as you can. (I see several of you are getting ready to run right now.) If you wanted to win, would you put these heavy weights on your legs to run the race? No, I don't think you would. I wouldn't either. You would take off all the extra weight you didn't need so that you could run the best race possible.

In our Bible story today, life is compared to a race. We are to run the race, to live our lives with patience and faith. That means we will occasionally go through hard and difficult times in the race, but if we keep our eyes on Jesus, who has run the race before us, he will give us the strength to win. To win is to know and enjoy God forever. Because the prize is ours through Jesus, we do not want to be weighed down with the ankle weights of hatred, jealousy, prejudice, or cruelty. We are to let these weights drop off as we run the race of life with joy and thanksgiving.—Gary D. Stratman

SECTION XI

A LITTLE TREASURY
OF ILLUSTRATIONS

SELF-ACCEPTANCE.   We can accept ourselves because Christ has accepted us for God's glory. Because he has already accepted other people, and accepts us, the whole landscape of life opens up before us in an endless vista. So where we accept one another, recognize one another, and affirm one another, we are on firm ground. We cannot go far enough. In the light of the life which God passionately affirms and accepts, no life is without value and no life is "second-class." The suffering of his love has transformed everything, and the more we go out of ourselves, the more we discover this and experience it.—Jürgen Moltmann[1]

VICTORIOUS LOVE.   The powerful love of God shall be victorious. This is the reason we dare to hope for the completion of our incomplete and broken lives and for the consummation of God's purposes for the whole of creation. Because we dare to hope in God, we refuse to go either the way of resignation or the way of retaliatory violence to achieve our goals. For resignation is hopeless, and violence only breeds more violence. Christian hope keeps alive and strong the struggle for justice and freedom. But it refuses to contribute to the spirit of revenge. Christians are called to bear witness to the "more excellent way" of love (1 Cor. 12:31), even when with heavy hearts they believe they are required to take up arms to defend human life against outrageous injustice and brutality.—Daniel L. Migliore[2]

HUMOR.   Full recognition of Christ's humor has been surprisingly rare. In many of the standard efforts to write the Life of Christ, there is no mention of humor at all, and when there is any, it is usually confined to a hint or two. Frequently there is not one suggestion that he ever spoke other than seriously. It is to Renan's credit that he sensed the existence of the humorous element in the Gospels and called it striking, though he did not develop his insight in detail. Tennyson, in pointing out the paradox that humor is generally most fruitful in the most solemn spirits, said, "You will even find it in the Gospel of Christ." In several authors of the twentieth century, we find a passing reference to the humorous side of Christ's teaching, though without development, in most cases. Characteristic is the reference of Harry Emerson Fosdick: "He never jests as Socrates does, but he often lets the ripple of a happy breeze play over the surface of his mighty deep."—Elton Trueblood[3]

---

[1]*The Power of the Powerless*
[2]*The Power of God*
[3]*The Humor of Christ*

424

RESURRECTION.   Unless the Resurrection shakes us, confuses and upsets us, we have not truly confronted it. Quantum mechanics tells us that our world is not at all what we ordinarily experience it to be. Light is both a particle and a wave. Matter consists of quanta of energy. Such ideas boggle our minds. They don't fit in our ordered and rational way of looking at things. The Resurrection does not fit into our ordinary perceptions of human power and importance and value. The Resurrection tells us that at the heart and center of the universe, love is reigning. Something deep within us resonates with this radical view of the nature of things, in spite of all the evidence to the contrary.—Morton Kelsey[4]

FAITH AS ACT.   Faith—one's conviction of the ultimate character and meaning of existence—is the resting place of the heart and the orienting guide of the mind. Faith forms, centers, and anchors integrity. Therefore, faith determines action; faith is manifest in action (and as we shall see, faith is constituted by action). When we recognize faith as the composing of what is true and trustworthy at the level of ultimacy, we recognize that faith is immediately related to doing. We human beings act in accordance with what we really trust—in contrast to what we may merely acclaim.—Sharon Parks[5]

MISTAKEN GUILT.   I had an experience some years ago that taught me something about the ways in which people make a bad situation worse by blaming themselves. One January, I had to officiate at two funerals on successive days for two elderly women in my community. Both had died "full of years," as the Bible would say; both had succumbed to the normal wearing out of the body after a long and full life. Their homes happened to be near each other, so I paid condolence calls to the two families on the same afternoon.

At the first home, the son of the deceased woman said to me, "If only I had sent my mother to Florida and gotten her out of this cold and snow, she would be alive today. It's my fault that she died." At the second home, the son of the other deceased woman said, "If only I hadn't insisted on my mother's going to Florida, she would be alive today. That long airplane ride, the abrupt change of climate, was more than she could take. It's my fault that she's dead."—Harold S. Kushner[6]

HOLY COMEDY.   It might be a jolt to pious sensibilities to call the *Magnificat* funny, but it is surely comic. I find that it has the same humorous surprise as Mr. Pompous brought low by the banana peel or Charlie Brown brought low because Lucy jerks the football out of the way when his punt is in full swing. Mary, rejoicing in God her Savior, shares "the courage of the comic." She can see that God "has scattered the proud in the imagination of their hearts; he has put down the mighty from their thrones, and exalted those of low degree" (Luke 2:51–52).—Marianne H. Micks[7]

---

[4]*Resurrection*
[5]*The Critical Years*
[6]*When Bad Things Happen to Good People*
[7]*Our Search for Identity*

BEING MERCIFUL.   Suppose that there was not one man who journeyed from Jericho to Jerusalem but that there were two, that both were overpowered by thieves, disabled, and that no one came traveling by. Suppose then that one of them knew of nothing else to do but groan, while the second one forgot and overcame his own suffering in order to speak comforting, friendly words or, something that involved great pain, dragged himself to a little creek in order to get a refreshing drink for the other. Or suppose that both were bereft of speech but one of them in silent prayer sighed to God for the other one also: was he not then merciful? If someone has cut off my hands, I cannot play the zither, and if someone has cut off my feet, I cannot dance, and if I lie disabled at the brink, I cannot throw myself into the sea to save another person's life, and if I lie with broken arm or leg, I cannot dash into the flames to save another's life: but for all that I can be merciful.—Søren Kierkegaard[8]

GOD'S HELP.   A friend of mine grew up in a home where he was told, "God helps those who help themselves." As a teenager he began with petty theft, then graduated to the more risky life of a car thief. Drugs and alcohol consumed him; more thievery became necessary to support his habits. The thought that "God helps those who help themselves" drove him to despair. Where and how would he begin helping himself? He broke resolutions to change almost as quickly as he made them; suicide seemed like an attractive alternative to his addictions. Not until he learned that God helps those who *cannot* help themselves was he converted and set free from his sinful lifestyle.—Erwin W. Lutzer[9]

FAITH AND SALVATION.   If God has a plan to save men and women who don't have personal faith in Christ, he has chosen not to reveal it. We must resist the temptation to make the Scriptures say what we think they should. Our role is to spread the gospel with the firm conviction that faith comes by hearing and people cannot believe what they do not know.—Erwin W. Lutzer[10]

ESCAPE TO GOD.   The genuine Christian can and does venture out into all kinds of exacting and even perilous activities, but all the time he knows that he has a completely stable and unchanging center of operations to which he can return for strength, refreshment, and recuperation. In that sense, he does "escape" to God, though he does not avoid the duties or burdens of life. His very escape fits him for the day-to-day engagement with life's strains and difficulties.—J. B. Phillips[11]

LOVE OF SELF.   The Gospel does not condemn love of oneself; it only requires us to love others as ourselves; it asserts the value of the human person as being the creation of God. To esteem oneself as such, while at the same time frankly recognizing one's sinfulness, is the essential precondition of the experience of God's grace.—Paul Tournier[12]

---

[8]*Works of Love*
[9]*Ten Lies About God*
[10]*Ten Lies About God*
[11]*Your God Is Too Small*
[12]*The Strong and the Weak*

NOT PERFECT.   I find to this day seven abominations in my heart: (1) Inclinings to unbelief. (2) Suddenly to forget the love and mercy that Christ manifesteth. (3) A leaning to the works of the law. (4) Wanderings and coldness in prayer. (5) To forget to watch for that I pray for. (6) Apt to murmur because I have no more, and yet ready to abuse what I have. (7) I can do none of those things which God commands me, but my corruptions will trust in themselves, "When I would do good, evil is present with me."—John Bunyan[13]

GOD'S LOVE.   On the whole, God's love for us is a much safer subject to think about than our love for him. Nobody can always have devout feelings; and even if we could, feelings are not what God principally cares about. Christian Love, either towards God or towards man, is an affair of the will. If we are trying to do his will, we are obeying the commandment, "Thou shalt love the Lord thy God." He will give us *feelings* of love if he pleases. We cannot create them for ourselves, and we must not demand them as a right. But the great thing to remember is that, though our feelings come and go, his love for us does not. It is not wearied by our sins or our indifference; and therefore it is quite relentless in its determination that we shall be cured of those sins, at whatever cost to us, at whatever cost to him.—C. S. Lewis[14]

ESPECIALLY FOR PREACHERS AND TEACHERS.   All the best reading is done with a pen in hand. The advantage is that the reader is himself active and doing something about the ideas. Little help comes to the passive observer or to the passive reader. We should underline striking sentences, query doubtful passages, and make our own index in the back of the book, so that later we can find significant sections with speed and ease. I have long been grateful to the man who started me on this practice twenty-five years ago.—Elton Trueblood[15]

ALREADY, NOT YET, AND AT HAND.   For Jesus himself the Kingdom of God was both "already" and "not yet"; it was both "now" and "yet to come." It was "now" with his own invasion of Satan's turf and the spoiling of his house. With the coming of Jesus the Kingdom of God has already been inaugurated; it has already penetrated the present. But inherent in its presence with Jesus was likewise its final and full consummation with the future coming of the Son of Man. The future is not something new, it is merely the consummation of what Jesus already began through his ministry, and finally and especially through his death, resurrection, and the gift of the Spirit. Thus the Kingdom, though still future, is already at hand.—Gordon D. Fee[16]

SERVICE OF JESUS CHRIST.   Brothers and sisters, there is no greater joy in all the Earth than the service of Jesus Christ. That service may cost us everything we have, but it gives us in return a new world of triumphant celebration. It will cost us our time, but it will give back the transcendent fullness of life. It will cost us our relationships, but it will give us back the sweetest loves ever known to humankind. It will cost us our pursuits in life, but it will give us

---

[13]*Grace Abounding to the Chief of Sinners*
[14]*Christian Behavior*
[15]*The Teacher*
[16]*Listening to the Spirit in the Text*

back the highest goals of human achievement. It will cost us our self-will, but it will give us back the glory of freedom. Is it worth it? All the saints of all times agree: yes, it is well worth it.—Paul C. McGlasson[17]

A SENSE OF AWE.   I met President Ronald Reagan once. My first reaction was not to say, "Hi, Ronnie! How's the Pres?" I knew he was just a human being, but there is something about the office of president that commands respect. I said, "It's nice to meet you, Mr. President." I mention this because I hear people say, "I can't wait till I can see God face-to-face. I'm just going to leap into his arms and give him a great big hug." But in Scripture, whenever someone came face-to-face with God (or even with an angel, one of God's messengers), the first reaction was not love but fear. There was a deep sense of awe and respect and even a genuine dread at the thought of being in the presence of someone so holy and powerful. When we come into the presence of the King of Kings and the Lord of the presidents, our appropriate response is one of wonderment and reverence.—Bob Russell[18]

JESUS' ETHIC.   *The centerpiece of Jesus' ethic is love:* the twofold command to love God and neighbor (Mark 12:29–31 par.) and the reminder that neighbors include even our enemies (Luke 10:25–37; cf. Luke 6:35). The gospel calls us to confront all tribalism, nationalism, or ethnocentrism that would value all allegiance to human groups above cross-cultural *agape* for all people and especially all fellow Christians. Unlike various negative prohibitions, the positive command to love can never be said to have been perfectly kept. Modeling our love upon God's leads us to reject every form of judgmentalism (Matt. 7:1) and to treat others exactly as we, in our best moments, would want to be treated (v. 12). Whether or not enemy-love leads to full-fledged pacifism, it certainly should stir us to move heaven and Earth to promote "just peacemaking," that is, doing everything within our power to reconcile alienated persons to God and to one another. In short, our lives are lived in loving service for others, at the risk of suffering and, if necessary, to the point of death (John 15:12–13).—Craig L. Blomberg[19]

LENGTH OF ETERNITY.   Suppose the ocean to be so enlarged as to include all the space between the Earth and the starry heavens. Suppose a drop of this water to be annihilated once in a thousand years; yet that whole space of duration, wherein this ocean would be annihilating, at the rate of one drop in a thousand years, would be infinitely less in proportion to eternity than one drop of water to that whole ocean.

Look then at those immortal spirits, whether they are in this or the other world. When they shall have lived thousands of thousands of years, yea, millions of millions of ages, their duration will be but just begun: They will be only upon the threshold of eternity!—John Wesley[20]

ENCOUNTERING CHRIST IN THE BIBLE.   The Bible can be used in a variety of ways. It can be treated as a collection of historical documents or as an anthology of ancient literature;

---

[17]*Canon and Proclamation*
[18]*When God Builds a Church*
[19]*Jesus and the Gospels*
[20]*The John Wesley Reader*

it can be regarded as a collection of proof-texts for one's own theological and philosophical presuppositions; but its distinctively Christian use is to be read and heard in the light of Jesus Christ. When he interprets the Scriptures, God himself is revealed; God's will for men and women is made known. Those, who read or hear the Bible with Jesus as their guide, will not be guilty of according it a superficial lip-service. They will not load it with empty praises. When they speak of its wonder and majesty and riches, their words will be genuine. They will have found in it strength for the present and hope for the future. They will have found there a direction in which to move on the voyage of life. Above all, they will have encountered there Jesus Christ himself.—Arthur Wainwright[21]

A CHRISTIAN INTERPRETATION.   The Bible needs a method of interpretation which is intelligible, honest, and unquestionably Christian. As the Church's Scripture, it needs to be understood and used by Christian people. It is not satisfactory for it to merely be in their possession, nor is it satisfactory for it to be read without understanding. A Bible which is read but not understood is of no more use than a Bible left unopened on a bookshelf. It is like a sealed tomb, concealing treasures that never see the light of day.—Arthur Wainwright[22]

POWER FOR LIFE.   The book of Acts is written so that assets need not stay frozen. This witness makes a simple affirmation: power for life is unloosed. It is a generous offer of an alternative. It is given to you. It is a dangerous chance. You can be on the side of the newness that God is now working. All our frozenness cannot stop the newness. Think of us; think of you; think of this church—beyond complacency, beyond despair. Our old habits of deathliness now are emptied of authority, because the new is under way. No more frightened hearts, but hearts alive, bodies restored, communities, families, the world—like the lame man, jumping up, leaping, singing, and praising God. It is the same one who used to sit disabled. It could be us!—Walter J. Brueggemann[23]

CONVERTS.   Very recently, a young priest told me in conversation, "I have already made seventy-two converts in six years of my priesthood." I said, "I would advise you to stop counting them, otherwise you might think you made them and not God."—Fulton J. Sheen[24]

OPPORTUNITY TO MEET CHRIST.   One day in 1942 in the French village of Le Chambon, the police of the Nazi puppet government pulled into town to round up all the Jews. "The police knew that Le Chambon had become a refuge for them, so they rousted everyone into the village square. The police captain stared straight into the face of the pastor of the Protestant church, Andre Trocme, 'warning him that if he did not give up the names of the Jews they had been sheltering in the village, he and his fellow pastor, as well as the families who had been caring for the Jews, would be arrested.'

"The pastor refused, and the police, after a thorough and frightening search, could find

---

[21]*Beyond Biblical Criticism*
[22]*Beyond Biblical Criticism*
[23]*The Threat of Life*
[24]*Treasure in Clay*

only one Jew. They loaded him into an otherwise empty bus. Before they drove off, 'a thirteen-year-old boy, the son of the pastor, pass[ed] a piece of his precious chocolate through the window to the prisoner, while twenty gendarms who were guarding the lone prisoner watched.' Then the rest of the villagers began 'passing their little gifts through the window until there were gifts all around him—most of them food in those hungry days of the German occupation of France.'"[25]

To prepare for Christ, we have to be like that thirteen-year-old boy who did not turn away from the evil that was in front of him but saw in it the opportunity to meet Christ. Jesus gives us the courage to go to the wilderness, to walk the rough places and uneven ground, because we know that he meets us there.—Stephens G. Lytch

UNSPEAKABLE LOVE.   Thomas Wolfe wrote a number of autobiographical novels. In one of these novels there is a character named George Weber who was very tall, like Thomas Wolfe. He was clearly writing about himself. George Weber was a writer living in New York City. Thomas Wolfe had lived in New York City for a while. Whenever George would become depressed and life would become difficult because his creativity as a writer had hit a dry period, he would go back home to North Carolina. Wolfe was also from North Carolina. Weber would return to a small cabin in the mountains to visit his mother. She would always be there to greet him. He and his mother would sit down on the top step of the porch. This huge bulk of a man would sit down beside his mother and lay his head in her lap. Neither said anything for a long time as his mother gently put her hand on his shoulder. Presently she would say, "George, it's going to be all right, whatever it is, it's going to be all right."

This Christmas, remember you can come back to God, lay your head on God's lap, and he will stroke you with the hand of his love and say, "It's okay. It is going to be all right. You do not have to face your problems alone. I am here, and I love you." There is unspeakable love in God's gift to us.—William Powell Tuck

CONSCIENCE.   Take note, then, all you who have a timid conscience, that you will not be saved by this or that work. For it will fare with you as with one who works in a sandpit: the more sand he shovels out the more falls upon him. That's why many have gone mad, as John Gerson says, so that they began to imagine things, one that he was a worm, another that he was a mouse, and so on. Just commit it to God and say, "Oh, my dear God, I have sinned, but I confess it to thee, I pour it out to thee and pray thee for help; do thou help me." That is what God wants of us.—Martin Luther

TOWARD OBEDIENCE.   When men would justify themselves by outward works, it is like covering a heap of filth with a clean linen cloth. Therefore let us put away the filthiness that is hidden in our hearts; I say, let us drive the evil from us, and then the Lord will accept our life: thus we may see wherein consists the true knowledge of God! When we understand this aright, it will lead us to live in obedience to his will.—John Calvin

---

[25]Philip Hallie, *Lest Innocent Blood Be Shed: The Story of the Village of Le Chambon and How Goodness Happened There* (New York: HarperCollins, 1979), p. 3, quoted in Craig Dykstra, *Growing in the Life of Faith: Education and Christian Practices* (Louisville, Ky.: Geneva Press, 1999), pp. 56–57.

A MINOR CLOUD.   That notable servant of Jesus Christ, Athanasius, who being exiled from Alexandria by that blasphemous, apostate, Julian the emperor, said unto his flock, who bitterly wept for his envious banishment, "Weep not, but be of good comfort, for this little cloud will suddenly vanish." He called both the emperor himself and his cruel tyranny a little cloud; and albeit there was small appearance of any deliverance to the Church of God, or of any punishment to have apprehended the proud tyrants, when the man of God pronounced these words, yet shortly after God did give witness that those words did not proceed from flesh nor blood, but from God's very Spirit. For not long after, being in warfare, Julian received a deadly wound, whether by his own hand, or by one of his own soldiers, the writers clearly conclude not; but casting his own blood against the heaven, he said, "At last Thou hast overcome, thou Galilean"; so in despite he termed the Lord Jesus. And so perished that tyrant in his own iniquity; the storm ceased, and the Church of God received new comfort.—John Knox (1513-1572)

SIN STAINS.   That is why I exhort both those recently deemed worthy of baptism and those who received this gift before. Those long since baptized I urge to cleanse away, by confession, tears, and most exact repentance, the filth they have already contracted. The newly baptized I exhort to keep the bloom of their luster and to keep watch over the beauty of their souls, so that they get no spot on them which can make them unclean. Do you not see how much care is taken by a man clad in a shining bright robe as he walks in the marketplace that no spot of mud splashes up to sully the beauty of his robe, even though this would do no harm to his soul? For the robe can be destroyed by moths and worn out with time. Besides, when it is dirty, it is easily washed clean with water. But in the case of the soul—and heaven forbid that it happen—if it ever should happen and the soul will receive some stain either from the tongue or the thoughts born in the mind, there straightway comes over the soul a great disgrace, a heavy burden, and a foul stench.—St. John Chrysostom

THE LORD'S PRAYER.   In our lives we are continually contracting what daily needs forgiveness. Those who are baptized and forthwith depart this life, come up from the font free of debt, and leave this world free of debt. But those who are baptized and are still imprisoned in this life, by reason of human frailty contract certain impurities, which even though they may not involve shipwreck, yet make it necessary to get rid of the bilge water. Otherwise, if it is not pumped out it seeps in little by little, until the whole ship is in danger of sinking. The offering of this prayer may be compared to the pumping out of bilge water.—St. Augustine

LONGING FOR GOD.   Although man has turned away his eyes from God and has gone astray, he still feels an eternal calling and yearning for him; however hard man tries to escape from it, he can find no peace because nothing except the one aim can fully satisfy him. It drives and draws him unconsciously into his innermost being. The soul longs for its rest in God in the same way as all material things eventually come to rest in their appropriate places: the stone on the ground and the fire in the air.—John Tauber

CHARITY.   Paul says, if he speaks with men's tongues and angel's tongues, and has not charity, he is as sounding brass and tinkling cymbal. It is known that preaching and other speech is the highest deed of man when it is done well. But however cleverly a man speaks in different languages of men—either English, French, Latin, or other languages—his voice is like a sound of brass that destroys himself unless he has charity by which he deserves bliss. For such men waste themselves and enlarge their pain. And in the same way, if a man speak in an angel's tongue, with clear voice or flowery words, but lacks charity with this, he is a tinkling cymbal; for he does not deserve heavenly bliss, but wastes himself to his own condemnation.—John Wyclif

REPROVING SIN.   I never heard or read of any considerable revival of religion which was not attended with a spirit of reproving. I believe it cannot be otherwise; for what is faith unless it work by love? Thus it was in every part of England, when the present revival of religion began about fifty years ago; all the subjects of that revival, all the Methodists so called, in every place, were reprovers of outward sin. And indeed so are all that, "being justified by faith, have peace with God through Jesus Christ." Such they are at first: and if they use that precious gift, it will never be taken away. Come, brethren! In the name of God, let us begin again! Rich or poor, let us all arise as one man! And in anywise, let every man "rebuke his neighbor, and not suffer sin upon him!" Then shall all Great Britain and Ireland know that we do not "go a warfare at our own cost." Yea, God shall bless us, and all the ends of the world shall fear him.—John Wesley

BEYOND RICHES.   Persons may do good *to the souls of others,* which is the most excellent way of doing good. Men may be, and oftentimes are, the instruments of spiritual and eternal good to others; and wherein any are so, they are the instruments of greater good to them than if they had given them the riches of the universe.—Jonathan Edwards

ARDENT SPIRITS.   A resort to ardent spirits as an alleviation of trouble results often in habits of confirmed intemperance. The loss of friends, perplexities of business, or the wreck of property bring upon the spirits the distractions of care and the pressure of sorrow; and instead of casting their cares upon the Lord, they resort to the exhilarating draught; but before the occasion for it has ceased, the remedy itself has become a calamity more intolerable than the disease. Before, the woes were temporary; now, they have multiplied, and have become eternal.—Lyman Beecher

DEATH DEFEATED.   I cannot trust the physician who plays upon the surface of my disease and throws over it the disguise of false coloring. I have more confidence to put in him who, like Christ the Physician of my soul, has looked the malady fairly in the face, has taken it up in all its extent and in all its soreness, has resolved it into its original principles, has probed it to the very bottom, and has set himself forward to combat with the radical elements of the disease. This is what the Savior has done with death. He has plucked it of its sting. He has taken a full survey of the corruption, and met it in every one quarter where its malignity operates. It was sin which constituted the virulence in the disease, and he hath extracted it. He hath put it away. He hath expiated the sentence; and the believer, rejoicing in the assurance that all is clear with God, serves him without fear in righteousness and in holiness all the days of his life. The sentence is no longer in force, against us who believe.—Thomas Chalmers

HINDRANCES.   It is but a vain thing to talk of going to heaven, if thou let thy heart be encumbered with those things that would hinder. Would you not say that such a man would be in danger of losing, though he run if he fill his pockets with stones, hang heavy garments on his shoulders, and get lumpish shoes on his feet? So it is here; thou talkest of going to heaven, and yet fillest thy pockets with stone—[that is,] fillest thy heart with this world, lettest that hang on thy shoulders, with its profits and pleasures. Alas! Alas! Thou art widely mistaken: if thou intendest to win, thou must strip, thou must lay aside every weight, thou must be temperate in all things. Thou must so run.—John Bunyan

EASTER GREETINGS.   Kenneth Woodward, that fine religion reporter, tries his best as a good journalist to disguise his faith in the Resurrection, but it sneaks through. He says, "That Jesus rose from the dead is a statement of Christian faith . . . and implies a bond of trust between those who live in the presence of Christ today and those who first carried the Easter message two thousand years ago."

There are several different ways of extending the greetings of the season to one another. "Happy Easter!" is the most familiar salutation. I have always envied the way one of my favorite professors was able to say, with a two-fisted handclasp and a clear gaze straight into the eyes, "A blessed feast of our Lord's Resurrection!" On the other end of the scale, we have hit a new low with "Have a nice Easter." To my ears this sounds something like saying to the astronaut leaving for Venus, "Have a nice trip."

The best Easter greeting, of course, is the oldest one: "Alleluia! Christ is risen!" to which the answer is, "He is risen indeed! Alleluia!"—Fleming Rutledge[26]

EGOTISM.   George Bush was one President who always kept his ego in check. When told that a company would be coming out with "presidential trading cards" for kids, he said, "I don't dare ask how many hundreds of George Bush cards you have to trade to get one Michael Jordan."—Bob Dole[27]

SAINTS.   It is only in the Church of God that those words, so wild politically, can ever be any more than a dream: "Liberty, Equality, and Fraternity." There you have them, where Jesus is; not in a republic, but in the kingdom of our Lord and Saviour Jesus Christ, where all rule and domination are vested in him, and all of us willingly acknowledge him as our glorious Head, and all we are brethren. Never fall into the idea that older believers were of a superior nature to ourselves. Do not talk of Saint Paul and Saint Matthew, and Saint Mark, unless you are prepared to speak of Saint William, and Saint Jane sitting over yonder, for if they be in Christ, they are as truly saints as those first saints were, and I ween there may be some who have attained even to higher saintship than many whom tradition has canonized. The heights of saintship are by grace open to us all, and the Lord invites us to ascend. Do not think that what the Lord wrought in the early saints cannot be wrought in you.—Charles H. Spurgeon

---

[26]*The Bible and The New York Times*
[27]*Great Political Wit*

GOD'S TIMETABLE.   Some C. S. Lewis scholars have written that *A Grief Observed* really shows that Jack lost his faith in God, but the book is actually one-third grief and two-thirds recovery. Jack's problem was that when his prayers of grief were not answered immediately, he believed God to be cruel and unjust: "I am not in much danger of ceasing to believe in God. The real danger is of coming to believe such dreadful things about him." Lewis finally came to see that his prayers were heard by a loving God, and that God's timetable of helping him was there all the time—he had to "let go" and give all to God, even his struggling prayers.—Perry Bramlett[28]

RETIREMENT.   I have an excellent friend, a medical colleague, who underwent an operation for a very painful condition. Naturally, when I went to visit him he talked about his experience. At the point when he was in greatest pain, he told me, the thought came to him that not only had he to accept his suffering, he had to "get inside it." I was struck by the expression. It meant so much more than the rather tame idea of acceptance, which too many people confuse with resignation. His expression evoked a much more vigorous reaction—like a courageous dive off the edge!

"Get inside it!" I have often quoted my friend's remark in seminars on preparation for retirement. A new page is to be turned, and it needs to be turned resolutely. One cannot read two pages at once. The resigned "got to put up with it" of those who only half-heartedly accept retirement—as well as the old age it heralds—leaves them passive, divided, and bitter. It is a matter of accepting the challenges of life, which always requires a fresh burst of enthusiasm, a vigorous effort at adaptation, a new personal development.—Paul Tournier[29]

---

[28]*C. S. Lewis: Life at the Center*
[29]*Creative Suffering*

CONTRIBUTORS AND ACKNOWLEDGMENTS

CONTRIBUTORS

Atkinson, Lowell M. Retired Methodist minister, Holiday, Florida

Berg, Martha. Student at North Park Theological Seminary, Chicago, Illinois

Brand, Rick. Pastor, First Presbyterian Church, Henderson, North Carolina

Cox, Ken. Pastor, First Baptist Church, New Boston, Texas

Crawford, James W. Pastor, Old South Church, Boston, Massachusetts

Cubine, William P. Adjunct professor, Department of Sociology, University of Louisville, Louisville, Kentucky

Dipboye, Larry. Pastor, First Baptist Church, Oak Ridge, Tennessee

Farmer, David Albert. Minister, Silverside Church, Wilmington, Delaware

Ferris, Theodore Parker. Former rector, Trinity Church, Boston, Massachusetts

Fink, Michael. Baptist minister and editor

Fribley, Peter. Presyterian minister

Gladstone, John N. Pastor emeritus, Yorkminster Park Baptist Church, Toronto, Ontario

Greene, Cheryl. Associate pastor, Ebenezer African Methodist Episcopal Church, Evanston, Illinois

Hagstrom, Dennis K. Minister, Advent Lutheran Church, Westminster, Colorado

Hammer, Randy. Columnist and Presbyterian pastor, Franklin, Tennessee

Harbour, Brian L. Pastor, First Baptist Church, Richardson, Texas

Harding, Joe A. Retired Methodist minister, Nashville, Tennessee

Huffman, John C. Retired Baptist minister, Louisville, Kentucky

Hull, David W. Pastor, First Baptist Church, Knoxville, Tennessee

Hull, William E. Professor, Sanford University, Birmingham, Alabama

Hummings, Bess Gibbs. Associate pastor, Epworth United Methodist Church, Durham, North Carolina

Hunsicker, Dave. Pastor, Hillside Memorial Christian Church, Fort Worth, Texas

Ivy, Audrea. Pastor, Woodlawn United Methodist Church, Chicago, Illinois

Killinger, John. President of the Mission for Biblical Literacy, Warrenton, Virginia

Litchfield, Hugh. Professor of Homiletics, North American Baptist Seminary, Sioux Falls, South Dakota

Lloyd, Samuel T., III. Rector, Trinity Church, Boston, Massachusetts

Lovette, Roger. Retired Baptist pastor, Birmingham, Alabama

Lytch, Stephens G. Pastor, Second Presbyterian Church, Louisville, Kentucky

Macleod, Donald. Retired professor of homiletics, Princeton Theological Seminary, Baltimore, Maryland

McElrath, Hugh T. Senior professor of church music, Southern Baptist Theological Seminary, Louisville, Kentucky

Murphy, Lael P. Associate minister, Old South Church, Boston, Massachusetts

Norén, Carol M. Professor of homiletics, North Park Theological Seminary, Chicago, Illinois

Parrent, Allan M. Adjunct professor, The School of Theology, University of the South, Sewanee, Tennessee

Poff, Robert L. Prison chaplain, Chillicothe, Ohio

Read, David H. C. Late minister emeritus, Madison Avenue Presbyterian Church, New York, New York

Sherman, Clark. Rector, St. James Episcopal Church, Bozeman, Montana

Shields, Bruce E. Director, Doctor of Ministry Program, Emmanuel School of Religion, Johnson City, Tennessee

Simmons, Paul D. Clinical professor, Department of Family and Community Medicine, School of Medicine, University of Louisville, Louisville, Kentucky

Stone, Lisa A. Pastor, Chestnut Hill United Methodist Church, Dandridge, Tennessee

Stout, Kenneth B. Professor of preaching and Christian ministry, Andrews University, Berrien Springs, Michigan

Strand, Tyler A. Dean, Cathedral of the Holy Trinity, Manila, Philippines

Stratman, Gary D. Pastor, First and Calvary Presbyterian Church, Springfield, Missouri

Thomason, William P. Author and sales representative for Westminster/John Knox Press, Louisville, Kentucky

Thompson, John. Minister of pastoral care, Venice Presbyterian Church, Venice, Florida

Tomlin, Carolyn R. Writer for a variety of publications, specializing in church curriculum materials, Jackson, Tennessee

Townsend, John H. Pastor emeritus, First Baptist Church, Los Angeles, California

Trotter, Mark. Retired pastor, First United Methodist Church, San Diego, California

Tuck, William Powell. Retired Baptist minister, Richmond, Virginia

Turner, William. Pastor, South Main Baptist Church, Houston, Texas

Vinson, Richard. Dean, Averett College, Danville, Virginia

Walsh, Albert J. D. Pastor, Heidelberg United Church of Christ, Heidelberg, Pennsylvania

Warner, Laceye. Assistant professor of evangelism, Garrett Evangelical Theological Seminary, Evanston, Illinois

Woods, Bob. Pastor, First Baptist Church, Granbury, Texas

ACKNOWLEDGMENTS

Excerpts from Hugh Litchfield, *Sermons on Those Other Special Days* (Nashville: Broadman Press, 1990), pp. 85–91.

Excerpts from Michael Fink in James C. Barry, ed., *Award Winning Sermons,* Vol. II (Nashville: Broadman Press, 1978), pp. 125–130.

Excerpts from Edward D. Johnson in James C. Barry, ed., *Award Winning Sermons,* Vol. IV (Nashville: Broadman Press, 1980), pp. 119–124.

Excerpts from Ralph L. Murray, *Christ and the City* (Nashville: Broadman Press, 1970), pp. 11–20.

INDEX OF CONTRIBUTORS

SERMON TITLE INDEX

Children's sermons are identified as (cs); sermon suggestions as (ss).

440

SCRIPTURAL INDEX

444

INDEX OF PRAYERS

INDEX OF MATERIALS
USEFUL AS CHILDREN'S STORIES
AND SERMONS NOT INCLUDED IN SECTION X

448

INDEX OF MATERIALS USEFUL
FOR SMALL GROUPS

TOPICAL INDEX

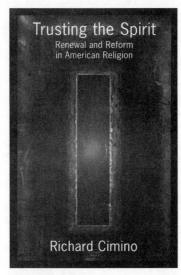

Trusting the Spirit
Renewal and Reform in American Religion
Richard Cimino
$21.95 Hardcover
ISBN: 0787951609

"Richard Cimino's well-researched case studies add immensely to our awareness of the substantial and increasing vigor of American religion. His book comes as another compelling rebuke to those still clinging to the passé claim that religion is declining and must soon die."

—Rodney Stark, professor of sociology
and comparative religion, University of Washington

Trusting the Spirit is an in-depth look at a range of current reform and renewal movements in traditional denominations that reveals what is—and is not—working to revitalize the institutions and spiritual lives of American Christians and Jews. As mainstream denominations struggle to retain members and also remain vibrant communities of faith, renewal and reform have emerged as important topics. *Trusting the Spirit* examines the main components of the renewal and reform process, describes their dynamics, and reveals how effective these organizations and movements have been within their traditions.

Going beyond description of these new organizations, Richard Cimino's journalistic approach takes readers inside each group to analyze their effectiveness in achieving their goals of spiritual and institutional change. Using interviews, observation, case studies, and analysis, Cimino shows how all the components of renewal and reform—the organization, the larger denomination, the congregation, and the individual members—interact at both local and national levels.

RICHARD CIMINO is editor and publisher of the much-quoted newsletter, *Religion Watch* (www.religionwatch.com), which researches trends in contemporary religion. He has worked extensively as a researcher and freelance writer for various publications, including *Christian Century* and Religion News Service. He is the author of *Against the Stream: The Adoption of Christian Faiths by Young Adults* and coauthor with Don Lattin of the groundbreaking *Shopping for Faith: American Religion in the New Millennium.*

[Price subject to change]

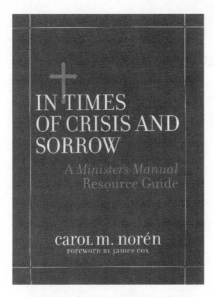

In Times of Crisis and Sorrow—A Minister's Manual Resource Guide

Carol M. Norén
Foreword by James W. Cox
$24.95 Hardcover
ISBN: 0787954029

The single most comprehensive reference for preaching in times of crisis and sorrow.

This unique reference book is designed to serve the large and established audience for the *Minister's Manual* by providing special resources for clergy. More than a funeral service manual, this resource helps pastors address personal, local, and national catastrophes in their congregations, such as natural disasters, premature or tragic death, and suicide. Unlike other preaching resources, *In Times of Crisis and Sorrow—A Minister's Manual Resource Guide* combines the best resources from 75 years of *Minister's Manuals* with new contextual material on theology, pastoral care, communities of faith, and types of services.

This reference also includes additional worship and liturgical material and is the only book on the market to provide theological reflection and rationale for what clergy believe and practice. Many books deal with funerals and grief in religious settings, but none have the broad coverage, theological integrity, ecumenical approach, and proven *Minister's Manual* resources of this invaluable desk reference for clergy.

This is the book that every preacher needs and that in hindsight all ministers wish they had when the unexpected crisis happens. In addition, this is an excellent resource for grief counselors and others in the helping professions.

CAROL M. NORÉN is an ordained minister in the United Methodist Church. A native of Chicago, she has served urban and suburban churches in the United States and also has been pastor of two inner-city churches and hospital chaplain in Manchester, England. She has taught at Princeton Theological Seminary, Duke Divinity School, and North Park Theological Seminary. In addition, she has been guest lecturer at denominational seminaries in Europe, Australia, and across the United States.

JAMES W. COX is a professor at Southern Baptist Theological Seminary in Louisville, Kentucky, and has been the editor of the *Minister's Manual* since 1984. He lives in Louisville.

[Price subject to change]

Leading Congregational Change

A Practical Guide for the
Transformational Journey
A Leadership Network Publication
Jim Herrington, Mike Bonem, and James H. Furr
$23.95 Hardcover
ISBN: 0787947652
$11.95 Paperback Workbook
ISBN: 0787948853

"Leading a church to change from being tradition- or program-driven to being purpose-driven is a task filled with all kinds of potentially explosive and divisive issues. This is a book you ought to read before you change anything."

—Rick Warren, author, *The Purpose-Driven Church*

"This book spotlights the universal principles for navigating the rapids of change between chaplaincy and mission. Identifying the simplicity—within the complexity—of this challenging leadership role, pastors and leaders learn how to go from hopeful to possible."

—Herb Miller, editor, *The Parish Paper*

"If you keep doing what you've been doing, you'll keep getting what you've been getting. Can you live with that?" For pastors and leaders whose answer to this challenge is no, here is a proven program to effect both personal and congregational transformation.

With this much-needed handbook, the authors brilliantly combine their experience guiding dozens of churches through the change process with both the study of Christian disciplines and the sophisticated understanding of such important business thinkers as John Kotter on leading change and Peter Senge on learning organizations. In this eminently readable book the authors have distilled their insights and practices into simple but powerful concepts for leading congregations, whether long established or recently formed, through profound change.

Leaders using this guide will also be interested in the companion *Leading Congregational Change Workbook*, which offers assessment questions, planning worksheets, activities, and case examples for each stage of the process.

JIM HERRINGTON is executive director of Mission Houston, an interdenominational, multicultural pastoral effort to transform the city of Houston.

MIKE BONEM is president and cofounder of Kingdom Transformation Partners, a church consulting and training firm based in Houston.

JAMES H. FURR is senior church consultant with Union Baptist Association and adjunct professor of sociology at Houston Baptist University.

[Price subject to change]